MW00851561

CLYMER®

YAMAHA

RHINO 700 • 2008-2012

The world's finest publisher of mechanical how-to manuals

P.O. Box 12901, Overland Park, Kansas 66282-2901

Copyright ©2012 Penton Business Media, Inc.

FIRST EDITION
First Printing April, 2012

Printed in U.S.A.

CLYMER and colophon are registered trademarks of Penton Business Media, Inc.

ISBN-10: 1-59969-541-3

ISBN-13: 978-1-59969-541-9

Library of Congress: 2012935398

AUTHOR: Ron Wright.

TECHNICAL PHOTOGRAPHY: Ron Wright.

*ASSISTANCE AND VEHICLE: Clawson Motorsports (**clawsonmotorsports.com**). Deek Garrison and Brad Wright.*

ILLUSTRATIONS: Steve Amos.

WIRING DIAGRAMS: Robert Meyer.

EDITOR: Steven Thomas.

PRODUCTION: Samantha Collins.

*COVER: Mark Clifford Photography (**markclifford.com**). Cover Rhino courtesy Bert's Mega Mall (**bertsmegamall.com**).*

All rights reserved. Reproduction or use, without express permission, of editorial or pictorial content, in any manner, is prohibited. No patent liability is assumed with respect to the use of the information contained herein. While every precaution has been taken in the preparation of this book, the publisher assumes no responsibility for errors or omissions. Neither is any liability assumed for damages resulting from use of the information contained herein. Publication of the servicing information in this manual does not imply approval of the manufacturers of the products covered.

All instructions and diagrams have been checked for accuracy and ease of application; however, success and safety in working with tools depend to a great extent upon individual accuracy, skill and caution. For this reason, the publishers are not able to guarantee the result of any procedure contained herein. Nor can they assume responsibility for any damage to property or injury to persons occasioned from the procedures. Persons engaging in the procedure do so entirely at their own risk.

Chapter One
General Information   1

Chapter Two
Troubleshooting   2

Chapter Three
Lubrication, Maintenance and Tune-up   3

Chapter Four
Engine Top End and Exhaust System   4

Chapter Five
Engine Lower End   5

Chapter Six
Clutch and Sheaves   6

Chapter Seven
Transmission and Shift Mechanism   7

Chapter Eight
Fuel Injection System   8

Chapter Nine
Electrical System   9

Chapter Ten
Liquid Cooling and Oil Cooler Systems   10

Chapter Eleven
Front Suspension and Steering   11

Chapter Twelve
Front Axles and Differential   12

Chapter Thirteen
Rear Suspension   13

Chapter Fourteen
Rear Axles and Final Drive   14

Chapter Fifteen
Brakes   15

Chapter Sixteen
Body   16

Index   17

Color Wiring Diagrams   18

CLYMER ®

Publisher Ron Rogers

EDITORIAL

Editorial Director
James Grooms

Editor
Steven Thomas

Associate Editor
Rick Arens

Authors
Ed Scott
Ron Wright
Michael Morlan
George Parise
Jay Bogart

Illustrators
Bob Meyer
Steve Amos
Errol McCarthy
Mitzi McCarthy

SALES

Sales Manager–Marine/I&T
Jay Lipton

Sales Manager–Powersport
Matt Tusken

CUSTOMER SERVICE

Customer Service Manager
Terri Cannon

Customer Service Representatives
Dinah Bunnell
Suzanne Johnson
April LeBlond
Sherry Rudkin

PRODUCTION

Director of Production
Dylan Goodwin

Production Manager
Greg Araujo

Senior Production Editors
Darin Watson
Adriane Wineinger

Associate Production Editors
Ashley Bally
Samantha Collins

 Penton

P.O. Box 12901, Overland Park, KS 66282-2901 • 800-262-1954 • 913-967-1719

More information available at *clymer.com*

CONTENTS

QUICK REFERENCE DATA IX

CHAPTER ONE
GENERAL INFORMATION 1

Manual organization
Warnings, cautions and notes
Safety
Serial numbers and information labels
Fasteners
Shop supplies

Tools
Measuring tools
Electrical system fundamentals
Service methods
Storage
Specifications

CHAPTER TWO
TROUBLESHOOTING 28

Starting the engine
Engine does not start
Poor engine performance
Fuel system
Electronic diagnostic system
Trouble codes
Charging system troubleshooting
Ignition system troubleshooting
Starting system troubleshooting
Engine
Engine lubrication

Cylinder leakdown test
Clutch troubleshooting
Transmission troubleshooting
Axles, differential and final drive unit
Drive shafts and middle gear unit
Electrical testing
Lighting and signal system troubleshooting
Front suspension and steering
Rear suspension
Brake system
Specifications

CHAPTER THREE
LUBRICATION, MAINTENANCE AND TUNE-UP 58

Tune-up
Pre-ride inspection
Fuel requirements
Battery
Air filter
Engine oil and filter
Engine oil pressure check
Front differential
Final drive oil
Cooling system
Spark plug
Valve clearance
Engine compression check
Fuel hose inspection
Breather hoses inspection
Exhaust system
Throttle body and air intake joint inspection
Accelerator cable adjustment

Ignition timing inspection
Select lever adjustment
Drive belt inspection
Brakes
Parking brake assembly
Engine mounts inspection
Control cables and pedals
Tires and wheels inspection
Wheel bearings
Steering system
Axle boots inspection
Front suspension
Rear suspension
Universal joint lubrication
Drain hoses
Fastener inspection
Engine break-in
Specifications

CHAPTER FOUR
ENGINE TOP END AND EXHAUST SYSTEM 87

Exhaust system
Cylinder head
Camshaft and rocker arms
Cam chain and guides

Valves and valve components
Cylinder
Piston and piston rings
Specifications

CHAPTER FIVE
ENGINE LOWER END 119

Servicing engine in frame
Engine
Balancer and oil pump gears
Oil pressure relief valve
Cam chain and guides
Crankcase
Crankcase seals and bearings
Relief valve and oil pipe adapter
Crankshaft

Balancer shaft
Oil pump
Middle gear bearing housing
Middle driven pinion gear bearing housing
Middle driven shaft
Middle gear assembly shim and lash adjustment
Universal joint
Shifting check
Specifications

CHAPTER SIX
CLUTCH AND SHEAVES. 164

Drive belt air duct assembly
Drive belt cover
Outer bearing housing
Drive belt

Primary and secondary sheaves
Left crankcase cover
Centrifugal clutch
Specifications

CHAPTER SEVEN
TRANSMISSION AND SHIFT MECHANISM 187

Select lever assembly
External shift mechanism
Transmission

Shift drum and forks
Specifications

CHAPTER EIGHT
FUEL INJECTION SYSTEM 199

Fuel injection (FI)
Fuel delivery system tests
Fuel tank
Fuel pump
Fuel level sender
Fuel injection system relay
Throttle body
Fuel rail and fuel injector
Idle speed control unit
Throttle position sensor
Engine control unit (ECU)

Intake air pressure sensor
Intake air temperature sensor
Coolant temperature sensor
Crankshaft position sensor
Speed sensor
Lean-angle sensor
Rollover valve
Air box
Air intake duct
Accelerator cable
Specifications

CHAPTER NINE
ELECTRICAL SYSTEM. 221

Electrical component replacement
Electrical connectors
Battery
Charging system
Regulator/rectifier
Right crankcase cover, stator coil and crankshaft
    position sensor
Flywheel, starter clutch and starter clutch gears
Ignition system
Ignition coil
Lean-angle sensor
Engine control unit (ECU)
Ignition timing

Starter
Starter relay
Lighting system
Meter assembly and indicator lights
Four-wheel-drive indicator and relays
Helmet/seat belt display (2009 and 2011-on models)
Cooling system
Load control relay
Switches
Diode
Auxiliary DC jack
Fuses
Specifications

CHAPTER TEN
COOLING SYSTEM AND OIL COOLER SYSTEMS 263

Cooling system safety
Cooling system inspection
Radiator
Cooling fan
Coolant reservoir

Thermostat
Water pump
Oil cooler lines and hoses
Oil cooler
Specifications

CHAPTER ELEVEN
FRONT SUSPENSION AND STEERING. 278

Front wheels
Front hub
Steering knuckle
Front control arms
Front shock absorbers
Steering wheel
Tie rod boots and tie rod ends

Steering gearbox, steering column and
    steering shaft
Toe-in adjustment
Tires
Wheel runout
Specifications

CHAPTER TWELVE
FRONT AXLES AND DIFFERENTIAL . . . . **.302**

Front axle
Front differential
Universal joint

Front drive shaft
Specifications

CHAPTER THIRTEEN
REAR SUSPENSIONS . . . . **.327**

Rear wheels
Tires
Rear hub
Rear knuckle

Stabilizer (2008-2009 models)
Rear control arms
Rear shock absorbers
Specifications

CHAPTER FOURTEEN
REAR AXLES AND FINAL DRIVE . . . . **.341**

Rear axle
Final drive unit

Rear drive shaft
Specifications

CHAPTER FIFTEEN
BRAKES . . . . **.367**

Brake service notes
Brake bleeding
Brake fluid flushing
Brake fluid draining
Brake pads
Brake caliper
Master cylinder

Parking brake caliper
Parking brake cable
Parking brake lever
Brake hose and brake line
Brake disc
Specifications

CHAPTER SIXTEEN
BODY . . . . **.398**

Plastic rivets
Blind rivets
Hood
Seats, seat supports and driver seat rail
Rear console
Front console
Corner panels and side panels
Center protector
Left protector
Right protector
Upper instrument panel

Lower instrument panel
Side doors
Seat belts and buckles
Cargo bed
Frame enclosure assembly
Front bumper
Skid plates
Pedal assembly
Floorboard
Specifications

INDEX . . . . **.414**

COLOR WIRING DIAGRAMS . . . . **.420**

QUICK REFERENCE DATA

VEHICLE INFORMATION

MODEL: _____ YEAR: _____

VIN NUMBER: _____

ENGINE SERIAL NUMBER: _____

KEY NUMBER: _____

TIRE AND WHEEL SPECIFICATIONS*

Tire	
Manufacturer	MAXXIS
Model	
Front	M951Y
Rear	M952Y
Size	
Front	25 × 8.00-12 NHS
Rear	25 × 10.00-12 NHS
Tire pressure (cold)	
Front	63-77 kPa (9-11 psi)
Rear	91-105 kPa (13-15 psi)
Wheels	
Size	
Front	12 × 6.0 AT
Rear	12 × 7.5 AT
Runout (radial and lateral)	2.0 mm (0.08 in.)

* Tire specifications are for original equipment tires only. Aftermarket tires may have different specifications.

OIL AND FLUID CAPACITIES

Radiator	2.35 L (2.48 qt.)
Coolant reservoir	
Amount between marks	0.21 L (0.22 qt.)
Total	0.32 L (0.34 qt.)
Engine oil	
Oil change only	2.00 L (2.11 qt.)
Oil and filter change	2.10 L (2.22 qt.)
Engine disassembly	3.00 L (3.18 qt.)
Final drive gear oil	
Oil change	250 ml (8.5 oz.)
Final drive gear disassembly	280 ml (9.5 oz.)
Front differential gear oil	
Oil change	180 ml (6.1 oz.)
Differential disassembly	200 ml (6.8 oz.)

RECOMMENDED LUBRICANTS, COOLANT AND FUEL

Air filter	Air filter oil
Brake fluid	DOT 4 brake fluid
Engine oil[2]	
Classification	
JASCO T 903 standard rating	MA
API rating	SG or higher
Viscosity	5W-30
30° F (0° C) or lower	
10-110° F (-10-43° C)	10W-40
50° F (10° C) or higher	20W-50
Engine coolant	
Type	Ethylene glycol containing anticorrosion inhibiters for aluminum engines

(continued)

RECOMMENDED LUBRICANTS, COOLANT AND FUEL (continued)

Engine coolant (continued)	
Mixture	50:50 (coolant/distilled water)
Final drive gear oil[1]	SAE80 API GL-4 hypoid gear oil
Front differential gear oil[1]	SAE80 API GL-4 hypoid gear oil
Fuel	Refer to text

1. Refer to Chapter One for additional information.
2. API SG or higher classified oils not specified as ENERGY CONSERVING II can be used. Refer to Chapter One for additional information.

MAINTENANCE AND TUNE-UP SPECIFICATIONS

Air filter type	Wet type element
Brake pad wear limit	
Front and rear	1.5 mm (0.06 in.)
Parking	1.0 mm (0.04 in.)
Brake pedal free play	0 mm (0 in.)
Engine compression	
Minimum	392 kPa (56.84 psi)
Standard	450 kPa (65.25 psi)
Maximum	504 kPa (73.08 psi)
Engine idle speed	1550-1650 rpm
Engine oil pressure (hot)	50.0 kPa (7.25 psi) @ 1600 rpm
Parking brake adjustment	
Number of clicks	1
Spark plug gap	0.8-0.9 mm (0.031-0.035 in.)
Spark plug type	NGK CPR7EA-9
Accelerator cable free play	0 mm (0 in.)
Tire wear limit	
Front and rear	3.0 mm (0.12 in.)
Valve clearance	
Intake	0.09-0.13 mm (0.0035-0.0051 in.)
Exhaust	0.16-0.20 mm (0.0063-0.0079 in.)
Drive-belt width	
Standard	33.3 mm (1.31 in.)
Service limit	30.0 mm (1.18 in.)

MAINTENANCE TORQUE SPECIFICATIONS

	N•m	in.-lb.	ft.-lb.
Brake rod locknut	17	–	12.5
Camshaft sprocket cover bolt	10	88	–
Coolant drain bolt	10	88	–
Differential oil fill plug	23	–	17
Differential oil drain bolt	10	88	–
Engine oil check bolt	10	88	–
Engine oil drain bolt	30	–	22
Engine oil filter	17	–	12.5
Final drive oil fill plug	23	–	17
Final drive oil drain bolt	20	–	15
Flywheel nut plug	10	88	–
Master cylinder mounting bolt	16	–	12
Parking brake lever nut	17	–	12.5
Shift rod locknut	15	–	11
Skid plate mounting bolts	7	62	–
Spark plug	13	115	–
Tailpipe mounting bolt	10	88	–
Thermostat cover air bleed bolt	10	88	–
Timing plug	6	53	–
Tie-rod end locknut	40	–	30
Valve adjust screw locknuts	14	–	10
Valve adjustment cover bolt	10	88	–
Water pump air bleed bolt	10	88	–
Wheel nuts	55	–	41

CHAPTER ONE

GENERAL INFORMATION

This detailed and comprehensive manual covers 2008-2009 and 2011-on 700 Rhino models.

The text provides complete information on maintenance, tune-up, repair and overhaul. Hundreds of photos and drawings guide the reader through every job. All procedures are in step-by-step format and designed for the reader who may be working on the vehicle for the first time.

MANUAL ORGANIZATION

A shop manual is a reference tool and, as in all Clymer manuals, the chapters are thumb-tabbed for easy reference. Important items are indexed at the end of the manual. Frequently used specifications and capacities from individual chapters are summarized in the *Quick Reference Data* at the front of the manual.

During some of the procedures there will be references to headings in other chapters or sections of the manual. When a specific heading is called out in a step it is *italicized* as it appears in the manual. If a sub-heading is indicated as being "in this section" it is located within the same main heading. For example, the sub-heading *Handling Gasoline Safely* is located within the main heading *SAFETY*.

This chapter provides general information on shop safety, tool use, service fundamentals and shop supplies. **Tables 1-8** at the end of this chapter provide general vehicle, mechanical and shop information.

Chapter Two provides methods for quick and accurate diagnoses of problems. Troubleshooting procedures present typical symptoms and logical methods to pinpoint and repair a problem.

Chapter Three explains routine maintenance and tune-up procedures.

Subsequent chapters describe specific systems, such as engine, clutch, transmission, fuel system, drive systems, suspension, brakes and body components.

Specification tables, when applicable, are located at the end of each chapter.

WARNINGS, CAUTIONS AND NOTES

The terms WARNING, CAUTION and NOTE have specific meanings in this manual.

A WARNING emphasizes areas where injury or even death could result from negligence. Mechanical damage may also occur. WARNINGS are to be taken seriously.

A CAUTION emphasizes areas where equipment damage could result. Disregarding a CAUTION could cause permanent mechanical damage, though injury is unlikely.

A NOTE provides additional information to make a step or procedure easier or clearer. Disregarding a NOTE could cause inconvenience, but would not cause equipment damage or injury.

SAFETY

Follow these guidelines and practice common sense to safely service the vehicle:

1. Do not operate the vehicle in an enclosed area. The exhaust gases contain carbon monoxide, an odorless, colorless and tasteless poisonous gas. Carbon monoxide levels build quickly in small enclosed areas and can cause unconsciousness and death in a short time. Make sure the work area is properly ventilated, or operate the vehicle outside.

2. Never use gasoline or any flammable liquid to clean parts. Refer to *Handling Gasoline Safely* and *Cleaning Parts* in this section.

3. Never smoke or use a torch in the vicinity of flammable liquids, such as gasoline or cleaning solvent.

4. Do not remove the radiator cap or cooling system hoses while the engine is hot. The cooling system is pressurized and the high temperature coolant may cause injury.

5. Dispose of and store coolant in a safe manner. Do not allow children or pets to open containers of coolant. Animals are attracted to antifreeze.

6. Avoid contact with engine oil and other chemicals. Most are known carcinogens. Wash your hands thoroughly after coming in contact with engine oil. If possible, wear a pair of disposable gloves.

7. If welding or brazing on the vehicle, remove the fuel tank and shocks to a safe distance at least 50 ft. (15 m) away.

8. Use the correct types and sizes of tools to avoid damaging fasteners.

9. Keep tools clean and in good condition. Replace or repair worn or damaged equipment.

10. When loosening a tight fastener, be guided by what would happen if the tool slips.

11. When replacing fasteners, make sure the new fasteners are the same size and strength as the originals. Refer to *Fasteners* in this chapter.

12. Keep the work area clean and organized.

13. Wear eye protection any time the safety of your eyes is in question. This includes procedures involving drilling, grinding, hammering, compressed air and chemicals.

14. Wear the correct clothing for the job. Tie up or cover long hair so it can not catch in moving equipment.

15. Do not carry sharp tools in clothing pockets.

16. Always have an approved fire extinguisher available. Make sure it is rated for gasoline (Class B) and electrical (Class C) fires.

17. Do not use compressed air to clean clothes, the vehicle or the work area. Debris may be blown into the eyes or skin. Never direct compressed air at anyone. Do not allow children to use or play with any compressed air equipment.

18. When using compressed air to dry rotating parts, hold the part so it cannot rotate. Do not allow the force of the air to spin the part. The air jet is capable of rotating parts at extreme speeds. The part may be damaged or disintegrate, causing serious injury.

19. Do not inhale the dust created by brake pad wear. These particles may contain asbestos. In addition, some types of insulating materials and gaskets may contain asbestos. Inhaling asbestos particles is hazardous to health.

20. Never work on the vehicle while someone is working under it.

21. When supporting the vehicle with the wheel(s) off the ground, make sure the vehicle is secure and cannot roll.

Handling Gasoline Safely

Gasoline is a volatile flammable liquid and is one of the most dangerous items in the shop. Because gasoline is used so often, many people forget that it is hazardous. Only use

gasoline as fuel for gasoline internal combustion engines. Keep in mind when working on a vehicle, gasoline is always present in the fuel tank, fuel line and carburetor. To avoid an accident when working around the fuel system, carefully observe the following precautions:

1. Never use gasoline to clean parts. Refer to *Cleaning Parts* in this section.

2. When working on the fuel system, work outside or in a well-ventilated area.

3. Do not add fuel to the fuel tank or service the fuel system while the vehicle is near open flames, sparks or where someone is smoking. Gasoline vapor is heavier than air, collects in low areas and is more easily ignited than liquid gasoline.

4. Allow the engine to cool completely before working on any fuel system component.

5. Do not store gasoline in glass containers. If the glass breaks, an explosion or fire may occur.

6. Immediately wipe up spilled gasoline with rags. Store the rags in a metal container with a lid until they can be properly disposed, or place them outside in a safe place for the fuel to evaporate.

7. Do not pour water onto a gasoline fire. Water spreads the fire and makes it more difficult to put out. Use a class B, BC or ABC fire extinguisher to extinguish the fire.

8. Always turn off the engine before refueling. Do not spill fuel onto the engine or exhaust system. Do not overfill the fuel tank. Leave an air space at the top of the tank to allow room for the fuel to expand due to temperature fluctuations.

Cleaning Parts

Cleaning parts is one of the more tedious and difficult service jobs performed in the home garage. Many types of chemical cleaners and solvents are available for shop use. Most are poisonous and extremely flammable. To prevent chemical exposure, vapor buildup, fire and injury, observe each product's warning label and note the following:

1. Read and observe the entire product label before using any chemical. Always know what type of chemical is being used and whether it is poisonous and/or flammable.

2. Do not use more than one type of cleaning solvent at a time. If mixing chemicals is required, measure the proper amounts according to the manufacturer.

3. Work in a well-ventilated area.

4. Wear chemical-resistant gloves that are appropriate for the chemical being used.

5. Wear safety glasses.

6. Wear a vapor respirator if the instructions call for it.

7. Wash hands and arms thoroughly after cleaning parts.

8. Keep chemicals away from children and pets, especially coolant.

9. Thoroughly clean all oil, grease and cleaner residue from any part that must be heated.

10. Use a nylon brush when cleaning parts. Metal brushes may cause a spark.

11. When using a parts washer, only use the solvent recommended by the manufacturer. Make sure the parts washer is equipped with a metal lid that will lower in case of fire.

Warning Labels

Most manufacturers attach information and warning labels to the vehicle. These labels contain instructions that are important to safety when operating, servicing, transporting and storing the vehicle Refer to the owner's manual for the description and location of labels. Order replacement labels from the manufacturer if they are missing or damaged.

SERIAL NUMBERS AND INFORMATION LABELS

The vehicle identification number (VIN) is stamped on the left side of the frame (**Figure 1**), behind the left rear tire.

The model identification number (**Figure 2**) is attached to the frame under the driver's seat.

The engine serial number (**Figure 3**) is stamped on the left crankcase, behind the left crankcase cover.

Record these numbers in the *Quick Reference Data* section in the front of the manual to have them available when ordering parts.

FASTENERS

WARNING
Do not install fasteners with a strength classification lower than what was originally installed by the manufacturer. Doing so may cause equipment failure and/or damage.

Proper fastener selection and installation is important to ensure the vehicle operates as designed and can be serviced efficiently. The choice of original equipment fasteners is not arrived at by chance. Make sure replacement fasteners meet the requirements.

Threaded Fasteners

Threaded fasteners secure most of the components on the vehicle. Most are tightened by turning them clockwise (right-hand threads). If the normal rotation of the component being tightened would loosen the fastener, it may have left-hand threads. If a left-hand threaded fastener is used, it is noted in the text.

Two dimensions are required to match the thread size of the fastener: the number of threads in a given distance and the outside diameter of the threads.

Two systems are currently used to specify threaded fastener dimensions: the U.S. Standard system and the metric system (**Figure 4**). Pay particular attention when working with unidentified fasteners; mismatching thread types can damage threads.

To ensure the fastener threads are not mismatched or cross-threaded, start all fasteners by hand. If a fastener is difficult to start or turn, determine the cause before tightening with a wrench.

Match fasteners by their length (L, **Figure 5**), diameter (D) and distance between thread crests (pitch, T). A typical metric bolt may be identified by the numbers, 8—1.25 × 130. This indicates the bolt has a diameter of 8 mm, the distance between thread crests is 1.25 mm and the length is 130 mm. Always measure bolt length as shown in L, **Figure 5** to avoid installing replacements of the wrong lengths.

If a number is located on the top of a metric fastener (**Figure 5**), this indicates the strength. The higher the num-

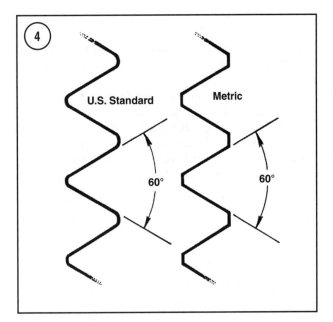

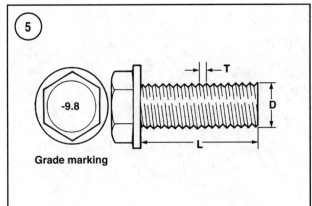

ber, the stronger the fastener. Typically, unnumbered fasteners are the weakest.

Many screws, bolts and studs are combined with nuts to secure particular components. To indicate the size of a nut, manufacturers specify the internal diameter and thread pitch.

The measurement across two flats on a nut or bolt indicates the wrench size.

Torque Specifications

The materials used in the manufacture of the vehicle may be subjected to uneven stresses if fasteners are not installed and tightened correctly. Improperly installed fasteners or ones that worked loose can cause extensive damage. It is essential to use an accurate torque wrench, as described in this chapter, with the torque specifications in this manual.

Specifications for torque are provided in Newton-meters (N•m), foot-pounds (ft.-lb.) and inch-pounds (in.-lb.). Refer to **Table 8** for general torque recommendations. To use **Table 8**, first determine the size of the fastener as described in *Threaded Fasteners* in this section. Torque specifications for specific components are at the end of the appropriate chapters. Torque wrenches are covered in *Tools* in this chapter.

Self-Locking Fasteners

Several types of bolts, screws and nuts incorporate a system that creates interference between the two fasteners. Interference is achieved in various ways. The most common type used is the nylon insert nut and a dry adhesive coating on the threads of a bolt.

Self-locking fasteners offer greater holding strength than standard fasteners, which improves their resistance to vibration. Self-locking fasteners cannot be reused. The materials used to form the lock become distorted after the

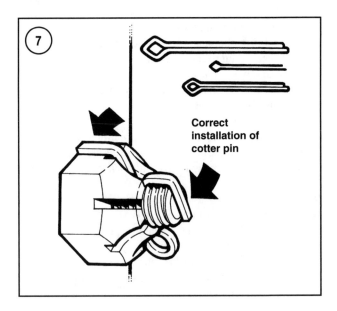

initial installation and removal. Do not replace self-locking fasteners with standard fasteners.

Some Yamaha fasteners are equipped with a threadlocking compound preapplied to the fastener threads (**Figure 6**). When replacing these fasteners, do not apply a separate threadlocking compound. When it is necessary to reuse one of these fasteners, remove the threadlocking compound residue from the threads. Then apply the threadlocking compound specified in the text.

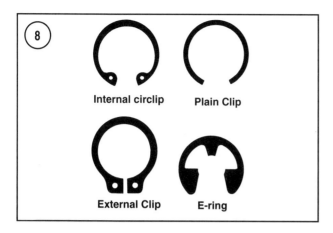

Internal circlip   Plain Clip

External Clip   E-ring

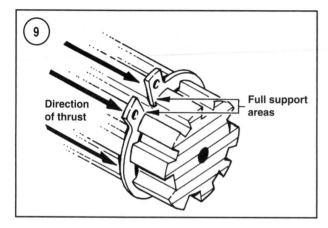

Direction of thrust

Full support areas

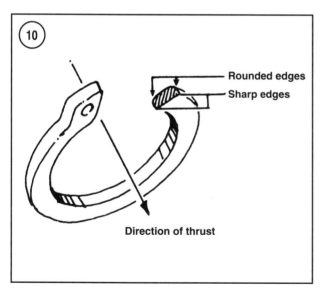

Rounded edges

Sharp edges

Direction of thrust

Washers

The two basic types of washers are flat washers and lockwashers. Flat washers are simple discs with a hole to fit a screw or bolt. Lockwashers are used to prevent a fastener from working loose. Washers can be used as spacers and seals or to help distribute fastener load and prevent the fastener from damaging the component.

As with fasteners, when replacing washers make sure the replacements meet the original specifications.

Cotter Pins

A cotter pin is a split metal pin inserted into a hole or slot to prevent a fastener from loosening. In certain applications, such as the rear axle, the fastener must be secured in this way. For these applications, a cotter pin and castellated (slotted) nut is used.

To use a cotter pin, first make sure the diameter is correct for the hole in the fastener. After correctly tightening the fastener and aligning the holes, insert the cotter pin through the hole and bend the ends over the fastener (**Figure 7**). Unless instructed to do so, never loosen a tightened fastener to align the holes. If the holes do not align, tighten the fastener just enough to achieve alignment.

Cotter pins are available in various diameters and lengths. Measure length from the bottom of the head to the tip of the shortest pin.

Snap Rings and E-clips

Snap rings (**Figure 8**) are circular-shaped metal retaining clips. They are required to secure parts and gears in place on parts such as shafts, pins or rods. External type snap rings are used to retain items on shafts. Internal type snap rings secure parts within housing bores. In some applications, in addition to securing the component(s), snap rings of varying thicknesses also determine endplay. These are usually called selective snap rings.

The two basic types of snap rings are machined and stamped snap rings. Machined snap rings (**Figure 9**) can be installed in either direction because both faces have sharp edges. Stamped snap rings (**Figure 10**) are manufactured with a sharp edge and round edge. When installing a stamped snap ring in a thrust application, install the sharp edge facing away from the part producing the thrust.

E-clips are used when it is not practical to use a snap ring. Remove E-clips with a flat blade screwdriver by prying between the shaft and E-clip. To install an E-clip, center it over the shaft groove and push or tap it into place.

Observe the following when installing snap rings:
1. Remove and install snap rings with snap ring pliers. Refer to *Tools* in this chapter.
2. In some applications, it may be necessary to replace snap rings after removing them.
3. Compress or expand snap rings only enough to install them. If overly expanded, they lose their retaining ability.
4. After installing a snap ring, make sure it seats completely.
5. Wear eye protection when removing and installing snap rings.

SHOP SUPPLIES

Lubricants and Fluids

Periodic lubrication helps ensure a long service life for any type of equipment. Using the correct type of lubricant is as important as performing the lubrication service, although in an emergency the wrong type is better than not using one. The following section describes the types of lubricants most often required. Make sure to follow the manufacturer's recommendations.

Engine oils

Engine oil for use in a four-stroke motorcycle engine is classified by three standards: the Japanese Automobile Standards Organization (JASO) T 903 certification standard, the American Petroleum Institute (API) service classification, and the Society of Automotive Engineers (SAE) viscosity index.

The JASO certification specifies the oil has passed requirements specified by Japanese motorcycle manufacturers. The JASO certification label (**Figure 11**) identifies which of the two separate classifications the oil meets. It also includes a registration number to indicate that the oil has passed all JASO certification standards for use in four-stroke motorcycle engines.

Two letters (**Figure 12**) are used to indicate the API service classification. A number or sequence of numbers and letter (10W-40 [**Figure 12**]) identify the oil's SAE viscosity rating. The API service classification and the SAE viscosity index are not indications of oil quality.

Viscosity is an indication of the oil's thickness. Thin oils have a lower number while thick oils have a higher number. Engine oils fall into the 5- to 50-weight range for single-grade oils.

Most manufacturers recommend multi-grade oil. These oils perform efficiently across a wide range of operating conditions. A W after the first number indicates that the oil is a multi-grade type and it shows the low-temperature viscosity.

Always use oil with a classification recommended by the manufacturer. Using oil with a different classification can cause clutch slippage and engine damage. Do not use oil with oil additives or oil with graphite or molybdenum additives. Do not use oil with a diesel specification of CD. Do not use vegetable, non-detergent or castor-based racing oils.

Use a high-quality motorcycle oil with a JASCO rating of MA or an API oil with an SG or higher classification that does not specify it as ENERGY CONSERVING II (**Figure 12**). Use SAE 10-40 oil for cool and warm climates and a heavier viscosity oil (20W-50) in hot climates.

Greases

Grease is lubricating oil with thickening agents added to it. The National Lubricating Grease Institute (NLGI) grades grease. Grades range from No. 000 to No. 6, with No. 6 being the thickest. Typical multipurpose grease is NLGI No. 2. For specific applications, manufacturers may recommend a water-resistant type grease or one with an additive, such as molybdenum disulfide (MoS_2).

JASO CERTIFICATION LABEL

Sales company oil code number

M001XXXXX

MA

OIL CLASSIFICATION
MA: Designed for high-friction applications
MB: Designed for low-friction applications

When rebuilding the clutch assemblies, Yamaha recommends the use of Yamalube Ultramatic Grease. Refer to Chapter Six.

Molybdenum oil solution

This is a 1:1 mixture of engine oil and molybdenum grease, which is used as an assembly lubricant during engine and chassis assembly to prevent wear and galling during start-up. Mix the solution in a clean container and cover with a removable cap to prevent contamination during storage. Apply the mixture with an acid brush.

Coolant

Coolant is a mixture of water and antifreeze used to dissipate engine heat. Ethylene glycol is the most common form of antifreeze used. Check the vehicle manufacturer's recommendations when selecting antifreeze, most require one specifically designed for use in aluminum engines. These types of antifreeze have additives that inhibit corrosion.

Only mix distilled water with antifreeze. Impurities in tap water may damage internal cooling system passages.

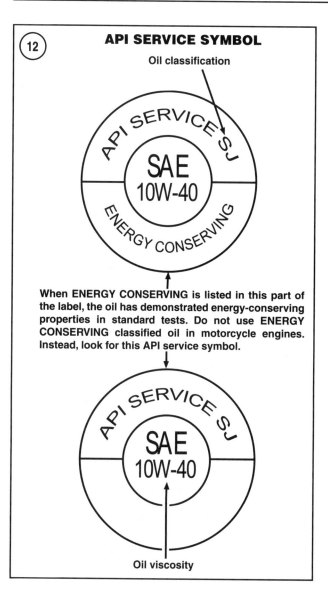

When oiling an aftermarket air filter, use the oil recommended by the manufacturer. Refer to Chapter Three.

Cleaners, Degreasers and Solvents

Many chemicals are available to remove oil, grease and other residue from the vehicle. Before using cleaning solvents, consider their uses and disposal methods, particularly if they are not water-soluble. Local ordinances may require special procedures for the disposal of many types of cleaning chemicals. Refer to *Cleaning Parts* in *Safety* in this chapter.

Use brake parts cleaner to clean brake system components when contact with petroleum-based products will damage seals. Brake parts cleaner leaves no residue. Use electrical contact cleaner to clean electrical connections and components without leaving any residue. Carburetor cleaner is a powerful solvent used to remove fuel deposits and varnish from fuel system components. Use this cleaner carefully; it may damage finishes.

Generally, degreasers are strong cleaners used to remove heavy accumulations of grease from engine and frame components.

Most solvents are designed to be used with a parts washing cabinet for individual component cleaning. For safety, use only nonflammable or high flash point solvents.

Gasket Sealant

Sealants are used in combination with a gasket, seal or occasionally alone. Follow the manufacturer's recommendation when using sealants. Use extreme care when choosing a sealant different from the type originally recommended. Choose sealants based on their resistance to heat, various fluids and their sealing capabilities.

One of the most common sealants is RTV, or room temperature vulcanizing, sealant. This sealant cures at room temperature over a specific time period. This allows the repositioning of components without damaging gaskets.

Moisture in the air causes the RTV sealant to cure. Always install the tube cap as soon as possible after applying RTV sealant. RTV sealant has a limited shelf life and will not cure properly if the shelf life has expired.

Keep partial tubes sealed and discard them if they have surpassed the expiration date. If there is no expiration date on a sealant tube, use a permanent marker and write the date on the tube when it is first opened. Manufacturers usually specify a shelf life of one year after a container is opened, though it is recommended to contact the sealant manufacturer to confirm shelf life.

Removing RTV sealant

Silicone sealant is used on many engine gasket surfaces. When cleaning parts after disassembly, a razor blade or gasket scraper is required to remove the silicone residue that cannot be pulled off by hand from the gasket surfaces.

API SERVICE SYMBOL

Oil classification

API SERVICE SJ

SAE 10W-40

ENERGY CONSERVING

When ENERGY CONSERVING is listed in this part of the label, the oil has demonstrated energy-conserving properties in standard tests. Do not use ENERGY CONSERVING classified oil in motorcycle engines. Instead, look for this API service symbol.

API SERVICE SJ

SAE 10W-40

Oil viscosity

Front differential and final drive gear oil

Gear oil is a thick oil specially formulated for differential and final drive units. Always use gear oil with a classification and viscosity rating of SAE 80 API GL-4. Hypoid gear oil with a GL-5 or GL-6 rating can also be used. Do not use engine oil or transmission oil recommended for two-stroke engines or automobiles.

Foam air filter oil

Foam filter oil is specifically designed to use on foam air filters. The oil is blended with additives making it easy to pour and apply evenly to the filter. Some filter oils include additives that evaporate quickly, making the filter oil very tacky. This allows the oil to remain suspended within the foam pores, trapping dirt and preventing it from being drawn into the engine.

Do not use engine oil as a substitute for foam filter oil. Engine oils do not remain in the filter. Instead, they are drawn into the engine, leaving the filter ineffective.

To avoid damaging gasket surfaces, use a silicone gasket remover to help soften the residue before scraping.

Applying RTV sealant

Clean all old sealer residue from the mating surfaces. Then inspect the mating surfaces for damage. Remove all sealer material from blind threaded holes; it can cause inaccurate bolt torque. Spray the mating surfaces with aerosol parts cleaner, and then wipe with a lint-free cloth. Because gasket surfaces must be dry and oil-free for the sealant to adhere, be thorough when cleaning and drying the parts.

Apply RTV sealant in a continuous bead 2-3 mm (0.08-0.12 in.) thick. Circle all the fastener holes unless otherwise specified. Do not allow any sealant to enter these holes. Assemble and tighten the fasteners to the specified torque within the time frame recommended by the RTV sealant manufacturer.

Gasket Remover

Aerosol gasket remover can help remove stubborn gaskets. This product can speed up the removal process and prevent damage to the mating surface when scraping gaskets. Most of these types of products are very caustic. Follow the gasket remover manufacturer's instructions for use. Note the following:

1. Depending on a gaskets thickness and other factors, the gasket remover will not always penetrate completely through the gasket with a single application. This becomes evident when attempting to remove the gasket as the gasket scraper may only remove an upper portion of the gasket. When this happens, reapply the gasket remover and repeat until the gasket can be easily removed. Do not force the tool through the gasket as it may damage the gasket surface. Damaged sealing surfaces leak.

2. To apply an aerosol gasket remover to the gasket surface when the engine is assembled, spray a small amount of gasket remover into a small container and then apply with an acid brush to the engine gasket surfaces. Block off engine areas as necessary with a paper towel.

3. Make sure and remove all gasket material and gasket remover from the engine and cover surfaces.

Threadlocking Compound

> *CAUTION*
> *Threadlocking compounds are anaerobic and damage most plastic parts and surfaces. Use caution when using these products in areas where plastic components are located.*

A threadlocking compound is a fluid applied to the threads of fasteners. After tightening the fastener, the fluid dries and becomes a solid filler between the threads. This makes it difficult for the fastener to work loose from vibra-

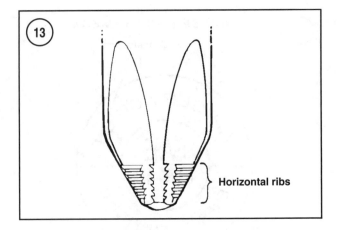

tion or heat expansion and contraction. Some threadlocking compounds also provide a seal against fluid leaks.

Before applying threadlocking compound, remove any old compound from both thread areas and clean them with aerosol parts cleaner. Use the compound sparingly. Excess fluid can run into adjoining parts.

Threadlocking compounds are available in various strengths, temperatures and repair applications.

TOOLS

Most of the procedures in this manual can be carried out with hand tools and test equipment familiar to the home mechanic. Always use the correct tools for the job. Keep tools organized and clean and store them in a tool chest with related tools organized together.

Quality tools are essential. The best are constructed of high-strength alloy steel. These tools are light, easy-to-use and resistant to wear. Their working surfaces are devoid of sharp edges and the tools are carefully polished. They have an easy-to-clean finish and are comfortable to use. Quality tools are a good investment.

When purchasing tools to perform the procedures covered in this manual, consider the tool's potential frequency of use. If a tool kit is just now being started, consider purchasing a tool set from a quality tool supplier. These sets are available in many tool combinations and offer substantial savings when compared to individually purchased tools. As work experience grows and tasks become more complicated, specialized tools can be added.

Some of the procedures in this manual specify special tools. In most cases, the tool is illustrated in use. Well-equipped mechanics may be able to substitute similar tools or fabricate a suitable replacement. However, in some cases, the specialized equipment or expertise may make it impractical for the home mechanic to attempt the procedure. When necessary, such operations are identified in the text with the recommendation to have a dealership or specialist perform the task. It may be less expensive to have a professional perform these jobs, especially when considering the cost of the equipment.

The manufacturer's part number is provided for many of the tools mentioned in this manual. These part numbers are

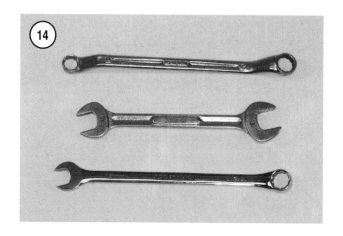

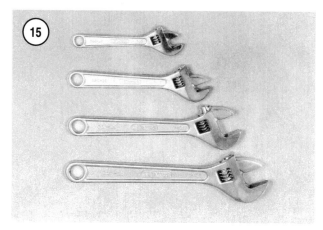

found on the driving faces or flutes of the screwdrivers tip (**Figure 13**). ACR Phillips II screwdrivers were designed as part of a manufacturing drive system to be used with ACR Phillips II screws, but they work well on all common Phillips screws. A number of tool companies offer ACR Phillips II screwdrivers in different tip sizes and interchangeable bits to fit screwdriver bit holders.

Another way to prevent camout and increase the grip of a Phillips screwdriver is to apply valve grinding compound or Permatex Screw & Socket Gripper onto the screwdriver tip. After loosening/tightening the screw, clean the screw recess to prevent possible contamination.

Wrenches

Open-end, box-end and combination wrenches (**Figure 14**) are available in a variety of types and sizes.

The number stamped on the wrench refers to the distance between the work areas. This size must match the size of the fastener head.

The box-end wrench is an excellent tool because it grips the fastener on all sides. This reduces the chance of the tool slipping. The box-end wrench is designed with either a 6- or 12-point opening. For stubborn or damaged fasteners, the 6-point provides superior holding ability by contacting the fastener across a wider area at all six edges. For general use, the 12-point works well. It allows the wrench to be removed and re-installed without moving the handle over such a wide arc.

An open-end wrench is fast and works best in areas with limited overhead access. It contacts the fastener at only two points, and is subject to slipping under heavy force or if the tool or fastener is worn. A box-end wrench is preferred in most instances, especially when breaking loose and applying the final tightness to a fastener.

The combination wrench has a box-end on one end, and an open-end on the other. This combination makes it a convenient tool.

Adjustable Wrenches

An adjustable wrench (**Figure 15**) can fit nearly any nut or bolt head that has clear access around its entire perimeter.

However, adjustable wrenches contact the fastener at only two points, which makes them more subject to slipping off the fastener. One jaw is adjustable and may loosen, which increases this possibility. Make certain the solid jaw is the one transmitting the force.

However, adjustable wrenches are typically used to prevent a large nut or bolt from turning while the other end is being loosened or tightened with a box-end or socket wrench.

Socket Wrenches, Ratchets and Handles

WARNING
Do not use hand sockets with air or impact tools; they may shatter and cause injury.

correct at the time of original publication. The publisher cannot guarantee the part number of the tools in this manual will be available in the future.

Screwdrivers

The two basic types of screwdrivers are the slotted tip (flat blade) and the Phillips tip. These are available in sets that often include an assortment of tip sizes and shaft lengths.

As with all tools, use the correct screwdriver. Make sure the size of the tip conforms to the size and shape of the fastener. Use them only for driving screws. Never use a screwdriver for prying or chiseling. Repair or replace worn or damaged screwdrivers. A worn tip may damage the fastener, making it difficult to remove.

Phillips-head screws are often damaged by incorrectly fitting screwdrivers. Quality Phillips screwdrivers are manufactured with their crosshead tip machined to Phillips Screw Company specifications. Poor quality or damaged Phillips screwdrivers can back out and round over the screw head (camout). Compounding the problem of using poor quality screwdrivers are Phillips-head screws made from weak or soft materials and screws initially installed with air tools.

The best type of screwdriver to use on Phillips screws is the ACR Phillips II screwdriver, patented by the Phillips Screw Company. ACR stands for the horizontal anti-camout ribs

Always wear eye protection when using impact or air tools.

Sockets that attach to a ratchet handle (**Figure 16**) are available with 6-point (A, **Figure 17**) or 12-point (B) openings and different drive sizes. The drive size indicates the size of the square hole that accepts the ratchet handle. The number stamped on the socket is the size of the work area and must match the fastener head.

As with wrenches, a 6-point socket provides superior-holding ability, while a 12-point socket needs to be moved only half as far to reposition it on the fastener.

Sockets are designated for either hand or impact use. Impact sockets are made of a thicker material for more durability. Compare the size and wall thickness of a 19-mm hand socket (A, **Figure 18**) and the 19-mm impact socket (B). Use impact sockets when using an impact driver or air tool. Use hand sockets with hand-driven attachments.

Various handles are available for sockets. The speed handle is used for fast operation. Flexible ratchet heads in varying lengths allow the socket to be turned with varying force and at odd angles. Extension bars allow the socket setup to reach difficult areas. The ratchet is the most versatile. It allows the user to install or remove the nut without removing the socket.

Sockets combined with any number of drivers make them undoubtedly the fastest, safest and most convenient tool for fastener removal and installation.

Impact Driver

WARNING
Do not use hand sockets with air or impact tools because they may shatter and cause injury. Always wear eye protection when using impact or air tools.

An impact driver provides extra force for removing fasteners by converting the impact of a hammer into a turning motion. This makes it possible to remove stubborn fasteners without damaging them. Impact drivers and interchangeable bits (**Figure 19**) are available from most tool suppliers. When using a socket with an impact driver, make sure the socket is designed for impact use. Refer to *Socket Wrenches, Ratchets and Handles* in this section.

Allen Wrenches

Allen, or setscrew wrenches, (**Figure 20**) are used on fasteners with hexagonal recesses in the fastener head. These wrenches are available in a L-shaped bar, socket and T-handle types. Allen bolts are sometimes called socket bolts.

Torx Fasteners

A Torx fastener head is a 6-point star-shaped pattern. Torx fasteners are identified with a T (internal) or E (exter-

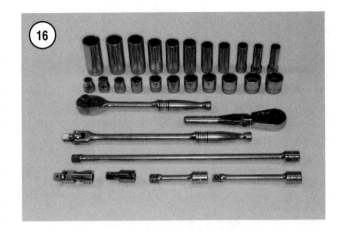

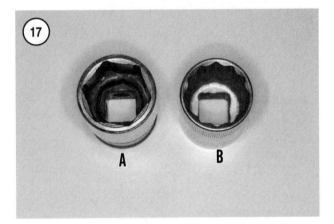

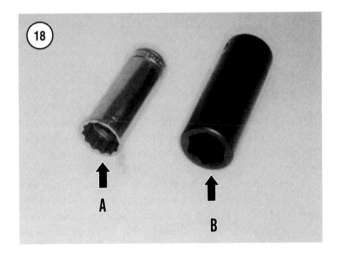

nal) and a number indicating their drive size. For example, T25 or E10. Torx drivers (A, **Figure 21**) are available in L-shaped bars, sockets and T-handles. Internal tamper-resistant Torx fasteners are also used and have a round shaft in the center of the fastener head. Internal tamper-resistance Torx fasteners require a Torx bit with a hole in the center of the bit (B, **Figure 21**).

Torque Wrenches

A torque wrench (**Figure 22**) is used with a socket, torque adapter or similar extension to tighten a fastener to

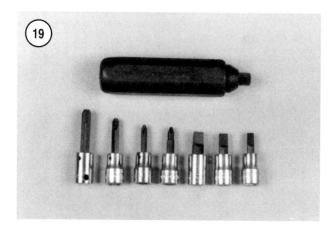

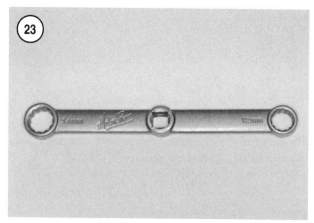

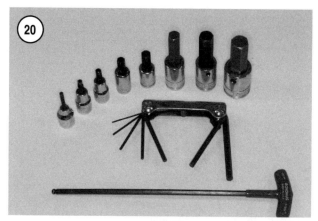

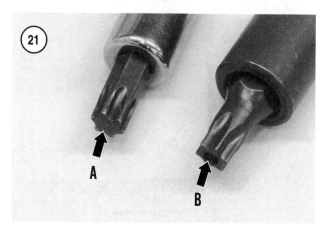

A

B

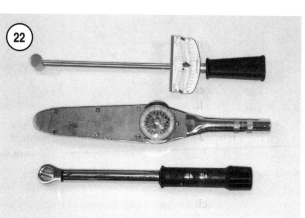

a measured torque. Torque wrenches come in several drive sizes (1/4, 3/8, 1/2 and 3/4) and have various methods of reading the torque value. The drive size indicates the size of the square drive that accepts the socket, adapter or extension. Common methods of reading the torque value are the reflecting beam, the dial indicator and the audible click. When choosing a torque wrench, consider the torque range, drive size and accuracy. The torque specifications in this manual provide an indication of the range required. A torque wrench is a precision tool that must be properly cared for to remain accurate. Store torque wrenches in cases or separate padded drawers within a toolbox. Follow the manufacturer's instructions for their care and calibration.

Torque Adapters

Torque adapters (**Figure 23**), or extensions, extend or reduce the reach of a torque wrench. Specific adapters are required to perform some of the procedures in this manual. These are available from the vehicle manufacturer, aftermarket tool suppliers, or can be fabricated to suit a specific purpose.

If a torque adapter changes the effective lever length, the torque reading on the wrench will not equal the actual torque applied to the fastener. It is necessary to recalibrate the torque setting on the wrench to compensate for the change of lever length. When a torque adapter is used at a right angle to the drive head, calibration is not required because the lever length has not changed.

To recalculate a torque reading when using a torque adapter, use the following formula, and refer to **Figure 24**.

$$TW = \frac{TA \times L}{L + A}$$

TW is the torque setting or dial reading on the wrench.

TA is the torque specification and the actual amount of torque that will be applied to the fastener.

A is the amount the adapter increases (or in some cases reduces) the effective lever length as measured along the centerline of the torque wrench.

L is the lever length of the wrench as measured from the center of the drive to the center of the grip.

The effective lever length is the sum of L and A.

Example:
TA = 20 ft.-lb.
A = 3 in.
L = 14 in.
$$TW = \frac{20 \times 14}{14 + 3} = \frac{280}{17} = 16.5 \text{ ft.-lb.}$$

In this example, the torque wrench would be set to the recalculated torque value (TW = 16.5 ft.-lb.). When using a beam-type wrench, tighten the fastener until the pointer aligns with 16.5 ft.-lb. In this example, although the torque wrench is pre set to 16.5 ft.-lb., the actual torque is 20 ft.-lb.

Pliers

Pliers come in a wide range of types and sizes. Pliers are useful for holding, cutting, bending, and crimping. Do not use them to turn fasteners unless they are designed to do so. **Figure 25** and **Figure 26** show several types of pliers. Each design has a specialized function. Slip-joint pliers are general-purpose pliers used for gripping and bending. Diagonal cutting pliers are needed to cut wire and can be used to remove cotter pins. Needlenose pliers are used to hold or bend small objects. Locking pliers (**Figure 26**) hold objects tightly. They have many uses ranging from holding two parts together, to gripping the end of a broken stud. Use caution when using locking pliers; the sharp jaws will damage the objects they hold.

Snap Ring Pliers

> *WARNING*
> *Snap rings can slip and fly off when removing and installing them. In addition, the snap ring pliers tips may break. Always wear eye protection when using snap ring pliers.*

Snap ring pliers (**Figure 27**) are specialized pliers with tips that fit into the ends of snap rings to remove and install them.

Snap ring pliers are available with a fixed action (either internal or external) or are convertible (one tool works on both internal and external snap rings). They may have fixed tips or interchangeable ones of various sizes and angles. For general use, select convertible type pliers with interchangeable tips.

Hammers

> *WARNING*
> *Always wear eye protection when using hammers. Make sure the hammer face is in good condition and the handle is not cracked. Select the correct hammer for the job and make sure to strike the object squarely. Do not use the handle or the side of the hammer to strike an object.*

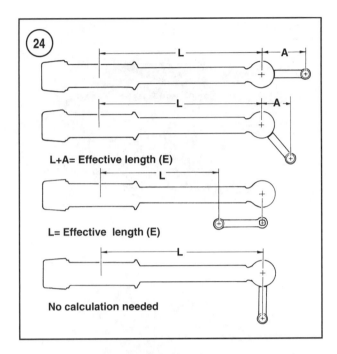

L+A= Effective length (E)

L= Effective length (E)

No calculation needed

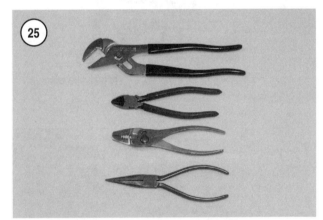

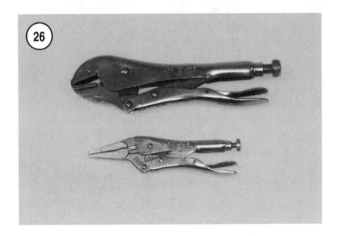

Various types of hammers are available to fit a number of applications. A ball-peen hammer is used to strike another tool, such as a punch or chisel. Soft-faced hammers are required when a metal object must be struck without damaging it. Never use a metal-faced hammer on engine and suspension components; damage will occur in most cases.

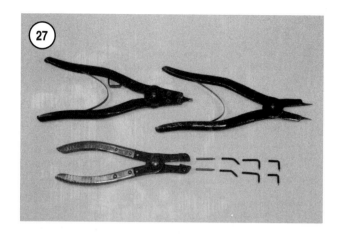

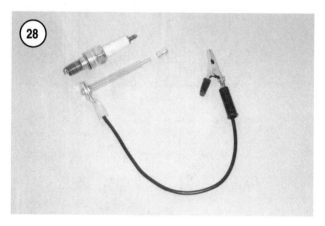

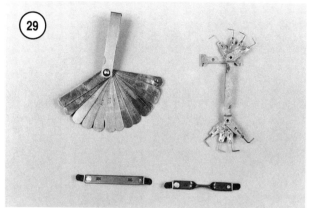

tool and cause inaccurate results. If any measurement is questionable, verify the measurement using another tool. A standard gauge is usually provided with measuring tools to check accuracy and calibrate the tool if necessary.

Accurate measurements are only possible if the mechanic possesses a feel for using the tool. Heavy-handed use of measuring tools produces less accurate results. Hold the tool gently by the fingertips so the point at which the tool contacts the object is easily felt. This feel for the equipment will produce more accurate measurements and reduce the risk of damaging the tool or component. Refer to the following sections for specific measuring tools.

Ignition Grounding Tool

Some test procedures in this manual require kicking the engine over without starting it. Do not remove the spark plug cap and crank the engine without grounding the plug cap. Doing so will damage the ignition system.

An effective way to ground the system is to fabricate the tool shown in **Figure 28** from a No. 6 screw, two washers and a length of wire with an alligator clip soldered on one end. To use the tool, insert it into the spark plug cap and attach the alligator clip to a known engine ground.

This tool is safer than a spark plug or spark tester because there is no spark firing across the end of the plug/tester to potentially ignite fuel vapor spraying from an open spark plug hole or leaking fuel component.

MEASURING TOOLS

The ability to accurately measure components is essential to successfully service many components. Equipment is manufactured to close tolerances, and obtaining consistently accurate measurements is essential.

Each type of measuring instrument is designed to measure a dimension with a certain degree of accuracy and within a certain range. When selecting the measuring tool, make sure it is applicable to the task.

As with all tools, measuring tools provide the best results if cared for properly. Improper use can damage the

Feeler Gauge

The feeler, or thickness gauge (**Figure 29**), is used for measuring the distance between two surfaces.

A feeler gauge set consists of an assortment of steel strips of graduated thicknesses. Each blade is marked with its thickness. Blades can be of various lengths and angles for different procedures.

A common use for a feeler gauge is to measure valve clearance. Wire (round) type gauges are used to measure spark plug gap.

Calipers

Calipers (**Figure 30**) are excellent tools for obtaining inside, outside and depth measurements. Although not as precise as a micrometer, they allow reasonable precision, typically to within 0.05 mm (0.001 in.). Most calipers have a range up to 150 mm (6 in.).

Calipers are available in dial, vernier or digital versions. Dial calipers have a dial readout that provides convenient reading. Vernier calipers have marked scales that must be compared to determine the measurement. The digital caliper uses a LCD to show the measurement.

Properly maintain the measuring surfaces of the caliper. There must not be any dirt or burrs between the tool and the object being measured. Never force the caliper closed around an object; close the caliper around the highest point so it can be removed with a slight drag. Some calipers re-

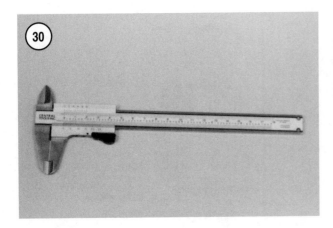

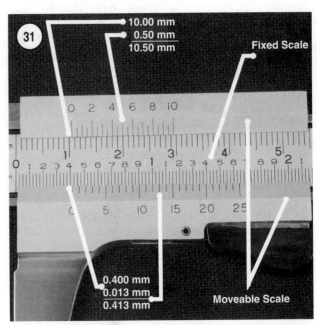

quire calibration. Always refer to the manufacturer's instructions when using a new or unfamiliar caliper.

To read a vernier caliper, refer to **Figure 31**. The fixed scale is marked in 1 mm increments. Ten individual lines on the fixed scale equal 1 cm. The moveable scale is marked in 0.05 mm (hundredth) increments. To obtain a reading, establish the first number by the location of the 0 line on the moveable scale in relation to the first line to the left on the fixed scale. In this example, the number is 10 mm. To determine the next number, note which of the lines on the movable scale align with a mark on the fixed scale. A number of lines will seem close, but only one will align exactly. In this case, 0.50 mm is the reading to add to the first number. The result of adding 10 mm and 0.50 mm is a measurement of 10.50 mm.

Micrometers

A micrometer (**Figure 32**) is an instrument designed for linear measurement using the decimal divisions of the inch or meter. While there are many types and styles of micrometers, most of the procedures in this manual call for an outside micrometer. The outside micrometer is used to measure the outside diameter of cylindrical forms and the thicknesses of materials.

A micrometer's size indicates the minimum and maximum size of a part that it can measure. The usual sizes are 0-25 mm (0-1 in.), 25-50 mm (1-2 in.), 50-75 mm (2-3 in.) and 75-100 mm (3-4 in.).

Micrometers that cover a wider range of measurements are available. These use a large frame with interchangeable anvils of various lengths. This type of micrometer offers a cost savings; however, its overall size may make it less convenient.

Adjustment

Before using a micrometer, check its adjustment as follows.

1. Clean the anvil and spindle faces.

2A. To check a 0-1 in. or 0-25 mm micrometer:

   a. Turn the thimble until the spindle contacts the anvil. If the micrometer has a ratchet stop, use it to ensure the proper amount of pressure is applied.

   b. If the adjustment is correct, the 0 mark on the thimble will align exactly with the 0 mark on the sleeve line. If the marks do not align, the micrometer is out of adjustment.

   c. Follow the manufacturer's instructions to adjust the micrometer.

2B. To check a micrometer larger than 1 in. or 25 mm, use the standard gauge supplied by the manufacturer. A standard gauge is a steel block, disc or rod that is machined to an exact size.

   a. Place the standard gauge between the spindle and anvil and measure its outside diameter or length. If the micrometer has a ratchet stop, use it to ensure the proper amount of pressure is applied.

   b. If the adjustment is correct, the 0 mark on the thimble will align exactly with the 0 mark on the sleeve line. If the marks do not align, the micrometer is out of adjustment.

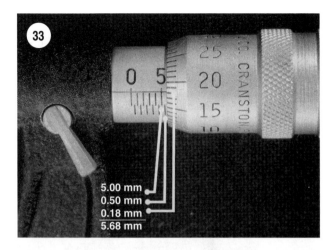

5.00 mm
0.50 mm
0.18 mm
5.68 mm

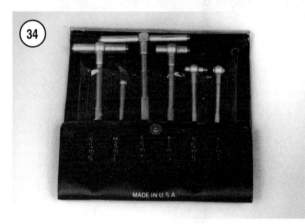

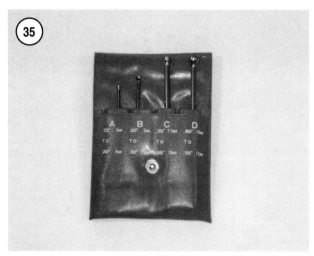

c. Follow the manufacturer's instructions to adjust the micrometer.

Care

Micrometers are precision instruments. They must be used and maintained with great care. Note the following:
1. Store micrometers in protective cases or separate padded drawers in a toolbox.
2. When in storage, make sure the spindle and anvil faces do not contact each other or another object. If they do, temperature changes and corrosion may damage the contact faces.
3. Do not clean a micrometer with compressed air. Dirt forced into the tool causes wear.
4. Lubricate micrometers to prevent corrosion.

Reading

When reading a micrometer, numbers are taken from different scales and added together.

For accurate results, properly maintain the measuring surfaces of the micrometer. There cannot be any dirt or burrs between the tool and the measured object. Never force the micrometer closed around an object. Close the micrometer around the highest point so it can be removed with a slight drag.

The standard metric micrometer is accurate to one one-hundredth of a millimeter (0.01 mm). The sleeve line is graduated in millimeter and half millimeter increments. The marks on the upper half of the sleeve line equal 1.00 mm. Each fifth mark above the sleeve line is identified with a number. The number sequence depends on the size of the micrometer. A 0-25 mm micrometer, for example, will have sleeve marks numbered 0 through 25 in 5 mm increments. This numbering sequence continues with larger micrometers. On all metric micrometers, each mark on the lower half of the sleeve equals 0.50 mm.

The tapered end of the thimble has 50 lines marked around it. Each mark equals 0.01 mm. One complete turn of the thimble aligns its 0 mark with the first line on the lower half of the sleeve line, or 0.50 mm.

When reading a metric micrometer, add the number of millimeters and half-millimeters on the sleeve line to the number of one one-hundredth millimeters on the thimble. Perform the following steps while referring to **Figure 33**.
1. Read the upper half of the sleeve line and count the number of lines visible. Each upper line equals 1 mm.
2. See if the half-millimeter line is visible on the lower sleeve line. If so, add 0.50 mm to the reading in Step 1.
3. Read the thimble mark that aligns with the sleeve line. Each thimble mark equals 0.01 mm.
4. If a thimble mark does not align exactly with the sleeve line, estimate the amount between the lines. For accurate readings in two-thousandths of a millimeter (0.002 mm), use a metric vernier micrometer.
5. Add the readings from Steps 1-4.

Telescoping and Small Hole Gauges

Use telescoping gauges (**Figure 34**) and small hole gauges (**Figure 35**) to measure bores. Neither gauge has a scale for direct readings. An outside micrometer must be used to determine the reading.

To use a telescoping gauge, select the correct size gauge for the bore. Compress the moveable post and carefully insert the gauge into the bore. Move the gauge in the bore to make sure it is centered. Tighten the knurled end of the

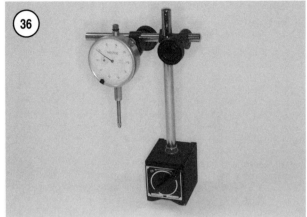

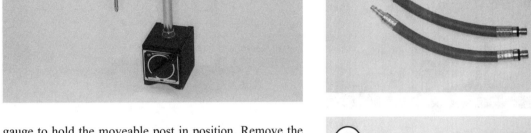

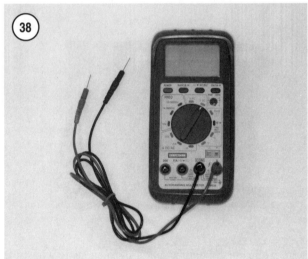

gauge to hold the moveable post in position. Remove the gauge and measure the length of the posts. Telescoping gauges are typically used to measure cylinder bores.

To use a small hole gauge, select the correct size gauge for the bore. Insert the gauge into the bore. Tighten the knurled end of the gauge to carefully expand the gauge fingers to the limit within the bore. Do not overtighten the gauge; there is no built-in release. Excessive tightening can damage the bore surface and tool. Remove the gauge and measure the outside dimension with a micrometer (**Figure 32**). Small hole gauges are typically used to measure valve guides.

Dial Indicator

A dial indicator (**Figure 36**) is a gauge with a dial face and needle used to measure variations in dimensions and movements. Measuring brake rotor runout is a typical use for a dial indicator.

Dial indicators are available in various ranges and graduations and with three types of mounting bases: magnetic, clamp or screw-in stud.

Cylinder Bore Gauge

A cylinder bore gauge is similar to a dial indicator. These typically consist of a dial indicator, handle and different length adapters (anvils) to fit the gauge to various bore sizes. The bore gauge is used to measure bore size, taper and out-of-round. When using a bore gauge, follow the manufacturer's instructions.

Compression Gauge

A compression gauge (**Figure 37**) measures combustion chamber (cylinder) pressure, usually in psi or kg/cm^2. The gauge adapter is either inserted and held in place or screwed into the spark plug hole to obtain the reading. Disable the engine so it will not start and hold the throttle in the wide-open position when performing a compression test. An engine that does not have adequate compression cannot be properly tuned. Refer to Chapter Three.

Multimeter

A multimeter (**Figure 38**) is an essential tool for electrical system diagnosis. The voltage function indicates the voltage applied or available to various electrical components. The ohmmeter function tests circuits for continuity, or lack of continuity, and measures the resistance of a circuit.

Some manufacturers' specifications for electrical components are based on results using a specific test meter. Results may vary if using a meter not recommend by the manufacturer. Such requirements are noted when applicable.

Ohmmeter (analog) calibration

Each time an analog ohmmeter is used or the scale is changed, the ohmmeter must be calibrated.

Digital ohmmeters do not require calibration.

1. Make sure the meter battery is in good condition.
2. Make sure the meter probes are in good condition.
3. Touch the two probes together and observe the needle location on the ohms scale. The needle must align with the 0 mark to obtain accurate measurements.
4. If necessary, rotate the meter ohms adjust knob until the needle and 0 mark align.

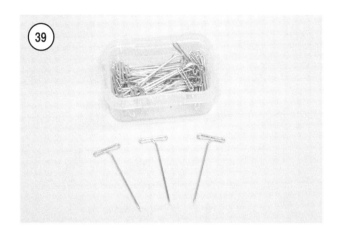

Back-probe pins

Many voltage and resistance tests are performed with the component connectors connected and locked together. On some connectors, the wires entering the connectors are protected by seals. To avoid damaging the connectors, wires and seals during testing, note the following:

1. Use test leads equipped with back-probe pins. These leads ends are smaller than typical test leads and mount onto standard meter leads. Sharpen the lead ends if blunt.

2. If back probe pins are not available, use T-pins (**Figure 39**) available from fabric and craft stores. These pins are sharp enough to push through the connector seals and the T-shaped head makes an ideal connection point for alligator test leads.

> *NOTE*
> *Back-probe pins referred to in this manual refers to both dedicated back probe-pins and T-pins.*

3. To use a back-probe pin when a connector is not disconnected from a component or another connector, slide it along side the wire and insert it into the seal from behind the connector until it contacts the terminal inside the connector. Make sure not to short circuit the pin by inserting it through two wires.

4. After completing the test, remove the back-probe pin and cover the pin hole in the seal with silicone sealant.

5. Back-probe pins can also be inserted into the front of a connector to contact the terminals when the connector halves have been disconnected for test purposes (**Figure 40**).

ELECTRICAL SYSTEM FUNDAMENTALS

A thorough study of the many types of electrical systems used in today's vehicles is beyond the scope of this manual. However, a basic understanding of voltage, resistance and amperage is necessary to perform diagnostic tests.

Refer to Chapter Two for troubleshooting.

Voltage

Voltage is the electrical potential or pressure in an electrical circuit and is expressed in volts. The more pressure (voltage) in a circuit, the more work can be performed.

Direct current (DC) voltage means the electricity flows in one direction. All circuits powered by a battery are DC circuits.

Alternating current (AC) means the electricity flows in one direction momentarily and then switches to the opposite direction. Alternator output is an example of AC voltage. This voltage must be changed or rectified to direct current to operate in a battery powered system.

Resistance

Resistance is the opposition to the flow of electricity within a circuit or component and is measured in ohms. Resistance causes a reduction in available current and voltage.

Resistance is measured in an inactive circuit with an ohmmeter. The ohmmeter sends a small amount of current into the circuit and measures how difficult it is to push the current through the circuit.

An ohmmeter, although useful, is not always a good indicator of a circuit's actual ability under operating conditions. This is due to the low voltage (6-9 volts) that the meter uses to test the circuit. The voltage in an ignition coil secondary winding can be several thousand volts. Such high voltage can cause the coil to malfunction, even though it tests acceptable during a resistance test.

Resistance generally increases with temperature. Perform all testing with the component or circuit at room temperature. Resistance tests performed at high temperatures may indicate false resistance readings and cause the unnecessary replacement of a component.

Amperage

Amperage is the unit of measure for the amount of current within a circuit. Current is the actual flow of electricity. The higher the current, the more work can be performed up to a given point. If the current flow exceeds the circuit or component capacity, the system will be damaged.

SERVICE METHODS

Many of the procedures in this manual are straightforward and can be performed by anyone reasonably competent with tools. However, consider previous experience carefully before performing any operation involving complicated procedures.

1. Front, in this manual, refers to the front of the vehicle. The front of any component is the end closest to the front of the vehicle. The left and right sides refer to the position of the parts as viewed by the driver sitting on the seat facing forward.

2. When servicing the vehicle, park it on a level surface and set the parking brake. If necessary, block the wheels so the vehicle cannot roll.

3. Label all parts for location and mark all mating parts for position. If possible, photograph or draw the number and thickness of any shim as it is removed. Identify parts by placing them in sealed and labeled plastic bags. It is possible for carefully laid out parts to become disturbed, making it difficult to reassemble the components correctly without a diagram.

4. Label disconnected wires and connectors. Do not rely on memory alone. Note how they are routed and the location of all clips and wire ties.

5. Protect finished surfaces from physical damage or corrosion. Keep gasoline and other chemicals off painted surfaces.

6. Use penetrating oil on frozen or tight bolts. Avoid using heat where possible. Heat can warp, melt or affect the temper of parts. Heat also damages the finish of paint and plastics. Refer to *Heating Components* in this section.

7. When a part is a press fit or requires a special tool for removal, the information or type of tool is identified in the text. Otherwise, if a part is difficult to remove or install, determine the cause before proceeding.

8. To prevent objects or debris from falling into the engine, cover all openings.

9. Read each procedure thoroughly and compare the figures to the actual components before starting the procedure. Perform the procedure in sequence.

10. Recommendations are occasionally made to refer service to a dealership or specialist. In these cases, the work can be performed more economically by the specialist than by the home mechanic.

11. The term *replace* means to discard a defective part and replace it with a new part. *Overhaul* means to remove, disassemble, inspect, measure, repair and/or replace parts as required to recondition an assembly.

12. Some operations require the use of a hydraulic press. If a press is not available, have these operations performed by a shop equipped with the necessary equipment. Do not use makeshift equipment that may damage the vehicle.

13. Do not direct high-pressure water at the steering assembly, fuel hoses, wheel bearings, suspension and electrical components. The water forces the grease out of the bearings and could damage the seals.

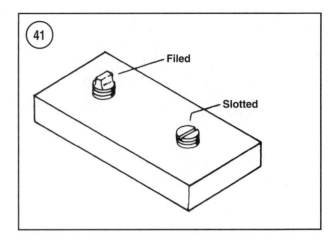

14. Repairs are much faster and easier if the vehicle is clean before starting work. Degrease the vehicle with a commercial degreaser; follow the directions on the container for the best results. Clean all parts with cleaning solvent. Refer to *Cleaning Parts* in *Safety* in this chapter.

15. If special tools are required, have them available before starting the procedure. When special tools are required, they will be described at the beginning of the procedure.

16. Make sure all shims and washers are reinstalled in the same location and position.

17. Whenever rotating parts contact a stationary part, look for a shim or washer.

18. Use new gaskets if there is any doubt about the condition of old ones.

19. If self-locking fasteners are used, replace them. Do not install standard fasteners in place of self-locking ones.

20. Use grease to hold small parts in place if they tend to fall out during assembly. Do not apply grease to electrical or brake components.

Heating Components

WARNING
Wear protective gloves to prevent burns and injury when heating parts.

CAUTION
Do not use a welding torch when heating parts. A welding torch applies excessive heat to a small area very quickly, which can damage parts.

A heat gun or propane torch is required to disassemble, assemble, remove and install many parts and components in this manual. Read the safety and operating information supplied by the manufacturer of the heat gun or propane torch while also noting the following:

1. The work area should be clean and dry. Remove all combustible components and materials from the work area. Wipe up all grease, oil and other fluids from parts. Check for leaking or damaged fuel system components. Repair or remove these parts before beginning work.

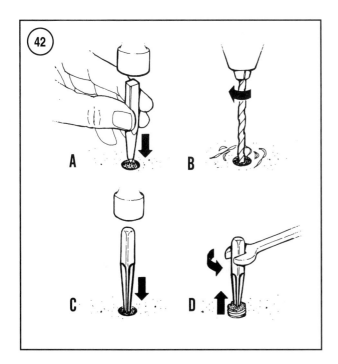

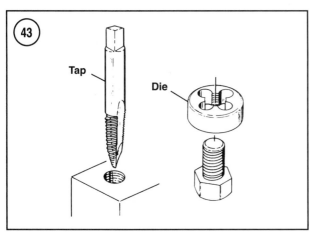

hot enough. Keep the heat in motion to prevent overheating.

Removing Frozen Fasteners

If a fastener cannot be removed, several methods may be used to loosen it. First, liberally apply penetrating oil, and let it penetrate for 10-15 minutes. Rap the fastener several times with a small hammer. Do not hit it hard enough to cause damage. Reapply the penetrating oil if necessary.

For frozen screws, apply penetrating oil as described, and then insert a screwdriver in the slot and rap the top of the screwdriver with a hammer. This loosens the rust so the screw can be removed in the normal way. If the screw head is too damaged to use this method, grip the head with locking pliers and twist it out.

If heat is required, refer to *Heating Components* in this section.

Removing Broken Fasteners

If the head breaks off a screw or bolt, several methods are available for removing the remaining portion. If a large portion of the remainder projects out, try gripping it with locking pliers. If the projecting portion is too small, file it to fit a wrench or cut a slot in it to fit a screwdriver (**Figure 41**).

If the head breaks off flush, use a screw extractor. To do this, center punch the exact center of the screw or bolt (A, **Figure 42**), and then drill a small hole in the screw (B) and tap the extractor into the hole (C). Back the screw out with a wrench on the extractor (D, **Figure 42**).

Repairing Damaged Threads

Occasionally, threads are stripped through carelessness or impact damage. Often the threads can be repaired by running a tap (for internal threads on nuts) or die (for external threads on bolts) through the threads (**Figure 43**). To clean or repair spark plug threads, use a spark plug tap.

If an internal thread is damaged, it may be necessary to install a Helicoil or some other type of thread insert. Follow the manufacturer's instructions when installing its insert.

Stud Removal/Installation

A stud removal tool (**Figure 44**) is available from most tool suppliers. This tool makes the removal and installation of studs easier. If one is not available and the threads on the stud are not damaged, thread two nuts onto the stud and tighten them against each other (**Figure 45**). Remove the stud by turning the lower nut.

1. Measure the height of the stud above the surface.
2. Thread the stud removal tool onto the stud and tighten it, or thread two nuts onto the stud.
3. Remove the stud by turning the stud remover or the lower nut.

2. Never use a flame near the battery, fuel tank, fuel lines or other flammable materials.
3. When using a heat gun, remember that the temperature can be in excess of 540° C (1000° F).
4. Have a fire extinguisher near the job.
5. Always wear protective goggles and gloves when heating parts.
6. Before heating a part installed on the vehicle, check areas around the part and those hidden that could be damaged or possibly ignite. Do not heat surfaces than can be damaged by heat. Shield materials near the part or area to be heated. For example, cables and wiring harnesses.
7. Before heating a part, read the entire procedure to make sure the required tools are available. This allows quick work while the part is at its optimum temperature.
8. Before heating parts, consider the possible effects. To avoid damaging a part, monitor the temperature with heat sticks or an infrared thermometer, if possible. Another way, though not as accurate, is to place tiny drops of water on the part. When the water starts to sizzle, the part is usually

4. Remove any threadlocking compounding compound from the threaded hole. Clean the threads with an aerosol parts cleaner.

5. Install the stud removal tool onto the new stud, or thread two nuts onto the stud.

6. Apply threadlocking compounding compound to the threads of the stud.

7. Install the stud and tighten with the stud removal tool or the top nut.

8. Install the stud to the height noted in Step 1 or its torque specification.

9. Remove the stud removal tool or the two nuts.

Hose Removal/Installation

When removing a stubborn hose, do not exert excessive force on the hose or fitting. Remove the hose clamp and carefully insert a small screwdriver or pick tool between the fitting and hose. Apply a spray lubricant under the hose and carefully twist the hose off the fitting. Clean the fitting of any corrosion or rubber hose material with a wire brush. Clean the inside of the hose thoroughly. Do not use any lubricant when installing the hose (new or old). The lubricant may allow the hose to come off the fitting, even with the clamp secure.

Bearings

Bearings are precision parts and must be maintained with proper lubrication and maintenance. If a bearing is damaged, replace it immediately. When installing a new bearing, make sure to prevent damaging it. Bearing replacement procedures are included in the individual chapters where applicable; however, use the following sections as a guideline.

Unless otherwise specified, install bearings with the manufacturer's mark or number facing outward.

Removal

While bearings are normally removed only when damaged, there may be times when it is necessary to remove a bearing that is in good condition. However, improper bearing removal will damage the bearing and maybe the shaft or case half. Note the following when removing bearings:

1. Before removing the bearings, note the following:
   a. Refer to the bearing removal/installation procedure in the appropriate chapter for any special instructions.
   b. Remove any seals that interfere with bearing removal. Refer to *Seal Removal/Installation* in this section.
   c. When removing more than one bearing, identify the bearings before removing them. Refer to the bearing manufacturer's numbers on the bearing.
   d. Note and record the direction in which the bearing numbers face for proper installation.
   e. Remove any set plates or bearing retainers before removing the bearings.

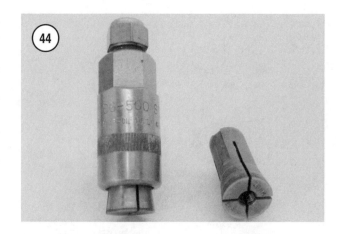

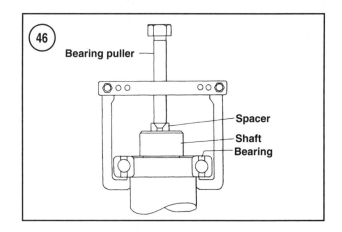

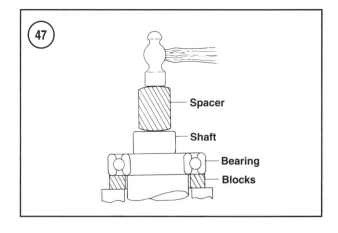

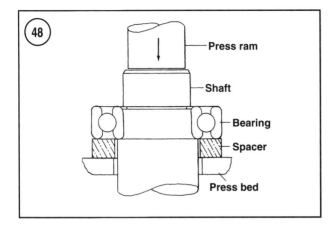

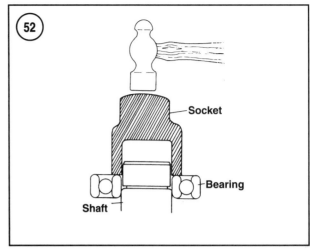

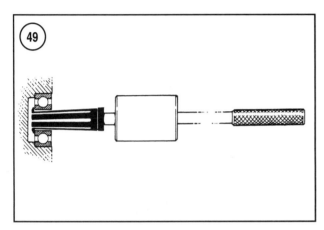

2. When using a puller to remove a bearing from a shaft, make sure the shaft is not damaged. Always place a piece of metal between the end of the shaft and the puller screw. In addition, place the puller arms next to the inner bearing race. Refer to **Figure 46**.

3. When using a hammer to remove a bearing from a shaft, do not strike the hammer directly against the shaft. Instead, use a brass or aluminum rod between the hammer and shaft (**Figure 47**) and make sure to support both bearing races with wooden blocks as shown.

4. The ideal method of bearing removal is with a hydraulic press. Note the following when using a press:

  a. Always support the inner and outer bearing races with a suitable size spacer (**Figure 48**). If only the outer race is supported, pressure applied against the balls and/or the inner race will damage them.

  b. Always make sure the press arm (**Figure 48**) aligns with the center of the shaft. If the arm is not centered, it may damage the bearing and/or shaft.

  c. The moment the shaft is free of the bearing, it will drop to the floor. Secure or hold the shaft to prevent it from falling.

  d. When removing bearings from a housing, support the housing with wooden blocks to prevent damage to gasket surfaces.

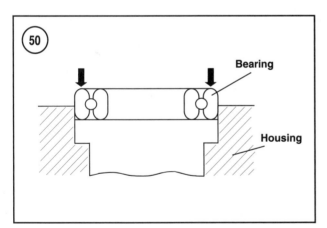

5. Use a blind bearing puller to remove bearings installed in blind holes (**Figure 49**).

Installation

1. When installing a bearing in a housing, apply pressure to the *outer* bearing race (**Figure 50**). When installing a bearing on a shaft, apply pressure to the *inner* bearing race (**Figure 51**).

2. When installing a bearing as described in Step 1, a driver is required. Never strike the bearing directly with a hammer or the bearing will be damaged. When installing a bearing, use a piece of pipe or a driver with a diameter that matches the bearing race. (**Figure 52**) shows the correct way to use a driver and hammer to install a bearing on a shaft.

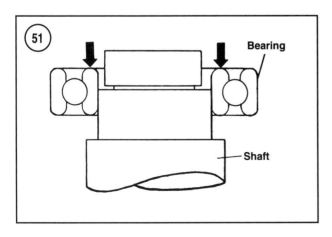

3. Step 1 describes how to install a bearing in a housing or over a shaft. However, when installing a bearing over a shaft and into the housing at the *same time*, a tight fit will be required for both outer and inner bearing races. In this situation, install a spacer underneath the driver tool so pressure is applied evenly across both races. Refer to **Figure 53**. If the outer race is not supported, the balls push against the outer bearing race and damage it.

Interference fit

1. Follow this procedure when installing a bearing over a shaft. When a tight fit is required, the bearing inside diameter will be smaller than the shaft. In this case, driving the bearing on the shaft using normal methods may cause bearing damage. Instead, heat the bearing before installation. Note the following:
   a. Secure the shaft so it is ready for bearing installation.
   b. Clean all residues from the bearing surface of the shaft. Remove burrs with a file.
   c. Fill a suitable pot or beaker with clean mineral oil. Place a thermometer rated above 120° C (248° F) in the oil. Support the thermometer so it does not rest on the bottom or side of the pot.
   d. Remove the bearing from its wrapper and secure it with a piece of heavy wire bent to hold it in the pot. Hang the bearing in the pot so it does not touch the bottom or sides of the pot.
   e. Turn the heat on and monitor the thermometer. When the oil temperature rises to approximately 120° C (248° F), remove the bearing from the pot and quickly install it. If necessary, place a socket on the inner bearing race and tap the bearing into place. As the bearing chills, it tightens on the shaft, so installation must be done quickly. Make sure the bearing is installed completely.

2. Follow this step when installing a bearing in a housing. Bearings are generally installed in a housing with a slight interference fit. Driving the bearing into the housing using normal methods may damage the housing or cause bearing damage. Instead, heat the housing before the bearing is installed. Note the following:
   a. Before heating the housing in this procedure, wash the housing thoroughly with detergent and water. Rinse and rewash the housing as required to remove all oil and chemicals.
   b. Heat the housing to approximately 100° C (212° F) with a heat gun or on a hot plate. Monitor temperature with an infrared thermometer, heat sticks or place tiny drops of water on the housing; if they sizzle and evaporate immediately, the temperature is correct. Heat only one housing at a time.
   c. If a hot plate is used, remove the housing and place it on wooden blocks.
   d. Hold the housing with the bearing side down and tap the bearing out with a suitable size socket and extension. Repeat for all bearings in the housing.

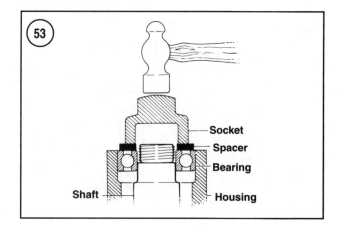

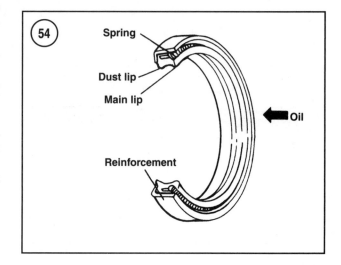

   e. Before heating the bearing housing, place the new bearing in a freezer, if possible. Chilling a bearing slightly reduces its outside diameter while the heated bearing housing assembly is slightly larger due to heat expansion. This makes bearing installation easier.
   f. While the housing is still hot, install the new bearing(s) into the housing. Install the bearings by hand, if possible. If necessary, lightly tap the bearing(s) into the housing with a socket placed on the outer bearing race (**Figure 50**). Do not install bearings by driving on the inner-bearing race. Install the bearing(s) until it seats completely.

Seal Removal/Installation

Seals (**Figure 54**) are used to contain oil, water, grease or combustion gasses in a housing or shaft. Improper removal of a seal can damage the housing or shaft. Improper installation of the seal can damage the seal.

1. Prying is generally the easiest and most effective method of removing a seal from the housing (**Figure 55**). When necessary, place a rag under the pry tool to prevent damage to the housing. When positioning the pry tool, do not allow the edge of the tool to contact the seal bore as the tool will score the bore wall.

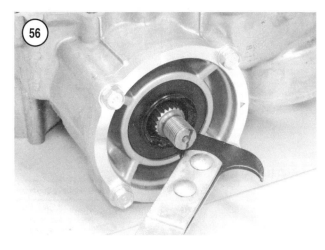

2. If a seal must be removed when there is a shaft installed in the housing, a seal puller (**Figure 56**) can be used.

3. Before installing a typical rubber seal, pack waterproof grease in the seal lips.

4. In most cases, install seals with the manufacturer's numbers or marks face out.

5. Install seals either by hand or with tools. Center the seal in its bore and attempt to install it by hand. If necessary, install the seal with a socket or bearing driver placed on the outside of the seal. Drive the seal squarely into the housing until it is flush with its mounting bore or at a position described in the text. Some large seals may require installation with a soft-faced hammer. When selecting a hammer, choose one with a smooth face to avoid cutting or damaging the seal.

STORAGE

Several months of non-use can cause a general deterioration of the vehicle. This is especially true in areas of extreme temperature variations. This deterioration can be minimized with careful preparation for storage. A properly stored vehicle is much easier to return to service.

Storage Area Selection

When selecting a storage area, consider the following:

1. The storage area must be dry. A heated area is best, but not necessary. It should be insulated to minimize extreme temperature variations.

2. If the building has large windows, mask them to keep sunlight off the vehicle.

3. Avoid storage areas close to saltwater.

4. Consider the area's risk of fire, theft or vandalism. Check with your insurer regarding vehicle coverage while in storage.

Preparing the Vehicle for Storage

The amount of preparation a vehicle should undergo before storage depends on the expected length of non-use, storage area conditions and personal preference. Consider the following list the minimum requirement:

1. Wash the vehicle thoroughly. Make sure all dirt, mud and road debris are removed.

2. Fill the fuel tank. Then add Yamaha Fuel Stabilizer and Conditioner (or equivalent) to the fuel tank. Add the specified amount as described on the container. Install the fuel cap.

3. Start the engine and run for a minimum of 5 minutes to allow the treated fuel to pass through the fuel system.

4. Drain the engine oil regardless of the driving time since the last service. Fill the engine with the recommended type and quantity of oil.

5. Remove the spark plug (Chapter Three). Pour a teaspoon (15-20 ml) of engine oil into the cylinder and turn the engine over as follows:

   a. Place a rag over the spark plug hole.
   b. Ground the ignition system with a grounding tool as described in *Tools* in this chapter.

NOTE
Do not reconnect the spark plug to the spark plug cap when turning the engine over.

   c. Disable the fuel pump by disconnecting the fuel pump electrical connector at the fuel pump as described in *Fuel Tank* in Chapter Eight.
   d. Operate the ignition switch to turn the engine over and distribute the oil into the cylinder. Turn the ignition switch off.
   e. Remove the rag and reinstall the spark plug and reconnect the spark plug cap.
   f. Reconnect the fuel pump electrical connector (Chapter Eight).

6. Remove the battery. Store it in a cool, dry location. Charge the battery once a month. Refer to *Battery* in Chapter Nine.

7. Lubricate the control cables as described in Chapter Eight and Chapter Fifteen.

8. Cover the exhaust and intake openings.

9. When storing in a coastal area (salt-air) or where there is high humidity, lightly coat exposed metal surfaces with oil. Do not coat rubber components with oil. Instead, use a protective substance designed for rubber products.

10. Inflate the front and rear tires to their recommended air pressure (Chapter Three).

11. If it is safe to do so, support the vehicle on a stand with the front and rear wheels off the ground.

Returning the Vehicle to Service

The amount of service required when returning a vehicle to service after storage depends on the length of non-use and storage conditions. In addition to performing the reverse of the above procedure, make sure the brakes, clutch, throttle and ignition switch work properly before operating the vehicle. Refer to Chapter Three and evaluate the service intervals to determine which areas require service while noting the following:

1. If the vehicle was stored for longer than two months and the fuel was not treated with a fuel-stabilizer, drain the fuel tank and refill with fresh gasoline.

2. If the vehicle was stored for longer than four months, change the engine oil.

3. Inflate the tires to the proper air pressure.

4. Check the coolant level.

5. Check the front differential and final drive oil levels.

6. Check the vehicle for insect and rodent nests.

7. Perform the *Pre-Ride Inspection* in Chapter Three.

8. Test-ride the vehicle slowly at first while checking the brakes and all controls for proper operation.

Table 1 MODEL CODE IDENTIFICATION

Year	Model Code Number	Specific Equipment Description
2008	5B41, 5B45 and 5B48	Oil damper shock absorbers and panel wheels
	5B49	Oil damper shock absorbers and cast wheels
	5B4B	Gas-oil damper shock absorbers and cast wheels
	5B4E	Gas-oil damper shock absorbers, cast wheels and overfenders
2009	5B4H, 5B4M and 5B4T	Oil damper shock absorbers and panel wheels
	5B4W	Oil damper shock absorbers and cast wheels
	5B4P	Gas-oil damper shock absorbers and cast wheels
	42S1	Gas-oil damper shock absorbers, cast wheels and overfenders
2010	–	
2011-on	No current listing available from manufacturer	

Table 2 GENERAL VEHICLE DIMENSIONS

	mm	in.
Ground clearance	280	11.0
Overall height		
5B41, 5B45, 5B49, 5B48, 5B4H, 5B4M and 5B4T	1853	73.0
5B4B, 5B4W and 5B4P	1901	74.8
5B4E and 42S1	1865	73.4
Overall length	2885	113.6
Overall width		
5B4E and 42S1	1516	59.7
All other models	1385	54.5
Seat height	818	32.2
Turning radius (minimum)	3900	154

Table 3 VEHICLE WEIGHT SPECIFICATIONS

	kg	lb.
With fuel and oil		
5B41, 5B45, 5B48, 5B4H, 5B4M and 5B4T	540	1190
All other models	548	1208

Table 4 CONVERSION FORMULAS

Multiply:	By:	To get the equivalent of:
Length		
Inches	25.4	Millimeter
Inches	2.54	Centimeter
Miles	1.609	Kilometer
Feet	0.3048	Meter
Millimeter	0.03937	Inches
Centimeter	0.3937	Inches
Kilometer	0.6214	Mile
Meter	3.281	Feet
Fluid volume		
U.S. quarts	0.9463	Liters
U.S. gallons	3.785	Liters
U.S. ounces	29.573529	Milliliters
Liters	0.2641721	U.S. gallons
Liters	1.0566882	U.S. quarts
Liters	33.814023	U.S. ounces
Milliliters	0.033814	U.S. ounces
Milliliters	1.0	Cubic centimeters
Milliliters	0.001	Liters
Torque		
Foot-pounds	1.3558	Newton-meters
Foot-pounds	0.138255	Meters-kilograms
Inch-pounds	0.11299	Newton-meters
Newton-meters	0.7375622	Foot-pounds
Newton-meters	8.8507	Inch-pounds
Meters-kilograms	7.2330139	Foot-pounds
Volume		
Cubic inches	16.387064	Cubic centimeters
Cubic centimeters	0.0610237	Cubic inches
Temperature		
Fahrenheit	$(°F - 32) \times 0.556$	Centigrade
Centigrade	$(°C \times 1.8) + 32$	Fahrenheit
Weight		
Ounces	28.3495	Grams
Pounds	0.4535924	Kilograms
Grams	0.035274	Ounces
Kilograms	2.2046224	Pounds
Pressure		
Pounds per square inch	0.070307	Kilograms per square centimeter
Kilograms per square centimeter	14.223343	Pounds per square inch
Kilopascals	0.1450	Pounds per square inch
Pounds per square inch	6.895	Kilopascals
Speed		
Miles per hour	1.609344	Kilometers per hour
Kilometers per hour	0.6213712	Miles per hour

Table 5 TECHNICAL ABBREVIATIONS

ABDC	After bottom dead center
API	American Petroleum Institute
ATDC	After top dead center
BBDC	Before bottom dead center
BDC	Bottom dead center
BTDC	Before top dead center
BARO	Barometric pressure sensor
C	Celsius (centigrade)
cc	Cubic centimeters
cid	Cubic inch displacement
CDI	Capacitor discharge ignition
cu. in.	Cubic inches
DC	Direct current
ECU	Engine control unit
EVAP	Evaporative emission
F	Fahrenheit
ft.	Feet
ft.-lb.	Foot-pounds
gal.	Gallons
H/A	High altitude
Hp	Horsepower
ICM	Ignition control module
in.	Inches
in.-lb.	Inch-pounds
I.D.	Inside diameter
ISC	Idle speed control unit
kg	Kilograms
kgm	Kilogram meters
km	kilometer
kPa	Kilopascals
L	Liter
LCD	Liquid-crystal display
LED	Light-emitting diode
m	Meter
MAG	Magneto
ml	Milliliter
mm	Millimeter
N•m	Newton-meters
O.D.	Outside diameter
OSHA	Occupational Safety and Health Administration
oz.	Ounces
psi	Pounds per square inch
pt.	Pint
qt.	Quart
RPM	Revolutions per minute
RTV	Room temperature vulcanization
TPS	Throttle position sensor
W	Watts

Table 6 METRIC TAP AND DRILL SIZES

Metric size	Drill equivalent	Decimal fraction	Nearest fraction
3 × 0.50	No. 39	0.0995	3/32
3 × 0.60	3/32	0.0937	3/32
4 × 0.70	No. 30	0.1285	1/8
4 × 0.75	1/8	0.125	1/8
5 × 0.80	No. 19	0.166	11/64
5 × 0.90	No. 20	0.161	5/32
6 × 1.00	No. 9	0.196	13/64
7 × 1.00	16/64	0.234	15/64
8 × 1.00	J	0.277	9/32
8 × 1.25	17/64	0.265	17/64
9 × 1.00	5/16	0.3125	5/16

(continued)

Table 6 METRIC TAP AND DRILL SIZES (continued)

Metric size	Drill equivalent	Decimal fraction	Nearest fraction
9 × 1.25	5/16	0.3125	5/16
10 × 1.25	11/32	0.3437	11/32
10 × 1.50	R	0.339	11/32
11 × 1.50	3/8	0.375	3/8
12 × 1.50	13/32	0.406	13/32
12 × 1.75	13/32	0.406	13/32

Table 7 METRIC, INCH AND FRACTIONAL EQUIVALENTS

mm	in.	Nearest fraction	mm	in.	Nearest fraction
1	0.0394	1/32	26	1.0236	1 1/32
2	0.0787	3/32	27	1.0630	1 1/16
3	0.1181	1/8	28	1.1024	1 3/32
4	0.1575	5/32	29	1.1417	1 5/32
5	0.1969	3/16	30	1.1811	1 3/16
6	0.2362	1/4	31	1.2205	1 7/32
7	0.2756	9/32	32	1.2598	1 1/4
8	0.3150	5/16	33	1.2992	1 5/16
9	0.3543	11/32	34	1.3386	1 11/32
10	0.3937	13/32	35	1.3780	1 3/8
11	0.4331	7/16	36	1.4173	1 13/32
12	0.4724	15/32	37	1.4567	1 15/32
13	0.5118	1/2	38	1.4961	1 1/2
14	0.5512	9/16	39	1.5354	1 17/32
15	0.5906	19/32	40	1.5748	1 9/16
16	0.6299	5/8	41	1.6142	1 5/8
17	0.6693	21/32	42	1.6535	1 21/32
18	0.7087	23/32	43	1.6929	1 11/16
19	0.7480	3/4	44	1.7323	1 23/32
20	0.7874	25/32	45	1.7717	1 25/32
21	0.8268	13/16	46	1.8110	1 13/16
22	0.8661	7/8	47	1.8504	1 27/32
23	0.9055	29/32	48	1.8898	1 7/8
24	0.9449	15/16	49	1.9291	1 15/16
25	0.9843	31/32	50	1.9685	1 31/32

Table 8 GENERAL TORQUE RECOMMENDATIONS[1, 2]

Size-mm	N·m	in.-lb.	ft.-lb.
5	3.4-5.9	30-43	–
6	5.9-7.8	52-69	–
8	14-19	–	10-14
10	25-34	–	18-25
12	44-61	–	32.5-45
14	73-98	–	54-72
16	115-155	–	83-115
18	165-225	–	125-165
20	225-325	–	165-240

1. Use this table for fasteners without a torque specifications.
2. Torque recommendations for dry, solvent cleaned threads.

CHAPTER TWO

TROUBLESHOOTING

The troubleshooting procedures described in this chapter provide typical symptoms and logical methods for isolating the cause(s). There may be several ways to solve a problem, but only a systematic approach will be successful in avoiding wasted time and possibly unnecessary parts replacement. Gather as much information as possible to aid in diagnosis. Never assume anything and do not overlook the obvious. Make sure the engine stop switch is in the run position and there is fuel in the tank. An engine needs the correct air/fuel mixture, compression and a spark at the correct time to run.

Learning to recognize symptoms makes troubleshooting easier. In most cases, expensive and complicated test equipment is not needed to determine whether repairs can be performed at home. On the other hand, be realistic and do not start procedures that are beyond your experience and equipment available. If the vehicle requires the attention of a professional, describe symptoms and conditions accurately and fully. The more information a technician has available, the easier it is to diagnose the problem.

Read *Safety* and *Service Methods* in Chapter One before servicing the vehicle in this chapter.

Table 1 and Table 2 are at the end of this chapter.

STARTING THE ENGINE

Starting Procedure

1. Turn the ignition key on. The engine trouble warning light and coolant temperature warning light (**Figure 1**) should turn on and then turn off.

> *CAUTION*
> *If the engine trouble warning light stays on or flashes, refer to **Electronic Diagnostic System** in this chapter.*

2. Apply the brake pedal.
3. Shift the select lever into neutral. The neutral indicator light should turn on.

> *NOTE*
> *If the transmission is in gear, the brake pedal must be pushed when starting the engine.*

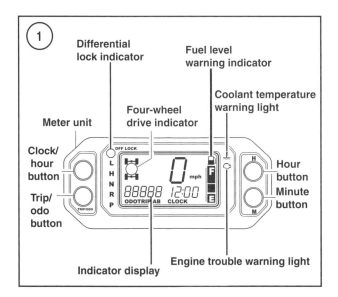

Differential lock indicator
Fuel level warning indicator
Coolant temperature warning light
Meter unit
Four-wheel drive indicator
Clock/ hour button
Hour button
Trip/ odo button
Minute button
Indicator display
Engine trouble warning light

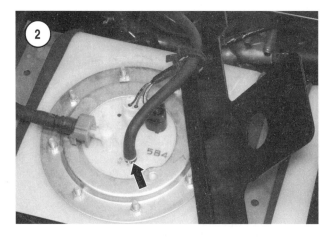

4. Turn the ignition key to START and start the engine. Release the key after the engine starts. Do not press the accelerator pedal when starting the engine.

NOTE
Do not operate the starter motor for more than 5 seconds at a time. Wait approximately 10 seconds between starting attempts.

CAUTION
Do not race the engine during the warm-up period. Excessive wear and potential engine damage can occur when the engine is not up to operating temperature.

ENGINE DOES NOT START

Identifying the Problem

If the engine does not start, perform the following steps in the following sequence. If the engine fails to start after performing these checks, refer to the troubleshooting procedures indicated in the steps. If the engine starts, but idles or runs roughly, refer to *Poor Engine Performance* in this chapter.

1. Turn the ignition switch on and check the engine trouble warning light (**Figure 1**). If the light flashes or stays on, refer to *Electronic Diagnostic System* (this chapter).

2. With the ignition switch on, check the fuel level warning indicator (**Figure 1**). There is sufficient fuel to start the engine if the lower E segment is still visible. If the E segment disappeared and the fuel level warning indicator is flashing, the fuel level in the tank is low. If the vehicle was driven with this indicator flashing, there may not be enough fuel in the tank.

3. Refer to *Starting the Engine* in this chapter to make sure all starting procedures are correct.

4. If the starter does not operate or turns over slowly, check the battery for loose or corroded terminals. If the cables and connections are good, test the battery as described in Chapter Nine. If the starter is turning over correctly, continue with Step 5.

NOTE
Push the clock/hour button on the meter assembly to display the voltage display mode on the meter assembly. If LO is displayed, the battery voltage is less than 10 volts. If HI is displayed, the battery voltage is above 16 volts.

5. If there is sufficient fuel in the fuel tank, remove the spark plug immediately after attempting to start the engine. The plug's insulator should be wet, indicating that fuel is reaching the engine. Note the following:

   a. If the plug tip is dry, fuel is not reaching the engine. A faulty fuel flow problem causes this condition. First check for a clogged fuel tank breather hose (**Figure 2**) at the fuel tank. Also check the opposite end of the breather hose where it is connected to the rollover valve (A, **Figure 3**). After checking/cleaning the breather hose, reattach the hose at the fuel tank but not at the rollover valve. Try to start the engine. If the engine now starts, check the rollover valve (Chapter Eight) and the upper breather hose (B, **Figure 3**).

NOTE
If the rollover valve was recently removed, make sure it is properly installed. Refer to Rollover Valve in Chapter Eight.

b. If the breather hose is clear and the engine doesn't start when the rollover valve is disconnected, refer to *Fuel Delivery System Tests* in Chapter Eight.

c. If there is fuel on the spark plug and the engine will not start, the engine may not have adequate spark. Continue with Step 6.

6. Make sure the spark plug cable is secure inside the cap. Push the cap back onto the plug and slightly rotate to clean the electrical connection between the plug and the connector. If the engine does not start, continue with Step 7.

NOTE
Remove the spark plug cap and check it for water.

NOTE
A cracked or damaged spark plug cap and cable can cause intermittent problems that are difficult to diagnose. If the engine occasionally misfires or cuts out, use a spray bottle to wet the spark plug cable and cap while the engine is running. Water that enters a damaged cap or cable causes an arc through the insulating material, causing an engine misfire.

7. Perform the *Spark Test* in this section. If there is a strong spark, perform Step 8.

8. If the fuel and ignition systems are working correctly, perform a leakdown test as described in this chapter and a cylinder compression test (Chapter Three). If the leakdown test indicates a problem or the compression is low, refer to *Low Compression* in *Engine* in this chapter.

Spark Test

Perform a spark test to determine if the ignition system is producing adequate spark. This test can be performed by removing the spark plug cap and then grounding a new spark plug against the engine. If available, a spark tester can also be used. Because the voltage required to jump the spark tester's gap is sufficiently larger than that of a normally gapped spark plug, the test results are more accurate than with a spark plug.

Perform this test when the engine is cold and it is at normal operating temperatures.

1. Remove the seats and rear console (Chapter Sixteen).
2. Make sure the battery is fully charges (Chapter Nine).
3. Disconnect the spark plug cap (Chapter Three) and leave the original spark plug in the cylinder head. Check for the presence of water in the plug cap.
4. Connect a separate new spark plug to the spark plug cap and ground it against the engine (**Figure 4**). If a spark tester is being used (Motion Pro part No. 08-122 [**Figure 5**]), ground it the same way. Position the spark plug/spark tester so the electrodes are visible.

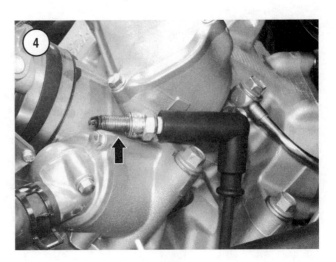

WARNING
Do not hold the spark plug or spark tester; a serious electrical shock may result.

5. With the transmission in neutral, turn the ignition switch on turn the key to turn the engine over. A fat blue spark must be evident between the spark plug/spark tester terminals.

6. If there is a spark, the ignition system is functioning properly. Check for one or more of the following possible malfunctions:

a. Remove and inspect the original spark plug (Chapter Three). If the plug appears fouled, install a new spark plug and repeat the spark test with the original spark plug.

b. Faulty fuel system component.

c. Flooded engine.

d. Engine damage (low compression).

7. If the spark was weak or if there was no spark, refer to *Ignition System Troubleshooting* in this chapter.

8. Reconnect the spark plug cap (Chapter Three).

9. Reinstall the rear console and seats (Chapter Sixteen).

Engine is Difficult to Start

1. After attempting to start the engine, remove the spark plug (Chapter Three) and check for the presence of fuel on the plug tip. Note the following:

a. If there is no fuel present of the fuel tip, continue with Step 2.

b. If there is fuel present on the fuel tip, go to Step 3.

c. If there is an excessive amount of fuel on the plug, check for a clogged or damaged air filter (Chapter Three). If the air filter is okay, the fuel pressure may be too high. Continue with Step 2.

2. Perform the *Fuel Delivery System Tests* in Chapter Eight. Note the following:

a. If the fuel pump operation is correct, go to Step 3.

b. If there is low fuel pressure, replace the fuel pump and retest.

c. If the fuel pressure is too high, the fuel pressure regulator is faulty. Replace the fuel pump and retest.

d. If fuel pump operation is faulty, replace the fuel pump and retest the fuel delivery system.

3. If the fuel operation is correct, refer to Chapter Eight and check for the following fuel system related problems:
   a. Plugged fuel tank breather hose.
   b. Contaminated fuel.
   c. Plugged or damaged rollover valve and connecting hose.
   d. Damaged fuel injection system relay.

4. Perform the spark test as described in this section Note the following:
   a. If the spark is weak or if there is no spark, go to Step 5.
   b. If the spark is good, go to Step 6.

5. If the spark is weak or if there is no spark, check the following:
   a. Fouled spark plug.
   b. Damaged spark plug.
   c. Loose or damaged spark plug wire.
   d. Loose or damaged spark plug cap.
   e. Faulty crankshaft position sensor.
   f. Faulty ignition coil.
   g. Faulty lean-angle sensor.
   h. Faulty ignition switch.
   i. Faulty gear position switch.
   j. Faulty brake light switch.
   k. Dirty or loose-fitting terminals.
   l. Damaged wiring.
   m. Faulty battery.
   n. Faulty ECU.

6. If the engine turns over but does not start, the engine compression is probably low. Check for the following possible malfunctions:
   a. Loose spark plug.
   b. Incorrect valve clearance.
   c. Leaking cylinder head gasket.
   d. Leaking base gasket.
   e. Bent or stuck valve(s).
   f. Incorrect valve timing.
   g. Worn cylinder and/or piston rings.
   h. Seized piston ring(s).
   i. Improperly installed piston ring(s) after engine reassembly.

7. If the spark is good, try starting the engine by following normal starting procedures. If the engine starts but then stops, check for the following conditions:
   a. Leaking or damaged intake tube.
   b. Contaminated fuel.
   c. Plugged or damaged rollover valve.
   d. Incorrect ignition timing.
   e. Faulty throttle position sensor.
   f. Faulty crankshaft position sensor.
   g. Defective fuel injector.

Starter Turns Over Correctly, but Engine Will Not Start

Perform the *Spark Test* in this section to isolate the problem to the ignition or fuel ignition system. If the ignition and fuel systems are working correctly, the engine has low compression. Refer to *Low Compression* in *Engine* this chapter.

Starter Does Not Turn Over

If the engine will not turn over, perform the following in order:

1. Refer to *Starting the Engine* in this chapter to make sure all starting procedures are correct.

NOTE
If the transmission is in gear, the brake pedal must be pushed when starting the engine.

2. Check the main, ignition, backup and signal system fuses (Chapter Nine).
3. Check the battery and battery cables (Chapter Nine).
4. Check all of the starting system connectors and wiring.
5. Test the following components as described in Chapter Nine:
   a. Starter.
   b. Starter relay.
   c. Ignition switch.
   d. Gear position switch.
   e. Brake light switch
   f. Load control relay.

6. Ignition system failure.
7. Check for engine damage:
   a. Sized piston.
   b. Seized camshaft.
   c. Seized crankshaft.

Starter Turns Over Slowly

For the starter to work correctly, the battery must be 75 percent charged and the battery cables must be clean and in good condition. Inspect and test the battery as described in Chapter Nine.

POOR ENGINE PERFORMANCE

If the engine runs, but performance is unsatisfactory, refer to the following section(s) that best describes the symptom(s). All models are equipped with a self-diagnostic engine management system. Refer to *Electronic Diagnostic System* in this chapter for identification of malfunctioning components that may cause a performance problem or to read trouble and diagnostic codes.

NOTE
*The ignition timing is not adjustable. If incorrect ignition timing is suspected, inspect the ignition timing as described in Chapter Three. If the timing is incorrect, a defective ignition system component is indicated. Refer to **Ignition System Troubleshooting** in this chapter.*

Engine Starts But Stalls and is Hard to Restart

Check for the following:
1. Clogged or damaged air filter
2. Plugged fuel tank breather hose.
3. Partially plugged or damaged rollover valve and connecting hose.
4. Plugged or damaged fuel supply hose.
5. Obstructed throttle body or fuel injector.
6. Flooded throttle body.
7. Contaminated or stale fuel.
8. Damaged fuel pump.
9. Intake air leak.
10. Faulty ECU.

Engine Backfires, Cuts Out or Misfires During Acceleration

A backfire occurs when fuel is burned or ignited in the exhaust system.
1. A lean air/fuel mixture can cause these engine performance problems. Check for the following conditions:
   a. Low fuel pressure.
   b. Clogged fuel injector.
   c. Vacuum leak.
   d. Damaged fuel pump.
2. Loose exhaust pipe-to-cylinder head connection.
3. Leaks in intake system.
4. Incorrect ignition timing: faulty ECU, crankshaft position sensor or damaged flywheel Woodruff key.
5. Faulty throttle position sensor.
6. Check the following engine components:
   a. Broken valve springs.
   b. Stuck or leaking valves.
   c. Worn or damaged camshaft lobes.
   d. Incorrect valve timing due to incorrect camshaft installation or a mechanical failure.

Poor Fuel Mileage

1. Incorrect fuel pressure (fuel pump/fuel pressure regulator).
2. Clogged fuel supply hose.
3. Dirty or clogged air filter.
4. Incorrect ignition timing.
5. Vacuum leak.

Incorrect Engine Idle Speed

Engine idle speed is determined by the idle speed control unit mounted on the throttle body and is not adjustable. Check the engine idle speed as described in *Ignition Timing Inspection* in Chapter Three. If incorrect, check the following:
1. Check for the following fuel system conditions:
   a. Clogged or damaged air filter.
   b. Incorrect throttle cable free play.
   c. Plugged, damaged or disconnected breather hoses.
   d. Plugged, damaged or disconnected vacuum hoses.
   e. Plugged fuel supply hose.
   f. Obstructed or defective fuel injector.
   g. Incorrect fuel pressure (fuel pump/fuel pressure regulator).
   h. Loose throttle body mounting bolts.
   i. Damaged throttle body to air filter housing gasket.
   j. Cracked or damaged intake tube.
   k. Flooded throttle body.
   l. Dirty or contaminated throttle body. Remove and clean the throttle body as described in Chapter Eight. Then reinstall the throttle body and recheck the idle speed. If the idle speed is still out of specifications, take the vehicle to a dealership for inspection.
2. Check for the following engine conditions:
   a. Incorrect valve clearance.
   b. Damaged valve springs or other valve train components.
   c. Restrictive exhaust system.
3. Check for the following electrical system conditions:
   a. Discharged or damaged battery.
   b. Fouled or damaged spark plug.
   c. Damaged secondary wire or spark plug cap. Loose or contaminated spark plug cap contact.
   d. Faulty ignition coil.
   e. Faulty crankshaft position sensor.
   f. Damaged flywheel Woodruff key (engine may also backfire).
   g. Faulty ECU.

Low Engine Power

1. Refer to *Clutch Troubleshooting* in this chapter. If the clutch and drive belt are in good condition, continue with Step 2.
2. Shift the transmission into neutral.

3. Support the vehicle on a workstand with the rear wheels off the ground, and then spin the rear wheels by hand. If the wheels spin freely, perform Step 4. If the wheels do not spin freely, check for the following conditions:

    a. Dragging brakes.

NOTE
After riding the vehicle, come to a stop on a level surface (in a safe area away from all traffic). Turn the engine off and shift the transmission into neutral. Push the vehicle forward. If the vehicle is harder to push than normal, check for dragging brakes.

    b. Damaged final drive.

4. Test drive the vehicle and accelerate lightly. If the engine speed increased according to throttle position, perform Step 6. If the engine speed did not increase, check for one or more of the following problems:

    a. Clogged or damaged air filter.
    b. Restricted fuel flow.
    c. Pinched fuel tank breather hose.
    d. Damaged rollover valve and/or connecting hose.
    e. Clogged or damaged muffler. Tap the muffler with a rubber mallet and check for loose or broken baffles.

NOTE
A clogged muffler or exhaust system will prevent some of the burned exhaust gases from exiting the exhaust port at the end of the exhaust stroke. This condition effects the incoming air/fuel mixture on the intake stroke and reduces engine power.

5. Check the ignition timing as described in Chapter Three. A decrease in power results when the plug fires later than normal.

6. Check for one or more of the following problems:

    a. Low engine compression.
    b. Worn spark plug.
    c. Fouled spark plug.
    d. Incorrect spark plug heat range.
    e. Weak ignition coil.
    f. Clogged or defective fuel injector.
    g. Incorrect ignition timing (defective ECU).
    h. Incorrect oil level (too high or too low).
    i. Contaminated oil.
    j. Worn or damaged valve train assembly.
    k. Engine overheating. Refer to *Engine Overheating* in this section.

7. If the engine knocks when it is accelerated or when running at high speed, check for one or more of the following possible malfunctions:

    a. Incorrect type of fuel.
    b. Lean fuel mixture.
    c. Incorrect (advanced) ignition timing (faulty ECU).

NOTE
Other signs of overly advanced ignition timing are engine overheating and hard or uneven engine starting.

    d. Excessive carbon buildup in combustion chamber.
    e. Worn piston and/or cylinder bore.

Poor Low Speed Performance

1. Refer to *Clutch Troubleshooting* in this chapter. If the clutch and drive belt are in good condition, continue with Step 2.

2. Check for damaged fuel body intake tube or loose throttle body and air filter housing hose clamps. These conditions will cause an air leak.

3. Perform the spark test as described in *Engine Does Not Start* in this chapter. Note the following:

    a. If the spark is good, go to Step 4.
    b. If the spark is weak, test the ignition system as described in *Ignition System Troubleshooting* in this chapter.

4. Check the ignition timing as described in Chapter Three. If ignition timing is correct, perform Step 5. If the timing is incorrect, test the ignition system components as described in Chapter Nine.

5. Refer to Chapter Eight and check the following fuel system components:

    a. Obstructed throttle body or defective fuel injector.
    b. Faulty throttle position sensor.
    c. Faulty intake air pressure sensor.

Poor High Speed Performance

1. Clogged or damaged air filter (Chapter Three).
2. Damaged fuel pump (Chapter Eight).
3. Check ignition timing as described in Chapter Three. If ignition timing is correct, perform Step 4. If the timing is incorrect, test the ignition system as described in *Ignition System Troubleshooting* in this chapter.
4. Check the valve clearance as described in Chapter Three. Note the following:

    a. If the valve clearance is correct, perform Step 5.
    b. If the clearance is incorrect, readjust the valves.

5. Incorrect valve timing and worn or damaged valve springs can cause poor high-speed performance. If the camshafts were timed just prior to the vehicle experiencing this type of problem, the cam timing may be incorrect. If the cam timing was not set or changed, and all of the other inspection procedures in this section failed to locate the problem, inspect the camshaft and valve assembly.

Engine Overheating

1. Cooling system:

    a. Low coolant level.
    b. Damaged fan motor.

c. Faulty thermostat (stuck closed).

d. Damaged water pump.

e. Clogged or damaged radiator. Because the oil cooler is mounted in front of the radiator, the area between the cooler and radiator can fill with mud and other debris and reduce the amount of air from entering the radiator.

f. Damaged coolant temperature sensor.

g. Air in cooling system. If the problem occurred right after changing the coolant, there could be air in the cooling system. If so, restart the engine and loosen the thermostat cover air bleed bolt (**Figure 6**) and note if air is escaping from around the bolt. If so, allow the bolt to remain loose until coolant flows steadily, then retighten the bolt. If coolant is escaping from around the bolt, the cooling system is probably bled of air. Refer to *Coolant Change* in *Cooling System* in Chapter Three.

NOTE
*If there is no air or coolant escaping from around the bolt, bleed the cooling system as described in **Cooling System** in Chapter Three.*

2. Ignition system:

a. Incorrect spark plug heat range.

b. Incorrect spark plug gap.

c. Faulty ECU.

3. Engine:

a. Low engine oil level.

b. Incorrect engine oil viscosity.

c. Incorrect engine oil type.

d. Broken oil pump drive chain. Because the water pump shaft meshes with the oil pump shaft, a broken chain will prevent both the oil pump and water pump from turning.

e. Heavy carbon buildup in engine combustion chambers and on piston crowns.

4. Fuel system:

a. Clogged or damaged air filter.

b. Loose throttle body mounting bolts.

c. Cracked, damaged or leaking intake tube joints.

d. Cracked intake tube.

5. Brake system:

a. Brake drag.

b. Parking brake drag.

Overcooling

If it takes a long time for the engine to warm up, check for a faulty thermostat (stuck open).

FUEL SYSTEM

If the starter turns over and there is a good spark at the spark plug, low fuel pressure may prevent fuel from being supplied to the engine. Troubleshoot fuel flow as follows:

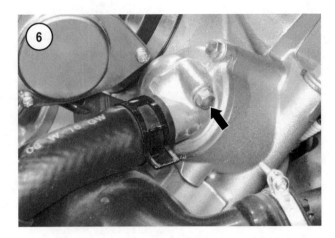

1. After attempting to start the engine, remove the spark plug (Chapter Three) and check for the presence of fuel on the plug tip. Note the following:

a. If the plug tip is dry, continue with Step 2.

b. If there is fuel present on the plug tip and the engine has spark, check for an excessive intake air leak or the possibility of contaminated or stale fuel.

NOTE
If the vehicle was not used for some time, and was not properly stored, the fuel may have gone stale, where lighter parts of the fuel have evaporated. Depending on the condition of the fuel, a no-start condition can result.

c. If there is an excessive amount of fuel on the plug, check for a clogged or damaged air filter or damaged fuel injector.

2. Check the main fuse, ignition fuse and fuel injection fuse (Chapter Nine). Also check the fuse and connector contacts for contamination and damage.

3. Check the fuel hoses for blocks or damage (Chapter Eight).

4. Check the rollover valve for damage (Chapter Eight).

5. Test the fuel injection system relay (Chapter Eight).

6. Check the fuel supply hose for damage. Note the following:

a. If the hose is good, go to Step 7.

b. Replace the hose if plugged or damaged. Then restart the engine to check its operation.

7. Perform the tests in *Fuel Delivery System Tests* in Chapter Eight. Note the following:

a. If the fuel pressure reading is correct, go to Step 8.

b. If the fuel pressure reading is too low or too high, replace the fuel pump and repeat the fuel pressure check.

8. Check the throttle body and fuel injector (Chapter Eight).

9. Check the fuel pump system wiring harness and connectors. Refer to Chapter Eight and to the wiring diagrams at the end of this manual.

10. If the problem has not been found, take the vehicle to a dealership and have them replace the ECU to determine whether the original ECU is faulty.

ELECTRONIC DIAGNOSTIC SYSTEM

The electronic control unit (ECU) includes a self-diagnostic function that monitors electrical components of the ignition and fuel injection systems. Whenever an error is detected, the ECU stores the malfunction and sets a trouble code. It also turns on the engine trouble warning light (**Figure 1**) in the meter panel. The engine trouble warning light will either stay on continuously or will blink depending on the fault.

Note that some malfunctions may not trigger a trouble code. If this occurs, refer to Chapter Nine and to the wiring diagrams at the end of this manual to assist in troubleshooting the problem.

Under normal conditions, the engine trouble warning light will turn on and then turn off after the ignition switch is turned on. If the warning light does not turn on as described, check for a faulty LED or other problem in the circuit. Refer to *Meter Assembly and Indicator Lights* in Chapter Nine.

Read through the following sections before beginning diagnostic system troubleshooting. Refer to Chapter Eight or Chapter Nine prior to replacing any component(s). If the procedures are not followed carefully, an incorrect diagnosis may occur. Do not overlook the possibility that something as simple as a loose or contaminated electrical connector or vacuum hose may be the source of a problem. If the source of a trouble code cannot be determined, take the vehicle to a dealership as soon as possible for troubleshooting and repair. Read *Electrical Component Replacement* in Chapter Nine.

Trouble Codes and Diagnostic Codes

There are two different types of codes:
1. Trouble codes. If a problem occurs within the system, the driver is notified by the engine trouble warning light. The engine trouble warning light remains on during operation or it blinks after the engine stops if a trouble code exists in the ECU. The vehicle may or may not be able to be started or ridden, depending on the type of malfunction. Refer to **Table 1** for trouble codes.
2. Diagnostic codes. After a trouble code is displayed, this can be cross-referenced to the two-digit diagnostic code, which can be read on the indicator display (**Figure 1**). Refer to *Reading Diagnostic Codes* in this section and to **Table 2** for diagnostic codes. Note that some trouble codes do not list a diagnostic code.

Reading Trouble Codes

1. If the engine trouble warning light (**Figure 1**) remains on during engine operation or it blinks after the engine stops, a trouble code exists in the ECU.
2. Come to a stop but do not turn the ignition switch off. The trouble code will now appear on the indicator display.

3. Read the trouble code displayed on the indicator display (**Figure 1**). The lowest numbered trouble code is displayed.
4. Turn the ignition switch off.

Reading Diagnostic Codes

Refer to **Figure 1**.
1. Make sure the ignition switch is turned off.
2. Disable the fuel pump by disconnecting the fuel pump electrical connector at the fuel pump as described in *Fuel Tank* in Chapter Eight.
3. Press and hold the CLOCK/HOUR and TRIP/ODO buttons simultaneously on the meter assembly, and then turn the ignition switch on. Continue to hold down the buttons for at least 8 seconds, then release them.

NOTE
All indicator display characters will disappear, then DIAG will appear on the indicator display.

4. When DIAG appears, press the CLOCK/HOUR and TRIP/ODO buttons simultaneously for at least 2 seconds to set the tool in diagnostic mode. Diagnostic code number d01 will appear on the indicator display.
5. Press the CLOCK/HOUR button for 1 second or longer to scroll up through the diagnostic codes (d01-d70). Press the TRIP/ODO button to scroll down.
6. Select the diagnostic code that applies to the item that was verified with the trouble code.
7. Refer to **Table 2** and verify the operation of the sensor/actuator by performing the instruction in the action column. Note the following:
   a. Sensor operation: Sensor data appears on the LCD screen.
   b. Actuator operation: Position the differential gear lock switch on the instrument panel to LOCK to actuate the actuator. If the differential gear lock switch is currently positioned in LOCK, first move it to 4WD, and then back to LOCK.
8. Turn the ignition switch off to cancel the diagnostic mode process.
9. Reconnect the fuel pump connector as described in *Fuel Tank* in Chapter Eight.

Fail-Safe Operation

When a problem with a sensor/actuator is detected by the ECU, the ECU processes the information and enters a preprogrammed specification for the sensor/actuator function. This fail-safe action, depending on the trouble code, may or may not allow vehicle operation. It also may be necessary to stop operation of the vehicle, depending on what area(s) of the system is affected.

If the engine trouble warning light stays on continuously, the vehicle may or may not operate, depending on the trouble code.

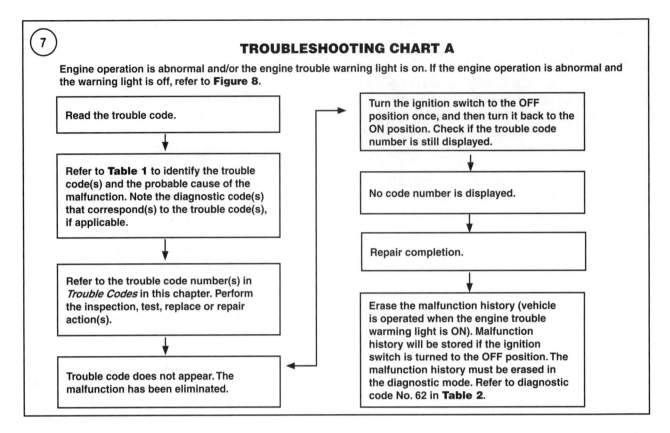

(7)

TROUBLESHOOTING CHART A

Engine operation is abnormal and/or the engine trouble warning light is on. If the engine operation is abnormal and the warning light is off, refer to **Figure 8**.

Read the trouble code.

↓

Refer to **Table 1** to identify the trouble code(s) and the probable cause of the malfunction. Note the diagnostic code(s) that correspond(s) to the trouble code(s), if applicable.

↓

Refer to the trouble code number(s) in *Trouble Codes* in this chapter. Perform the inspection, test, replace or repair action(s).

↓

Trouble code does not appear. The malfunction has been eliminated.

Turn the ignition switch to the OFF position once, and then turn it back to the ON position. Check if the trouble code number is still displayed.

↓

No code number is displayed.

↓

Repair completion.

↓

Erase the malfunction history (vehicle is operated when the engine trouble warming light is ON). Malfunction history will be stored if the ignition switch is turned to the OFF position. The malfunction history must be erased in the diagnostic mode. Refer to diagnostic code No. 62 in **Table 2**.

If the engine trouble light is blinking or stays on and the vehicle stops and cannot be restarted, or the vehicle will not start after it was turned off, one or more of the following trouble codes may exist:

1. No. 12: Crankshaft position sensor.
2. No. 30: Lean-angle sensor (latch up detected).
3. No. 41: Lean-angle sensor (open or short circuit).
4. No. 50: ECU internal malfunction (memory check error).

TROUBLE CODES

General Information

1. Refer to **Figure 7** and **Figure 8** for an outline of the diagnostic steps. Refer to **Figure 7** if a trouble code is present. Refer to **Figure 8** if an abnormal engine condition is occurring and no trouble code is present.
2. Use the trouble code information (**Table 1**) and, if appropriate, diagnostic code information (**Table 2**), along with the corresponding data on the indicator display (**Figure 1**) to diagnose the fault(s). Refer to the following trouble codes in this section by specific individual trouble codes for testing procedures.
3. When checking the pins and wires in a sensor connector for possible damage, also check the corresponding pins and wires in the ECU connectors. Refer to the correct wiring diagram at the end of this manual to identify the ECU wiring harness color codes used for a particular sensor.
4. If a problem cannot be found, the ECU may be faulty. However, before purchasing a new ECU, take the vehicle

to a dealership and have them troubleshoot the system and substitute the ECU with a new one to verify the problem.

Trouble Code 12: Normal Signals are Not Received from the Crankshaft Position Sensor

Refer to Chapter Nine.

1. Check the crankshaft position sensor electrical connector for any loose or pulled-out pins.
2. Check the ECU electrical connectors for the same conditions described in Step 1.
3. Check the gray and black/blue wires between the crankshaft position sensor and ECU for an open or short circuit.
4. Make sure the crankshaft position sensor is properly installed. Check for a loose mounting bolt. Also check the exposed part of the wiring harness that is located behind the flywheel for damage. This will require flywheel removal as described in Chapter Nine.
5. Test the crankshaft position sensor as described in Chapter Nine.
6. To check if the problem has been corrected, start the engine and run at idle speed. Note the following:
   a. If no fault code is displayed, the problem has been corrected. Erase the diagnostic code(s) as described in **Figure 7**.
   b. If the fault code reappears, a problem still exists. Repeat the troubleshooting procedure or take the vehicle to a dealership and have them substitute the ECU with a known good ECU.
7. When the problem has been corrected, crank the engine to reinstate the crankshaft position sensor.

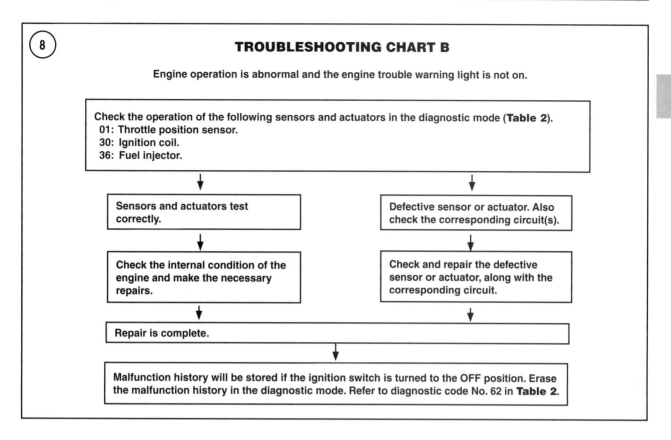

TROUBLESHOOTING CHART B

Engine operation is abnormal and the engine trouble warning light is not on.

Check the operation of the following sensors and actuators in the diagnostic mode (**Table 2**).
01: Throttle position sensor.
30: Ignition coil.
36: Fuel injector.

Sensors and actuators test correctly.

Defective sensor or actuator. Also check the corresponding circuit(s).

Check the internal condition of the engine and make the necessary repairs.

Check and repair the defective sensor or actuator, along with the corresponding circuit.

Repair is complete.

Malfunction history will be stored if the ignition switch is turned to the OFF position. Erase the malfunction history in the diagnostic mode. Refer to diagnostic code No. 62 in **Table 2**.

Trouble Code 13 Open or Short Circuit Detected in the Intake Air Pressure Sensor (Diagnostic Code No. 03)

Refer to Chapter Eight.
1. Check the intake air pressure sensor electrical connector for any loose or pulled-out pins.
2. Check the ECU electrical connectors for the same conditions described in Step 1.
3. Check the black/blue, pink and blue wires between the intake air pressure sensor and ECU for an open or short circuit.
4. Make sure the intake air pressure sensor is properly installed. Check for a loose mounting bolt.
5. Institute diagnostic code No. 03 to display the intake air temperature. Operate the accelerator pedal while starting the engine. If the display value changes, the intake air temperature sensor is working correctly. If the display value does not change, test the intake air pressure sensor as described in Chapter Eight.
6. To check if the problem has been corrected, start the engine and run at idle speed. Note the following:
   a. If no fault code is displayed, the problem has been corrected. Erase the diagnostic code(s) as described in **Figure 7**.
   b. If the fault code reappears, a problem still exists. Repeat the troubleshooting procedure or take the vehicle to a dealership and have them substitute the ECU with a different ECU.
7. When the problem has been corrected, turn the ignition switch on to reinstate the intake air pressure sensor.

Trouble Code 14: Clogged or Detached Hose in the Intake Air Pressure Sensor (Diagnostic Code No. 03)

Refer to Chapter Eight.
1. Check the sensor for a disconnected, plugged or damaged hose. Check both ends of the hose. Also check the sensor hose port for blockage.
2. Make sure the intake air pressure sensor is properly installed.
3. Check the intake air pressure sensor electrical connector for any loose or pulled-out pins.
4. Check the ECU electrical connector for any loose or pulled-out black/blue, pink or blue pins.
5. Institute diagnostic code No. 03 to display the intake air temperature. Operate the accelerator pedal while pushing the ignition switch. If the display value changes, the intake air temperature sensor is working correctly. If the display value does not change, test the intake air pressure sensor as described in Chapter Eight.
6. To check if the problem has been corrected, start the engine and run at idle speed. Note the following:
   a. If no fault code is displayed, the problem has been corrected. Erase the diagnostic code(s) as described in **Figure 7**.
   b. If the fault code reappears, a problem still exists. Repeat the troubleshooting procedure or take the vehicle to a dealership and have them substitute the ECU with a known good ECU.
7. When the problem has been corrected, start the engine and allow to run at idle speed to reinstate the intake air pressure sensor.

Trouble Code 15: Open or Short Circuit Detected in the Throttle Position Sensor (Diagnostic Code No. 01)

Refer to Chapter Eight.

1. Check the throttle position sensor for any loose mounting screws. If the sensor is loose, readjust as described in Chapter Eight. If the sensor screws are tight, continue with Step 2.
2. Check the throttle position sensor connector at the sensor. The connector must be locked in place.
3. Disconnect the throttle position sensor electrical connector and check for any loose or pulled-out pins.
4. Check the blue, yellow and black/blue wires between the throttle position sensor and ECU for an open or short circuit.
5. Check the 26-pin ECU electrical connector for any loose or pulled-out blue, yellow or black/blue pins.
6. Using back-probe pins at the throttle position sensor electrical connector, connect the positive voltmeter lead to the yellow wire and the negative lead to the black/blue wire. Refer to *Back Probe Pins* in *Measuring Tools* in Chapter One. Turn the ignition switch on. The correct voltage reading is 0.67 volts. If the voltage is incorrect, loosen the sensor mounting screws and adjust the sensor until the specified voltage reading is obtained. Tighten the screws and recheck the adjustment. If the correct voltage reading cannot be obtained, continue with Step 7.

NOTE
The 0.67 voltage reading is the closed throttle voltage signal. A piece of carbon or other debris on the throttle blade or in the throttle bore inside the throttle body can affect the adjustment. If the throttle body is removed, check the throttle blade and bore for contamination.

7. Institute diagnostic code No. 01 to display the throttle angle. With the throttle fully closed, the throttle angle on the indicator display should read between 15 and 20. If the reading is incorrect, test and adjust the throttle position sensor as described in Chapter Eight.
8. To check if the problem has been corrected, start the engine and run at idle speed. Note the following:
   a. If no fault code is displayed, the problem has been corrected. Erase the diagnostic code(s) as described in **Figure 7**.
   b. If the fault code reappears, a problem still exists. Repeat the troubleshooting procedure or take the vehicle to a dealership and have them substitute the ECU with a known good ECU.
9. When the problem has been corrected, turn the ignition switch on to reinstate the throttle position sensor.

Trouble Code: 16 Stuck Throttle Position Sensor Detected (Diagnostic Code No. 01)

Refer to Chapter Eight.

1. Check the throttle position sensor for any loose mounting screws. If the sensor is loose, readjust as described in Chapter Eight. If the sensor screws are tight, continue with Step 2.
2. Check the throttle position sensor connector at the sensor. The connector must be locked in place.

NOTE
Make sure the throttle blade inside the throttle body is closed when the accelerator pedal is at rest. A piece of carbon or other debris on the throttle blade or in the throttle bore inside the throttle body can affect the adjustment. If the throttle body is removed, check the throttle blade and bore for contamination.

3. Institute diagnostic code No. 01 to display the throttle angle. With the throttle fully closed, the throttle angle on the indicator display should read between 15 and 20. If the reading is incorrect, test and adjust the throttle position sensor as described in Chapter Eight.
4. To check if the problem has been corrected, start the engine and run at idle speed. Note the following:
   a. If no fault code is displayed, the problem has been corrected. Erase the diagnostic code(s) as described in **Figure 7**.
   b. If the fault code reappears, a problem still exists. Repeat the troubleshooting procedure or take the vehicle to a dealership and have them substitute the ECU with a known good ECU.
5. When the problem has been corrected, start the engine and run at idle speed. Then increase the engine speed to a high rpm with the accelerator pedal to reinstate the throttle position sensor.

Trouble Code 21 Open or Short Circuit Detected in the Coolant Temperature Sensor (Diagnostic Code No. 6)

Refer to *Cooling System* in Chapter Nine.

1. Make sure the coolant temperature sensor is properly installed.
2. Check the black/blue and green/ yellow wires between the coolant temperature sensor and ECU for an open or short circuit.
3. Check the coolant temperature sensor electrical connector for any loose or pulled-out pins.
4. Check the ECU electrical connectors for the same conditions described in Step 3.
5. Institute diagnostic code No. 06 to display the coolant temperature. Then measure the actual coolant temperature with an infrared thermometer and compare the temperature readings. If there is a significant difference in the two temperature readings, remove and test the coolant temperature sensor as described in *Cooling System* in Chapter Nine.
6. To check if the problem has been corrected, start the engine and run at idle speed. Note the following:
   a. If no fault code is displayed, the problem has been corrected. Erase the diagnostic code(s) as described in **Figure 7**.

b. If the fault code reappears, a problem still exists. Repeat the troubleshooting procedure or take the vehicle to a dealership and have them substitute the ECU with a known good ECU.

7. When the problem has been corrected, turn the ignition switch on to reinstate the coolant temperature sensor.

Trouble Code 22 Open or Short Circuit Detected in the Intake Air Temperature Sensor (Diagnostic Code No. 5)

Refer to Chapter Eight.

1. Make sure the intake air temperature sensor is properly installed.

2. Check the black/blue and brown/white wires between the intake air temperature sensor and ECU for an open or short circuit.

3. Check the intake air temperature sensor electrical connector for any loose or pulled-out pins.

4. Check the ECU electrical connectors for the same conditions described in Step 3.

5. Institute diagnostic code No. 05 to display the intake air temperature. Then measure the actual ambient air temperature with a thermometer and compare the temperature readings. If there is a significant difference in the two temperature readings, remove and test the intake air temperature sensor as described in Chapter Eight.

6. To check if the problem has been corrected, start the engine and run at idle speed. Note the following:

a. If no fault code is displayed, the problem has been corrected. Erase the diagnostic code(s) as described in **Figure 7**.

b. If the fault code reappears, a problem still exists. Repeat the troubleshooting procedure or take the vehicle to a dealership and have them substitute the ECU with a known good ECU.

7. When the problem has been corrected, turn the ignition switch on to reinstate the intake air temperature sensor.

Trouble Code 30: Vehicle Turned Over (Diagnostic Code No. 08)

Refer to Chapter Nine.

1. Park the vehicle on a level surface.

2. Check the lean-angle sensor for loose mounting bolts. Also check the wiring harness and connector for pinched or damaged wires.

3. Check the blue, yellow/green and black/blue wires between the lean-angle sensor and the 26-pin ECU connector for an open or short circuit.

4. Check the lean-angle sensor electrical connector for any loose or pulled-out pins.

5. Check the ECU electrical connectors for the same conditions described in Step 4.

6. Institute diagnostic code No. 08 to display the current lean-angle voltage reading. When the vehicle is sitting upright, the correct reading is 3.55-4.45 volts. When the

vehicle is inclined more than 65°, the correct reading is 0.65-1.35 volts. If the voltage reading is incorrect for the vehicle's resting position, test the lean-angle sensor as described in Chapter Nine.

7. To check if the problem has been corrected, start the engine and run at idle speed. Note the following:

a. If no fault code is displayed, the problem has been corrected. Erase the diagnostic code(s) as described in **Figure 7**.

b. If the fault code reappears, a problem still exists. Repeat the troubleshooting procedure or take the vehicle to a dealership and have them substitute the ECU with a known good ECU.

8. When the problem has been corrected, turn the ignition switch first to the OFF, then to the ON position.

Trouble Code 33 Malfunction Detected in the Primary Lead of the Ignition Coil (Diagnostic Code No. 30)

Refer to Chapter Nine.

1. Check the orange wire between the ignition coil connector and the black ECU 18-pin connector for an open or short circuit.

2. Check the brown/red wire between the ignition coil connector and ignition switch connector for an open or short circuit.

3. Check the ignition coil, ECU and ignition switch connectors for any loose or pulled-out pins.

4. Reconnect all of the connectors. Disconnect the spark plug cap, then install a spark tester into the ignition coil and ground it against the engine. Institute diagnostic code No. 30. When doing so the spark tester should fire 5 times in one second intervals. The engine trouble warning light should also flash 5 times. If there was no spark at the tester, remove and test the ignition coil as described in Chapter Nine.

5. To check if the problem has been corrected, start the engine and run at idle speed. Note the following:

a. If no fault code is displayed, the problem has been corrected. Erase the diagnostic code(s) as described in **Figure 7**.

b. If the fault code reappears, a problem still exists. Repeat the troubleshooting procedure or take the vehicle to a dealership and have them substitute the ECU with a known good ECU.

6. When the problem has been corrected, start the engine and operate the engine at idle speed to reinstate the indicator display.

Trouble Code 37 Engine Idle Speed is Too High (Diagnostic Code No. 54)

Refer to Chapter Eight.

1. Check for a blown backup fuse (Chapter Nine).

2. If the throttle valve does not close completely, a high engine idle can result. Perform the following:

a. Check the accelerator cable adjustment (Chapter Three).

b. Check the throttle valve and throttle bore for carbon or other contamination.

c. Check the throttle body for damage.

3. Check for a disconnected idle speed control unit hose or a disconnected connector. Both conditions can cause the idle speed control unit to be stuck in its open position.

NOTE
To check if the idle speed control unit is stuck open, start and run the engine at idle speed. Then touch the idle speed control unit with your hand and turn the ignition switch off. The unit should vibrate for approximately 3 seconds when the switch is turned off. If not, the idle speed control unit is stuck open.

4. Check for an open or short circuit in the wiring harness. Check for continuity in the white/green, red/green, brown/blue, pink/blue and red/white wires between the idle speed control unit connector and the two ECU connectors.

5. Institute diagnostic code No. 54. This actuates and closes the idle speed control unit. Then start the engine, which the unit will then open (operation takes approximately 12 seconds). Turning this time, touch the idle speed control unit with your hand. The unit will vibrate when its valve opens. Turn the engine off. If the error code reappears, replace the throttle body assembly, or refer to vehicle to a dealership for further testing.

6. When the problem has been corrected, turn the ignition switch on and then off. Then start the engine. The system is reinstated if the engine idle speed is within specification (1550-1650 rpm).

Trouble Code 39 Open or Short Circuit Detected in the Fuel Injector (Diagnostic Code No. 36)

Refer to Chapter Eight.

1. Make sure the fuel injector is properly installed.

2. Check the red wire between the fuel injector connector and the 18-pin ECU connector. Check the red/blue wire between the fuel injector, 26-pin ECU connector and the fuel injection system relay. Check the wires for an open or short circuit.

3. Check the fuel injector and ECU connectors for any loose or pulled-out pins.

4. Institute diagnostic code No. 36. When doing so the fuel injector should activate (audible click) 5 times in 1 second intervals. Check by listening to the fuel injector. Replace the fuel injector if it did not operate as described.

5. To check if the problem has been corrected, start the engine and run at idle speed. Note the following:

a. If no fault code is displayed, the problem has been corrected. Erase the diagnostic code(s) as described in **Figure 7**.

b. If the fault code reappears, a problem still exists. Repeat the troubleshooting procedure or take the

vehicle to a dealership and have them substitute the ECU with a known good ECU.

6. When the problem has been corrected, crank the engine to reinstate the indicator display.

Trouble Code 41 Open or Short Circuit Detected in the Lean-Angle Sensor (Diagnostic Code No. 08)

Refer to Chapter Nine.

1. Make sure the lean-angle sensor is properly installed. Check for loose mounting bolts.

2. Check the blue, yellow/green and black/blue wires between the lean-angle sensor and the 26-pin ECU connector for an open or short circuit.

3. Check the lean-angle sensor and 26-pin ECU electrical connectors for any loose or pulled-out pins.

4. Institute diagnostic code No. 08 to display the current lean-angle voltage reading. When the vehicle is sitting upright, the correct reading is 3.55-4.45 volts. When the vehicle is inclined more than 65°, the correct reading is 0.65-1.35 volts. If the voltage reading is incorrect for the vehicle's resting position, test the lean-angle sensor as described in Chapter Nine.

5. To check if the problem has been corrected, start the engine and run at idle speed. Note the following:

a. If no fault code is displayed, the problem has been corrected. Erase the diagnostic code(s) as described in **Figure 7**.

b. If the fault code reappears, a problem still exists. Repeat the troubleshooting procedure or take the vehicle to a dealership and have them substitute the ECU with a known good ECU.

6. When the problem has been corrected, turn the ignition switch on to reinstate the indicator display.

Trouble Code 42 Normal Signals are not Received from the Speed Sensor (Diagnostic Code No. 07)

Refer to Chapter Eight.

1. Make sure the speed sensor is properly installed. Check for loose mounting bolts.

2. Check the blue, white and black/blue wires between the speed sensor and the 26-pin ECU connector for an open or short circuit.

NOTE
The blue/yellow wire leading out of the speed sensor changes to a solid blue wire at the harness connector.

3. Check the speed sensor and 26-pin ECU electrical connectors for any loose or pulled-out pins.

4. The gear that detects vehicle speed may be damaged. Check for any clicking or other abnormal noise from the transmission that may indicate a gear problem.

5. Support the vehicle with the rear wheels off the ground. Institute diagnostic code No. 07 and rotate the rear wheels. The number on the indicator display should increase as

the rear wheels are rotated. The numbers do not reset until number 999 is reached. The number does not reset when the wheels stop turning. If the number does not increase, replace the speed sensor and retest.

6. To check if the problem has been corrected, start the engine and run at idle speed. Note the following:

    a. If no fault code is displayed, the problem has been corrected. Erase the diagnostic code(s) as described in **Figure 7**.

    b. If the fault code reappears, a problem still exists. Repeat the troubleshooting procedure or take the vehicle to a dealership and have them substitute the ECU with a known good ECU.

7. When the problem has been corrected, start the engine and run the vehicle at a speed between 12-19 mph (20-30 km/h) to reinstate the indicator display.

Trouble Code 43 Abnormal Power to the Fuel Injector and Fuel Pump (Diagnostic Code No. 09)

Refer to Chapter Eight.

1. Check the red/blue wire between the fuel pump, 26-pin ECU and fuel injection system relay connectors for a short or open circuit.

2. Check the brown/black wire between the fuel injection system relay and the starter relay for a short or open circuit.

3. Check the electrical connectors at the red/yellow and brown/black wire electrical connectors (refer to Step 1 and Step 2) for any loose or pulled-out pins.

4. Institute diagnostic code No. 09 to display the fuel pump voltage. Record this voltage and compare to the actual battery voltage. If the battery voltage is lower, recharge the battery and retest. If there is no fuel pump voltage and all of the wires and connectors are in good condition, test the fuel injection system relay as described in Chapter Eight.

5. To check if the problem has been corrected, start the engine and run at idle speed. Note the following:

    a. If no fault code is displayed, the problem has been corrected. Erase the diagnostic code(s) as described in **Figure 7**.

    b. If the fault code reappears, a problem still exists. Repeat the troubleshooting procedure or take the vehicle to a dealership and have them substitute the ECU with a known good ECU.

6. When the problem has been corrected, start the engine and run at idle speed to reinstate the indicator display.

Trouble Code 44 Error is Detected While Reading or Wiring on the EEPROM (Diagnostic Code No. 60)

1. Execute diagnostic code 60 and read the codes on the indicator display. Error code 00 indicates there is no faulty code history stored in memory. Error code 01 indicates that an error history code is stored in memory.

2. Start the engine and run at idle speed. Note the following:

    a. If no fault code is displayed, the problem has been corrected. Erase the diagnostic code(s) as described in **Figure 7**.

    b. If the fault code reappears, a problem still exists. Take the vehicle to a dealership and have them substitute the ECU with a known good ECU to see whether the problem still exists.

3. When the problem has been corrected, turn the ignition switch on to reinstate the indicator display.

Trouble Code 46 Abnormal Power to the ECU

1. Disconnect both ECU connectors and check for any loose or pulled-out pins.

2. Test the battery as described in Chapter Nine. Recharge or replace the battery if necessary and retest.

3. Test the charging system as described in Chapter Nine. Note the following:

    a. If the charging system is normal, continue with Step 4.

    b. If the charging system is not normal, troubleshoot the system as described in this chapter.

4. Check for an open or short circuit in the following wires:

    a. Red wire between the positive battery lead and the main fuse connector.

    b. Red wire between the main fuse connector and ignition fuse.

    c. Red/black wire between the ignition fuse and ignition switch.

5. To check if the problem has been corrected, start the engine and run at idle speed. Note the following:

    a. If no fault code is displayed, the problem has been corrected. Erase the diagnostic code(s) as described in **Figure 7**.

    b. If the fault code reappears, a problem still exists. Repeat the troubleshooting procedure.

6. When the problem has been corrected, start the engine and run at idle speed to reinstate the indicator display.

Trouble Code 50 ECU Internal Failure

NOTE
When the malfunction occurs in the ECU, the trouble code number may not appear on the indicator display.

1. Replace the ECU with a known good unit as described in Chapter Eight.

2. Turn the ignition switch on to reinstate the indicator display.

CHARGING SYSTEM TROUBLESHOOTING

Whenever there is a problem with the charging system, follow the troubleshooting procedures in order to help isolate the problem. If a test indicates that a component is working properly, reconnect the electrical connections (if disconnected) and proceed to the next step. Systematically work through the troubleshooting checklist until the problem is found. Repair or replace the defective parts as described in the appropriate section of the manual.

1. Check the main fuse (Chapter Nine).
2. Check and charge the battery (Chapter Nine). When the battery is fully charged, perform a load test as described in *Battery* in Chapter Nine to make sure the battery is in good condition and is not the problem.
3. Perform the current draw test as described in *Charging System* in Chapter Nine.
4. Perform the charging voltage test as described in *Charging System* in Chapter Nine. Note the following:
    a. If the charging voltage is not within specification, continue with Step 5.
    b. If the charging voltage is within specification, the charging system is working correctly.
5. Check the stator coil resistance (Chapter Nine).
6. Check the wiring and connectors for the entire charging system.
7. If the battery is good and the problem has not been located, replace the regulator/rectifier as described in Chapter Nine and repeat the charging voltage test.
8. Once a repair has been made, repeat the charging voltage test (Chapter Nine) to confirm the charging system is working correctly.

IGNITION SYSTEM TROUBLESHOOTING

If the engine trouble warning light stays on or flashes, refer to *Electronic Diagnostic System* in this chapter. Otherwise, perform the following steps in order:

1. Check the main, ignition and backup fuses (Chapter Nine).
2. Check and charge the battery (Chapter Nine). When the battery is fully charged, perform a load test as described under *Battery* in Chapter Nine to make sure the battery is in good condition and is not the problem.
3. Check for a worn or fouled spark plug (Chapter Three).
4. Perform the spark test as described in *Engine Does Not Start* in this chapter:
    a. If there is a strong spark at the spark plug, the ignition system is working correctly.
    b. If there is no spark or the spark is weak, continue with Step 5.
5. Check for a loose or damaged spark plug cap. Test the spark plug cap resistance as described in *Ignition Coil* in Chapter Nine.
6. Test the ignition coil (Chapter Nine).
7. Test the ignition switch (Chapter Nine).
8. Test the crankshaft position sensor (Chapter Nine).
9. Test the lean-angle sensor (Chapter Nine).
10. Carefully check all of the ignition system wiring and connectors for corrosion, damaged pins, loose pins or other damage. Refer to the wiring diagram at the end of this manual.

11. If the problem has not been found, have a dealership replace the ECU and retest.

STARTING SYSTEM TROUBLESHOOTING

When the ignition is turned on and the ignition switch is operated, current is transmitted from the battery to the starter relay. When the relay is activated, it activates the starter solenoid that mechanically engages the starter with the engine.

A starting system problem may be electrical or mechanical. Refer to *Engine Will Not Start* in this chapter for general troubleshooting procedures to help isolate the starting problems.

1. Check the main, backup, ignition and signal system fuses (Chapter Nine).
2. Check and charge the battery (Chapter Nine). When the battery is fully charged, perform a load test as described in *Battery* in Chapter Nine to make sure the battery is in good condition and is not the problem.

> *WARNING*
> *Step 3 will produce sparks. Make sure the area around the battery and test area is free of all flammable gas and other chemicals and materials and there are no fuel leaks on the vehicle.*

3. Use an auxiliary battery and apply battery voltage directly to the starter. Connect the positive lead to the starter motor cable and the negative lead to a good ground away from the fuel system. The starter should turn when battery voltage is directly applied.
    a. If the starter does not turn, disassemble and inspect the starter as described in Chapter Nine.
    b. If the starter turns, continue with Step 4.
4. Test the starter relay (Chapter Nine).
5. Test the load control relay (Chapter Nine).
6. Test the ignition switch (Chapter Nine).
7. Test the brake light switch (Chapter Nine).
8. Test the gear position switch (Chapter Nine).
9. Check all of the starting system wiring and connectors for corrosion, damaged pins, loose pins or other damage.
10. Replace the diode (Chapter Nine).
11. If the problem has not been found, have a dealership replace the ECU and retest.

ENGINE

Exhaust Smoke

The color of the exhaust can help diagnose engine problems or operating conditions.

Black

Black smoke is an indication of a rich air/fuel mixture where an excessive amount of fuel is being burned in the combustion chamber. Check for a leaking fuel injector or flooded throttle body as described in Chapter Eight.

Blue

Blue smoke indicates the engine is burning oil in the combustion chamber as it leaks past worn piston rings and/or worn valve stem seals. Excessive oil consumption is another indicator of an engine that is burning oil. Perform a compression test (Chapter Three) to isolate the problem.

White or steam

It is normal to see white smoke or steam from the exhaust after first starting the engine in cold weather. This is actually condensation formed by the engine during combustion. Once the engine heats up to normal operating temperature, the water evaporates and exits the engine through the crankcase vent system. However, if the vehicle is ridden for short trips or repeatedly started and stopped without reaching operating temperature, water will start to collect in the crankcase. As this water mixes with the oil in the crankcase, sludge is produced. Sludge can eventually cause engine damage as it circulates through the lubrication system and blocks off oil passages.

Low Compression

Problems with the engine top end will affect engine performance and drivability. When the engine is suspect, perform the leakdown procedure in this chapter and make a compression test as described in Chapter Three. Interpret the results as described in each procedure to troubleshoot the suspect area. A loss of engine compression can occur through the following areas:
1. Valves:
   a. Incorrect valve adjustment.
   b. Incorrect valve timing.
   c. Worn or damaged valve seats (valve and/or cylinder head).
   d. Bent valves.
   e. Weak or broken valve springs.
   f. Valve stuck open.
2. Cylinder head:
   a. Loose spark plug or damaged spark plug hole.
   b. Damaged cylinder head gasket.
   c. Warped or cracked cylinder head.

Preignition

Preignition is the premature burning of fuel and is caused by hot spots in the combustion chamber. Glowing deposits in the combustion chamber, inadequate cooling or an overheated spark plug can all cause preignition. This is first noticed as a power loss but eventually causes damage to the internal parts of the engine because of higher combustion chamber temperatures.

Detonation

Commonly called spark knock or fuel knock, detonation is the violent explosion of fuel in the combustion chamber before the proper time of ignition. Engine damage can result. Use of low octane gasoline is a common cause of detonation.

Even when using a high octane gasoline, detonation can occur. Other causes are over-advanced ignition timing, lean air/fuel mixture at or near full throttle, inadequate engine cooling or the excessive accumulation of carbon deposits in the combustion chamber (cylinder head and piston crown).

Power Loss

Refer to *Poor Engine Performance* in this chapter.

Noises

Unusual noises are often the first indication of a developing problem. Investigate any new noises as soon as possible. Something that may be a minor problem, if corrected early, could prevent the possibility of more extensive damage.

Use a mechanic's stethoscope or a small section of hose held near your ear (not directly on your ear) with the other end close to the source of the noise to isolate the location. Determining the exact cause of a noise can be difficult. If this is the case, consult with a professional mechanic to determine the cause. Do not disassemble major components until all other possibilities have been eliminated.

Consider the following when troubleshooting engine noises:
1. Knocking or pinging during acceleration is caused by using a lower octane fuel than recommended. It may also be caused by poor fuel. Pinging can also be caused by an incorrect spark plug heat range or carbon buildup in the combustion chamber.
2. Slapping or rattling noises at low speed or during acceleration may be caused by excessive piston-to-cylinder wall clearance (piston slap). Piston slap is easier to detect when the engine is cold and before the piston has expanded. Once the engine has warmed up, piston expansion reduces piston-to-cylinder clearance.
3. Knocking or rapping while decelerating is usually caused by excessive rod bearing clearance.
4. Persistent knocking and vibration occurring every crankshaft rotation is usually caused by worn rod or main bearing(s). It can also be caused by broken piston rings or a damaged piston pin.
5. A rapid on-off squeal may be a compression leak around the cylinder head gasket or spark plug.
6. For a valve train noise, check the following:
   a. Excessive valve clearance.
   b. Worn or damaged camshaft.
   c. Worn or damaged valve train components.

d. Valve sticking in guide.
e. Broken valve spring.
f. Low oil pressure.
g. Clogged oil passage.
7. For rattles, start checking where the sound is coming from.

ENGINE LUBRICATION

An improperly operating engine lubrication system will quickly lead to engine seizure. Check the engine oil level end pressure as described in Chapter Three. Oil pump service is described in Chapter Five.

High Oil Consumption or Excessive Exhaust Smoke

1. Worn valve guides.
2. Worn or damaged piston rings.

Low Oil Pressure

1. Low oil level.
2. Worn or damaged oil pump.
3. Clogged oil filter.
4. Clogged oil strainer (mounted on bottom of oil pump).
5. Internal oil leak.
6. Broken oil pump drive chain.
7. Damaged oil pump drive or driven sprockets.

High Oil Pressure

1. Oil pressure relief valve stuck closed.
2. Clogged oil filter.
3. Clogged oil gallery.

Oil Level Too Low

1. Oil level not maintained at the correct level.
2. External oil leaks.
3. Worn piston rings.
4. Worn cylinder.
5. Worn valve guides.
6. Worn valve stem seals.
7. Piston rings incorrectly installed during engine overhaul.

Oil Contamination

1. Worn or damaged piston ring.
2. Oil and filter not changed at specified intervals or when operating conditions demand more frequent changes.

CYLINDER LEAKDOWN TEST

A cylinder leakdown test can locate engine problems from leaking valves, a blown head gasket or broken, and

worn or stuck piston rings. This test is performed by applying compressed air to the cylinder and then measuring the leak percentage or pressure loss.

Follow the manufacturer's directions along with the following information.
1. Start and run the engine until it is warm. Turn it off.
2. Remove the spark plug (Chapter Three).

NOTE
With the fuel tank installed in the frame, the flywheel timing marks cannot be viewed. Align the camshaft sprocket index mark with the cylinder head boss as described in Step 3. If this does not work, remove the fuel tank (Chapter Eight) and use the procedures in **Cylinder Head** *in Chapter Four to set the engine at TDC on its compression stroke.*

3. Set the piston to top dead center (TDC) on its compression stroke as described in Chapter Three in *Valve Clearance*.

WARNING
The crankshaft may rotate when compressed air is applied to the cylinder. Remove any tools attached to the end of the crankshaft.

4. Thread the test adapter into the spark plug hole. Connect the air compressor hose to the tester (**Figure 9**).
5. Apply compressed air to the leakdown tester. Read the leak rate on the gauge and interpret the results as follows:
   a. 0 to 5%: Engine is in excellent condition.
   b. 6 to 14%: Engine is in good condition.
   c. 15 to 22%: Engine is in poor condition. While the engine can operate in this condition, performance is greatly reduced.
   d. 23% and higher: Engine is suffering from severe wear and possible damage. Engine overhaul is required.

NOTE
If the engine is showing a 100% loss from the engine, the piston is probably not at TDC its compression stroke. If the timing marks are

aligned, turn the crankshaft 360° and realign the timing marks (Step 3).

6. With air pressure still applied to the cylinder, listen for air escaping from the following areas. If necessary, use a mechanic's stethoscope to pinpoint the source.

    a. Air leaking through the exhaust pipe indicates a leaking exhaust valve.

    b. Air leaking through the throttle body indicates a leaking intake valve.

    c. Air leaking through the crankcase breather tube suggests worn piston rings or a worn cylinder bore.

    d. Remove the radiator cap. If the coolant is bubbling and air is escaping through the radiator cap opening, the cylinder head gasket is leaking. This can be caused by a damaged head gasket or a warped cylinder head or cylinder block.

7. Remove the leakdown tester.

8. Record the results in the back of this manual for future reference.

CLUTCH TROUBLESHOOTING

Clutch service is covered in Chapter Six.

Engine Runs But Vehicle Will Not Move When In Gear

Drive belt

1. Worn or damaged drive belt.
2. Drive belt is slipping between sheaves.

Primary pulley slider and primary pulley cam

1. Worn or damaged primary pulley slider.
2. Worn or damaged primary pulley cam.
3. Damaged transmission.

Vehicle Moves When In Gear But Under Hesitation or Jerking

Drive belt

1. Drive belt contaminated with grease.
2. Drive belt is slipping between sheaves.

Clutch shoe

1. Clutch shoe is worn, bent or damaged.

Primary sliding sheave

1. Worn pin.
2. Worn pin groove.
3. Faulty primary sliding sheave operation.

Clutch Slips

1. Worn or damaged clutch shoe.
2. Loose, worn or damaged clutch shoe spring.
3. Seized primary sliding sheave.

Poor Engine Performance (Clutch Problem)

1. Drive belt slipping, worn or damaged.
2. Primary fixed sheave worn or damaged.
3. Primary pulley weights worn or damaged.
4. Primary sliding sheave worn or damaged.
5. Secondary fixed sheave worn or damaged.
6. Secondary sliding sheave worn or damaged.

TRANSMISSION TROUBLESHOOTING

Transmission symptoms are sometimes difficult to distinguish from clutch symptoms. Before working on the transmission, make sure the clutch is not causing the problem. Refer to Chapter Seven for select lever and transmission service procedures and to identify the parts called out in the following procedures.

Before troubleshooting the clutch or transmission, turn the ignition switch on and shift the transmission into the low gear, high gear, neutral and reverse. Make sure the shift indicator light for each position comes on when the gear position is made. If not, adjust the select lever (Chapter Three).

Difficult Shifting

Refer to *Clutch Troubleshooting* in this chapter.

Difficult Shifting to All Positions

Select lever

1. Incorrect select lever adjustment.
2. Damaged shift rod.
3. Loose or missing shift arm mounting bolt.
4. Loose shift arm-to-shift shaft engagement. Shoulders on both parts are damaged.

External shift mechanism

1. Loose or missing shift arm mounting bolt.
2. Loose shift arm-to-shift shaft engagement. Shoulders on both parts are damaged.
3. Damaged shift shaft.
4. Damaged shift lever 1.
5. Damaged shift lever 1 spring.
6. Damaged shift lever 2.
7. External shift mechanism incorrectly assembled (problem started after reassembly).

Select Lever Does Not Move or is Jammed

1. Damaged shift lever assembly.
2. Seized or damaged external shift mechanism.
3. Seized shift fork.
4. Bent shift fork shaft.
5. Damaged shift drum grooves.
6. Seized transmission gear.
7. Debris lodged in shift drum grooves.
8. Transmission incorrectly assembled (problem started after engine rebuild).

Jumps Out of Gear

1. Excessive shift drum thrust play.
2. Worn or damaged shift drum grooves.
3. Worn or damaged shift forks.
4. Worn gear dogs or slots.
5. Bent shift fork shaft.
6. Damaged shift fork assembly spring.
7. Damaged or missing shift fork shaft snap rings.
8. Debris lodged in shift drum grooves.

Excessive Gear Noise

1. Worn or damaged transmission bearings.
2. Worn or damaged gears.
3. Excessive gear backlash.

AXLES, DIFFERENTIAL AND FINAL DRIVE UNIT

Problems with the axles, differential and final drive unit are often accompanied by noise. If damage to one of these units is suspected, try to isolate where the sound originates. Support the vehicle with the wheels off the ground. Turn the axles and feel the exterior of the differential and final drive unit. Excessive wear or damage can often be felt through the parts, especially an irregular knock as the parts are rotated. Also, immediately after operating the machine, feel the components for excessive heat, particularly around the axle and shaft bearings. Use an infrared thermometer to compare temperatures from the operating surfaces.

Refer to Chapter Twelve and Chapter Fourteen to identify the components.

Symptoms of Damage

The following are likely symptoms of damage to the axles, differential or final drive unit.
1. Excessive play in the axle.
2. Axle binding and vibration.
3. Locked axle.
4. A low-pitch rumble or high-pitch whine when the vehicle is in motion.
5. A delayed knock or metallic sound that quickly follows acceleration or deceleration.

Possible Causes of Damage

The following are possible causes of damage to the axles, differential or final drive unit.
1. Worn or damaged CV joints.
2. Bent axle.
3. Seized or damaged wheel bearing(s).
4. Seized or damaged differential/final drive unit bearing.
5. Broken or damaged teeth in differential drive unit.
6. Incorrect gear lash in differential/final drive unit.
7. Debris lodged between differential/final drive unit parts.

DRIVE SHAFTS AND MIDDLE GEAR UNIT

Problems with the drive shafts and middle gear components are difficult to diagnose without removing and inspecting the parts. Always try to isolate where the sound originates before assuming the drive shafts or middle gear components are damaged. Inspect the axles, differential and final drive unit before disassembling the drive shafts and middle gear unit.

Refer to Chapter Five to identify the middle gear components.

Symptoms of Damage

The following are likely symptoms of damage to the drive shaft and/or middle gear components.
1. A low-pitch rumble or high-pitch whine when the machine is in motion.
2. A delayed knock or metallic sound that quickly follows acceleration or deceleration.
3. Binding or erratic machine movement, accompanied by inconsistent engine speed.
4. Lock drive shafts, with no power going to either axle.

Possible Causes of Damage

The following are possible causes of damage to the drive shaft and/or middle gear components.
1. Stripped or slipping drive shaft splines and couplers.
2. Bent drive shaft.
3. Seized or damaged middle gear unit bearing.
4. Broken or damaged teeth in middle gear unit.
5. Improper gear lash in middle gear unit.
6. Debris lodged between middle gear unit parts.

ELECTRICAL TESTING

This section describes electrical troubleshooting and the use of test equipment.

Never assume anything and do not overlook the obvious, such as a blown fuse or an electrical connector that has separated. Test the simplest and most obvious items first and try to make tests at easily accessible points on the vehicle. Make sure to troubleshoot systematically.

Refer to the color wiring diagrams at the end of this manual for component and connector identification. Use the wiring diagrams to determine how the circuit should work by tracing the current paths from the power source through the circuit components to ground. Also check any circuits that share the same fuse, ground or switch. If the other circuits work properly and the shared wiring is good, the cause must be in the wiring used only by the suspect circuit. If all related circuits are faulty at the same time, the probable cause is a poor ground connection or a blown fuse(s).

Preliminary Checks and Precautions

Before starting any electrical troubleshooting, perform the following:
1. Inspect the fuse for the suspected circuit, and replace it if blown. Refer to Chapter Nine.
2. Test the battery (Chapter Nine). Make sure it is fully charged and the battery leads are clean and securely attached to the battery terminals.
3. Electrical connectors are often the cause of electrical system problems. Inspect the connectors as follows:
   a. Disconnect each electrical connector in the suspect circuit and make sure there are no bent terminals in the electrical connector. A bent terminal will not connect to its mate, causing an open circuit.
   b. Make sure the terminals are pushed all the way into the connector. If not, carefully push them in with a narrow blade screwdriver or a terminal tool.
   c. Check the wires where they attach to the terminals for damage.
   d. Make sure each terminal is clean and free of corrosion. Clean them, if necessary, and pack the connectors with dielectric grease.
   e. Push the connector halves together. Make sure the connectors are fully engaged and locked together.
   f. Never pull the wires when disconnecting a connector. Pull only on the connector housing.
4. Never use a self-powered test light on circuits that contain solid-state devices. The solid-state devices may be damaged.

Intermittent Problems

Problems that do not occur all the time can be difficult to isolate during testing. For example, when a problem only occurs when the vehicle is ridden over rough roads (vibration) or in wet conditions (water penetration). Note the following:
1. Vibration. This is a common problem with loose or damaged electrical connectors.
   a. Perform a continuity test as described in the appropriate service procedure or in *Continuity Test* in this section.
   b. Lightly pull or wiggle the connectors while repeating the test. Do the same when checking the wiring har-

ness and individual components, especially where the wires enter a housing or connector.
   c. A change in meter readings indicates a poor connection. Find and repair the problem or replace the part. Check for wires with cracked or broken insulation.

NOTE
An analog ohmmeter is useful when making this type of test. Slight needle movements are visibly apparent, which indicate a loose connection.

2. Heat. This is a common problem with connectors or joints that have loose or poor connections. As these connections heat up, the connection or joint expands and separates, causing an open circuit. Other heat related problems occur when a component starts to fail as it heats up.
   a. Troubleshoot the problem to isolate the circuit.

CAUTION
A heat gun will quickly raise the temperature of the component being tested. Do not apply heat directly to the ECU or use heat in excess of 60° C (140° F) on any electrical component.

   b. To check a connector, perform a continuity test as described in the appropriate service procedure or in *Continuity Test* in this section. Then repeat the test while heating the connector with a heat gun. If the meter reading was normal (continuity) when the connector was cold, and then fluctuated or read infinity when heat was applied, the connection is bad.
   c. To check a component, allow the engine to cool, and then start and run the engine. Note operational differences when the engine is cold and hot.
   d. If the engine will not start, isolate and remove the suspect component. Test it at room temperature and again after heating it. A change in meter readings indicates a temperature problem.
3. Water. When the problem occurs when riding in wet conditions or in areas with high humidity, start and run the engine in a dry area. Then, with the engine running, spray water onto the suspected component/circuit. Water-related problems often stop after the component heats up and dries.

Test Light or Voltmeter

Use a test light to check for voltage in a circuit. Attach one lead to ground and the other lead to various points along the circuit. It does not make a difference which test lead is attached to ground. The bulb lights when voltage is present.

Use a voltmeter in the same manner as the test light to find out if voltage is present in any given circuit. The voltmeter, unlike the test light, also indicates how much voltage is present at each test point.

Voltage test

Unless otherwise specified, make all voltage tests with the electrical connectors still connected. Insert the test leads into the backside of the connector and make sure the test lead touches the electrical terminal within the connector housing. If the test lead only touches the wire insulation, it will cause a false reading. Back probe pins can be used for these tests. Refer to *Back Probe Pins* in *Measuring Tools* in Chapter One.

Always check both sides of the connector because one side may be loose or corroded, thus preventing electrical flow through the connector. This type of test can be performed with a test light or a voltmeter.

1. Attach the voltmeter negative test lead to a confirmed ground location. If possible, use the battery ground connection. Make sure the ground is not insulated.

2. Attach the voltmeter positive test lead to the point to be tested (**Figure 10**).

3. Turn the ignition switch on. If using a test light, the test light will come on if voltage is present. If using a voltmeter, note the voltage reading. The reading should be within 1 volt of battery voltage. If the voltage is less there is a problem in the circuit.

Voltage drop test

The wires, cables, connectors and switches in the electrical circuit are designed to carry current with low resistance. This ensures current can flow through the circuit with a minimum loss of voltage. Voltage drop indicates where there is resistance in a circuit. A higher-than-normal amount of resistance in a circuit decreases the flow of current and causes the voltage to drop between the source and destination in the circuit.

Because resistance causes voltage to drop, a voltmeter is used to measure voltage drop when current is running through the circuit. If the circuit has no resistance, there is no voltage drop so the voltmeter indicates 0 volts. The greater the resistance in a circuit, the greater the voltage drop reading.

To perform a voltage drop:

1. Connect the positive meter test lead to the electrical source (where electricity is coming from).

2. Connect the voltmeter negative test lead to the electrical load (where the electricity is going). Refer to **Figure 11**.

3. If necessary, activate the component(s) in the circuit.

4. Read the voltage drop (difference in voltage between the source and destination) on the voltmeter. Note the following:

    a. The voltmeter should indicate 0 volts. If there is a drop of 1 volt or more, there is a problem within the circuit. A voltage drop reading of 12 volts indicates an open in the circuit.

    b. A voltage drop of 1 or more volts indicates that a circuit has excessive resistance.

    c. For example, consider a starting problem where the battery is fully charged but the starter turns over

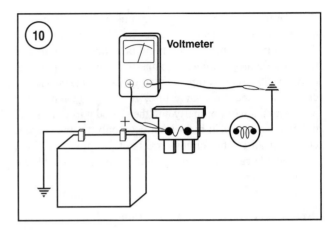

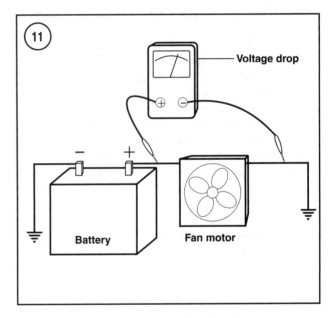

slowly. Voltage drop would be the difference in the voltage at the battery (source) and the voltage at the starter (destination) as the engine is being started (current is flowing through the battery cables). A corroded battery cable would cause a high voltage drop (high resistance) and slow engine cranking.

    d. Common sources of voltage drop are loose or contaminated connectors and poor ground connections.

Testing For a Short with a Voltmeter

A test light may also be used.

1. Remove the blown fuse from the fuse panel.

2. Connect the voltmeter across the fuse terminals in the fuse panel. Turn the ignition switch on and check for battery voltage.

3. With the voltmeter attached to the fuse terminals, wiggle the wiring harness relating to the suspect circuit at approximately 15.2 cm (6 in.) intervals. Start next to the fuse panel and work systematically away from the panel. Note the voltmeter reading while progressing along the harness.

4. If the voltmeter reading changes (test light blinks), there is a short-to-ground at that point in the harness.

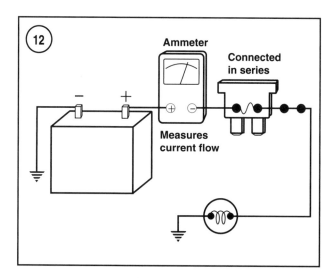

Ammeter

Use an ammeter to measure the flow of current (amps) in a circuit (**Figure 12**). When connected in series in a circuit, the ammeter determines if current is flowing through the circuit and if that current flow is excessive because of a short in the circuit. Current flow is often referred to as current draw. Comparing actual current draw in the circuit or component to current draw specification (if specified by the manufacturer) provides useful diagnostic information.

Self-powered Test Light

A self-powered test light can be constructed from a 12-volt light bulb, a pair of test leads and a 12-volt battery. When the test leads are touched together the light bulb should go on.

Use a self-powered test light as follows:
1. Touch the test leads together to make sure the light bulb goes on. If not, correct the problem.
2. Disconnect the vehicle's battery or remove the fuse(s) that protects the circuit to be tested. Do not connect a self-powered test light to a circuit that has power applied to it.
3. Select two points within the circuit where there should be continuity.
4. Attach one lead of the test light to each point.
5. If there is continuity, the test light bulb will come on.
6. If there is no continuity, the test light bulb will not come on, indicating an open circuit.

Ohmmeter

> *CAUTION*
> *To prevent damage to the ohmmeter, never connect it to a circuit that has power applied to it. Always disconnect the battery negative lead before using an ohmmeter.*

Use an ohmmeter to measure the resistance (in ohms) to current flow in a circuit or component.

Ohmmeters may be analog type (needle scale) or digital type (LCD or LED readout). Both types of ohmmeters have a switch that allows the user to select different ranges of resistance for accurate readings. The analog ohmmeter also has a set-adjust control which is used to zero or calibrate the meter (digital ohmmeters do not require calibration). Refer to the ohmmeter's instructions to determine the correct scale setting.

Use an ohmmeter by connecting its test leads to the circuit or component to be tested. If an analog meter is used, it must be calibrated by touching the test leads together and turning the set-adjust knob until the meter needle reads zero. When the leads are uncrossed, the needle should move to the other end of the scale, indicating infinite resistance.

During a continuity test, a reading of infinite resistance indicates there is an open in the circuit or component. A reading of zero indicates continuity, that is, there is no measurable resistance in the circuit or component. A measured reading indicates the actual resistance to current flow that is present in that circuit. Even though resistance is present, the circuit has continuity.

Continuity test

Perform a continuity test to determine the integrity of a circuit, wire or component. A circuit has continuity if it forms a complete circuit; that is if there are no opens in either the electrical wires or components within the circuit. A circuit with an open, on the other hand, has no continuity.

This type of test can be performed with a self-powered test light or an ohmmeter. An ohmmeter gives the best results.
1. Disconnect the negative battery cable or disconnect the test circuit/component from its power source.
2. Attach one test lead (test light or ohmmeter) to one end of the part of the circuit to be tested.
3. Attach the other test lead to the other end of the part or the circuit to be tested.
4. The self-powered test light comes on if there is continuity. An ohmmeter reads 0 or low resistance if there is continuity. A reading of infinite resistance indicates no continuity; the circuit is open.
5. If testing a component, note the resistance and compare this to the specification if available.

Testing for short with an ohmmeter

An analog ohmmeter or one with an audible continuity indicator works best for short testing. A self-powered test light may also be used.
1. Disconnect the negative battery cable.
2. If necessary, remove the blown fuse from the fuse panel.
3. Connect one test lead of the ohmmeter to the load side (battery side) of the fuse terminal in the fuse panel.

4. Connect the other test lead to a confirmed ground location. Make sure the ground is not insulated. If possible, use the battery ground connection.

5. Wiggle the wiring harness relating to the suspect circuit at approximately 15.2 cm (6 in.) intervals. Watch the ohmmeter while progressing along the harness.

6. If the ohmmeter needle moves or the ohmmeter beeps, there is a short-to-ground at that point in the harness.

Jumper Wire

Use a jumper wire to bypass a potential problem and isolate it to a particular point in a circuit. If a faulty circuit works properly with a jumper wire installed, an open exists between the two jumped points in the circuit.

To troubleshoot with a jumper wire, first use the wire to determine if the problem is on the ground side or the load side of a device. Test the ground by connecting the wire between the lamp and a good ground. If the lamp comes on, the problem is the connection between the lamp and ground. If the lamp does not come on with the wire installed, the lamp's connection to ground is good, so the problem is between the lamp and the power source.

To isolate the problem, connect the wire between the battery and the lamp. If it comes on, the problem is between these two points. Next, connect the wire between the battery and the fuse side of the switch. If the lamp comes on, the switch is good. By successively moving the wire from one point to another, the problem can be isolated to a particular place in the circuit.

Note the following when using a jumper wire:

1. Make sure the wire gauge (thickness) is the same as that used in the circuit being tested. Smaller gauge wire rapidly overheats and could melt.

2. Make sure the jumper wire has insulated alligator clips. This prevents accidental grounding (sparks) or possible shock. Install an inline fuse/fuse holder in the jumper wire.

3. A jumper wire is a temporary test measure. Do not leave a jumper wire installed as a permanent solution. This creates a fire hazard.

4. Never use a jumper wire across any load (a component that is connected and turned on). This would cause a direct short and blow the fuse(s).

LIGHTING AND SIGNAL SYSTEM TROUBLESHOOTING

When troubleshooting lighting and signal system components, first check the fuses, battery and ignition switch as described in Chapter Nine. If these are all good, follow the steps in the appropriate section:

CAUTION
*The ECU and meter assembly are expensive. Be sure the part to be replaced is faulty before purchasing a new one. Most dealerships do not accept returned electrical components. Refer to **Electrical Component Replacement** in Chapter Nine.*

Brake Light Does Not Operate

1. Check for a blown bulb.

2. Test the brake light switch as described in *Switches* in Chapter Nine.

3. Perform the *Taillight/Brake Light Voltage Test* in *Lighting System* in Chapter Nine.

4. Check the brake light and signal system wiring for damaged or contaminated connectors or frayed or damaged wiring.

Headlights or Taillights Fail to Operate

1. Check for a blown main, headlight or ignition fuse (Chapter Nine).

2. Test the battery as described in *Switches* in Chapter Nine.

3. Test the ignition switch as described in *Switches* in Chapter Nine.

4. Test the light switch (Chapter Nine).

5. Test the load control relay (Chapter Nine).

6. When testing for an inoperative headlight, also perform for the following:

   a. *Headlight Voltage Test* in *Lighting System* in Chapter Nine.

   b. *Headlight Relay Testing/Removal/Installation* in *Lighting System* in Chapter Nine.

7. Check the wiring harness assembly and connectors used in the lighting system. Refer to the wiring diagrams at the end of this manual.

Brake Light, Warning Light or Indicator Light Fail to Operate

1. Check for a blown backup, ignition or signal system fuse (Chapter Nine).

2. Test the battery (Chapter Nine).

3. Test the ignition switch as described in *Swtiches* in (Chapter Nine).

4. Test the load control relay (Chapter Nine).

5. Check the wiring harness assembly and connectors used in the lighting system. Refer to the wiring diagrams at the end of this manual.

Any Indicator Light Fails to Operate

Perform the appropriate test in *Indicator Light and Circuit Testing* in *Meter Assembly and Indicator Lights* Chapter Nine.

FRONT SUSPENSION AND STEERING

Steering is Sluggish

1. Tire pressure too low.
2. Damaged tire(s).
3. Damaged steering gearbox, steering column or steering shaft.
4. Damaged tie rods.
5. Incorrect steering adjustment.
6. Worn or damaged front axles.
7. Incorrectly installed steering or suspension components.
8. Damaged frame.

Vehicle Steers to One Side

1. Incorrect steering adjustment.
2. Tire pressure unequal.
3. Damaged tires or wheels.
4. Bent tie rod.
5. Bent suspension arm.
6. Damaged shock absorber.
7. Damaged steering bearings.
8. Damaged front hub.
9. Bent frame.
10. Incorrect wheel alignment.

Front Wheel Wobble

1. Loose wheel nuts.
2. Damaged wheel.
3. Loose or damaged wheel studs.
4. Wheel improperly installed.
5. Tire improperly seated on wheel rim.
6. Damaged steering bearings.
7. Excessive wheel bearing play in steering knuckle.
8. Damaged front hub.

Front End Too Soft

1. Weak or damaged front shock absorber spring.
2. Damaged shock absorber (leaking damper).

Front End Too Stiff

1. Seized or damaged suspension arm pivot bolts.
2. Damaged suspension arm(s).
3. Shock absorber damper rod bent or seized.
4. Aftermarket spring installed with too stiff spring rate.

Front Suspension Noise

1. Loose suspension or steering fasteners.
2. Damaged suspension or steering component.
3. Suspension arms binding.
4. Damaged shock absorber(s).

REAR SUSPENSION

Rear Wheel Wobble

1. Loose wheel nuts.
2. Damaged wheel.
3. Loose or damaged wheel studs.
4. Wheel improperly installed.
5. Tire improperly seated on wheel rim.
6. Damaged rear hub.
7. Damaged rear axle.
8. Damaged knuckle bearings.

Rear Axle Hard to Turn

1. Dragging parking brake.
2. Dragging wheel brake(s).
3. Bent rear axle.
4. Damaged knuckle bearings.
5. Damaged final drive unit.

Rear End Too Soft

1. Incorrect shock absorber adjustment.
2. Weak or damaged shock absorber spring.
3. Damaged shock absorber (leaking damper).

Rear End Too Stiff

1. Incorrect shock absorber adjustment.
2. Shock absorber damper rod bent or seized.
3. Aftermarket spring installed with too stiff spring rate.

Rear Suspension Noise

1. Loose suspension fasteners.
2. Damaged suspension component.
3. Worn or damaged suspension linkage bearing(s).
4. Damaged shock absorber.

BRAKE SYSTEM

The brake system is critical to driving performance and safety. Always check the brake operation before driving the vehicle. Inspect the front and rear brakes frequently and repair any problem immediately. When replacing or refilling the brake fluid, use only DOT 4 brake fluid from a closed container. Refer to Chapter Three and Chapter Fifteen for brake inspection and service.

Refer to *Parking Brake* in this section to troubleshoot the parking brake assembly.

Soft or Spongy Brake Pedal

Quickly operate the brake pedal and check to see if the pedal travel distance increases. If the pedal travel does increase while being operated, or feels soft or spongy, there may be air in the brake lines. In this condition, the brake system is not capable of producing sufficient brake force. When an increase in pedal travel is noticed or when the brake feels soft or spongy, check the following possible causes:

1. Air in system.

NOTE
If the brake level in the reservoir drops too low, air can enter the hydraulic system through the master cylinder. Air can also enter the system from loose or damaged hose fittings. Air in the hydraulic system causes a soft or spongy brake pedal action. This condition is noticeable and reduces brake performance. When it is suspected that air has entered the system, bleed the brakes as described in Chapter Fifteen.

2. Low brake fluid level.

NOTE
As the brake pads wear, the brake fluid level in the master cylinder reservoir drops. Whenever adding brake fluid to the reservoirs, visually check the brake pads for wear. If it does not appear that there is an increase in pad wear, check the brake hoses, lines and banjo bolts for leaks.

3. Leak in the brake system.
4. Contaminated brake fluid.
5. Plugged brake fluid passages.
6. Damaged brake pedal assembly.
7. Worn or damaged brake pads.
8. Worn or damaged brake disc.
9. Warped brake disc.
10. Contaminated brake pads and disc.
11. Worn or damaged master cylinder cups and/or cylinder bore.
12. Worn or damaged brake caliper piston seals.
13. Contaminated master cylinder assembly.
14. Contaminated brake caliper assembly.
15. Brake caliper not sliding correctly on fixed shafts.
16. Sticking master cylinder piston assembly.
17. Sticking brake caliper pistons.

Brake Drag

When the brakes drag, the brake pads are not capable of moving away from the brake disc when the brake pedal is released. Any of the following causes, if they occur, would prevent correct brake pad movement and cause brake drag.

1. Warped or damaged brake disc.
2. Brake caliper not sliding correctly on fixed shafts.
3. Sticking or damaged brake caliper pistons.
4. Worn or damaged brake caliper seals.
5. Contaminated brake pads and disc.

6. Plugged master cylinder port.
7. Contaminated brake fluid and hydraulic passages.
8. Restricted brake hose joint.
9. Loose brake disc mounting bolts.
10. Damaged or misaligned wheel.
11. Incorrect wheel alignment.
12. Incorrectly installed brake caliper.

Hard Pedal Operation

When the brakes are applied and there is sufficient brake performance but the operation of the brake pedal feels excessively hard, check for the following possible causes:

1. Clogged brake hydraulic system.
2. Sticking caliper piston.
3. Sticking master cylinder piston.
4. Glazed or worn brake pads.
5. Mismatched brake pads.
6. Damaged brake pedal.
7. Brake caliper not sliding correctly on fixed shafts.
8. Worn or damaged brake caliper seals.

Brakes Grab

1. Damaged brake pad pin bolt. Look for steps or cracks along the pad pin bolt surface.
2. Contaminated brake pads and disc.
3. Incorrect wheel alignment.
4. Warped brake disc.
5. Loose brake disc mounting bolts.
6. Brake caliper not sliding correctly on fixed shafts.
7. Mismatched brake pads.
8. Damaged wheel bearings.

Brake Squeal or Chatter

1. Contaminated brake pads and disc.
2. Incorrectly installed brake caliper.
3. Warped brake disc.
4. Incorrect wheel alignment.
5. Mismatched brake pads.
6. Incorrectly installed brake pads.
7. Loose brake system fasteners.

Leaking Brake Caliper

1. Damaged dust and piston seals.
2. Damaged cylinder bore.
3. Loose banjo bolt.
4. Missing or damaged banjo bolt washers.
5. Damaged banjo bolt threads in caliper body.

Leaking Master Cylinder

1. Damaged piston secondary seal.
2. Damaged piston circlip/circlip groove.

3. Worn or damaged master cylinder bore.
4. Loose banjo bolt.
5. Missing or damaged banjo bolt washers.
6. Damaged banjo bolt threads in master cylinder body.
7. Loose or damaged reservoir cap and/or diaphragm.

Parking Brake

This is a mechanical system that locks the parking brake disc mounted on the rear drive shaft.

Parking brake does not work

If the parking brake will not hold the vehicle when applied, note the following:
1. Check the parking brake lever, caliper and cable for damage.
2. Make sure the parking brake disc mounting bolts are tight and the disc is not warped or damaged.
3. Check for worn or damaged parking brake pads as described in Chapter Three.
4. Check the parking brake adjustment as described in Chapter Three.
5. If necessary, remove and service the parking brake caliper as described in Chapter Fifteen.

Parking brake drags

To check for a dragging parking brake, perform the following:
1. Shift the transmission into neutral and block the front wheels so the vehicle cannot roll.
2. Raise the vehicle so the rear wheels are off the ground.
3. Apply the parking brake. The rear wheels should not turn.
4. Release the parking brake. The rear wheels should turn.
5. If the parking brake drags, perform the following:
   a. Check the parking brake lever, caliper and cable for damage.
   b. Check for contaminated or damaged parking brake pads as described in Chapter Three.
   c. Make sure the parking brake disc mounting bolts are tight and the disc is not warped or damaged.
   d. Check the parking brake adjustment as described in Chapter Three.
   e. Check for a damaged barking brake caliper as described in Chapter Fifteen.
   f. Check for a damaged rear drive shaft as described in Chapter Fourteen.

Table 1 and Table 2 are on the following pages.

Table 1 TROUBLE CODES

Trouble code number	Symptoms	Probable cause of malfunction	Diagnostic code number
12	1. Normal signals are not received from the crankshaft position sensor. 2. Engine is unable to start.	1. Open or short circuit in wiring harness. 2. Defective crankshaft position sensor. 3. ECU malfunction. 4. Improperly installed sensor.	–
13	1. Intake air pressure sensor open or short circuit detected. 2. Engine is able to start.	1. Open or short circuit in the wiring harness. 2. Defective intake air pressure sensor. 3. ECU malfunction	03
14	1. Faulty intake air pressure sensor hose system. 2. Engine is able to start.	1. Hose is detached, clogged or damaged. 2. Defective intake air pressure sensor. 3. ECU malfunction.	03
15	1. Throttle position sensor open or short circuit detected. 2. Engine is able to start.	1. Open or short circuit in wiring harness. 2. Defective throttle position sensor. 3. ECU malfunction. 4. Improperly installed throttle position sensor.	01
16	1. Stuck throttle position sensor detected. 2. Engine is able to start.	1. Stuck throttle position sensor. 2. ECU malfunction.	01
21	1. Coolant temperature sensor open or short circuit detected. 2. Engine is able to start.	1. Defective coolant temperature sensor. 2. Open or short circuit in wire harness. 3. ECU malfunction. 4. Improperly installed coolant temperature sensor.	06
22	1. Intake air temperature sensor, open or short circuit detected. 2. Engine is able to start.	1. Defective intake air temperature sensor. 2. Open or short circuit in wiring harness. 3. ECU malfunction. 4. Improperly installed intake air temperature sensor.	05
30	1. Vehicle has overturned. 2. Engine is unable to start.	1. Vehicle overturned. 2. ECU malfunction. 3. Lean angle sensor malfunction. 4. Incorrectly installed lean angle sensor.	08
33	1. Ignition coil primary lead malfunction detected. 2. Engine is unable to start.	1. Defective ignition coil. 2. Open or short circuit in wiring harness. 3. ECU malfunction. 4. Ignition cut-off circuit component malfunction.	30
37	1. Engine idle speed is too high. 2. Engine is able to start.	1. Blown backup fuse. 2. Incorrect throttle cable adjustment. 3. Damaged throttle cable. 4. Open circuit in wiring harness. 5. Idle speed control valve is stuck in open position. 6. Throttle body contamination. 7. Throttle body malfunction. 8. ECU malfunction.	54
39	1. Open circuit detected in the fuel injector. 2. Engine is unable to start.	1. Open or short circuit in wiring harness. 2. Injector improperly installed. 3. Injector malfunction.	36

(continued)

Table 1 TROUBLE CODES (continued)

Trouble code number	Symptoms	Probable cause of malfunction	Diagnostic code number
41	1. Lean-angle sensor open or short circuit detected. 2. Engine is unable to start.	1. Open or short circuit in wiring harness. 2. Defective lean-angle sensor. 3. ECU malfunction.	08
42	1. No signals are received from the speed sensor. 2. Engine is able to start.	1. Open or short circuit in wiring harness. 2. Defective speed sensor. 3. Malfunction in the speed sensor detected. 4. Defective neutral switch. 5. Malfunction in the engine side of the neutral switch. 6. ECU malfunction.	07
43	1. Fuel pump and fuel injector battery voltage failure. 2. Engine is able to start.	1. Open or short circuit in wiring harness. 2. ECU malfunction.	09
44	1. An error is detected while reading or writing on EEPROM.	1. ECU malfunction.	60
46	1. Fuel injection battery voltage failure. 2. Engine is able to start.	1. Charging system malfunction.	–
50	1. Faulty ECU memory. 2. Engine is unable to start.	1. ECU malfunction	–
Er-1	1. No signals received from the ECU. 2. Engine is unable to start.	1. Open or short circuit in wiring harness. 2. ECU malfunction.	–
Er-2	1. No signals are received from the ECU. 2. Engine is unable to start.	1. Open or short circuit in wiring harness. 2. ECU malfunction.	–
Er-3	1. Data from the ECU cannot be received correctly. 2. Engine unable to start.	1. Open or short circuit in wiring harness. 2. ECU malfunction.	–
Er-4	1. Non-registered data has been received from the meter unit. 2. Meter unit malfunction. 3. ECU malfunction.	1. Open or short circuit in wiring harness.	–

Table 2 DIAGNOSTIC CODES

Diagnostic code number	Component	Indicator display[1]	Description of action code
01	Throttle angle	15-20° (fully closed) 95-100° (fully open)	Check with throttle fully closed. Check with throttle fully open.

(continued)

Table 2 DIAGNOSTIC CODES (continued)

Diagnostic code number	Component	Indicator display[1]	Description of action code
03	Pressure difference[2]	Intake air pressure	Displayed value must change when throttle is operated while starting engine.
05	Intake air temperature	Intake air temperature	Compare the actual ambient temperature with indicator display.
06	Coolant temperature	Coolant temperature	Compare the actual coolant temperature with the indicator display.
07	Vehicle speed pulse	0-999	The number should increase from 0-999 as the rear wheels are turned by hand; resets to 0 after reaching 999.
08	Lean-angle sensor	3.55-4.45 volts (upright) 0.65-1.35 volts (overturned)	Remove the lean angle sensor and tilt it more than 65° and recheck indicator display.
09	Fuel system voltage	Approximately 12.0 volts	Compare the actual battery voltage reading with the indicator display. If the actual battery voltage is lower, recharge the battery and retest.
21	Gear position switch	Displays that the switch is on or off	Neutral: on. In gear: off.
30	Ignition coil	Engine trouble warning light flashes five times	Use a spark checker to check the engine spark.
36	Fuel injector	Actuates the fuel injector five times on one second intervals.	Check that the injectors clicks.
48	False code	No fault has occurred.	No service required.
50	Fuel injection system relay	Engine trouble warning light flashes five times (the warning light is off when the relay is on and the light is on when the relay is off).	Check for the sound of the fuel injection relay operating five times when the engine switch is in the ON position.
51	Radiator fan motor motor relay	Actuates the radiator fan motor relay (the engine warning light cycles five times as follows: 5 seconds per cycle (2 seconds ON, 3 seconds OFF).	Check for the sound of the radiator fan motor operating five times.
54	Idle speed	Actuates the idle speed control unit for 12 seconds. The engine warning light also lights.	Check that the idle speed control unit vibrates.
60	EEPROM fault Code display	00 display indicates normal operation. 01 indicates a history exists in memory.	–
61	Malfunction history code display	No history: 00 Fault code history: fault codes 12-50[3]	–

(continued)

Table 2 DIAGNOSTIC CODES (continued)

Diagnostic code number	Component	Indicator display[1]	Description of action code
62	Malfunction history code eraser	Displays trouble code(s) of a malfunction that has occurred once and that has been corrected.	With the ignition switch turned on, set the differential gear lock switch to 4WD and then to LOCK.

1. The indicator display is the small digital screen on the meter assembly face.
2. Atmospheric pressure and intake air pressure.
3. If more than one code is stored, the meter display lists all code numbers in two second intervals. When all of the codes have been displayed, the cycle repeats.

CHAPTER THREE

LUBRICATION, MAINTENANCE AND TUNE-UP

This chapter describes lubrication, maintenance and tune-up procedures. Procedures that require more than minor disassembly or adjustment are covered in the appropriate chapter.

Tables 1-6 are at the end of this chapter. **Table 1** lists the recommended lubrication and maintenance intervals. If the vehicle is operated in severe conditions, it may be appropriate to reduce the interval between some maintenance items. **Table 5** lists maintenance and tune-up specifications.

Read *Safety* and *Service Methods* in Chapter One before servicing the vehicle in this chapter.

TUNE-UP

Perform the maintenance tasks in **Table 1** at the specified intervals.

The frequency of tune-ups depends on vehicle usage. Creating a record that contains the type of operation and when tune-ups occur will help establish the frequency for future tune-ups.

As a guideline, the following items may be included in a tune-up:
1. Air filter inspection or cleaning.
2. Engine oil and filter change.
3. Spark plug inspection or replacement.
4. Valve adjustment.
5. Engine compression.
6. Cooling system inspection.
7. Fuel system inspection.
8. Ignition timing check.
9. Drive belt inspection.
10. Brake system inspection.
11. Wheels and tires inspection.
12. Steering component inspection.
13. Suspension component inspection
14. Fastener inspection.

PRE-RIDE INSPECTION

Perform the following checks before driving the vehicle. If a component requires service, refer to the appropriate section or chapter.

WARNING
When performing any service work to the engine or cooling system, never remove the radiator cap, coolant drain bolt or disconnect any hose while the engine and radiator are hot. Scalding fluid and steam may be blown out under pressure and cause serious injury.

NOTE
To check inside the engine compartment, remove the rear console as described in Chapter Sixteen.

1. Inspect the fuel line and fittings for leaks.
2. Check the fuel level. Check for leaks.
3. Check the engine oil level. Check for leaks.
4. Check the coolant level. Check for leaks.
5. Check the differential and final drive units for oil leaks. If leaks are detected, check the oil level.
6. Check the front and rear axle boots for damage.
7. Push and release the accelerator pedal. It must move smoothly and return to its idle position when released.
8. Check the brake fluid in the brake reservoir. Add DOT 4 brake fluid if necessary.
9. Make sure the brake pedal operates properly with no binding.
10. Check parking brake operation and free play.
11. Check that the seat belts are in good condition and engage and release properly. Check the harness assembly for fraying, wear, damage and loose or missing fasteners. Remove any dirt and other debris from the seat belt components that could affect operation. Check that the seat belt moves smoothly when pulled and retracts under its own operation when released. Check each belt assembly.
12. Check the steering for proper operation. Service the steering assembly if excessive play or damage is noted.
13. Turn the ignition switch on and check all lights and switches for proper operation.
14. Check the tires for excessive wear and damage.
15. Check the tire pressure.
16. Check the steering, suspension and brake assembly for loose or missing fasteners. Check the engine for loose or missing fasteners.
17. Check the exhaust system for looseness or damage.
18. Make sure all loads are properly secured in the bed.

FUEL REQUIREMENTS

The engine is designed to operate on unleaded gasoline that has a pump octane number ([R+m]/2) of 86 or higher or a research octane number of 91 or higher. Unleaded fuel (automotive grade) is recommended. This fuel produces

fewer engine emissions and spark plug deposits. Using a gasoline with a lower octane number can cause pinging or spark knock and lead to engine damage.

When choosing gasoline and filling the fuel tank, note the following:

1. In some areas of the United States and Canada, oxygenated fuels are used to reduce exhaust emissions. If using oxygenated fuel, make sure it meets the minimum octane requirements. Oxygenated fuels can damage plastic and paint. Do not spill fuel onto the fuel tank during filling. Wipe up spills with a soft cloth.
2. Do not use any fuel containing more than 10 percent ethanol.
3. Do not use any fuel containing methanol as it may cause engine starting, fuel and performance related problems.

BATTERY

The original equipment battery is a maintenance-free type. Maintenance-free batteries do not require periodic electrolyte inspection and water cannot be added. Refer to Chapter Nine for battery service.

AIR FILTER

Inspect and service the air filter at the intervals specified in **Table 1**. Never run the engine without a properly oiled and installed air filter element. Likewise, running the engine with a dry or damaged air filter element allows unfiltered air to enter the engine.

NOTE
It is a good idea to have one or more pre-oiled air filters stored in plastic bags that can be installed when operating in severe dust or sand conditions. Do not attempt to clean an air filter and reuse it unless there is enough time to properly dry the filter. A filter that was damp when oiled will not trap fine dust. Make sure the filter element is dry before oiling it.

Air Box Inspection Hose

Periodically check the inspection hose mounted at the bottom of the air box (**Figure 1**). Whenever there is water and/or dust in this hose, clean the air filter and the air filter housing, regardless of the service intervals listed in **Table 1**. Remove the inspection hose to drain the air box of water and other contaminants.

Air Filter

Removal/installation

1. Open the hood (Chapter Sixteen).
2. Turn and remove the two plastic rivets and remove the air box shroud (A, **Figure 2**).

3. Release the spring clamps (B, **Figure 2**) and remove the air box cover (C). Inspect the O-ring installed in the cover and replace if flattened or damaged.

4. Remove the air filter (**Figure 3**).

5. Check inside the air box for dirt and other debris that may have passed through or around the air filter.

6. Wipe the inside of the air box with a clean rag. If the air box cannot be cleaned while it is installed on the vehicle, remove and then clean it as described in Chapter Eight.

7. If the air filter will not be immediately installed, either reinstall the air box cover or cover the intake opening with a plastic bag.

8. Clean and reoil the air filter element as described in this section.

9. Apply thick grease to the filter's sealing surface (**Figure 4**).

10. Install the air filter into the air box, making sure its sealing surface seats squarely against the air box. Check for any gaps between the filter and air box surfaces.

CAUTION
When installing the air box cover, make sure it does not knock the filter off its mounting position on the air box and cause an air leak.

11. Install the air box cover by inserting its two projections into the holders on the air box housing (**Figure 5**).

12. Hold the cover down (C, **Figure 2**) and secure in place with the spring clamps (B). Check that each clip is properly installed.

13. Install the air box shroud (A, **Figure 2**) and secure with the two rivets.

14. Close the hood.

Cleaning and reoiling

1. Remove the air filter as described in this section.

2. Hold the air filter element and remove the holder (**Figure 6**).

3. Before cleaning the air filter element, check it for brittleness, separation or other damage. Replace the element if it is excessively worn or damaged. If there is no visible damage, clean the air filter element as follows.

WARNING
Do not clean the air filter element or holder with gasoline.

CAUTION
Do not wring or twist the filter element when cleaning it. This could damage filter pores or tear the filter element loose at a seam and allow unfiltered air to enter the engine.

4. Soak the air filter element in a container filled with a high flash point solvent, kerosene or an air filter cleaning solution. Gently squeeze the filter to dislodge and remove the oil and dirt from the filter pores. Swish the filter around in the cleaner while repeating this step several times, then remove the air filter and set it aside to dry. If using an aftermarket air filter element, follow the manufacturer's instructions.

5. Fill a clean pan with warm soapy water and submerge the filter. Soak and squeeze the filter several times until is is clean and there is no dirt or other debris visible in the filter pores.

6. Rinse the filter element under warm water while gently squeezing it.

7. Repeat these steps until there are no signs of dirt being rinsed from the filter element.

8. After cleaning the filter element, inspect it and replace it if it is torn or damaged. Do not run the engine with a dam-

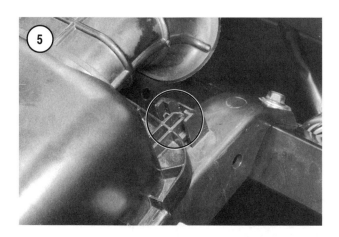

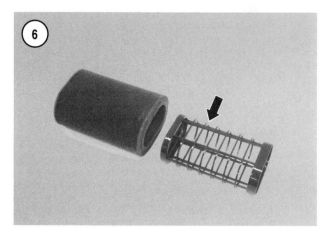

aged air filter element, as it allows dirt to enter and damage the engine.

9. Set the air filter element aside and allow it to dry thoroughly.

CAUTION
A filter that was damp when oiled will not trap fine dust. Make sure the filter element is dry before oiling it.

CAUTION
Do not use engine oil to lubricate the foam air filter. Foam air filter oil is specifically formulated for easy and thorough application into the filter pores and provides a tacky viscous medium to filter air borne contaminants. Engine oil is too thin to remain suspended in the filter and will be drawn into the engine, allowing dirt to pass through the filter.

10. Properly oiling an air filter element is a messy job. Wear a pair of disposable rubber gloves when performing this procedure. Oil the filter element as follows:

   a. Place the air filter element into a one gallon-sized storage bag.

   b. Pour foam air filter oil into the bag and onto the filter element to soak it.

   c. Gently squeeze and release the filter element, from the outside of the bag, to soak the filter oil into the fil-

ter element pores. Repeat until all of the filter's pores are saturated.

   d. Remove the filter element from the bag and check the pores for uneven oiling. Light or dark areas on the filter indicate this. If necessary, work more oil into the filter and repeat substep c.

   e. When the filter is oiled evenly, squeeze the filter a final time to remove excess oil.

   f. Remove the air filter element from the bag.

11. Align and install the filter element over the holder.

12. Install the air filter element as described in this chapter.

13. Pour the left over oil from the bag back into the bottle for future use.

ENGINE OIL AND FILTER

Change the engine oil and filter at the intervals specified in **Table 1**.

Engine Oil Selection

Refer to *Shop Supplies* in Chapter One. Make sure the viscosity is appropriate for the anticipated ambient temperatures (**Table 4**).

NOTE
There are a number of ways to discard used oil safely. The easiest way is to pour it from the drain pan into a gallon plastic container for disposal. Many service stations and oil retailers accept used oil for recycling. Do not discard oil in household trash or pour it onto the ground.

Engine Oil Level Check

Check the engine oil level when the engine is cold. If the engine is hot, turn the engine off and wait a minimum of 10 minutes for the oil to drain back into the crankcase to ensure an accurate reading. If the engine was just started, run it long enough for the oil to warm up sufficiently and then turn the engine off and wait a minimum of 10 minutes.

1. Park the vehicle on a level surface.

2. Remove the rear console (Chapter Sixteen).

3. Remove the dipstick (**Figure 7**) and wipe it clean.

4. Reinsert the dipstick until it seats fully into the dipstick tube.

5. Remove the dipstick. The oil level should be between the upper and lower marks on the on the knurled side of the dipstick (**Figure 8**). The oil level should not exceed the upper mark.

6. If the oil level is near or below the low level mark, add the specified oil (**Table 4**) through the dipstick tube to correct the level. Add oil in small quantities and check the level often. When the proper level is reached, reinstall the dipstick. Do not overfill.

7. After starting and running the engine, check the oil level again.

8. Install the rear console (Chapter Sixteen).

Engine Oil and Filter Change

NOTE
Warming the engine heats the oil so it flows freely and carries out contamination and sludge.

1. Park the vehicle on a level surface.
2. Remove the rear console (Chapter Sixteen).
3. Raise the cargo bed.

WARNING
The engine, exhaust system and oil are hot. Work carefully when removing the oil drain bolt and oil filter to avoid contacting the oil or hot engine parts.

4. Clean the area around the oil drain bolt and oil filter.
5. Place a clean drip pan under the crankcase and remove the oil drain bolt and gasket (**Figure 9**).
6. Remove the oil filler dipstick (**Figure 7**) to help speed up the flow of oil. Allow the oil to drain completely.
7. To replace the oil filter, perform the following:
   a. Install a socket type oil filter wrench squarely onto the oil filter (**Figure 10**) and turn the filter counterclockwise until oil begins to run out, then remove the oil filter.
   b. Hold the filter over the drain pan and pour out any remaining oil, then place the old filter in a plastic bag and dispose of it properly.
   c. Clean the oil filter sealing surface on the crankcase. Do not allow any dirt or other debris to enter the engine.
   d. Lubricate the rubber seal and threads on the new oil filter with clean engine oil.
   e. Install the new oil filter onto the threaded fitting on the crankcase. Tighten the filter by hand until it contacts the crankcase. Then tighten an additional 3/4 turn. If using the oil filter socket, tighten the oil filter to 17 N•m (12.5 ft.-lb.).
8. Install the oil drain bolt (**Figure 9**) and new gasket and tighten to 30 N•m (22 ft.-lb.).
9. Insert a funnel into the dipstick tube and fill the engine with the correct weight (**Table 4**) and quantity of oil (**Table 3**).
10. Remove the funnel and install the dipstick (**Figure 7**).
11. Start the engine and let it idle for several minutes.
12. Check the oil filter and drain bolt for leaks.
13. Turn the engine off after a minimum of 10 minutes and check the oil level as described in this section. Adjust the oil level if necessary.
14. Check the engine oil pressure as described in this chapter.
15. Install the rear console (Chapter Sixteen).

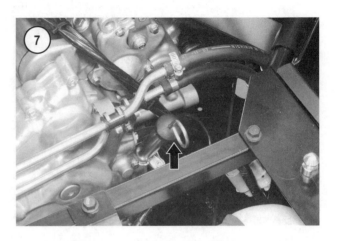

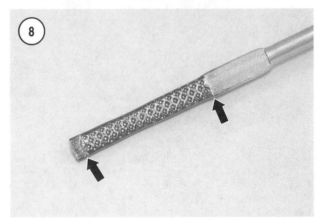

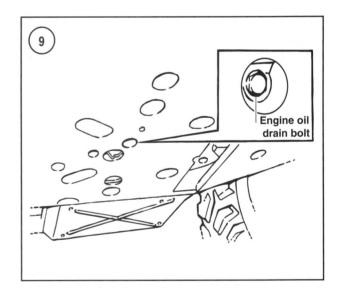

ENGINE OIL PRESSURE CHECK

WARNING
The engine and oil are hot during this procedure. Work carefully to avoid contacting the oil or hot engine parts.

Check the engine oil pressure after changing the engine oil, reassembling the engine or when troubleshooting the lubrication system.

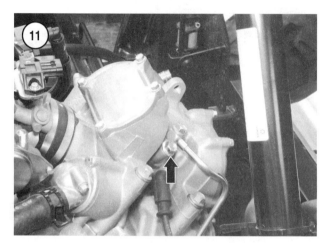

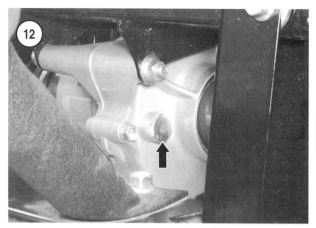

1. Remove the rear console (Chapter Sixteen).
2. Loosen the engine oil check bolt (**Figure 11**) at the cylinder head. Do not remove it.
3. Start the engine and run at idle speed. Oil should seep from the bolt within one minute.
4. If no oil seeps from the bolt within one minute, turn the engine off to prevent damage. Then inspect the oil filter, oil lines and oil pump for damage.
5. Turn the engine off and tighten the engine oil check bolt to 10 N•m (88 in.-lb.).
6. Install the rear console (Chapter Sixteen).

FRONT DIFFERENTIAL

WARNING
Prolonged contact with used gear oil may cause skin cancer. Minimize contact with gear oil.

Gear Oil Selection

Refer to *Shop Supplies* in Chapter One for general gear oil information. Refer to **Table 4**.

Oil Level Check

1. Park the vehicle on level ground.

2. Wipe the area around the oil fill plug and remove it (**Figure 12**) and its gasket.
3. The oil level must be to the bottom edge of the oil fill plug hole.

NOTE
*Refer to **Oil Change** in this section for tips on making a funnel to add oil to the front differential.*

4. If the oil level is low, add the recommended type gear oil (**Table 4**) to correct the level.

NOTE
Because of the limited working area around the oil fill plug, a syringe works well when adding a small amount of gear oil to the front differential.

5. Clean the plug. If necessary, replace the washer on the plug.
6. Install and tighten the oil fill plug to 23 N•m (17 ft.-lb.).

Oil Change

Change the front differential oil at the intervals specified in **Table 1**.

NOTE
*To help fill the front differential with gear oil, use a funnel with an attached hose. The funnel shown in **Figure 13** was made from a discarded hypoid gear oil container (Pro Honda Shaft Drive Oil) and a length of hose attached to the container's tapered filler cap. The hose is secured to the cap with a clamp. Because hypoid oil is thick and pours slowly, use as large a hose as possible that will fit inside the oil fill plug hole. Cut out one side of the container for filling (**Figure 14**). To use the funnel, remove the left front wheel and secure the funnel in place with a plastic tie (**Figure 15**). Cover the brake caliper with a plastic sheet to prevent any spilled oil from contacting the brake disc and pads.*

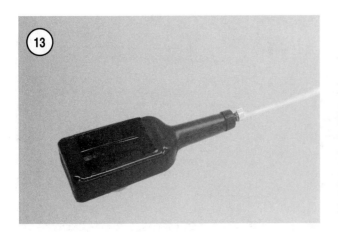

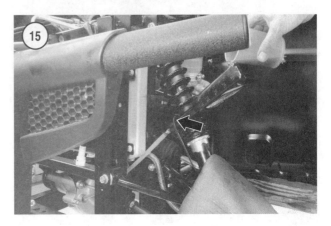

1. Drive the vehicle several miles to warm the oil in the front differential.

2. Park the vehicle on level ground and set the parking brake.

3. Remove the front skid plate (Chapter Sixteen).

4. Clean the area around oil filler plug and drain bolt.

5. Place a drain pan under the final drive unit.

NOTE
Before removing the drain bolt, clean its Allen head recess to avoid stripping the bolt.

6. Remove the oil fill plug (**Figure 12**) and the drain bolt (**Figure 16**) to drain the oil.

7. Clean the drain bolt. If necessary, replace the washer on the bolt.

8. Install and tighten the oil drain bolt to 10 N•m (88 in.-lb.).

9. Add the recommended type gear oil (**Table 4**) to bring the oil level to the bottom edge of the oil fill plug hole. **Table 3** lists front differential oil capacity.

NOTE
Because of the limited working area around the oil fill plug, a syringe works well when adding a small amount of gear oil to the front differential.

10. Clean the oil fill plug. If necessary, replace the washer on the plug.

11. Install and tighten the oil fill plug to 23 N•m (17 ft.-lb.).

12. Start the engine and drive the vehicle, then check for oil leaks.

13. Install the front skid plate, washers and bolts and tighten to 7 N•m (62 in.-lb.).

FINAL DRIVE OIL

WARNING
Prolonged contact with used gear oil may cause skin cancer.

NOTE
*Refer to **Front Differential** in this chapter for tips on making a funnel to add oil to the final drive.*

Gear Oil Selection

Refer to *Shop Supplies* in Chapter One for general gear oil information. Refer to **Table 4**.

Oil Level Check

1. Park the vehicle on level ground.

2. Wipe the area around the oil fill plug (**Figure 17**) and remove it and its O-ring.

3. The oil level must be to the bottom edge of the oil fill plug hole.

4. If the oil level is low, add the recommended type gear oil (**Table 4**) to correct the level.

NOTE
Because of the limited working area around the oil fill plug, a syringe works well when adding a small amount of gear oil to the final drive.

5. Clean the plug. If necessary, replace the O-ring on the plug.

6. Install and tighten the oil fill plug to 23 N•m (17 ft.-lb.).

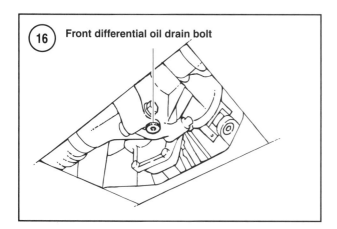

16 Front differential oil drain bolt

17

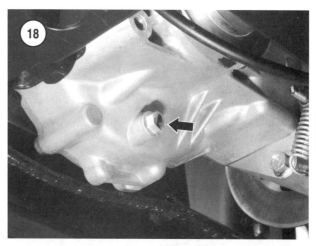

18

Oil Change

Change the final drive oil at the intervals specified in **Table 1**.

1. Drive the vehicle several miles to warm the oil in the final drive.

2. Park the vehicle on level ground and set the parking brake.

3. Remove the rear skid plate (Chapter Sixteen).

4. Clean the area around the oil filler plug and drain bolt.

5. Place a drain pan under the final drive unit.

6. Remove the oil fill plug (**Figure 17**) and the drain bolt (**Figure 18**) to drain the oil.

7. Clean the drain bolt. If necessary, replace the washer on the bolt.

8. Install and tighten the oil drain bolt to 20 N•m (15 in.-lb.).

9. Add the recommended type gear oil (**Table 4**) to bring the oil level to the bottom edge of the oil fill plug hole. **Table 3** lists final drive oil capacity.

NOTE
Because of the limited working area around the oil fill plug, a syringe works well when adding a small amount of gear oil to the final drive.

10. Clean the oil fill plug. If necessary, replace the O-ring on the plug.

11. Install and tighten the oil fill plug to 23 N•m (17 ft.-lb.).

12. Start the engine and drive the vehicle, then check for oil leaks.

13. Install the rear skid plate, washers and bolts and tighten to 7 N•m (62 in.-lb.).

COOLING SYSTEM

Service the cooling system at the intervals in **Table 1**.

WARNING
Never remove the radiator cap, the coolant drain plug or disconnect any coolant hose while the engine and radiator are hot. Scalding fluid and steam may blow out under pressure and cause serious injury.

CAUTION
Be careful not to spill antifreeze on painted surfaces as it damages the surface. Wash immediately with soapy water and rinse thoroughly with clean water.

Coolant

Use only a high quality ethylene glycol-based antifreeze compounded for aluminum engines. Mix the antifreeze with water in a 50:50 ratio. **Table 3** lists coolant capacity. When mixing antifreeze with water, make sure to use only distilled (or purified) water. Never use tap or salt water as this damages engine parts. Distilled water is available at supermarkets and drug stores.

Inspection

Refer to *Cooling System Inspection* and *Water Pump Seal Check* in *Water Pump* in Chapter Ten.

Coolant Check

1. Park the vehicle on level ground.

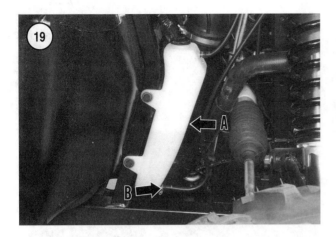

2. When the engine is cold, the coolant level must be between the minimum and maximum level marks on the reservoir (A, **Figure 19**).

3. If the level is low, remove the reservoir cap and add a sufficient amount of specified coolant (**Table 4**). Reinstall the reservoir cap.

Coolant Change

Drain and refill the cooling system at the interval listed in **Table 1**.

> *WARNING*
> *Antifreeze is classified as an environmental toxic waste by the EPA and cannot be legally disposed of by flushing down a drain or pouring it onto the ground. Place antifreeze in a suitable container and dispose of it according to local EPA regulations. Do not store coolant where it is accessible to children or animals.*

> *WARNING*
> *Change the engine coolant when the engine is cold.*

1. Remove the rear console (Chapter Sixteen).
2. Open the hood (Chapter Sixteen).
3. Remove the coolant reservoir cap. Then disconnect the hose (B, **Figure 19**) and drain the coolant into a drain pan. Flush the reservoir with clean water. Reconnect the hose and secure with its clamp.
4. Remove the radiator cap (**Figure 20**).
5. Place a drain pan underneath the right side of the engine.
6. Remove the coolant drain bolt (A, **Figure 21**) and the water pump air bleed bolt (B) and their sealing washers from the water pump cover and drain the coolant.

> *NOTE*
> *If it is necessary to flush the cooling system with water, remove the radiator (Chapter Ten) then turn it over to remove all of the coolant.*

7. Install the coolant drain bolt (A, **Figure 21**) and a new washer and tighten to 10 N•m (88 in.-lb.).

8. Refill the cooling system with the specified coolant (**Table 4**) through the radiator filler neck.

9. Refill the coolant reservoir (A, **Figure 19**) to its maximum level mark and install the reservoir cap.

> *NOTE*
> *Make sure to maintain a high coolant level in the radiator while bleeding air/coolant through the water pump and thermostat housing bleed bolt holes in the following steps.*

10. When coolant flows out of the water pump air bleed bolt hole, install the bolt (B, **Figure 21**) with a new washer and tighten to 10 N•m (88 in.-lb.).

11. Loosen, do not remove, the thermostat cover air bleed bolt (**Figure 22**) to allow air to escape from the cooling system. When coolant begins to drain through the bleed hole, tighten the bolt to 10 N•m (88 in.-lb.).

> *NOTE*
> *If there is no air or coolant passing through the thermostat cover bleed hole, raise the vehicle front end with a jack. Coolant should soon drain through the bleed hole. During this step, have an assistant continue to slowly add coolant to the radiator to maintain a high coolant level. When coolant begins to flow continuously from the hole, tighten the bolt as*

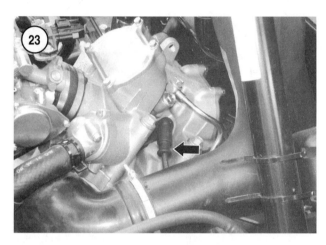

*described in Step 12. Then lower the vehicle
so the front wheels are on the ground. Top off
the radiator with coolant if necessary.*

12. Start the engine and allow it to run at idle speed for 10 minutes. Check for coolant leaks.
13. Press and release the accelerator pedal a minimum of five times to continue bleeding air from the cooling system.
14. Add coolant to the top of the radiator filler neck.
15. Turn the engine off.
16. Recheck the coolant level in the radiator after the engine has cooled down. If necessary, add coolant to the top of the radiator filler neck.
17. Install the radiator cap.
18. Reverse Steps 1 and 2.

SPARK PLUG

Inspect and replace the spark plug at the service intervals specified in **Table 1**.

Removal

CAUTION
Careful removal of the spark plug is important in preventing grit from entering the combustion chamber. It is also important to know how to remove a plug that is seized, or is re-

*sistant to removal. Forcing a seized plug can
destroy the threads in the cylinder head.*

1. Remove the rear console (Chapter Sixteen).
2. Grasp the plug cap (**Figure 23**) and twist it slightly to break it loose, then pull it from the spark plug.
3. Blow any dirt that has accumulated around the spark plug.

CAUTION
*Dirt that falls through the spark plug hole
causes rapid engine wear.*

CAUTION
*The porcelain cover, found on the top of the
spark plug, actually extends into the plug to
prevent the spark from grounding through the
plug's metal body and threads. The porcelain
cover can be easily damaged from mishandling. Make sure the spark plug socket fits the
plug fully before turning the plug.*

4. Fit a spark plug wrench onto the spark plug, then remove it by turning the wrench counterclockwise. If the plug is seized or drags excessively during removal, stop and perform the following:
   a. Apply penetrating lubricant and allow it to stand for about 15 minutes.
   b. If the plug is completely seized, apply moderate pressure in both directions with the wrench. Only attempt to break the seal so lubricant can penetrate under the spark plug and into the threads. If this does not work, and the engine can still be started, install the spark plug cap and start the engine. Allow to completely warm up. The heat of the engine may be enough to expand the parts and allow the plug to be removed.
   c. When a spark plug is loose, but drags excessively during removal, apply penetrating lubricant around the spark plug threads. Turn the plug in (clockwise) to help distribute the lubricant onto the threads. Slowly remove the plug, working it in and out of the cylinder head while continuing to add lubricant. Do not reuse the spark plug.
   d. Inspect the threads in the cylinder head for damage. Clean and true the threads with a spark plug thread-chaser. Apply a thick grease onto the thread-chaser threads before using it. The grease will help trap some of the debris cut from the threads to prevent it from falling into the engine.

NOTE
*Damaged spark plug threads will require removal of the cylinder head (Chapter Four)
and repair.*

5. Inspect the spark plug as described in this section.

Gap Measurement

Use a wire feeler gauge when measuring spark plug gap.

1. If installing a new spark plug, remove it from the box. The small terminal adapter installed on the end of the plug is not used with the stock spark plug cap.

2. Refer to the spark plug gap listed in **Table 5**. Select the correct size wire feeler gauge and try to slide it past the gap between both electrodes (**Figure 24**). If there is a slight drag as the wire gauge passes through the gap, the setting is correct. If the gap is incorrect, adjust it with the spark plug gauge tool (**Figure 25**).

Installation

1. Wipe a small amount of antiseize compound onto the plug threads before installing the spark plug. Do not allow the compound to contact the electrodes.

> *NOTE*
> *Do not overtighten the spark plug. This may crush the gasket and cause a compression leak or damage the cylinder head threads.*

2. Screw the spark plug in by hand until it seats. Very little effort should be required; if force is necessary, the plug may be cross-threaded. Unscrew it and try again. When the spark plug is properly seated, tighten it to 13 N•m (115 in.-lb.).

3. Align and press the plug cap (**Figure 23**) onto the spark plug.

4. Install the rear console (Chapter Sixteen).

Selection

If the engine is run in hot climates, at high speed or under heavy loads for prolonged periods, a spark plug with a colder heat range may be required. A colder plug quickly transfers heat away from its firing tip and to the cylinder head. This is accomplished by a short path up the ceramic insulator and into the body of the spark plug (**Figure 26**). By transferring heat quickly, the plug remains cool enough to avoid overheating and preignition problems. If the engine is run slowly for prolonged periods, this type of plug will foul and result in poor performance. A colder plug will not cool down a hot engine.

If the engine is run in cold climates or at a slow speed for prolonged periods, a spark plug with a hotter heat range may be required. A hotter plug slowly transfers heat away from its firing tip and to the cylinder head. This is accomplished by a long path up the ceramic insulator and into the body of the plug (**Figure 26**). By transferring heat slowly, the plug remains hot enough to avoid fouling and buildup. If the engine is run in hot climates for fast or prolonged periods, this type of plug will overheat, cause preignition problems and possible melt the electrode. Damage to the piston and cylinder assembly is possible.

When running a stock engine, changing to a different heat range plug is normally not required. Changing to a different heat range plug may be necessary when operating a vehicle with a modified engine. This type of change

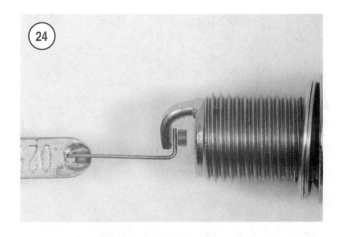

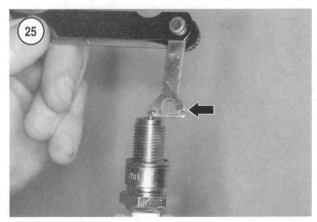

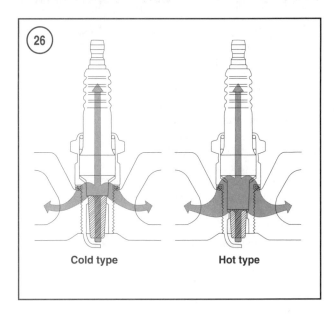

Cold type   Hot type

is usually based on a recommendation made by the engine builder. Experience in spark plug reading is also required when trying to determine if a different heat range plug is required. When installing a different heat range plug, go one step hotter or colder from the specified plug (**Table 5**). Do not try to correct fuel injection or ignition problems by using a different spark plug. This will only compound the existing problem(s) and possibly lead to severe engine damage.

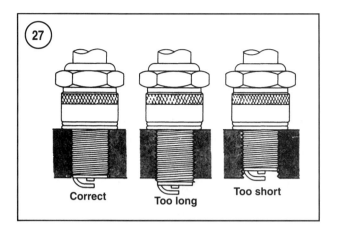

Correct   Too long   Too short

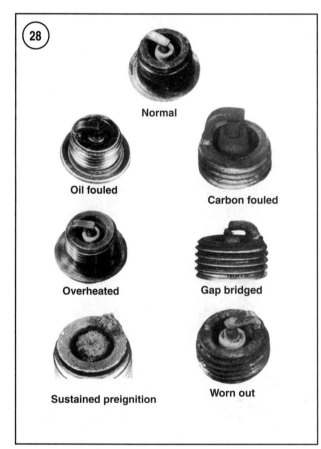

Normal

Oil fouled   Carbon fouled

Overheated   Gap bridged

Sustained preignition   Worn out

The reach (length) of a plug is also important (**Figure 27**). A shorter than normal plug causes hard starting, reduce engine performance and carbon buildup on the exposed cylinder head threads. These same conditions can occur if the correct length plug is used without a gasket. Trying to thread a spark plug into threads with carbon buildup may damage the threads in the cylinder head.

Reading/Inspection

The spark plug is an excellent indicator of how the engine is operating. By correctly evaluating the condition of the plug, engine problems can be diagnosed. To correctly read a spark plug, perform the following:

1. Refer to *Installation* in this section when removing and installing the spark plug during this procedure.

2. If a new plug was installed, drive the vehicle for approximately 15 to 20 minutes so it will begin to color. Then continue with Step 3.

3. Accelerate on a straight road at full throttle. Then come to a stop and turn the engine off.

4. Remove the spark plug and examine its firing tip while noting the following:

a. Inspect the spark plug with a magnifying glass or spark plug reader.

b. Refer to **Figure 28** and the following paragraphs provide a description, as well as common causes for each of the conditions.

CAUTION
In all cases, when a spark plug is abnormal, find the cause of the problem before continuing engine operation. Severe engine damage is possible when abnormal plug readings are ignored.

Normal condition

The porcelain insulator around the center electrode is clean and colorless. There should be a gray ring around the center electrode where it separates from the porcelain. No erosion or rounding of the electrodes or abnormal gap is evident. This indicates an engine that has proper fuel mixture and ignition timing. This heat range of plug is appropriate for the conditions in which the engine has been operated. The plug can be reused.

Oil fouled

The plug is wet with black, oily deposits on the electrodes and insulator. The electrodes do not show wear. Replace the spark plug.
1. Clogged air filter.
2. Faulty fuel system.
3. Faulty ignition component.
4. Spark plug heat range too cold.
5. Low engine compression.
6. Engine not properly broken in.

Carbon fouled

The plug is black with a dry, sooty deposit on the entire plug surface. This dry sooty deposit is conductive and can create electrical paths that bypass the electrode gap. This often results in misfiring of the plug. Replace the spark plug.
1. Rich fuel mixture.
2. Faulty fuel system.
3. Spark plug heat range too cold.
4. Clogged air filter.
5. Faulty ignition component.
6. Low engine compression.

Overheating

The plug is dry and the insulator has a white or light gray cast. The insulator may also appear blistered. The electrodes may have a burnt appearance and there may be metallic specks on the center electrode and porcelain. This material is being removed from the piston crown. Replace the spark plug.

1. Lean fuel mixture.
2. Faulty fuel system.
3. Spark plug heat range too hot.
4. Faulty ignition component.
5. Air leak at the exhaust pipe or intake tube.
6. Overtightened spark plug.
7. No crush washer on spark plug.
8. Spark plug heat range too hot.

Gap bridging

The plug is clogged with deposits between the electrodes. The engine may run with a bridged spark plug, but it will misfire. Replace the spark plug.

1. Incorrect oil type.
2. Incorrect fuel or fuel contamination.
3. Excessive carbon deposits in combustion chamber.

Preignition

The plug electrodes are severely eroded or melted. This condition can lead to severe engine damage. Replace the spark plug.

1. Faulty ignition system component.
2. Spark plug heat range too hot.
3. Air leak.
4. Excessive carbon deposits in combustion chamber.

Worn out

The center electrode is rounded from normal combustion. There is no indication of abnormal combustion or engine conditions.

VALVE CLEARANCE

Check the valve clearance at the intervals in **Table 1**.

Inspection

Refer to **Table 5** for valve clearance specifications.

NOTE
Do not check or adjust the valve clearance when the air or engine temperature is above 35° C (95°F).

1. Remove the following as described in Chapter Sixteen:
   a. Seats.

   b. Rear console.
   c. Center protector.
2. Remove air duct 2 as described in *Drive Belt Air Duct Assembly* in Chapter Six.
3. Disconnect the intake air pressure sensor (**Figure 29**).
4. Disconnect the breather hose at the cylinder head (A, **Figure 30**).
5. Remove the valve adjustment covers (B, **Figure 30**) and their O-rings.
6. Remove the camshaft sprocket cover (C, **Figure 30**) and O-ring.
7. Remove the flywheel nut plug and O-ring with a 14 mm hex wrench (**Figure 31**).

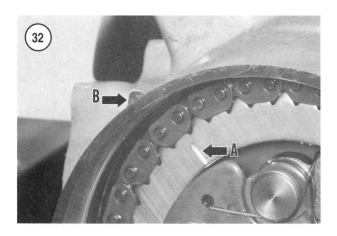

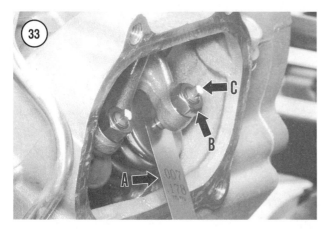

c. If there is too much or too little drag, adjust the valve clearance as described in this section.

11. When the clearance of each valve is within specification, reverse Steps 1-8 while noting the following:

   a. Reinstall the spark plug as described in this chapter.

   b. Replace leaking or damaged plug and cover O-rings. Lubricate the O-rings with oil.

   c. Tighten the flywheel nut plug to 10 N•m (88 in.-lb.).

   d. Tighten the camshaft sprocket cover mounting bolts to 10 N•m (88 in.-lb.).

   e. Tighten the valve adjustment cover mounting bolts to 10 N•m (88 in.-lb.).

Adjustment

1. Set the cylinder at TDC on its compression stroke as described in *Inspection* in this section.

2. Loosen the locknut (B, **Figure 33**) on the valve adjust screw.

3. Turn the valve adjust screw (C, **Figure 33**) with a 3 mm wrench until the valve clearance (slight drag on feeler gauge) is correct.

4. Hold the valve adjust screw (C, **Figure 33**) to prevent it from turning and tighten the locknut (B) to 14 N•m (10 ft.-lb.).

5. Recheck the valve clearance as described in this section. If the clearance changed when the locknut was tightened, loosen the locknut and readjust the valve clearance. Repeat until the valve clearance is correct after the locknut is tightened.

ENGINE COMPRESSION CHECK

An engine compression test checks the internal condition of the engine (piston rings, piston, head gasket, valves and cylinder). It is a good idea to check compression at each tune-up, record it and compare it with the reading obtained at the next tune-up.

Use a screw-in type compression gauge with a flexible adapter. Before using the gauge, check that the rubber gasket on the end of the adapter is not cracked or damaged; this gasket seals the cylinder to ensure accurate compression readings.

1. Make sure the battery is fully charged to ensure proper engine cranking speed. Refer to Chapter Nine. If the starter does not turn the engine over fast enough, the compression reading will be incorrect.

2. Run the engine until it reaches normal operating temperature, then turn it off.

3. Remove the rear console (Chapter Sixteen).

4. Remove the spark plug as described in this chapter.

5. Lubricate the threads of the compression gauge adapter with a small amount of antiseize compound and carefully thread the gauge into the spark plug hole. Tighten the hose by hand to form a good seal (**Figure 34**).

8. Remove the spark plug as described in this chapter. This will make it easier to turn the engine by hand.

9. The engine must be set at top dead center (TDC) on its compression stroke before removing the sprocket bolts and cam sprocket. Perform the following:

NOTE
With the fuel tank installed in the frame, the flywheel timing marks cannot be viewed.

   a. Fit a 22-mm socket onto the flywheel nut and turn the crankshaft counterclockwise until the camshaft sprocket index mark (A, **Figure 32**) aligns with the cylinder head boss (B).

   b. Verify the engine is at TDC on its compression stroke by trying to move the intake and exhaust rocker arms to see if they have a valve clearance, indictating the intake and exhaust valves are closed. If not, turn the crankshaft one revolution counterclockwise and realign the marks. Move each rocker arm by hand. There should now be some movement or free play.

10. Measure the clearance of the exhaust and intake valves as follows:

   a. Refer to **Table 5** to select the correct feeler gauges for the valve to be checked.

   b. Insert the feeler gauge (A, **Figure 33**) between the valve adjusting screw and the end of the valve stem. When the clearance is correct, there is a slight drag on the feeler gauge when it is inserted and withdrawn.

CAUTION
*When the spark plug lead is disconnected, the electronic ignition will produce the highest voltage possible. This can damage the ignition control module (ICM). To protect the ignition system, install a grounding tool in the spark plug cap. Refer to **Ignition Grounding Tool** in **Tools** in Chapter One. Do not crank the engine more than necessary.*

6. Have an assistant press the accelerator pedal fully to open the throttle while operating the starter to turn the engine over. Read the compression gauge until there is no further rise in pressure. The compression reading should increase on each stroke. Record the reading.

7. Refer to **Table 5** for the standard compression pressure reading. If the compression reading is low, go to Step 8. If the compression reading is high, go to Step 9.

8. A low compression reading can be caused by the following:
    a. Incorrect valve adjustment.
    b. Worn piston rings, piston or cylinder bore.
    c. Leaking valve seat(s).
    d. Damaged cylinder head gasket.

To isolate the problem to a valve or ring problem, perform a wet compression test. Pour about a teaspoon of engine oil into the spark plug hole. Repeat the compression test and record the reading. If the compression increases significantly, the valves are good but the rings are defective. If compression does not increase, the valves require servicing.

NOTE
An engine with low compression cannot be tuned to maximum performance.

9. A high compression reading can be caused by excessive carbon deposits on the piston crown or combustion chamber.

10. Reverse the steps to complete installation. Reinstall the spark plug as described in this chapter.

FUEL HOSE INSPECTION

Inspect the fuel hose at the intervals specified in **Table 1**.

Remove the rear console (Chapter Sixteen) and inspect the fuel hose (A, **Figure 35**) for cracks, leaks, soft spots and deterioration. Make sure each end of the hose is properly installed

WARNING
A leaking fuel hose may cause a fire; do not start the engine with a leaking or damaged fuel hose.

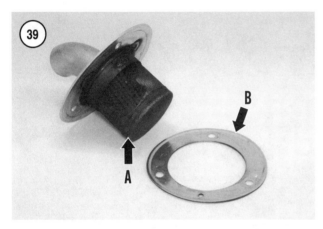

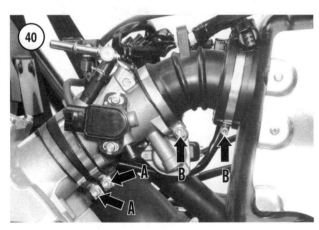

BREATHER HOSES INSPECTION

Inspect the crankcase and throttle body breather hoses at the intervals specified in **Table 1**. At the same time, inspect the front differential and final drive breather hoses.

1. Remove the rear console (Chapter Sixteen).
2. Inspect the following hoses for cracks, soft spots and deterioration:
    a. Crankcase breather hose (B, **Figure 35**). Make sure both hose ends are secured tightly.
    b. Throttle body breather hose (C, **Figure 35**). Make sure the hose open end is free of all debris.
    c. Front differential breather hose (**Figure 36**). Make sure the hose open end is free of all debris.

    d. Final drive breather hose (**Figure 37**). Make sure the hose open end is free of all debris.
3. Replace the hose and hose clamps if damaged.

EXHAUST SYSTEM

Refer to Chapter Four for service and repair procedures.

Inspection

Inspect the exhaust system at the intervals specified in **Table 1**.
1. Inspect the exhaust pipe for cracks or dents that could alter performance. Refer all repairs to a dealership.
2. Check all of the exhaust pipe springs, fasteners and mounting points for loose or damaged parts.

Spark Arrestor Cleaning

Clean the spark arrestor at the intervals specified in **Table 1**.
Perform the following procedure when the exhaust system is cold.
1. Remove the bolts (A, **Figure 38**), tailpipe (B) and gasket.
2. Clean the spark arrestor screen (A, **Figure 39**) and the exposed area inside the muffler with a wire brush. Replace the spark arrestor if the screen is damaged.
3. Replace the gasket (B, **Figure 39**) if leaking or damaged.
4. Installation is the reverse of these steps.
    a. Tighten the tailpipe mounting bolts (A, **Figure 38**) to 10 N•m (88 in.-lb.).
    b. Start the engine. While wearing welding gloves and goggles, hold a clean, dry shop cloth next to the tailpipe (blocking the exhaust opening) while an assistant accelerates the engine approximately 20 times. This creates backpressure and forces carbon deposits out of the exhaust.
    c. Turn the engine off.

THROTTLE BODY AND AIR INTAKE JOINT INSPECTION

Inspect the throttle body and air intake joint at the intervals specified in **Table 1**.
1. Remove the rear console (Chapter Sixteen).
2. Inspect the front intake tube hose clamps (A, **Figure 40**) and the air intake duct joint hose clamps (B) for looseness or damage.
3. Check the front intake tube and air intake duct joint for cracks and other damage.
4. Replace damaged parts.

ACCELERATOR CABLE ADJUSTMENT

1. Remove the rear console (Chapter Sixteen).

2. Remove the screws and the accelerator cable housing cover and O-ring (A, **Figure 41**) from the left side of the throttle body.

3. Check the accelerator cable slack at the point indicated in B, **Figure 41**. There should be no slack and the throttle valve should be closed against the throttle stop screw (C, **Figure 41**). If adjustment is necessary, continue with Step 4.

4. Loosen the accelerator cable adjuster locknut (A, **Figure 42**) and turn the adjuster (B) to adjust the accelerator cable. Tighten the locknut and recheck the adjustment (Step 3).

5. Start the engine and then press the accelerator pedal several times. With the engine running at idle speed, make sure the throttle valve is closed against the throttle stop screw (C, **Figure 41**). Readjust the accelerator cable if necessary.

> *NOTE*
> *If the correct free play cannot be achieved, the accelerator cable may be damaged or stretched to the point where it needs to be replaced. Replace the accelerator cable as described in Chapter Eight.*

6. Install the O-ring (A, **Figure 41**) and accelerator cable housing and tighten the screws securely.

7. Install the rear console (Chapter Sixteen).

8. Start the engine and check the engine idle speed and accelerator pedal operation again. If the idle sounds high, inspect and readjust the accelerator cable.

IGNITION TIMING INSPECTION

The engine control unit (ECU) is not adjustable. However, checking the ignition timing can provide diagnostic information. If an ignition related problem is suspected, check the ignition timing to confirm proper ignition system operation. Also check the ignition timing after installing a new ignition system component to make sure it is working correctly.

1. Check the accelerator cable free play as described in this chapter. Adjust if necessary.

2. Start the engine and warm to normal operating temperature, then turn the engine off.

3. Remove the fuel tank (Chapter Eight).

4. Remove the timing plug (**Figure 43**) and its O-ring from the right crankcase cover.

5. Connect a shop tachometer to the engine following the manufacturer's instructions.

6. Connect a timing light onto the cylinder spark plug wire following the manufacturer's instructions.

7. Start the engine and check the idle speed (**Table 5**).

8. Aim the timing light at the timing hole and pull the trigger. The ignition timing is correct if the firing range mark on the flywheel aligns with the index mark (**Figure 44**) in

the timing hole while the engine is running at idle speed. Turn the engine off.

9. If the ignition timing is correct, the ignition system is working correctly. If the ignition timing is incorrect, there is a problem with one or more ignition system components. Refer to Chapter Two.

10. Disconnect the timing light and tachometer.

11. Replace the timing plug O-ring if leaking or damaged. Lubricate the O-ring with lithium grease.

12. Install and tighten the timing plug to 6 N•m (53 in.-lb.).

13. Install the fuel tank (Chapter Eight).

SELECT LEVER ADJUSTMENT

If the shifting becomes rough or hard, adjust the shift rod length to see if the shifting can be improved. There is no standard adjustment position.

1. Remove the rear console (Chapter Sixteen).

2. Draw an alignment mark on top of the shift rod (A, **Figure 45**) to be used as a reference when adjusting the shift rod.

> *NOTE*
> *Always shift the transmission when the vehicle is at a complete stop and the engine is running at normal idle speed.*

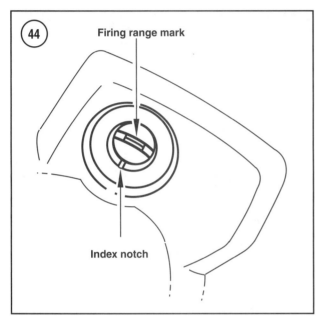

Firing range mark

Index notch

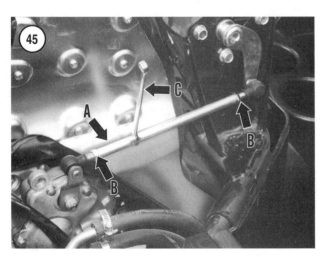

3. Turn the ignition switch on and shift the transmission into NEUTRAL. The neutral indicator light should turn on.

4. Loosen the locknuts (B, **Figure 45**) and adjust the shift rod length with a wrench on the shift rod flats (C). Tighten the locknuts to 15 N•m (11 ft.-lb.).

5. With the engine running at idle speed, shift the transmission into gear or reverse and then back into neutral while comparing the shifting with the previous shifting position. Make sure the correct indicator light turns on for each shifting position. Repeat if additional adjustment is required.

6. Tighten the shift rod locknuts to 15 N•m (11 ft.-lb.).

7. Install the rear console (Chapter Sixteen).

DRIVE BELT INSPECTION

At the intervals specified in **Table 1**, remove the drive belt cover and inspect the drive belt as described in Chapter Six.

BRAKES

Inspect the brake system at the intervals specified in **Table 1.** Immediately inspect the brake components when their operating condition has changed or when abnormal noises are detected.

Bleeding the brakes, replacing the brake pads and servicing the brake components is covered in Chapter Fifteen.

Refer to *Parking Brake Assembly* in this chapter to service the parking brake assembly.

Brake System Inspection

If any damage is detected during the following checks, refer to Chapter Fifteen for brake system repair procedures and specifications.

1. Apply the brake pedal. If the pedal feels soft, air has probably entered the brake system; diagnose and repair the system, then bleed the brake system (Chapter Fifteen).

2. Support the vehicle so the wheels (either front or back) are off the ground.

3. Inspect the front and rear discs for:

    a. Scoring—If scoring is evident, remove the wheels and inspect the brake discs.

    b. Drag—Turn each wheel and check for drag on the disc. Light drag on the disc is acceptable. If the drag is heavy, troubleshoot and repair the brake system.

    c. Runout—This is the lateral movement of the disc as it spins. Runout can be detected by turning a wheel and listening for uneven drag on the disc. A pulsating drag usually indicates disc warp (or damaged brake pads). If warp is suspected, measure it with a dial indicator (Chapter Fifteen). If the disc is not warped, look for loose brake disc mounting fasteners, a damaged caliper or damaged hub.

    d. Disc thickness—Measure the thickness of all discs.

4. Check brake lines and hoses for proper routing and connection. Look for binding, leaking, chafing, cracks or other defects. Replace any damaged hoses and correct other defects, if found.

5. Check the brake fluid level as described in this section.

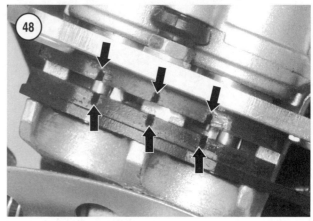

Brake Fluid Level Check

The brake reservoir is marked with MAX (A, **Figure 46**) and MIN (B) level marks. The brake fluid level in the master cylinder reservoir must be kept above the MIN (minimum) level mark. If the fluid level is low, check for loose or damaged brake lines, hoses or banjo bolts. If there are no visible fluid leaks, check the brake pads for excessive wear. As the brake pads wear, the caliper pistons move farther out of the bores, thus causing the brake fluid level to drop in the reservoir. Also, check the master cylinder bore and the brake caliper piston areas for signs of leaking brake fluid. If there is a fluid leak, the seals inside the component are damaged and the component must be overhauled. Check the brake pads for wear as described in this section. Refer to Chapter Fifteen for brake service not covered in this section.

WARNING
If the reservoir is empty, or if the brake fluid level is so low that air is entering the brake system, the brake system must be bled as described in Chapter Fifteen. Simply adding brake fluid to the reservoir does not restore the brake system to its full effectiveness.

1. Park the vehicle on level ground.
2. Open the hood (Chapter Sixteen).
3. Clean the master cylinder cap and reservoir before removing the cover to avoid contaminating the reservoir and brake fluid.
4. Observe the brake fluid level through the reservoir on the master cylinder reservoir. The brake fluid level must be above the MIN level mark (B, **Figure 46**).
5. If the level is low, remove the cap and diaphragm. The diaphragm (**Figure 47**) should be attached to the cap.

WARNING
Use brake fluid clearly marked DOT 4 and specified for disc brakes. Others may vaporize and cause brake failure. Do not intermix different brands or types of brake fluid, as they may not be compatible. Do not intermix a silicone-based (DOT 5) brake fluid, as it

can cause brake component damage leading to brake system failure.

CAUTION
Be careful when handling brake fluid. Do not spill it on painted or plastic surfaces, as it will damage them. Wash the area immediately with soap and water and rinse thoroughly.

6. Add DOT 4 brake fluid up to the MAX (maximum) level mark.

NOTE
*When adding brake fluid to the reservoir, inspect the master cylinder reservoir diaphragm (**Figure 47**) for tearing, cracks or other damage. A damaged diaphragm will allow moisture to enter the reservoir and contaminate the brake fluid.*

7. Install the cap with the diaphragm and tighten securely.
8. Close the hood.

Front Brake Pad Wear Check

Check the brake pads at the intervals specified in **Table 1**, when the brake fluid level in the reservoir has dropped or whenever any scrapping or grinding noises are heard at either caliper.

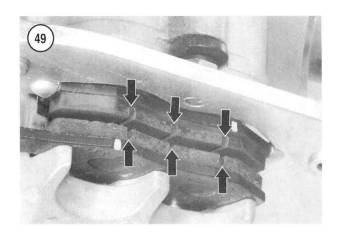

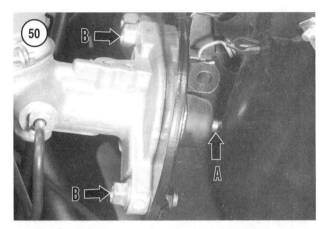

NOTE
Do not disconnect the brake hose at the caliper.

1. Remove the front brake calipers (Chapter Fifteen).
2. Replace the brake pads when the pad material is almost worn down to the bottom of the indicator grooves in the pad material (**Figure 48**) or when the brake pad thickness is 1.5 mm (0.06 in.) or less.
3. Inspect the pads for oil or grease contamination, uneven wear and damage. Uneven wear may indicate that the caliper brackets are binding in the caliper. This will require cleaning of the brackets and possible replacement of the rubber boots or other components.

4. If one set of brake pads are worn, replace the brake pads in both front calipers as described in Chapter Fifteen.
5. If the brake pads are not excessively worn but there is still excessive noise coming from a caliper(s) or the brakes do not feel right, inspect the brake pads and calipers as described in Chapter Fifteen.
6. Install the front brake calipers (Chapter Fifteen).

Rear Brake Pad Wear Check

Check the brake pads at the intervals specified in **Table 1**, when the brake fluid level in the reservoir has dropped or whenever any scrapping or grinding noises are heard at either caliper.

NOTE
Do not disconnect the brake hose at the caliper.

1. Remove the rear brake calipers (Chapter Fifteen).
2. Replace the brake pads when the pad material is almost worn down to the bottom of the indicator grooves in the pad material (**Figure 49**) or when the brake pad thickness is 1.5 mm (0.06 in.) or less.
3. Inspect the pads for oil or grease contamination, uneven wear and damage. Uneven wear may indicate that the caliper brackets are binding in the caliper. This will require cleaning of the brackets and possible replacement of the rubber boots or other components.
4. If one set of brake pads are worn, replace the brake pads in both rear calipers as described in Chapter Fifteen.
5. If the brake pads are not excessively worn but there is still excessive noise coming from a caliper(s) or the brakes do not feel right, inspect the brake pads and calipers as described in Chapter Fifteen.
6. Install the rear brake calipers (Chapter Fifteen).

Brake Pedal Adjustment

The brake rod (A, **Figure 50**) must lightly contact the master cylinder piston when at rest, resulting in zero brake pedal free play. Check by applying the brake pedal. If there is free play, adjust the brake pedal as follows:
1. Make sure the master cylinder mounting bolts (B, **Figure 50**) are tightened to 16 N•m (12 ft.-lb.).
2. Make sure the brake return spring is installed and in good condition.
3. Apply the brake several times and allow the pedal to come to rest.
4. Loosen the brake rod locknut (A, **Figure 51**) turn the brake rod (B) until it lightly contacts the master cylinder piston and there is zero clearance. Hold the brake rod and tighten the locknut to 17 N•m (12.5 ft.-lb.).
5. Check the adjustment and readjust if necessary.

Rear Brake Light Switch Adjustment

1. Turn the ignition switch on.

2. Depress the brake pedal while someone watches the brake light. The brake light should come on just before feeling pressure at the brake pedal. If necessary, adjust the switch by performing the following:

  a. Open the hood (Chapter Sixteen).
  b. Hold the switch body (A, **Figure 52**) and turn the adjusting nut (B) to adjust the switch. Do not turn the switch body.
  c. Make sure the brake light comes on when the pedal is depressed and goes off when the pedal is released. Readjust if necessary.

3. Turn the ignition switch off.

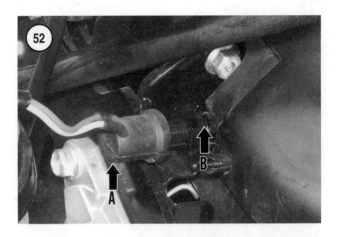

Disc Brake Hose Removal/Installation

Replace the brake hoses at the interval specified in **Table 1** or when they become swollen or damaged. Refer to Chapter Fifteen for service procedures.

Brake Fluid Change

Every time the reservoir cap is removed from the master cylinder, a small amount of dirt and moisture enters the brake system. The same thing happens if a leak occurs or any part of the hydraulic system is loosened or disconnected. Dirt can clog the system and cause unnecessary wear. Water in the brake fluid can vaporize at high brake system temperatures, impairing the hydraulic action and reducing the brake's stopping ability.

To maintain peak performance, change the brake fluid every year and whenever rebuilding a caliper or master cylinder. To change brake fluid, follow the brake fluid draining procedure in Chapter Fifteen.

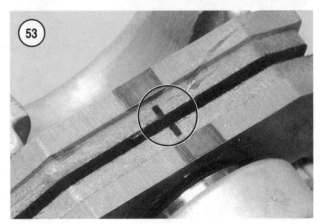

Brake Caliper and Master Cylinder Seal Removal/Installation

Replace the seals in the brake caliper and master cylinder at the interval specified in **Table 1**. Refer to Chapter Fifteen for service procedures.

PARKING BRAKE ASSEMBLY

Parking Brake Pad Wear Check

Check the parking brake pads at the intervals specified in **Table 1** or whenever any scrapping or grinding noises are heard at the parking brake caliper.

1. Remove the parking brake caliper (Chapter Fifteen).
2. Replace the parking brake pads when the pad material is almost worn down to the bottom of the indicator grooves in the pad material (**Figure 53** and **Figure 54**) or when the parking brake pad thickness is 1.0 mm (0.04 in.) or less.
3. Inspect the pads for oil or grease contamination, uneven wear and damage.
4. Install the parking brake caliper (Chapter Fifteen).

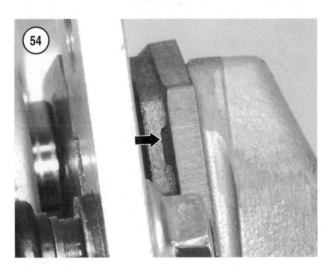

5. Set the parking brake and check its operation.

Parking Brake Disc Check

Inspect the parking brake disc for damage.

Parking Brake Cable Adjustment

The parking brake cable adjustment is determined by the number of clicks heard when operating the parking brake lever.

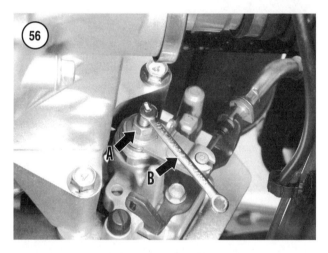

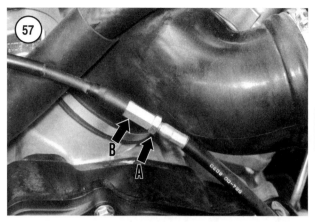

3

1. Pull the parking brake and count the clicks. The parking brake is properly adjusted when there is one click. If there is more than one click, continue with Step 2.

2. Shift the transmission into low gear.

3. Remove the rear console (Chapter Sixteen).

4. Block the front wheels so the vehicle cannot roll.

5. Support the vehicle and remove the right rear wheel (Chapter Thirteen).

6. Raise the bed (Chapter Sixteen).

7. Perform the following adjustment at the parking brake caliper:

   a. Release the parking brake lever.

   b. Disconnect the return spring (**Figure 55**).

   c. Loosen the parking brake lever nut (A, **Figure 56**).

   d. Using a 5 mm open end wrench (B, **Figure 56**), turn the pushrod in until it bottoms, then back out 3/4 turn.

   e. Tighten the parking brake lever nut (A, **Figure 56**) to 17 N•m (12.5 ft.-lb.).

NOTE
*A torque adapter can be used to tighten the nut. Refer to **Torque Adapters** in **Tools** in Chapter One for additional information.*

   f. Install the return spring (**Figure 55**).

8. Adjust the parking brake cable free play as follows:

   a. Make sure the parking brake lever is released.

   b. Slide the cover away from the parking brake locknut and adjuster.

   c. Loosen the parking brake cable adjuster locknut (A, **Figure 57**) and turn the adjuster (B) to adjust the parking brake lever travel.

   d. Set the parking brake lever and count the clicks. If it clicks more than one time, repeat the adjustment.

   e. When the parking brake lever clicks one time when applied, hold the adjuster and tighten the locknut.

   f. Recheck the adjustment.

9. Reinstall the right rear wheel (Chapter Thirteen).

10. Perform the following:

   a. Block the front wheels so the vehicle cannot roll, if necessary.

   b. Raise the vehicle so both rear wheels are off the ground.

   c. Shift the transmission into neutral.

   d. Release the parking brake and turn the rear wheels to make sure the parking brake does not drag.

   e. Apply the parking brake and lower the rear wheels onto the ground.

11. Turn the ignition switch on. Make sure the parking brake indicator illuminates when the parking brake lever is applied.

12. Turn the ignition switch off.

ENGINE MOUNTS INSPECTION

At the intervals specified in **Table 1**, check the engine mounts for cracks and other damage. Check the nuts and bolts for looseness. Refer to Chapter Five for torque specifications.

CONTROL CABLES AND PEDALS

Inspection/Lubrication

Periodically remove and lubricate the control cables with a cable lubricant or engine oil. Then remove the pedals and lubricate the pedal pivot surfaces with lithium grease.

Remove the cables by referring to the cable replacement procedure in Chapter Eight (accelerator cable) and Chapter Fifteen (parking brake cable). Before lubricating the cables, inspect the cable sheath for cracks, splitting and other damage. Inspect the cable ends for fraying and other signs of damage. Check the cable operation by holding the sheath and then sliding the cable. Replace the cable(s) if damaged.

To access the accelerator pedal and brake pedal, refer to the pedal removal/installation procedures in Chapter Sixteen.

TIRES AND WHEELS

Tire Pressure

WARNING
Always inflate both tire sets (front and rear) to the correct air pressure. If the vehicle is run with unequal air pressures, the vehicle may run toward one side, causing poor handling.

Check and set the tire pressure to maintain good traction and handling and to prevent rim damage. **Table 2** lists the standard tire pressure for the front and rear wheels. Check the tire pressure when the tires are cold.

Tire Inspection

WARNING
Do not ride the vehicle with damaged or excessively worn tires. A tire in this condition can cause loss of control. Replace damaged or severely worn tires immediately.

Inspect tires daily for excessive wear, cuts, abrasions or punctures. If a nail or other object is found in a tire, mark the location with a light crayon before removing it. Service the tires as described in Chapter Eleven.

To gauge tire wear, inspect the height of the tread knobs. If the average tread knob height measures 3 mm (0.2 in.) or less (**Figure 58**), replace the tire as described in Chapter Eleven.

Wheels Inspection

Check the wheels for cracks, dents and other damage. Rim damage may be sufficient to cause an air leak or affect wheel alignment. Improper wheel alignment can cause vibration and result in an unsafe riding condition.

Make sure the wheel nuts are tightened securely on each wheel. Tighten the wheel nuts in a crossing pattern to 55 N•m (41 ft.-lb.).

Refer to Chapter Eleven to measure wheel runout at the intervals specified in **Table 1**.

WHEEL BEARINGS INSPECTION

Inspect the front and rear wheel bearings at the intervals specified in **Table 1**. To replace the seals and wheel bearings, refer to *Steering Knuckle* in Chapter Eleven or *Rear Knuckle* in Chapter Thirteen.

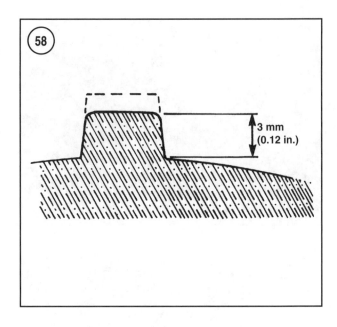

1. Support the vehicle so the front wheels are off the ground.
2. Grab the wheel at two points and rock it. There should be no play at the wheel bearings. If any movement can be seen or felt, check the wheel bearings for excessive wear or damage.

WARNING
A faulty ball joint can cause excessive front wheel movement. Determine whether wheel movement is due to faulty bearings or ball joints. Refer to Chapter Eleven.

3. Repeat for the rear wheels.

STEERING SYSTEM

Inspect the steering components and perform the required services at the intervals specified in **Table 1**. If any of the components are damaged or the steering fasteners are loose, refer to Chapter Eleven for the correct service procedures and torque specifications.

Steering Column and Steering Shaft Inspection

1. Support the vehicle on level ground and set the parking brake.
2. Inspect all components of the steering system. Repair or replace damaged components as described in Chapter Eleven.
3. Make sure the front axle nuts are tight and that all cotter pins are in place.
4. Check that the cotter pins are in place on all other steering components. If any cotter pin is missing, check the nut for looseness. Tighten the nut to the specified torque and install a new cotter pin as described in Chapter Eleven.
5. Check the steering wheel alignment and the steering wheel nut for tightness as described in Chapter Eleven.

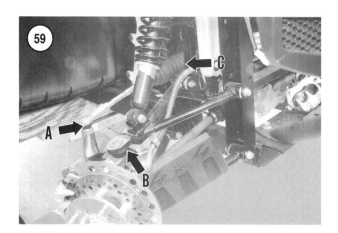

6. Check the steering shaft play as follows:
   a. Support the vehicle with the front wheels off the ground.
   b. To check steering shaft radial play, move the steering wheel from side to side (without attempting to move the wheels). If radial play is excessive, the steering column and/or the steering shaft assembly may be loose or damaged. Check the steering shaft and steering column as described in Chapter Eleven.
   c. To check steering column thrust play, lift up and then push down on the steering wheel. If there is excessive thrust play, check the steering column mounting bolts for looseness. If the bolts are tightened properly, check the steering column for damage.

Steering Gearbox, Tie Rod and Boot Inspection

The steering gearbox, tie rods and tie rod ends must be in good condition for proper steering operation. All handling and steering shaft movement is transferred through the tie rods to the front wheels. The tie rod ends are permanently sealed and do not require periodic lubrication.

1. Inspect both tie rod ends as follows:
   a. Turn the steering wheel fully to the left until it stops. Then try to move the steering wheel. Repeat by turning the wheel fully to the right. If there is any play,

replace the tie rod ends (A, **Figure 59**) as described in Chapter Eleven.
   b. Inspect the rubber boots for tears and other damage.
   c. Grasp the tie rod end and check for looseness or dryness, indicating a worn ball joint.
   d. Make sure the cotter pins are in place and the nuts are tightened to specification.
2. Park the vehicle with all four wheels on the ground and position the steering wheel with the front wheels pointing forward. Grasp the sides of each front wheel and attempt to push them back and forth. If there is any looseness, check the ball joints on the upper (B, **Figure 59**) and lower arms for damage. If the ball joints are good, the wheel bearings may be worn or damaged.
3. Check the boots (C, **Figure 59**) installed on the steering gearbox for tearing or loose or damaged clamps.
4. If any wear or damage is detected in Steps 1-3, refer to Chapter Eleven for service procedures and torque specifications.

Toe-In Adjustment

Refer to Chapter Eleven.

Steering Knuckle Boot Inspection

Inspect the boot (A, **Figure 60**) on the steering knuckle ball joints for tearing and other damage. If necessary, replace the steering knuckle ball joint(s) as described in Chapter Eleven. The ball joint is permanently sealed and does not require periodic lubrication.

Front Upper Arm Boot Inspection

Inspect the boot (B, **Figure 60**) on the front arm ball joints for tearing and other damage. If necessary, replace the front upper arm ball joint(s) as described in Chapter Eleven. The ball joint is permanently sealed and does not require periodic lubrication.

AXLE BOOTS INSPECTION

Check the front and rear axle boots (C, **Figure 60**, typical) for tearing and other damage at the intervals in **Table 1**. Check for signs of grease that may have leaked out of the boots. At the same time check for loose or damaged boot clamps. If necessary, refer to Chapter Twelve or Chapter Fourteen for service procedures to replace the boots(s).

FRONT SUSPENSION

Inspect and lubricate the front suspension components at the intervals specified in **Table 1**. If any of the components are loose or damaged, refer to Chapter Eleven for the service procedures and torque specifications.

Shock Absorber Inspection

Inspect the shock absorbers at the intervals specified in **Table 1**.

1. Check the front shock absorbers for oil leaks, a bent damper rod or other damage.
2. If necessary, adjust or service the shock absorbers as described in Chapter Eleven.

Front Arm Inspection and Lubrication

1. Remove the front wheels as described in Chapter Eleven.
2. Check for loose front suspension components.
3. Check the tightness of the front suspension fasteners.
4. Remove the front upper and lower arms and inspect the bushings. Clean and lubricate the pivot bolts with lithium grease.

REAR SUSPENSION

Inspect and lubricate the rear suspension components at the intervals specified in **Table 1**. If any of the components are loose or damaged, refer to Chapter Thirteen for the service procedures and torque specifications.

Rear Knuckle Pivot Lubrication

Lubricate the rear knuckle grease fittings (**Figure 61**) at the intervals in **Table 1** with lithium grease.

Shock Absorber Inspection

1. Check the rear shock absorbers for oil leaks, a bent damper rod or other damage.
2. If necessary, adjust or service the shock absorbers as described in Chapter Thirteen.

Rear Arm Inspection and Lubrication

1. Remove the rear wheel as described in Chapter Thirteen.
2. Check for loose rear suspension components.
3. Check the tightness of the rear suspension fasteners.

4. Remove the rear upper and lower arms and inspect the bushings. Clean and lubricate the pivot bolts with lithium grease.

UNIVERSAL JOINT LUBRICATION

Lubricate the front differential universal joint (**Figure 62**) and the middle driven pinion gear bearing housing universal joint (**Figure 63**) grease fittings at the intervals in **Table 1** with lithium grease.

DRAIN HOSES

Inspect the drain hoses whenever the machine has been operated in wet conditions, particularly deep water.

Air Filter Housing

Refer to *Air Filter* in this chapter.

Air Intake Duct

The inspection hose is located at the front, lower part of the air intake duct, directly behind the steering gearbox (**Figure 64**). Remove the inspection hose to drain the air intake duct.

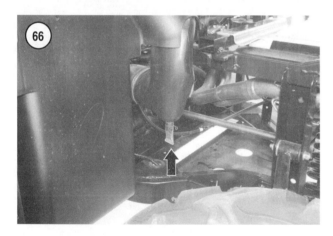

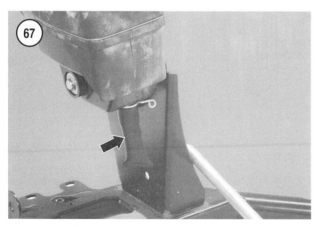

Drive Belt Cover

The drive belt drain plug is located on the left side of the engine at the bottom of the drive belt cover (**Figure 65**). Remove the rear console (Chapter Sixteen) to access the drain. Pull the drain plug and drain water and other contaminants from the cover.

Rear Air Duct

Raise the bed (Chapter Sixteen) to access the rear air duct inspection hose (**Figure 66**). Remove the inspection hose to drain the rear air duct.

Select Lever Assembly

The select lever inspection hose is mounted on the left side of the select lever assembly. **Figure 67** shows the select lever assembly removed to identify the hose position. Remove the rear console (Chapter Sixteen) to access the inspection hose (**Figure 67**). Remove the inspection hose to drain the select lever assembly.

FASTENERS INSPECTION

At the intervals specified in **Table 1**, check for loose or missing chassis and engine fasteners. Check that all steering and suspension assembly cotter pins are installed and locked in place. Check that all hose clamps, guides and safety clips are correctly installed.

ENGINE BREAK-IN

The performance and service life of a new or reconditioned engine depends greatly on a careful and sensible break-in for the first 20 hours of engine operation.

1. Observe the following conditions when breaking in the engine.
   a. If possible, operate the vehicle on flat ground. Do not run in sand, mud or up hills. This will overload and possibly overheat the engine.
   b. Avoid hard acceleration for longer than 2-3 seconds at a time. After hard acceleration, lower the engine speed considerably and for a sufficient amount of time to reduce the build-up of heat in the engine.
2. Perform the *Pre-Ride Inspection* in this chapter.
3. Service the air filter as described in this chapter.
4. Check the engine oil level.
5. Make sure the cooling system is full and bled of all air.

NOTE
Check the spark plug frequently. Refer to the spark plug chart in this chapter to identify spark plug condition.

6. Start the engine and allow it to warm up. During this time, check for proper idle speed and leaks.

7. For the first 10 hours of operation, use no more than one-half throttle. Vary the speed as much as possible within this throttle range. Avoid running the machine at a steady speed. After every hour of operation, allow the engine to cool for 10 minutes.

8. For the next 10 hours of operation, use no more than three-fourths throttle. Vary the speed as much as possible within this throttle range.

9. At the end of the first month, 200 mile (320km) or 20 hour break-in period, perform the service items in **Table 1**.

Table 1 MAINTENANCE AND LUBRICATION SCHEDULE*

Every 20-40 hours or more often when operating in wet and dusty conditions
  Clean and service the air filter.
First month, 200 miles (320 km) or 20 hours
  Check the valve clearance and adjust if necessary.
  Check the spark plug condition and gap. Replace if necessary.
  Check the cooling system for leaks and damage.
  Change the engine oil and filter.
  Check the final gear oil. Check for oil leaks.
  Change the differential gear oil. Check for oil leaks.
  Check the brake fluid level.
  Check the front and rear brake pad wear.
  Check the front and rear brake systems for leaks or loose or missing fasteners.
  Check the parking brake assembly for damage or missing parts.
  Check the parking brake pad wear.
  Check the parking brake operation and free-play measurement.
  Check the accelerator pedal operation and accelerator cable adjustment.
  Measure the drive belt width. Check the belt for damage.
  Check the wheels for excessive runout and damage. Check wheel balance and adjust if necessary.
  Check the wheel bearings for excessive play or damage.
  Check the steering system operation and for excessive looseness.
  Check the toe-in and adjust if necessary.
  Check the front and rear axle boots for damage.
  Check all chassis fasteners and other components for looseness or damage.
3 months, 750 miles (1200 km) or 75 hours
  Check the spark plug condition and gap. Replace if necessary.
  Check the cooling system for leaks and damage.
  Check the brake fluid level.
  Check the front and rear brake pad wear.
  Check the front and rear brake systems for leaks or loose or missing fasteners.
  Check the parking brake assembly for damage or missing parts.
  Check the parking brake pad wear.
  Check the parking brake operation and free-play measurement.
  Check the accelerator pedal operation and accelerator cable adjustment.
  Check the steering system operation and for excessive looseness.
  Check the toe-in and adjust if necessary.
  Check all chassis fasteners and other components for looseness or damage.
  Check throttle body and intake joint.
6 months, 1500 miles (2400 km) or 150 hours
  Repeat 3 month, 750 miles (1200 km) or 75 hour checks.
  Check the fuel hose for cracks, missing clamps or other damage.
  Check the valve clearance and adjust if necessary.
  Check the breather hoses for cracks, missing clamps or other damage.
  Check the exhaust system for leaks, loose or missing fasteners or damage.
  Clean the spark arrestor.
  Check the cooling system for leaks and damage.
  Change the engine oil and filter.
  Lubricate the rear knuckle pivot grease fittings.
  Lubricate the universal joint grease fittings.
  Check the engine mounts for damage or loose or missing fasteners.
  Check the stabilizer bushings for cracks and other damage.
  Check all chassis fasteners and other components for looseness or damage.
  Measure the drive belt width. Check the belt for damage.
  Check the front and rear shock absorbers for leaks and damage. Check for loose or missing fasteners.

(continued)

Table 1 MAINTENANCE AND LUBRICATION SCHEDULE* (continued)

12 months, 3000 miles (4800 km) or 300 hours
  Repeat 6 months, 1500 miles (2400 km) or 150 hour checks.
Every 12 months, 3000 miles (4800 km) or 150 hours
  Change the final drive gear oil. Check for oil leaks.
  Change the differential oil. Check for oil leaks.
  Check the front and rear axle boots for damage.
Every two years
  Change the engine coolant.
  Replace the master cylinder seals and piston assemblies.
  Replace the brake caliper seals.
Every four years
  Replace the brake hoses or earlier if cracked or damaged.

*Consider this schedule a guide to general maintenance and lubrication intervals. Harder than normal use and exposure to mud, water, and high humidity will require more frequent attention to most maintenance items.

Table 2 TIRE INFLATION PRESSURE*

	kPa	psi
Front	63-77	9-11
Rear	91-105	13-15

*Tire specifications are for original equipment tires only. After market tires may have different specifications.

Table 3 OIL AND FLUID CAPACITIES

Radiator	2.35 L (2.48 qt.)
Coolant reservoir	
Amount between marks	0.21 L (0.22 qt.)
Total	0.32 L (0.34 qt.)
Engine oil	
Oil change only	2.00 L (2.11 qt.)
Oil and filter change	2.10 L (2.22 qt.)
Engine disassembly	3.00 L (3.18 qt.)
Final drive gear oil	
Oil change	250 ml (8.5 oz.)
Final drive gear disassembly	280 ml (9.5 oz.)
Front differential gear oil	
Oil change	180 ml (6.1 oz.)
Differential disassembly	200 ml (6.8 oz.)

Table 4 RECOMMENDED LUBRICANTS, COOLANT AND FUEL

Air filter	Air filter oil
Brake fluid	DOT 4 brake fluid
Engine oil[2]	
Classification	
JASCO T 903 standard rating	MA
API rating	SG or higher
Viscosity	5W-30
30° F (0° C) or lower	
10-110° F (-10-43° C)	10W-40
50° F (10° C) or higher	20W-50
Engine coolant	
Type	Ethylene glycol containing anticorrosion inhibiters for aluminum engines
Mixture	50:50 (coolant/distilled water)
Final drive gear oil[1]	SAE80 API GL-4 hypoid gear oil

(continued)

Table 4 RECOMMENDED LUBRICANTS, COOLANT AND FUEL (continued)

Front differential gear oil[1]	SAE80 API GL-4 hypoid gear oil
Fuel	Refer to text

1. Refer to Chapter One for additional information.
2. API SG or higher classified oils not specified as ENERGY CONSERVING II can be used. Refer to Chapter One for additional information.

Table 5 MAINTENANCE AND TUNE-UP SPECIFICATIONS

Air filter type	Wet type element
Brake pad wear limit	
Front and rear	1.5 mm (0.06 in.)
Parking	1.0 mm (0.04 in.)
Brake pedal free play	0 mm (0 in.)
Engine compression	
Minimum	392 kPa (56.84 psi)
Standard	450 kPa (65.25 psi)
Maximum	504 kPa (73.08 psi)
Engine idle speed	1550-1650 rpm
Engine oil pressure (hot)	50.0 kPa (7.25 psi) @ 1600 rpm
Parking brake adjustment	
Number of clicks	1
Spark plug gap	0.8-0.9 mm (0.031-0.035 in.)
Spark plug type	NGK CPR7EA-9
Accelerator cable free play	0 mm (0 in.)
Tire wear limit	
Front and rear	3.0 mm (0.12 in.)
Valve clearance	
Intake	0.09-0.13 mm (0.0035-0.0051 in.)
Exhaust	0.16-0.20 mm (0.0063-0.0079 in.)
Drive belt width	
Standard	33.3 mm (1.31 in.)
Service limit	30.0 mm (1.18 in.)

Table 6 MAINTENANCE TORQUE SPECIFICATIONS

	N•m	in.-lb.	ft.-lb.
Brake rod locknut	17	–	12.5
Camshaft sprocket cover bolt	10	88	–
Coolant drain bolt	10	88	–
Differential oil fill plug	23	–	17
Differential oil drain bolt	10	88	–
Engine oil check bolt	10	88	–
Engine oil drain bolt	30	–	22
Engine oil filter	17	–	12.5
Final drive oil fill plug	23	–	17
Final drive oil drain bolt	20	–	15
Flywheel nut plug	10	88	–
Master cylinder mounting bolt	16	–	12
Parking brake lever nut	17	–	12.5
Shift rod locknut	15	–	11
Skid plate mounting bolts	7	62	–
Spark plug	13	115	–
Tailpipe mounting bolt	10	88	–
Thermostat cover air bleed bolt	10	88	–
Timing plug	6	53	–
Tie-rod end locknut	40	–	30
Valve adjust screw locknuts	14	–	10
Valve adjustment cover bolt	10	88	–
Water pump air bleed bolt	10	88	–
Wheel nuts	55	–	41

ENGINE TOP END AND EXHAUST SYSTEM

This chapter covers the exhaust system and the engine top end. Refer to Chapter Three to adjust the valve clearance. Read *Safety* and *Service Methods* in Chapter One.

Tables 1-4 are at the end of this chapter.

EXHAUST SYSTEM

Refer to *Exhaust System* in Chapter Three to service the spark arrester.

Refer to **Figure 1**.

Removal

1. Remove the cargo bed (Chapter Sixteen).
2. Remove the center protector (Chapter Sixteen).
3. Remove the bolts and the heat protector (**Figure 2**).

WARNING
*The springs are strong and can be difficult to disconnect. Wear gloves to protect hands and use a spring tool (A, **Figure 3**) or equivalent.*

NOTE
*To prevent the rear exhaust pipe from moving rearward when disconnecting the springs, place a wooden pry bar between the rear exhaust pipe and frame (B, **Figure 3**). Otherwise, the springs will pull the exhaust pipe rearward, thus making it more difficult to disconnect the springs.*

4. Use a spring tool to disconnect and remove the springs.

5. Insert a thin screwdriver between the damper (**Figure 4**) and frame bracket and pry the damper off of the frame bracket. If the damper is hardened or stuck, spray it with a WD-40 or an equivalent to prevent it from tearing and ease removal.
6. Remove the rear exhaust pipe (C, **Figure 3**).
7. Remove the muffler mounting bolts (A, **Figure 5**). Then turn the muffler inward so the brackets on the muffler clear the frame mounting brackets and remove the muffler (B, **Figure 5**) through the rear side of the frame.
8. Remove the nuts (**Figure 6**) securing the front exhaust pipe to the cylinder head. Then slide the flanges off of the exhaust pipe studs and remove the front exhaust pipe (**Figure 7**).

NOTE
*If a flange will not slide off of the studs, the nuts were over tightened and bent the flange. This may have also bent one or both studs. However, do not drive the flange off as this may damage the stud threads. Instead, remove the stud. Either install two nuts onto one of the studs. Tighten the two nuts together, making sure the outer nut is fully installed on the stud. Then turn the inner nut (**Figure 8**) to remove the stud. Now slide the flange off the remaining stud and remove the front exhaust pipe. Or use a stud remover. Refer to **Serive Methods** in Chapter One.*

9. Pry the gaskets (17, **Figure 1**) from the cylinder head exhaust ports and discard them.
10. If necessary, remove the bolts and the muffler mounting brackets (A, **Figure 9**).
11. Inspect as described in this section.

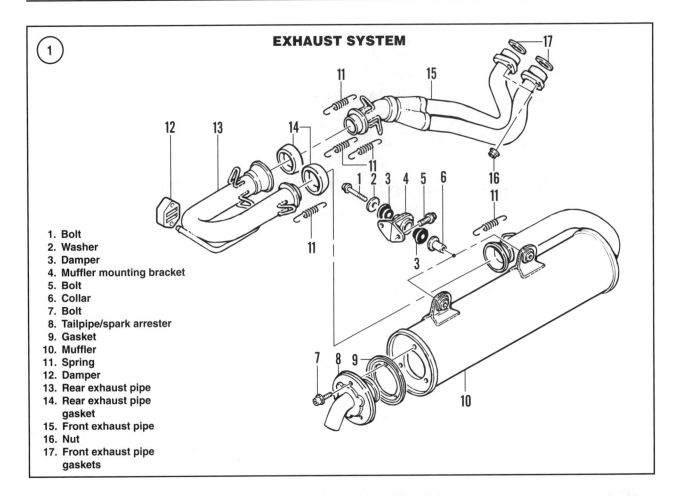

EXHAUST SYSTEM

1. Bolt
2. Washer
3. Damper
4. Muffler mounting bracket
5. Bolt
6. Collar
7. Bolt
8. Tailpipe/spark arrester
9. Gasket
10. Muffler
11. Spring
12. Damper
13. Rear exhaust pipe
14. Rear exhaust pipe
    gasket
15. Front exhaust pipe
16. Nut
17. Front exhaust pipe
    gaskets

Installation

1. If removed, install the muffler mounting brackets (A, **Figure 9**) and tighten the mounting bolts to 30 N•m (22 ft.-lb.). Install the mounting brackets so that the collar (B, **Figure 9**) will seat against the muffler.

2. Apply a few dabs of grease onto one side of the new front exhaust pipe gaskets (17, **Figure 1**) and seat them into the exhaust ports with the grease side resting against the cylinder head. The grease will hold the gaskets in place and burn off soon after starting the engine.

3. Install the front exhaust pipe (**Figure 7**) and secure in place with the flanges and nuts (**Figure 6**). Tighten the nuts finger-tight.

4. Install the muffler (B, **Figure 5**) and secure with the two mounting bolts and washers (A). Tighten the bolts finger-tight.

5. Install a gasket (**Figure 10**) onto the front exhaust pipe and rear exhaust pipe (**Figure 11**), if removed.

6. Install the rear exhaust pipe while installing the damper (**Figure 12**) over the frame bracket.

7. Check the exhaust pipe and muffler alignment to make sure none of the parts are binding, especially where the front exhaust pipe assembly is attached to the cylinder head.

8. Install the springs between the spring hooks connecting the rear exhaust pipe to the front exhaust pipe and muffler. Make sure each spring is connected fully on both ends.

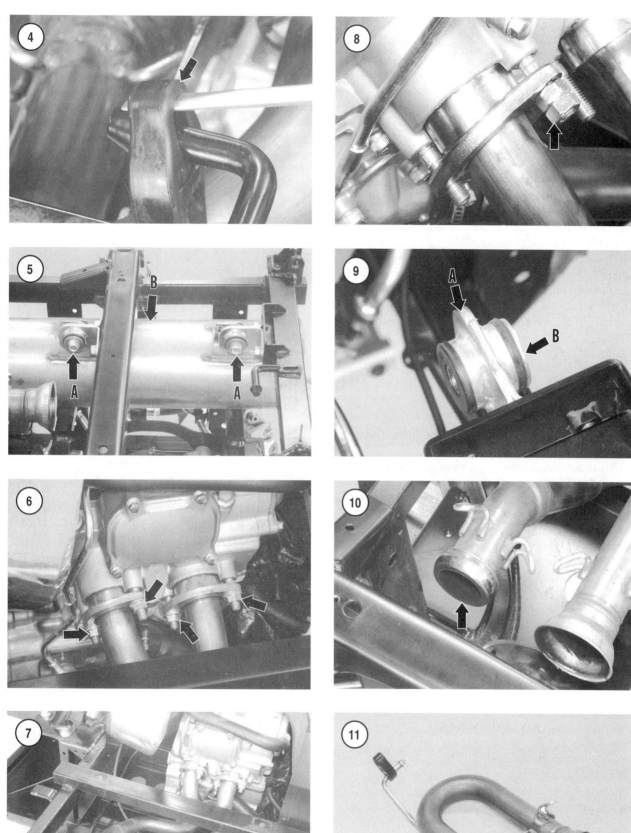

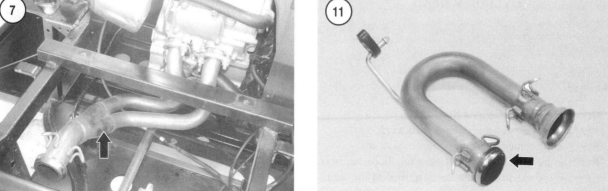

CAUTION
Do not overtighten the front exhaust pipe nuts as doing so may damage the flange on the exhaust pipe(s) or the studs.

NOTE
A 12-mm box-end torque adapter will be required to reach some of the front exhaust pipe nuts when using a torque wrench. Refer to **Torque Adapters** *in* **Tools** *Chapter.*

9. Tighten the front exhaust pipe nuts (**Figure 6**) evenly and in a crossing pattern to compress the exhaust pipe gasket. Then tighten the nuts to 20 N•m (15 ft.-lb.).

10. Tighten the muffler mounting bolts (A, **Figure 5**) to 20 N•m (15 ft.-lb.).

11. Install the heat protector (**Figure 2**) and tighten its mounting bolts to 8 N•m (71 in.-lb.).

12. Start the engine and allow it to run long enough burn off the grease previously installed on the gaskets. Then continue to run the engine and check the exhaust system for leaks.

13. Install the center protector (Chapter Sixteen).

14. Install the cargo bed (Chapter Sixteen).

Inspection

1. Inspect the exhaust pipes for damage. Refer damage to a dealership.

2. Replace the rear exhaust pipe gaskets (**Figure 10** and **Figure 11**) if leaking or damaged.

3. Replace the mounting bracket dampers (3, **Figure 1**) if damaged.

4. Replace the rear exhaust pipe damper (12, **Figure 1**) if damaged.

5. Check the springs for gaps between the coils when the springs are at rest. Then check the spring hooks for damage.

6. Clean the exhaust pipe nuts and check for damage.

7. Clean the cylinder head studs and check for looseness or damage. If a stud was removed earlier, replace it as described in *Service Methods* in Chapter One. Install the stud end with the short-length threaded side into the cylinder head.

CYLINDER HEAD

The cylinder head can be removed with the engine mounted in the frame.

Removal

1. Remove the seats (Chapter Sixteen).

2. Remove the rear console (Chapter Sixteen).

3. Remove the center protector (Chapter Sixteen).

4. Remove the drive belt air duct assembly (Chapter Six).

5. Remove the exhaust system as described in this chapter.

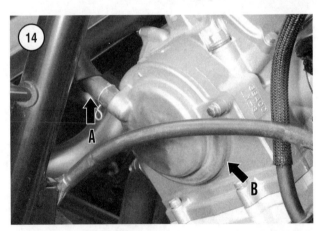

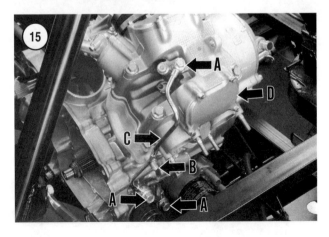

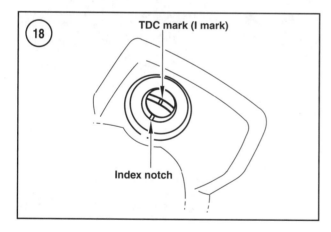

TDC mark (I mark)

Index notch

6. Remove the fuel tank (Chapter Eight).

7. Drain the engine oil (Chapter Three).

8. Drain the coolant (Chapter Three).

9. Remove the throttle body (Chapter Eight).

10. Loosen the clamp and disconnect the radiator hose (A, **Figure 13**) from the thermostat cover.

11. Disconnect the coolant temperature sensor connector (B, **Figure 13**).

12. Disconnect the breather hose at the cylinder head (A, **Figure 14**).

13. Remove the camshaft sprocket cover (B, **Figure 14**) and O-ring.

14. Remove the banjo bolts (A, **Figure 15**) and washers, mounting bolt (B) and the oil delivery pipe (C).

15. Remove the valve adjustment covers (D, **Figure 15**) and their O-rings.

16. Remove the timing plug (A, **Figure 16**) and the flywheel nut plug (B).

17. Remove the spark plug (Chapter Three). This will make it easier to turn the engine by hand.

18. The engine must be set at top dead center (TDC) on its compression stroke before removing the sprocket bolts and cam sprocket. Perform the following:

　a. Fit a 22-mm socket onto the flywheel nut (**Figure 17**) and turn the crankshaft counterclockwise until the TDC mark on the flywheel is aligned with the index notch in the timing hole (**Figure 18**).

　b. Verify that the camshaft sprocket index mark (A, **Figure 19**) aligns with the cylinder head boss (B). If these marks are not aligned, turn the crankshaft one revolution counterclockwise and realign the flywheel TDC mark with the index notch.

　c. When the camshaft sprocket and flywheel marks are properly aligned, all rocker arms will have a valve clearance, indicating that the intake and exhaust valves are closed. Move each rocker arm by hand. There should be some movement or free play.

NOTE
If the camshaft sprocket index mark does not align with the cylinder head boss when the flywheel TDC mark is aligned with the index notch in the timing hole, the cam timing is incorrect. Inspect the cam chain, sprockets and cam chain tensioner assembly for damage as described in this section.

19. Loosen, but do not remove, the cam chain tensioner cap bolt (A, **Figure 20**).

20. Remove the cam chain tensioner mounting bolts (B, **Figure 20**) and hose guide (C) and remove the tensioner (D) from the cylinder block.

21. Secure the cam chain with wire. This will prevent the chain from falling into the cylinder chain tunnel.

22. Hold the flywheel nut with a socket and loosen the camshaft sprocket bolts (A, **Figure 21**).

NOTE
If the decompressor assembly will be re-moved later, loosen, but do not remove, the two mounting bolts (B, Figure 21).

23. Remove the camshaft sprocket bolts (A, **Figure 21**). Then separate the camshaft sprocket (C, **Figure 21**) from the camshaft and remove it.

NOTE
The camshaft and both rocker arms can be removed with the cylinder head mounted in the frame as described in Camshaft and Rocker Arms in this chapter.

24. Perform the following to loosen and remove the cylinder head bolts and nuts in numerical order:
   a. Loosen the two cylinder head Allen bolts on the side of the engine (1 and 2, **Figure 22**).
   b. Loosen the lower cylinder head bolts (**Figure 23**) at the front and rear of the engine (3 and 4, **Figure 22**).
   c. Using a crossing pattern, loosen each of the upper cylinder head mounting bolts a half turn at a time until all of the bolts are loose (5, 6, 7 and 8, **Figure 22**).
   d. Remove all of the bolts and washers.

25. Tap the cylinder head with a rubber mallet to break it free from the head gasket.

26. Remove the cylinder head.

27. Remove and discard the cylinder head gasket (A, **Figure 24**).

28. Remove the two dowel pins (B, **Figure 24**) from the top of the cylinder block.

29. If necessary, remove the front cam chain guide (**Figure 25**).

30. Cover the cylinder block with a clean shop rag.

31. If necessary, remove the camshaft and rocker arms as described in this chapter.

32. If wear or damage is evident on the timing chain or guides, refer to *Cam Chain and Guide* in Chapter Five.

33. Inspect as described in this section.

Installation

1. Remove all gasket material from the cylinder head, cylinder block and cam chain tensioner mating surfaces.

2. If removed, install the rocker arm and shafts and camshaft as described in this chapter.

3. If removed, install the front cam chain guide (**Figure 25**) into the cylinder head.

4. Install the two cylinder head dowel pins (B, **Figure 24**).

5. Install a new cylinder head gasket (A, **Figure 24**) over the dowel pins.

6. Install the cylinder head and direct the cam chain and its wire through the cylinder head chain tunnel.

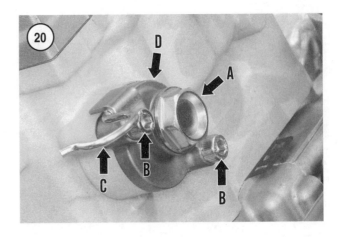

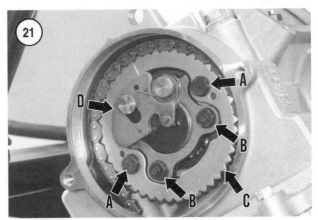

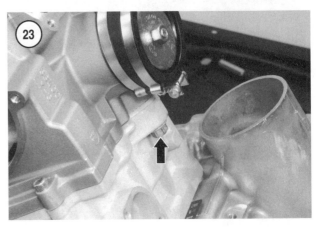

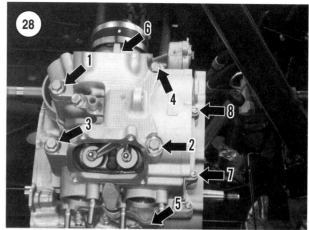

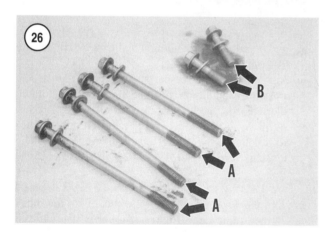

7. Lubricate the upper cylinder head bolt threads, flanges and washers (A, **Figure 26**) with molybdenum disulfide grease.

8. Lubricate the lower cylinder head bolt threads and washers (B, **Figure 26**) with engine oil.

> *NOTE*
> *Two different length cylinder head mounting bolts are used. The longer mounting bolts are installed on the clutch side of the engine. The shorter bolts have the No. 12 marked on their bolt heads and are installed on the alternator side of the engine.*

9. Install the cylinder head mounting bolts and washers and tighten in numerical order as follows:

> *NOTE*
> *A 12-mm torque adapter will be required to tighten the lower cylinder head mounting bolts when using a torque wrench. **Figure 27** shows the Motion Pro torque wrench adapter (part No. 08-0134) being used. Refer to **Torque Adapters** in **Tools** in Chapter One for a description of these tools and how to use them with a torque wrench.*

a. Initially tighten bolts 1-6 (**Figure 28**) in the order shown and in several steps to 18 N•m (13 ft.-lb.).

b. Then tighten bolts 1-4 (**Figure 28**) to the final specification of 35 N•m (26 ft.-lb.).

c. Then tighten bolts 5 and 6 (**Figure 28**) to the final specification of 38 N•m (28 ft.-lb.).

d. Tighten bolts 7 and 8 (**Figure 28**) to 10 N•m (88 in.-lb.).

> *CAUTION*
> *The cam chain must be kept tight against its sprocket when turning the crankshaft. Otherwise, the chain can roll off the sprocket and bind in the lower end, causing chain damage.*

10. Make sure the camshaft is positioned so the decompressor cam is at the top as shown in **Figure 29**. This will

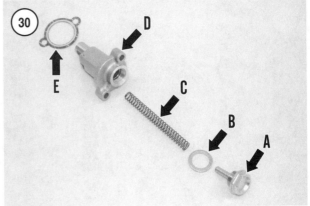

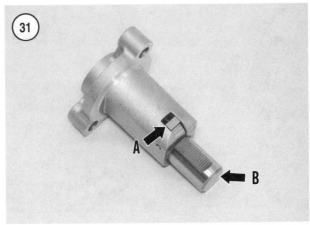

position the camshaft lobes at the bottom. If not, rotate the camshaft.

11. If the crankshaft was rotated away from TDC, perform the following:

a. Lift the cam chain and make sure it is engaged with the crankshaft sprocket. Hold the chain in this position when turning the crankshaft.

b. With a socket on the flywheel nut (**Figure 17**), turn the crankshaft counterclockwise and align the TDC mark on the flywheel with the index notch in the timing hole (**Figure 18**). This will place the piston at TDC.

12. Remove the safety wire from the top of the cam chain and reconnect it lower on the chain so it may be removed after installing the cam sprocket.

13. Align the cam sprocket so that its timing mark is facing out and is positioned up. Then, install the cam chain onto the cam sprocket, making sure the exhaust side of the cam chain is kept tight as it is slipped over the sprocket.

14. Place the cam sprocket onto the camshaft and install the cam sprocket mounting bolts (A, **Figure 21**) finger-tight.

15. Verify that the cam sprocket timing mark (A, **Figure 19**) aligns with the cylinder head boss (B). If not, remove the sprocket and reposition it on the cam chain.

NOTE
The cam sprocket and decompressor mounting bolts will be tightened after the cam chain tensioner is installed and the engine rotated several times to ensure the cam timing is correct.

16. Install the cam chain tensioner as follows:

a. Remove the cam chain tensioner cap bolt (A, **Figure 30**), washer (B) and spring (C) from the tensior (D).

b. Depress the cam chain tensioner one-way cam (A, **Figure 31**) and push the tensioner rod (B) into the tensioner body until it stops and locks in place. Refer to A, **Figure 32**.

c. Install a new gasket (B, **Figure 32**) onto the cam chain tensioner so the raised sealer bead is toward the tensioner end.

d. Install the cam chain tensioner body (D, **Figure 20**) and hose guide (C) and tighten the mounting bolts to 10 N•m (88 in.-lb.).

e. Install the spring, washer and cap bolt (**Figure 33**). Push the cap bolt into position and then thread it into the tensioner body. As the cap bolt is pushed into position, the tensioner rod is adjusted outward until it contacts the cam chain. Tighten the cam chain tensioner cap bolt (A, **Figure 20**) to 20 N•m (15 ft.-lb.).

17. Turn the crankshaft *counterclockwise* several times, then align the TDC mark on the flywheel with the index notch in the timing hole (**Figure 18**). Verify that the cam sprocket timing mark (A, **Figure 19**) aligns with the cylinder head boss (B). If not, the camshaft timing is incorrect.

18. Hold the flywheel nut with a socket and tighten the camshaft sprocket bolts (A, **Figure 21**) to 20 N•m (15 ft.-lb.).

19. Hold the flywheel nut with a socket and tighten the decompressor assembly bolts (B, **Figure 21**) to 20 N•m (15 ft.-lb.). Then check that the decompressor weight cam (D, **Figure 21**) moves and returns freely.

20. Check the valve clearance (Chapter Three).

21. Install the spark plug and tighten to 13 N•m (115 in.-lb.).

NOTE
In Steps 22-25, lubricate all plug and cover O-rings with lithium grease.

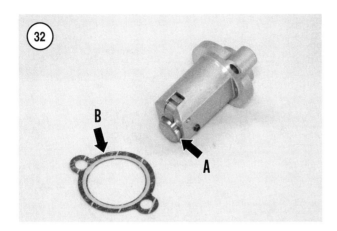

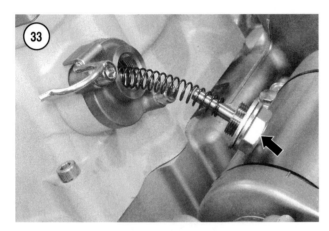

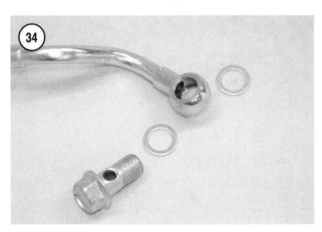

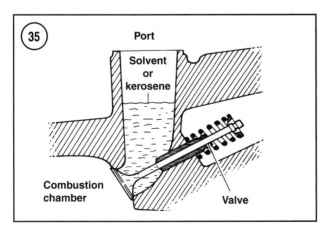

Port

Solvent
or
kerosene

Combustion
chamber

Valve

22. Tighten the flywheel nut plug (B, **Figure 16**) to 10 N•m (88 in.-lb.).

23. Tighten the timing plug (A, **Figure 16**) to 6 N•m (53 in.-lb.).

24. Tighten the camshaft sprocket cover (B, **Figure 15**) mounting bolts to 10 N•m (88 in.-lb.).

25. Tighten the valve adjustment cover mounting bolts to 10 N•m (88 in.-lb.).

26. Install the oil pipe (C, **Figure 15**) and the oil pipe mounting bolt (B). Tighten the mounting bolt finger-tight.

27. Install the oil pipe banjo bolts with new washers on both sides of each fitting (**Figure 34**). Tighten the banjo bolts (A, **Figure 15**) to 35 N•m (26 ft.-lb.).

28. Tighten the oil pipe mounting bolt to 10 N•m (88 in.-lb.).

29. Reconnect the breather hose at the cylinder head (A, **Figure 14**).

30. Reconnect the coolant temperature sensor connector (B, **Figure 13**).

31. Reconnect the radiator hose (A, **Figure 13**) at the thermostat cover.

32. Install the throttle body assembly (Chapter Eight).

33. Refill the engine with oil (Chapter Three).

34. Install the fuel tank (Chapter Eight).

35. Install the exhaust system as described in this chapter.

36. Install the drive belt air duct assembly (Chapter Six).

37. Install the center protector (Chapter Sixteen).

38. Refill the engine with coolant and bleed the cooling system (Chapter Three).

39. Install the rear console (Chapter Sixteen).

40. Install the seats (Chapter Sixteen).

Inspection

Cylinder head

1. Before removing the valves from the cylinder head, perform a solvent test to check the valve face-to-valve seat seal.

   a. Support the cylinder head with the exhaust port facing up (**Figure 35**). Pour solvent or kerosene into the port. Check the combustion chamber for fluid leaking past the exhaust valves. There should be no fluid leaking into the combustion chamber.

   b. Repeat Step 2 for the intake valves.

   c. If the combustion chamber is wet, one or more valves are not seating correctly.

   d. If there is a leak, check for a damaged valve stem, valve seat and/or face, or possibly a cracked combustion chamber.

2. Remove the spark plug.

3. Remove the 6-mm oil check bolt and gasket from the cylinder head.

4. Clean the cylinder head and cylinder block gasket surfaces. Do not scratch the gasket surface. If the gasket residue is hard to remove, place a solvent soaked rag across the cylinder head gasket surface to soften the deposits.

CAUTION
Cleaning the combustion chamber with the valves removed can damage the valve seat surfaces. A damaged or even slightly scratched valve seat will cause poor valve seating.

5. Before removing the valves, remove all carbon deposits from the combustion chamber (**Figure 36**) with a wire brush. To protect the cylinder head surface, place the two dowel pins and the old head gasket onto the cylinder head and hold in place while cleaning the combustion chamber. Do not damage the head, valves or spark plug threads.

6. Examine the spark plug threads in the cylinder head for damage. If damage is minor or if the threads are contaminated with carbon, use a spark plug thread tap to clean the threads following the manufacturer's instructions. If thread damage is severe, repair the head by installing a steel thread insert.

CAUTION
When using a tap to clean the spark plug threads, lubricate the tap with an aluminum tap cutting fluid or kerosene.

7. Clean the entire head in solvent and flush both oil passages. Dry the cylinder head with compressed air.

8. Reinstall the 6-mm oil check bolt and a new gasket and tighten to 10 N•m (88 in.-lb.).

9. Plug the oil hose fitting on top of the cylinder head to prevent debris from entering the oil passage before the hose is attached.

CAUTION
If the cylinder head was bead blasted, cleaning grit must be removed from all head areas.

10. Check for cracks in the combustion chamber (**Figure 36**) and exhaust port. A cracked head must be replaced.

11. Examine the piston crown. The crown should show no signs of wear or damage. If the crown appears pecked or spongy-looking, check the spark plug, valves and combustion chamber for aluminum deposits. If these deposits are found, the cylinder is overheating.

CAUTION
Do not clean the piston crown while the piston is installed in the cylinder. Carbon scraped from the top of the piston may fall between the cylinder wall and piston and onto the piston rings. Because carbon grit is very abrasive, premature cylinder, piston and ring wear will occur. If the piston crown has a thick deposit of carbon, remove and clean the piston as described in this chapter. Excessive carbon buildup on the piston crown reduces piston cooling, raises engine compression and causes overheating.

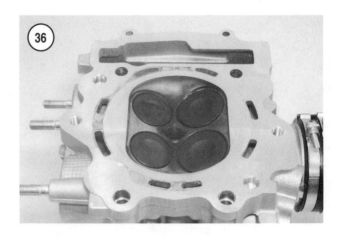

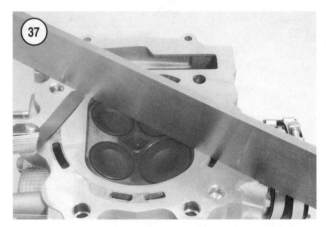

12. Measure cylinder head warp with a feeler gauge and a straightedge (**Figure 37**). Check at several locations. Maximum allowable warp is listed in **Table 2**. If the warp exceeds this limit, the cylinder head must be resurfaced or replaced.

13. Check the exhaust pipe studs for looseness or thread damage. Slight thread damage can be repaired with a thread file or die. If thread damage is severe, replace the damaged stud(s) as described in *Service Methods* in Chapter One. Install the stud end with the short-length threaded side (**Figure 38**) into the cylinder head.

14. Check the valves and valve guides as described in *Valves and Valve Components* in this chapter.

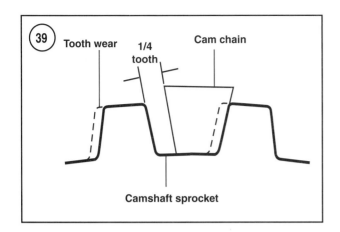

Tooth wear   1/4   Cam chain
tooth
Camshaft sprocket

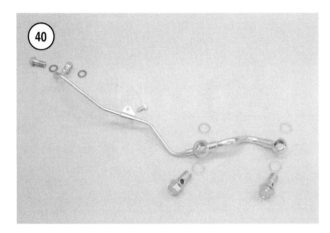

does not bind. Also make sure when it is locked in placed it cannot move in by hand.

4. Replace the cam chain tensioner if damaged, if the cam chain jumped teeth on the sprocket or if the cam chain and sprockets are severely worn.

Oil pipe

1. Flush the oil pipe and banjo bolts (**Figure 40**) with solvent and dry with compressed air.
2. Inspect the oil pipe for cracks, bending and other damage.
3. Replace damaged banjo bolts.

CAMSHAFT AND ROCKER ARMS

A single camshaft is mounted in the cylinder head. The chain-driven camshaft is supported by ball bearings. One bearing is permanently installed on the camshaft. The other bearing is pressed into the cylinder head. A decompressor assembly on the camshaft opens the exhaust valves during starting. The camshaft and both rocker arms can be removed with the cylinder head installed on the engine, or after cylinder head removal.

Tools

A slide hammer bolt (Yamaha YU-01083-1 or equivalent) and weight (Yamaha part No. YU-01083-3 or equivalent) are required to remove the rocker arm shafts from the cylinder head. A suitable tool may also be fabricated using a threaded shaft with M6 × 1.00 mm threads and a suitable weight that can slide on the shaft.

Camshaft and Rocker Arms Removal

1. Remove the mounting bolts (A, **Figure 41**), and then remove the decompressor weight assembly (B).
2. Remove the retaining bolts (A, **Figure 42**), and then remove the retainer (B).

> *NOTE*
> *Mark the rocker arm shafts and rocker arms so they may be installed in their original positions.*

3. Thread the slide hammer (A, **Figure 43**) fully into one of the rocker arm shafts. Secure the cylinder head, then operate the slide hammer to remove the rocker arm shaft (B). Then remove the rocker arm (C, **Figure 43**).
4. Repeat Step 3 to remove the opposite rocker arm shaft and rocker arm. Refer to **Figure 44**.
5. Slide the camshaft and bearing (**Figure 45**) out of the cylinder head.

> *NOTE*
> *The opposite camshaft bearing is pressed into the cylinder head. Do not remove this bearing unless damaged.*

Camshaft sprocket and cam chain

1. Inspect the camshaft sprocket for broken or chipped teeth. If the upper sprocket is damaged, check the lower sprocket mounted on the crankshaft (Chapter Five) for damage.
2. Fit the camshaft sprocket onto the cam chain and check for wear. If there is more than 1/4 tooth wear as shown in **Figure 39**, replace the sprocket and cam chain as a set. Replace the lower sprocket and cam chain as described in Chapter Five.

Cam chain tensioner

A damaged cam chain tensioner will allow the cam chain to jump one or more teeth and resulting in severe engine damage if a valve contacts the piston.

> *NOTE*
> *The cap bolt washer is not available separately.*

1. Clean and dry the cam chain tensioner assembly (**Figure 30**). Discard the gasket (E, **Figure 30**).
2. Inspect the spring (C, **Figure 30**) for cracks, bending or uneven gaps between the coils.
3. Depress the lock (A, **Figure 31**) and push the tensioner rod (B) into the tensioner body until it stops and locks in place. Make sure the tensioner rod moves smoothly and

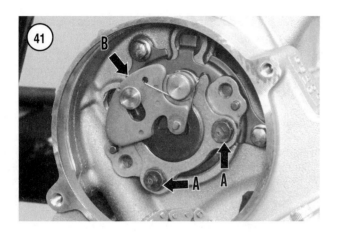

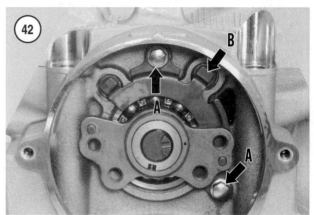

6. Remove the decompressor shaft (A, **Figure 46**) and de-compressor pin (B) from the camshaft.

7. Inspect the camshaft, decompressor assembly, rocker arms and shafts as described in this section.

Camshaft Inspection

Refer to **Table 2**. Replace worn or damaged parts as described in this section.

1. Clean the camshafts in solvent and dry thoroughly. Flush the camshaft oil passages with solvent and compressed air.

2. Check the cam lobes (A, **Figure 47**) for wear. Replace the camshaft if the lobes are pitted, scored or damaged.

3. Check the camshaft journal (B, **Figure 47**) for wear or scoring. If wear or damage is noted, check the bearing inside the cylinder head for damage as described in this section.

4. Turn the camshaft bearing (C, **Figure 47**) by hand check for smooth, quiet operation. Try to push the bearing in and out to check for axial play (**Figure 48**). Slight play is normal. Try to push the bearing up and down to check for radial play (**Figure 48**). Any radial play should be difficult to feel. If play is easily felt, the bearing is worn out and the camshaft must be replaced. This bearing is not available separately.

5. Support the camshaft between centers (lathe or truing stand) and measure runout with a dial indicator stem placed against the bearing. Replace the camshaft if the runout is out of specification.

6. Measure each cam lobe height and base diameter (**Figure 49**) with a micrometer.

Left Camshaft Bearing
Inspection/Removal/Installation

The left camshaft bearing (**Figure 50**) is pressed inside the cylinder head and can be replaced separately.

1. Inspect the bearing for any visible damage.

2. Turn the bearing inner race and check for smooth, quiet operation. Try to push the bearing inner race in and out to check for axial play (**Figure 48**). Slight play is normal. Try to push the bearing inner race up and down to check for

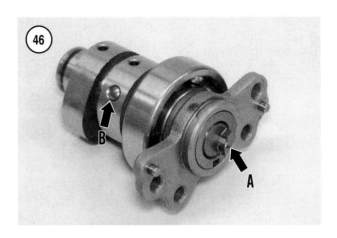

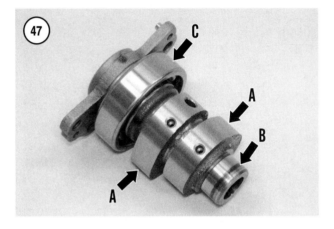

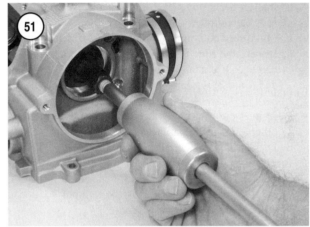

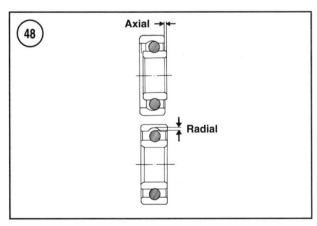

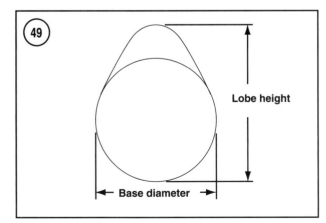

radial play (**Figure 48**). Any radial play should be difficult to feel. If play is easily felt, the bearing is worn out and must be replaced.

3. Replace the bearing as follows:
   a. Mount a 20-mm collet onto a blind bearing puller. Insert the collet through the bearing and tighten it to lock against the backside of the bearing (**Figure 51**). Operate the puller and remove the bearing. Discard the bearing.
   b. Clean the bearing bore of all corrosion. Then inspect for cracks and other damage.
   c. Lubricate the open side of the bearing with engine oil.
   d. Support the cylinder head and then drive or press the new bearing into the bore with its closed side facing toward the camshaft (**Figure 50**). Make sure the bearing is fully seated in its bore.

Decompressor Inspection

1. Inspect the decompressor weight assembly (**Figure 52**) as follows:
   a. Make sure the decompressor weight (A, **Figure 52**) moves under spring tension. If not, check the tension spring (**Figure 53**) for damage. If the tension spring is good but there is binding, check the pivots for damage.

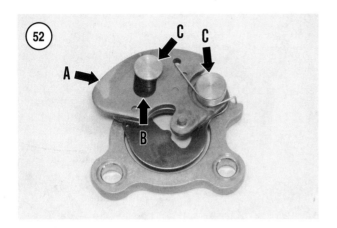

b. Inspect the groove (B, **Figure 52**) in the weight for scoring and other damage.

c. Make sure both pins (C, **Figure 52**) are tight.

d. Inspect the pin (**Figure 54**) on the weight plate for damage. If damage is noted, inspect the outer shaft end (Step 2) for damage.

2. Inspect the shaft (A, **Figure 55**) as follows:

a. Inspect the bearing surfaces for scoring, bluing and other damage. All surfaces must be smooth.

b. Inspect both engagement ends for damage.

3. Inspect the pin (B, **Figure 55**) as follows:

a. Inspect the bearing surfaces for scoring, bluing and other damage. The pin must be smooth so it can move freely in the camshaft bore.

b. Inspect the engagement notch for damage.

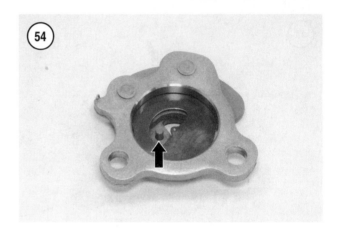

Rocker Arms and Shafts Inspection

1. Clean all parts in solvent. Dry with compressed air.

2. Inspect the rocker arm roller (A, **Figure 56**) for damage. Make sure the roller turns freely without excessive play or roughness.

3. Inspect the adjusters (B, **Figure 56**). Check for flat spots, uneven wear and scoring. Replace the valve adjuster if damaged.

4. Inspect the rocker arm shaft (C, **Figure 56**) for wear or scoring.

5. Calculate rocker arm shaft clearance as follows:

a. Measure the rocker arm inside diameter and record the measurement.

b. Measure the rocker arm shaft outside diameter and record the measurement.

c. Subtract the measurement in sub-step b from the measurement in sub-step a to determine rocker arm shaft clearance. Replace the worn parts if clearance exceeds the specification in **Table 2**.

6. Repeat for the other rocker arm assembly.

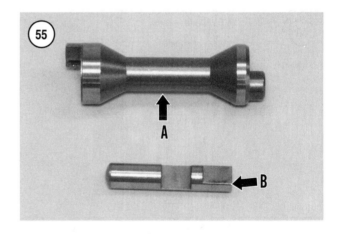

Camshaft and Rocker Arms Installation

1. If the left camshaft bearing (**Figure 50**) was not replaced, make sure the original bearing is seated fully in the cylinder head.

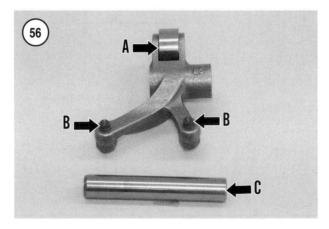

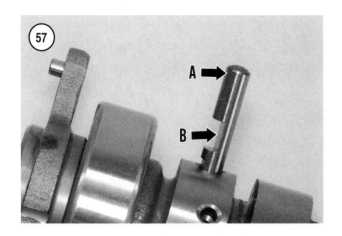

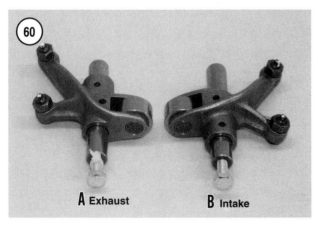

A Exhaust **B Intake**

2. Install the decompressor shaft (A, **Figure 55**) and pin (B) into the camshaft as follows:

  a. Lubricate the decompressor shaft and pin with engine oil.

  b. Install the pin (A, **Figure 57**) into the camshaft with its rounded end facing out. Then position the pin so that its notch (B, **Figure 57**) is facing toward the camshaft's sprocket end.

  c. Insert the shaft (A, **Figure 46**) into the camshaft so that its boss end enter first. Then engage the boss end of the shaft into the notch in the pin as shown in **Figure 58**. Rotating the shaft (A, **Figure 46**) should raise and lower the pin (B). If not, remove the parts and reinstall.

3. Lubricate the cam lobes with molybdenum disulfide oil. Lubricate the bearing with engine oil.

4. Install the camshaft so the flanges are positioned as shown in **Figure 59**. This positions the camshaft with the lobes facing down.

> *NOTE*
> *The decompressor shaft can slide out of the camshaft if the head is tilted.*

5. Lubricate each rocker arm shaft and rocker arm bore and roller with engine oil. Lubricate the valve stem ends with molybdenum disulfide oil.

> *CAUTION*
> *Install the rocker arms and shafts in their original positions. **Figure 60** identifies the rocker arms: exhaust (A) and intake (B).*

6. Install the rocker arm shaft so the threaded end faces out. Thread the puller bolt fully into the rocker arm, then partially drive the rocker arm shaft into the cylinder head and position the rocker arm in the cylinder head (**Figure 61**). The valve adjusters on the rocker arm must face out.

7. Continue to drive the rocker arm shaft through the cylinder head until it aligns and enters the rocker arm and then bottoms.

8. Repeat Steps 6 and 7 to install the remaining rocker arm assembly.

9. Install the bearing retainer (A, **Figure 62**). Apply a medium-strength threadlocking compound onto the bearing

retainer mounting bolt threads and tighten (B, **Figure 62**) to 10 N•m (88 in.-lb.).

10. Mount the decompressor weight assembly (A, **Figure 63**) on the camshaft so the pin on the weight plate properly engages the shaft slot as shown in **Figure 64**. Install the mounting bolts (B, **Figure 63**) and tighten finger-tight. Final tightening will take place after the cylinder head is installed on the engine and the cam chain is installed on the cam sprocket.

11. Install the cylinder head and cam sprocket as described in this chapter.

CAM CHAIN AND GUIDE

The cam chain is driven by a sprocket on the alternator side of the crankshaft. Refer to Chapter Five for cam chain service.

VALVES AND VALVE COMPONENTS

A valve spring compressor is required to remove and install the valve springs.

Valve Removal

1. Remove the cylinder head as described in this chapter.

2. Identify the individual valve assemblies (**Figure 65**) so they can be reinstalled in their original position.

3. Install a valve spring compressor squarely over the upper retainer with the other end of the tool placed against the valve head (**Figure 66**). Handle the tool carefully to avoid damaging the cylinder head gasket surface.

4. Tighten the valve spring compressor until the valve keepers (**Figure 67**) separate and remove them.

5. Gradually loosen the valve spring compressor and remove it from the head. Remove the upper retainer (A, **Figure 68**) and valve spring (B).

> *CAUTION*
> *Remove any burrs from the valve stem groove (**Figure 69**) before removing the valve; otherwise, the valve guide may be damaged as the valve stem passes through it as described in this section.*

> *NOTE*
> *If a valve is difficult to remove, it may be bent, causing it to stick in its valve guide. This condition will require valve and valve guide replacement.*

6. Remove the valve from its guide while rotating it slightly.

7. Use a pair of pliers to pull the oil seal (A, **Figure 70**) off the valve guide and discard it.

8. Remove the spring seat (B, **Figure 70**).

9. Repeat for the remaining valves.

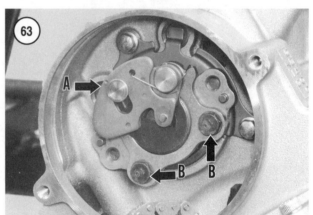

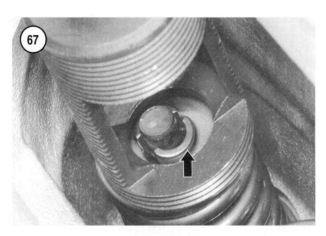

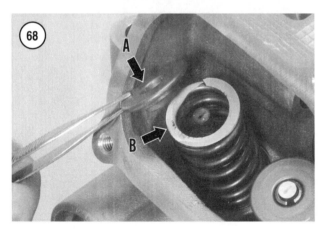

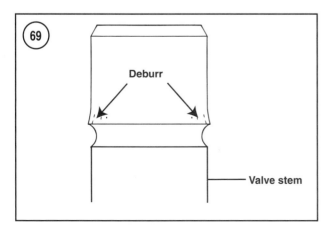

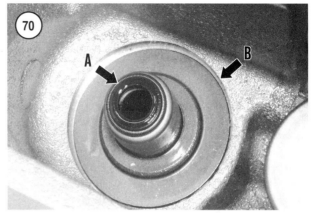

10. Service the valve assembly and valve seats as described in this section.

Valve Installation

Install the valves and their components in their original locations as recorded during removal.

1. Install the spring seat (B, **Figure 70**) with its shoulder facing up.

2. Lubricate the inside of a new oil seal and the oil seal lip with molybdenum disulfide oil. Then align and push the seal straight down the valve guide until it snaps into the groove in the top of the guide (A, **Figure 70**). Check that the oil seal is centered and seats squarely on top of the guide. If the seal is cocked to one side, oil will leak past the seal during engine operation. If it is necessary to remove a new seal, do not reuse it.

3. Install the valve as follows:

    a. Coat the valve stem with molybdenum disulfide oil.

    b. Lubricate the groove on the top of the valve with engine oil.

    c. Install the valve partway into its guide. Then hold the valve stem seal in place and slowly turn the valve as it enters the seal. Continue turning the valve until it is installed all the way.

    d. Make sure the valve moves up and down smoothly.

4. Install the valve spring with the tightly wound spring coils facing down toward the spring seat (**Figure 71**).

5. Install the retainer (A, **Figure 68**) on top of the valve spring.

> *CAUTION*
> *To avoid loss of spring tension, do not compress the spring any more than necessary when installing the valve keepers.*

6. Compress the valve spring with a valve spring compressor tool and install the valve keepers (**Figure 67**) around the valve stem and into the hole in the top of the retainer. Then slowly release tension on the valve spring while watching the movement of the retainer and keepers. Make sure the keepers fit into the groove in the valve stem. Gently tap the upper retainer with a plastic hammer to ensure the keepers are fully seated in the valve stem groove.

7. Repeat for the remaining valves.

8. After installing the cylinder head and camshaft, check the valve clearance as described in Chapter Three.

Valve Inspection

Valve components

Refer to **Table 2**. Replace parts that are damaged or out of specification as described in this section.

1. Clean the valve components in solvent. Do not damage the valve seating surface.

2. Inspect the valve face (A, **Figure 72**) for burning, pitting or other signs of wear. Unevenness of the valve face is an indication that the valve is not serviceable. If the wear on a valve is too extensive to be corrected by hand-lapping the valve into its seat, replace the valve. The face on the valve cannot be ground. Replace the valve if defective.

3. Measure the valve margin thickness, the distance between the top of the valve and the top of the valve face, with a micrometer.

4. Inspect the valve stems for wear and roughness. Check the valve keeper grooves for damage.

5. Place the valve on V-blocks and measure valve stem runout with a dial indicator.

6. Measure each valve stem outside diameter with a micrometer (**Figure 73**). Note the following:

   a. If a valve stem is out of specification, discard the valve.

   b. If a valve stem is within specification, record the measurement so it can be used to determine the valve stem-to-guide clearance in Step 7.

7. Insert each valve into its respective valve guide and move it up and down by hand. The valve should move smoothly.

8. Measure each valve guide inside diameter at the top, center and bottom (**Figure 74**). Record the measurements and use the largest bore diameter measurement when determining its size.

   a. If a valve guide is out of specification, replace it as described in this section.

   b. If a valve guide is within specification, record the measurement so it can be used to determine the valve stem-to-guide clearance in Step 7.

9. Subtract the valve stem outside diameter measurement from the valve guide inside diameter measurement to determine the valve stem-to-guide clearance. Note the following:

   a. If the clearance is out of specification, determine if a new guide would bring the clearance within specification.

   b. If the clearance would be out of specification with a new guide, replace the valve and guide as a set.

10. Check the valve springs as follows:

   a. Inspect each spring for any cracks or other visual damage.

   b. Measure the free length of each valve spring (**Figure 75**).

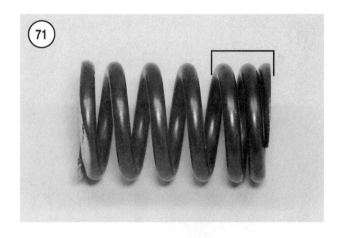

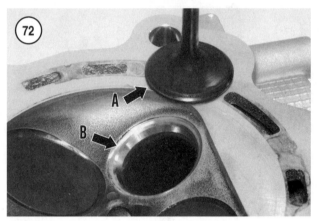

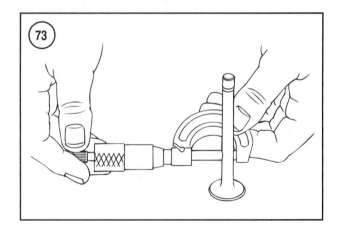

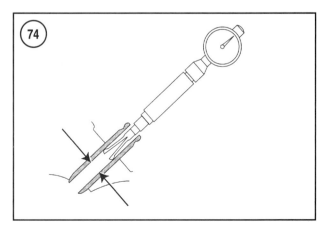

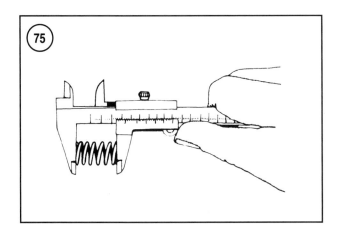

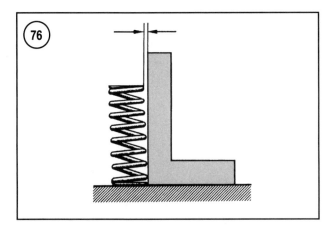

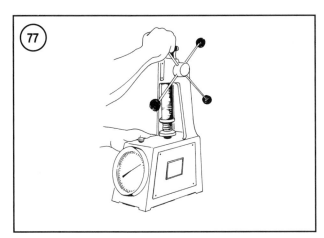

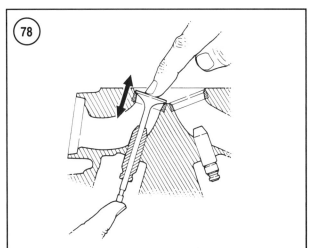

c. Stand the spring vertically, and then place a square next to the spring (**Figure 76**) to check for distortion or tilt.

d. Using a spring compression tool (**Figure 77**), compress the springs at the height specified in **Table 2** and measure the valve spring pressure. Replace the springs if out of specification.

e. Replace weak or defective springs.

11. Check the valve keepers for cracks and any surface spots. Replace in pairs.

12. Inspect the spring retainer and spring seat for damage.

13. Inspect the valve seats as described in this section.

Valve seat

The most accurate method for checking the valve seat is to use a marking compound (machinist's dye), available from auto parts and tool stores. Marking compound is used to locate high or irregular spots when checking or making close fits. Follow the manufacturer's directions.

NOTE
Because of the close operating tolerances within the valve assembly, the valve stem and guide must be within tolerance as described in this section; otherwise, the inspection results will be inaccurate.

1. Remove the valves as described in this section.

2. Clean the valve (A, **Figure 72**) and valve seat (B) mating areas with contact cleaner.

3. Clean all carbon deposits from the valve face with solvent and dry thoroughly.

4. Spread a thin layer of marking compound evenly on the valve face.

5. Slowly insert the valve into its guide and tap the valve against its seat several times (**Figure 78**) without spinning it.

6. Remove the valve and examine the impression left by the marking compound. If the impression on the valve or in the cylinder head is not even and continuous, and the valve seat width (**Figure 79**) is not within the specified tolerance listed in **Table 2**, the valve seat in the cylinder head must be reconditioned.

7. Examine the valve seat in the cylinder head (B, **Figure 72**). It should be smooth and even with a polished seating surface.

8. If the valve seat is not in good condition, recondition the valve seat as described in this section.

NOTE
The valve guides must be in good condition and serviced, if necessary, before regrinding the valve seats.

9. Repeat for the other valves.

Valve Guide Removal/Installation

Tools

The following Yamaha tools (or equivalents) are required to remove and install the valve guides. Confirm part numbers with a Yamaha dealership before ordering them.
1. 6.0 mm valve guide remover (part No. YM-04064-A/90890-04064).
2. 6.0 valve guide installer (part No. YM-04065-A/90890-04065).
3. 6.0 valve guide reamer (part No. YM-04066/90890-04066).

Procedure

1. Remove all of the valves and valve guide seals from the cylinder head as described in this section.
2. Place the new valve guides in the freezer for approximately one hour prior to heating the cylinder head. The freezing temperature will shrink the new guides slightly and ease installation refer to *Service Methods* in Chapter One.
3. Measure the valve guide projection height above the cylinder head surface with a vernier caliper (**Figure 80**). Record the projection height for each valve guide and compare to the valve guide projection height specification in **Table 2**.

> *WARNING*
> *Wear protective gloves to prevent burns.*

> *CAUTION*
> *Do not heat the cylinder head with a torch. The direct heat can destroy the case hardening of the valve guide and may warp the cylinder head.*

4. Place the cylinder head in an oven or on a hot plate and heat to a temperature of 100° C (212° F).
5. Remove the cylinder head from the oven or hot plate and place on wooden blocks with the combustion chamber facing up.
6. From the combustion chamber side of the head, drive out the valve guide with the valve guide remover (**Figure 81**). Quickly repeat this step for each guide to be replaced. Reheat the head as required. Discard the valve guides after removing them.

> *CAUTION*
> *Do not attempt to remove the valve guides if the head is not hot enough. Doing so may damage the valve guide bore in the cylinder head and require replacement of the head.*

7. Allow the head to cool.
8. Inspect and clean the valve guide bores. Check for cracks or any scoring along the bore wall.

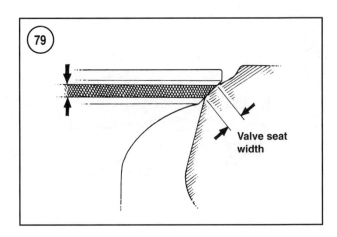

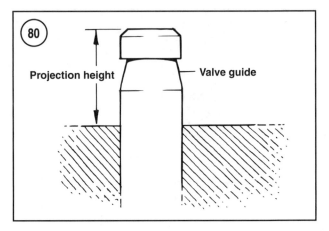

9. Reheat the cylinder head as described in Step 4. Then set it on wooden blocks with the combustion chamber facing down. The valve guide is installed from the spring side.
10. Using the valve guide installer, drive the new valve guide into the cylinder head until the projection height (**Figure 80**) of the valve guide is within the specification in **Table 2**.
11. Repeat to install the remaining valve guides.
12. Allow the head to cool to room temperature.
13. Ream each valve guide as follows:
   a. Coat the valve guide and valve guide reamer with cutting oil.

> *CAUTION*
> *Always rotate the valve guide reamer in the same direction when installing and removing it from the guide. If the reamer is rotated in the opposite direction, the guide will be damaged and require replacement.*

> *CAUTION*
> *Do not allow the reamer to tilt. Keep the tool square to the hole and apply even pressure and twisting motion during the entire operation.*

   b. Insert the reamer into the top of the valve guide (spring side) and start rotating it by keeping it aligned squarely with the guide. Continue rotating the ream-

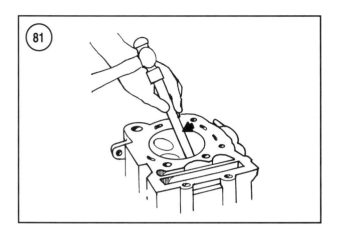

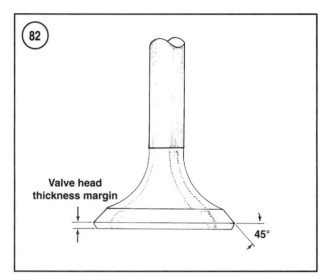

Valve head
thickness margin

45°

in this chapter. The valve and seat angle is 45° (**Figure 82**). No other angles are cut above or below the valve face.

> *CAUTION*
> *Work slowly and make light cuts during reconditioning. Excessive valve seat cutting will lower the valves into the cylinder head, which will affect valve adjustment and may require cylinder head replacement.*

> *NOTE*
> *Follow the manufacturer's instructions when using valve seat cutters.*

1. Carefully rotate and insert the solid pilot into the valve guide. Be sure the pilot is correctly seated.
2. Install the 45° cutter onto the valve tool and lightly cut the seat to remove roughness.
3. Measure the valve seat width (**Figure 79**). Compare the measurement to the specification in **Table 2**.
4. When the valve seat width is within specification, clean the valve seat and valve mating areas with contact cleaner and allow to dry.
5. Spread a thin layer of marking compound evenly on the valve seat.
6. Slowly insert the valve into its guide. Support the valve with two fingers (**Figure 78**) and tap the valve up and down in the cylinder head several times. Do not rotate the valve or a false reading will result.
7. Remove the valve and evaluate where the seat has contacted the valve:
   a. The seat contact should be in the center of the valve face area.
   b. If the seat is high on the valve face area, the valve head may not be within specification, or the seat diameter in the cylinder head is excessive. Refer further inspection to a dealership.
   c. If the seat is low on the valve face area, the valve may need to be machined so it fits lower in the seat. Do not continue to cut the valve seat in the cylinder head in order to accommodate the valve. If the seat diameter is excessive, replace the cylinder head. Refer further inspection to a dealership.
8. When the seat width is correct, lap the valve as described in this section.

Valve Lapping

Valve lapping restores the valve seat without machining if the surfaces are not excessively worn. Lap valves and seats that have been inspected and are within specification or when the seats have been reconditioned.
1. Smear a light coating of fine grade valve lapping compound on the valve face seating surface. Then lubricate the valve stem with molybdenum disulfide oil.
2. Insert the valve into the head.
3. Wet the suction cup of the lapping stick and stick it onto the head of the valve. Spin the tool in both directions, while pressing it against the valve seat and lap the valve to the

er to work it slowly down through the entire length of the guide. Stop occasionally and apply additional cutting oil during the procedure.
   c. While rotating the reamer in the same direction, withdraw the reamer from the valve guide.
   d. Clean the reamer of all chips and relubricate with cutting oil before starting on the next guide. Repeat for each guide as required.
14. Thoroughly clean the cylinder head and all valve components in solvent, then with soap and hot water to remove all cutting residue. Rinse in cold water. Dry with compressed air.
15. Measure the valve guide inside diameter. The measurement must be within the specification listed in **Table 2**.
16. Apply engine oil to the valve guides to prevent rust.
17. Lubricate a valve stem with engine oil and pass it through its valve guide, verifying that it moves without any roughness or binding.
18. Reface the valve seats as described in *Valve Seat Reconditioning* in this section.

Valve Seat Reconditioning

Before reconditioning the valve seats, inspect and measure them as described in *Valve Seat* in *Valve Inspection* in seat (**Figure 83**). Every 5 to 10 seconds, lift and rotate the valve 180° in the valve seat. Continue until the gasket surfaces on the valve and seat are smooth and equal in size.

4. Closely examine the valve seat in the cylinder head (B, **Figure 72**). It should be smooth and even with a smooth, polished seating ring. Identify each lapped valve so it will be installed in the correct seat during assembly.

5. Repeat Steps 1-4 for the other valves.

6. Thoroughly clean the cylinder head and all valve components in solvent, then with detergent and hot water. Rinse in cold water and dry with compressed air. Lubricate the valve guides to prevent rust. Any abrasive allowed to remain in the head will cause premature wear and damage to other engine parts.

7. After cleaning the cylinder head and valve components in detergent and hot water, apply a light coat of engine oil to all bare metal surfaces to prevent rust formation.

8. After valve installation, perform a solvent test as described in this chapter. If leaking is detected, remove that valve and repeat the lapping process.

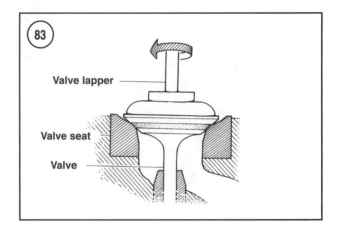

CYLINDER

The cylinder and piston can be removed with the engine mounted in the frame.

Removal

CAUTION
When rotating the crankshaft, pull up the cam chain so it does not bind.

1. Remove the cylinder head as described in this chapter.

2. If the engine is mounted in the frame, disconnect the coolant hose at the cylinder head (**Figure 84**).

3. Remove the lower cylinder mounting bolts (A, **Figure 85**).

4. Remove the upper cylinder mounting bolts (B, **Figure 85**).

5. Raise the cylinder with the piston. Then slide the cylinder off the piston while holding the piston with one hand just before it clears the cylinder to prevent it from falling and possibly damaging the piston rings.

6. Remove the dowel pins (A, **Figure 86**).

7. Remove and discard the base gasket (B, **Figure 86**).

8. Cover the piston and crankcase opening.

9. Clean and inspect the cylinder as described in this section.

Installation

CAUTION
When rotating the crankshaft, pull up the cam chain so it does not bind.

1. If removed, install the piston and rings as described in this chapter.

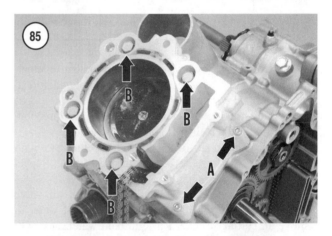

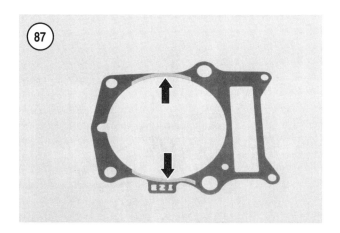

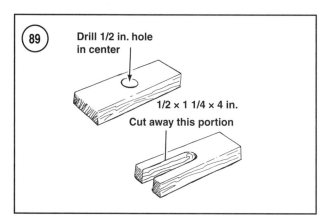

Drill 1/2 in. hole in center

1/2 × 1 1/4 × 4 in.

Cut away this portion

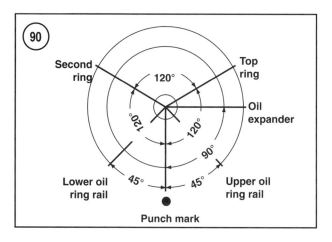

Second ring

Top ring

120°

Oil expander

120°

120°

90°

Lower oil ring rail

45°

45°

Upper oil ring rail

Punch mark

CAUTION
Make sure the piston pin circlips have been properly installed.

2. Install the dowel pins (A, **Figure 86**) and a new base gasket (B). Install the base gasket with its raised sealer beads (**Figure 87**) facing down.

3. Install a piston holding fixture (**Figure 88**) under the piston. If necessary, fabricate a wooden piston holding fixture from a piece of wood (**Figure 89**).

4. Lubricate the cylinder wall, piston and rings with engine oil. Liberally lubricate the oil control rings and spacer with oil.

5. Stagger the piston ring end gaps around the piston as shown in **Figure 90**. Refer to *Piston and Piston Rings* in this chapter.

6. Lower the cylinder onto the piston, routing the cam chain and rear chain guide through the chain tunnel. Compress each piston ring by hand as it enters the cylinder. Do not force the cylinder past the rings. Push the cylinder down until it bottoms on the piston holding fixture.

7. Remove the piston holding fixture and push the cylinder down into place over the dowel pins and against the base gasket.

8. Install the lower cylinder mounting bolts (A, **Figure 85**) and tighten finger-tight.

9. Pull up on the cam chain and rotate the crankshaft counterclockwise. The piston must move up and down in the bore with no binding or roughness. If there is any interference, a piston ring may have broken during cylinder installation.

10. Lubricate the bolt threads, bolt flanges and washers on the upper cylinder mounting bolts with engine oil (**Figure 91**).

11. Install the upper cylinder mounting bolts and washers (B, **Figure 85**) and tighten in a crossing pattern in two steps:
 a. Initially tighten to 15 N•m (11 ft.-lb.).
 b. Finally tighten to 50 N•m (37 ft.-lb.).

12. Tighten the lower cylinder mounting bolts (A, **Figure 85**) to 10 N•m (88 in.-lb.).

13. Install the cylinder head as described in this chapter.

14. If the engine is mounted in the frame, align the paint mark on the coolant hose with the raised boss on the hose nozzle. Then tighten the hose clamp (**Figure 84**).

15. Install the cylinder head as described in this chapter.

Inspection

Refer to **Table 3**. Replace the cylinder if it is out of specifications or damaged.

1. Soak the cylinder block surfaces in solvent, then carefully remove gasket material from the top and bottom mating surfaces with a scraper. Do not nick or gouge the gasket surfaces or leakage will result.

2. Wash the cylinder block in solvent. Dry with compressed air.

3. Check the dowel pin holes for cracks or other damage.

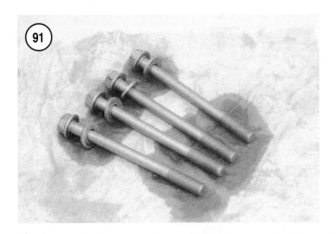

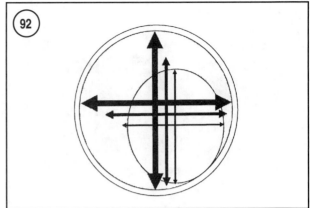

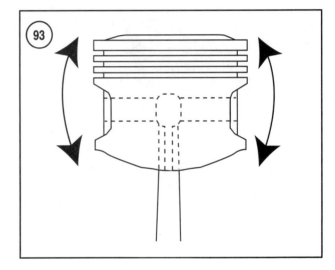

4. Measure the cylinder bore inside diameter with a bore gauge or inside micrometer at the points shown in **Figure 92**. Measure in line with the piston pin and 90° to the pin. Use the largest measurement to determine cylinder bore. Also check for taper and out-of-round. If the cylinder bore diameter, taper or out-of-round is greater than specifications, replace the cylinder, piston and rings as a set.

5. Determine piston-to-cylinder clearance as described in *Piston Clearance* in *Piston and Piston Rings* in this chapter.

6. Refer to *Piston and Piston Rings* in this chapter to determine if the cylinder is within specification. The cylinder must be deglazed to accommodate new piston rings. Cylinder glaze appears as a hard, shiny surface and is removed by a cylinder hone. As the hone deglazes the cylinder, a crosshatch pattern is left on the cylinder bore. The pattern provides a uniform surface, capable of spreading oil and allowing the rings to seat and seal against the cylinder. When deglazing the cylinder, apply plenty of honing lubricant to the hone and cylinder surface. Do not run the hone at high speed, or the crosshatch pattern will not develop. Move the hone at a moderate and consistent rate in an up and down motion for a time period specified by the manufacturer. Proper movement speed of the hone is achieved when a 45° crosshatch pattern is visible on the cylinder wall.

> *CAUTION*
> *A combination of soap and hot water is required to completely clean the cylinder walls. Solvent and kerosene cannot wash fine grit out of cylinder crevices. Any grit left in the cylinder will cause the piston rings and other engine parts to wear unnecessarily.*

7. After the cylinder has been serviced, clean the cylinder as follows:
   a. Wash the cylinder in hot soapy water.
   b. Also wash out any fine grit material from the cooling passages surrounding the cylinder.
   c. After washing the cylinder, wipe the cylinder wall with a clean white cloth. It should *not* show any traces of grit or debris. If the rag is the slightest bit

dirty, the wall is not thoroughly cleaned and must be washed again.
   d. When the cylinder wall is clean, lubricate it with clean engine oil to prevent rust.
   e. Wrap the cylinder until engine reassembly.

PISTON AND PISTON RINGS

Piston Removal

> *CAUTION*
> *When rotating the crankshaft, pull up the cam chain so it cannot bind.*

1. Remove the cylinder as described in this chapter.

2. Before removing the piston, hold the rod and attempt to rock the piston as shown in **Figure 93**. Any rocking motion (do not confuse with the normal sliding motion) indicates wear on the piston pin, pin bore, rod bushing, or a combination of all three.

3. Block off the crankcase below the piston with a clean shop cloth to prevent the piston pin circlips from falling into the crankcase.

4. Support the piston with a piston holder fixture

5. Remove a circlip (**Figure 94**) from the side of the piston opposite the cam chain side.

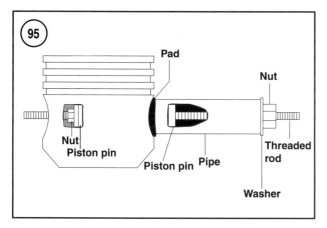

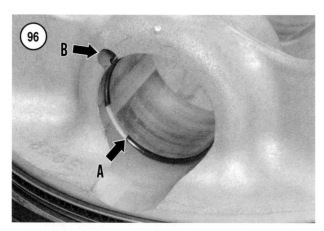

4

CAUTION
The piston pin operates with a sliding fit and can be removed by hand. However, problems such as varnish on the piston pin, a burred pin bore or circlip groove, or a damaged piston can make it difficult to remove the piston pin. Do not drive the pin out as the piston and connecting rod assembly may be damaged.

6. Push the piston pin out of the piston by hand. If the pin is tight, use a homemade tool (**Figure 95**) to remove it after removing the circlip. Do not drive the piston pin out as this may damage the piston pin, connecting rod or piston. Heat can also be used to ease removal. Heat the piston crown and not the side of the piston with a heat gun.

7. Lift the piston off the connecting rod.

8. Inspect the piston, piston pin and piston rings as described in this section.

Piston Installation

CAUTION
When rotating the crankshaft, pull up the cam chain so it cannot bind.

1. Make sure the crankcase gasket surface is clean.

2. Install the piston rings onto the piston as described in this chapter.

CAUTION
Never install used circlips. Severe engine damage could occur. Circlips fatigue and distort during removal, even though they appear reusable.

3. Install a new piston circlip into the piston on its cam chain side. Make sure the gap (A, **Figure 96**) does not align with the notch (B) on the piston and the circlip seats in the groove completely.

4. Coat the connecting rod small end, piston pin and its bore in the piston with engine oil.

5. Start the piston pin into the open piston pin bore.

6. Position the piston onto the connecting rod so the punch mark (A, **Figure 97**) stamped on the piston crown faces toward the exhaust side of the engine. Make sure the two intake valve notches (B, **Figure 97**) on the piston crown face the intake side of the engine.

CAUTION
The piston must be installed correctly to accommodate piston pin offset and prevent the valves from striking the piston. Failure to install the piston correctly can cause engine damage.

7. Align the piston with the rod, then push the piston pin through the connecting rod and into the other side of the piston. Center the piston pin in the piston.

8. Block off the crankcase below the piston with a clean shop cloth to prevent the circlip from falling into the crankcase.

9. Install the second new circlip (**Figure 94**) so the gap (A, **Figure 96**) does not align with the notch (B, **Figure 96**) on the piston. The first circlip was installed in Step 3. Make sure both circlips seat in the piston grooves completely.

Piston Inspection

1. Remove the piston rings as described in this section.
2. Soak the piston in solvent to soften the carbon deposits.

CAUTION
Do not wire brush the piston skirt.

3. Clean the carbon from the piston crown with a soft scraper or wire wheel mounted in a drill. A thick carbon buildup reduces piston cooling and results in detonation and piston damage.

4. After cleaning the piston, examine the crown. The crown must show no signs of wear or damage. If the crown appears pecked or spongy-looking, also check the spark plug, valves and combustion chamber for aluminum deposits. If these deposits are found, the engine is overheating.

5. Examine each ring groove for burrs, dented edges or other damage. Pay particular attention to the top compression ring groove as it usually wears more than the others. Because the oil rings are bathed in oiled, these rings and grooves wear little compared to compression rings and their grooves. If there is evidence of oil ring groove wear or if the oil ring is tight and difficult to remove, the piston skirt may have collapsed due to excessive heat. Replace the piston.

6. Clean the oil control holes (A, **Figure 98**) in the piston.

7. Check the piston skirts (B, **Figure 98**) for cracks or other damage. If the piston shows signs of partial seizure bits of aluminum built up on the piston skirt), replace the piston and inspect the cylinder bore for the same material.

NOTE
If the piston skirt is worn or scuffed unevenly from side-to-side, the connecting rod may be bent or twisted.

8. Check the piston circlip grooves (C, **Figure 98**) for cracks or other damage.

9. Measure piston-to-cylinder clearance as described in *Piston Clearance* in this section.

Piston Pin Inspection

Refer to **Table 3**. Replace the piston pin if out of specification or if it shows damage as described in this section.
1. Clean and dry the piston pin.
2. Inspect the piston pin for chrome flaking, cracks and bluing (overheating).

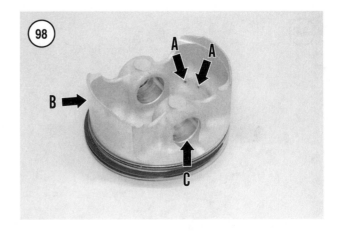

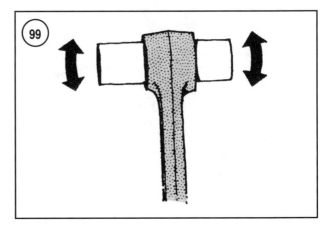

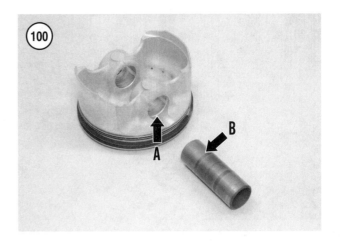

3. Oil the piston pin and install it in the piston. Slowly rotate the piston pin and check for tightness or excessive play.

4. Lubricate the piston pin with oil and install it in the connecting rod. Rotate the piston pin and check for radial play (**Figure 99**).

5. Measure the piston pin bore (A, **Figure 100**) inside diameter. Replace the piston if the bore diameter is too large.

6. Measure the piston pin (B, **Figure 100**) outside diameter.

7. Subtract the piston pin bore inside diameter from the piston pin outside diameter. The difference is the piston-to-

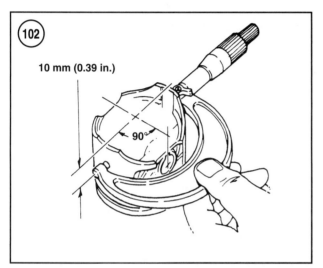

10 mm (0.39 in.)

90°

piston pin clearance. Replace the piston and piston pin if the clearance exceeds the service limit.

Connecting Rod Small End Inspection

Inspect the connecting rod small end (**Figure 101**) for cracks, scoring and bluing (overheating).

If the connecting rod is damaged, replace it as described in *Crankshaft* in Chapter Five.

Piston Clearance

Calculate the clearance between the piston and cylinder to determine if the parts can be reused. Clean and dry the piston and cylinder before measuring.

1. Measure the piston diameter 10 mm (0.39 in.) up from the bottom edge of the piston skirt and 90° to the direction of the piston pin (**Figure 102**). Record the measurement.
2. Determine the bore inside diameter as described in *Cylinder* in this chapter.
3. Subtract the piston diameter from the largest bore diameter. The difference is piston-to-cylinder clearance. If clearance exceeds the service limit in **Table 3**, determine if the piston, cylinder or both are worn. If the cylinder is worn, replace the piston, piston rings and cylinder as a set.

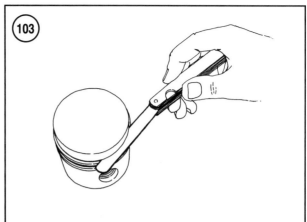

Piston Ring Inspection/Removal

A 3-ring type piston and ring assembly is used. The top and second rings are compression rings. The lower ring is an oil control ring assembly consisting of two ring rails and a spacer.

Refer to the specifications in **Table 3**. Replace the piston rings as a set if out of specification or if they show damage as described in this section.

1. Measure the side clearance of each ring in its groove with a flat feeler gauge (**Figure 103**):
   a. If the clearance is greater than specified, replace the rings. If the clearance is still excessive with new rings, replace the piston.
   b. If the clearance is too small, check the ring and ring groove for carbon and oil residue. Carefully clean the ring without removing any metal from its surface. Clean the piston ring groove as described in this section.

NOTE
To help identify the piston rings if they will be reused, mark the top side of each ring with a paint marker. Also identify the top and second compression rings. The top ring is marked with the letter R. The second ring is marked with the letters RN. However, these marks may not be visible on used rings. The oil ring rails are not marked. However, marking them ensures they will be reinstalled facing in their original direction.

2. Remove the compression rings with a ring expander tool or spread the ring ends by hand (**Figure 104**). Store the rings in order of removal and with the upper side of the ring facing up.
3. Remove the oil ring assembly by first removing the upper and then the lower ring rails. Remove the spacer.
4. Remove carbon and oil residues from the piston ring grooves (**Figure 105**) with a broken piston ring. Do not remove aluminum material from the ring grooves as this will increase the side clearance.
5. Inspect the ring grooves for burrs, nicks or broken or cracked lands. Replace the piston if necessary.

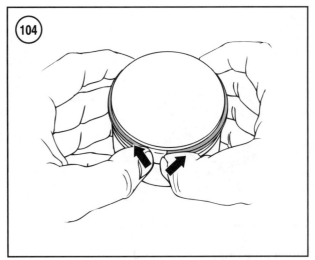

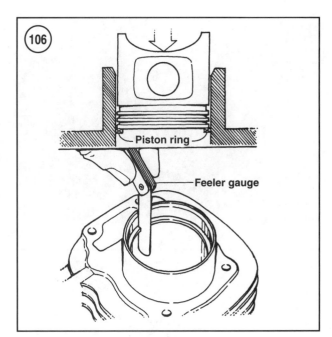

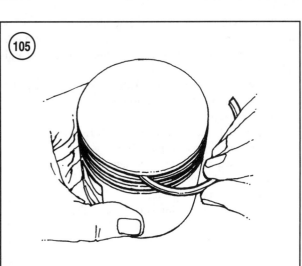

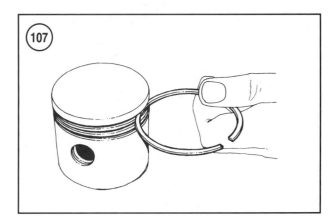

6. Check the end gap of each ring. Insert the ring 50 mm (1.97 in.) down from the top of the cylinder and square it with the cylinder wall by tapping it with the piston (**Figure 106**). Measure the end gap with a feeler gauge. Replace the rings as a set if any gap is too large. If the gap on the new ring is smaller than specified, hold a small file in a vise. Then grip the ends of the ring with your fingers and slowly enlarge the gap.

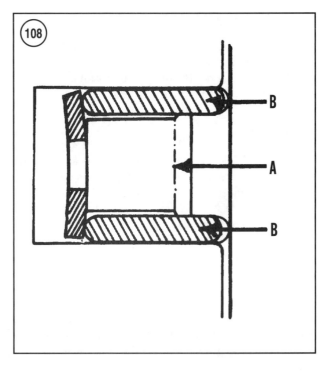

NOTE
When measuring the oil control ring end gap, measure the upper and lower ring rail end gaps only. Do not measure the spacer.

7. Roll each compression ring around its piston groove (**Figure 107**) to check for binding. Repair minor binding with a fine-cut file.

Piston Ring Installation

1. When installing new piston rings, hone or deglaze the cylinder wall. This will help the new rings to seat in the cylinder. Refer to *Cylinder* in this chapter or refer this ser-

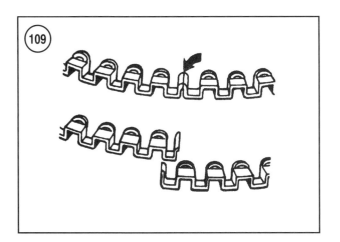

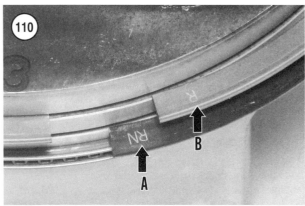

vice to a dealership. After honing, measure the end gap of each ring and compare to the dimensions in **Table 3**.

2. Clean the cylinder as described in *Inspection* in *Cylinder* in this chapter.

3. Clean and dry the piston and rings.

4. Install the piston rings as follows:

   a. Install the oil ring assembly into the bottom ring groove. Install the spacer first (A, **Figure 108**), and then the bottom and top ring rails (B). Make sure the ends of the spacer butt together (**Figure 109**). They should not overlap. If reassembling used parts, install the ring rails in their original positions.

   b. Install the compression rings with a ring expander tool or by spreading the ring ends by hand (**Figure 104**).

   c. Install the second compression ring with its RN mark (A, **Figure 110**) facing up.

   d.Install the top compression ring with its R mark (B, **Figure 110**) facing up.

5. If new parts were installed, follow the *Engine Break-In* procedure in Chapter Three.

Table 1 GENERAL ENGINE SPECIFICATIONS

Bore × stroke	102 × 84 mm (4.02 × 3.31 in.)
Camshaft drive system	Chain drive
Chain tensioner	Automatic
Compression ratio	9.20:1
Displacement	686 cc (41.86 cu. in.)
Engine type	4-stroke, liquid cooled, SOHC, single
Lubrication system	Wet sump
Timing chain	
Model	98XRH2010
Links	126

Table 2 CYLINDER HEAD AND VALVE SERVICE SPECIFICATIONS

	New mm (in.)	Service limit mm (in.)
Cylinder head warp	–	0.03 (0.0012)
Camshafts		
Base diameter		
intake	36.950-37.050 (1.4547-1.4587)	36.850 (1.4508)
exhaust	36.983-37.082 (1.4560-1.4600)	36.882 (1.4520)
Lobe height		
intake	42.481-42.581 (1.6725-1.6764)	42.381 (1.6685)
exhaust	43.129-43.229 (1.6980-1.7019)	43.029 (1.6941)
Runout	–	0.015 (0.0006)
Rocker arm and rocker arm shaft		
Rocker arm inside diameter	12.000-12.018 (0.4724-0.4731)	–
Rocker arm shaft outside diameter	11.981-11.991 (0.4717-0.4721)	–
Rocker arm shaft clearance	0.009-0.037 (0.0004-0.0015)	
Valves		
Valve head diameter		
Intake	37.90-38.10 (1.4921-1.5000)	–
Exhaust	31.90-32.10 (1.2559-1.2638)	–
Valve face width	2.26 (0.089)	–
Valve seat width	1.00-1.20 (0.0394-0.0472)	1.60 (0.0630)
Valve margin thickness	0.80-1.20 (0.0315-0.0472)	–
Valve stem runout	–	0.040 (0.0016)
Valve stem diameter		
Intake	5.975-5.990 (0.2352-0.2358)	5.945 (0.2341)
Exhaust	5.960-5.975 (0.2346-0.2352)	5.930 (0.2335)
Valve guide inside diameter	6.000-6.012 (0.2362-0.2367)	6.050 (0.2382)
Valve stem-to-guide clearance		
Intake	0.010-0.037 (0.0004-0.0015)	0.080 (0.0032)
Exhaust	0.025-0.052 (0.0010-0.0020)	0.100 (0.0039)
Valve guide projection height above cylinder head	12.7-13.1 (0.500-0.516)	–
Valve springs		
Free length	40.38 (1.59)	38.36 (1.51)
Installed length	35.00 (1.38)	–
Pressure	171.0-197.0 N @ 35 mm (38.44-44.29 lb. @ 1.38 in.)	–
Spring tilt	–	2.5°/1.8 (2.5°/0.071)

Table 3 PISTON, RINGS AND CYLINDER SPECIFICATIONS

	New mm (in.)	Service limit mm (in.)
Cylinder		
Inside diameter	102.000-102.010 (4.0157-4.0161)	102.080 (4.0189)
Maximum taper	–	0.050 (0.0020)
Out-of-round	–	0.050 (0.0020)
Piston		
Diameter	101.955-101.970 (4.0140-4.0146)	–
Measuring position*	10.0 (0.39)	–
Piston-to-cylinder clearance	0.030-0.055 (0.0012-0.0022)	0.13 (0.0051)
Piston pin bore inside diameter	23.004-23.015 (0.9057-0.9061)	23.045 (0.9073)
Piston pin		
Outside diameter	22.991-23.000 (0.9052-0.9055)	22.971 (0.9044)
Piston-to-piston pin clearance	0.004-0.024 (0.0002-0.0009)	0.074 (0.0029)
Piston rings		
Ring type		
Top	Barrel	
Second	Taper	
Side clearance		
Top and second	0.030-0.070 (0.0012-0.0028)	0.12 (0.0047)
Oil ring	0.060-0.150 (0.0024-0.0059)	–
End gap		
Top	0.20-0.35 0.008-0.014)	0.60 (0.024)
Second	0.75-0.90 (0.030-0.035)	1.25 (0.049)
Oil ring	0.20-0.70 (0.008-0.028)	–
Thickness		
Top and second	1.20 (0.05)	–

*Refer to text.

Table 4 ENGINE TOP END TORQUE SPECIFICATIONS

	N•m	in.-lb.	ft.-lb.
Bearing retainer mounting bolt*	10	88	–
Cam chain tensioner body mounting bolt	10	88	–
Cam chain tensioner cap bolt*	20	–	15
Camshaft sprocket cover	10	88	–
Camshaft sprocket mounting bolt	20	–	15
Cylinder bolts*			
Upper bolts	50	–	37
Cylinder bolts* (continued)			
Lower bolts	10	88	–
Cylinder head bolts*			
Upper bolts	35	–	26
Lower bolts	38	–	28
Side bolts	10	88	–
Decompressor assembly mounting bolt	20	–	15

(continued)

Table 4 ENGINE TOP END TORQUE SPECIFICATIONS (continued)

	N•m	in.-lb.	ft.-lb.
Flywheel nut plug	10	88	–
Front exhaust pipe nuts*	20	–	15
Heat protector mounting bolt	8	71	–
Muffler bracket mounting bolt	30	–	22
Muffler mounting bolt	20	–	15
Oil check bolt	10	88	–
Oil pipe banjo bolt	35	–	26
Oil pipe mounting bolt	10	88	–
Spark plug	13	115	–
Timing plug	6	53	–
Valve adjustment cover mounting bolt	10	88	–
*Refer to text.			

CHAPTER FIVE

ENGINE LOWER END

This chapter provides service procedures for lower end components. These include the crankcase, crankshaft, connecting rod, oil pump and middle gear assembly. This chapter also includes removal and installation procedures for the transmission and internal shift mechanism assemblies. However, service procedures for these components are described in Chapter Seven.

Read *Safety* and *Service Methods* in Chapter One.

Table 1 and **Table 2** are at the end of this chapter.

SERVICING ENGINE IN FRAME

1. The following components can be serviced with the engine mounted in the frame:
   a. Camshaft and cylinder head.
   b. Cylinder and piston.
   c. Throttle body.
   d. Alternator and starter clutch.
   e. Clutch, primary drive and external shift linkage.
   f. Starter motor.
   g. Thermostat.
   h. Water pump.
   i. Exhaust system.
2. The following components require engine removal for service:
   a. Crankshaft.
   b. Transmission and internal shift mechanism.
   c. Oil pump.
   d. Middle gear assembly.

ENGINE

Preliminary Information

Before servicing the engine, note the following:
1. Review *Service Methods* and *Measuring Tools* in Chapter One.
2. Prior to removing and disassembling the engine, clean the engine. Keep the work environment as clean as possible
3. Viewed from the engine's flywheel side, crankshaft rotation is counterclockwise.
4. Throughout the text there are references to the left and right side of the engine. This refers to the engine as it is mounted in the frame, not how it may sit on the workbench.
5. Always replace worn or damaged fasteners with those of the same size, type and torque requirements. If a specific torque value is not in **Table 2**, refer to the general torque recommendations table at the end of Chapter One.
6. Store parts and assemblies in well-marked plastic bags and containers. Use masking tape and a permanent, waterproof marking pen to label parts.
7. Use a box of assorted size and color vacuum hose identifiers, such as those shown in **Figure 1** (Lisle part No. 74600), to identify hoses and fittings during engine re-

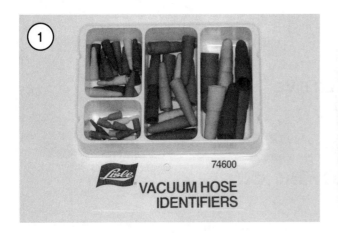

moval and disassembly. Automotive and aftermarket parts suppliers carry this kit, or similar equivalents.

8. Use a vise with protective jaws to hold parts.

9. Use special tools where noted or suitable equivalents.

10. Use a press or special tools when force is required to remove and install parts. Do not try to pry, hammer or otherwise force them on or off.

11. Replace all O-rings and seals during reassembly. Apply a small amount of grease to the inner lips of each new seal to prevent damage when the engine is first started.

12. If possible, take photographs of hose and wire routing before engine removal.

Removal

The engine is difficult to remove and install as a complete assembly. If possible, lighten the engine by removing its subassemblies while it is mounted in the frame.

1. Disconnect the negative battery cable from the battery (Chapter Nine). Place an insulator over the cable end so it cannot fall back across the battery and reconnect itself.

2. Remove the cargo bed (Chapter Sixteen).

3. Remove the seats (Chapter Sixteen).

4. Remove the rear and front consoles (Chapter Sixteen).

5. Remove the right seat support (Chapter Sixteen).

6. Remove the left seat support (Chapter Sixteen).

7. Remove the driver seat rail (Chapter Sixteen).

8. Remove the left, right and center protectors (Chapter Sixteen).

9. Remove both corner and side panels (Chapter Sixteen).

10. Remove the fuel tank (Chapter Eight).

11. Remove air duct 1 and air duct 2 (Chapter Six).

12. Drain the engine oil (Chapter Three).

13. Drain the engine coolant (Chapter Three).

14. Disconnect the spark plug lead at the spark plug.

15. Disconnect the cylinder head breather hose (**Figure 2**).

16. Remove the throttle body (Chapter Eight).

17. Loosen the clamp and disconnect the radiator hose (A, **Figure 3**) from the thermostat cover.

18. Disconnect the coolant temperature sensor connector (B, **Figure 3**).

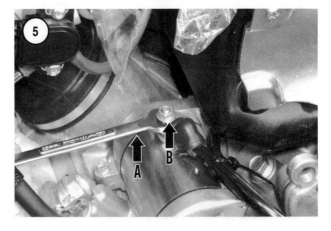

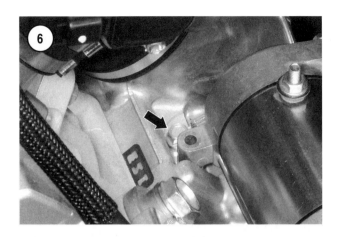

5

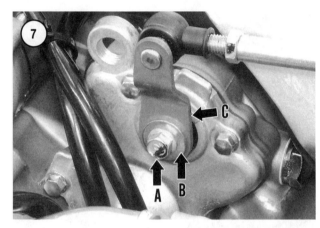

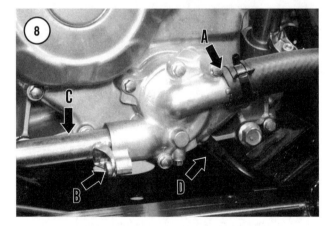

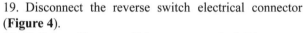

19. Disconnect the reverse switch electrical connector (**Figure 4**).

20. Pull the rubber cap off the starter terminal. Disconnect the starter cable by holding the inner nut with a wrench (A, **Figure 5**) and removing the outer nut (B). Holding the inner nut prevents the terminal bolt from turning and damaging the insulator installed inside the starter.

21. Remove the bolt (**Figure 6**) and disconnect the engine ground cable at the engine.

22. Remove the shift arm mounting bolt (A, **Figure 7**), washer (B) and remove the shift arm (C) from the shift shaft.

23. Loosen the hose clamp and disconnect the inlet hose (A, **Figure 8**) at the water pump.

24. Remove the bolt (B, **Figure 8**) securing the outlet pipe to the engine and remove the pipe (C) from the water pump.

25. Loosen the hose clamp and disconnect the outlet hose (**Figure 9**) at the cylinder block, then and remove the outlet pipe/hose assembly.

26. Open the clamp and disconnect the breather hose (D, **Figure 8**) at the water pump.

27. Loosen the hose clamps and disconnect the inlet (A, **Figure 10**) and outlet oil hoses (B) at the oil pipes. Plug the oil hoses and oil pipes to prevent debris from entering them.

28. Disconnect the electrical connectors secured to the passenger seat rail. Refer to **Figure 11**:

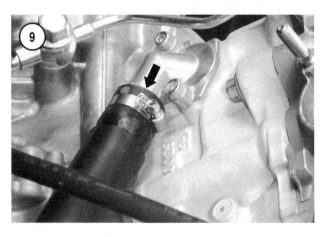

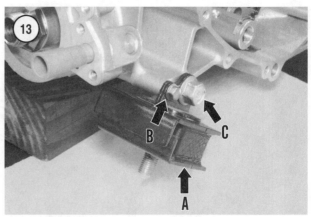

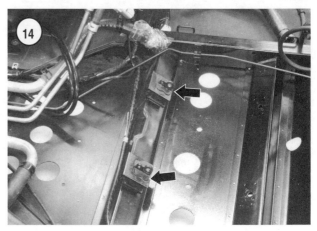

NOTE
Refer to the wiring diagram at the end of this manual to identify the different electrical connectors by their wire colors.

  a. Speed sensor electrical connector.
  b. Alternator connectors.
  c. Crankshaft position sensor electrical connector.

29. Remove the front differential and disconnect the front drive shaft from the engine as described in Chapter Twelve.

30. Remove the final drive unit and disconnect the rear drive shaft from the engine as described in Chapter Fourteen.

31. Remove the drive belt cover (Chapter Six).

32. Disconnect the gear position switch electrical connector (A, **Figure 12**).

33. If the engine will be disassembled, remove the following to help lighten the engine and ease removal:

  a. Cylinder head, cylinder and piston (Chapter Four).
  b. Clutch assembly (Chapter Six).
  c. Alternator cover and flywheel (Chapter Nine).
  d. Starter (Chapter Nine).

34. Check the engine for any remaining hoses or electrical connectors that were not disconnected and disconnect them now. If desired, remove any additional components that will make engine removal and handling easier.

NOTE
*The engine is secured to the frame with four engine mounts (A, **Figure 13**). Two bolts (6-mm [B, **Figure 13**] and 10-mm [C]) secure the engine mount to the engine. The 6-mm bolt is secured with a threadlocking compound. A nut located underneath the vehicle secures the engine mount to the frame.*

35. Working underneath the vehicle, remove the nuts securing the two rear engine mounts to the frame. These mounts will be remain on the engine (A, **Figure 13**).

36. Working inside the engine compartment, remove the two bolts (B and C, **Figure 12**) securing the two front engine mounts to the engine. These mounts will remain attached to the frame when the engine is removed.

NOTE
If removing an assembled engine, use an engine hoist to lift it out of the frame.

37. With one or more assistants, remove the engine from the frame.

38. Remove the nuts securing the front engine mounts (**Figure 14**) to the frame and remove the mounts.

Inspection

1. Inspect the frame for cracks or other damage. If found, have the frame inspected by a dealership.

2. Touch up the frame with paint as required.

3. Inspect all engine mounts (A, **Figure 13**) for cracks, damper separation and other damage. Make sure the bottom stud is tight. Replace damaged engine mounts.

4. Inspect the engine mount fasteners for corrosion and thread damage. Clean each fastener in solvent. Remove all threadlocking compound residue from the fastener threads where used. Replace worn or damaged fasteners.

5. Inspect and replace any damaged vacuum hoses.

6. Inspect the wiring harness for signs of damage that may have occurred when removing the engine. Repair damaged wires as required.

7. Inspect all of the coolant and oil line pipes and hoses for damage (**Figure 15**). Replace damaged pipes and hoses as described in Chapter Ten.

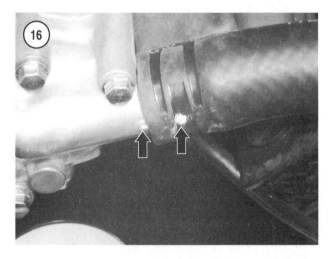

8. Inspect the brake lines for dents, creasing or other damage. Replace damaged brake lines as described in Chapter Fifteen.

Installation

CAUTION
Make sure the engine mount fastener threads are clean and dry. Do not oil them.

1. Install and tighten the rear engine mounts onto the engine as follows:
   a. Position one of the rear engine mounts (A, **Figure 13**) against the engine.
   b. Apply a medium-strength threadlocking compound onto the 6-mm bolt threads (B, **Figure 13**) and install the bolt finger tight.
   c. Tighten the 10-mm bolt to 42 N•m (31 ft.-lb.).
   d. Tighten the 6-mm bolt to 10 N•m (88 in.-lb.).
   e. Repeat for the other rear engine mount.
2. Install the front engine mounts into the holes in the frame (**Figure 14**) so the end with the 6-mm bolt holes faces toward the front of the vehicle. Install the nuts finger-tight.

NOTE
If necessary, use an engine hoist to install the engine into the frame.

3. Install the engine in the frame so the engine fits between the front mounts and the rear mount studs fit through the frame holes.
4. Install the nuts onto the rear engine mount studs but do not tighten them.
5. Apply a medium-strength threadlocking compound onto the 6-mm bolt threads and install the bolt through one of the front engine mounts and tighten finger-tight. Then install the 10-mm bolt finger-tight. Repeat for the other front engine mount.
6. Tighten the engine mount fasteners in the following order:
   a. Tighten the front engine mount nuts to 42 N•m (31 ft.-lb.).
   b. Tighten the front engine mount 10-mm bolts to 42 N•m (31 ft.-lb.).
   c. Tighten the front engine mount 6-mm bolts to 10 N•m (88 in.-lb.).
   d. Tighten the rear engine mount nuts to 42 N•m (31 ft.-lb.).
7. Reverse Steps 1-33 in *Removal* in this section to complete engine installation, plus the following steps.
8. Clean electrical connections and apply dielectric grease before reconnecting.
9. Tighten the engine ground cable mounting bolt (**Figure 6**) to 10 N•m (88 in.-lb.).
10. When connecting the coolant hoses onto the cylinder block (**Figure 9**) and water pump (A, **Figure 8**), align the paint mark on each hose with the raised boss on the cylinder block hose nozzle and water pump (**Figure 16**, typical). Then install and tighten the hose clamps.
11. Install the shift arm by aligning its flats with the flats on the shift shaft (**Figure 17**). Apply a medium-strength threadlocking compound onto the shift arm mounting bolt threads and install the bolt (A, **Figure 7**) and washer (B). Tighten the bolt to 14 N•m (10 ft.-lb.).
12. Lubricate a new O-ring with grease and install it onto the outlet pipe. Tighten the outlet pipe mounting bolt (B, **Figure 8**) to 10 N•m (88 in.-lb.).
13. If the oil filter was removed, install a new oil filter (Chapter Three).
14. Fill the engine with oil (Chapter Three).

5

15. Reconnect the negative battery cable at the battery (Chapter Nine).

16. Refill and bleed the cooling system (Chapter Three). Check the coolant hoses and pipes for leaks.

17. Start the engine and continue the cooling system bleeding procedure (Chapter Three). Also check for coolant, oil and fuel leaks.

18. Operate all controls and adjust as needed.

19. Turn the ignition switch on and shift the transmission into the low gear, high gear, neutral and reverse. Make sure the shift indicator light for each position comes on when the gear position is made. If not, adjust the select lever (Chapter Three).

20. Slowly test ride the vehicle to ensure all systems are operating correctly.

21. If the engine top end was rebuilt, refer to *Engine Break-In* in Chapter Three.

22. Perform an engine compression check (Chapter Three) and record the results for future reference.

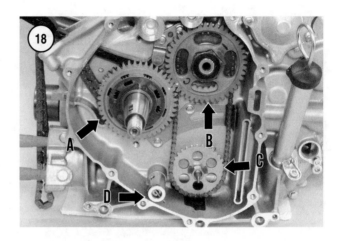

BALANCER AND OIL PUMP GEARS

This section services the balancer drive (A, **Figure 18**) and driven (B) gears, oil pump driven gear (C) and chain. These parts can be serviced with the engine mounted in the frame.

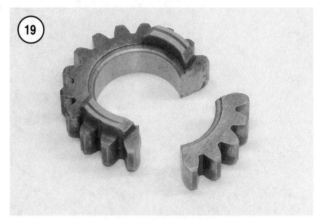

Tools

A gear holder is required to lock the balancer drive and driven gears when turning the balancer driven gear nut. A gear holder can be made by cutting a section of gear teeth (**Figure 19**) from a discarded gear, using a small hand grinder and cut-off wheel as follows:

1. If possible, select a gear with a large inside diameter. This will reduce the amount of material that must be cut through.

2. Mark the number of gear teeth to be removed, then mount the gear in a vise.

WARNING
Using a cut-off wheel and hand grinder as described in this procedure will cause flying particles. Wear proper eye protection.

3. Cut through the gear with a hand grinder and cut-off wheel (**Figure 20**) at the marks made in Step 2. If the gear holder is too long, shorten it with a bench grinder.

WARNING
The gear holder and gear will be hot. Allow them to cool before handling them.

Removal

1. Remove the flywheel, starter clutch and starter clutch gear assembly (Chapter Nine).

2. If necessary, remove the oil pressure relief valve (D, **Figure 18**) by sliding it out of the crankcase. Store the valve in a clean plastic bag.

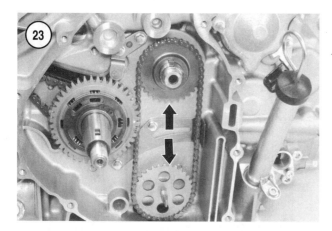

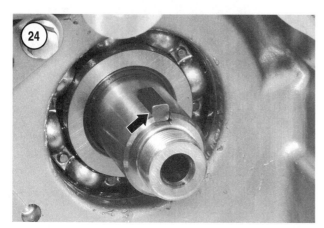

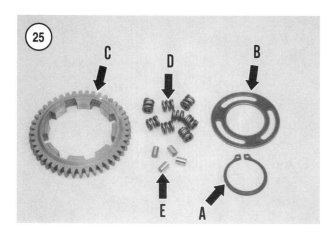

3. Remove the balancer driven gear (B, **Figure 18**) and oil pump driven gear (C) as follows:

    a. Bend the lockwasher tab (A, **Figure 21**) away from the balancer driven gear locknut.

    b. Lock the drive and driven gears with a gear holder as shown in B, **Figure 21**.

    c. Remove the locknut (C, **Figure 21**) and lockwasher.

    d. Bend the lockwasher tab (A, **Figure 22**) away from the oil pump driven gear locknut.

    e. With the gear holder still locking the two gears, remove the locknut (B, **Figure 22**) and lockwasher.

    f. Remove the gear holder.

    g. Slide the gears and chain off the shafts (**Figure 23**).

    h. Remove the key (**Figure 24**) from the balancer shaft.

NOTE
If the crankshaft is rotated with the balancer driven gear removed, turn the balancer shaft as required to prevent it from jamming against the crankshaft.

4. Remove the balancer drive gear (A, **Figure 18**) as follows:

NOTE
*The balancer drive gear consists of a snap ring (A, **Figure 25**), plate (B), gear (C), springs (D) and pins (E). Take care when removing the gear assembly to prevent the springs and pins from falling inside the engine.*

    a. Place a rag underneath the balancer drive gear to prevent any springs and pins from falling into the lower engine openings.

    b. Remove the snap ring (A, **Figure 26**) and plate (B).

    c. Place a plastic bag over the gear (**Figure 27**). Then pull the gear from the boss. The bag will catch any springs and pins that dislodge from the buffer boss.

    d. Pry and remove any remaining springs and pins from the buffer boss.

NOTE
*The buffer boss (**Figure 28**) is permanently installed on the crankshaft. If the boss is*

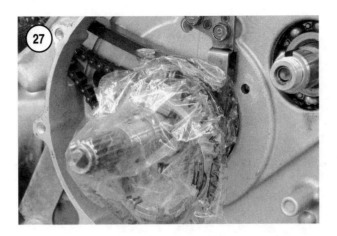

damaged, replace the crankshaft or have a dealership replace the right crankshaft half and rebuild the crankshaft.

5. Inspect as described in this section.

Installation

1. Install the balancer drive gear as follows:
   a. Install the pins and springs into the balancer drive gear. Alternate the pins in the springs; the arrows in **Figure 28** indicate the positions of the four pins. Use pliers to lightly compress the springs while inserting them into the gear.

   b. Align the timing mark on the balancer drive gear with the hole in the buffer boss (**Figure 29**). Then slowly and carefully push the gear (**Figure 30**) and spring the assemblies into the buffer boss. Work around the gear, pressing the springs into the boss until all parts are seated.
   c. Install the plate (B, **Figure 26**) and a new snap ring (A). Install the snap ring with its flat edge facing out. Make sure the snap ring seats in the groove completely.

2. Install the balancer driven gear and oil pump driven gear as follows:
   a. Install the key (**Figure 24**) into the balancer shaft.
   b. Assemble the chain and two gears. The short shoulder on the balancer driven gear should face out (A, **Figure 31**). The marks on the oil pump driven gear should face out (B, **Figure 31**).
   c. Install the gear and chain assembly by aligning the timing mark on the balancer driven gear with the timing mark on the balancer drive gear (**Figure 32**). Also align the keyway in the driven gear with the key installed in the balancer shaft.
   d. Install the oil pump driven gear by aligning it with the oil pump shaft (**Figure 33**).
   e. Install a new balancer shaft lockwasher by inserting its tab into the slot in the gear. Refer to **Figure 34**.
   f. Install a new oil pump shaft lockwasher and seat it against the driven gear (A, **Figure 22**). The tabs on the lockwasher must face out.

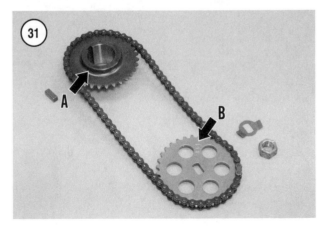

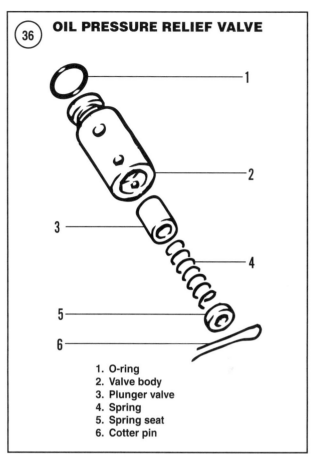

OIL PRESSURE RELIEF VALVE

1. O-ring
2. Valve body
3. Plunger valve
4. Spring
5. Spring seat
6. Cotter pin

g. Lubricate the threads on the balancer shaft and oil pump shaft and both locknuts with engine oil. Install both nuts finger-tight.

h. Place the gear holder at the bottom of the drive and driven gears (A, **Figure 35**) and tighten the driven gear locknut (B) to 80 N•m (58 in.-lb.). Bend the lockwasher tab against the locknut.

i. With the gear holder still in place, tighten the oil pump driven gear locknut (B, **Figure 22**) to 22 N•m (16 ft.-lb.). Bend the lockwasher tab against the locknut.

j. Remove the gear holder.

3. If removed, lubricate the oil pressure relief valve O-ring with grease and install it into the crankcase (D, **Figure 18**). Replace the O-ring if cracked or damaged. Refer to *Oil Pressure Relief Valve* in this chapter.

4. Install the starter idler gear assembly, starter clutch and flywheel (Chapter Nine).

OIL PRESSURE RELIEF VALVE

An oil pressure relief valve (**Figure 36**) is installed in the lubrication system to limit excessive oil pressure. When the oil pressure is operating at normal levels, the plunger valve is closed so that no oil can escape through the valve body relief holes. When the oil pressure becomes too high, it forces the plunger valve toward the spring seat and opens relief holes in the valve body. Oil can then drain through

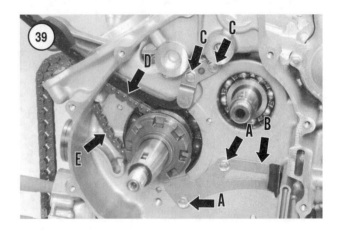

the relief holes and back into the crankcase, which reduces oil pressure to an acceptable level. If the plunger valve is stuck closed, high oil pressure will result. If the plunger valve is stuck open, low oil pressure will result and possibly cause engine seizure.

The oil pressure relief valve can be disassembled for inspection, but replacement parts other than the O-ring are unavailable.

The oil pressure relief valve can be serviced with the engine mounted in the frame.

Removal/Inspection/Installation

1. Remove the flywheel cover (Chapter Nine).
2. Remove the oil pressure relief valve (**Figure 37**) by pulling it out of the crankcase bore.
3. Remove and discard the O-ring (**Figure 38**).
4. Clean the valve in solvent and dry with compressed air.
5. If necessary, inspect the oil pressure relief valve (**Figure 36**) as follows:

NOTE
The internal parts are under spring tension.

   a. Remove and discard the cotter pin, then remove the spring seat, spring, and plunger valve.
   b. Clean and dry the parts. Do not scratch the plunger valve or valve bore.
   c. Inspect the spring for cracks and unevenly spaced spring coils. Do not attempt to stretch or repair the spring as this will change the relief valve pressure setting and possibly cause engine damage. Replace the valve assembly if the spring appears damaged, stretched or worn.
   d. Inspect the valve and the valve body bore surfaces for cracks, scoring and other damage. The valve must slide through the bore smoothly with no roughness or binding. Replace the valve assembly if the surfaces show wear or damage.
   e. If the valve assembly does not show any wear or damage, lubricate the valve and bore with new engine oil. Then install the valve with its open side facing the spring. Then install the spring, spring seat and secure with a new cotter pin that is the same size

as the original. Bend the cotter pin arms over to lock it.

CAUTION
Make sure to use a new cotter pin and to lock it carefully. If the cotter pin should fail and allow the spring and plunger valve to release from the valve, the engine may seize from a lack of oil pressure.

6. Lubricate a new O-ring (**Figure 38**) with lithium grease and install it onto the valve groove.
7. Push the valve (**Figure 37**) into the crankcase bore.
8. Install the flywheel cover (Chapter Nine).

CAM CHAIN AND GUIDES

The cam chain and guides are located behind the flywheel. The front chain guide can be removed after cylinder head removal (Chapter Four). The cam chain and rear chain guide can be replaced with the engine mounted in the frame.

Removal/Inspection/Installation

1. Remove the cylinder head and cylinder head gasket (Chapter Four).
2. Remove the balancer and oil pump gears as described in this chapter.

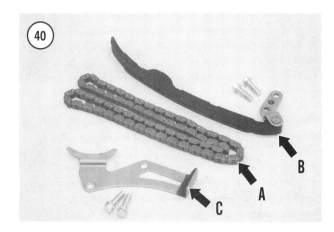

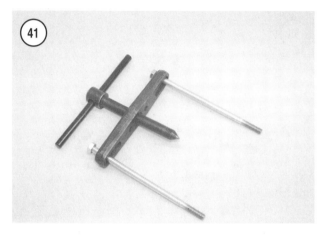

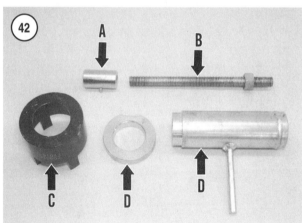

3. Remove the cam chain stopper mounting bolts (A, **Figure 39**) and the chain stopper (B).

4. Remove the rear cam chain guide mounting bolts (C, **Figure 39**) and the guide (D).

5. Remove the cam chain (E, **Figure 39**).

6. Clean and dry all parts. Remove all threadlocking compound residue from the mounting bolt and crankcase threads.

7. Inspect the cam chain (A, **Figure 40**) for wear and damage. Check for excessive play between the links, indicating worn rollers and pins. If chain replacement is necessary, also inspect the crankshaft drive sprocket and camshaft driven sprocket.

8. Inspect the guides (B, **Figure 40**) for excessive wear (grooves), cuts or other damage. Replace both front and rear guides as a set.

9. Check the cam chain stopper (C, **Figure 40**) for damage.

NOTE
If the chain guides and cam chain are damaged, replace them as well as the cam chain tensioner as a set.

10. Installation is the reverse of removal. Note the following:

   a. Apply a medium-strength threadlocking compound onto the cam chain guide mounting bolt threads and tighten to 10 N•m (88 in.-lb.).

   b. Apply a medium-strength threadlocking compound onto the cam chain stopper mounting bolt threads and tighten to 10 N•m (88 in.-lb.).

CRANKCASE

The following procedures detail the disassembly and reassembly of the crankcase while servicing the following components:

1. Middle driven shaft.
2. Middle driven pinion gear bearing housing and gear.
3. Reverse idle gear assembly.
4. Input shaft.
5. Output shaft.
6. Shift drum.
7. Balancer shaft.
8. Middle gear bearing housing and gears.
9. Oil pump.
10. Crankshaft.
11. Crankcase bearings.

The crankcase halves are made of cast aluminum alloy. Do not hammer or excessively pry on the cases. The cases will fracture or break. The cases are aligned and sealed at the joint by dowels and a gasket sealer.

Tools

The crankshaft is a press fit in the right crankcase main bearing and requires special tools for removal and installation. The following Yamaha special tools or their equivalents can be used:

1. Crankshaft removal tool: part No. YU-01135-B (**Figure 41**).

2. The following Yamaha tools are used as an assembly to install the crankshaft:

   a. Adapter No.13: part No. YU-04059 (A, **Figure 42**).

   b. Nut and bolt: part No. YU-90060 (B, **Figure 42**).

   c. Pot spacer: part No. YM-91044 (C, **Figure 42**).

   d. Installer pot and spacer: part No. YU-90058 (D, **Figure 42**).

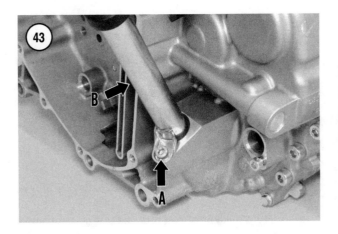

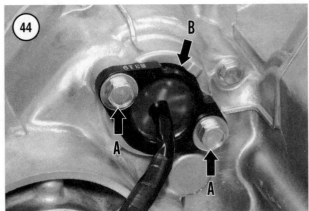

Disassembly

Identify parts or make written notes as required to help with reassembly. Note any damaged or worn parts.

Reference to the left or right side of the engine refers to the engine as it is mounted in the frame, not on the workbench.

1. Prior to disassembly of the crankcase, remove the following parts if not removed during engine removal:

   a. Starter (Chapter Nine).

   b. Clutch (Chapter Six).

NOTE
*Before removing the external shift mechanism, perform **Shifting Check** in this chapter to confirm the transmission is shifting properly. If the engine is being disassembled to service a shifting problem, the results obtained in the procedure may help diagnose the problem.*

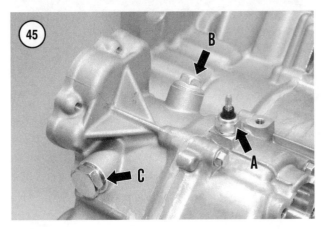

   c. External shift mechanism (Chapter Seven).

   d. Piston (Chapter Four).

   e. Oil pressure relief valve as described in this chapter.

   f. Torque limiter as described in *Flywheel, Starter Clutch and Starter Gears* in Chapter Nine.

   g. Starter idle gear (Chapter Nine).

   h. Flywheel (Chapter Nine).

   i. Balancer and oil pump gears as described in this chapter.

   j. Cam chain and rear guide as described in this chapter.

   k. Speed sensor (Chapter Nine).

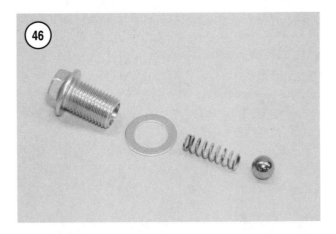

2. Remove the dipstick tube mounting bolt (A, **Figure 43**), tube (B) and O-ring.

3. Remove the gear position switch mounting bolts (A, **Figure 44**), switch (B) and O-ring.

4. Remove the reverse switch (A, **Figure 45**) and its gasket.

5. Remove the bolt and washer (B, **Figure 45**) and the shift drum detent assembly. Refer to **Figure 46**.

NOTE
*The plug bolt (C, **Figure 45**) does not require removal unless loose or its gasket is leaking.*

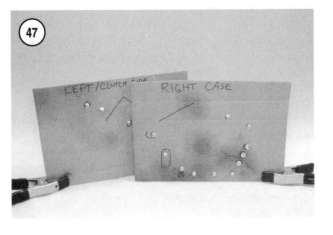

6. Draw an outline of the left and right crankcase halves on a piece of cardboard and punch a hole along the outline for each crankcase assembly bolt (**Figure 47**). Place the bolts into their respective holes after removal. If necessary, make any additional notes on the cardboard to help with reassembly.

7. Loosen the left (**Figure 48**) and right (**Figure 49**) crankcase bolts. Loosen each bolt one-fourth turn, working in a crossing pattern. Remove all bolts from the right crankcase.

8. Place the engine on wooden blocks with the left crankcase facing up. Remove the bolts from the left crankcase. The crankshaft, balancer shaft and transmission components will remain in the right crankcase half. The crankshaft is a press fit and will be removed after the other components.

9. Separate and remove the left crankcase while noting the following:

CAUTION
Do not hammer or pry on areas of the engine cases that are not reinforced. Do not pry on gasket surfaces. If the left crankcase is tight, check for an installed crankcase mounting bolt or a seized shaft.

a. Begin tapping upward on the left the crankcase to break the sealer bond.

b. Because the input shaft is supported by two bearings in the left case half, the shaft can bind as the left crankcase is being removed. Tap the shaft to free it and ease left crankcase removal.

c. Two dowel pins are used for case half alignment and can bind crankcase separation if corroded. These are found at the front and rear of the engine.

d. Make sure the left crankcase remains parallel with the right crankcase during its removal (**Figure 50**).

e. Remove the left crankcase (A, **Figure 51**). Account for the washer (B, **Figure 51**) installed on the output shaft and reinstall it onto the shaft, if necessary.

10. Remove the two dowel pins (A, **Figure 52**).

11. Remove the balancer shaft (B, **Figure 52**).

12. Remove the four bolts and lift out the middle gear bearing housing (C, **Figure 52**). Inspect and service the bearing housing as described in this chapter.

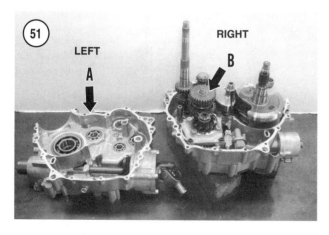

13. Remove the transmission as follows:

NOTE
Refer to Chapter Seven to identify the gears called out in this step.

a. Lift the reverse idler gear shaft (**Figure 53**), then tilt it toward the outside and remove it from the crankcase. The gear is secured to the shaft with snap rings and the gear and shaft will come out as an assembly.

b. Lift the input shaft, then tilt it toward the outside (**Figure 54**) and remove it from the crankcase.

c. Remove the washer (A, **Figure 55**), high gear (B, **Figure 55**), collar (A, **Figure 56**) and washer (B, **Figure 56**) from the output shaft

d. Turn the shift drum and shift the output shaft into neutral. Neutral can be confirmed when the gear dogs on the clutch dog and middle drive gear are free.

NOTE
*Neutral can also be confirmed by viewing the shift drum detent ramps through the detent hole (**Figure 57**) in the crankcase. Refer to **Figure 58** to identify the shift drum's neutral position detent ramp. Turn the shift drum until the neutral detent ramp is visible.*

e. Pull the shift fork shaft up (**Figure 59**) until it is free from its bore in the crankcase. Then pivot the shift

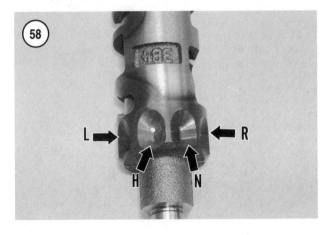

5

fork away from the shift drum and remove the shift drum (**Figure 60**).

   f. Lift and remove the output shaft and shift forks as an assembly (**Figure 61**).

14. Remove the three mounting bolts (A, **Figure 62**) and the oil pump and its gasket. Do not loosen the Phillips screw (B, **Figure 62**) unless the pump will be disassembled.

15. Remove the crankshaft as follows:

NOTE
*Refer to **Tools** in this section for a description of the tools required to remove the crankshaft.*

   a. Install the flywheel nut (A, **Figure 63**) onto the end of the flywheel.

   b. Attach the crankshaft separating tool (B, **Figure 63**) to the right crankcase. Thread the bolts fully into the crankcase.

   c. Lubricate the separating tool center bolt and crankshaft end with grease.

   d. Set the crankcase upright. Then while holding the crankshaft, tighten the center bolt to push the crankshaft and its main bearing out of the crankcase.

16. Remove the spacer/crank seal assembly (**Figure 64**) from the left crankcase.

17. Remove the input shaft collar (A, **Figure 65**) from the left crankcase.

18. Remove the middle driven pinion gear bearing housing (A, **Figure 66**) and the middle driven shaft (B) from the left crankcase as described in this chapter.

19. Inspect the crankcase halves, input shaft seal, bearing and the other components removed in this procedure as described in this chapter. Inspect the transmission as described in Chapter Seven.

Assembly

1. Install the middle driven shaft (A, **Figure 66**) and middle driven pinion gear bearing housing (B) as described in this chapter.

2. Make sure all of the crankcase oil passages are clean.

3. Lubricate the crankcase bearings with engine oil.

4. Install the spacer/crank seal assembly (**Figure 67**) as follows:

    a. Lubricate the two crank seals on the spacer with engine oil. Make sure seal ends are hooked together as shown in A, **Figure 67**.

    b. Install the spacer/crank seal assembly with its shoulder (B, **Figure 67**) facing out. Refer to **Figure 64**.

CAUTION
Do not force the spacer into the crankcase. If the spacer will not slide into place, one or both crank seals are improperly installed.

5. Lubricate the input shaft seal lip (**Figure 68**) with grease.

6. Install the input shaft collar as follows:

    a. Lubricate a new O-ring with grease and install it in the inner collar groove (B, **Figure 65**). Make sure the O-ring seats squarely in the groove and is not twisted.

    b. Install the collar with its flat side facing out (A, **Figure 65**).

7. Install the crankshaft as follows:

CAUTION
Do not use a hammer to drive the crankshaft bearing into the crankcase.

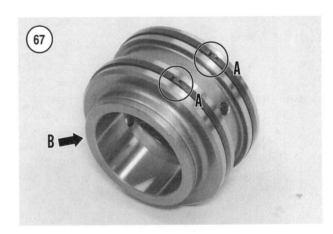

    a. Refer to *Tools* in this section to identify the crankshaft installation tools.

    b. Lubricate the bolt threads (B, **Figure 42**) with a high-pressure lubricant or anti-seize. This will help turn the bolt and ease crankshaft installation when pressing its bearing into the crankcase.

    c. Install two of the cylinder block mounting bolts (A, **Figure 69**) into the left crankcase.

    d. Lubricate the right crankcase main bearing bore (B, **Figure 69**) with engine oil.

    e. Place the crankshaft (A, **Figure 70**) on wooden blocks with its right side facing up.

    f. Thread the adapter (B, **Figure 70**) onto the crankshaft.

    g. Place the right crankcase over the crankshaft so that its bearing bore is resting on the crankshaft bearing. Have an assistant hold the crankcase in place.

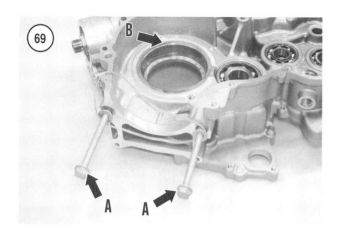

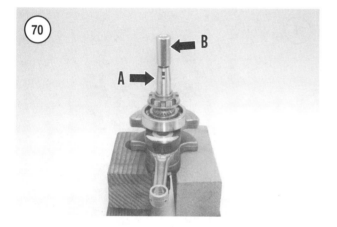

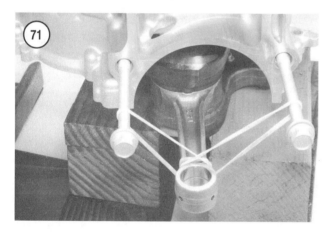

h. Secure the connecting rod at TDC with a large rubber band wrapped around the rod and the two bolts as shown in **Figure 71**. The rubber band will help to control the connecting rod and prevent it from catching against the crankcase gasket surface when installing the crankshaft.

i. Thread the bolt (A, **Figure 72**) fully into the adapter.

j. Place the pot spacer (B, **Figure 72**) over the bolt. The pot spacer must seat parallel to the crankcase.

k. Install the spacer (C, **Figure 72**) and installer pot (D) over the bolt and center them into the pot spacer. Make sure the pin on the adapter enters the groove in the installer pot. Then, install the nut onto the bolt.

CAUTION
Make sure the crankcase and crankshaft bearing remains centered. If the bearing enters the bore at an angle, loosen the nut and realign the parts before damaging the bore.

l. Hold the installer pot and tighten the nut to press the bearing into the crankcase. At the same time, make sure the connecting rod remains centered so that it does not catch against and damage the crankcase gasket surface. Continue to tighten the nut until the bearing bottoms inside the bearing bore (**Figure 73**).

m. Remove the tools and rubber band from the crankshaft. Then turn the crankshaft by hand, making sure it turns freely and there is no binding or roughness.

8. Position the right crankcase on wooden blocks with the crankshaft facing up.

9. Install the oil pump as follows:

a. Lubricate the rotors with new engine oil. Turn the shaft to distribute the oil on the rotors and bore surfaces.

b. Install a new gasket, making sure the oil passage hole in the gasket aligns with the oil passage hole in the pump.

c. Install the oil pump and tighten the mounting bolts (A, **Figure 62**) to 10 N•m (88 in.-lb.).

d. Reach underneath the crankcase and turn the oil pump shaft by hand to check for any binding or roughness.

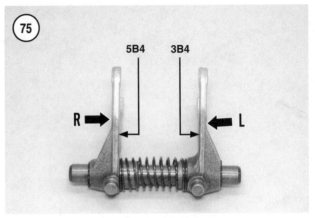

10. Install the output shaft as follows:
   a. If installed, remove the washer (A, **Figure 74**), high gear (B), collar (C) and washer (D) from the output shaft (E).
   b. Refer to **Figure 75** to identify the shift forks.
   c. Mesh the R (right) shift fork with the clutch dog groove and the L (left) shift fork with the middle drive gear groove (**Figure 76**). Because the shift forks are under spring tension, the right shift fork will slide the clutch dog toward the top of the shaft.
   d. Install the output shaft and shift forks as an assembly (**Figure 77**).
   e. Lift the shift forks (and not the shift fork shaft) as required to install the shift fork pins into the shift drum grooves while sliding the shift drum into position (**Figure 78**). Make sure the shift fork shaft and shift drum are both bottomed in the case half.
   f. Install the collar (A, **Figure 79**), washer (B, **Figure 79**), high gear (A, **Figure 80**) and washer (B, **Figure 80**).

11. Install the input shaft (A, **Figure 81**) and mesh it with the output shaft.

12. Install the reverse idler gear shaft (B, **Figure 81**) and mesh it with the input and output shafts.

13. Install the middle gear bearing housing (A, **Figure 82**). Apply a medium-strength threadlocking compound onto the mounting bolt threads and tighten to 32 N•m (24 ft.-lb.).

14. Install the balancer shaft (B, **Figure 82**).

15. Lubricate all exposed shaft bearing surfaces with engine oil. Also lubricate the bearings in the left crankcase with engine oil.

16. Clean all crankcase gasket mating surfaces with electrical contact cleaner or Isopropyl alcohol and allow to dry.

NOTE
The sealer recommended in Step 17 is thin and runs easily. Make sure it does not contact any of the bearings or oil passages.

17. Apply a thin coat of semi-drying liquid gasket (Yamabond No. 4, Hondabond 4 or ThreeBond 1104 or

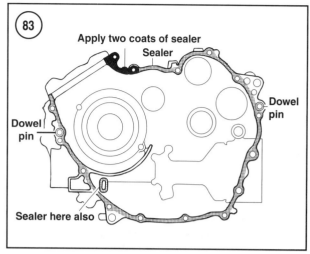

equivalent) to all mating surfaces on both crankcase halves (**Figure 83**). Apply two coats of sealer to the area identified in **Figure 83**.

18. Install the two dowel pins (C, **Figure 82**) in the right crankcase.

19. Position the connecting rod at TDC so it does not interfere with crankcase installation.

20. Install the left crankcase squarely onto the right crankcase. The crankcase may go all the way down by hand pressure. However, if necessary tap the case with a soft-faced mallet while making sure the dowel pins engage the mating holes. Continue until the left crankcase seats on the right crankcase. The gasket surfaces must be flush all the way around the case halves. Now make sure all shafts rotate freely; there must be no binding.

> *CAUTION*
> *If the crankcase halves do not fit together completely, do not pull them together with the crankcase bolts. Separate the crankcase halves and investigate the cause of the interference. If the output shaft was disassembled, make sure a gear was not installed backward. Do not risk damage by trying to force the crankcases together.*

21. Install the crankcase bolts as follows:

> *NOTE*
> *Make sure the crankcase mounting bolt and crankshaft threads are clean and dry.*

   a. Use the cardboard templates made during disassembly to identify the crankcase bolts.
   b. Install the left crankcase bolts (**Figure 84**) finger-tight.
   c. Turn the engine over so the right side faces up.
   d. Install the right crankcase bolts (**Figure 85**) finger-tight.

22. Tighten the crankcase bolts as follows:

   a. Tighten all of the right and then left crankcase 6-mm bolts in a crossing pattern to 10 N•m (88 in.-lb.).

b. Tighten the right crankcase 8-mm crankcase bolts to 26 N•m (19 ft.-lb.).

c. Make sure the input shaft collar (A, **Figure 86**) and spacer/crank seal assembly (**Figure 87**) is properly seated in the left crankcase.

d. Turn all of the shafts; there must be no binding.

23. If removed, install the plug bolt (C, **Figure 45**) and a new washer and tighten to 18 N•m (13 ft.-lb.).

24. Install the shift drum detent assembly in the order shown in **Figure 46**. Install a new washer and tighten the shift drum detent bolt (B, **Figure 45**) to 18 N•m (13 ft.-lb.).

25. Install the reverse switch (A, **Figure 45**) with a new washer and tighten to 17 N•m (12 ft.-lb.).

26. Lubricate a new O-ring with grease and install it on the gear position switch. Install the switch with its notched side facing up (B, **Figure 44**) and tighten the mounting bolts to 7 N•m (62 in.-lb.).

27. Lubricate a new O-ring with grease and install it on the dipstick tube. Install the dipstick tube (B, **Figure 43**) and mounting bolt (A) and tighten to 10 N•m (88 in.-lb.).

28. Perform *Shifting Check* in this chapter.

29. Reverse the procedures in Step 1 in *Disassembly* in this section to complete assembly.

Inspection

1. Remove all sealer residue from the gasket surfaces with solvent and a scraper. Remove sealer residue from the threaded holes in both case halves with a small brush.

2. Temporarily rinse the cases in solvent to remove the sealer residue. Recheck the gasket surfaces and reclean if necessary.

3. Remove and discard the input shaft seal as described in this chapter.

4. When the gasket surfaces are clean, clean the crankcase halves with solvent. Thoroughly flush the oil passage bores with solvent.

5. Inspect the crankcases for fractures around all mounting and bearing bosses, stiffening ribs and threaded holes. If repair is required, refer inspection to a dealership.

6. Using clean solvent, flush each bearing.

7. Check all threaded holes for damage or debris buildup. Clean threads with the correct size metric tap. Lubricate the tap with kerosene or aluminum tap fluid. Clean all debris from the threads. Rinse again with solvent.

8. Dry the crankcase halves with compressed air. Blow through all oil passages and oil holes.

> *WARNING*
> *When drying a bearing with compressed air, do not allow the inner bearing race to spin. The air can spin the bearing at excessive speed, possibly damaging the bearing.*

9. Lightly oil the engine bearings with new engine oil before inspecting their condition. A dry bearing will exhibit more sound and looseness than a properly lubricated bearing.

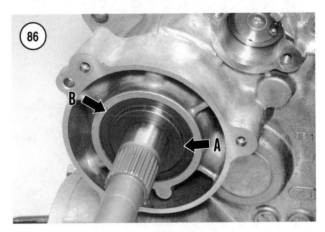

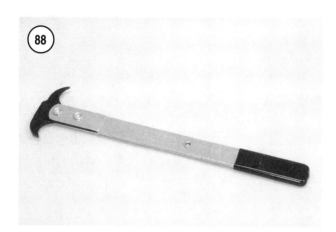

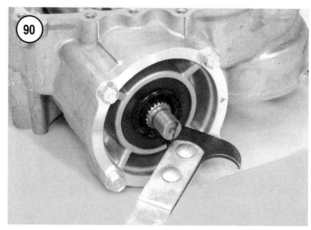

10. Inspect the bearings for roughness, pitting, galling and play. Replace any bearing that is not in good condition. Always replace the opposite bearing at the same time. Refer to *Crankcase Seals and Bearings* in this chapter.

CRANKCASE SEALS AND BEARINGS

Refer to *Service Procedures* in Chapter One for general bearing and seal removal and installation techniques.

Input Shaft Seal Removal/Installation

Engine in frame

> *NOTE*
> *If the input shaft collar can be removed from the crankcase, it is possible to replace this seal without having to disassemble the engine. However, the collar is equipped with an O-ring and can be difficult to remove.*

1. Remove the clutch assembly (Chapter Six).
2. Remove the input shaft collar (A, **Figure 86**). Remove the O-ring and clean the collar. Lubricate a new O-ring with grease and install it in the collar groove. Make sure the O-ring sits squarely in the collar groove.
3. Pry the seal out at different positions with a seal removal tool (**Figure 88**, typical) until it starts to move and then

remove it. Do not insert the tool so deeply that it damages the seal bore.
4. Lubricate the lips of a new seal with grease.
5. Carefully slide the seal over the input shaft and tap it into the crankcase with its flat side facing out (B, **Figure 86**). Install the seal until its outer edge is flush with the crankcase.
6. Install the input shaft collar (A, **Figure 86**) with its flat side facing out. Push the collar into the seal until it bottoms.

Engine disassembled

1. Using a suitable seal removal tool, extract the seal (**Figure 89**) from the crankcase.
2. Pack the lip of a new seal with grease.
3. Install the seal with its closed side facing out until its outer edge is flush with the crankcase.

Bearing Housing and Middle Driven Shaft Seals

If the bearing housing and middle driven shaft components will not be removed, the seals installed at the front and rear of the engine can be replaced as follows:
1. If replacing the bearing housing seal, remove the universal joint as described in this chapter.
2. If replacing the middle driven shaft seal, remove the drive shaft coupling gear as described in *Middle Gear Assembly* in this chapter.
3. Pry the seal out at different positions with a seal removal tool until it starts to move and then remove it. Do not insert the tool so deeply that it damages the seal bore. Refer to **Figure 90** or **Figure 91**.
4. Lubricate the lips of a new seal with grease.
5. Slide the seal over the shaft and tap it into the crankcase with its flat side facing out. Install the seal until its outer edge is 1.0-1.5 mm (0.039-0.0-59 in.) below the seal bore edge. Refer to **Figure 92** or **Figure 93**.

Crankcase Bearings Removal/Installation

1. When replacing crankcase bearings, note the following:

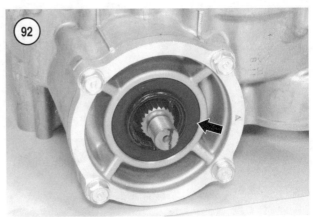

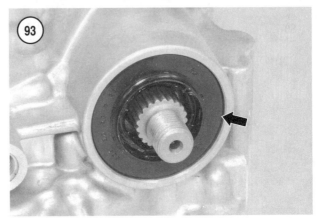

a. The input shaft bearings installed in the left crank-case are secured with a bearing retainer (**Figure 94**). After removing the bolts, remove all threadlocking compound residue from the bolt and case half threads. Apply a medium-strength threadlocking compound to the bolt threads and tighten to 10 N•m (88 in.-lb.).

b. Identify and record the size code of each bearing before it is removed from the crankcase. This will eliminate confusion when installing the new bearings.

c. Record the orientation of each bearing in its bore. Note if the size code faces toward the inside or outside of the case half.

d. Heat the crankcase area around the bearing or bearing bore to approximately 80° C (176° F) before removing and installing the bearing. Refer to *Service Methods* in Chapter One for additional information on bearing service.

e. Remove bearings that are only accessible from one side with a blind bearing puller (**Figure 95**). The puller is fitted through the bearing, then expanded to grip the back-side of the bearing.

2. The left crankcase half houses the following bearings:
   a. Main bearing (A, **Figure 96**).
   b. Balancer shaft bearing (B, **Figure 96**).
   c. Output shaft bearing (C, **Figure 96**).
   d. Input shaft bearing (D, **Figure 96**).

3. The right crankcase half houses the following bearings:
   a. Input shaft bearing (A, **Figure 97**).
   b. Output shaft bearing (B, **Figure 97**).
   c. Balancer shaft bearing (C, **Figure 97**).
   d. Crankshaft bearing insert (D, **Figure 97**).
   e. Middle drive shaft bearing (E, **Figure 97**).

RELIEF VALVE AND OIL PIPE ADAPTER

Relief Valve Removal/Installation

A relief valve is installed in the oil pipe adapter that opens to allow oil to flow when the oil filter is severely restricted and cannot flow oil. However, the oil flowing through the relief valve is unfiltered. Change the oil and filter at intervals specified in Chapter Three.

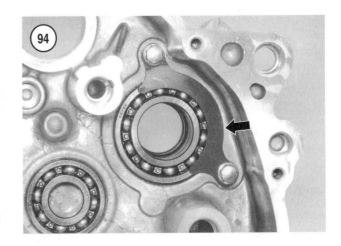

1. If the engine is mounted in the frame, drain the engine oil (Chapter Three).

2. Remove the oil filter.

3. Remove the snap ring (**Figure 98** and A, **Figure 99**), washer (B, **Figure 99**), spring (C, **Figure 99**) and relief valve (D, **Figure 99**). Discard the snap ring.

4. Clean and inspect for worn or damaged parts.

5. Check the relief valve bore for contamination. If necessary, remove the oil pipe adapter as described in this section so the bore can be thoroughly cleaned

6. Installation is the reverse of these steps. Install a new snap ring with its flat side facing out. Make sure the snap ring seats in the groove completely.

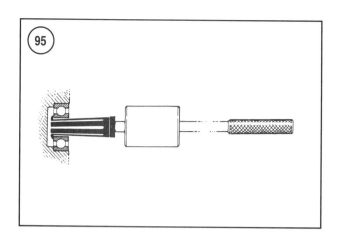

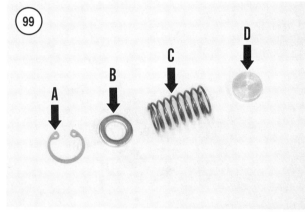

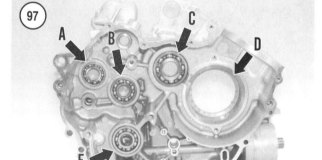

Oil Pipe Adapter Removal/Installation

The oil pipe adapter can be removed for replacement or to replace its O-ring if leaking.

1. Remove the relief valve as described in this section.
2. Support the right crankcase and remove the oil pipe adapter bolt (A, **Figure 100**).
3. Remove the oil pipe adapter (B, **Figure 100**) and discard its O-ring.
4. Clean and dry the adapter. Also clean its mating surface on the crankcase.

CRANKSHAFT

The crankshaft is removed and installed as described in *Disassembly* and *Reassembly* in *Crankcase* in this chapter.

Inspection

Handle the crankshaft carefully during inspection. Do not place the crankshaft where it could accidentally roll off the workbench. The crankshaft is an assembly-type, with its two halves joined by the crankpin. The crankpin is pressed into the flywheels and aligned, both vertically and horizontally, with calibrated equipment. If the crankshaft assembly shows signs of wear, or is out of alignment, have a dealership inspect the crankshaft. The crankshaft can also be rebuilt. Inspect the crankshaft assembly as follows:

1. Clean the crankshaft with solvent while thoroughly flushing its oil passages (A and B, **Figure 101**).
2. Dry the crankshaft and oil passages with compressed air.
3. Inspect the crankshaft bearing surfaces (C, **Figure 101**) for scoring, heat discoloration or other damage. Repair minor damage with 320 grit carborundum cloth. If the bearing surfaces show damage, check the mating inner bearing races for damage.
4. Inspect the splines (D, **Figure 101**), buffer boss (A, **Figure 102**), sprocket (B, **Figure 102**), bearing (C, **Figure 102**) shaft taper and keyway (D, **Figure 102**) for wear or damage. Note the following:

    a. If the splines are damaged, check the clutch carrier splines for damage.

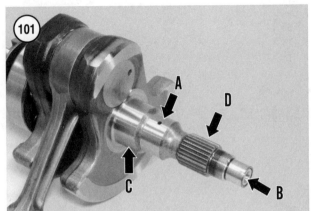

b. If the buffer boss is damaged, inspect the balancer drive gear, springs and pins as described in this chapter.

c. If the sprocket is damaged, check the cam chain, upper cam sprocket, chain guides and cam chain tensioner for damage.

d. If the bearing is damaged, either replace or rebuild the crankshaft by replacing its right crank wheel assembly.

e. If the shaft taper or keyway is damaged, check the flywheel taper and keyway for damage.

5. Inspect the connecting rod small end (A, **Figure 103**) as described in *Piston and Piston Rings* in Chapter Four.

6. Refer to **Table 1** and inspect the connecting rod big (B, **Figure 103**) as follows:

a. Hold the crankshaft and turn the rod by hand. If there is any roughness or grinding, the bottom rod end bearing and connecting rod has suffered some type of damage. Refer further inspection to a dealership.

b. Slide the connecting rod to one side and measure the connecting rod side clearance with a flat feeler gauge (**Figure 104**).

c. Support the crankshaft on a set of V-blocks and position the pointer of a dial indicator in the middle of the connecting rod lower end (**Figure 105**). Hold the crankshaft securely and then move the connecting rod as shown in **Figure 105** to measure the big end radial clearance.

d. Support the crankshaft and measure the small end free play as shown in **Figure 106**.

7. Measure the crankshaft width along its machined surfaces (**Figure 107**). If the width is out of specification (**Table 1**), have a dealership inspect and possibly true the crankshaft.

CAUTION
*Do not place the crankshaft between centers to measure runout. Doing so may damage the oil plug (B, **Figure 101**) in the right end of the crankshaft.*

8. Place the crankshaft on a set of V-blocks at the points indicated in **Figure 108**. Rotate the crankshaft and measure crankshaft runout with a dial indicator at the two points

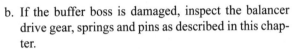

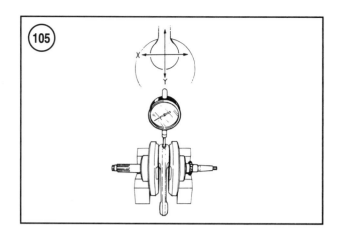

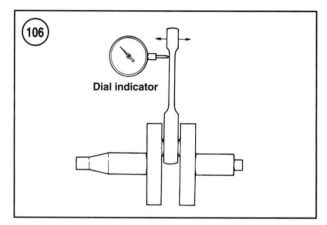

Dial indicator

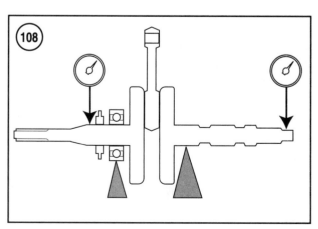

indicated in **Figure 108**. If the runout exceeds the service limit in **Table 1**, have a dealership evaluate and possibly true the crankshaft.

BALANCER SHAFT

The engine uses a rotating balancer to dampen engine vibration. The balancer weight is synchronized with the crankshaft and is driven by a gear located on the right end of the crankshaft. The balancer shaft is removed during crankcase disassembly.

Inspection

1. Install the balancer shaft into its crankcase bearings and check for play between the parts.
2. Inspect the bearing surfaces (A, **Figure 109**), keyway (B) and threads (C) for damage.
3. Inspect the fit of the gear, key and nut on the balancer shaft.

OIL PUMP

The oil pump is chain-driven by the balancer shaft. The oil pump shaft not only operates the rotors in the oil pump, but also drives the water pump. The tang at the exposed end of the oil pump shaft engages with the back of the water pump. If the oil pump is badly worn, it cannot maintain oil pressure.

The oil pump can be disassembled for inspection, but individual replacement parts other than the gasket are not available.

The oil pump is removed during crankcase disassembly.
1. Check the pump screen (A, **Figure 110**) for sealer and other debris. Carefully clean by picking the material off the screen, making sure not to damage or penetrate the screen. If the screen is clogged, disassemble the pump as described in this section and back flush the screen with solvent.
2. Turn the oil pump shaft (B, **Figure 110**) to check rotor operation. If the rotors turn roughly or if there is binding, replace the oil pump assembly.

Disassembly/Assembly

Refer to **Figure 111**.

> *NOTE*
> *The oil pump assembly screw (1, **Figure 111**) is tight and difficult to remove. Make sure to secure the pump body when loosening and tightening the screw.*

1. Either secure the oil pump into the right crankcase with its mounting bolts or bolt the pump onto a wooden block (A, **Figure 112**) secured in a vise.
2. Loosen the screw (B, **Figure 112**) with a Phillips bit mounted in a hand impact driver.

5

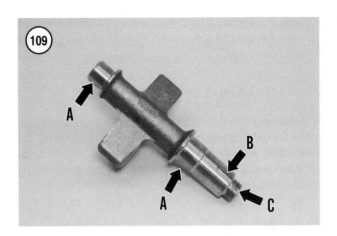

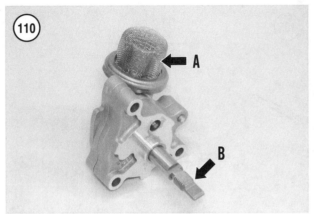

NOTE
Identify the inner and outer rotors so they can be reinstalled facing their original direction.

3. Disassemble the oil pump as shown in **Figure 111**.

4. Inspect the oil pump assembly as described in this section.

5. Lubricate the rotors, rotor bores and shaft with engine oil. Do not lubricate the screw or the screw threads in the housing.

6. Install the outer rotor (5, **Figure 111**) into the housing so it faces in its original direction as identified during disassembly.

7. Install the drive pin (6, **Figure 111**) into the shaft, then install the inner rotor (4) over the shaft and engage its slot with the pin. Make sure the rotor faces in its original direction.

8. Install the inner rotor and shaft by meshing the inner rotor into the outer rotor. Make sure the pin remains in the slot in the inner rotor.

9. Install the cover and the screw finger-tight. Secure the oil pump and tighten the screw to 5 N•m (44 in.-lb.).

10. Turn the oil pump shaft (B, **Figure 110**). If there is any binding or roughness, disassemble the oil pump and inspect the parts as described in this section.

Inspection

Refer to **Table 1**. If any measurement is out of specification, or if any component is damaged, replace the oil pump assembly. Replacement parts are not available.

1. Clean and dry all parts.

2. Inspect the housing cover and housing for cracks and other damage.

3. Check the rotors and bore surfaces for scoring and other damage.

4. Inspect the pump screen for damage.

5. Inspect the shaft and drive pin for cracks or other damage.

6. Install the rotors into the housing and facing in their original direction.

7. Measure the axial clearance between the rotors and pump housing with a straightedge and flat feeler gauge (**Figure 113**).

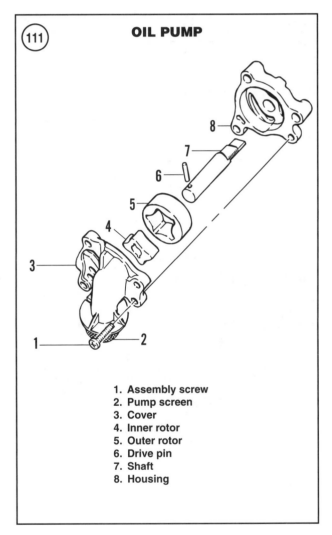

OIL PUMP

1. Assembly screw
2. Pump screen
3. Cover
4. Inner rotor
5. Outer rotor
6. Drive pin
7. Shaft
8. Housing

8. Install the drive pin into the shaft and install the shaft and pin into the inner rotor. Turn the inner rotor until one of its tips aligns directly with a ramp on the outer rotor. Then measure the tip clearance between the inner and outer rotors with a flat feeler gauge (**Figure 114**). Turn the inner rotor and measure the clearance at each tip position.

9. Measure the side clearance between the outer rotor and housing bore with a flat feeler gauge (**Figure 115**). Measure at different locations around the bore and outer rotor.

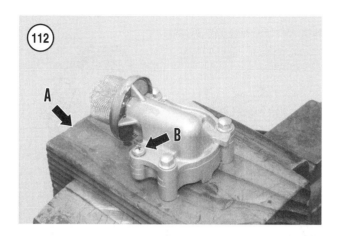

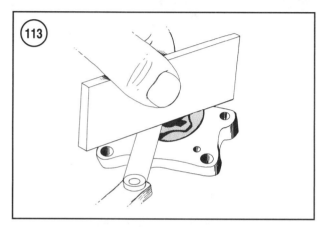

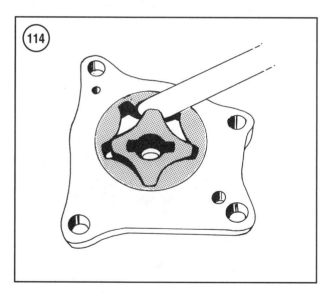

MIDDLE GEAR BEARING HOUSING

This section services the middle drive pinion gear, bearing, middle drive shaft and middle driven gear. Refer to **Figure 116**.

Removal/Installation

The middle gear bearing housing assembly is removed and installed in *Crankcase* in this chapter.

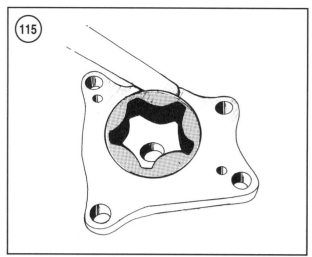

Cleaning/Inspection

NOTE
*Before cleaning the middle gear bearing housing or the middle drive pinion gear, record the number on the gear teeth (**Figure 117**). This number is required when shimming the middle gear assembly. Because this number is painted on, it may be completely removed when cleaning. If the number is not visible or is removed during cleaning, consult a dealership. The bearing housing shim number is permanently scribed into the housing.*

1. Clean and dry the housing assembly. Relubricate the bearing with engine oil.
2. Inspect the middle gear bearing housing assembly (**Figure 118**) for cracks and other damage.
3. Check the gear teeth on both gears for damage and pitting.
4. Check for loose bearing retainer screws. These screws are secured with a threadlocking compound .
5. Inspect the bearing by rotating the gears. The shaft should turn smoothly with no axial or radial play. If the shaft turns roughly, replace the bearing as described in this section.

Disassembly/Assembly

Refer to **Figure 116**.
1. Lock the middle drive shaft in a vise with soft jaws.
2. Grind the flattened portion of the locknut to weaken it. Do not grind through the nut.
3. Loosen and remove the nut (A, **Figure 118**). Discard the nut.
4. Remove the middle drive pinion gear (B, **Figure 118**) and the shims.

NOTE
Do not press the gear off the drive shaft. These parts are assembled and purchased as a set.

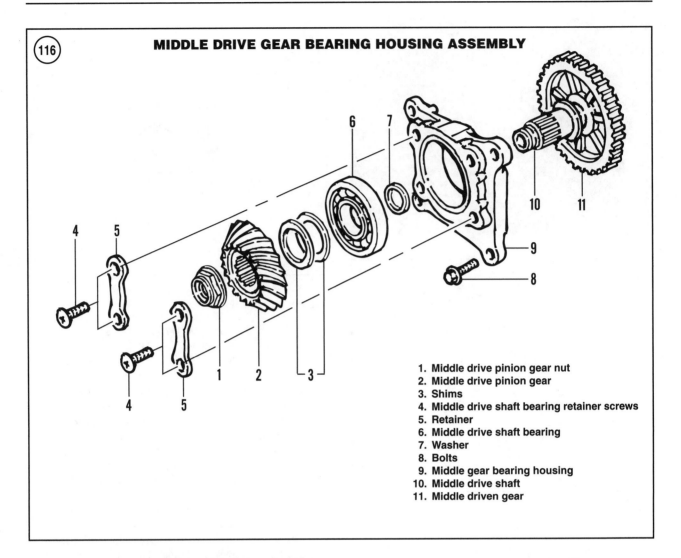

MIDDLE DRIVE GEAR BEARING HOUSING ASSEMBLY

1. Middle drive pinion gear nut
2. Middle drive pinion gear
3. Shims
4. Middle drive shaft bearing retainer screws
5. Retainer
6. Middle drive shaft bearing
7. Washer
8. Bolts
9. Middle gear bearing housing
10. Middle drive shaft
11. Middle driven gear

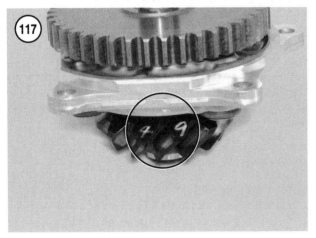

5. Remove the middle drive shaft and driven gear assembly. Replace the shaft and gear as an assembly if either part is damaged.

6. To replace the bearing, perform the following:

   a. Remove the screws (C, **Figure 118**) and both bearing retainers (D). Discard the screws.

   b. Support the housing in a press bed and press out the bearing. Refer to *Service Methods* in Chapter One.

c. Remove the washer. Replace the washer if damaged.

d. Clean and dry the housing and inspect the bearing bore for cracks and other damage.

e. Install the washer and press in the new bearing.

f. Install the bearing retainers. Apply a medium-strength onto the screw threads and tighten to 29 N•m (21 ft.-lb.).

7. Lubricate the bearing with engine oil.

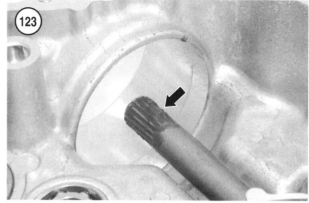

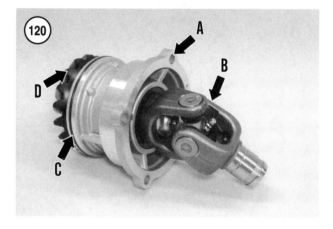

8. Install the middle drive shaft and gear assembly.
9. Install the shims and the middle drive pinion gear.
10. Lock the middle drive shaft in a vise with soft jaws.
11. Install a new middle drive pinion gear nut (A, **Figure 118**) and tighten to 190 N•m (140 ft.-lb.).
12. Perform the *Middle Gear Assembly Shim and Lash Adjustment* in this chapter.
13. Stake a portion of the nut into the notch in the shaft (**Figure 119**).

MIDDLE DRIVEN PINION GEAR BEARING HOUSING

This section services the middle driven pinion gear and bearings installed in the bearing housing (A, **Figure 120**). Service the universal joint (B, **Figure 20**) as described in this chapter.

Removal/Installation

1A. If the middle driven pinion gear bearing housing will be disassembled, remove the universal joint as described in *Universal Joint* in this chapter.
1B. If the middle driven pinion gear bearing housing will not be disassembled, do not remove the universal joint from the bearing housing.

NOTE
*The housing can be difficult to slide out of the crankcase because of the large O-ring (C, **Figure 120**) installed around its shoulder. If necessary, tap and turn the housing to remove it.*

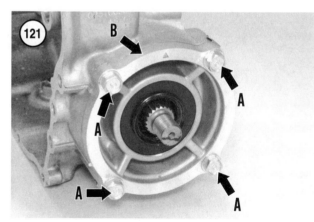

2. Remove the bolts (A, **Figure 121**) securing the middle driven pinion bearing housing to the left crankcase. After removing the bolts, remove the shims (**Figure 122**) installed between the housing and crankcase. Then remove the housing (B, **Figure 121**).
3. Clean and inspect the housing as described in this section.
4. Lubricate the middle driven shaft splines (**Figure 123**) with molybdenum disulfide oil.
5. Lubricate a new O-ring with lithium grease and install it into the housing groove (C, **Figure 120**).

6. Note the number on each shim. If two different thickness shims are used, align them with each other as shown in **Figure 124**. Then align the shim sets as shown in **Figure 125**.

7. Install the bearing housing with its triangle mark (A, **Figure 126**) facing up and by engaging the splines on the middle driven shaft with the splines in the middle driven pinion gear. Install the housing squarely while turning it so that the edge of the crankcase does not cut the housing O-ring. Then continue to turn and push the housing into the crankcase until it almost contacts the crankcase. Install the shim sets so that the tabs on the shims are positioned at the two bolt hole positions identified in B, **Figure 126**. Then push the housing all the way into the crankcase.

8. Hold the shims in place by hand and install the mounting bolts, making sure they fully engage the slots in the shims. Then tighten the mounting bolts to 25 N•m (18 ft.-lb.) in a crossing pattern. Check again that the shims are fully seated between the housing and crankcase.

9. If removed, install the universal joint assembly as described in this chapter.

Cleaning/Inspection

> *NOTE*
> *Before cleaning the middle driven pinion gear bearing housing and gear (*Figure 127*), record the individual number sets on the housing and gear teeth. These numbers are required when shimming the middle gear assembly. Because these number sets are painted on, they may be completely removed when cleaning. If the numbers are not visible or are removed during cleaning, consult a dealership.*

1. Clean and dry the housing assembly. Relubricate the bearing with engine oil.

2. Inspect the middle gear bearing housing assembly (A, **Figure 120**) for cracks and other damage. Check the O-ring groove for damage.

3. Check the gear teeth (D, **Figure 120**) on for damage and pitting.

4. Inspect the bearings by rotating the gear. The shaft should turn smoothly with no axial or radial play. If the shaft turns roughly, replace the bearings as follows.

Disassembly/Reassembly

Refer to **Figure 127**.

Tools

1. The Yamaha middle gear bearing retainer wrench (YM-04128 [**Figure 128**]) is required to removal and install the bearing retainer (4, **Figure 127**).

2. A blind bearing removal tool is required to remove the front and rear bearings (3 and 5, **Figure 127**).

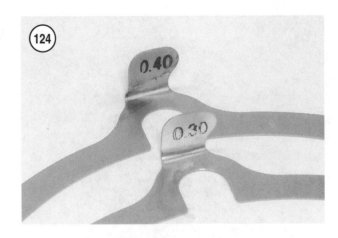

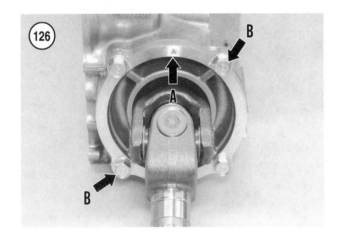

3. A press is required to remove and install the middle driven pinion gear.

Procedure

1. Remove the seal (8, **Figure 127**) with a seal removal tool.

2. Place the housing in a press with the gear's threaded end facing up. A, **Figure 129** shows a bearing splitter used to support the housing.

3. Place a driver (B, **Figure 129**) over middle driven pinion gear so that it rests on the gear's shoulder and not the threads.

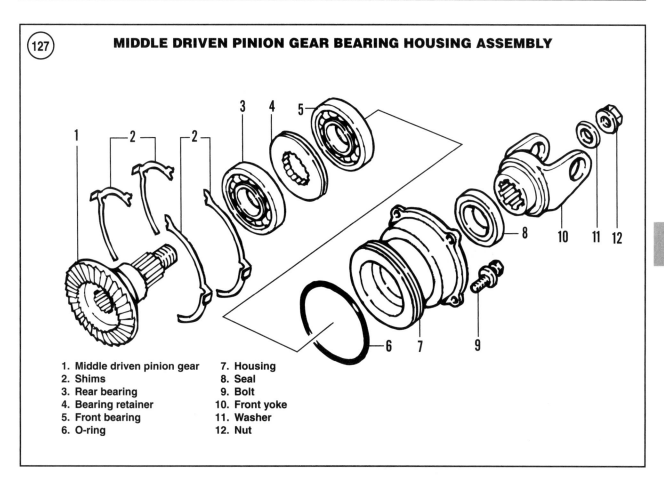

MIDDLE DRIVEN PINION GEAR BEARING HOUSING ASSEMBLY

1. Middle driven pinion gear
2. Shims
3. Rear bearing
4. Bearing retainer
5. Front bearing
6. O-ring
7. Housing
8. Seal
9. Bolt
10. Front yoke
11. Washer
12. Nut

5

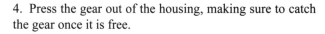

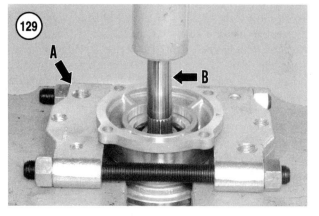

4. Press the gear out of the housing, making sure to catch the gear once it is free.

NOTE
The front and rear bearings are different. Make sure to note which side of each bearing faces out.

5. Remove the rear bearing (3, **Figure 127**) as follows:
   a. Bolt the housing onto a wooden block (A, **Figure 130**) or metal plate, then secure the block or plate in a vise.
   b. Mount a collet onto a blind bearing puller (B, **Figure 130**). Insert the collet through the bearing and tighten

it to lock against the backside of the bearing. Operate the puller and remove the bearing. Discard the bearing.

NOTE
The bearing retainer uses left-hand threads.

NOTE
The bearing retainer is tightened to a high torque specification. Make sure the housing is held securely when loosening and tightening the retainer.

6. Using the middle gear bearing retainer wrench (**Figure 128**) turn the bearing retainer (4, **Figure 127**) clockwise and remove it from the housing.

7. Repeat Step 5 to remove the front bearing

8. Clean and inspect the housing. Remove all threadlocking compound residue from the housing and bearing retainer threads.

9. Inspect the bearing bores for scoring and other damage.

10. Inspect the bearing retainer for damage.

11. Inspect the gear for the following:
   a. Worn or chipped teeth (A, **Figure 131**). If the gear teeth are damaged, inspect the mating gear teeth for damage.
   b. Twisted or damaged splines (B, **Figure 131**). If these splines are damaged, inspect the splines on the middle driven shaft for damage.
   c. Cracked, scored or overheated bearing surfaces (A, **Figure 132**).
   d. Twisted or damaged splines (B, **Figure 132**). If these splines are damaged, check the splines in the universal joint for damage.
   e. Damaged threads (C, **Figure 132**).

12. Support the housing in press and press in the front bearing until it bottoms.

13. Support the housing on the wooden block or metal plate used during disassembly.

14. Apply a medium-strength threadlocking compound onto the bearing retainer threads. Install the bearing retainer by turning it counterclockwise and tighten to 130 N•m (96 ft.-lb.).

15. Press the rear bearing into the housing until it bottoms

16. Lubricate the lips of a new seal with grease and install the seal so that the outer edge of the seal is 1.0-1.5 mm (0.039-0.0-59 in.) below the seal bore edge (**Figure 133**).

17. Support the housing in a press and press the middle driven pinion gear into the housing until it bottoms against the outer bearing. Turn the gear to make sure it turns freely.

18. Perform the *Middle Gear Assembly Shim and Lash Adjustment* in this chapter.

MIDDLE DRIVEN SHAFT

This section services the coupling gear, bearing and middle driven shaft (**Figure 134**) installed in the left crankcase. Before starting work, read this entire section. Obtain the special tools necessary or appropriate substitutes. A threadlocking compound is used on the coupling gear nut and the bearing retainer and both fasteners can be difficult to loosen and tighten.

Tools

The following tools are required to remove and install the middle driven shaft. The tools are shown in the text.

1. The Yamaha gear holder (part No. YM-01229) is required to hold the coupling gear when loosening and tightening the coupling gear nut.

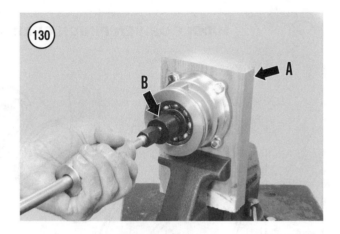

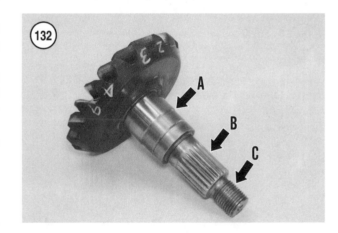

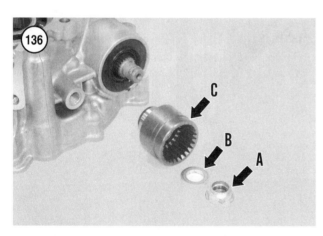

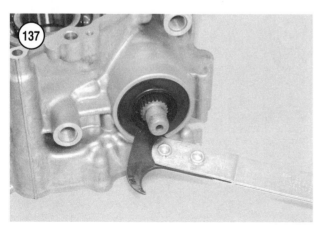

2. The Yamaha ring nut wrench (part No. YM-38404) is required to loosen and tighten the bearing retainer.

Removal/Inspection/Installation

> *CAUTION*
> *When removing the middle driven shaft assembly, handle the crankcase carefully to avoid damaging its gasket surfaces. Place the crankcase on a rubber mat when supporting it.*

> *NOTE*
> *The coupling gear nut is tightened to a high torque specification. Loosen the nut with an impact wrench, if available.*

1. Hold the coupling gear with the gear holder (**Figure 135**) and loosen the nut. Then remove the nut (A, **Figure 136**), washer (B) and coupling gear (C).

2. Remove the seal with a seal removal tool (**Figure 137**).

> *NOTE*
> *The bearing retainer uses left-hand threads.*

3. Using the ring nut wrench (A, **Figure 138**), turn the bearing retainer (B, **Figure 138**) *clockwise* and remove it from the crankcase.

4. Tap the middle driven shaft with a wooden block and hammer and remove it and its bearing (**Figure 139**) from the crankcase.

5. Remove all threadlocking compound residue from the shaft, nut and case threads. Then clean the shaft, bearing and bearing retainer in solvent.

6. Inspect the shaft (A, **Figure 140**) for damaged threads and splines.

7. Hold the shaft and turn the bearing (B, **Figure 140**). The bearing should turn smoothly with no axial or radial play. If the bearing turns roughly, replace the shaft and bearing.

> *NOTE*
> *The shaft and bearing are purchased as an assembly. The bearing is not available separately.*

8. Before installing the shaft, check that the bearing is bottomed against the shaft shoulder. If not, perform the following:

   a. Place a bearing driver (A, **Figure 141**) against the bearing (B) so that it rests on the bearing's inner race. Refer to *Service Methods* in Chapter One. Support the shaft in a press and press on the bearing until it bottoms against the shaft's shoulder.

   b. Hold the shaft and turn the bearing to make sure it was not damaged.

9. Install the shaft and bearing as follows:

   a. Install the shaft and bearing into the crankcase, then support the crankcase in a press so the bearing is facing up.

b. Center the bearing in its bore. Then place a bearing driver against the bearing so it rests on the bearing's outer race (**Figure 142**). Refer to *Service Methods* in Chapter One.

c. Press in the bearing until it bottoms.

d. Turn the shaft to make sure the bearing was not damaged during installation.

10. Apply a medium-strength threadlocking compound onto the bearing retainer threads, then install the bearing retainer (B, **Figure 138**) by turning it *counterclockwise* until it contacts the bearing. Tighten the bearing retainer to 80 N•m (59 ft.-lb.) using the ring nut wrench (A, **Figure 138**).

11. Install a new seal as follows:

a. Lubricate the lips of a new seal with grease.

b. Carefully position the seal and tap it into the crankcase with its flat side facing out. Install the seal until its outer edge is 1.0-1.5 mm (0.039-0.0-59 in.) below the seal bore edge (**Figure 143**).

12. Lubricate the coupling gear (C, **Figure 136**) shoulder with grease and install it through the seal and onto shaft splines. Turn the coupling gear when installing it through the seal to avoid damaging the seal's lip and dislodging the garter spring.

13. Install the washer and seat it against the coupling gear.

14. Apply a medium-strength threadlocking compound onto the coupling gear nut. Thread the nut onto the shaft finger-tight.

NOTE
The coupling gear nut is tightened to a high torque specification, which makes it difficult to hold the gear holder and crankcase when tightening the nut. Use the setup in Step 15 to support the crankcase and gear holder when tightening the nut.

15. Place the crankcase (A, **Figure 144**) on a rubber mat that is on the floor. Then place a thick pad (B, **Figure 144**) across the top of the crankcase. Install the gear holder into the coupling gear and position its handle so that it rests against the floor as shown in C, **Figure 144**. Kneel down so that a knee is touching the thick pad. Then use your body weight to hold the crankcase and the gear holder in place and tighten the nut to 190 N•m (140 ft.-lb.).

16. Turn the shaft to make sure there is no binding or roughness.

MIDDLE GEAR ASSEMBLY SHIM AND LASH ADJUSTMENT

When the crankcase, middle drive pinion gear, middle driven pinion gear or either bearing housing are replaced, the gear assembly must be properly shimmed to create the correct clearance between the parts. Also check clearance whenever wear is evident on original parts that are being reused.

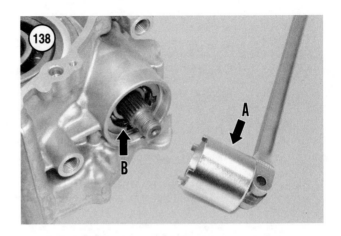

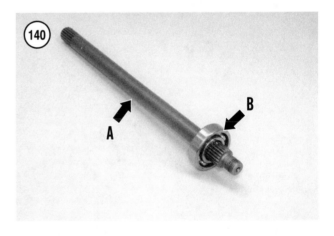

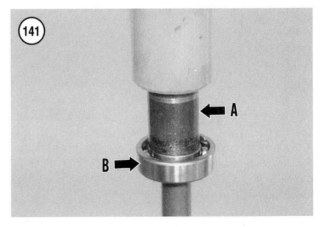

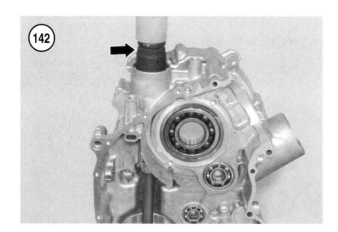

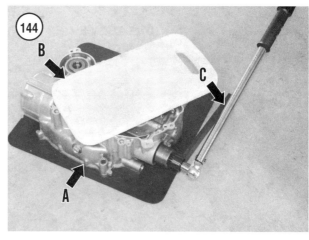

b. Round 3-7 to 5.
c. Round 8 and 9 to 10.
9. After rounding the result, the correct shim size is 1.40 mm thick. Drive pinion shims are available in 0.50, 0.55, 0.60, 0.70, 0.80, 0.90 and 1.00 mm thicknesses. In the example, 0.50 and 0.90 thickness shims are required.
10. Install the correct thickness shims (3, **Figure 145**) on the middle drive pinion gear shaft.
11. Perform the *Middle Gear Lash Measurement* in this section.

Middle Driven Pinion Gear Shim Selection

1. Determine the middle driven pinion gear shim size with the formula: $B = f - g + h - i - j - 0.02$.
2. Note the number (shown as a decimal) on the driven gear bearing housing (f, **Figure 150**). In the example, the number is -0.09. Positive numbers are added to 77.5. Negative numbers are subtracted from 77.5. The result is the *f* variable of the shim formula, or 77.41.

NOTE
*Replacing parts in the middle driven pinion gear assembly may change the overall length of the assembly from its standard length of 77.5 mm. If replacing parts, make sure to measure the length of the middle driven pinion gear assembly as shown in **Figure 151**; measure from the bearing housing's inner shoulder to the gear's flat surface next to its bore (**Figure 152**). Do not measure from the top of the gear teeth. Replace the overall length measurement for the **f** variable of the shim formula if it differs from 77.5 mm.*

3. Note the number (shown as a decimal) on the inside of the middle driven pinion gear (g, **Figure 152**). In the example, the number is .07. Positive numbers are added to 49.0. Negative numbers are subtracted from 49.0. The result is the *g* variable of the shim formula, or 49.07.
4. Note the first number (shown as a decimal) on the outside of the middle driven pinion gear (h, **Figure 153**). In the example, the number is -.02. Positive numbers are add-

Shim thicknesses are determined by using the numbers marked on the bearing housings, crankcase and on the gears themselves, and then applying the numbers into formulas.
Refer to **Figure 145** and **Figure 146** to identify the bearing housings, shims and gears.

Middle Drive Pinion Gear Shim Selection

1. Determine the middle drive pinion gear shim size with the formula: $A = e + d + a - c - b - k$.
2. Note the number (shown as a decimal) on the drive gear bearing housing (a, **Figure 147**). In the example, the number is + 0.02. Positive numbers are added to 0.9. Negative numbers are subtracted from 0.9. The result is the *a* variable of the shim formula.
3. The number 17.0 is the *b* variable of the shim formula.
4. The number 55.0 is the *c* variable of the shim formula.
5. Note the middle number (shown as decimal) on the left crankcase (d, **Figure 148**). In the example, the number is 65.00. This is the *d* variable of the shim formula.
6. Note the middle number (shown as a decimal) on the right crankcase (e, **Figure 149**). In the example, the number is 9.0. This is the *e* variable of the shim formula.
7. The number 1.5 is the *k* variable of the shim formula.
8. The example equation is now: $A = 9.0 + 65.00 + 0.92 - 55.0 - 17.0 - 1.5$. The result is $A = 1.42$. Round the numeral in the hundredths position as follows:
   a. Round 0-2 to 0.

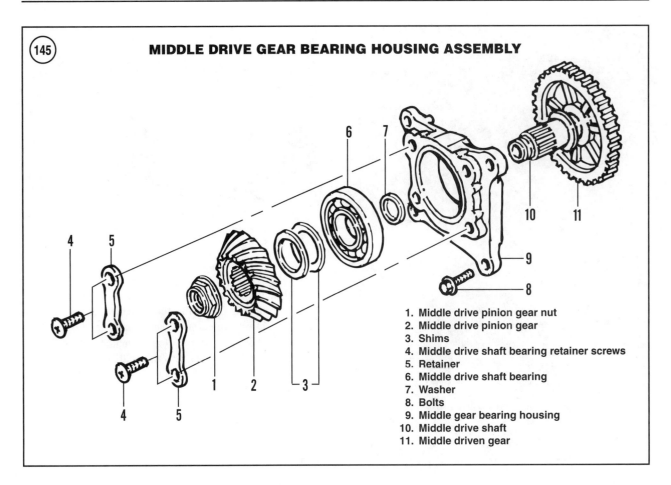

145 **MIDDLE DRIVE GEAR BEARING HOUSING ASSEMBLY**

1. Middle drive pinion gear nut
2. Middle drive pinion gear
3. Shims
4. Middle drive shaft bearing retainer screws
5. Retainer
6. Middle drive shaft bearing
7. Washer
8. Bolts
9. Middle gear bearing housing
10. Middle drive shaft
11. Middle driven gear

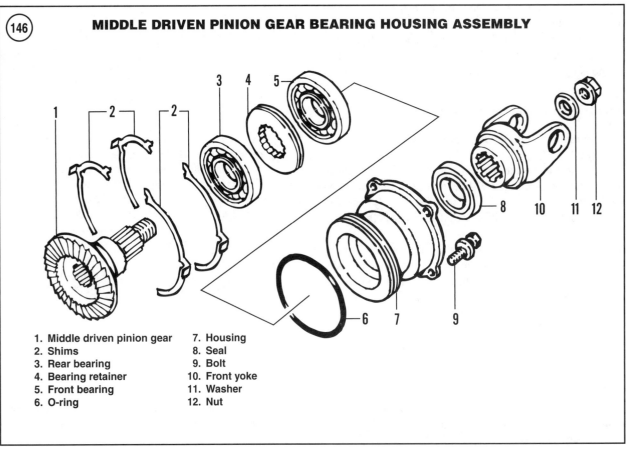

146 **MIDDLE DRIVEN PINION GEAR BEARING HOUSING ASSEMBLY**

1. Middle driven pinion gear
2. Shims
3. Rear bearing
4. Bearing retainer
5. Front bearing
6. O-ring
7. Housing
8. Seal
9. Bolt
10. Front yoke
11. Washer
12. Nut

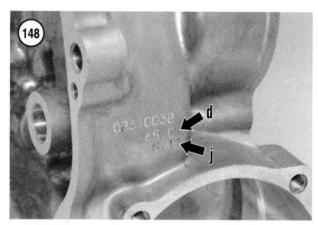

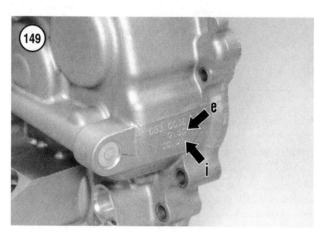

ed to 80.5. Negative numbers are subtracted from 80.5. The result is the *h* variable of the shim formula, or 80.48.

5. Note the lower number on the right crankcase (i, **Figure 149**). In the example, the number is 100.01. This is the *i* variable of the shim formula.

6. Note the lower number on the left crankcase (j, **Figure 148**). In the example, the number is 8.11. This is the *j* variable of the shim formula.

7. The example equation is now: B = 77.41 − 49.07 + 80.48 − 100.01 − 8.11 − 0.02. The result is: B = 0.68. Round the numeral in the hundredths position as follows:

    a. Round 0-2 to 0.

    b. Round 3-7 to 5.

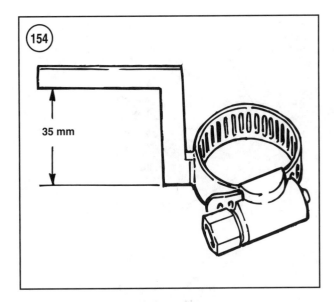

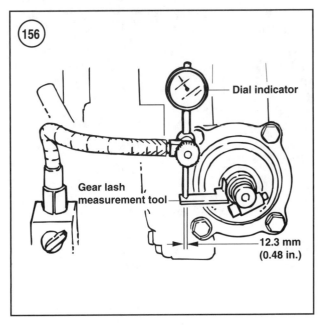

c. Round 8 and 9 to 10.

8. After rounding the result, the correct shim size is 0.70 mm thick. Driven pinion shims are available in 0.10, 0.15, 0.20, 0.30, 0.40, 0.50 and 0.60 mm thicknesses. In the example, 0.30 and 0.40 thickness shims are required.

9. Install the correct thickness shims (2, **Figure 146**) when assembling the middle driven pinion gear bearing housing.

10. Perform the *Middle Gear Lash Measurement* in this section.

Middle Gear Lash Measurement

After the middle gear assemblies are installed in both crankcase housings, check middle gear lash to verify the shim selection. Gear lash is measured with a gear lash measurement tool (Yamaha part No. YM-01467 [**Figure 154**]) or its equivalent, and a dial indicator.

1. With the middle driven pinion gear bearing housing installed in the left crankcase and the middle drive gear bearing housing installed in the right crankcase, temporarily assembly the two crankcase halves. Install the dowel pins and several bolts to hold the crankcase halves together.

2. In the right crankcase, lock the middle driven gear into position. Wrap the tip of a screwdriver with a shop cloth and insert the tool through the speed sensor hole on the outside of the crankcase (**Figure 155**). Work the tool into the gear so it cannot move when measuring lash.

3. Clamp the gear lash measurement tool onto the middle driven pinion gear shaft (**Figure 156**). Position the tool so the arm can contact the dial indicator.

4. Position a dial indicator in contact with the measurement tool and 12.3 mm (0.48 in.) from the end of the tool's arm (**Figure 156**). Make sure the dial indicator is stable and set to read gear lash in both directions. Zero the gauge on the dial indicator.

5. Gently rotate the middle driven shaft (**Figure 134**) clockwise until lash between the parts is eliminated. Note the dial indicator reading.

6. Gently rotate the middle driven shaft (**Figure 134**) in the opposite direction until lash between the parts is eliminated. Note the dial indicator reading.

7. Add the indicator readings in Step 5 and 6 to determine the differential gear lash and record the number.

8. Remove the screwdriver and rotate the middle driven shaft 90°. Lock the middle driven gear into place, and repeat the check. Measure the gear lash at every 90° until the shaft has rotated one full turn (four total measurements).

9. Determine the average reading of the four checks. Middle gear lash should be 0.10-0.30 mm (0.0040-0.012 in.). If necessary, adjust the shim size for either or both the middle drive pinion gear (2, **Figure 145**) and the middle driven pinion gear (1, **Figure 146**).

10. After installation of the replacement shim(s), repeat the lash adjustment procedure to verify the middle gear lash is within specification.

UNIVERSAL JOINT

The universal joint assembly installed on the middle driven pinion gear shaft consists of a front yoke, rear yoke,

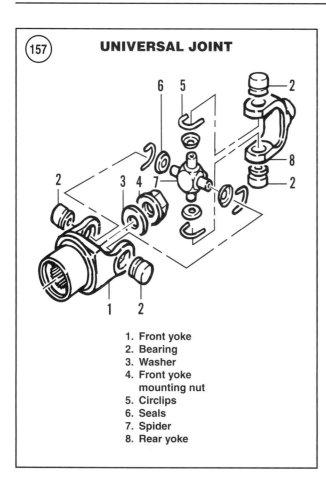

UNIVERSAL JOINT

1. Front yoke
2. Bearing
3. Washer
4. Front yoke
   mounting nut
5. Circlips
6. Seals
7. Spider
8. Rear yoke

spider, four bearings, four circlips and four seals (**Figure 157**). To remove the universal joint, it is partially disassembled by removing two opposing circlips and then pressing the two opposing bearings out of the front yoke. This will free the spider so the rear yoke/spider assembly can be removed from the front yoke. The front yoke is secured to the pinion gear shaft and can then be removed.

> *NOTE*
> *The seals (6, **Figure 157**) and small O-rings installed on each bearing (2) are not available separately. If reusing these parts, handle them carefully during all procedures.*

Tools

1. One of the following tools (or equivalent) is required to hold the front yoke (1, **Figure 157**) when loosening and tightening the nut (4):
   a. The Yamaha universal joint holder (part No. YM-04062). This tool fits around the front yoke and uses two pins to hold the yoke in place.
   b. The Yamaha joint holder (part No.YM-04062-3 [A, **Figure 158**]). This tool has been modified to hold the front yoke with a bolt (B, **Figure 158**) and machined collar (C) along with the pin (D) that is part of the original tool. Fabricate the collar so that it fits between the holder and into one side of the yoke. Then thread the inside of the collar to accept the bolt. The bolt should be long enough to thread all the way through the collar. This tool is shown in the following sections.

2. A hydraulic press and suitable adapters are required to remove and install the universal joint bearings.

Removal

1. Remove the engine as described in this chapter.

> *NOTE*
> *The universal joint can be removed with the middle driven pinion gear bearing housing either installed on or removed from the engine.*

> *WARNING*
> *Because the circlips (A, **Figure 159**) may fly off when removed, wear goggles or other eye protection.*

> *NOTE*
> *Note the direction the grease nipple (A, **Figure 160**) faces so that the spider can be installed with the nipple facing in the same direction.*

2. Using a metal rod and hammer, remove a circlip (**Figure 159**) by driving it off one of the bearings. Refer to B, **Figure 160**.

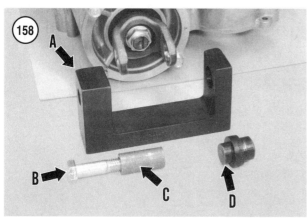

3. Repeat Step 2 to remove the circlip from the opposing bearing.

4. Support the housing in a press. Then support the front yoke with a piece of pipe (A, **Figure 161**) and with an inside diameter large enough to accept the bearing.

5. Position a driver with an outside diameter that is small enough to pass through the yoke between the press ram and bearing (B, **Figure 161**).

> *CAUTION*
> *Before operating the press, check that the two circlips for the bearings being removed were previously removed.*

> *NOTE*
> *In Step 6, press the upper bearing just far enough to remove the lower bearing from the yoke. If the upper bearing is pressed too far, it will fall through to the inside of the yoke. Because the upper bearing must be pressed out in the same manner as the lower bearing, having to realign the bearing with the yoke bore and spider can be difficult if the parts are damaged or corroded.*

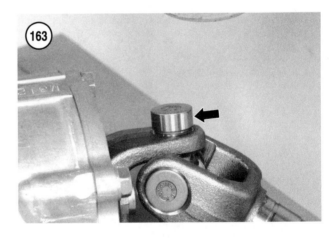

6. Press the upper bearing (**Figure 162**) into the yoke to press the lower bearing out of the yoke and into the pipe. Refer to **Figure 163**.

7. Reposition the universal joint so that the upper bearing in Step 6 is now at the bottom. Center the spider in the yoke and press against the spider (**Figure 164**) to press the bearing into the pipe. Remove the bearing (A, **Figure 165**) and the rear yoke assembly (B).

8. Remove the two seals (A, **Figure 166**).

9. If necessary, repeat Steps 2-8 to remove the remaining two bearings, spider and seals (B, **Figure 166**).

10. Remove the front yoke (1, **Figure 157**) as follows:
   a. If using joint holder part No. 04062, secure it across the front yoke with the two pins (**Figure 167**).
   b. If using joint holder part No. 04062-3 (A, **Figure 168**), secure it across the front yoke with the pin (B), machined collar (C) and bolt (D).
   c. Lock the joint holder in a vise while using a thick blanket to protect the housing from damage. Then loosen the front yoke mounting nut (E, **Figure 168**).

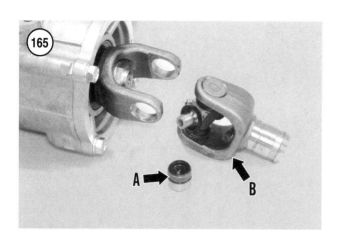

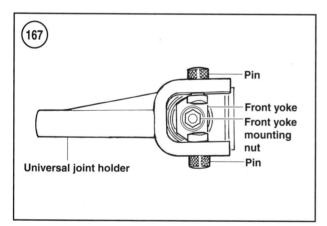

Pin
Front yoke
Front yoke
mounting
nut
Pin
Universal joint holder

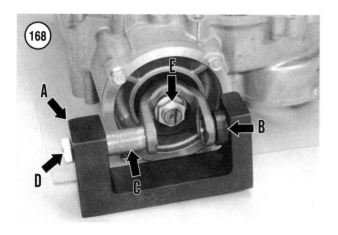

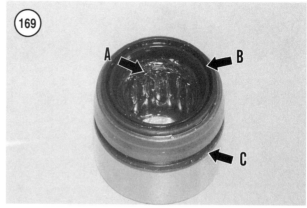

d. Remove the joint holder and housing from the vise. Then remove the joint holder, nut, washer and front yoke.

Inspection

1. Clean and dry all parts. Discard the circlips.
2. Inspect the yoke and spider bearing surfaces for cracks, scoring and other damage. Remove burrs with a fine-cut file.
3. Inspect the yoke housing for cracks and other damage.
4. Inspect the bearing housing and needles (A, **Figure 169**) for corrosion and other damage. If the bearing is contaminated, the seal (B, **Figure 169**) at the top of the bearing is probably distorted or damaged. Then inspect the O-ring (C, **Figure 159**) for damage. Discard the bearing if these parts are damaged or the bearing is corroded. Repeat for each bearing.
5. Remove all threadlocking compound residue from the pinion shaft and front yoke mounting nut threads.

Installation

1. Install a new housing seal (A, **Figure 170**) as described in *Crankcase Seals and Bearings* in this chapter. Lubricate the seal lips with lithium grease.
2. Install the front yoke (B, **Figure 170**) by aligning its splines with the shaft splines. Then turn the yoke to make sure the seal lips are seating squarely against the yoke and are not distorted.
3. Install the washer (C, **Figure 170**) and seat it against the front yoke. Then apply a medium-strength threadlocking compound onto the front yoke mounting nut (D, **Figure 170**) and install the nut finger-tight.
4. Secure the front yoke with the same tool used during removal and tighten the front yoke mounting nut (E, **Figure 168**) to 150 N•m (111 ft.-lb.). Remove the joint holder and housing from the vise. Turn the yoke to make sure the shaft turns smoothly.
5. If reusing the bearings, lubricate the needles with lithium grease.
6. Before installing the bearings slide each bearing over one of the spider arms to make sure the needles are posi-

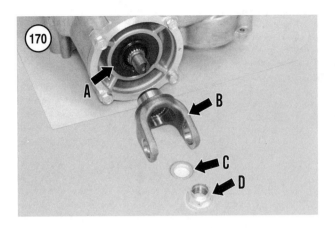

tioned against the inside of the bearing. If not, reposition the needles and recheck. The bearings should slide smoothly over the spider arm.

NOTE
*Steps 7-11 can be used to install both sets of bearings when assembling the universal joint assembly. The following photographs show assembly with the spider already installed in the rear yoke. However, if the spider was removed from the rear yoke, assemble these parts first, making sure to align the spider so the grease fitting (**Figure 171**) is accessible when the universal joint is installed on the engine.*

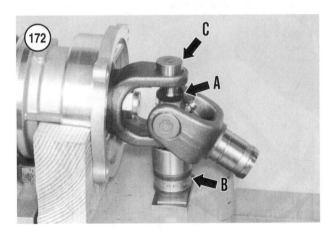

7. Install a cupped seal on each opposing spider arm with the cup side facing away from the spider (A, **Figure 166**).
8. Support the assembly in a press. Slip the spider (A, **Figure 172**) into the yoke while supporting the bottom of the yoke with a piece of pipe (B). Center the bearing (C, **Figure 172**) into the yoke bore and over the spider arm.

WARNING
Because the circlips may fly off when being installed, wear goggles or other eye protection.

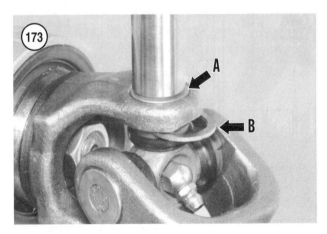

CAUTION
Make sure the bearing is aligned squarely with the yoke bore. Otherwise, the bearing may enter the bore at an angle and damage the yoke. If a bearing starts moving smoothly and then tightens as it is being installed, it is probably entering the yoke at an angle. When installing a bearing set, the second or opposing bearing will be harder to align squarely with the yoke.

NOTE
Install new circlips in Steps 9 and 10.

9. Using a driver on top of the bearing press the bearing into the yoke until the top of the bearing is almost flush with the top of the yoke (A, **Figure 173**). Then check the circlip fit (B, **Figure 173**) between the bearing shoulder and the side of the yoke. If there is not enough clearance, continue to press the bearing into the yoke until the circlip

can be tapped in place until it bottoms completely against the bearing (**Figure 174**).

10. Turn the universal joint over and repeat Steps 8 and 9 to install the opposing bearing and circlip.

11. After both circlips are installed, pivot the rear yoke up and down and side to side to compare the tension movement in both directions. Tension movement in both directions should be approximately the same. If the rear yoke feels tight in one or both directions, examine the circlips by trying to pry them sideways with a screwdriver (do not try to remove them) at their middle section. If a circlip feels looser than the other, support the yoke in the press with the loose circlip side down and carefully press the upper bearing until it just moves slightly. A feeler gauge can also be used to compare circlip tightness. Repeat until the yoke movement feels the same in both directions.

SHIFTING CHECK

This check uses the gear position and reverse switches to check transmission shifting. An ohmmeter or test light is required. This check should be performed after reassembling the crankcase halves.

> *NOTE*
> *Perform this check while standing at the engine's front end while the engine is mounted on a workbench.*

1. Make sure the following are installed on the engine:
   a. Reverse switch (Chapter Nine).
   b. Gear position switch (Chapter Nine).
   c. Shift shaft and shift lever. Refer to *External Shift Mechanism* in Chapter Seven.

2. Connect the negative ohmmeter lead to ground on the engine (A, **Figure 175**).

3. Connect the positive lead to the gear position switch (B, **Figure 175**) blue terminal. Turn the input shaft (C, **Figure 175**) forward (or clockwise if standing on the left side of the engine) and turn the shift lever bolt with a socket (D) until the shift shaft and shift index marks align as shown in **Figure 176**. This shifts the transmission into neutral and the ohmmeter should read continuity. The universal joint (E, **Figure 175**) at the front of the engine should not turn when the input shaft is turned.

4. Connect the positive ohmmeter lead to the gear position switch gray terminal. Turn the input shaft forward and turn the shift lever bolt clockwise until the ohmmeter reads continuity. This indicates the transmission is in high gear and the universal joint at the front of the engine should turn clockwise. **Figure 177** shows the shift lever and shift shaft in high gear.

5. Connect the positive ohmmeter lead to the gear position switch white terminal. Turn the input shaft forward and turn the shift lever bolt clockwise until the ohmmeter reads continuity. This indicates the transmission is in low gear and the universal joint at the front of the engine should turn clockwise. **Figure 178** shows the shift lever and shift shaft in low gear.

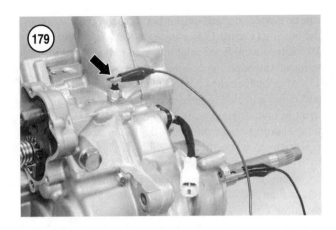

6. Connect the positive ohmmeter lead to the reverse switch (**Figure 179**) mounted on top of the engine. Turn the input shaft forward and turn the shift lever bolt counterclockwise until the ohmmeter reads infinity. This indicates the transmission is in reverse and the universal joint at the front of the engine should turn counterclockwise. **Figure 180** shows the shift lever and shaft in reverse.

Table 1 ENGINE LOWER END SPECIFICATIONS

	New mm (in.)	Service limit mm (in.)
Connecting rod		
Big end radial clearance	0.010-0.025 (0.0004-0.0010)	–
Side clearance	0.350-0.650 (0.0138-0.0256)	1.0 (0.04)
Small end free play	0.16-0.40 (0.0063-0.0157)	–
Crankshaft		
Runout	–	0.030 (0.0012)
Width	74.95-75.00 (2.951-2.953)	–
Middle gear lash	0.10-0.30 (0.0040-0.012)	–
Oil pump		
Axial clearance	0.03-0.10 (0.0012-0.0039)	0.17 (0.0067)
Side clearance	0.09-0.17 (0.0035-0.0067)	0.24 (0.0094)
Tip clearance	Less than 0.12 (0.0047)	0.20 (0.0079)

Table 2 ENGINE LOWER END TORQUE SPECIFICATIONS

	N•m	in.-lb.	ft.-lb.
Cam chain guide mounting bolt*	10	88	–
Cam chain stopper mounting bolt*	10	88	–
Crankcase mounting bolts*			
6-mm	10	88	–
8-mm	26	–	19
Dipstick tube mounting bolt	10	88	–
Driven gear locknut*	80	–	58
Engine ground cable mounting bolt	10	88	–
Engine mount bolts			
6-mm*	10	88	–
10-mm	42	–	31
Engine mount nuts	42	–	31
Front yoke mounting nut*	150	–	111
Gear position switch	7	62	–
Input shaft bearing retainer mounting bolt*	10	88	–
Middle drive pinion gear nut*	190	–	140
Middle drive shaft bearing retainer screw*	29	–	21
Middle driven pinion gear bearing housing			
mounting bolt	25	–	18
Middle driven pinion gear bearing retainer*	130	–	96
Middle driven shaft bearing retainer*	80	–	59
Middle driven shaft coupling gear mounting nut*	190	–	140
Middle gear bearing housing mounting bolt*	32	–	24
Oil pipe adapter bolt	68	–	50
Oil pump assembly mounting screw	5	44	–
Oil pump driven gear locknut*	22	–	16
Oil pump mounting bolts	10	88	–
Outlet pipe mounting bolt at water pump	10	88	–
Plug bolt	18	–	13
Reverse switch	17	–	12
Shift arm mounting bolt*	14	–	10
Shift drum detent bolt	18	–	13

*Refer to text.

5

CHAPTER SIX

CLUTCH AND SHEAVES

This chapter covers the drive belt air ducts, outer bearing housing, drive belt, primary sheave, secondary sheave, centrifugal clutch and covers. Read *Safety* and *Service Methods* in Chapter One before servicing the vehicle in this chapter.

Tables 1-3 are at the end of this chapter.

DRIVE BELT AIR DUCT ASSEMBLY

Air duct 1 is shown in A, **Figure 1**. Air duct 2 is shown in B, **Figure 1**.

Removal/Installation

Air duct 1

Figure 2 shows air duct 1 assembly.

1. Remove the following as described in Chapter Sixteen:
    a. Seats.
    b. Rear console.
    c. Lift corner panel and left side panel.
    d. Left seat support.
    e. Driver seat rail.
    f. Left support.
2. Loosen the hose clamp (A, **Figure 3**) securing the rear joint to the front air duct 1. Remove the rear air duct 1 housing (B, **Figure 3**).
3. Loosen the hose clamp (A, **Figure 4**) securing the front joint to the drive belt cover. Then remove the two mounting bolts (B, **Figure 4**) and front air duct 1 housing (C).
4. If necessary, loosen the hose clamps securing the front joint and rear joint to the air ducts.
5. Replace the damper plate (5, **Figure 2**) or protector cover (6) if missing or damaged.
6. Installation is the reverse of removal. Note the following:
    a. Align the tab on the front joint between the two raised projections on the front air duct 1 (**Figure 5**).

    b. Align the raised projection on the front air duct 1 with the tab on the rear joint (**Figure 6**).
    c. Tighten the front air duct 1 mounting bolts to 7 N•m (62 in.-lb.).

Air duct 2

1. Remove the center protector (Chapter Sixteen).
2. Loosen the hose clamp securing the front joint to the engine.
3. Remove the two rivets securing the air duct 2 to the frame and remove air duct 2 (**Figure 7**).
4. If necessary, loosen the hose clamps securing the air duct 2 to the front joint.
5. Installation is the reverse of removal. Note the following:
    a. Align the projection on the front joint with the rib on the crankcase.
    b. Align the tab on the front joint between the two raised projections on air duct 2.

DRIVE BELT COVER

Removal/Installation

NOTE
Anytime the drive belt cover is removed, inspect the drive belt as described in this chapter.

1. Remove the following as described in Chapter Sixteen:
    a. Seats.
    b. Rear console.
    c. Lift corner panel and left side panel.
    d. Left seat support.
    e. Driver seat rail.
2. Remove air duct 1 as described in this chapter

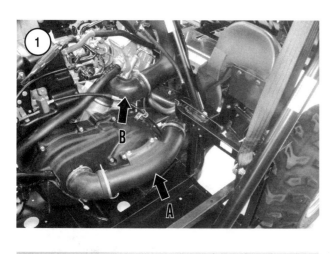

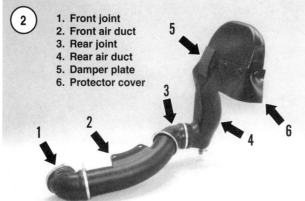

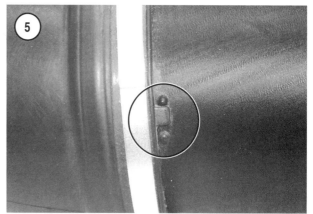

1. Front joint
2. Front air duct
3. Rear joint
4. Rear air duct
5. Damper plate
6. Protector cover

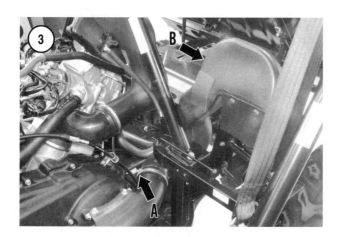

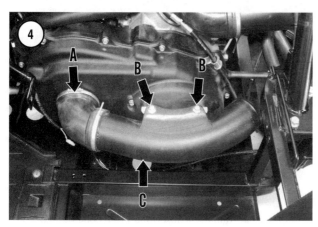

3. Remove the bolts and the drive belt cover (A, **Figure 8**) and its gasket. Note the position of the parking brake cable bracket (B, **Figure 8**).

4. If the air duct 1 mounting bracket (C, **Figure 8**) is removed, tighten the mounting bolts to 10 N•m (88 in.-lb.).

NOTE
The drive belt and sheaves should be dry. If there is oil inside the drive belt cover, check the clutch housing as described in this chapter for an oil leak.

5. Installation is the reverse of removal. Note the following:
    a. Replace the cover gasket if damaged.
    b. Install the gaskets onto the cover before installing the cover.
    c. Tighten the drive belt cover mounting bolts to 10 N•m (88 in.-lb.).

OUTER BEARING HOUSING

The outer bearing housing (**Figure 9**) fits over the primary sheave. A bearing inside the housing supports the outer end of the clutch housing shaft. The clutch housing is located behind the primary sheave.

Removal/Installation

1. Remove the drive belt cover as described in this chapter.

2. Unbolt and remove bearing housing (**Figure 9**). Account for the two dowel pins.

3. Perform the *Inspection/Bearing Replacement* in this section.

4. Installation is the reverse of removal. Note the following:
    a. Install the dowel pins.
    b. Install the two longer mounting bolts at the dowel pin mounting holes.
    c. Tighten the outer bearing housing mounting bolts to 10 N•m (88 in.-lb.).

Inspection/Bearing Replacement

1. Inspect the outer bearing housing for cracks and other damage.

2. Inspect the bearing and seal. If the bearing does not operate smoothly, replace the bearing and seal as follows:
    a. Remove the bolt (A, **Figure 10**) and cover (B).
    b. Remove and discard the seal (**Figure 11**).
    c. Remove the bearing with a blind bearing removal tool and a 10-mm collet (**Figure 12**). Support the outer bearing housing carefully when removing the bearing.
    d. Clean the bore and check for cracks, scoring and other damage. If any damage is noted, replace the outer bearing housing.

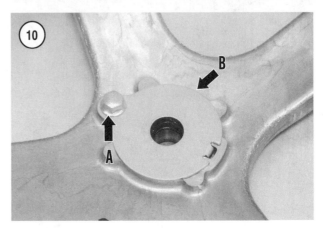

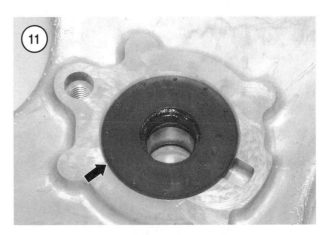

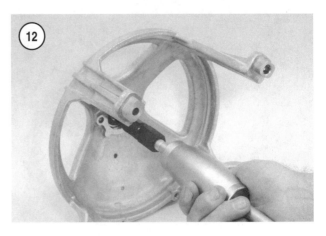

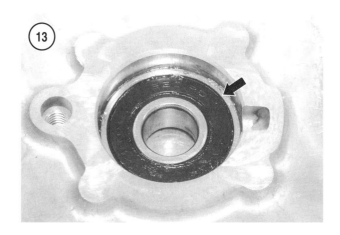

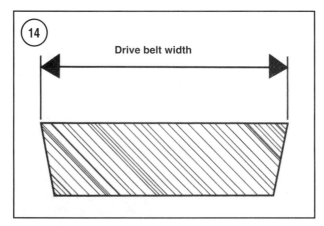

Drive belt width

e. Install the new bearing in a freezer for a minimum of two hours.

f. If the bearing is open on one side, lubricate the bearing rollers with engine oil.

g. Support the outer bearing housing on a wooden block, either in a press or on a workbench.

h. Place the new bearing in the housing with its closed side facing out. Carefully align the bearing with its bore.

i. Refer to *Service Methods* in Chapter One and drive or press the new bearing into the bearing housing until it bottoms (**Figure 13**). Then turn the bearing inner race to make sure it turns smoothly and that the bearing was not damaged during installation.

j. Lubricate the lips of a new oil seal with grease and install the seal with its closed side facing out (**Figure 11**). Install the seal until it is flush with the outer housing bore edge.

k. Install the cover (B, **Figure 10**) by aligning its notch with the groove in the outer bearing housing. Install the bolt (A, **Figure 10**) and tighten to 10 N•m (88 in.-lb.).

DRIVE BELT

Anytime the drive belt cover is removed, inspect the condition of the drive belt.

Inspection

1. Remove the drive belt cover as described in this chapter

2. Remove the outer bearing housing as described in this chapter

3. Measure the width of the belt at its widest point (**Figure 14**). Replace the belt if the width is less than the specified service limit (**Table 1**).

4. Inspect the drive belt (**Figure 15**) for wear, cracks, contamination (grease and oil) and damaged teeth. The belt should be dry and in good condition.

5. If necessary, replace the drive belt as described in this section.

6. Reverse Step 1 and Step 2.

Removal/Installation

1. Remove the drive belt cover as described in this chapter

2. Remove the outer bearing housing as described in this chapter

3. Locate the directional arrow on the drive belt. If the arrow is not visible, mark the top of the drive belt with an arrow pointing rearward.

NOTE
With the fan installed, only one bolt can be used in Step 4.

4. Thread a 6—1.0 × 80-mm bolt (Yamaha part No. 90101-06018) into the sheave hub (**Figure 16**). Tighten the bolt until the sheave is fully spread and the drive belt is loose.

5. Rotate the drive belt (**Figure 17**) forard and over the secondary sheave (A, **Figure 18**).

6. Remove the drive belt from the primary sheave (B, **Figure 18**).

> *NOTE*
> *If the drive belt is difficult to remove, a weight may have fallen out of place in the primary sheave. This will prevent the primary sheaves from separating all the way and prevent the belt from loosening enough to remove it.*

7. Clean the secondary and primary sheave surfaces with electrical contact cleaner or Isopropyl alcohol and allow to dry.

8. Locate the arrow on the drive belt (**Figure 19**). Then install the drive belt over the primary sheave, then the secondary sheave with its arrow pointing rearward, when the arrow is at the top of the sheaves.

9. Remove the bolt (**Figure 16**) from the secondary sheave. When doing so the secondary sheave will tighten. While loosening the bolt, it is helpful to rotate the secondary sheave to help the belt to rise to the top of the sheave.

10. Reverse Step 1 and Step 2.

PRIMARY AND SECONDARY SHEAVES

A primary clutch holder (Yamaha part No. YS-01880-A [A, **Figure 20**] or equivalent) is required to hold the sheaves when loosening and tightening their mounting nuts.

Removal

1. Remove the drive belt cover as described in this chapter.

2. Remove the outer bearing housing as described in this chapter.

3. Locate the directional arrow on the drive belt (**Figure 19**). If the arrow is not visible, mark the top of the drive belt with an arrow pointing rearward.

4. Hold the outside of the primary sheave with a clutch holder (A, **Figure 20**).

5A. Loosen the secondary sheave mounting nut (B, **Figure 20**). If the secondary sheave slips, perform the following:

    a. Loosen the mounting nut with an impact wrench.

    b. If an impact wrench is not available, perform Step 5B.

5B. Hold the secondary sheave with a clutch holder as follows:

    a. If the belt is on the top edge of the secondary sheave, install a 6-mm bolt (**Figure 16**) and spread the sheave to loosen the belt as described in *Removal/ Installation* in *Drive Belt* in this chapter. When the belt is loose, slide it down and away from the sheave's upper edge.

    b. Mount the clutch holder (**Figure 21**) on the outer edge of the secondary sheave and loosen the mounting nut (B, **Figure 20**).

c. Remove the 6-mm bolt (**Figure 16**) from the secondary sheave. When doing so the secondary sheave will tighten. While loosening the bolt, it is helpful to rotate the secondary sheave to help the belt to rise to the top of the sheave.

6. Loosen the primary sheave mounting nut and remove the primary sheave as follows:

    a. Reinstall the clutch holder (A, **Figure 20**) onto the primary sheave if it was moved in Step 5B.

NOTE
*If the primary sheave will not be serviced, make sure to push against the sheave's pulley cam (A, **Figure 22**) when loosening and removing the mounting nut and when removing the primary sheave to prevent an internal weight from falling out of position. If this happens, the primary sheave will have to be disassembled and the weight repositioned as described in this section.*

    b. Loosen the primary sheave mounting nut (C, **Figure 20**).

    c. Push the pulley cam (A, **Figure 22**), then remove the nut, washer and the primary sheave assembly (B). Place the primary sheave on the workbench with the pulley cam facing up.

    d. Remove the collar (**Figure 23**) if it remained on the crankshaft and did not stay in the primary sheave.

7. Remove the drive belt (A, **Figure 24**) and the primary fixed sheave (B).

8. Remove the secondary sheave nut (A, **Figure 25**), fan (B, **Figure 25**), spacer (**Figure 26**) and secondary sheave (C, **Figure 24**).

9. Disassemble and inspect the primary sheave and secondary sheave as described in this section.

Installation

1. Clean the secondary and primary sheave surfaces with electrical contact cleaner or Isopropyl alcohol and allow to dry.

2. Clean the transmission input shaft (A, **Figure 27**) and the clutch housing shaft (B). Then lightly lubricate

the shafts and splines with grease (Yamalube Ultramatic Grease or equivalent). Do not lubricate the threads on the end of the shafts.

3. Install the primary fixed sheave (B, **Figure 24**) onto the clutch housing shaft with its belt surface facing outward.

4. Spread the secondary sheave by installing one or two 6—1.0 × 50 mm bolts into the sheave hub (A, **Figure 28**). Tighten the bolt(s) until the sheave is fully spread.

5. Locate the directional arrow on the drive belt. Then install the drive belt (B, **Figure 28**) over the secondary sheave so the arrow will be pointing toward the rear (**Figure 19**) when the sheave is installed over the transmission input shaft.

6. Install the secondary sheave (**Figure 29**) over the transmission input shaft. Make sure the directional arrow on the drive belt is facing toward the rear.

7. Install the primary sheave as follows:
   a. If the primary sheave was not serviced, lubricate the sheave's bore with grease (Yamalube Ultramatic Grease or equivalent).
   b. Lubricate the inside of the collar with Yamalube Ultramatic Grease. Then slide the collar (**Figure 23**) over the clutch housing shaft. Make sure the grease does not contact the primary fixed sheave surface.
   c. Pick up the primary sheave while applying pressure on the pulley cam and install it over the collar while continuing to hold the pulley cam inward (**Figure 30**).
   d. Check that splines on the clutch housing shaft are visible past the pulley cam as shown in **Figure 31**. If not, a weight(s) has moved out of position. Disassemble the primary sheave and reposition the weight(s) as described in this section. If the splines are visible, continue with substep e.
   e. Install the washer over the clutch housing shaft and center it on the splines (**Figure 32**). Then install the primary sheave mounting nut (**Figure 33**) finger-tight, making sure the washer remains centered on the splines.

> *NOTE*
> *Because only a short section of the splines are accessible, it is easy for the washer to slide off the splines. Recheck the washer's position after installing and tightening the nut.*

   f. Hold the primary sheave with a clutch holding tool (A, **Figure 20**) and tighten the primary sheave mounting nut (C, **Figure 20**) to 140 N•m (103 ft.-lb.).

8. Complete secondary sheave installation by performing the following:
   a. Install the spacer (**Figure 26**).
   b. Install the fan (B, **Figure 25**) so it fits over the splines on the transmission input shaft and with its marked side facing out.
   c. Install the secondary sheave mounting nut (A, **Figure 25**) and tighten to 100 N•m (74 ft.-lb.).
   d. If the secondary sheave slips and the nut cannot be tightened, perform Step 5B in *Removal* in this sec-

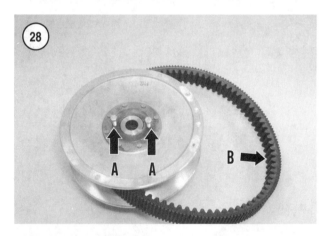

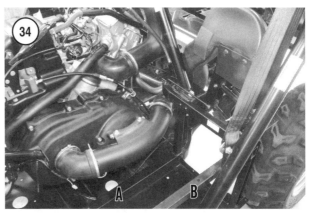

tion to hold the secondary sheave and tighten the nut to 100 N•m (74 ft.-lb.). Remove the clutch holding tool.

9. Install the outer bearing housing as described in this chapter.

10. Install the drive belt cover as described in this chapter.

Primary Sheave

The primary sheave is mounted on the clutch housing shaft and consists of two major pieces. The fixed sheave (A, **Figure 34**) is a single plate that remains in one position on the shaft, while the sliding sheave (B) can move toward or away from the fixed sheave, depending on shaft speed. As shaft speed increases, centrifugal weights inside the sliding sheave push it toward the fixed sheave. This forces the drive belt higher in the sheave assembly. As shaft speed decreases, the weights apply less force and the belt moves lower in the sheave assembly. This raising and lowering of the belt works in conjunction with the secondary sheave to provide variable gear ratios.

Refer to **Figure 35**.

Disassembly

1. Remove the collar (1, **Figure 35**) if it remained in the sliding sheave assembly.

2. Remove the screws and washers (A, **Figure 36**) from the cap (B). Then pry the cap off the sheave (**Figure 37**). Resistance from the O-ring (5, **Figure 35**) at the perimeter of the sheave will be felt during removal.

3. Remove the O-ring (A, **Figure 38**) and the pulley cam (B).

4. Remove the sliders (**Figure 39**) attached to the pulley cam.

5. Remove the weights (A, **Figure 40**) from the sheave.

6. Remove the seals (A, **Figure 41**) from the sheave bore.

Inspection

1. Clean and dry all parts. Remove grease from all parts.

2. Inspect the sliding sheave as follows:

   a. Inspect the sheave bore (B, **Figure 41**) for scoring or other damage. If damage is noted, inspect the collar for the same conditions.

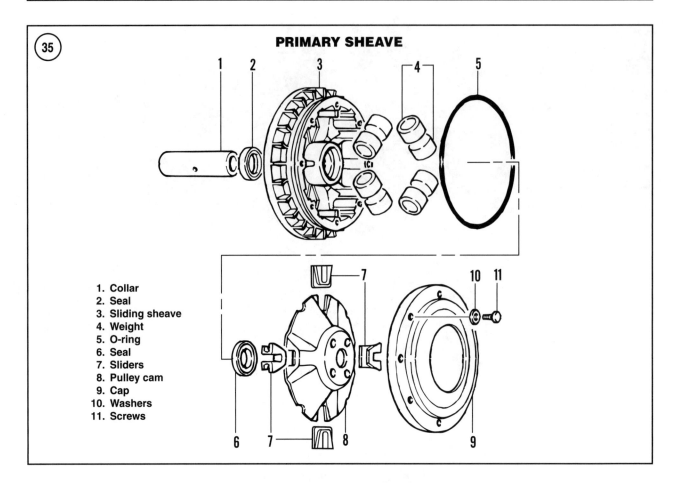

PRIMARY SHEAVE

1. Collar
2. Seal
3. Sliding sheave
4. Weight
5. O-ring
6. Seal
7. Sliders
8. Pulley cam
9. Cap
10. Washers
11. Screws

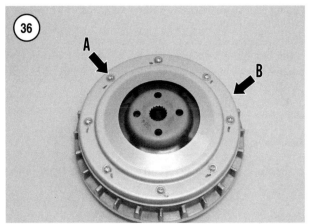

   b. Inspect the pulley cam (C, **Figure 41**) and slider (D) contact areas for scoring and other damage.

3. Inspect the pulley cam as follows:

   a. Inspect the weight ramps (A, **Figure 42**) for uneven wear and scoring. If the ramps appear unequally worn, the weights are not uniformly engaging or applying even pressure.

   b. Inspect the slider grooves (B, **Figure 42**) for cracks and other damage.

4. Replace the sliders (**Figure 39**) if the inner face is worn or damaged. The sliders must be in good condition so the sliding sheave does not drag or jam against the pulley cam.

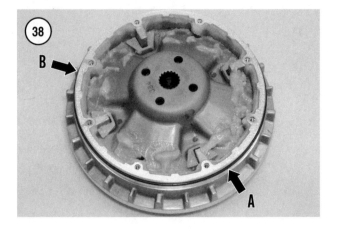

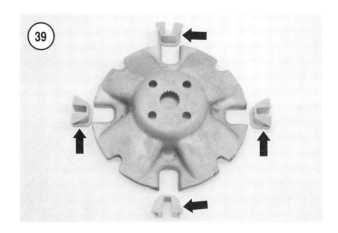

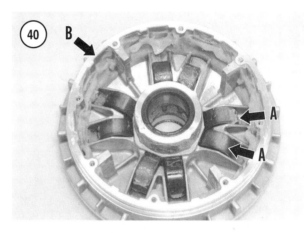

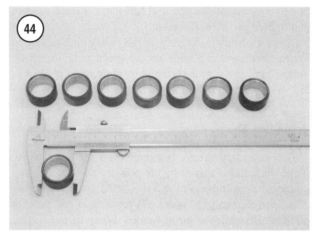

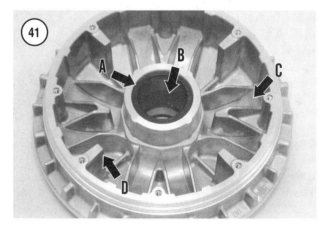

5. Inspect and measure the weights (**Figure 43**) as follows:

    a. Inspect the coating material on the top and side of the weights for excessive wear, tearing or other damage.

    b. Measure the weights outside diameter (**Figure 44**) and compare to the specifications in **Table 1**. Replace the weights as a set if any are too small.

6. Inspect the cap and mounting hardware for damage.

7. Inspect the belt operating surface on each sheave for damage. The surfaces must be smooth.

Assembly

> *NOTE*
> *Use Yamalube Ultramatic Grease when grease is called for in the following steps.*

1. Install a new seal (**Figure 45**) into each side of the sliding sheave bore with their closed side facing out. Install the seals until they bottom.

2. Lubricate the inside of the collar (1, **Figure 35**) and the sheave bore with grease.

3. Lubricate the weight contact surfaces inside the sliding sheave (B, **Figure 40**) with grease.

4. Lubricate the weights on their outer and side surfaces with grease and install them into the sliding sheave as shown in A, **Figure 40**.

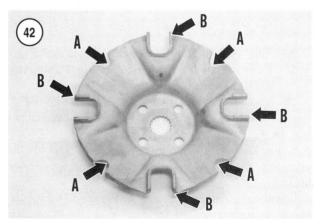

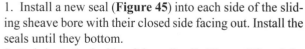

5. Install the sliders (**Figure 39**) into the pulley cam grooves. The side of the slider with the angled shoulders (**Figure 46**) must face up.

> *NOTE*
> *When installing the pulley cam in Step 6, make sure the weights are positioned against the inside of the sliding sheave as shown in A, **Figure 40**.*

6. Install the pulley cam (B, **Figure 38**) so the sliders engage the shoulders in the sliding sheave.

7. Lubricate a new O-ring with grease and install it into the sliding sheave groove (A, **Figure 38**).

8. Install the cap (B, **Figure 36**) over the sliding sheave and O-ring. Install the screws (A, **Figure 36**)and washers and tighten to 3 N•m (26 in.-lb.).

9. Store the sliding sheave with the pulley cam facing up. When handling the sliding sheave, keep pressure on the pulley cam. If the pulley cam does not remain pushed in, the weights may fall out of position.

Secondary Sheave

The secondary sheave is mounted on the transmission input shaft and is driven by the primary sheave. The secondary sheave consists of two sheave halves and a spring. The fixed sheave (A, **Figure 47**) remains in one position on the shaft, while the spring-loaded sliding sheave (B) can move away from or toward the fixed sheave. At low sheave speed, the sheave halves are pressed together by the spring and the drive belt is seated near the outer edge of the assembly. As sheave speed increases, the drive belt is driven downward, pushing the sliding sheave outward and compressing the spring. As sheave speed decreases, the spring forces the sliding sheave back toward the outer edge of the assembly. The raising and lowering of the belt works in conjunction with the primary sheave to provide variable gear ratios.

Refer to **Figure 48**.

Tools

The following tools are required when servicing the secondary sheave assembly.

1. Locknut wrench (Yamaha part No. YM-01348): A, **Figure 49**.

2. Fixed bracket, washer and compressor nut (Yamaha part No. YM-04135): B, **Figure 49**.

3. Spring compressor (Yamaha part No. YM-04134): C, **Figure 49**.

Disassembly

> *WARNING*
> *Do not disassemble the secondary sheave without the proper tools. The sheave nut, upper spring seat and spring are under high*

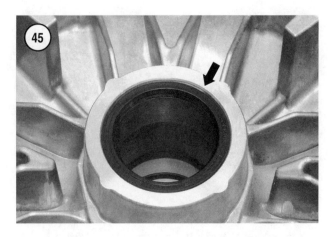

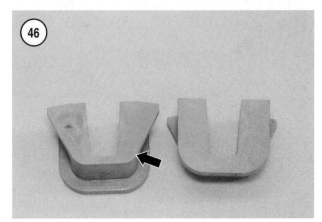

*spring pressure and can cause personal injury. Refer to **Tools** in this section.*

1. Slide the fixed bracket (A, **Figure 50**) through the secondary sheave and bolt it to the fixed sheave. Use the two bolt holes (B, **Figure 50**) near the sheave bore.

2. Clamp the fixed bracket securely in a vise (**Figure 51**). Lubricate the fix bracket threads in the area above and below the sheave nut with an anti-seize lubricant.

3. Center the spring compressor (A, **Figure 52**) over the upper spring seat and install the washer and compressor nut (B).

4. Tighten the compressor nut (A, **Figure 53**) until the spring is compressed enough to loosen the secondary

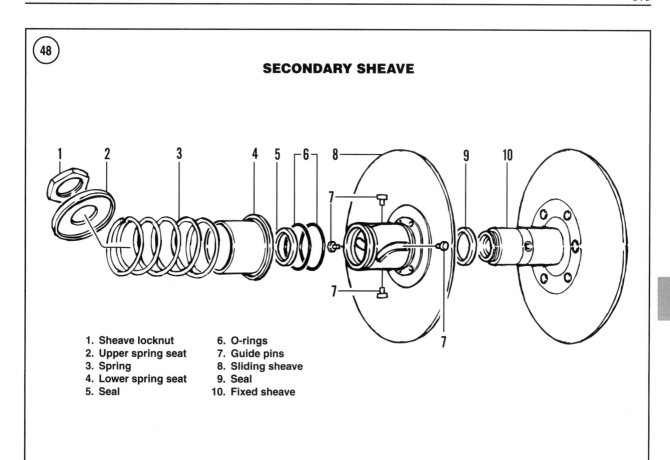

SECONDARY SHEAVE

1. Sheave locknut
2. Upper spring seat
3. Spring
4. Lower spring seat
5. Seal
6. O-rings
7. Guide pins
8. Sliding sheave
9. Seal
10. Fixed sheave

6

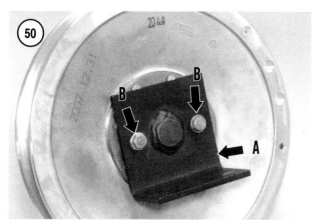

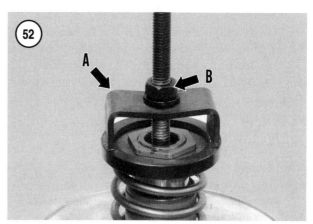

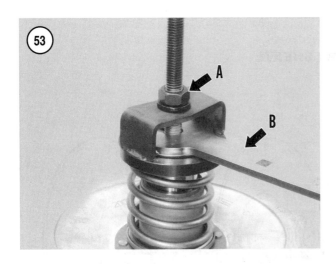

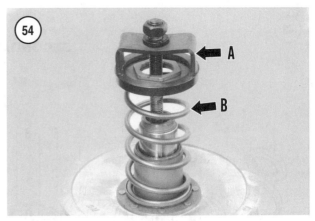

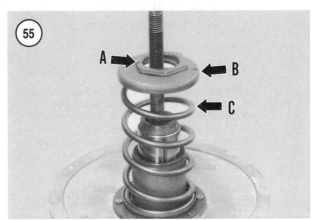

sheave locknut with the locknut wrench (B). Continue to loosen the locknut until it is free of the threads on the fixed sheave.

5. Loosen the compressor nut to relieve pressure on the spring compressor (A, **Figure 54**) and the spring (B) is relaxed.

6. Remove the nut, washer and spring compressor.

7. Remove the secondary sheave locknut (A, **Figure 55**), upper spring seat (B) and spring (C).

8. Use a screwdrive (A, **Figure 56**) and pry the lower spring seat up (B) and then twist it to slide it off the fixed sheave.

9. Remove the guide pins (**Figure 57**).

10. Remove the sliding sheave (**Figure 58**).

11. Remove and discard the O-rings (A, **Figure 59**) installed in the sliding sheave grooves.

12. Remove and discard the seals (B, **Figure 59**) installed in the sliding sheave bore.

13. Remove the fixed bracket from the vise. Then remove the bolts and the fixed sheave.

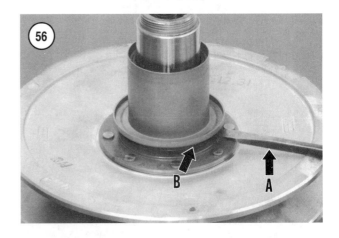

Inspection

1. Clean and dry all parts.

2. Measure the spring free length (**Figure 60**) and compare to the specifications in **Table 1**.

3. Assemble the sheaves and guide pins. Then hold the fixed sheave and slide the sliding sheave to inspect the action of the guide pins and cam grooves (**Figure 61**). The two sheaves should operate smoothly. Replace the guide pins (**Figure 62**) if wear is evident. Replace both sheaves if the cam grooves (C, **Figure 59**) are excessively worn or the parts are excessively loose.

4. Inspect the spring seats for damage.

5. Inspect the secondary sheave locknut for cracks and other damage. Then check the locknut and fixed sheave threads for damage.

6. Inspect the belt operating surface on each sheave for damage. The surfaces must be smooth.

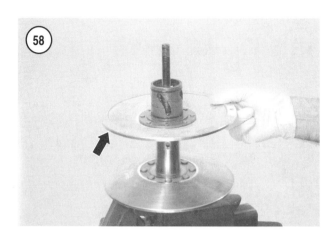

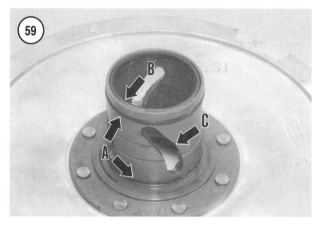

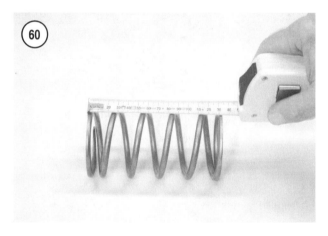

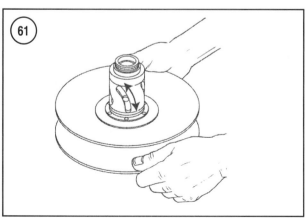

Assembly

WARNING
Do not assemble the secondary sheave with-
out the proper tools. The sheave nut, upper
spring seat and spring are under high spring
pressure and can cause personal injury. Refer
to ***Tools*** *in this section.*

NOTE
Use assembly lube (Bel-Ray Assembly Lube
or equivalent) when lubrication is called for
in the following steps.

1. Lubricate the fixed sheave bore (A, **Figure 63**) and
guide pin holes (B).
2. Secure the fixed bracket to the fixed sheave with the two
mounting bolts (B, **Figure 50**) and clamp the fixed bracket
in a vise as shown in **Figure 64**.
3. Install a new seal in each side of the sliding sheave bore
with their flat sides facing out (B, **Figure 59**). Lubricate
the seal lips.
4. Lubricate two new O-rings and install into the grooves
in the sliding sheave (A, **Figure 59**).
5. Lubricate the sliding sheave grooves (C, **Figure 59**) and
bore.
6. Clean the belt surfaces on both sheaves with electrical
contact cleaner or Isopropyl alcohol and allow to dry.
7. Install the sliding sheave (**Figure 58**) over the fixed
sheave.

8. Lubricate the guide pins (**Figure 57**) and install them through the sliding sheave grooves and into the holes in the fixed sheave (**Figure 65**). Then slide the sliding sheave to make sure it moves smoothly.

9. Install the lower spring seat (**Figure 66**) over the sliding sheave until it bottoms.

10. Clean and dry the secondary sheave locknut and fixed sheave threads.

11. Install the spring (C, **Figure 55**) and upper spring seat (B) and place the secondary sheave locknut (A) on top of the spring seat.

12. Place the spring compressor (A, **Figure 67**) on the upper spring seat and install the washer and compressor nut. Tighten the compressor nut (B, **Figure 67**) to compress the spring. Continue until the upper spring seat bottoms on the shoulder on the sliding sheave. Then thread the secondary sheave locknut (C, **Figure 67**) onto the sheave by hand and tighten-finger tight.

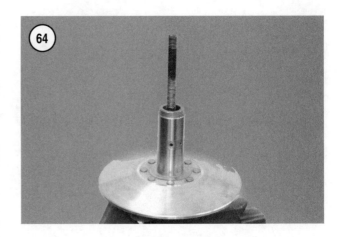

NOTE
*In Step 13, the locknut wrench is used as a torque adapter to tighten the secondary sheave locknut. Refer to **Torque Adapters** in **Tools** in Chapter One for additional information on using torque adapters with a torque wrench.*

13. Install the locknut wrench (A, **Figure 68**) onto the secondary sheave locknut so that it is centered between the spring compressor. Then mount a torque wrench at a 90° angle (B, **Figure 68**) into the square hole in the locknut wrench that is closest to the locknut and tighten the locknut to 90 N•m (66 ft.-lb.). Remove the locknut wrench.

14. Check the secondary sheave locknut to make sure it is not cracked or damaged. If the locknut is in good condition, continue with Step 15. If the locknut is damaged, loosen and remove the locknut and repeat the steps to install a new locknut.

15. Slowly loosen the compressor nut until it can be turned by hand, then remove the compressor nut, washer and spring compressor.

16. Remove the fixed block from the vise and remove the two bolts (B, **Figure 50**) and the secondary sheave assembly.

LEFT CRANKCASE COVER

Removal/Installation

1. Remove the primary and secondary sheaves as described in this chapter.

2. Remove the bolts from the center and perimeter of the left crankcase cover (**Figure 69**).

3. Remove the cover and gaskets.

4. Inspect the cover and gaskets (**Figure 70**) for damage.

5. Clean the clutch and transmission shaft compartments.

6. Installation is the reverse of these steps, plus the following:

    a. Install the gaskets onto the cover.

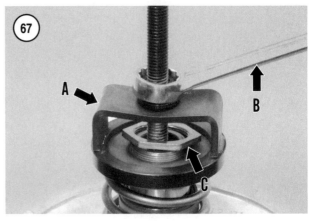

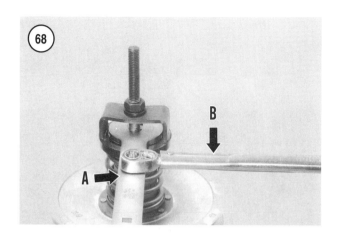

b. Tighten the left crankcase cover mounting bolts to 10 N•m (88 in.-lb.).

CENTRIFUGAL CLUTCH

The centrifugal clutch assembly is located in a housing (A, **Figure 71**) at the end of the crankshaft and transmits power to the primary sheave. The clutch consists of a clutch housing and a centrifugal shoe assembly that is locked to the crankshaft. As engine speed is raised, the shoe assembly centrifugally expands, engaging with the clutch housing. As the engine speed is lowered, the shoe assembly contracts and disengages from the clutch housing.

The clutch is also equipped with a one-way clutch, located between the clutch housing and shoe assembly. The one-way clutch provides engine braking when the shoe assembly is disengaged from the clutch housing, as when descending a hill at idle speed.

Removal

1. Remove the left crankcase cover as described in this chapter

2. Check the general condition of the one-way clutch before removing the clutch from the engine. Check the one-way clutch as follows:

    a. Turn the clutch housing shaft (B, **Figure 71**) counterclockwise. The shaft should turn freely.

    b. Turn the clutch housing shaft clockwise. The shaft should lock.

    c. If the one-way clutch fails either test, remove and inspect the one-way clutch as described in this section.

3. Drain the engine oil (Chapter Three).

4. Loosen the clutch housing bolts in several steps in a crossing pattern. Then remove the bolts and clutch housing (A, **Figure 71**). Remove the two dowel pins.

5. Remove the one-way clutch (**Figure 72**) if it did not come off with the clutch housing.

6. Remove the clutch locknut as follows:

    a. Turn the crankshaft until the staked portion on the clutch locknut is accessible (**Figure 73**).

b. Wrap a piece of tape around the end of the crankshaft and secure it with a plastic-tie (**Figure 74**). The tape will prevent metal debris from entering the oil hole in the end of the crankshaft.

c. Carefully grind the staked portion of the clutch locknut with a small grinding stone to weaken it. Do not grind through the nut or the crankshaft will be damaged. Remove the tape from the end of the crankshaft and spray the clutch locknut with electrical contact cleaner.

d. Hold the shoe assembly with a clutch holding tool (Yamaha part No. YM-91042 [A, **Figure 75**] or equivalent).

CAUTION
The area between the shoe assembly and crankcase where the clutch holding tool grips the top of the shoe assembly is very narrow. Make sure to carefully lock and secure the clutch holding tool so that it cannot slip and damage the shoe surface or crankcase. An impact gun will ease removal of the nut.

NOTE
The clutch locknut uses left-hand threads.

e. Turn the clutch locknut *clockwise* to loosen and remove it. Discard the locknut.

f. Remove the clutch holding tool.

7. Remove the shoe assembly (B, **Figure 75**).

8. Remove the gasket from the crankcase. Make sure none of the gasket residue falls into the crankcase.

9. Inspect and service the clutch housing, shoe assembly and one-way clutch as described in this section.

Installation

1. Make sure the crankcase and clutch housing gasket surfaces are clean.

2. Make sure the spacer (A, **Figure 76**) is seated against the crankshaft main bearing.

3. Clean the exposed end of the crankshaft (B, **Figure 76**) and allow to dry.

CAUTION
*Make sure there is no debris remaining in the crankcase/clutch housing area (C, **Figure** 76) that could fall into the crankcase.*

4. Lubricate the clutch housing, clutch housing bearing, one-way clutch and shoe assembly areas identified in **Figure 77** with engine oil.

NOTE
If installing a new shoe assembly, soak the new shoe surfaces with engine oil.

5. Install the shoe assembly (B, **Figure 75**) over the crankshaft with the one-way clutch shoulder (C) facing out.

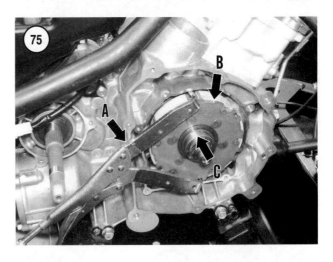

6. Install and tighten the clutch locknut (**Figure 73**) as follows:

NOTE
The clutch locknut uses left-hand threads.

a. Lubricate the crankshaft threads and the threads and seating surfaces on a new clutch locknut with molybdenum disulfide oil. Turn the clutch locknut *counterclockwise* to install it on the crankshaft and tighten finger-tight.

b. Hold the shoe assembly with a clutch holding tool (A, **Figure 75**).

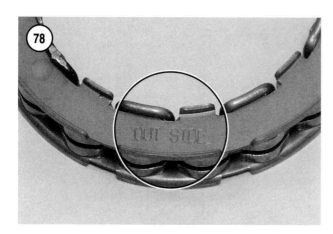

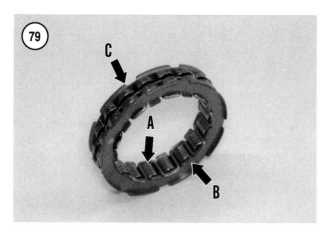

CAUTION
The area between the shoe assembly and crankcase where the clutch holding tool grips the top of the shoe assembly is very narrow. Make sure to carefully lock and secure the clutch holding tool so that it cannot slip and damage the shoe surface or crankcase.

   c. When the clutch holding tool is secure, tighten the clutch locknut to 190 N•m (140 ft.-lb.).

   d. Use a punch and stake a portion of the clutch locknut shoulder into the groove in the crankshaft (**Figure 73**).

7. Install the one-way clutch with the word OUT SIDE (**Figure 78**) facing away from the shoe assembly. Refer to **Figure 72**.

8. Install the two dowel pins and a new gasket.

9. Install the clutch housing, making sure to engage it with the dowel pins.

10. Install the two longer mounting bolts through the dowel pins holes, then install the remaining bolts and tighten finger-tight.

11. Tighten the clutch housing mounting bolts in a crossing pattern to 10 N•m (88 in.-lb.).

12. Check the one-way clutch for proper operation:

   a. Turn the clutch housing shaft (B, **Figure 71**) counterclockwise. The shaft should turn freely.

   b. Turn the clutch housing shaft clockwise. The shaft should lock.

   c. If the one-way clutch fails either test, it is either damaged or installed incorrectly. Remove and inspect the one-way clutch as described in this section.

13. Refill the engine with the correct type and quantity oil (Chapter Three).

14. Install the left crankcase cover as described in this chapter.

Inspection

1. Clean the parts in solvent and dry with compressed air.

2. If the one-way clutch is damaged, replace the one-way clutch and clutch housing as a set. Inspect the one-way clutch as follows:

   a. Inspect the clutch sprags (A, **Figure 79**) for scoring, wear and heat damage. Make sure the retainer spring (B, **Figure 79**) firmly holds the sprags in place.

   b. Make sure each sprag is free to pivot and that all sprags are resting in the same position.

   c. Inspect the clutch cage (C, **Figure 79**) for cracks and damage.

   d. Test the one-way clutch. Install the one-way clutch with the word OUT SIDE (**Figure 78**) facing away from the shoe assembly. Insert the shoe assembly into the clutch housing. Hold the shoe assembly and turn the housing shaft. The shaft should turn clockwise as viewed in **Figure 80** and lock when turned counterclockwise.

3. Inspect the clutch housing and bearing housing:

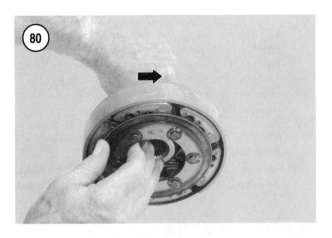

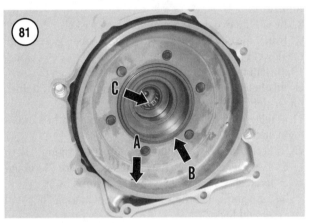

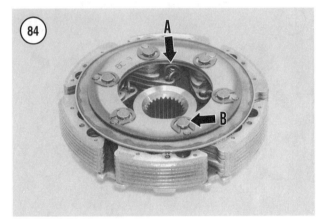

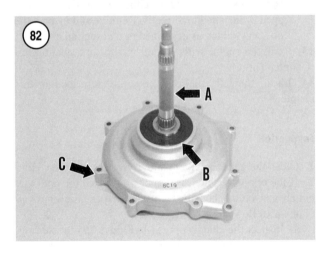

a. Inspect the clutch shoe contact area (A, **Figure 81**) for scoring, wear and heat damage.

b. Inspect the one-way clutch contact area (B, **Figure 81**) for scoring, wear and heat damage.

c. Inspect the needle bearing (C, **Figure 81**). The rollers should be smooth and polished with no flat spots, burrs or other damage. Inspect the bearing cage for cracks or other damage. If damaged, replace the bearing as described in this section.

NOTE
If the needle bearing is damaged, check the mating end of the crankshaft for damage.

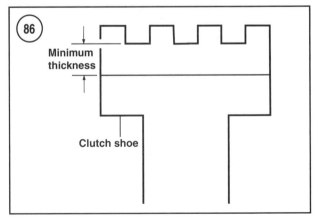

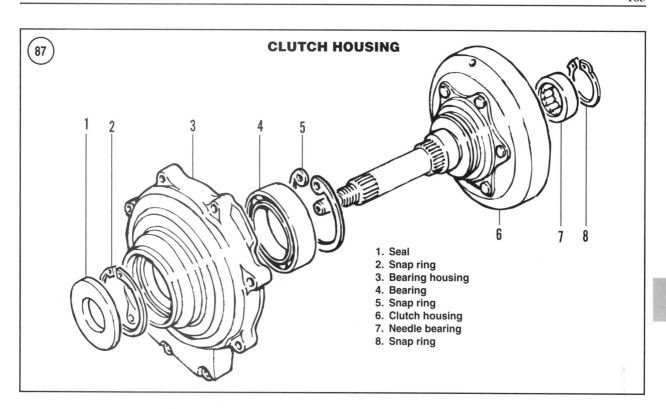

CLUTCH HOUSING

1. Seal
2. Snap ring
3. Bearing housing
4. Bearing
5. Snap ring
6. Clutch housing
7. Needle bearing
8. Snap ring

d. Check the clutch housing shaft (A, **Figure 82**) for damaged threads and splines.

e. Rotate the clutch housing shaft (A, **Figure 82**) and check for smooth operation. If the clutch housing turns roughly, replace the clutch housing bearing as described in this section.

f. If the clutch housing oil seal (B, **Figure 82**) is leaking oil or appears damaged, replace it as described in this section.

g. Inspect the bearing housing (C, **Figure 82**) for damage.

4. Inspect the clutch shoe assembly:

   a. Inspect the splines (A, **Figure 83**), guides and one-way clutch contact area (B) for damage.

   b. Inspect the springs (A, **Figure 84**), levers, pivots and E-clips (B). Look for broken or weak springs. Inspect the pivots for tightness and missing E-clips. Make sure all shoes are equally seated. If not, check for worn or jammed levers, pivots and springs.

c. Inspect the shoes (**Figure 85**) for wear, heat damage and contamination. Measure the shoe thickness (**Figure 86**) and compare to specifications in **Table 2**. Replace the shoe assembly if the shoes are worn to the service limit or when the grooves are no longer visible.

Clutch Housing Overhaul

Refer to **Figure 87**.

NOTE
*The oil seal (1, **Figure 87**) can be replaced without having to remove the clutch housing.*

1. Carefully drill a 1/8 in. hole through the middle of the oil seal (**Figure 88**). Then insert a seal puller into the hole and pry the oil seal out of the housing (**Figure 89**). Check the seal bore for damage.

NOTE
If additional service is not required, go to Step 7 to install the new seal.

2. Remove the snap ring (**Figure 90**) from the groove in the clutch housing and remove the clutch housing (A, **Figure 91**). Seperate the clutch housing (A, **Figure 91**) from the bearing housing (B).

NOTE
The Motion Pro Blind Bearing and Bushing Remover (part No. 08-0292) is used to remove the bearing in Step 3.

3. Replace the needle bearing (7, **Figure 87**) as follows:

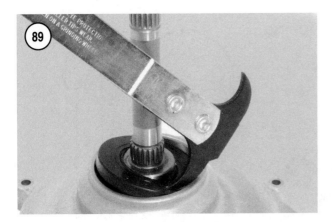

a. Remove and discard the snap ring (A, **Figure 92**).

b. Insert a 15 mm bearing collet (**Figure 93**) into the needle bearing (B, **Figure 92**). Expand the collet to lock it against the bearing.

c. Support the clutch housing and remove the bearing with the blind bearing remover (**Figure 93**). Discard the bearing.

d. Inspect the bearing bore for scoring, cracks and other damage.

e. Align the new bearing with the bearing bore and press or drive the bearing into the bore. Then turn the bearing needles to make sure the bearing was not damaged during installation.

f. Install a new snap ring (A, **Figure 92**) into the clutch housing groove with its flat side facing out. Make sure the snap ring seats in the groove completely.

g. Lubricate the bearing needles with engine oil.

4. Replace the bearing (4, **Figure 87**) as follows:

a. Remove the snap ring (A, **Figure 94**) from the groove in the bearing housing and discard it.

b. Support the bearing housing in a press, and use a bearing friver (**Figure 95**) to remove the bearing.

c. Inspect the bearing bore for damage.

d. Align the new bearing with the bearing bore and press (**Figure 96**) or drive the bearing into the bore. Then turn the bearing inner race (B, **Figure 94**) to make sure the bearing was not damaged during installation.

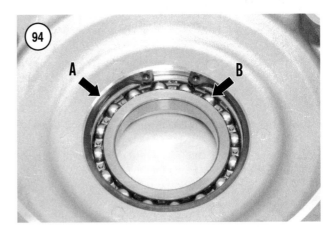

e. Install a new snap ring (A, **Figure 94**) into the bearing groove with its flat side facing out. Make sure the snap ring seats in the groove completely.

f. Lubricate the bearing with engine oil.

5. Install the clutch housing through the bearing.

6. Install a new snap ring (**Figure 90**) into the clutch housing groove with its flat side facing out (**Figure 97**). Turn the clutch housing to make sure it turns freely and that the snap ring is properly installed and seated in its groove.

7. Install a new seal as follows:

a. Lubricate the lips of a new seal with grease.

b. Install the seal over the clutch shaft with its flat side facing out. Position the seal so it squarely contacts the shoulder (**Figure 98**) on the clutch housing.

c. Carefully tap around the seal with a plastic hammer (**Figure 99**), making sure it enters the seal bore squarely. Install the seal until its outer surface is flush with the seal bore upper surface.

d. Turn the clutch housing to make sure the seal lip (**Figure 100**) seats evenly around the clutch housing shoulder.

Table 1, Table 2 and Table 3 are on the following page.

Table 1 DRIVE BELT AND SHEAVE SPECIFICATIONS

Drive belt width	
New	33.3 mm (1.31 in.)
Service limit	30.0 mm (1.18 in.)
Primary sheave weight outside diameter	
New	30.0 mm (1.18 in.)
Service limit	29.5 mm (1.16 in.)
Secondary sheave spring free length	
New	130.6 mm (5.14 in.)
Service limit	128.0 mm (5.04 in.)

Table 2 CLUTCH SPECIFICATIONS

Type	Wet, centrifugal automatic
Clutch shoe thickness	
New	1.5 mm (0.06 in.)
Service limit	1.0 mm (0.04 in.)
Clutch-in revolution	1850-2250 rpm
Clutch-stall revolution	3500-4100 rpm

Table 3 CLUTCH AND SHEAVE TORQUE SPECIFICATIONS

	N•m	in.-lb.	ft.-lb.
Air duct 1 mounting bracket mounting bolts	10	88	–
Cap screws	3	26	–
Clutch housing mounting bolts	10	88	–
Clutch locknut (centrifugal clutch)*	190	–	140
Drive belt cover mounting bolts	10	88	–
Front air duct 1 mounting bolts	7	62	–
Left crankcase cover mounting bolts	10	88	–
Outer bearing housing bearing cover mounting bolt	10	88	–
Outer bearing housing mounting bolt	10	88	–
Primary sheave mounting nut	140	–	103
Secondary sheave mounting nut	100	–	74
Secondary sheave locknut	90	–	66

*Refer to text.

CHAPTER SEVEN

TRANSMISSION AND SHIFT MECHANISM

This chapter covers the transmission and shift mechanisms. This includes the select lever assembly, external shift mechanism and transmission. To service the transmission, remove the engine and seperate the crankcase as described in Chapter Five.

Read *Safety* and *Service Methods* in Chapter One before servicing the vehicle in this chapter.

Table 1 and **Table 2** are at the end of this chapter.

SELECT LEVER ASSEMBLY

NOTE
If poor shifting is occurring or the shift indicator lights do not come on to indicate gear engagement, check the select lever adjustment (Chapter Three) before servicing the select lever components.

Removal/Installation

Refer to **Figure 1**.
1. Remove the rear console (Chapter Sixteen).
2. Remove the shift arm mounting bolt (A, **Figure 2**), washer (B) and remove the shift arm (C) from the shift shaft.
3. Remove the select lever assembly mounting bolts (A, **Figure 3**) and the select lever assembly (B).
4. Installation is the reverse of removal. Note the following:
   a. Tighten the select lever assembly mounting bolts to 15 N•m (11 ft.-lb.).
   b. Install the shift arm by aligning its flats with the flats on the shift shaft (**Figure 4**).

   c. Apply a medium-strength threadlocking compound onto the shift arm mounting bolt threads and tighten to 14 N•m (10 ft.-lb.).
   d. Turn the ignition switch on and shift the transmission from neutral into high gear, low gear and reverse. Make sure the shift indicator light for each position comes on when the gear change is made. If not, adjust the select lever (Chapter Three).

Inspection

The select lever assembly is a sealed unit and should not be disassembled. Inspect the boot and shift arm for damage.

EXTERNAL SHIFT MECHANISM

The external shift mechanism (**Figure 1**) links the action of the select lever to the transmission. When the select lever is shifted, the external shift mechanism rotates the transmission shift drum to the appropriate gear position.

Removal

1. If the engine is mounted in the frame, perform the following:
   a. Remove the rear console (Chapter Sixteen).
   b. Shift the transmission into neutral.
   c. Remove the shift arm mounting bolt (A, **Figure 2**), washer (B) and remove the shift arm from the shift shaft.
   d. Remove the wiring harness from the guide on the shift cover.

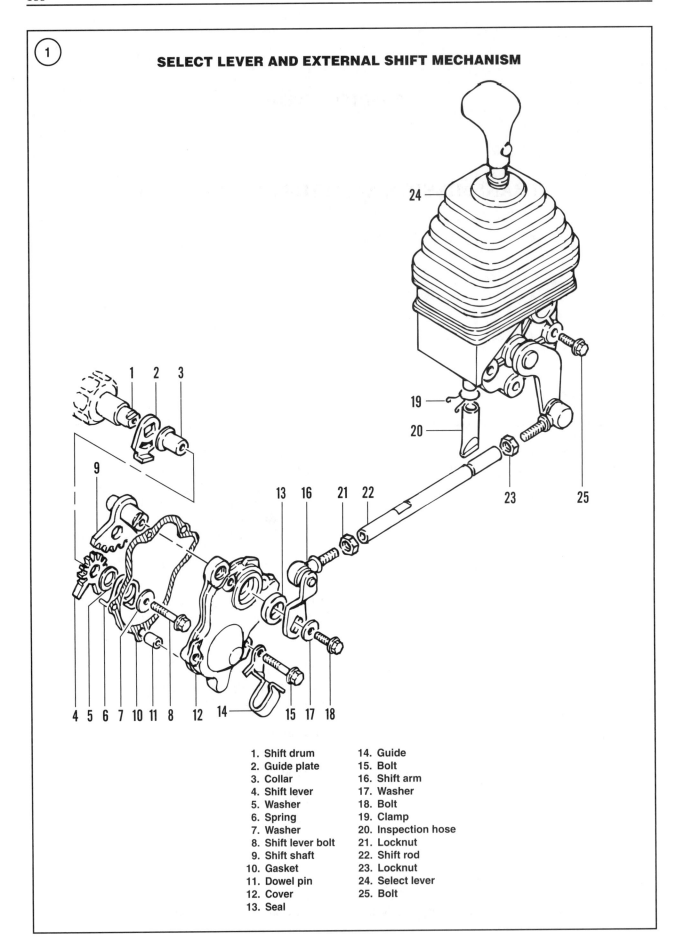

① **SELECT LEVER AND EXTERNAL SHIFT MECHANISM**

1. Shift drum
2. Guide plate
3. Collar
4. Shift lever
5. Washer
6. Spring
7. Washer
8. Shift lever bolt
9. Shift shaft
10. Gasket
11. Dowel pin
12. Cover
13. Seal
14. Guide
15. Bolt
16. Shift arm
17. Washer
18. Bolt
19. Clamp
20. Inspection hose
21. Locknut
22. Shift rod
23. Locknut
24. Select lever
25. Bolt

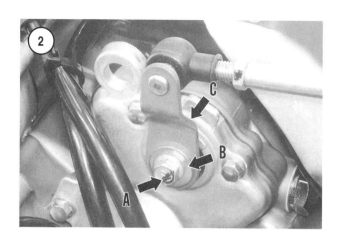

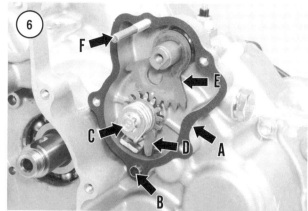

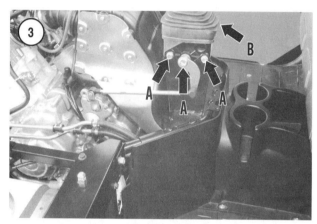

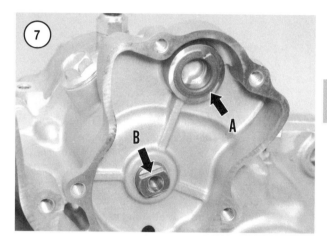

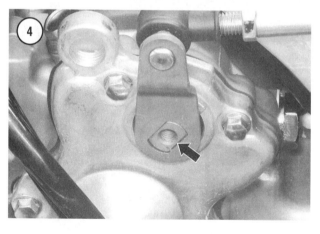

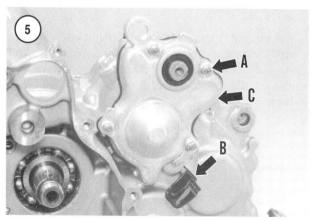

NOTE
The following photographs show the service performed with the engine removed from the frame for clarity.

2. Remove the shift cover mounting bolts (A, **Figure 5**) and wiring harness guide (B). Then push the shift shaft to hold it in place and remove the shift cover (C, **Figure 5**).

3. Remove the gasket (A, **Figure 6**) and dowel pin (B).

4. Remove the shift lever bolt and washer (C, **Figure 6**), shift lever (D) and shift shaft (E).

5. Inspect the components as described in this section.

Installation

1. Lubricate the bushing (A, **Figure 7**) with engine oil.

2. Install the shift lever by aligning its flats (**Figure 8**) with the flats on the shift drum (B, **Figure 7**). Refer to D, **Figure 6**.

3. Install the shift lever bolt and washer (C, **Figure 6**) and tighten to 14 N•m (10 ft.-lb.).

4. Install the shift shaft (E, **Figure 6**) by aligning its punch mark between the two punch marks on the shift lever. Refer to **Figure 9**.

5. Lubricate the shift lever and shift shaft gear teeth with engine oil.

6. Install the dowel pin (B, **Figure 6**) and a new gasket (A).

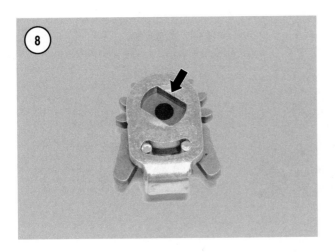

NOTE
*A separate bolt with its head cut off (F, **Figure** 6) can be used as an alignment stud to help align the gasket with the cover.*

7. Lubricate the cover seal lips with grease and install the cover, wiring harness guide (B, **Figure 5**) and mounting bolts. Remove the alignment stud (F, **Figure 6**) if used.

8. Tighten the shift cover mounting bolts to 10 N•m (88 in.-lb.).

9. If the engine is installed in the frame, reverse Step 1 in *Removal* in this section. Note perform the following:

    a. Install the shift arm by aligning its flats with the flats on the shift shaft (**Figure 4**).

    b. Apply a medium-strength threadlocking compound onto the shift arm mounting bolt threads and tighten to 14 N•m (10 ft.-lb.).

    c. Turn the ignition switch on and shift the transmission from neutral into high gear, low gear and reverse. Make sure the shift indicator light for each position comes on when the gear change is made. If not, adjust the select lever (Chapter Three).

Inspection

1. Clean and dry all parts.

2. Inspect the shift lever (A, **Figure 10**) and shift shaft (B) gear teeth for wear or damage.

3. Check all pivot surfaces for scoring, cracks and other damage.

4. If the shift lever is damaged or requires inspection of the assembled parts, perform the following:

    a. Refer to **Figure 1** and remove the spring, washer, shift lever, collar and guide plate.

    b. Replace any worn damaged parts.

    c. Refer to **Figure 1** to assemble the parts. Lubricate the collar (3, **Figure 1**) with lithium grease. Make sure the index mark on the shift lever face away from the guide plate. Position the spring (C, **Figure 10**) so that its arms engage the slot in the guide plate.

5. Inspect the shift cover bushing for scoring, cracks and other damage. If damaged, replace the cover.

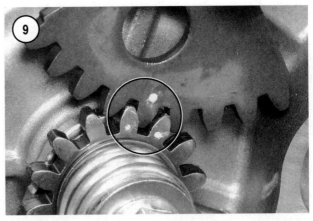

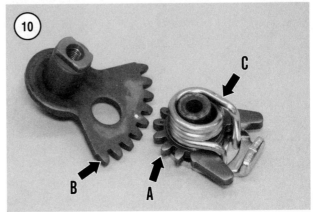

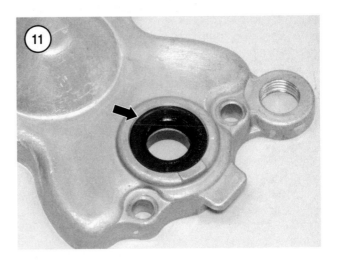

6. Pry the seal (**Figure 11**) out of the shift cover and discard it. Clean the seal bore and check for damage. Lubricate the lips of a new seal with grease and install the seal with its flat side facing out. Install the seal until it bottoms in its bore.

TRANSMISSION

Operation

The engine is equipped with a dual-range, constant-mesh transmission, plus a gear driven reverse gear. The transmis-

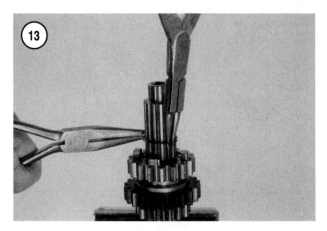

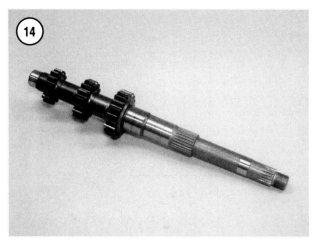

sion shafts, shift forks and shift drum are located in the right crankcase housing (**Figure 12**).

The gears on the input shaft (A, **Figure 12**) are fixed in position, and are meshed with their free-wheeling, high or low-range gear on the output shaft (B). Similarly, the reverse gear on the input shaft is fixed, while the output shaft gear freewheels. To make the high/low gear ranges active, the dog clutch on the output shaft slides laterally and locks against the selected gear. Since the dog clutch is splined to the output shaft, the selected gear range becomes active and the output shaft turns.

Reverse gear is activated by the dogs on the side of the middle drive gear. The splined drive gear not only engages and disengages reverse, but transfers all power from the output shaft (forward and reverse) to the middle drive gear unit, located below the transmission.

To engage and disengage the gears, the dog clutch and middle drive gear are moved by shift forks. The shift forks are guided by the shift drum, which is controlled by the select lever. As the select lever is operated, the shift drum rotates and guides the forks to engage or disengage the gears on the output shaft.

Service

1. The engine crankcase must be separated to remove the transmission and shift assembles. Refer to *Crankcase* in Chapter Five.

2. As the output shaft is disassembled, store the individual parts in a divided container, or make an identification mark on each part to indicate orientation.

3. Install new snap rings during reassembly. Because snap rings fatigue and distort when removed, do not reuse them, although they may appear to be in good condition.

4. To install new snap rings without distorting them, perform the following:

   a. Open the new snap ring with a pair of snap ring pliers while holding the back of the snap ring with a pair of pliers (**Figure 13**).

   b. Slide the snap ring down the shaft and seat it into its correct groove.

   c. This technique can also be used to remove the snap rings from a shaft once they are free from their grooves.

Input Shaft

The input shaft gears are fixed onto the input shaft (**Figure 14**). Inspect as described in this section.

Output Shaft

Refer to **Figure 15**.

Disassembly

> *CAUTION*
> *The snap rings, splined washers and thrust washers used on the output shaft are stamped types. One edge is rounded, while the other is sharp (**Figure 16**). The side with the sharp edge, referred to as the flat side, must be installed so the flat side always faces away from the part producing the thrust. The sharp edge prevents the snap ring from rolling out of its groove when thrust is applied. Note the direction of all the snap rings, splined washers and thrust washers before removal. When installing new ones they must face in their original direction.*

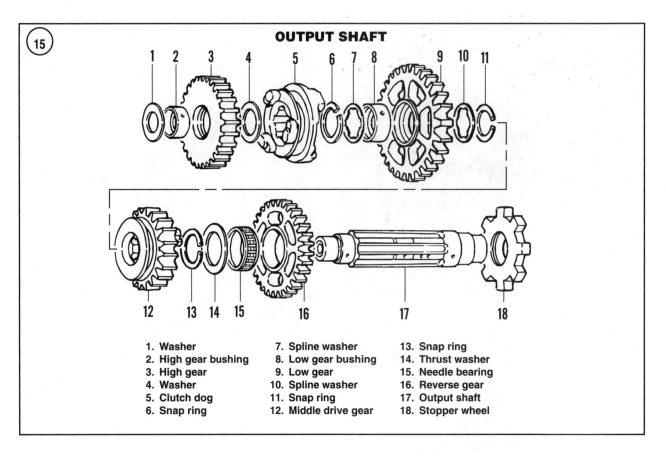

OUTPUT SHAFT

1. Washer
2. High gear bushing
3. High gear
4. Washer
5. Clutch dog
6. Snap ring
7. Spline washer
8. Low gear bushing
9. Low gear
10. Spline washer
11. Snap ring
12. Middle drive gear
13. Snap ring
14. Thrust washer
15. Needle bearing
16. Reverse gear
17. Output shaft
18. Stopper wheel

NOTE
Parts 1-4 in **Figure 15** *were removed during crankcase disassembly in Chapter Five.*

1. Remove the clutch dog.
2. Remove the snap ring and splined washer.
3. Remove low gear and its bushing.
4. Remove the splined washer and snap ring.
5. Remove the middle drive gear.
6. Remove the snap ring and thrust washer.
7. Remove reverse gear and its needle bearing.

NOTE
The stopper wheel (A, **Figure 17**) *is a press fit. Do not remove unless replacement is necessary.*

8. To remove the stopper wheel, perform the following:
   a. Support the stopper wheel in a press with a bearing splitter (A, **Figure 18**).
   b. Using a bearing driver (B, **Figure 18**) on top of the output shaft, press the output shaft out of the stopper wheel.
9. Inspect the output shaft assembly as described in *Inspecton* in this section.

Assembly

Before beginning assembly, have three *new* snap rings on hand. Throughout the procedure, the orientation of parts is made in relationship to the stopper wheel (A, **Figure 17**).

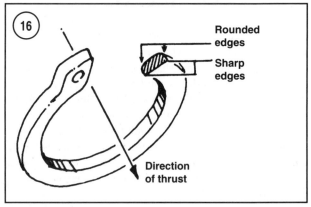

Rounded edges
Sharp edges
Direction of thrust

1. Clean and dry all parts before assembly. Make sure all of the oil holes and the inside of the output shaft are clean.
2. Lubricate the mating bushing, gear and shaft surfaces with molybdenum disulfide oil before assembly.
3. If the stopper wheel was removed, install it as follows:
   a. Support the output shaft with a hollow driver as shown in A, **Figure 19**.
   b. Place the stopper wheel onto the output shaft with its shoulder side (B, **Figure 17**) facing up (away from shaft).
   c. Place a bearing driver on top of the stopper wheel (B, **Figure 19**) and press the stopper wheel onto the output shaft until it bottoms against the shaft's upper shoulder.
4. Install the reverse gear needle bearing (A, **Figure 20**) and reverse gear (B) onto the output shaft (C). The gear

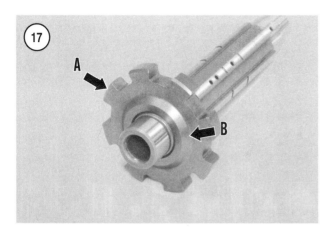

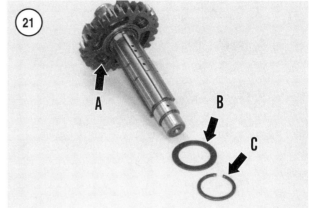

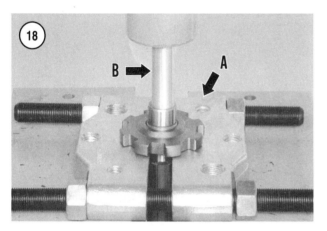

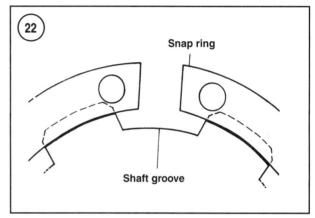

Snap ring

Shaft groove

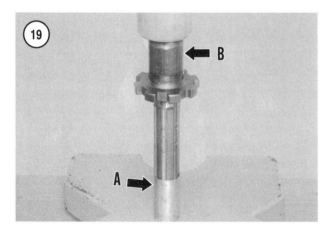

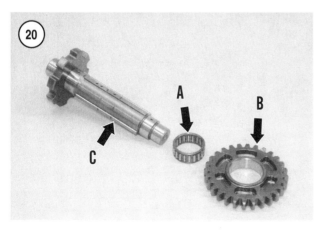

7

dog holes (A, **Figure 21**) on the reverse gear must face away from the stopper wheel.

CAUTION
*Install all of the output shaft snap rings so their ends align with a groove in the splines (**Figure 22**).*

5. Install the thrust washer (B, **Figure 21**) and a new snap ring (C) onto the shaft. The snap ring (**Figure 23**) must seat fully in the groove in the shaft.

6. Spin reverse gear, making sure there is no excessive roughness or binding.

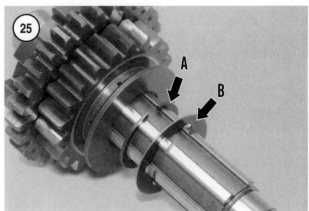

7. Install the middle drive gear (A, **Figure 24)** with it shift fork groove facing away from the stopper wheel. Make sure the gear and shaft oil holes align as shown in B, **Figure 24**.

8. Install a new snap ring into the shaft groove (A, **Figure 25**).

9. Install the spline washer (B, **Figure 25**) and seat it next to the snap ring.

10. Install the low gear bushing (A, **Figure 26**) and low gear (B) onto the output shaft. The gear dog holes (A, **Figure 27**) on low gear must face away from the stopper wheel.

11. Install the spline washer (B, **Figure 27**) and seat it next to low gear.

12. Install a new snap ring into the shaft groove (C, **Figure 27**).

13. Spin low gear, making sure there is no excessive roughness or binding.

14. Install the clutch dog with its larger outside diameter shoulder (**Figure 28**) facing the stopper wheel.

NOTE
*Parts 1-4 in **Figure 15** are installed during transmission installation in Chapter Five.*

15. Compare the assembled shaft assembly with **Figure 29**.

16. Wrap a heavy rubber band around the end of the shaft to prevent parts from sliding off the shaft.

Reverse Idle Gear Assembly

Disassembly/assembly

The original reverse idle gear assembly shown in **Figure 30** has been replaced with the reverse idle gear set shown in **Figure 31**. Whenever the crankcase is disassembled, it is suggested to install the new gear assembly. The new style parts are also available in a replacement kit.

Refer to *Inspection* in this section.

CAUTION
If the original reverse idle gear assembly will be reused, note that part numbers for the as-

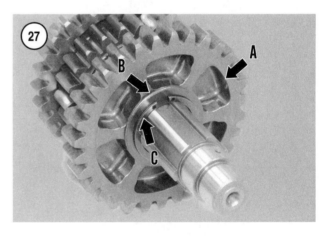

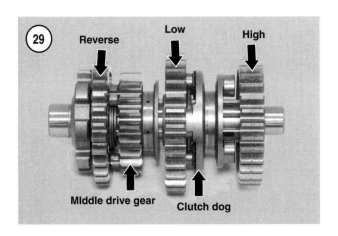

Reverse | Low | High
Middle drive gear | Clutch dog

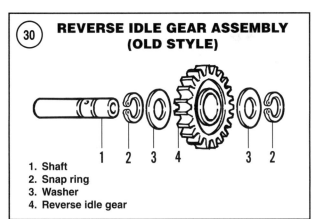

REVERSE IDLE GEAR ASSEMBLY (OLD STYLE)

1. Shaft
2. Snap ring
3. Washer
4. Reverse idle gear

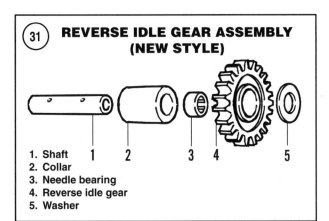

REVERSE IDLE GEAR ASSEMBLY (NEW STYLE)

1. Shaft
2. Collar
3. Needle bearing
4. Reverse idle gear
5. Washer

sembly (**Figure 30**) are no longer listed. If the original reverse gear assembly is disassembled, it will be necessary to reassemble the gear assembly with the original snap rings. Snap rings can be damaged during removal and installation.

Inspection

Replace worn or damaged parts as described in this section.

NOTE
Maintain the alignment of the output shaft components when cleaning and inspecting the parts.

1. Inspect the input shaft (**Figure 32**) for:
   a. Worn or damaged splines.
   b. Missing, broken or chipped gear teeth.
   c. Worn or damaged bearing surfaces.
   d. Damaged threads.
2. Inspect the output shaft (**Figure 33**) for:
   a. Worn or damaged splines.
   b. Worn or damaged bearing surfaces.
   c. Cracked or rounded snap ring grooves.
   d. Excessive runout. Place the output shaft on V-blocks and check runout with a dial indicator. Replace the output shaft if runout exceeds 0.06 mm (0.0024 in.).

CAUTION
Do not attempt to straighten a bent input or output shaft.

3. Inspect the reverse idle gear assembly (**Figure 30** or **Figure 31**) for:
   a. Missing, broken or chipped gear teeth.
   b. Worn or damaged shaft surface.
   c. Damaged needle bearing rollers (**Figure 31**).
   d. Damaged collar (**Figure 31**).
4. Check the splines on the clutch dog and middle drive gear and the bore on the stationary gears for excessive wear or damage.
5. To check stationary gears for wear, install them and their bushing or needle bearing on the output shaft and in

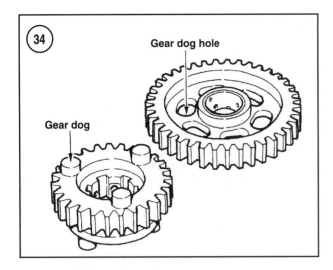

Gear dog hole

Gear dog

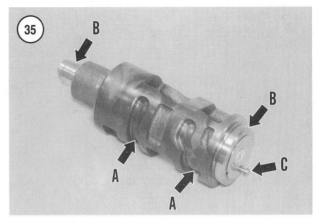

their original operating position. If necessary, use the old snap rings to secure them in place. Then spin the gear by hand. The gear should turn smoothly. A rough turning gear indicates heat damage. Check for a dark blue color or galling on the operating surfaces. Rocking indicates excessive wear, either to the gear, bushing, needle bearing or shaft.

6. To check the clutch dog and middle drive gear, install them on the output shaft and in their original operating position. The clutch dog and gear should slide back and forth without any binding or excessive play.

NOTE
The side of the gear dogs that carries the engine load will wear and eventually become rounded. The unloaded side of the dogs remains unworn. Rounded dogs cause the transmission to jump out of gear.

7. Check the dogs and dog holes (**Figure 34**) on the clutch dog and gears for excessive wear, rounding, cracks or other damage. Any wear on the dogs and mating recesses should be uniform. If the dogs are not worn evenly, the remaining dogs will be overstressed and possibly fail.

8. Check engaging output shaft gears and the clutch dog by installing mating parts on the output shaft and in their original operating position, then twist the parts together to engage the dogs. Check for positive engagement in both directions. If damage is evident, also inspect the condition of the shift forks, as described in this chapter.

9. Check for worn or damaged shift fork grooves. Check the clutch dog and middle drive gear grooves and mating shift forks.

10. Check the low gear and high gear bushings for:
   a. Severely worn or damaged bearing surface.
   b. Worn or damaged bore.
   c. Cracked or scored gear bore (on the mating gear).

11. Check the reverse gear needle bearing (15, **Figure 15**). The rollers should be smooth and polished with no flat spots, burrs or other damage. Inspect the bearing cage for cracks or other damage. Replace the bearing if necessary.

12. Inspect the spline washers. The teeth in the washer should be uniform and show no signs of thrust wear.

13. Inspect the thrust washers. The washers should be smooth and show no signs of thrust wear or heat damage (bluing).

SHIFT DRUM AND FORKS

When shifting the transmission, the shift drum and fork assembly engage and disengage the gears on the transmission output shaft. Gear shifting is controlled by the shift forks, which are guided by cam grooves in the shift drum.

The shift drum grooves, shift forks and mating clutch dog and gear grooves must be in good condition. Too much wear between the parts will cause poor engagement of the gears. This can lead to premature wear of the gear dogs and other parts.

Shift Drum Inspection

1. Clean and dry the shift drum.

2. Inspect the shift drum grooves (A, **Figure 35**). The grooves should be a uniform width with no signs of roughness or damage. Worn grooves can prevent complete gear engagement, which can cause rough shifting.

3. Check the journals (B, **Figure 35**) on each end of the shift drum for excessive wear, scoring or overheating (blue discoloration). Fit the shift drum into each crankcase and check for play, binding or roughness.

4. Check the shift drum detent holes (**Figure 36**) for cracks, excessive wear or other damage.

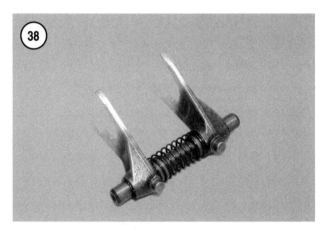

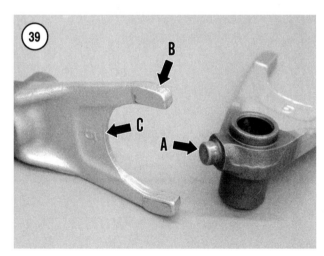

5. Check the shift drum detent assembly (**Figure 37**) for:
   a. Cracked, damaged or weak spring.
   b. Cracked or damaged detent ball.
6. Check the neutral pin (C, **Figure 35**) for damage. The pin is spring-loaded and should return when pressed and released. If damage is noted, perform the following:
   a. Remove the screw, side plate, pin and spring.
   b. Inspect and replace the damaged part(s). Replace the screw if the Torx shoulders were damaged during screw removal.
   c. Remove all threadlocking compound from the screw and shift drum threads if previously used.

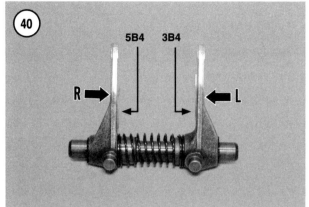

   d. Install the spring, pin and side plate. Fit the groove in the side plate around the pin.
   e. Apply a medium-strength threadlocking compound onto the screw and tighten securely.

Shift Fork and Shaft Inspection

1. If the shift fork assembly (**Figure 38**) is in good condition, it is not necessary to disassemble the parts. If parts are worn, or if the cause of poor shifting is unknown, remove the snap rings and disassemble the parts. Inspect and assemble the parts as described in the following steps.
2. Make sure the guide pin (A, **Figure 39**) is symmetrical with no flat spots. Make sure the pin passes through the mating groove on the shift drum without binding or excessive looseness.
3. Make sure the shift fork claw (B, **Figure 39**) is not worn. The claw surfaces must be smooth with no signs of excessive wear, bending, cracks, scored surface, heat discoloration or other damage. A polished appearance at the contact points is normal.
4. Make sure the radius and sides (C, **Figure 39**) are not worn. If wear is evident (scored surface), the fork is binding in the groove. This could be caused by a worn or damaged fork bore, shift drum, clutch dog or gear. The shift fork shaft may be bent or damaged.
5. Check the shift fork shaft for bending or other damage. Install each shift fork on the shaft and slide it back and forth. Each shift fork must slide smoothly with no binding or tight spots. If any fork binds, check the shaft for bending by rolling it on a flat surface.
6. Inspect the spring for cracks, unevenly spaced coils or other damage.
7. Assemble the shift fork assembly:
   a. Install a new snap ring on one end of the shaft.
   b. Install the shift forks and spring. Install the shift forks so the 3B4 mark on the left shift fork faces the 5B4 mark on the right shift fork (**Figure 40**).
   c. Install a new snap ring in the remaining snap ring groove. Make sure the spring seats over the shoulders on both shift forks.
   d. Make sure both snap rings seat in their grooves completely.

Table 1 TRANSMISSION SPECIFICATIONS

Primary reduction system	Drive belt
Reverse gear ratio	23/14 × 28/23 (2.00)
Secondary reduction ratio	41/21 × 17/12 x 33/9 (10.142)
Secondary reduction system	Shaft drive
Single speed automatic	2.380-0.783:1
Sub-transmission ratio	
Low	31/16 (1.938)
High	31/21 (1.476)
Transmission type	Drive belt automatic
Output shaft runout limit	0.06 mm (0.0024 in.)

Table 2 TRANSMISSION AND SHIFT MECHANISM TORQUE SPECIFICATIONS

	N•m	in.-lb.	ft.-lb.
Shift arm mounting bolt*	14	–	10
Shift lever bolt	14	–	10
Select lever assembly mounting bolts	15	–	11
Shift cover mounting bolts	10	88	–
*Refer to text.			

CHAPTER EIGHT

FUEL INJECTION SYSTEM

The fuel system consists of the fuel tank, fuel pump, fuel pump relay, fuel injector, throttle body, ECU and associated electrical components and wiring.

Air filter service is covered in Chapter Three.

Read *Safety* and *Service Methods* in Chapter One before servicing the vehicle in this chapter.

Tables 1-3 are at the end of this chapter.

FUEL INJECTION (FI)

This section describes the components and operation of the electronic fuel injection (FI) system. The FI system consists of a fuel delivery system and electronic control system. Refer to **Figure 1**.

Components in the fuel delivery system include the fuel tank, fuel pump, fuel pressure regulator, fuel filter, fuel pump relay and fuel injector. The fuel pump resides in the fuel tank and directs fuel to the fuel injector at a regulated pressure of 324 kPa (47 psi). The fuel injector is mounted on the throttle body, which is attached to the intake tube. The fuel pressure regulator and fuel filter are a permanent part of the fuel pump and are not serviceable.

The electronic control system consists of the electronic control unit (ECU) and sensors (**Figure 1**). The ECU determines the output of the fuel injector, as well as controlling ignition timing.

Refer to *Fuel System* in Chapter Two for fuel injection system troubleshooting procedures.

Engine Control Unit (ECU) and Sensors

The engine control unit (ECU) is mounted inside the electrical box, mounted at the front, right side of the vehicle. The ECU contains a program map that determines the optimum fuel injection and ignition timing based on input from the sensors.

1. The throttle position sensor (TPS), located on the throttle body and attached directly to the throttle shaft, indicates throttle angle. The ECU determines the air volume entering the engine based on input from this sensor.

2. The intake air temperature sensor is mounted on the air intake duct. The ECU determines the air density and adjusts the injector opening time based on input from this sensor.

3. The intake air pressure sensor is mounted on the throttle body. The sensor monitors atmospheric pressure and sends this information to the ECU.

4. The idle speed control (ISC) unit is permanently mounted on the throttle body. Using different inputs, the ECU adjusts and maintains idle speed by varying the volume of air that is delivered to the engine. There is no manual idle speed adjustment.

5. The crankshaft position sensor is located inside the right crankcase cover. The sensor provides engine speed and crankshaft position to the ECU.

6. The speed sensor is mounted on the right side of the engine and informs the ECU of vehicle speed.

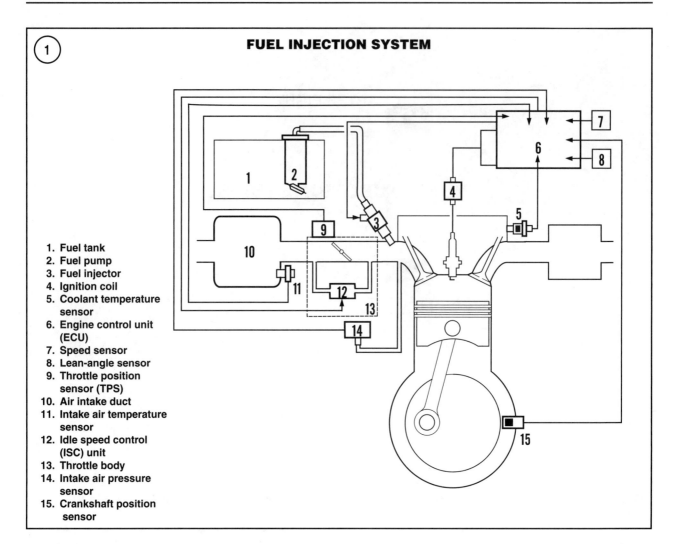

FUEL INJECTION SYSTEM

1. Fuel tank
2. Fuel pump
3. Fuel injector
4. Ignition coil
5. Coolant temperature sensor
6. Engine control unit (ECU)
7. Speed sensor
8. Lean-angle sensor
9. Throttle position sensor (TPS)
10. Air intake duct
11. Intake air temperature sensor
12. Idle speed control (ISC) unit
13. Throttle body
14. Intake air pressure sensor
15. Crankshaft position sensor

7. The lean-angle sensor, located at the front of the vehicle, interrupts the ignition and shuts off the engine if the vehicle lean angle exceeds 60-70° from vertical.

8. The coolant temperature sensor is located in the cylinder head. The ECU adjusts the injector opening time based on input from this sensor.

Fuel Delivery System

Fuel pump

The fuel pump is located inside the fuel tank.

Fuel pressure regulator

A fuel pressure regulator within the fuel pump unit maintains fuel pressure at 324 kPa (46.1 psi).

Fuel injector

The multiple-orifice fuel injector consists of a solenoid plunger, needle valve and housing. The injector operates at a constant pressure.

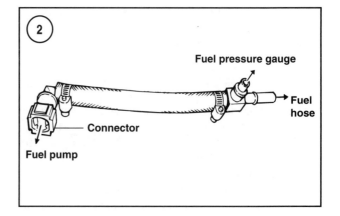

Fuel pressure gauge

Fuel hose

Connector

Fuel pump

Throttle Body

The throttle body is attached to the intake tube at the cylinder. Mounted on the throttle body are the throttle position sensor (TPS) and the idle speed control (ISC) unit.

Fuel Injection System Fuse

The fuel injection system is protected by a 10 amp fuse. Refer to Chapter Nine.

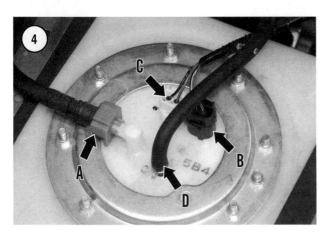

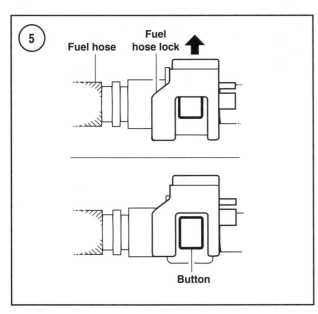

Fuel hose   Fuel
hose lock

Button

FUEL DELIVERY SYSTEM TESTS

The following tests evaluate the performance of the fuel delivery system (fuel pump and fuel pressure regulator).

WARNING
Before disconnecting the fuel fittings and hoses, turn the ignition switch off and allow the system to internally release fuel pressure.

WARNING
*Fuel will spill and fuel vapors will be present when performing this procedure. Because gasoline is extremely flammable, perform this procedure away from all open flames, including appliance pilot lights and sparks. Do not smoke or allow someone who is smoking in the work area as an explosion and fire may occur. Always work in a well-ventilated area. Wipe up spills immediately. Keep a fire extinguisher nearby. Refer to **Safety** in Chapter One.*

WARNING
Always wear eye protection when working on the fuel system.

Fuel Pump Operation Test

Make sure the battery and ignition switch are working correctly. Refer to Chapter Nine.
1. Remove the passenger seat (Chapter Sixteen).
2. Turn the ignition switch on and listen for operation of the fuel pump.
3. If no sound is heard, check the fuel injection system fuse (Chapter Nine).
4. If the fuse is good, test the fuel injection system relay as described in this chapter and the lean-angle sensor (Chapter Nine). If both of these components are within specification, replace the fuel pump. If the fuel pump is okay, replace the ECU with a known-good unit and retest.

Fuel Pressure Test

The following procedure requires a fuel pressure adapter (Yamaha part No. YM-03176 [**Figure 2**] or an equivalent) and fuel pressure gauge (Yamaha part No. YU-03153 or an equivalent).
1. Remove the passenger seat (Chapter Sixteen).
2. Remove the bolts and the damper plate (**Figure 3**). Do not remove the breather hose or wiring harness from the clamp on the bottom of the damper plate.
3. Disconnect the fuel hose (A, **Figure 4**) at the fuel pump fitting as follows:
   a. Place a rag underneath the fuel hose fitting to catch spilled fuel.
   b. Slide the fuel hose lock in the direction shown in **Figure 5** until it stops. The lock will remain on the fuel hose.
   c. Push the two buttons (**Figure 5**) on the fuel hose, then pull the fuel hose and disconnect it from the fuel pump.
4. Connect the fuel pressure adapter (**Figure 2**) between the fuel pump and fuel hose using the ends of the adapter identified in **Figure 2**. Slide the adapter's connector over the fuel pump fitting until it clicks, then slide the lock down to lock it. Repeat when connecting the fuel hose connector (A, **Figure 4**) to the adapter.

5. Connect the fuel pressure gauge onto the adapter fitting identified in **Figure 2**. Slide the fuel gauge connector over the adapter fitting until it clicks, then slide the lock down to lock it.

6. Remove the rag from underneath the fuel tank and dispose of properly.

> *WARNING*
> *Wipe up all spilled fuel underneath the fuel tank before starting the engine.*

7. Start the engine and run it at idle. Read the fuel pressure and compare with the specification in **Table 2**.

8A. If the fuel pressure is less than specified, check for a leak in the fuel system or a plugged or damaged hose. If no external problem is found, replace the fuel pump as described in this chapter and retest.

8B. If the fuel pressure exceeds specification, the fuel pressure regulator is faulty. Replace the fuel pump as described in this chapter.

9. Place a rag underneath the fuel hose and remove the fuel pressure gauge and adapter.

10. Reconnect the fuel hose (A, **Figure 4**) onto the fuel pump, then slide the lock down to lock the hose in place (**Figure 5**).

11. Turn the ignition switch on to pressurize the system and check for leaks. Turn the ignition switch off.

> *WARNING*
> *Do not start the engine if the fuel hose is leaking.*

12. Install the damper plate (**Figure 3**) and tighten the mounting bolts to 16 N•m (12 ft.-lb.).

13. Reinstall the passenger seat (Chapter Sixteen).

FUEL TANK

Removal/Installation

> *WARNING*
> *Work in a well ventilated area that is free of all sparks and pilot lights.*

1. Disconnect the negative battery cable (Chapter Nine).
2. Remove the following as described in Chapter Sixteen:
   a. Seats.
   b. Rear console.
   c. Front console.
   d. Right side panel and right corner panel.
   e. Right protector.
   f. Passenger seat support.
3. Remove the bolts and the damper plate (**Figure 3**). Disconnect the wiring harness from the clamp on the bottom of the damper plate.
4. Disconnect the following at the fuel pump:
   a. Fuel sender connector (B, **Figure 4**).
   b. Fuel pump connector (C, **Figure 4**).
   c. Breather hose (D, **Figure 4**).

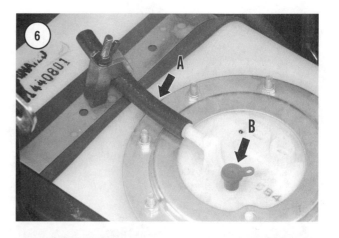

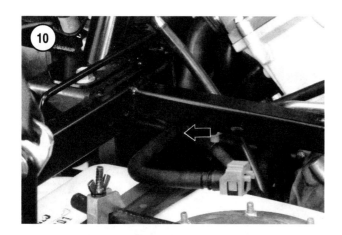

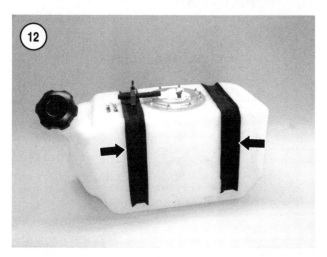

7. Remove the outer and inner fuel tank mounting bracket bolts (**Figure 7**).

8. Pry the mounting brackets (**Figure 8**) away from the rubber straps placed across the top and side of the fuel tank.

9. Slide the fuel tank toward the right side of the vehicle until it stops, then unhook the mounting brackets from the hooks on the left side of the fuel tank and remove them.

NOTE
Because the fuel cap must be removed when removing the tank, siphon as much fuel out of the tank as possible. Because the fill spout will be pointing down during fuel tank removal, any fuel remaining in the tank will spill out.

10. Using a siphon, drain the fuel tank (**Figure 9**). Tilt the tank to remove as much fuel from the tank as possible.

NOTE
Even with the right rear wheel removed, the fuel tank cannot be removed from the rear of the vehicle.

11. Open the clamp (**Figure 10**) and reroute the fuel hose so it does not interfere with fuel tank removal.

12. Remove the fuel cap. Then cover the fuel tank filler opening with a thick plastic bag and secure with a plastic-tie.

13. Pivot the tank upward (**Figure 11**) and remove it through the passenger compartment.

14. Remove the plastic from the filler tank opening and reinstall the fuel cap.

15. Inspect the rubber straps (**Figure 12**) for looseness or damage. Replace or reinstall the rubber straps if necessary. Secure the rubber straps in place with a rubber adhesive.

16. Installation is the reverse of removal. Note the following:

    a. Reconnect the fuel hose (A, **Figure 4**) onto the fuel pump, then slide the lock down to lock the hose in place (**Figure 5**).

    b. Tighten the fuel tank mounting bracket bolts to 30 N•m (22 ft.-lb.).

    c. Turn the ignition switch on to pressurize the system and check for leaks. Turn the ignition switch off.

WARNING
Do not start the engine if the fuel hose is leaking.

    d. Install the damper plate (**Figure 3**) and tighten the mounting bolts to 16 N•m (12 ft.-lb.).

WARNING
Do not overfill the tank. During hot weather, fuel expansion can cause fuel to leak from the fuel tank.

5. Disconnect the fuel hose (A, **Figure 4**) at the fuel pump fitting as follows:

    a. Place a rag underneath the fuel hose fitting to catch spilled fuel.

    b. Slide the fuel hose lock in the direction shown in **Figure 5** until it stops. The lock will remain on the fuel hose.

    c. Push the two buttons (**Figure 5**) on the fuel hose, then pull the fuel hose and disconnect it from the fuel pump.

6. Plug the fuel hose (A, **Figure 6**) and breather hose (B) openings.

FUEL PUMP

NOTE
Other than the mounting ring and gasket at the top of the fuel pump, there are no replacement parts available for the fuel pump assembly. It must be replaced as a unit.

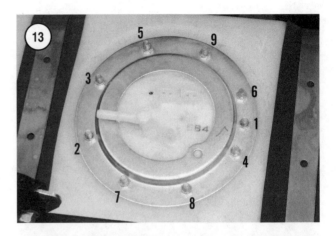

Removal/Installation

The fuel pump can be removed with the fuel tank mounted in the frame.

1. Disconnect the hoses and connectors at the fuel pump and drain the fuel tank as described in *Fuel Tank* in this chapter.

2. Evenly loosen in several steps the fuel pump mounting plate nuts in the numerical order shown in **Figure 13**. Then remove the nuts and the mounting plate.

3. Lift the fuel pump straight up (**Figure 14**), then tilt it forward so the fuel level sender can clear the tank opening, then remove the fuel pump.

4. Cover the fuel tank opening.

5. Remove and discard the gasket (**Figure 15**) at the top of the fuel pump.

6. Clean the gasket surface on the top of the fuel tank.

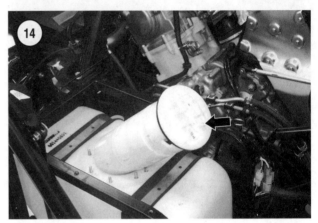

7. Make sure the three rubber dampers are installed on the bottom of the fuel pump.

8. Install the fuel pump by tilting the pump and inserting the fuel lever sender (**Figure 16**) into the front part of the tank. When the fuel level sender is inside the tank, align the fuel pump and slide it through the fuel tank opening. The clearance between the middle of the fuel pump and tank opening is small.

9. When the fuel pump is bottomed inside the tank, install the mounting plate on top of the fuel pump by aligning the hole in the plate with the pin on the pump (**Figure 17**). Then align the holes in the mounting plate with the studs in the tank. Push the mounting plate down to seat the pump gasket against the tank, then hold in place and install the nuts hand-tight. The top of the tank is spring loaded and will rise up when released.

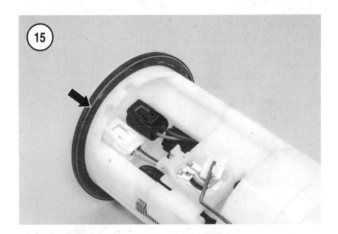

10. Tighten the nuts in several steps in the numerical order shown in **Figure 13** to 8 N•m (71 in.-lb.).

11. Reverse Step 1 to complete installation. Turn the ignition switch on to pressurize the system and check for leaks. Turn the ignition switch off.

WARNING
Do not start the engine if there are any fuel leaks.

WARNING
Do not overfill the tank. During hot weather, fuel expansion can cause fuel to leak from the fuel tank.

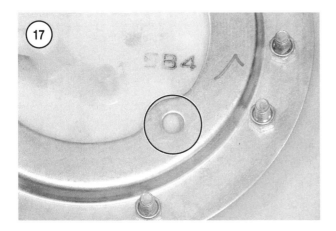

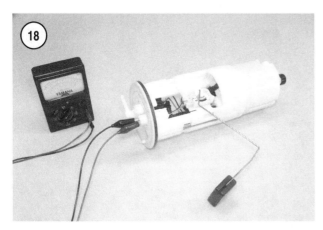

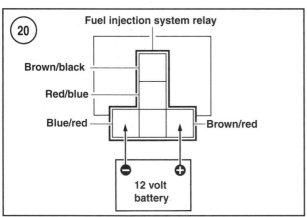

Fuel injection system relay

Brown/black

Red/blue

Blue/red — — Brown/red

12 volt battery

FUEL LEVEL SENDER

The fuel level sender is permanently attached to the fuel pump.

Testing

1. Remove the fuel pump as described in this chapter.
2. Place the fuel pump on a clean surface with the fuel level sender accessible.
3. Measure resistance across the fuel level sensor connector. Connect the positive ohmmeter lead to the orange/black terminal wire and the negative lead to the black/white terminal wire (**Figure 18**).
4. Raise and lower the fuel level sender float while reading the ohmmeter and compare the resistance readings to the specifications in **Table 2**. Replace the fuel pump if either resistance reading is out of specification.

FUEL INJECTION SYSTEM RELAY

The fuel injection system relay controls power to the fuel pump and fuel injector. The ECU controls relay operation. The fuel injection system relay is located in the electrical box at the front of the vehicle.

Removal/Installation

1. Open the hood and remove the electrical box cover.
2. Pull the fuel injection system relay (**Figure 19**) to disconnect it from the wiring harness.
3. Installation is the reverse of removal.

Testing

1. Remove the relay as described in this section.
2. Disconnect the wire harness from the relay.
3. Use an ohmmeter and check the continuity of the relay as follows (**Figure 20**):
    a. Use jumpers to connect the positive battery terminal to the brown/red terminal and the negative battery terminal to the blue/red terminal on the relay.
    b. Connect the positive ohmmeter lead to the brown/black terminal and the negative ohmmeter lead to the red/blue terminal on the relay.
    c. The unit should have continuity while voltage is applied.
4. Replace the relay if there is no continuity.

THROTTLE BODY

Removal

1. Remove the seats and rear console (Chapter Sixteen).
2. Disconnect the breather hose (**Figure 21**) at the air intake duct and set aside.

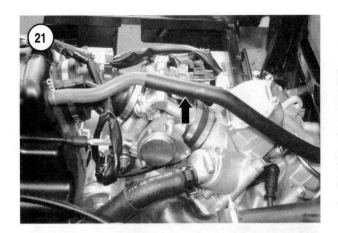

3. Disconnect the intake air pressure sensor connector (A, **Figure 22**).

4. Disconnect the idle speed control unit electrical connector (B, **Figure 22**).

5. Remove the screws and the accelerator cable housing cover (C, **Figure 22**) and O-ring.

6. Disconnect the accelerator cable as follows:

   a. Loosen the accelerator cable adjuster locknut (A, **Figure 23**) and turn the adjuster (B) to loosen the accelerator cable.

NOTE
*The accelerator cable is secured to the cable guide with a brass collar (**Figure 24**). Place a rag underneath the throttle body to help catch the collar if it falls off the end of the cable.*

   b. Have an assistant push down and hold the cable guide at the throttle body. Because of the strong spring pressure, use a piece of metal (A, **Figure 25**) to hold the cable guide in place.

   c. Use needle nose pliers and pull the brass collar out of the cable guide. If necessary, work the cable out of the cable guide to help with removal of the cable collar, then disconnect the cable (B, **Figure 25**). When the cable is free, remove the brass collar (**Figure 26**).

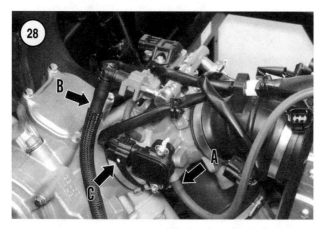

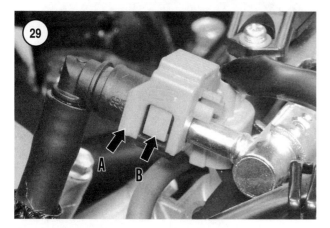

d. Turn the cable adjuster (**Figure 27**) to disconnect it from the threaded cable collar attached to the throttle body. When the adjuster is free, remove it and the cable from the throttle body.

7. Disconnect the throttle body breather hose (A, **Figure 28**).

8. Disconnect the fuel hose (B, **Figure 28**) at the throttle body fitting as follows:

    a. Place a rag underneath the fuel hose fitting to catch spilled fuel.

    b. Slide the fuel hose lock up (A, **Figure 29**) until it stops. The lock will remain on the fuel hose.

    c. Push the two buttons (B, **Figure 29**) on the fuel hose, then pull the fuel hose and disconnect it from the throttle body.

9. Disconnect the throttle position sensor electrical connector (C, **Figure 28**).

10. Disconnect the fuel injector electrical connector (**Figure 30**).

11. Remove the wiring harness bundle from the clamp on the top of the air duct (A, **Figure 31**) and set aside.

12. Loosen the two air intake duct joint hose clamps (B, **Figure 31**).

13. Push the air intake duct joint toward the rear to disconnect it from the throttle body, then twist and remove it from the air intake duct (**Figure 32**).

14. Loosen the front intake tube hose clamp bolt (A, **Figure 33**) and remove the throttle body assembly

15. To remove the intake tube (A, **Figure 34**), loosen the rear hose clamp (B, **Figure 33**) and remove the intake tube.

16. Plug the intake opening to avoid dropping objects into the cylinder head.

17. Clean and inspect the throttle body as described in this section.

Installation

1. Remove the plug from the intake opening. Then check there is no debris in the cylinder head.

2. Install the intake tube by aligning the slot in the tube with the raised boss on the cylinder head (B, **Figure 34**). Tighten the rear hose clamp bolt (B, **Figure 33**) securely.

3. Make sure the hose clamps properly fit around the locating tubes (C, **Figure 33**) on the intake tube.

4. Install the throttle body by inserting the tab on the throttle body into the notch in the intake tube (**Figure 35**). Tighten the front hose clamp bolt (A, **Figure 33**) securely.

5. Install the air intake duct joint into the air intake duct (**Figure 32**) and reconnect it onto the throttle body. Also make sure air intake duct joint shoulder is not pinched. Then align the raised shoulder on the air intake duct joint between the two round tabs on the air intake duct (**Figure 36**). Recheck the alignment and tighten the two hose clamps (B, **Figure 31**) securely.

6. Position the wiring harness beside the throttle body while aligning the electrical connectors with their positions on the throttle body. Make sure the connectors are not twisted. Then install the wiring harness bundle so that the section with the white tape fits into the clamp on top of the air intake duct (A, **Figure 31**).

7. Reconnect the fuel injector electrical connector (**Figure 30**).

8. Reconnect the throttle position sensor electrical connector (C, **Figure 28**).

9. Reconnect the fuel hose (B, **Figure 28**) onto the throttle body, then slide the lock down to lock the hose in place (**Figure 37**).

10. Reconnect the throttle body breather hose (A, **Figure 28**).

11. Reconnect the accelerator cable as follows:

> *NOTE*
> *Before reconnecting the accelerator cable, inspect the cable end for fraying and other damage. Also check the outer sheath for bending, creases or other damage. If damaged, replace the cable as described in this chapter.*

   a. Insert the cable end through the collar, then thread the cable adjuster onto the collar until it bottoms against the nut on the collar.

   b. Pull the cable (B, **Figure 25**) until all of the slack is removed, then have an assistant push down and hold the cable guide in place with a piece of metal (A).

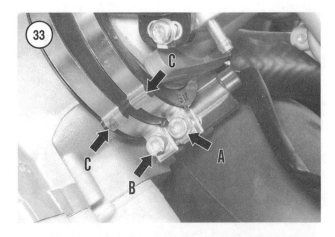

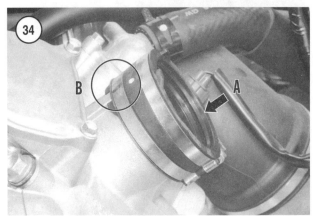

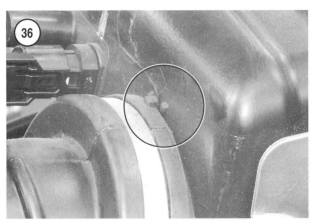

c. Lubricate the cable end and brass collar with lithium grease and install the collar onto the cable end (**Figure 26**).

d. Route the cable around the cable guide and fit the brass collar into the hole in the throttle wheel, then release the throttle wheel. Make sure the cable is routed through the guide in the throttle wheel and the brass collar fits tightly into the hole (**Figure 24**).

e. Adjust the accelerator cable as described in Chapter Three. Make sure the accelerator cable adjuster locknut (A, **Figure 23**) is tight after adjusting the accelerator cable.

12. Install the O-ring, accelerator cable housing cover (C, **Figure 22**) and secure with the screws. Tighten the screws securely.

13. Reconnect the idle speed control unit electrical connector (B, **Figure 22**).

14. Reconnect the intake air pressure sensor electrical connector (A, **Figure 22**).

15. Reconnect the breather hose (**Figure 21**) at the air intake duct.

16. Install the rear console and seats (Chapter Sixteen).

17. Shift the transmission into neutral and start the engine. Make sure the engine idles properly.

Cleaning/Inspection

1. The throttle body is pre-set by the manufacturer. Do not disassemble the throttle body in any way other than as described in this section.

2. Do not loosen the idle speed control unit screws (A, **Figure 38**) or attempt to adjust the idle speed screw (B). Doing so may cause throttle and idle valve synchronization failure.

3. The throttle position sensor (A, **Figure 39**) and intake air pressure sensor (B) can be serviced as described in this chapter.

4. Check intake air pressure sensor hose (C, **Figure 39**) for damage. Make sure the hose is connected onto the throttle body and sensor ports.

5. Clean the throttle body with a fuel injection cleaner. Do not use caustic carburetor cleaning chemicals. Plug all openings before cleaning.

6. Do not clean the sensors, seals or plastic parts with any chemical cleaner.

7. Do not push against the throttle valve (**Figure 40**) to open it. Turn the throttle shaft to open the valve.

8. Do not damage the throttle valve or throttle valve bore as this may cause the engine to idle roughly.

10. Inspect the throttle body for cracks or other damage that could admit unfiltered air.

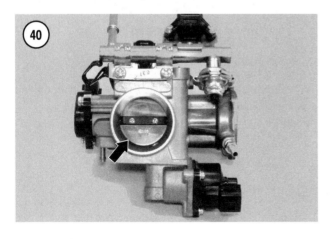

FUEL RAIL AND FUEL INJECTOR

Preliminary Inspection

The fuel injector can be checked as follows:

8

1. Remove the console (Chapter Sixteen).
2. Start the engine and allow to idle.
3. Use a mechanic's stethoscope and listen for operating sounds at the fuel injector.
4. If the injector is quiet, replace it as described in this section.
5. Look and feel around the fuel injector where it enters the throttle body and fuel rail. Check for any leaks.

Removal/Installation

1. Remove the throttle body as described in this chapter.
2. Disconnect the intake air pressure sensor hose (C, **Figure 39**) at the throttle body.
3. Remove the screws (A, **Figure 41**) and lift the fuel rail (B) while also removing the fuel injector from the throttle body.
4. Remove the fuel injector (A, **Figure 42**) from the fuel rail (B).
5. Remove the fuel injector seal (A, **Figure 43**) from the throttle body and discard it. The O-ring (B, **Figure 43**) installed on the fuel injector is not available separately.
6. Install a new fuel injector seal (A, **Figure 43**) into the throttle body with its flat side facing out.
7. Install the fuel injector (A, **Figure 42**) into the fuel rail with its connector terminal aligned with the U-shaped guide (A, **Figure 42**).
8. Install the fuel rail by inserting the fuel injector into its seal.
9. Install the two screws (A, **Figure 41**) securing the fuel rail to the throttle body and tighten securely.
10. Reconnect the intake air pressure sensor hose (C, **Figure 39**) at the throttle body.
11. Install the throttle body as described in this chapter.
12. Turn the ignition switch on to activate the fuel pump for a few seconds, then turn the ignition switch off when the fuel pump stops running. When the fuel pump runs, fuel pressure rises in the fuel system. Repeat this sequence two times. Then turn the ignition switch off and check for fuel leaks around the fuel injector, fuel rail and pressure regulator. Repair any leaks before starting the engine.

Inspection

1. Replace the intake air pressure hose (C, **Figure 39**) if damaged.
2. Inspect the fuel injector and its O-ring (B, **Figure 43**) for damage. The O-ring is not available separately.
3. Inspect the injector nozzle (C, **Figure 43**) for carbon buildup.
4. Check the fuel injector terminals (D, **Figure 43**) and the wiring harness connector for corrosion or damage.
5. Make sure the fuel injector mounting bore in the fuel rail is clean.
6. Inspect the fuel rail (B, **Figure 42**) for damage.

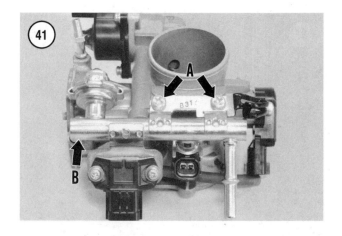

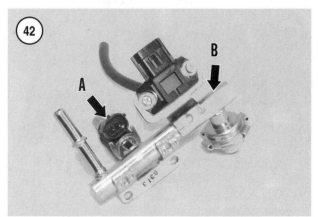

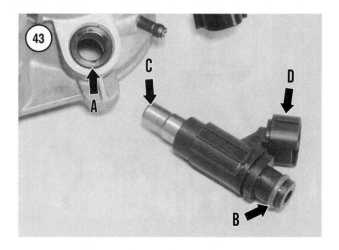

IDLE SPEED CONTROL UNIT

Removal/Installation

The idle speed control unit (A, **Figure 38**) is preset and permanently mounted onto the throttle body and must not be adjusted or removed.

THROTTLE POSITION SENSOR

Adjustment

1. Remove the rear console (Chapter Sixteen).

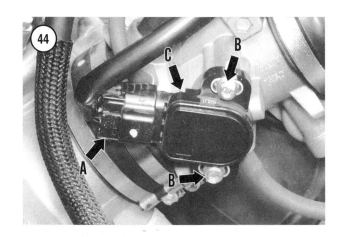

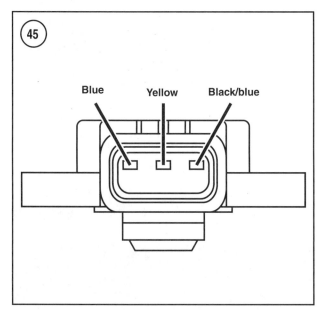

2. Make marks on the throttle position sensor and throttle body so the sensor can be reinstalled in its original position.

3. Disconnect the throttle position sensor connector (A, **Figure 44**).

4. Remove the sensor mounting screws (B, **Figure 44**).

5. Pull out and remove the throttle position sensor (C, **Figure 44**) and its O-ring.

6. Installation is the reverse of these steps, plus the following:

    a. Make sure the tab on the sensor fits into the slot in the throttle body shaft.

    b. Adjust the sensor as described in this section.

Testing

1. Remove the throttle position sensor as described in this section.

2. Connect the positive lead of an ohmmeter to the blue (**Figure 45**) terminal on the sensor and the negative lead to the black/blue terminal on the sensor.

3. The ohmmeter should indicate the maximum resistance listed in **Table 2**. Replace the throttle position sensor if the resistance is not within specification.

ENGINE CONTROL UNIT (ECU)

Testing

> *NOTE*
> *The ECU is expensive. Be sure the ECU is faulty before purchasing a new unit. Most dealerships do not accept returned electrical components. Refer to **Electrical Component Replacement** in Chapter Nine.*

Test specifications for the engine control unit (ECU) are not available. Determining whether the ECU is faulty requires eliminating other possible causes through troubleshooting. Refer to Chapter Two for troubleshooting procedures.

Removal/Installation

The engine control unit is mounted inside the electrical box.

1. Open the hood and remove the electrical box cover (Chapter Nine).

2. Disconnect the negative battery cable at the battery (Chapter Nine).

3. Remove the mounting bolts (A, **Figure 46**) and remove the ECU (B) from the electrical box.

4. Disconnect the two connectors (**Figure 47**) at the ECU.

5. Installation is the reverse of removal.

6. Install the ECU with its lower mounting flange inserted into the mating flange slot in the bottom of the electrical box.

2. Using back probe pins, insert the voltmeter test leads into the connector (A, **Figure 44**) so the positive lead contacts the yellow wire and the negative lead contacts the black/blue wire. Refer to *Back Probe Pins* in *Measuring Tools* in Chapter One.

3. Start and run the engine at idle speed.

4. Observe the voltmeter reading. The specified voltage is 0.68 volts. If the voltage is not within specification, perform Step 5.

5. Loosen the mounting screws (B, **Figure 44**) and slowly rotate the throttle position sensor until the voltage reading is within specification.

6. Tighten the mounting screws securely.

7. Turn the ignition switch off.

8. Disconnect the tester leads and remove the back probe pins. Apply silicone sealant over the pin holes in the two wires.

9. Install the rear console (Chapter Sixteen).

Removal/Installation

1. Remove the rear console (Chapter Sixteen).

INTAKE AIR PRESSURE SENSOR

The intake air pressure sensor is mounted on the throttle body.

Removal/Installation

1. Remove the rear console (Chapter Sixteen).
2. Disconnect the connector (A, **Figure 48**).
3. Remove the mounting screws and sensor (B, **Figure 48**).
4. Installation is the reverse of removal. Tighten the mounting screws securely.

Output Voltage Test

1. Remove the rear console (Chapter Sixteen).

NOTE
The connector must remain attached to the intake air pressure sensor during this test.

2. Using back probe pins, insert the voltmeter test leads into the connector (A, **Figure 48**) so the positive lead contacts the pink wire and the negative lead contacts the black/blue wire. Refer to *Back Probe Pins* in *Measuring Tools* in Chapter One.
3. Turn the ignition switch on and measure the output voltage. It should be within the specifications in **Table 2**. Replace the sensor if it fails the voltage test.
4. Disconnect the tester leads and remove the back probe pins. Apply silicone sealant over the pin holes in the two wires.
5. Install the rear console (Chapter Sixteen).

INTAKE AIR TEMPERATURE SENSOR

The intake air temperature sensor is mounted on the air intake duct.

CAUTION
The intake air temperature sensor is sensitive to shock. Handle it carefully.

Removal/Installation

1. Remove the rear console (Chapter Sixteen).
2. Disconnect the breather hose at the air intake duct.
3. Disconnect the connector (A, **Figure 49**).
4. Remove screw and sensor (B, **Figure 49**).
5. Installation is the reverse of removal. Tighten the screw securely..

Resistance Test

1. Remove the intake air temperature sensor as described in this section.

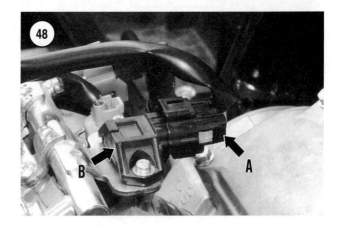

NOTE
Refer to the wiring harness connector to identify the sensor terminals in Step 2.

2. Connect the positive ohmmeter leads across brown/white sensor terminal and the negative lead across the black/blue sensor terminal.

NOTE
Do not allow the air temperature terminals or test leads to get wet.

3. Support the intake air temperature sensor and a thermometer rated higher than the test temperature in a pan of water. The intake air temperature sensor and thermometer

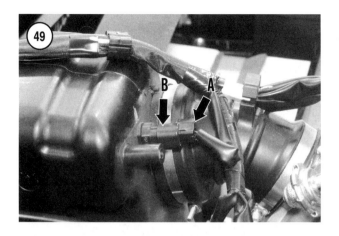

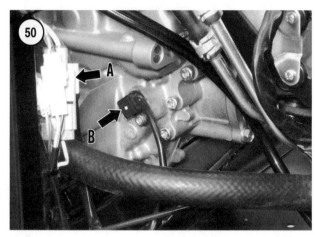

must not touch the sides or bottom of the pan or a false reading will result.

CAUTION
Protect the ohmmeter leads from heat damage.

4. Gradually heat the water to a temperature above the test temperature listed in **Table 2**.
5. Allow the water to cool while checking the resistance between the terminals on the sensor at the temperature specified in **Table 2**.
6. If the resistance reading does not match the specification listed in **Table 2** at the specified temperature, replace the sensor.

COOLANT TEMPERATURE SENSOR

Refer to *Cooling System* in Chapter Nine for replacement and testing procedures.

CRANKSHAFT POSITION SENSOR

Refer to Chapter Nine for replacement and testing procedures.

SPEED SENSOR

The speed sensor is mounted on the front, right side of the engine.

Removal/Installation

1. Remove the passenger seat (Chapter Sixteen).
2. Remove the rear console (Chapter Sixteen).
3. Disconnect the white speed sensor connector (A, **Figure 50**).
4. Remove the mounting screw and the speed sensor (B, **Figure 50**). Discard the O-ring.
5. Installation is the reverse of removal. Lubricate a new O-ring with lithium grease and install on the speed sensor. Tighten the mounting screw to 10 N•m (88 in.-lb.).

Voltage Test

1. Remove the passenger seat (Chapter Sixteen).
2. Remove the rear console (Chapter Sixteen).
3. Support the vehicle with the rear wheels off the ground.
4. Locate the white speed sensor connector (A, **Figure 50**).
5. Using back probe pins, insert the voltmeter test leads into the harness end of the speed sensor connector so the positive lead contact the white terminal and the negative lead contacts the black/blue terminal. Refer to *Back Probe Pins* in *Measuring Tools* in Chapter One.
6. Turn the ignition switch on and slowly rotate the rear wheels while observing the voltmeter.
7. The speed sensor is operating properly if the voltage cycles between 0.6 and 4.9 volts per each revolution of the wheel. Replace the speed sensor if the voltage is not withing specification.
8. Turn the ignition switch off and lower the rear wheels onto the ground.
9. Disconnect the tester leads and remove the back probe pins. Apply silicone sealant over the pin holes in the two wires.
10. Reverse Steps 1-3.

LEAN-ANGLE SENSOR

Refer to Chapter Nine for testing and replacement procedures.

ROLLOVER VALVE

Removal/Installation

1. Remove the passenger seat (Chapter Sixteen).
2. Remove the rear console (Chapter Sixteen).
3. Open the clamps securing the rollover valve (**Figure 51**) in place. The lower hose is connected to the fuel tank.
4. Label and disconnect the upper and lower hoses at the rollover valve and remove the valve.
5. Inspect the rollover valve housing for cracks and other damage.
6. Installation is the reverse of these steps. Install the rollover valve with its UP mark facing up.

Test

If the engine is not receiving fuel (spark plug tip is dry when checked), disconnect the fuel tank-to-rollover breather hose at the rollover valve (**Figure 51**) and try to start the engine. If the engine starts, the rollover is probably damaged or its breather hose is plugged.

AIR BOX

Removal/Installation

1. Open the hood.
2. Turn and remove the two plastic rivets and remove the air box shroud (A, **Figure 52**).
3. Remove the bolts (B, **Figure 52**) and collars securing the air box to the frame.
4. Before loosening the hose clamp at the bottom of the air box, note the alignment tab on the left side of the air box joint and where it aligns with the two raised tabs on the air box. Loosen the hose clamp securing the air box joint to the bottom of the air box.
5. Remove the air box assembly (C, **Figure 52**). Cover the opening on the bottom of the air box with a plastic bag.
6A. If the air box joint (**Figure 53**) will be removed, note the alignment tab on the left side of the air box joint and where it aligns with the two raised tabs on the air intake duct. Loosen the hose clamp and remove the air box joint. Cover the air duct opening with a plastic bag.
6B. If the air box joint (**Figure 53**) will not be removed, cover its opening with a plastic bag.
7. Installation is the reverse of removal. Make sure the alignment tabs on the air box joint align with the raised tabs on the air box and air intake duct. Tighten the hose clamps securely.

AIR INTAKE DUCT

The air intake duct (**Figure 54**) connects the air box to the throttle body assembly.

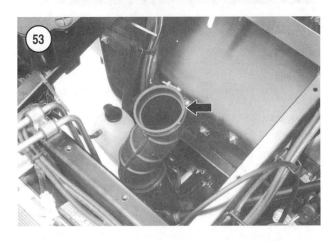

Removal/Installation

1. Remove the following as described in Chapter Sixteen:
   a. Seats.
   b. Rear console.
   c. Front console.
   d. Corner panels and side panels.

> *NOTE*
> *Note all wiring harness and cable routing paths alongside the air intake duct so they can be routed and repositioned following their original paths.*

2. Disconnect the ignition coil electrical connectors located underneath the driver's seat.

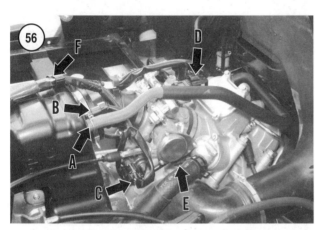

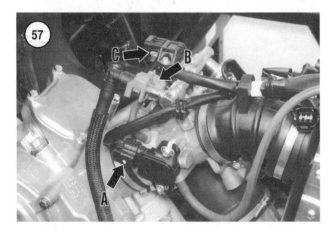

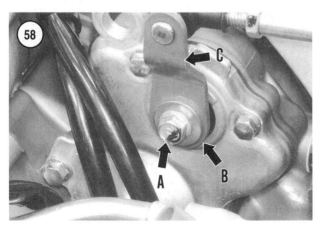

3. Remove the air box and air box joint as described in this chapter.

4. Disconnect the parking brake electrical connector (A, **Figure 55**).

5. Remove the two bolts (B, **Figure 55**) securing the parking brake bracket to the seat support bracket.

NOTE
If the throttle body will also be removed, remove it first as described in this chapter.

6. Disconnect the breather hose (A, **Figure 56**) at the air intake duct.

7. Disconnect the intake air temperature sensor electrical connector (B, **Figure 56**).

8. Disconnect the idle speed control unit electrical connector (C, **Figure 56**).

9. Disconnect the intake air pressure sensor electrical connector (D, **Figure 56**).

10. Disconnect the coolant temperature electrical connector (E, **Figure 56**).

11. Disconnect the throttle position sensor electrical connector (A, **Figure 57**).

NOTE
*If the fuel hose interferes with the fuel injector electrical connector removal in Step 12, disconnect the fuel hose (B, **Figure 57**) at the throttle body as described in **Throttle Body** in this chapter.*

12. Disconnect the fuel injector electrical connector (C, **Figure 57**).

13. Remove the wiring harness bundle (F, **Figure 56**) from the clamp on top of the air intake duct.

14. Remove the shift arm mounting bolt (A, **Figure 58**), washer (B) and remove the shift arm (C) from the shift shaft.

NOTE
Note the accelerator cable routing before removing it from the clamp in Step 15.

15. Open the clamp securing the accelerator cable to the seat support bracket (A, **Figure 59**).

16. Disconnect the gear position switch electrical connector (B, **Figure 59**).

NOTE
Before removing the wiring harness clamp in Step 17, note how the wiring harness is routed through the seat support bracket.

17. Disconnect the clamp (**Figure 60**) securing the wiring harness bundle to the seat support bracket.
18. Remove the seat support bracket mounting bolts.
19. Disconnect the reverse switch electrical connector (**Figure 61**). Note how the switch wiring harness is routed through the seat support bracket.
20. Remove the seat support bracket (A, **Figure 62**) by disconnecting it from the rubber damper (B) mounted on the air intake duct.
21. Loosen the hose clamp (**Figure 63**) securing the air intake duct joint to the air intake duct.
22. Remove the coolant reserve tank mounting bolts. It is not necessary to remove the coolant reserve tank.
23. Remove the two air intake duct mounting bolts (**Figure 64**).

NOTE
If removing the engine, the air intake duct can remain in the frame by repositioning it as necessary.

24. Remove the air intake duct assembly.

NOTE
If the front air duct mounting bolt brackets interfere with removal, it will be necessary to loosen or remove some of the floorboard panels as described in Chapter Sixteen.

25. Installation is the reverse of removal. Note the following:
   a. Check the inside of the air intake duct for any debris.
   b. Align the raised shoulder on the air intake duct joint between the two round tabs on the air intake duct (**Figure 65**). Tighten the clamp securely.
   c. Tighten the air intake duct mounting bolts (**Figure 64**) to 7 N•m (62 in.-lb.).
   d. Tighten the seat support bracket mounting bolts (**Figure 66**) to 32 N•m (24 ft.-lb.).
   e. Install the shift guide by aligning its flats with the flats on the shift shaft (**Figure 67**). Then apply a medium-strength threadlocking compound onto the shift arm mounting bolt (A, **Figure 58**) threads and tighten to 14 N•m (10 ft.-lb.).
   f. Turn the ignition switch on and shift the transmission from neutral into hight gear, low gear and reverse. Make sure the shift indicator light for each position comes on when the gear change is made. If not, adjust the select lever (Chapter Three).

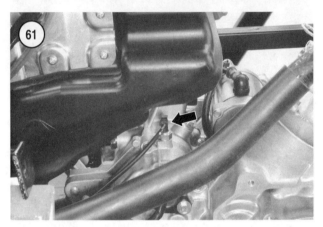

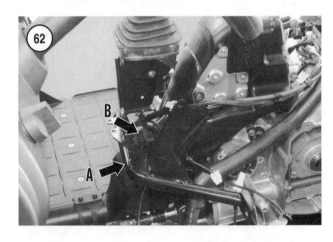

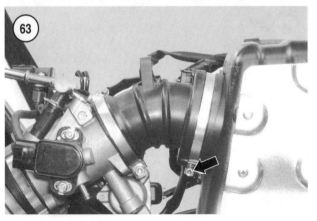

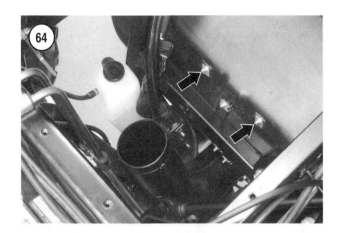

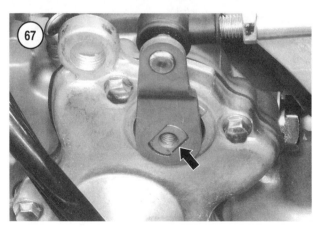

8

ACCELERATOR CABLE

Removal/Installation

NOTE
The following cable and clamp information was noted on a 2009 model. Note that the clamps and routing on your vehicle may differ, possibly due to manufacturing changes or changes made by a previous owner.

1. Remove the following as described in Chapter Sixteen:
   a. Seats.
   b. Rear console.

NOTE
*The accelerator cable passes through a cable guide welded to the frame, which is located underneath the left side of the front console (**Figure 68**). If the accelerator cable can be guided through this cable guide during replacement, removal of the center console is not required.*

   c. Front console (if necessary).
2. Remove the air box as described in this chapter.
3. Note the accelerator cable routing from the pedal to the throttle body.
4. Remove the screws and the accelerator cable housing cover and O-ring at the throttle body.
5. Loosen the accelerator cable adjuster locknut (A, **Figure 69**) and turn the adjuster (B) to loosen the accelerator cable.

NOTE
*The accelerator cable is secured to the cable guide with a brass collar (**Figure 70**). Place a rag underneath the throttle body to help catch the cable collar if it falls off the end of the cable.*

   a. Have an assistant push down and hold the cable guide at the throttle body. Because of the strong spring pressure, use a piece of metal (A, **Figure 71**) to hold the cable guide in place.

b. Use needle nose pliers and pull the brass accelerator cable collar out of the cable guide. If necessary, work the cable out of the cable guide to help remove the cable collar and disconnect the cable (B, **Figure 71**). When the cable is free, remove the brass collar (**Figure 72**).

c. Turn the cable adjuster (**Figure 73**) to disconnect it from the threaded cable collar attached to the throttle body. When the adjuster is free, remove it and the cable from the throttle body.

d. Tie a length of strong string to this end of the cable. Make sure the string is longer than the replacement cable.

6. Open the reusable plastic tie clamps. Reusable plastic tie clamps are used in two places. To open the clamp, lift the clamp's short tab with a screwdriver, then push the longer clamp arm (**Figure 74**). Open the clamp far enough to allow the accelerator cable assembly to pass through.

7. Open the ring clamp (**Figure 75**) near the front master cylinder with a screwdriver.

8. Cut the plastic tie (**Figure 76**) securing the accelerator cable to the radiator hose on the left side of the vehicle, underneath the master cylinder.

9. Disconnect the accelerator cable at the pedal as follows:

NOTE
At the pedal, the end of the accelerator cable consists of an aluminum plate soldered to the

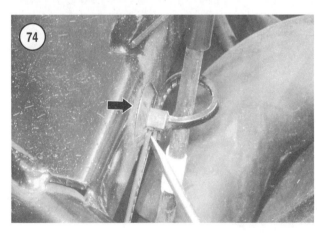

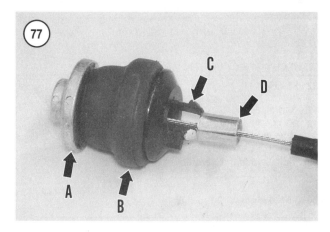

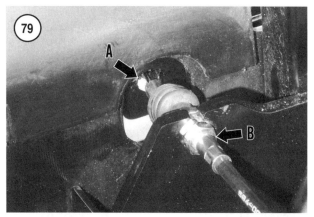

cable (A, **Figure 77**), rubber boot (B) and a plastic rivet (C) that locks onto the pedal. All of these parts are located on the outside of the pedal and are not replaceable. A 6-mm steel hex shaft (D, **Figure 77**) is permanently fixed to the cable and is located between the plastic rivet and the boot covering the front cable adjuster assembly.

a. Working on the front side of the pedal, pinch the arms on the plastic rivet and slide the cable through the notch (**Figure 78**) in the right side of the pedal. It may be easier to work through the firewall (A, **Figure 79**) at the front side of the vehicle when attempting to pinch the arms on the plastic rivet.

NOTE
The cable holder serviced in Step 10 is mounted on a notch machined into the front master cylinder mounting bracket. The holder is not an adjuster.

10. From inside the front compartment, loosen the cable holder locknut (B, **Figure 79**) and then turn the nut until the nut and lockwasher are free of the holder. Then press the pedal all the way down and remove the cable through the hole in the firewall.

11. Remove the accelerator cable while making sure the string follows the original cable routing path.

12. Compare the new and old cables.

13. Installation is the reverse of removal. Note the following:

    a. When attaching the cable holder, make sure the lockwasher is positioned on the same side of the mounting bracket as the locknut. Tighten the locknut securely.

    b. Attach the accelerator cable at the pedal by sliding the cable through the cable notch in the pedal, then push the rivet to lock it in place. Note that there is a shoulder on one of the rivet arms. Install and lock the rivet so the shoulder engages the slot (**Figure 78**) in the accelerator pedal. Then look through the hole (A, **Figure 79**) in the front side of the firewall and make sure both rivet arms are locked against the pedal.

    c. Lubricate the rear cable end and brass collar with lithium grease and install the collar onto the cable end (**Figure 72**).

d. Route the cable around the cable guide and fit the brass collar into the hole in the throttle wheel, then release the throttle wheel. Make sure the cable is routed through the guide in the throttle wheel and the brass collar fits tightly into the hole (**Figure 70**).

e. Replace the cover O-ring if leaking or damaged.

f. Adjust the accelerator cable as described in Chapter Three. Make sure the accelerator cable adjuster locknut (A, **Figure 69**) is tight after adjusting the accelerator cable.

Table 1 FUEL INJECTION GENERAL SPECIFICATIONS

ECU	
Manufacturer	Mitsubishi
Model	F8T83871
Engine idle speed	1500-1650 rpm
Fuel injector	
Manufacturer	Nippon
Model	E252019
Fuel injection system relay	
Manufacturer	Matsushita
Model	ACM33211
Coil resistance	96.0 ohms
Fuel pump	
Manufacturer	AISAN
Model	5B4
Type	Electrical
Throttle body	
Manufacturer	Mikuni
Model	41EHS
Intake vacuum	40.0 kPa (11.8 in./HG)
Water temperature	80-90° C (176-194° F)
Oil temperature	60-70° C (140-158° F)

Table 2 FUEL INJECTION SYSTEM TEST SPECIFICATIONS

Fuel pressure	324 kPa (47 psi)
Fuel level sender resistance	
Full (float up)	19.00-21.00 ohms
Empty (float down)	137.00-143.00 ohms
Intake air pressure sensor output voltage	3.75-4.25 volts
Intake air temperature sensor resistance	290-390 ohms @ 80° C (176° F)
Speed sensor output voltage	0.6 and 4.9 volts per revolution. Refer to text.
Throttle position sensor	
Output voltage at idle	0.68 volts
Resistance	3080-5720 ohms @ 20° C (68° F)

Table 3 FUEL SYSTEM TORQUE SPECIFICATIONS

	N•m	in.-lb.	ft.-lb.
Air intake duct mounting bolts	7	62	–
Damper plate mounting bolt	16	–	12
Fuel pump mounting plate nuts*	8	71	–
Fuel tank mounting bracket bolt	30	–	22
Seat support bracket mounting bolt	32	–	24
Shift arm mounting bolt threads*	14	–	10
Speed sensor mounting screw	10	88	–

*Refer to text.

CHAPTER NINE

ELECTRICAL SYSTEM

Read *Safety* and *Service Methods* in Chapter One before servicing the vehicle in this chapter.

Tables 1-9 are at the end of this chapter.

ELECTRICAL COMPONENT REPLACEMENT

Most dealerships and parts suppliers will not accept the return of any electrical part. If you cannot determine the exact cause of any electrical system malfunction, have a dealership retest that specific system to verify your test results. If you purchase a new electrical component(s), install it, and then find that the system still does not work properly, you will probably not be able to return the unit for a refund.

Consider any test result carefully before replacing a component that tests only slightly out of specification, especially resistance. A number of variables can affect test results dramatically. These include the testing meter's internal circuitry, ambient temperatures and conditions under which the vehicle has been operated. All instructions and specifications have been checked for accuracy; however, successful test results depend largely upon individual accuracy.

ELECTRICAL CONNECTORS

Corrosion-causing moisture can enter electrical connectors and cause poor electrical connections leading to component failure. Troubleshooting an electrical circuit with one or more corroded electrical connectors can be time-consuming and frustrating. Before reconnecting electrical connectors, pack them with a dielectric grease compound. Do not use a substitute that may interfere with the current flow within the electrical connector. Do not use silicone sealant.

BATTERY

A sealed, maintenance-free battery is installed on all models. The battery electrolyte level cannot be serviced. When replacing the battery, use a sealed type; do not install a non-sealed battery. Never attempt to remove the sealing cap from the top of the battery. The battery does not require periodic electrolyte inspection or refilling. Refer to **Table 1** for battery specifications.

To prevent accidental shorts that could blow a fuse when working on the electrical system, always disconnect the negative battery cable from the battery as described in *Removal/Installation* in this section.

Safety Precautions

> *WARNING*
> *Although the battery is a sealed type, protect your eyes, skin and clothing; electrolyte is corrosive and can cause severe burns and permanent injury. The battery case may be cracked and leaking electrolyte. If electrolyte gets into your eyes, flush your eyes thoroughly with clean, running water and get imme-*

diate medical attention. Always wear safety goggles when servicing the battery.

WARNING
While batteries are being charged, highly explosive hydrogen gas forms in each cell. Some of this gas escapes through a vent opening and may form an explosive atmosphere in and around the battery. This condition can persist for several hours. Sparks, an open flame or a lighted cigarette can ignite the gas, causing an internal battery explosion and possible serious injury.

NOTE
Recycle the old battery. When replacing the old battery, be sure to turn in the old battery at that time. The lead plates and the plastic case can be recycled. Most dealerships accept old batteries in trade when purchasing a new one. Never place an old battery in household trash; it is illegal, in most states, to place any acid or lead (heavy metal) contents in landfills.

1. Do not disconnect live circuits at the battery. A spark usually occurs when a live circuit is broken.
2. Do not smoke or permit any open flame near any battery being charged or which has been recently charged.
3. Take care when connecting or disconnecting a battery charger. Be sure the power switch is turned off before making or breaking connections. Poor connections are a common cause of electrical arcs, which cause explosions.
4. Keep children and pets away from the charging equipment and battery.

Removal/Installation

The battery is installed in the electrical box.
1. Read *Safety Precautions* in this section.
2. Turn the ignition switch off.
3. Open the hood.
4. Turn the plastic screws (A, **Figure 1**) and remove the electrical box cover (B).
5. Disconnect the negative battery lead (A, **Figure 2**), then the positive lead (B) from the battery terminals.

NOTE
If only the negative battery terminal is being disconnected, insulate the negative battery cable so it cannot accidentally reconnect the battery circuit.

6. Disconnect the rubber strap (C, **Figure 2**) and remove the battery.
7. After servicing the battery, install it by reversing these removal steps. Note the following:
   a. Coat the battery leads with dielectric grease or petroleum jelly.

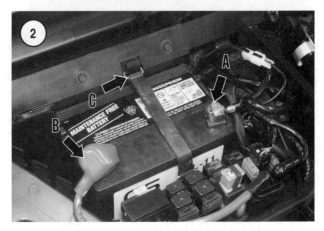

   b. Always connect the positive cable first (B, **Figure 1**), then the negative cable (A).

CAUTION
Be sure the battery cables are connected to their proper terminals. Connecting the battery backward reverses the polarity and damages components in the electrical system. When installing a replacement battery, make sure the negative and positive battery terminals are in the same positions.

Cleaning/Inspection

The battery electrolyte level cannot be serviced. Never attempt to remove the sealing bar cap from the top of the battery (**Figure 3**). The battery does not require periodic electrolyte inspection or refilling.
1. Read *Safety Precautions* in this section.
2. Remove the battery from the vehicle as described in this section. Do not clean the battery while it is mounted in the vehicle.
3. Clean the battery case (**Figure 3**) with a solution of warm water and baking soda. Rinse thoroughly with clean water.
4. Inspect the physical condition of the battery. Look for bulges or cracks in the case, leaking electrolyte or corrosion buildup.

5. Check the battery terminal bolts, spacers and nuts for corrosion and damage. Clean parts with a solution of baking soda and water and rinse thoroughly. Replace if damaged.

6. Check the battery cable clamps for corrosion and damage. If corrosion is minor, clean the battery cable clamps with a stiff brush. Replace excessively worn or damaged cables.

NOTE
If the battery cables are replaced, route the negative battery cable over the positive battery cable. Do not route the positive battery cable over the top of the starter relay.

Voltage Test

Static

Use a digital voltmeter to test the battery while it is mounted on the vehicle. Refer to **Table 1** for battery voltage readings.

1. Read *Safety Precautions* in this section.
2. Turn the ignition switch off.
3. Open the hood.
4. Turn the plastic screws (A, **Figure 1**) and remove the electrical box cover (B).

NOTE
To prevent false test readings, do not test the battery if the battery terminals are corroded. Remove and clean the battery and terminals as described in this section, then install and test the battery.

5. Connect a digital voltmeter between the battery positive (+) and negative (–) leads.
   a. If the battery voltage is 12.8 volts or higher, the battery is fully charged.
   b. If the battery voltage is below 12.7 volts or less, the battery is undercharged and requires charging.
6. If the battery is undercharged, charge it as described in this section. Then test the charging system as described in this chapter.

Starting

This procedure tests the batteries capacity when starting the vehicle.
1. Read *Safety Precautions* in this section.
2. Open the hood.

NOTE
To prevent false test readings, do not test the battery if the battery terminals are corroded. Remove and clean the battery and terminals as described in this section, then install and test the battery.

3. Connect a digital voltmeter between the battery positive (+) and negative (–) leads.
4. Start the vehicle while reading the voltmeter. If the voltage drops below 9.5 volts, recharge the battery as described in this section and then repeat the test. If the voltage still drops below 9.5 volts, replace the battery.

Load Test

Low load test

1. Remove the seat (Chapter Fourteen).
2. Connect a digital voltmeter between the battery positive (+) and negative (–) leads.
3. Turn the ignition switch on while making sure the headlights are on.
4. The voltmeter should read a minimum of 11.5 volts. If the voltage reading is lower, charge the battery as described in this section.
5. Turn the ignition switch off and disconnect the voltmeter.

High load test

This test requires a battery load tester. This load test checks the battery's performance with a current draw or load applied and is the best indication of battery condition. When using a load tester, follow the manufacturer's instructions.

Charging

Refer to *Battery Initialization* in this section if the battery is new.

To recharge a maintenance-free battery, a digital voltmeter and a charger with an adjustable or automatically variable amperage output are required. If this equipment is not available, have the battery charged by a shop with the proper equipment. Excessive voltage and amperage from an unregulated charger can damage the battery and shorten service life.

The battery should only self-discharge approximately one percent of its given capacity each day. If a battery not in use, without any loads connected, loses its charge within one week after charging, the battery is defective.

If the vehicle is not used for long periods, an automatic battery charger with variable voltage and amperage outputs is recommended for optimum battery service life.

WARNING
During the charging process, highly explosive hydrogen gas is released from the battery. Charge the battery only in a well-ventilated area away from any open flames including pilot lights on home gas appliances. Do not allow any smoking in the area. Never check the charge of the battery by connecting screwdriver blades or other metal objects between the terminals; the resulting spark can ignite the hydrogen gas.

CAUTION
Always remove the battery from the vehicle as described in this section before connecting the battery charger. Never recharge a battery in the vehicle; corrosive gasses emitted during the charging process will damage surfaces.

1. Remove the battery as described in this section.
2. Measure the battery voltage as described in *Voltage Test* in this section. Locate the voltage reading in **Table 2** to determine the battery state of charge.

NOTE
If the voltage reading is low, internal resistance in the battery may prevent it from recovering when following normal charging attempts. When a battery's state of charge is 11.5 volts or less, it is necessary to increase the charging voltage of the battery by applying a low current rate to allow the battery to recover. This will require an adjustable battery charger with a separate amp and volt meter. However, some battery chargers can do this automatically by diagnosing and recovering deep-discharged batteries. These chargers can also charge and maintain batteries during all normal battery service without overcharging or overheating the battery. Refer to the charger manufacturer's instructions and specifications for making this test.

3. Clean the battery terminals and case as described in this section.
4. Connect the positive (+) charger lead to the positive battery terminal and the negative (−) charger lead to the negative battery terminal.
5. Charge the battery following the manufacturer's instructions. Set the charger at 12 volts and switch it on. Charge the battery at a slow charge rate of 1/10 its given capacity. To determine the current output in amps, divide the battery amp hour capacity by 10. Refer to the charging current specification in **Table 1**.

NOTE
When using an adjustable battery charger, follow the manufacturer's instructions. Do not use a larger output battery charger or increase the charge rate on an adjustable battery charger to reduce charging time. Doing so can cause permanent battery damage.

6. After the battery has been charged for 4-5 hours, turn the charger off, disconnect the leads and allow the battery to set for a minimum of 30 minutes. Then check the battery with a digital voltmeter and compare to the voltage specifications in **Table 2**.

Battery Storage

When the vehicle is ridden infrequently or put in storage for an extended amount of time, the battery must be periodically charged to ensure it will be capable of working correctly when returned to service. Use an automatic battery charger with variable voltage and amperage outputs.
1. Remove the battery as described in this section.
2. Clean the battery and terminals as described in this section.
3. Inspect the battery case as described in this section. Replace the battery if the case is leaking or damaged.
4. Clean the electrical box in the vehicle.
5. Charge the battery to 100%. Store the battery in a cool dry place. Continue to charge the battery once a month when stored in temperatures below 16° C (60°F) and every two weeks when stored in temperatures above 16° C (60°F).

Battery Initialization

A new battery must be fully charged before installation. Failure to do so reduces the life of the battery. Using a new battery without an initial charge causes permanent battery damage. That is, the battery will never be able to hold more than an 80% charge. Charging a new battery after it has been used will not bring its charge to 100%. When purchasing a new battery from a dealership or parts store, verify its charge status. If necessary, have them perform the initial or booster charge before accepting the battery.

CHARGING SYSTEM

The charging system supplies power to operate the engine and electrical system components and keeps the battery charged. The charging system consists of the battery, alternator and a regulator/rectifier. Refer to the appropriate wiring diagram at the end of this manual.

Alternating current generated by the alternator is rectified to direct current. The regulator/rectifier maintains constant voltage to the battery and additional electrical loads, such as lights or ignition, despite variations in engine speed and load.

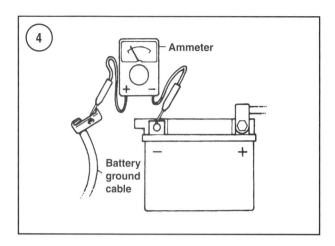

b. Faulty voltage regulator/rectifier.
c. Short circuit in the system.
d. Loose, dirty or faulty electrical connectors.
e. Aftermarket electrical accessories added to the electrical system.

6. To find the short circuit that is causing the excessive current draw, refer to the wiring diagram at the end of this book. Then disconnect different electrical connectors one by one while monitoring the ammeter. When the current drain rate returns to an acceptable level, the faulty circuit is indicated. Test the circuit further to find the problem.
7. Disconnect the ammeter.
8. Reconnect the negative battery cable as described in this section.

Troubleshooting

Refer to Chapter Two.

Current Draw Test

A short circuit will increase current draw and drain the battery. Adding electrical accessories can also drain the battery. While the manufacturer does not provide current draw specifications for models covered in this manual, the test can be used to troubleshoot for shorts and to check the current draw of accessories added to the electrical system.

NOTE
When installing electrical accessories, do not wire them into a live circuit where they stay on all the time. Refer to the accessory manufacturer's instructions.

NOTE
Perform this test before and after adding electrical accessories to determine base line readings that can be referred to if charging system problems occur at a later time.

1. Turn the ignition switch off.
2. Disconnect the negative battery cable at the battery as described in this chapter.

CAUTION
Before connecting the ammeter into the circuit, set the meter to its highest amperage scale. This prevents a large current flow from damaging the meter or blowing the meter's fuse.

3. Connect an ammeter between the negative battery cable and the negative battery terminal (**Figure 4**). Do *not* turn the ignition switch on once this connection is made.
4. Switch the ammeter to its lowest scale and note the current draw reading.
5. If the current draw seems excessive, consider the following probable causes:
   a. Damaged battery.

Charging Voltage Test

To obtain accurate test results, the battery must be fully charged. Refer to *Voltage Test* in *Battery* in this chapter.
1. Start and run the engine until it reaches normal operating temperature, then turn the engine off.
2. Connect a shop tachometer to the spark plug lead following the manufacturer's instructions.
3. Connect a digital voltmeter to the battery terminals (positive-to-positive and negative-to-negative). To prevent a short, make sure the voltmeter leads attach firmly to the battery terminals.

CAUTION
Do not disconnect either battery cable when making this test. Doing so may damage the voltmeter or electrical accessories.

4. Start the engine and allow it to idle. Turn the headlight to HI beam. Gradually increase engine speed to 5000 rpm and read the voltage indicated on the voltmeter. The voltmeter should read 14.0 volts.

NOTE
*If the battery is often discharged, but the charging voltage tested normal during Step 4, the battery may be damaged. Perform a load test as described in **Battery** in this chapter.*

5. If the voltage reading is incorrect, note the following:
   a. If the charging voltage is too low, check for an open or short circuit in the charging system wiring harness, an open or short in the alternator, high resistance in the alternator-to-battery cable or a damaged regulator/rectifier.
   b. If the charging voltage is too high, check for a poor regulator/rectifier ground, damaged regulator/rectifier or a damaged battery.

REGULATOR/RECTIFIER

Removal/Installation

1. Turn the ignition switch off.

2. Open the hood.

3. Disconnect the connectors (A, **Figure 5**) at the regulator/rectifier.

4. Remove the two regulator/rectifier mounting bolts and the regulator/rectifier (B, **Figure 5**).

5. Installation is the reverse of removal. Note the following:

   a. Tighten the regulator/rectifier mounting bolts securely.

   b. Clean the electrical terminals.

   c. Apply dielectric grease to the connectors.

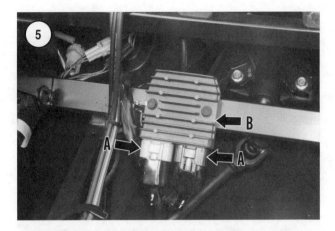

RIGHT CRANKCASE COVER, STATOR COIL AND CRANKSHAFT POSITION SENSOR

The stator coil and crankshaft position sensor are mounted inside the right crankcase cover.

Stator Coil Resistance Test

The stator coil is mounted inside the right crankcase cover and can be tested while the cover is mounted on the engine. Perform this test when the engine is cold.

1. Remove the following as described in Chapter Sixteen:

   a. Seats.

   b. Rear console.

   c. Front console.

   d. Right corner panel and right side panel.

2. Disconnect the gray 2-pin and gray 1-pin alternator connectors containing the white wires (**Figure 6**).

3. Measure the resistance between each white wire on the alternator side of the connectors. Note the resistance reading for each check and refer to **Table 3** for the specified stator coil resistance. Replace the stator if any resistance reading is not within specification.

4. Check for continuity between the stator coil and ground as follows:

   a. Ground one of the ohmmeter leads to the engine (or right crankcase cover, if removed).

   b. Touch the other lead to each white wire. There should be no continuity. If continuity exists, indicating a short, replace the stator coil/crankshaft position sensor assembly.

NOTE
Before replacing the stator/crankshaft position sensor assembly, check the electrical wires to and within the electrical connector for any opens or poor connections.

5. Reverse Step 1 and Step 2.

Crankshaft Position Sensor Resistance Test

The crankshaft position sensor is mounted inside the right crankcase cover and can be tested while the cover is mounted on the engine. Perform this test when the engine is cold.

1. Remove the following as described in Chapter Sixteen:

   a. Seats.

   b. Rear console.

   c. Front console.

   d. Right corner panel and right side panel.

2. Disconnect the crankshaft position sensor 2-pin connector containing the gray and black wires (**Figure 6**).

3. Use an ohmmeter and measure crankshaft position sensor resistance as follows:

   a. Connect the positive ohmmeter lead to grey terminal and the negative ohmmeter lead to the black terminal. Note the resistance reading.

   b. Refer to **Table 4** for the resistance specification.

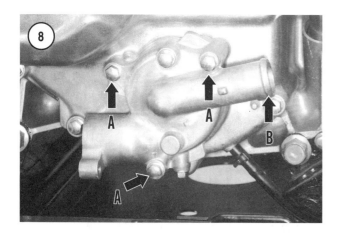

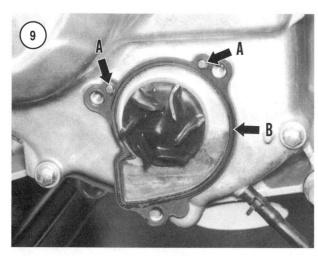

c. Replace the stator/crankshaft position sensor assembly if the resistance reading is not within specification.

NOTE
Before replacing the stator/crankshaft position sensor assembly, check the electrical wires to and within the electrical connector for any opens or poor connections.

4. Reverse Step 1 and Step 2.

Right Crankcase Cover

Removal

1. Remove the following as described in Chapter Sixteen:
   a. Seats.
   b. Rear console.
   c. Front console.
   d. Right corner panel and right side panel.
2. Drain the engine oil (Chapter Three).
3. Drain the coolant (Chapter Three).
4. Remove the rear inlet and outlet oil lines and hoses as described in *Oil Cooler Lines and Hoses* in Chapter Ten.
5. Loosen the hose clamp and disconnect the inlet hose (A, **Figure 7**) at the water pump.

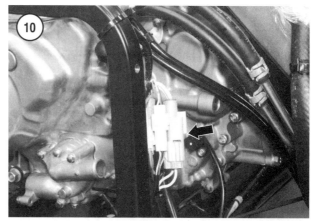

6. Remove the bolt (B, **Figure 7**) securing the outlet pipe to the engine and remove the pipe (C) and its O-ring from the water pump.
7. Open the clamp and disconnect the breather hose (D, **Figure 7**) at the water pump.

NOTE
The right crankcase cover can be removed without removing the water pump cover. However, the lower water pump cover mounting bolt must be removed. When installing the right crankcase cover, the water pump cover must be removed so the impeller can be turned to engage its shaft with the oil pump shaft.

8. Remove the bolts (A, **Figure 8**) and the water pump cover (B). Then remove the two dowel pins (A, **Figure 9**) and gasket (B).
9. Perform the following:
   a. Note the alternator wiring harness routing.
   b. Remove any clamps securing the alternator wiring harness to the frame.
   c. Disconnect the gray 2-pin and gray 1-pin alternator connectors containing the white wires (**Figure 10**).
   d. Disconnect the crankshaft position sensor 2-pin connector containing the gray and black wires (**Figure 10**).
10. Place several paper towels or rags underneath the right crankcase cover to catch some of the oil that will drain out when the cover is removed.

NOTE
To ensure that the right crankcase cover bolts are correctly located during assembly, make an outline of the right crankcase cover on a piece of cardboard. Punch holes in the cardboard at the same locations as the bolts. Place the bolts in their respective holes.

11. Loosen the bolts securing the right crankcase cover (A, **Figure 11**) to the engine 1/4 turn at a time until all of the bolts are loose. Then remove the bolts and the oil pipe holder (B, **Figure 11**). Remove the cover by lightly tapping it to loosen it from the engine. Do not pry the cover off.

Magnetic force will pull the cover back toward the crank-case during its removal.

> *NOTE*
> *The torque limiter (A, **Figure 12**) may come off with the cover.*

12. Account for the two dowels pins (B, **Figure 12**) that may remain in the crankcase or cover.

13. Remove all gasket residue from the cover and crank-case mating surfaces.

14. If necessary, service the stator coil and crankshaft po-sition sensor as described in this section.

15. Do not clean the cover or stator coils in solvent. Wipe the coils with a clean rag.

Installation

1. Remove all threadsealer residue from the bolt and crankcase threads. Spray the crankcase bolt holes with con-tact cleaner to remove all oil residue Make sure the threads are clean and dry.

2. Clean the cover and crankcase mating surfaces.

3. Make sure the starter drive gears are properly installed and meshed together as described in *Flywheel, Starter Clutch and Starter Clutch Gears* in this chapter.

4A. If the grommets were removed from the cover, apply a silicone sealer onto the grommets and push them into the cover (**Figure 13**). Then apply sealer to both outer surfac-es.

4B. If the grommets were not removed, apply a silicone sealer onto the exposed grommet surface (**Figure 13**).

5. Install the two dowel pins (B, **Figure 12**).

6. Install a new cover gasket.

7. Check the flywheel for any metal objects that it may have picked up during service and remove them.

8. Align and install the cover, making sure it engages both dowel pins (B, **Figure 12**) while turning the impeller to align its slot with the oil pump shaft (C). Then check that the cover seats flush against the gasket.

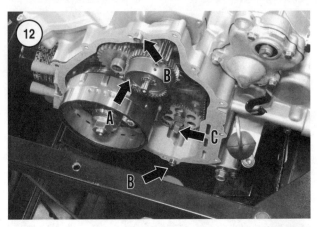

> *CAUTION*
> *Do not try to pull the cover into place with its mounting bolts. When properly installed the cover will seat flush against the gasket. If not, either the dowel pins are incorrectly installed or the impeller is not properly aligned with the oil pump shaft.*

9. Tighten the right crankcase cover mounting bolts in a crossing pattern and in several steps to 10 N•m (88 in.-lb.).

10. Make sure the electrical connectors are free of corro-sion and then reconnect them. Check the wiring harness routing.

11. Install the water pump cover as follows:

   a. Install the two dowel pins (A, **Figure 9**) and a new gasket.

   b. Install the cover (B, **Figure 8**) and tighten the mount-ing bolts (A) to 10 N•m (88 in.-lb.).

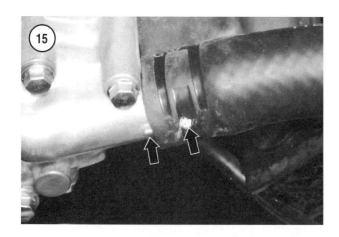

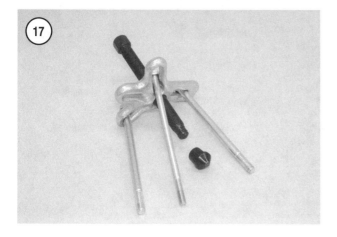

12. Connect the breather hose (D, **Figure 7**) at the water pump. Secure the hose with its clamp.

13. Lubricate a new O-ring with grease and install it onto the outlet pipe (**Figure 14**). Then install the outlet pipe into the water pump cover and tighten the mounting bolt (B, **Figure 7**) to 10 N•m (88 in.-lb.).

14. Connect the inlet hose by aligning its paint mark with the raised boss on the water pump (**Figure 15**). Then install and tighten the hose clamp.

15. Reverse Steps 1-4 to complete installation. Note the following:

    a. Refill the engine with oil (Chapter Three).

    b. Refill and bleed the cooling system (Chapter Three).

    c. Start the engine and check for oil and coolant leaks.

Stator Coil and Crankshaft Position Sensor Removal/Installation

1. Remove the right crankcase cover as described in this section.

2. Remove the bolts and the wire harness guide plate (A, **Figure 16**). Note the stator coil and crankshaft position sensor wire harness routing before removing them.

3. Remove the stator coil (B, **Figure 16**) and crankshaft position sensor (C) mounting bolts.

4. Pull the grommets out of the cover and remove the stator coil and crankshaft position sensor.

NOTE
Do not separate the stator coil and crankshaft position sensor wiring harnesses. Both components are assembled as a complete assembly.

5. Clean and dry the right crankcase cover. Clean the mounting bolt holes of all threadlocking compound residue.

6. Installation is the revere of removal. Note the following:

    a. Apply a medium-strength threadlocking compound onto the stator coil and crankshaft position sensor mounting bolts and tighten to 7 N•m (62 in.-lb.).

    b. Apply a medium-strength threadlocking compound onto the wiring harness guide plate mounting bolts and tighten to 7 N•m (62 in.-lb.).

    c. Make sure to seal the grommets as described in *Right Crankcase Cover* in this section.

FLYWHEEL, STARTER CLUTCH AND STARTER CLUTCH GEARS

The flywheel (alternator rotor) is mounted on the right end of the crankshaft. The starter clutch is mounted on the back of the flywheel. The starter clutch gears engage the starter with the starter clutch.

Tools

The following tools or their equivalents are required to remove the flywheel (alternator rotor):

1. Flywheel puller, (Yamaha part No. YU-33270-B [**Figure 17**], or equivalent).

2. Flywheel holder, (Yamaha part No. YS-01880-A, or equivalent).

Removal

1. Remove the right crankcase cover as described in this chapter.

2. Remove the torque limiter (A, **Figure 18**).

3. Remove the starter idle gear shaft (B, **Figure 18**) and gear (C).

NOTE
Mount the flywheel holder onto the flywheel so that it does not contact the raised projections.

4. Hold the flywheel with a flywheel holder (A, **Figure 19**) and turn the flywheel mounting nut (B) to loosen it. Then remove the nut and washer.

5. Install the puller by threading the three long puller bolts (A, **Figure 20**) fully into the starter clutch threaded holes. These bolts must fully engage the threads in the starter clutch; otherwise, the threads may be damaged when pressure is applied against them.

6. Install a metal protector (B, **Figure 20**) against the end of the crankshaft, then tighten the puller's pressure bolt against the protector.

CAUTION
Do not try to remove the flywheel without the correct puller. Any attempt to do so may damage the starter clutch, flywheel and crankshaft.

CAUTION
If normal flywheel removal attempts fail, do not force the puller. Excessive force will strip the starter clutch threads, causing expensive damage. Take the engine to a dealership for flywheel removal.

7. Hold the flywheel with the flywheel holder and tighten the puller's pressure bolt (C, **Figure 20**) until the flywheel pops off the crankshaft taper. Remove the flywheel with the tool attached.

8. Remove the Woodruff key (A, **Figure 21**).

9. Remove the starter clutch gear (B, **Figure 21**) if necessary.

10. Remove the washer (**Figure 22**).

11. Inspect the components as described in this section.

Installation

1. Lubricate the washer (**Figure 22**) with engine oil and install it over the crankshaft.

2. Lubricate the starter clutch gear bore and shoulder with engine oil. Then install the gear over the crankshaft with its shoulder side facing out (B, **Figure 21**).

3. Install the Woodruff key (A, **Figure 21**) into the crankshaft keyway.

4. Lubricate the starter clutch (A, **Figure 23**) mounted in the backside of the flywheel with engine oil.

5. Clean the crankshaft outer taper and the flywheel inner taper (B, **Figure 23**) with contact cleaner to remove all oil. Allow both tapers to dry before installing the flywheel.

6. Align the flywheel keyway with the Woodruff key and install the flywheel. At the same time rotate the starter clutch gear clockwise while installing the flywheel to engage the starter clutch. Check that the Woodruff key aligns with the flywheel keyway.

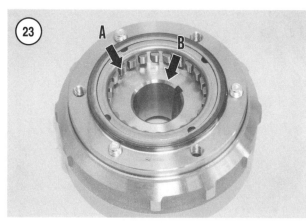

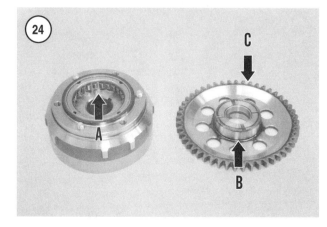

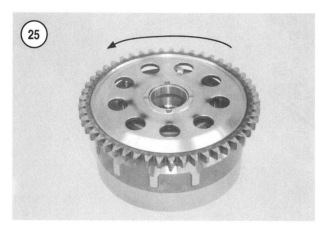

7. Lubricate the flywheel nut threads and seating surfaces and washer with engine oil and install the nut finger-tight.

8. Hold the flywheel with the flywheel holder (A, **Figure 19**) and tighten the flywheel nut (B) to 60 N•m (44 ft.-lb.).

9. Remove the flywheel holder.

10. Lubricate the starter idle gear shaft and gear and the torque limiter shaft surfaces with engine oil.

11. Install the starter idle gear (C, **Figure 18**) with its larger gear facing out. Then install the shaft (B, **Figure 18**), making sure the shaft bottoms in the crankcase.

12. Install the torque limiter, meshing it with the starter idle gear and the starter shaft as shown in A, **Figure 18**.

13. Install the right crankcase cover as described in this chapter.

Inspection

1. Clean the flywheel/starter clutch assembly and the starter clutch gears in solvent and dry with compressed air.

2. Check the flywheel for cracks or breaks.

> *WARNING*
> *Replace a cracked or chipped flywheel. A damaged flywheel can fly apart at high engine speeds, throwing metal fragments into the engine. Do not repair or reinstall a damaged flywheel.*

3. Check the flywheel tapered bore and the crankshaft taper for pitting and other damage.

4. Inspect the flywheel keyway for damage.

5. Inspect the starter clutch assembly as follows:
   a. Inspect the one-way clutch roller cage (A, **Figure 24**) for overheating, pitting or flaking. If damaged, replace the starter clutch as described in this section. Inspect the starter clutch gear shoulder (B, **Figure 24**) for the same conditions.
   b. Inspect the starter clutch gear (C, **Figure 24**) for damaged gear teeth. Then inspect the operating surfaces for pitting, cracks and other damage.
   c. If there is no visible damage, perform Step 6 to check the starter clutch operation.

6. Insert the starter clutch gear into the starter clutch. Hold the flywheel and try to turn the gear clockwise and then counterclockwise. The gear should only turn *counterclockwise* (**Figure 25**). If the gear turns clockwise, replace the starter clutch as described in this section.

7. Inspect the starter idle gear and shafts for:
   a. Broken or chipped gear teeth.
   b. Worn or scored gear bores.
   c. Pitted or damaged shaft surfaces.

8. Inspect the torque limiter for:

> *NOTE*
> *Do not disassemble the torque limiter. Replacement parts are not available.*

   a. Broken or chipped gear teeth.
   b. Pitted or damaged shaft surfaces.

9. Inspect the flywheel nut and washer for damage. Both parts are made of hardened material. Replace only with original equipment parts.

Starter Clutch Removal/Installation

1. Secure the flywheel with the flywheel holder used to remove the flywheel. Then remove the starter clutch mounting bolts (**Figure 26**).

2. Remove the starter clutch and its outer race from the flywheel.

3. Clean and dry all parts. Remove all thread sealer residue from the mounting bolt threads.

4. Install the starter clutch into the outer race so the flange on the starter clutch fits into the outer race as shown in **Figure 27**. The arrow mark (**Figure 28**) on the outer race must face away from the flywheel.

5. Install the starter clutch onto the flywheel so the arrow is visible and faces in the direction shown in **Figure 28**.

6. Apply a medium-strength threadlocking compound to the threads on the three mounting bolts and install the bolts in alternate positions (**Figure 26**). Tighten the mounting bolts to 30 N•m (22 ft.-lb.).

7. Lubricate the starter clutch gear shoulder and starter clutch rollers with engine oil.

8. Insert the starter clutch gear into the starter clutch. Hold the flywheel and try to turn the gear clockwise and then counterclockwise. The gear should only turn *counterclockwise* (**Figure 25**). If the gear turns clockwise, the starter clutch was installed incorrectly.

IGNITION SYSTEM

The ignition system consists of the crankshaft position sensor, main fuse, ignition fuse, ignition switch, battery, backup fuse, ECU, ignition coil, lean-angle sensor, spark plug and the frame ground. Refer to the appropriate sections in this chapter to sevice individual components. Refer to Chapter Three for spark plug removal/installation procedures. Refer to the wiring diagram at the end of this manual to identify the wire harness colors and connectors.

Refer to **Table 4**.

Ignition System Precautions

When working on the vehicle, note the following to protect ignition system components:

1. Never disconnect any of the electrical connections while the engine is running.

2. Keep all electrical connections clean and tight. Apply dielectric grease to all electrical connectors before reconnecting them. This will help seal out moisture.

3. When operating the starter with the spark plug removed, make sure the spark plug or a spark tester is installed in the plug cap, and that the plug or tester is grounded. If not, excessive resistance may damage the ECU. Refer to *Spark Test* in *Engine Does Not Start* in Chapter Two.

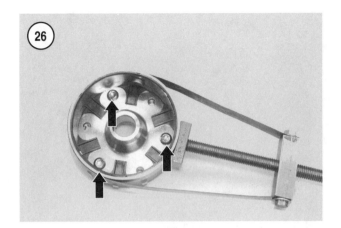

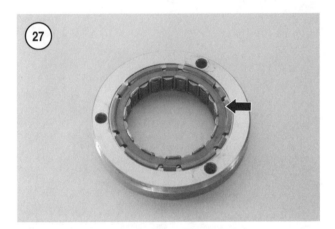

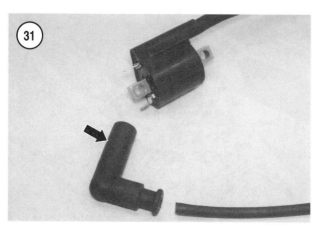

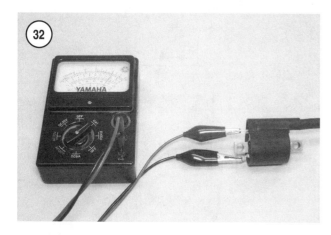

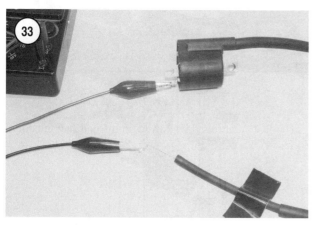

4. Make sure all ignition system components are mounted correctly.

Troubleshooting

Refer to Chapter Two.

IGNITION COIL

Refer to *Ignition System* in this chapter.

Removal/Installation

1. Remove the rear console (Chapter Sixteen).
2. Disconnect the spark plug cap (A, **Figure 29**) from the spark plug.
3. Remove the clamp securing the secondary wire to the parking brake cable (B, **Figure 29**).
4. Identify and disconnect the primary connectors (**Figure 30**) at the ignition coil.
5. Unbolt and remove the ignition coil.
6. Installation is the reverse of these steps. Note the following:
    a. Make sure the primary terminals on the ignition coil are free of corrosion.
    b. Tighten the ignition coil mounting bolts to 7 N•m (62 in.-lb.).

Testing

The ignition coil can be tested while installed on the vehicle.
1. Remove the rear console (Chapter Sixteen).
2. Disconnect the spark plug cap (B, **Figure 29**) from the spark plug.
3. Identify and disconnect the primary connectors (**Figure 30**) at the ignition coil.
4. Hold the secondary wire and unscrew the spark plug cap (**Figure 31**) from the secondary wire.
5. If necessary, remove the ignition coil as described in this section.
6. Use an ohmmeter and check primary coil resistance as follows:
    a. Measure resistance across the two primary coil terminals on the ignition coil as shown in **Figure 32**.
    b. Replace the ignition coil if the primary resistance is not within specifications (**Table 4**).
7. Use an ohmmeter and check secondary coil resistance as follows:
    a. Measure resistance across the brown/red terminal and the secondary wire lead as shown in **Figure 33**.
    b. Replace the ignition coil if the secondary coil resistance is not within specifications (**Table 4**).
8. Use an ohmmeter and check spark plug cap resistance as follows:
    a. Measure resistance between each end of the cap as shown in **Figure 34**.

b. Replace the spark plug cap if the resistance is not within specification (**Table 4**).

9. Reverse Steps 1-4.

Spark Plug Cap Removal/Installation

Hold the secondary wire and then loosen and unscrew the plug cap (**Figure 31**). The secondary wire cannot be replaced separately. If damaged, replace the ignition coil. Inspect the terminal inside the cap and the exposed secondary wires for corrosion and damage. Reverse to install.

LEAN-ANGLE SENSOR

Whenever the lean-angle sensor is activated, the ECU cuts off power to the fuel pump, ignition system and fuel injector circuits.

To reset the sensor, position the vehicle on all four wheels on level ground. Turn the ignition switch off, and then turn it back on.

The lean-angle sensor is mounted at the front, center of the vehicle, in front of the lower instrument panel.

Refer to *Ignition System* in this chapter.

Testing/Removal/Installation

1. Open the hood.
2. Unbolt and remove the lean-angle unit (A, **Figure 35**) from its mounting position. Do not disconnect the sensor connector (B, **Figure 35**).
3. Using back probe pins, insert the voltmeter test leads into the connector so the positive lead contacts the yellow/green terminal and the negative lead contacts the black/blue terminal. Refer to *Back Probe Pins* in *Measuring Tools* in Chapter One.
4. Turn the ignition switch on.
5. Hold the lean angle sensor in a level position with its UP mark facing up (**Figure 36**). Perform the following output voltage tests while reading the voltmeter:
    a. Hold the sensor at an angle less than 65°, the voltmeter should read 3.55-4.45 volts.
    b. Tilt the sensor at an angle greater than 65°, the voltmeter should read 0.65-1.35 volts.
    c. If either measurement is out of specification, replace the lean angle sensor.
6. Turn the ignition switch off.
7. Install the lean angle sensor (A, **Figure 35**) with its UP mark facing up. Tighten the mounting bolts securely.
8. Close the hood.

> *NOTE*
> *If there is no spark after installing the lean-angle sensor, make sure the sensor is correctly installed.*

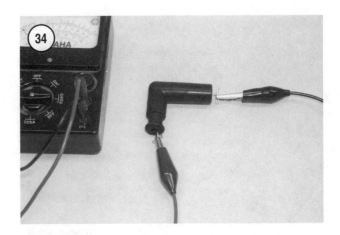

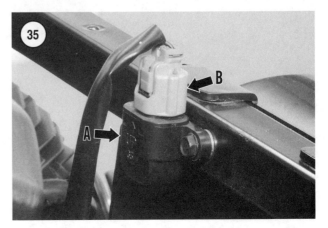

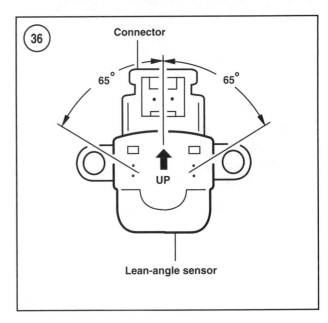

ENGINE CONTROL UNIT (ECU)

The ECU controls the ignition timing and fuel injection. Refer to Chapter Eight.

IGNITION TIMING

Refer to Chapter Three.

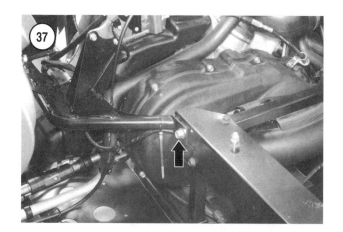

STARTER

The starting system consists of the starter, relay, main fuse, backup fuse, signal system fuse, ignition fuse, ignition switch, battery, diode, ECU, gear position switch, brake light switch, load control relay and frame ground

The starter will only operate when the transmission is in neutral or if the brake pedal is pressed when the transmission is in gear. Refer to *Starting The Engine* in Chapter Two.

CAUTION
Do not operate the starter for more than 5 seconds at a time. Wait approximately 10 seconds between starting attempts.

Starter Removal/Installation

1. Set the parking brake.
2. Disconnect the negative battery cable at the battery as described in this chapter.
3. Remove the following as described in Chapter Sixteen:
    a. Seats.
    b. Rear console.
    c. Left and right side panel/corner panel assemblies.
    d. Front console.
4. Remove the seat support bracket left side mounting bolt (**Figure 37**).
5. Loosen the seat support bracket right side mounting bolt (**Figure 38**). Do not remove the bolt.
6. Disconnect the breather hose (A, **Figure 39**) at the air intake duct.
7. Disconnect the intake air temperature sensor electrical connector (B, **Figure 39**).
8. Remove the wiring harness bundle from the clamp on the air intake duct joint (A, **Figure 40**). Then loosen the two hose clamps (B, **Figure 40**) and remove the joint from inside the air intake duct (**Figure 41**). Cover the throttle body and air intake duct openings with plastic bags.

NOTE
The insulator described in Step 9 cannot be purchased separately. If this part is damaged, the starter must be replaced.

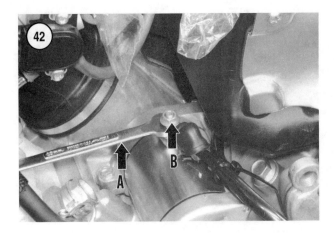

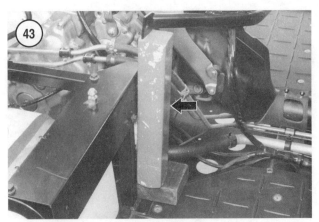

9. Disconnect the starter cable by holding the inner nut with a wrench (A, **Figure 42**) and removing the outer nut (B). Holding the inner nut prevents the terminal bolt from turning and damaging the insulator installed inside the starter.

10. Cut the plastic-tie securing the starter cable and engine ground cables together. Pull the starter cable back out of the way and reposition the engine ground cable so it does not interfere with the front starter mounting bolt.

CAUTION
When lifting the seat support bracket, check all of the wiring harness and cable routing to make sure these parts are not pulled sharply or damaged. If necessary, disconnect the connectors and cables.

11. Lift the seat support bracket and support it with wooden blocks (**Figure 43**) to access the starter mounting bolts.

12. Remove the starter mounting bolts (**Figure 44**).

13. Remove the engine ground cable mounting bolt (**Figure 45**) and reposition the cable.

14. Push the starter toward the left side to disconnect it from the engine, then lift and remove the starter (**Figure 46**).

15. Installation is the reverse of removal. Note the following:

   a. Replace the starter O-ring if damaged.
   b. Lubricate the starter O-ring with grease.
   c. Tighten the starter mounting bolts (**Figure 44**) to 10 N•m (88 in.-lb.).
   d. Tighten the engine ground cable mounting bolt (**Figure 45**) to 10 N•m (88 in.-lb.).
   e. Clean the starter cable end and install it onto the starter terminal. Hold the inner nut on the starter terminal with a wrench (A, **Figure 42**) and tighten the outer nut to 5 N•m (44 in.-lb.).
   f. Secure the starter cable to the ground cable with a new plastic-tie.
   g. Install the air intake duct joint into the air intake duct (**Figure 41**) and reconnect it onto the throttle body. Also make sure air intake duct joint shoulder is not pinched. Then align the raised shoulder on the air intake duct joint between the two round tabs on the air

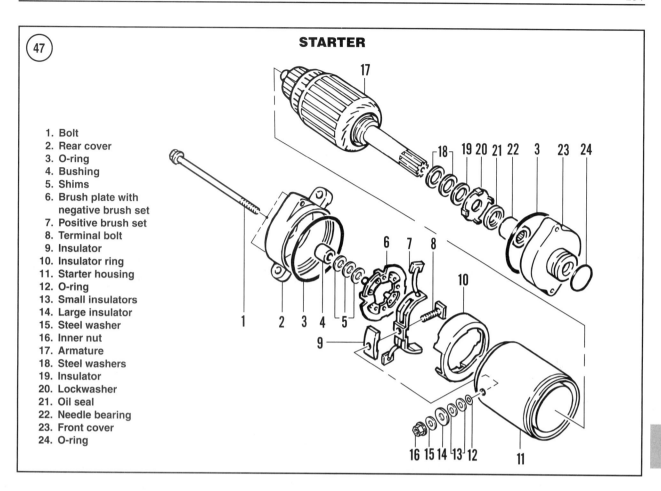

STARTER

1. Bolt
2. Rear cover
3. O-ring
4. Bushing
5. Shims
6. Brush plate with negative brush set
7. Positive brush set
8. Terminal bolt
9. Insulator
10. Insulator ring
11. Starter housing
12. O-ring
13. Small insulators
14. Large insulator
15. Steel washer
16. Inner nut
17. Armature
18. Steel washers
19. Insulator
20. Lockwasher
21. Oil seal
22. Needle bearing
23. Front cover
24. O-ring

9

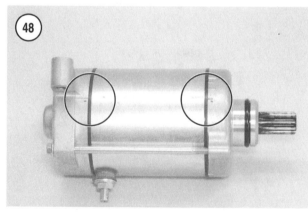

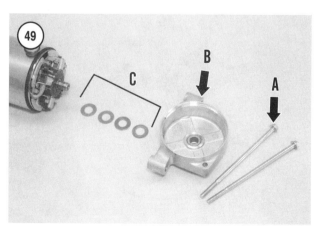

intake duct (C, **Figure 40**). Recheck the alignment and tighten the two hose clamps securely (B, **Figure 40**).

h. Install the wiring harness bundle so that the section with the white tape (A, **Figure 40**) fits into the clamp on top of the air intake duct.

i. Tighten the seat support bracket mounting bolts to 32 N•m (24 ft.-lb.).

Disassembly

Refer to **Figure 47**.

1. Find the alignment marks across the armature housing and both end covers (**Figure 48**). If necessary, scribe or paint the marks to identify them.
2. Remove the bolts (A, **Figure 49**).

CAUTION
The number of shims used in each starter varies. The shims and washers must be re-installed in their correct order and number. Failing to install the correct number of shims and washers may increase armature end play and cause the starter to draw excessive current. Record the thickness and alignment of each shim and washer removed during disassembly.

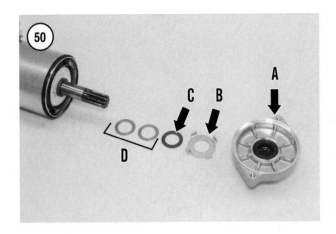

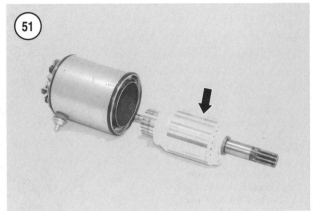

NOTE
If disassembling the starter to only check brush condition, remove only the rear cover. The brushes can be inspected and the cover installed if further disassembly is not required. When doing so, locate and reinstall the shims onto the armature shaft in the order they were removed.

3. Remove the rear cover (B, **Figure 49**) and shims (C).

4. Remove the front cover (A, **Figure 50**) and the lockwasher (B).

NOTE
Do not remove the seal from the front cover. It is not available as a replacement part.

5. Remove the insulated washer (C, **Figure 50**) and shim(s) (D).

6. Remove the armature (**Figure 51**) from the housing.

7. Before removing the brush holder, test the brushes and terminal bolt as follows:

NOTE
*The positive brushes have insulated sleeves (A, **Figure 52**) installed over their wire leads. The negative brush wire leads (B, **Figure 52**) do not.*

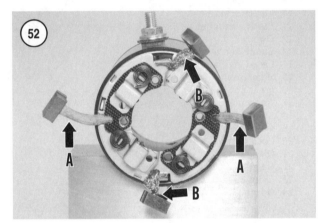

a. Check for continuity between the terminal bolt and each positive brush (**Figure 53**). There should be continuity. If there is no continuity, replace the positive brush holder during reassembly.

b. Check for continuity between the terminal bolt and starter housing (**Figure 54**). There should be no continuity. If there is continuity, check for damaged, missing or improperly installed insulators. Compare the alignment of the installed insulators before removing them.

c. Check for continuity between the positive (A, **Figure 55**) and negative (B) brushes. There should be no continuity. If there is continuity, check the positive brush wires for damaged insulation sleeves. The insulation sleeves must be installed through the brush holder plate so the positive brush wires cannot short out.

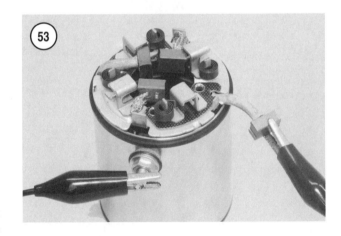

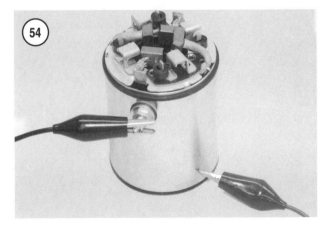

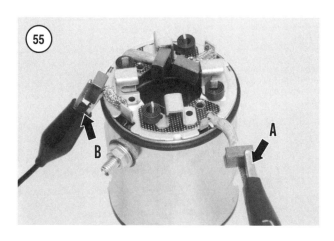

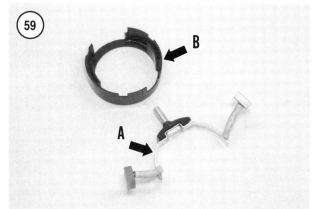

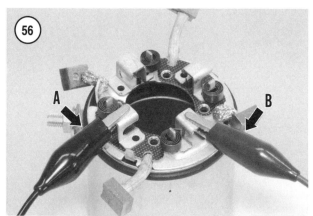

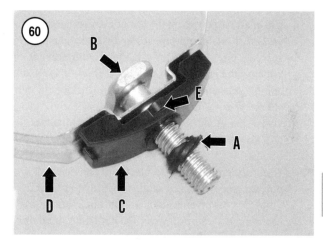

9

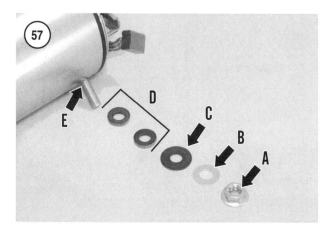

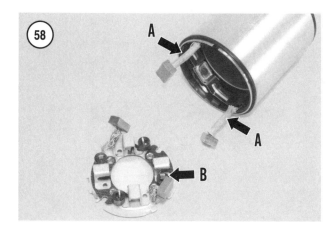

d. Check for continuity between the positive (A, **Figure 56**) and negative (B) brush holders on the brush plate. There should be no continuity. If there is continuity, the brush holder plate is shorted and should be replaced.

8. Remove the inner nut (A, **Figure 57**), steel washer (B), large insulator (C) and the two small insulators (D). Remove the O-ring if accessible or remove it after removing the terminal bolt (E, **Figure 57**).

9. Straighten the positive brush wires (A, **Figure 58**) and remove the brush plate (B) with the negative brushes attached. Do not damage the insulation sleeves on the positive brush wires.

10. Remove the positive brush set (A, **Figure 59**) and insulator ring (B).

11. Remove the O-ring (A, **Figure 60**) and separate the terminal bolt (B), insulator (C) and positive brush holder (D).

12. Clean all grease, dirt and carbon from the armature, starter housing and end covers as described in *Inspection* in this section.

Inspection

NOTE
Some internal and external starter components are available separately. If a damaged part is not available, the starter must be re-

placed as an assembly. Refer to a dealership for replacement parts.

1. The internal parts in a used starter are often contaminated with carbon and copper dust released from the brushes and commutator. Because a starter can be damaged from improper cleaning, note the following:

> *NOTE*
> *A dirty or rough commutator will result in poor brush contact and cause rapid brush wear. In addition, carbon dust resulting from brush wear accumulates between commutator segments and partially shorts out starter current.*

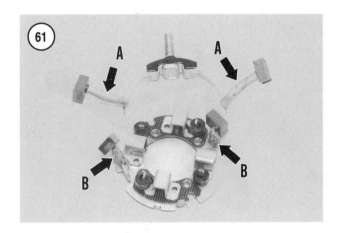

   a. Clean all parts (except the armature, insulated washers, brush plate and brushes and starter housing) in solvent. Use a rag lightly damped with solvent to wipe off the armature, insulated washers, brush plate and brushes and the starter housing (inside and outside).

   b. Use a fine grade sandpaper to clean the brushes. Do not use emery cloth as its fibers may insulate the brushes.

   c. Use only crocus cloth to clean the commutator. Do not use emery cloth or sandpaper. Any abrasive material left on or embedded in the commutator may cause excessive brush wear. Do not leave any debris on or between the commutator bars.

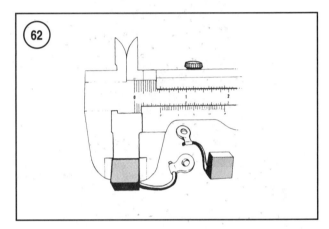

2. Replace the starter housing O-rings if damaged.

> *NOTE*
> *The bushing, seal and bearing used in the end covers are not available separately.*

3. Inspect the bushing in the front cover for wear or damage.

4. Inspect the seal and needle bearing in the rear cover for damage. Do not remove the seal to check the bearing.

5. Check the lockwasher, shims and insulated washers for damage.

6. Inspect the brushes (A and B, **Figure 61**) as follows:

   a. Inspect each brush for cracks and other damage.

   b. Inspect the insulation sleeves on the positive brushes (A, **Figure 61**) for tearing and other damage.

   c. Check each brush where it is fixed to its holder (A or B, **Figure 61**) for looseness or damage.

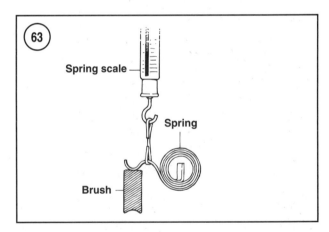

   d. Measure the length of each brush (**Figure 62**). If the length of any one brush is out of specification (**Table 5**), replace the brush plate and positive brush set (**Figure 61**) as the brushes are permanently fixed in place. Soldering is not required.

> *NOTE*
> *Worn brushes or weak springs can cause poor brush contact, resulting in starter malfunction.*

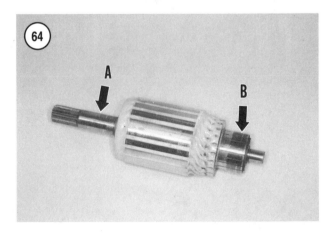

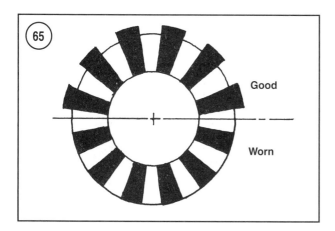

65

Good

Worn

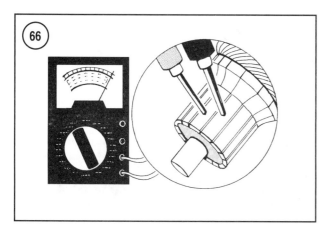

66

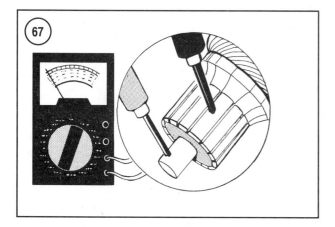

67

68

7. Inspect the brush springs for damage. Brush spring force is listed in **Table 5** and can be measured with a tension gauge (**Figure 63**). The springs can be considered serviceable if they snap the brushes firmly in position. If the springs are weak or damaged, replace the brush set.

8. Inspect the armature (A, **Figure 64**):
   a. Inspect both shafts for scoring and other damage.
   b. Inspect the windings for obvious damage.
   c. To check the armature for a short circuit, have it tested on a growler by a dealership or an automotive electrical repair shop.

9. Inspect the commutator (B, **Figure 64**):
   a. Inspect the commutator bars for visual damage.
   b. Clean the commutator surface as described in Step 1.
   c. The mica must be below the surface of the copper bars. On a worn commutator the mica and copper bars may be worn to the same level (**Figure 65**).
   d. If the mica level is too high or if its shape is too narrow or V-shaped, undercut the mica with a hacksaw blade.
   e. Inspect the commutator copper bars for discoloration. If a pair of bars are discolored, grounded armature coils are indicated.
   f. Measure the commutator outside diameter and compare to the specifications in **Table 5**. Replace the armature if the commutator outside diameter is less than the service limit.
   g. Check for continuity across all adjacent pairs of commutator bars (**Figure 66**). There should be continuity across all pairs of bars. If an open circuit exists between a pair of bars, replace the armature.
   h. Check for continuity between the armature shaft and each commutator bar (**Figure 67**). There should be no continuity. If there is continuity, replace the armature.
   i. Check for continuity between the armature coil core and each commutator bar (**Figure 68**). There should be no continuity. If there is continuity, replace the armature.

10. Inspect the starter housing for cracks or other damage. Then inspect for loose, chipped or damaged magnets.

Assembly

1. Install the terminal bolt through the positive brush holder, then install the insulator (E, **Figure 60**) and O-ring (A). The insulator has a pin on one side. When installing the terminal bolt assembly, the pin on the insulator must be facing up.

2. Install the positive brush holder into the insulator ring so the pin on the insulator is facing up (away from the insulator ring). Then install the assembly into the housing (**Figure 69**).

3. Install the brush plate by aligning the tab on the plate with the notch in the housing (**Figure 70**). At the same time position the two positive brush wires (A, **Figure 52**) in the

notches in the plate. Make sure the wires are not pinched between the plate and housing.

NOTE
Reinstall all parts in the order described to insulate the positive brushes from the housing.

4. Slide the O-ring (A, **Figure 60**) onto the terminal bolt until it fits squarely in the hole in the starter housing (E, **Figure 57**). Then install the two small insulators (D, **Figure 57**), large insulator (C), steel washer (B) and inner nut (A). Tighten the inner nut to 11 N•m (97 in.-lb.).

5. Perform the continuity checks described in Step 7 in *Disassembly* in this section to check the positive brushes and terminal bolt for proper installation.

6. Install the brushes into their holders as follows:
   a. To keep spring pressure off the four brushes when installing the armature, insert strips of stiff plastic between each spring and brush holder (**Figure 71**).

NOTE
*One side of each brush is machined with a groove (**Figure 72**). The groove side faces toward the spring and not the commutator.*

   b. Install the brushes (**Figure 72**) into their holders.

NOTE
In Step 7, magnetic force will pull the armature against the coils inside the starter housing. Hold the armature tightly when installing it to avoid damaging the coils or brushes.

7. Install the armature into the starter housing until the commutator is aligned with the brush holders. Then remove the plastic strips to release the brush springs and allow them to push the brushes against the commutator. Check that each brush seats squarely against the commutator and the brush wires are properly routed (**Figure 73**).

8. Install the shims (C, **Figure 49**) onto the armature shaft.

9. Install the O-ring onto the commutator side of the starter housing.

10. Apply a thin coat of grease onto the armature shaft.

11. Install the rear cover (B, **Figure 49**) over the armature shaft and seat it against the O-ring/housing. Align the index mark on the rear cover with the mark on the housing (**Figure 48**).

12. Install the O-ring onto the front side of the starter housing.

13. Lubricate the front cover oil seal lips and bearing with grease.

14. Refer to **Figure 50** and install the front cover as follows:
   a. Install the steel shims (D, **Figure 50**) onto the armature shaft. The number of shims on the starter may differ from the number of shims shown.
   b. Install the insulator (C, **Figure 50**) and seat against the shims.

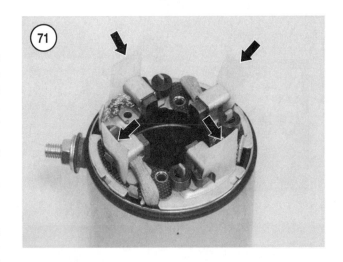

   c. Align and install the lockwasher (B) onto the front cover.
   d. Install the front cover by aligning the index mark on the cover with the mark on the housing (**Figure 48**). Set the cover against the O-ring/housing.

15. Install the starter assembly bolts and tighten to 5 N•m (44 in.-lb.).

NOTE
If one or both bolts will not pass through the starter, the end covers and/or the brush plate are installed incorrectly.

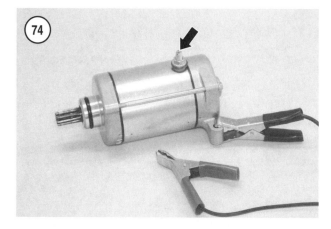

16. Lubricate the O-ring with grease and install it into the front cover groove.

17. Hold the starter and turn the armature shaft by hand. The armature should turn with some resistance, but should not bind or lockup. If the armature does not turn properly, disassemble the starter and check the shim, insulated washer and lockwasher alignment.

CAUTION
Because of the large amount of current that will flow from the battery to the starter, use a large diameter cable when making the connection. To avoid damaging the starter, do not leave the battery connected for more than a few seconds.

18. Use an auxiliary battery and apply battery voltage directly to the starter. Clamp the negative terminal to the starter housing and then briefly touch the positive terminal to the terminal bolt (**Figure 74**). The starter should turn when battery voltage is applied directly to the terminal bolt. If the starter did not turn, disassemble and inspect the starter as described in this section.

STARTER RELAY

The starter relay connects the battery to the starter. The relay is designed to temporarily carry the high electrical load between the parts during starting. The relay is activated when the key in the ignition switch is turned.

Removal/Installation

1. Turn the ignition switch off.
2. Open the hood.
3. Turn the plastic screws and remove the electrical box cover as described in *Battery* in this chapter.
4. Disconnect the negative battery cable as described in this chapter.
5. Disconnect the starter relay switch electrical connector (A, **Figure 75**).
6. Remove the bolts and disconnect the red (A, **Figure 76**) and black (B) cables at the starter relay.
7. Lift and remove the starter relay and its holder from the frame mount.
8. Installation is the reverse of these steps. Clean the battery and starter cable leads as described in this chapter before connecting them to the relay.

Testing

1. Remove the starter relay as described in this section.
2. Connect an ohmmeter to the red and black cable terminals on the relay (A, **Figure 77**).
3. Connect the positive terminal of a fully charged 12-volt battery to the starter relay blue/yellow terminal (B, **Figure 77**).

9

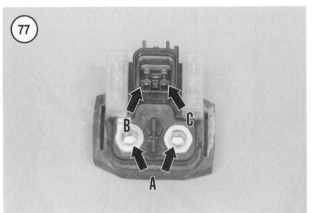

4. Observe the meter and momentarily touch the negative battery terminal to the red/yellow terminal (C, **Figure 77**) and note the following:

   a. If the meter reads continuity, the relay is in good condition.

   b. If the meter shows a resistance reading, the relay is faulty.

LIGHTING SYSTEM

Refer to **Table 6** for bulb specifications. Always use the specified bulb. Using the wrong size bulb produces a dim light or causes the bulb to burn out prematurely.

Headlight Adjustment

Refer to **Figure 78**.

1. Turn the adjusting screw clockwise to raise the headlight beam.

2. Turn the adjusting screw counterclockwise to lower the headlight beam.

Headlight Bulb Removal/Installation

> *WARNING*
> *If the headlight just burned out or it was just turned off it will be hot. Do not touch the bulb until it cools off.*

> *CAUTION*
> *A quartz-halogen bulb is used. Because traces of oil on the glass will reduce the life of the bulb, do not touch the bulb glass. Clean any oil or other chemicals from the bulb glass with an alcohol-moistened cloth.*

1. Raise the hood.

2. Remove the outer cover (**Figure 79**) from the headlight housing.

3. Remove the inner bulb holder cover (**Figure 80**) and set it aside in the headlight housing. This cover cannot be removed separately.

4. Push the headlight bulb holder in and turn counterclockwise to align its three tabs with the three notches in the

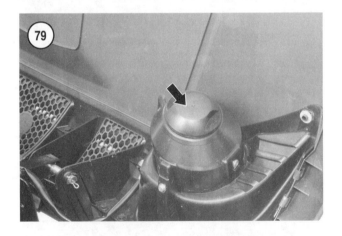

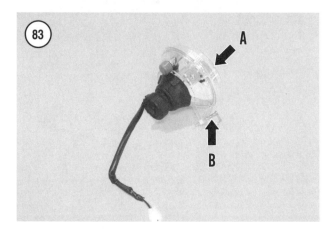

headlight assembly. Lift the bulb holder out and set aside in the headlight housing.

5. Remove the bulb (A, **Figure 81**).

6. Installation is the reverse of these steps. Note the following:

   a. Align the tab (B, **Figure 81**) on the bulb with the notch in the headlight housing.

   b. Align the three tabs on the bulb holder with the three notches in the headlight housing, the push the holder and turn it clockwise until it stops.

   c. Make sure the inner bulb holder cover fits securely around the headlight housing.

   d. Turn the ignition switch on. Then turn the headlight switch on and check the headlight operation in both the LO and HI positions. Turn the ignition switch off.

Headlight Housing/Lens Removal/Installation

1. Remove the three screws (A, **Figure 82**) securing the housing to the front grill. Note that the screw threaded into the headlight adjuster uses a flat washer.

2. Remove the outer housing (B, **Figure 82**) and the lens assembly (A, **Figure 83**).

3. Installation is the reverse of removal. Note the following:

   a. Align the headlight adjuster (B, **Figure 83**) with the channel in the front grill.

   b. Turn the ignition switch on. Then turn the headlight switch on and check the headlight operation in both the LO and HI positions. Turn the ignition switch off.

Headlight Voltage Test

If the headlight(s) does not turn on but the bulb(s) and fuses are in good working order, check for voltage at the headlight connector(s) as follows:

1. Open the hood.

2. Disconnect the headlight electrical connector (**Figure 84**).

3. Turn the light switch to LO and check the voltage at the headlight wiring harness side connector as follows:

   a. Connect the voltmeter negative test lead to the black terminal.

   b. Connect the voltmeter positive test lead to the green terminal.

   c. Turn the ignition switch on. The voltmeter should read battery voltage.

4. Turn the light switch to HI, and check the voltage at the headlight wiring harness side connector as follows:

   a. Connect the voltmeter negative test lead to the black terminal.

   b. Connect the voltmeter positive test lead to the yellow terminal.

   c. Turn the ignition switch on. The voltmeter should read battery voltage.

9

5. If the system fails either test, the wiring between the ignition switch and the headlight connector is defective. Make the necessary repairs.

Headlight Relay
Testing/Removal/Installation

The headlight relay is mounted in the electrical box.
1. Turn the ignition switch off.
2. Open the hood.
3. Turn the plastic screws and remove the electrical box cover.
4. Disconnect the headlight relay (B, **Figure 75**).
5. Test the high beam relay circuit as follows:
   a. Connect the positive ohmmeter lead to the headlight relay blue terminal (A, **Figure 85**) and the negative lead to the yellow terminal (B).
   b. Connect the positive terminal of a fully charged 12-volt battery to the headlight relay yellow terminal (C, **Figure 85**).
   c. Observe the meter and momentarily touch the negative battery terminal to the black terminal (D, **Figure 85**). There should be continuity with battery voltage applied to the relay.
6. Test the low beam relay circuit as follows:
   a. Connect the positive ohmmeter lead to the headlight relay blue terminal (A, **Figure 85**) and the negative lead to the green terminal (E).
   b. Connect the positive terminal of a fully charged 12-volt battery to the headlight relay yellow terminal (C, **Figure 85**).
   c. Observe the meter and momentarily touch the negative battery terminal to the black terminal (D, **Figure 85**). There should be continuity with battery voltage applied to the relay.
7. Replace the relay if it fails any portion of this test.
8. Installation is the reverse of these steps. Start the engine and check the headlight operation.

Taillight/Brake Light Bulb
Removal/Installation

1. Remove the rivets along the top and bottom rear side of the cargo bed panel. Refer to Chapter Sixteen. Then remove the nuts and bolts at the front, center portion of the panel. Refer to **Figure 86**.
2. Raise the bed.
3. Remove the cargo bed panel (A, **Figure 87**) with the taillight/brake light wiring harness attached (B).
4. Turn the bulb holder (**Figure 88**) counterclockwise and remove it from the panel.
5. Push the bulb (A, **Figure 89**) and turn it counterclockwise to remove it from the bulb holder (B).
6. Installation is the reverse of removal. Note the following:
   a. Tighten the cargo bed panel mounting bolts/nuts to 7 N•m (62 in.-lb.).

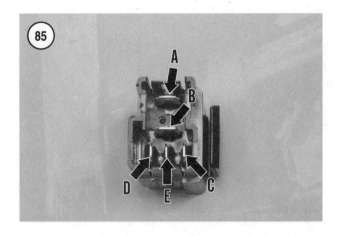

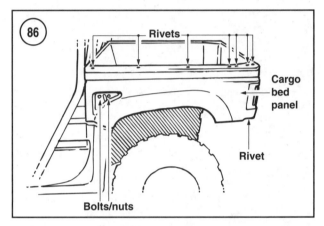

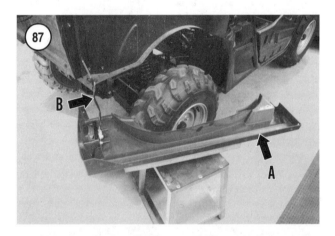

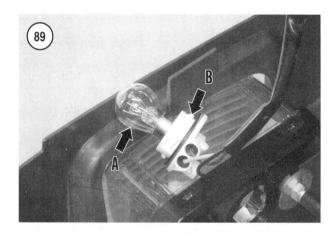

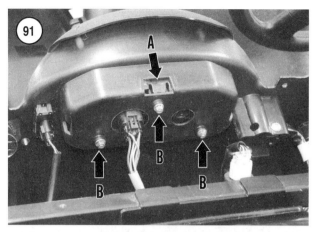

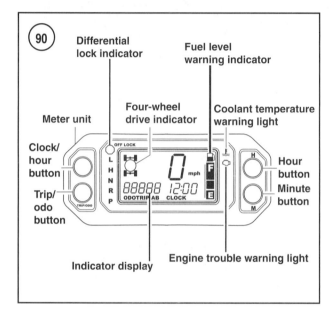

Differential lock indicator

Fuel level warning indicator

Four-wheel drive indicator

Coolant temperature warning light

Meter unit

Clock/ hour button

Trip/ odo button

Hour button

Minute button

Indicator display

Engine trouble warning light

b. Turn the ignition switch on and check the taillight and rear brake light operation.

c. Turn the ignition switch off.

Taillight/Brake Light Voltage Test

If the taillight/brake light do not turn on or operate and the rear brake light switch is properly adjusted and in good condition, check for voltage at the taillight/brake light connector(s) as follows:

1. Remove the taillight/brake light bulb holder as described in this section

2. Test the taillight circuit as follows:

a. Using back probe pins, insert the voltmeter test leads into the bulb holder (B, **Figure 89**) so the positive lead contacts the blue wire and the negative lead contacts the black wire. Refer to *Back Probe Pins* in *Measuring Tools* in Chapter One.

b. Turn the ignition switch on. The voltmeter should read battery voltage.

c. If there is no voltage reading, the wiring between the ignition switch and taillight/brake light connector is defective. Make the necessary repairs.

3. Test the brake light circuit as follows:

a. Using back probe pins, insert the voltmeter test leads into the connector (B, **Figure 89**) so the positive lead contacts the yellow wire and the negative lead contacts the black wire. Refer to *Back Probe Pins* in *Measuring Tools* in Chapter One.

b. Turn the ignition switch on and press the brake pedal. The voltmeter should read battery voltage.

c. If there is no voltage reading, the wiring between the ignition switch and taillight/brake light connector is defective. Make the necessary repairs.

4. Installation is the reverse of these steps. Disconnect the tester leads and remove the back probe pins. Apply silicone sealant over the pin holes in the wires.

METER ASSEMBLY AND INDICATOR LIGHTS

The meter assembly (**Figure 90**) is equipped with the following:

1. Clock.
2. Fuel gauge.
3. Voltage display.
4. Engine operating meter.
5. Two trip meters.
6 Speedometer.
7. Odometer.
8. Indicator lights.

Removal/Installation

1. Remove the upper instrument panel (Chapter Sixteen).
2. Disconnect the electrical connector (A, **Figure 91**) at the meter assembly.
3. Remove the nuts (B, **Figure 91**) and the meter assembly.
4. Installation is the reverse of removal.

Indicator Light and Circuit Testing

Indicator lights for the differential lock, engine trouble, coolant temperature, parking, reverse, neutral, high-range indicator and low-range indicator are mounted in the meter assembly. Individual lights are not available. If an indicator fails to operate, perform the following to isolate the problem to the wiring harness, individual electrical component, ECU or meter assembly. If the problem is with the meter assembly, it must be replaced. The meter assembly and its internal multifunction meter assembly and LEDs are not serviceable.

Indicator circuit test

If the brake light, a warning light or indicator light fails to operate, perform the following tests in order. If a problem is not found in a step, continue with the following step. If a problem is found, repair or replace the component and retest.

> *NOTE*
> *If the brake light does not operate, refer to **Taillight/Brake Light Bulb Removal/Installation** and **Taillight/Brake Light Voltage Test** in **Lighting System** in this chapter. If a problem is not found, proceed to Step 1.*

1. Check for a blown main, backup, ignition or signal system fuse as described in this chapter.
2. Test the battery as described in this chapter.
3. Test the ignition switch as described in this chapter.
4. Test the load control relay as described in this chapter.
5. If a problem has not been found, check the individual circuit for damaged wiring or dirty or damaged connectors. If the wiring and connectors are good, perform the individual component test(s) in this section. Refer to the correct wiring diagram at the end of this manual to identify the individual connectors and wiring for the individual components.

Neutral, high-range and low-range indicator voltage test

1. Test the gear position switch as described in *Switches* in this chapter.
2. Check the wiring and connectors between the gear position switch and the ECU. Then check the yellow/blue wire and connectors between the ECU and the meter assembly.
3. Disconnect the meter connector (A, **Figure 91**). Turn the ignition switch on and check for battery voltage between the brown/yellow (+) and black/white (−) wiring harness connector terminals (**Figure 92**).
    a. Yes. The power circuit to the meter assembly is good. Replace the meter assembly and retest. If there is still a problem, replace the ECU with a known-good unit and retest.
    b. No. Check the wiring between the ignition switch and meter assembly for an open circuit.

Park indicator voltage test

1. Test the parking brake switch as described in *Switches* in this chapter.
2. Check the blue/black wire and connectors between the parking brake switch and ECU. Then check the yellow/blue wire and connectors between the ECU and meter assembly.
3. Disconnect the meter connector (A, **Figure 91**). Turn the ignition switch on and check for battery voltage between the brown/yellow (+) and black/white (−) wiring harness connector terminals (**Figure 92**).
    a. Yes. The power circuit to the meter assembly is good. Replace the meter assembly and retest. If there is still a problem, replace the ECU with a known-good unit and retest.
    b. No. Check the wiring between the ignition switch and meter assembly for an open circuit.

Reverse indicator voltage test

1. Test the reverse switch as described in *Switches* in this chapter.
2. Check the green/white wire and connectors between the reverse switch and ECU. Then check the yellow/blue wire and connectors between the ECU and meter assembly.
3. Disconnect the meter connector (A, **Figure 91**). Turn the ignition switch on and check for battery voltage between the brown/yellow (+) and black/white (−) wiring harness connector terminals (**Figure 92**).
    a. Yes. The power circuit to the meter assembly is good. Replace the meter assembly and retest. If there is still a problem, replace the ECU with a known-good unit and retest.
    b. No. Check the wiring between the ignition switch and meter assembly for an open circuit.

Differential gear lock indicator and/or four-wheel- drive indicator voltage test

If the differential lock indicator and/or the four-wheel-drive indicator do not light, perform the following:
1. Test the gear motor as described in *Gear Motor Removal/Testing/Installation* in *Front Differential* in Chapter Twelve. Note the following:
    a. If the gear motor is okay, continue with Step 2.
    b. If the gear motor is damaged, replace the gear motor as described in *Front Differential* in Chapter Twelve.
2. Check the wiring and connectors between the on-command four-wheel-drive motor switch and differential gear lock switch and ECU. Then check the yellow/blue wire and connectors between the ECU and meter assembly.
3. Disconnect the meter connector (A, **Figure 91**). Turn the ignition switch on and check for battery voltage between the brown/yellow (+) and black/white (−) wiring harness connector terminals (**Figure 92**).

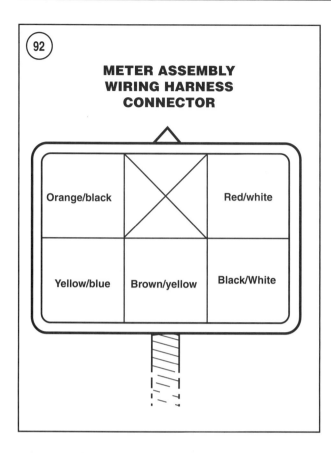

METER ASSEMBLY WIRING HARNESS CONNECTOR

Orange/black | Red/white

Yellow/blue | Brown/yellow | Black/White

Fuel meter voltage test

1. Test the fuel level sender as described in Chapter Eight.
2. Check the red/blue wire and connectors between the fuel pump and ECU. Then check the orange/black wire and connectors between the fuel pump and meter assembly.
3. Disconnect the meter connector (A, **Figure 91**). Turn the ignition switch on and check for battery voltage between the brown/yellow (+) and black/white (–) wiring harness connector terminals (**Figure 92**).
   a. Yes. The power circuit to the meter assembly is good. Replace the meter assembly with a known-good unit and retest.
   b. No. Check the wiring between the ignition switch and meter assembly for an open circuit.

Speedometer voltage test

1. Test the speed sensor as described in Chapter Eight.
2. Check the wiring harness and connectors between the speed sensor and ECU. Then check the yellow/blue wire and connectors between the ECU and meter assembly.
3. Disconnect the meter connector (A, **Figure 91**). Turn the ignition switch on and check for battery voltage between the brown/yellow (+) and black/white (–) wiring harness connector terminals (**Figure 92**).
   a. Yes. The power circuit to the meter assembly is good. Replace the meter assembly with a known-good unit and retest.
   b. No. Check the wiring between the ignition switch and meter assembly for an open circuit.

a. Yes. The power circuit to the meter assembly is good. Replace the meter assembly and retest. If there is still a problem, replace the ECU with a good-known unit and retest.
b. No. Check the wiring between the ignition switch and meter assembly for an open circuit.

NOTE
*Additional testing for the four-wheel-drive indicator is found in **Four-Wheel-Drive Indicator and Relays** in this chapter.*

Coolant temperature warning light voltage test

1. Test the coolant temperature sensor as described in *Cooling System* in this chapter.
2. Check the green/yellow wire and connectors between the coolant temperature sensor and the ECU. Then check the yellow/blue wire and connectors between the ECU and meter assembly.
3. Disconnect the meter connector (A, **Figure 91**). Turn the ignition switch on and check for battery voltage between the brown/yellow (+) and black/white (–) wiring harness connector terminals (**Figure 92**).
   a. Yes. The power circuit to the meter assembly is good. Replace the meter assembly and retest. If there is still a problem, replace the ECU with a known-good unit and retest.
   b. No. Check the wiring between the ignition switch and meter assembly for an open circuit.

FOUR-WHEEL-DRIVE INDICATOR AND RELAYS

Preliminary Testing

If the vehicle is changed from two-wheel-drive to four-wheel-drive and the four-wheel-drive indicator (**Figure 90**) does not turn on, perform the tests in this section in order. If a problem is not found in a step, continue with the following step. If a problem is found, repair or replace the component and retest.

1. Check the main fuse, ignition fuse and four-wheel-drive motor fuse as described in this chapter.
2. Test the battery as described in this chapter.
3. Test the ignition switch as described in *Switches* in this chapter.
4. Test the four-wheel-drive motor relays (1, 2 and 3) as described in this section.
5. Test the on-command four-wheel-drive motor switch and differential gear lock switch as described in *Switches* in this chapter.
6. Test the gear motor as described in *Front Differential* in Chapter Twelve.
7. If the problem has not been found, replace the ECU with a known-good unit and retest.

Four-Wheel-Drive Motor Relays
Testing/Removal/Installation

NOTE
When making the following tests, observe the ohmmeter and momentarily touch the negative battery terminal to the specified relay terminal.

Relay 1

The four-wheel-drive motor relay 1 is mounted in the electrical box.
1. Turn the ignition switch off.
2. Open the hood.
3. Turn the plastic screws and remove the electrical box cover as described in *Battery* in this chapter.
4. Disconnect and remove relay 1 (A, **Figure 93**).
5. Connect test leads to the relay as follows:
   a. Ohmmeter positive test lead (A, **Figure 94**).
   b. Ohmmeter negative test lead (B, **Figure 94**).
   c. Jumper from 12-volt battery positive terminal (C, **Figure 94**).
   d. Jumper from 12-volt battery negative terminal (D, **Figure 94**).
6. There should be continuity with battery voltage applied to the relay.
7. Disconnect the test leads.
8. Connect test leads to the relay as follows:
   a. Ohmmeter positive test lead (A, **Figure 94**).
   b. Ohmmeter negative test lead (E, **Figure 94**).
   c. Jumper from 12-volt battery positive terminal (C, **Figure 94**).
   d. Jumper from 12-volt battery negative terminal (D, **Figure 94**).
9. There should be continuity with battery voltage applied to the relay.
10. Disconnect the test leads.
11. Replace the relay if it fails any portion of this test.

Relay 2

The four-wheel-drive motor relay 2 is mounted in the electrical box.
1. Turn the ignition switch off.
2. Open the hood.
3. Turn the plastic screws and remove the electrical box cover as described in *Battery* in this chapter.
4. Disconnect and remove relay 2 (B, **Figure 93**).
5. Connect test leads to the relay as follows:
   a. Ohmmeter positive test lead (A, **Figure 95**).
   b. Ohmmeter negative test lead (B, **Figure 95**).
   c. Jumper from 12-volt battery positive terminal (C, **Figure 95**).
   d. Jumper from 12-volt battery negative terminal (D, **Figure 95**).
6. There should be continuity with battery voltage applied to the relay.
7. Disconnect the test leads.

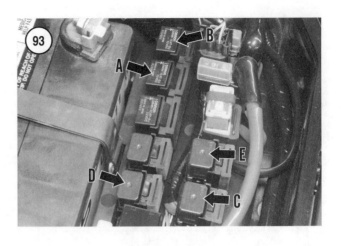

93

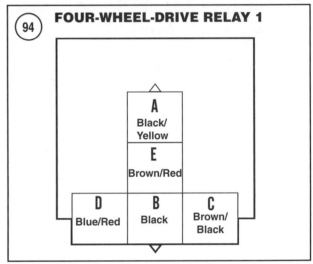

94 **FOUR-WHEEL-DRIVE RELAY 1**

A
Black/Yellow

E
Brown/Red

D
Blue/Red

B
Black

C
Brown/Black

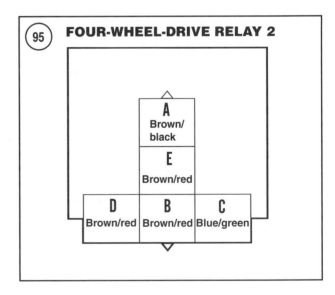

95 **FOUR-WHEEL-DRIVE RELAY 2**

A
Brown/black

E
Brown/red

D
Brown/red

B
Brown/red

C
Blue/green

8. Connect test leads to the relay as follows:
   a. Ohmmeter positive test lead (A, **Figure 95**).
   b. Ohmmeter negative test lead (E, **Figure 95**).
   c. Jumper from 12-volt battery positive terminal (C, **Figure 95**).
   d. Jumper from 12-volt battery negative terminal (D, **Figure 95**).

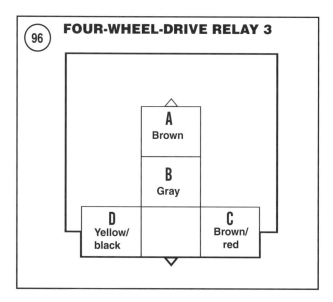

96 FOUR-WHEEL-DRIVE RELAY 3

A
Brown

B
Gray

D
Yellow/
black

C
Brown/
red

97

98

9. There should be continuity with battery voltage applied to the relay.

10. Disconnect the test leads.

11. Replace the relay if it fails any portion of this test.

Relay 3

The four-wheel-drive motor relay 3 is mounted in the electrical box.

1. Turn the ignition switch off.

2. Open the hood.

3. Turn the plastic screws and remove the electrical box cover as described in *Battery* in this chapter.

4. Disconnect and remove relay 3 (C, **Figure 93**).

5. Connect test leads to the relay as follows:
   a. Ohmmeter positive test lead (A, **Figure 96**).
   b. Ohmmeter negative test lead (B, **Figure 96**).
   c. Jumper from 12-volt battery positive terminal (C, **Figure 96**).
   d. Jumper from 12-volt battery negative terminal (D, **Figure 96**).

6. There should be continuity with battery voltage applied to the relay.

7. Disconnect the test leads.

8. Replace the relay if it fails any portion of this test.

HELMET/SEAT BELT DISPLAY (2009 AND 2011-ON MODELS)

The helmet/seat belt display turns on when the ignition switch is turned to ON and will remain on even when the seat belts are fastened. If the display does not turn on, test as described:

Testing/Removal/Installation

1. Remove the hood (Chapter Sixteen).

2. Remove the upper instrument panel (Chapter Sixteen).

3. Disconnect the electrical connector at the display (**Figure 97**).

4. Use an ohmmeter and check for continuity across the display terminals:
   a. Yes. The display is good. Continue with Step 5.
   b. No. Replace the display and retest.

5. Check for voltage at the display wiring harness connector as follows:
   a. Connect the voltmeter negative test lead to the black connector terminal.
   b. Connect the voltmeter positive test lead to the brown/yellow connector terminal.
   c. Turn the ignition switch on. The voltmeter should read battery voltage.
   d. Turn the ignition switch off.
   e. If there is no voltage reading, check the wiring between the display and ignition switch for an open circuit.

6. To remove the display (**Figure 98**), push it through the panel toward the driver's compartment.

7. Installation is the reverse of removal. Turn the ignition switch to ON and make sure the display turned on.

COOLING SYSTEM

Radiator Fan Motor Testing

1. Raise the hood.

2. Disconnect the cooling fan electrical connector (**Figure 99**).

3. Connect a fully charged 12-volt battery to the connector as follows:

   a. Positive battery lead to the blue terminal.

   b. Negative battery lead to the black terminal.

4. The cooling fan should operate. If it is faulty, replace it as described in Chapter Ten.

5. Reconnect the electrical connector and close the hood.

Cooling Fan Relay
Testing/Removal/Installation

The cooling fan relay is mounted in the electrical box.

1. Turn the ignition switch off.

2. Open the hood.

3. Turn the plastic screws and remove the electrical box cover as described in *Battery* in this chapter.

4. Disconnect and remove the cooling fan relay (D, **Figure 93**).

5. Connect test leads to the relay as follows:

   a. Ohmmeter positive test lead (A, **Figure 100**).

   b. Ohmmeter negative test lead (B, **Figure 100**).

   c. Jumper from 12-volt battery positive terminal (C, **Figure 100**).

   d. Jumper from 12-volt battery negative terminal (D, **Figure 100**).

6. There should be continuity with battery voltage applied to the relay.

7. Disconnect the test leads.

8. Replace the relay if it fails this test.

Cooling Fan Circuit Breaker
Testing/Removal/Installation

A circuit breaker protects the fan circuit. The circuit breaker is contained in a small vinyl pack attached to the fan relay wires next to the battery.

1. Open the hood.

2. Disconnect the negative battery cable as described in this chapter.

3. Remove the tape from around the circuit breaker (**Figure 101**) and disconnect the leads.

4. Using an ohmmeter, measure the resistance between the circuit breaker leads.

5. If the resistance is greater than 0.5 ohms, replace the circuit breaker.

6. Installation is the reverse of removal.

Coolant Temperature Sensor

Removal/installation

1. Drain the cooling system (Chapter Three).

2. Disconnect the electrical connector (**Figure 102**) from the sensor.

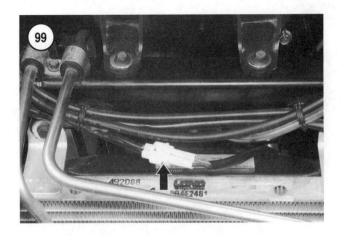

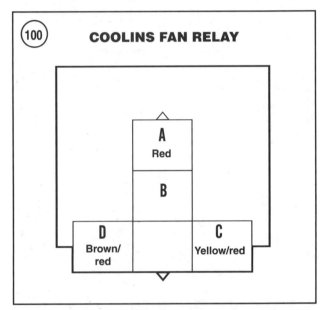

COOLINS FAN RELAY

A — Red
B
D — Brown/red
C — Yellow/red

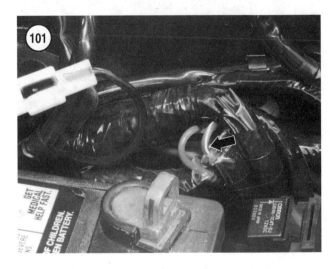

3. Unscrew and remove the sensor and washer from the cylinder head.

4. Install a new washer onto the sensor.

5. Install the coolant temperature sensor and tighten to 18 N•m (13 ft.-lb.).

6. Connect the electrical connector to the sensor.

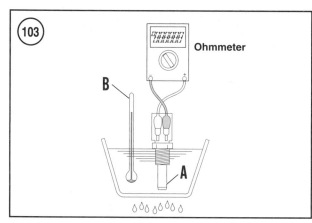

Ohmmeter

B

A

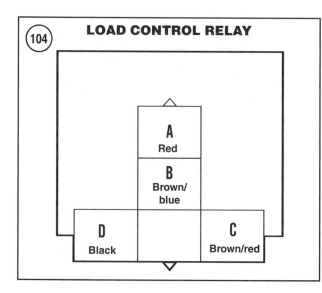

LOAD CONTROL RELAY

A
Red

B
Brown/
blue

D
Black

C
Brown/red

7. Refill and bleed the cooling system (Chapter Three).

Testing

> *NOTE*
> *Make sure the sensor terminals do not get wet.*

1. Place the sensor (A, **Figure 103**) in a pan filled with the coolant specified in Chapter Three. Support the sensor

so the threads are covered with the coolant and the sensor does not contact the pan.

2. Place a shop thermometer (B, **Figure 103**) in the pan. Use a thermometer that is rated higher than the test temperature (**Table 7**).

3. Connect an ohmmeter to the terminals on top of the sensor.

4. Heat the coolant to a temperature above the test temperature listed in **Table 7**.

5. Allow the coolant to cool while checking resistance between the terminals on the sensor at the temperature specified in **Table 7**.

6. If the resistance test results do not match the specifications listed in **Table 7**, replace the sensor.

LOAD CONTROL RELAY

Testing/Removal/Installation

The load control relay is located in the electrical box.
1. Turn the ignition switch off.
2. Open the hood.
3. Turn the plastic screws and remove the electrical box cover as described in *Battery* in this chapter.
4. Disconnect the load control relay (E, **Figure 93**).
5. Connect the positive ohmmeter lead to the load control relay red terminal (A, **Figure 104**) and the negative lead to the brown/blue terminal (B).
6. Connect the positive terminal of a fully charged 12-volt battery to the load control relay brown/red terminal (C, **Figure 104**).
7. Observe the meter and momentarily touch the negative battery terminal to the black terminal (D, **Figure 104**) and note the following:
   a. If the meter reads continuity, the relay is in good condition.
   b. If the meter shows a resistance reading, the relay is faulty.
8. Installation is the reverse of these steps.

SWITCHES

Continuity Testing

Test switches for continuity with an ohmmeter or a self-powered test light. Refer to *Tools* in Chapter One. Disconnect the switch connector and check continuity at the terminals on the switch side of the connector. Operate a switch in each of its operating positions and compare the results with the switch continuity diagram, if used, or follow the steps in the specific procedure in this section.

To use a switch continuity diagram, refer to **Figure 105**. It illustrates which terminals should have continuity when the switch is in a certain position. The line on the continuity diagram indicates there should be continuity between the black/white and black/yellow terminals when the switch button is pressed and there should be no continuity between these terminals when the button is released. When

9

the button is pressed, an ohmmeter connected between these terminals should indicate little or no resistance (a test lamp should light). When the button is released, there should be no continuity between the same terminals. An ohmmeter should indicate infinite resistance (a test lamp should not light).

Refer to the wiring diagram at the end of this manual for specific wire colors and continuity diagrams (if used).

Precautions

When testing switches, note the following:
1. First check the fuses as described in this chapter.
2. Disconnect the negative battery cable at the battery as described in this chapter if the switch is not disconnected from the circuit.

> *CAUTION*
> *Do not attempt to start the engine with the battery disconnected.*

3. When separating two connectors, pull on the connector housings and not the wires.
4. After locating a defective circuit, check the connectors to make sure they are clean and properly connected. Check all wires going into a connector housing to make sure each wire is properly positioned and the wire ends are not loose.
5. Before disconnecting two connectors, check them for any locking tabs or arms that must be pushed or opened. If two connectors are difficult to separate, do not force them as damage may occur.
6. When reconnecting electrical connector halves, push them together until they click or snap into place.
7. When replacing switches, make sure the wiring harness is properly routed and secured in place.

Ignition Switch

Testing

Refer to *Continuity Testing* in this section.

Removal/installation

1. Remove the upper instrument panel (Chapter Sixteen).
2. Remove the nut (**Figure 106**) securing the switch to the instrument panel.
3. Remove switch and disconnect electrical connector.
4. Installation is the reverse of removal. Note the following:
   a. Install the switch by aligning the tab on the switch with the notch in the lower instrument panel.
   b. If installing a new ignition switch, record the new key number in the *Quick Reference Data* section at the front of this manual.
   c. After completing installation, check the switch operation.

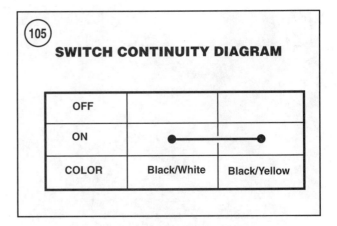

SWITCH CONTINUITY DIAGRAM

OFF		
ON	●————————●	
COLOR	Black/White	Black/Yellow

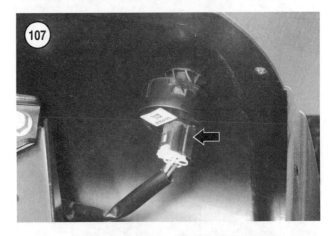

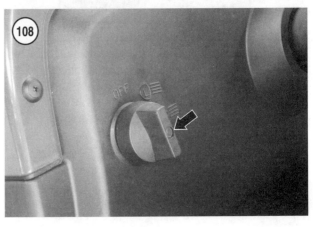

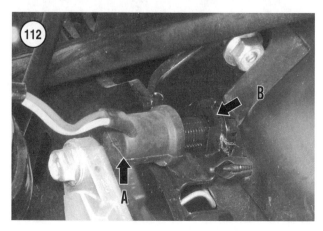

Light Switch

Testing

Refer to *Continuity Testing* in this section.

Removal/installation

1. Remove the upper instrument panel (Chapter Sixteen).
2. Disconnect the connector (**Figure 107**) at the switch.
3. Remove the switch handle (**Figure 108**) and the switch.
4. Installation is the reverse of removal. Note the following:
   a. Install the switch by aligning the tab on the switch with the notch in the instrument panel.
   b. After completing installation, check the switch operation.

On-Command Four-Wheel-Drive Motor Switch and Differential Gear Lock Switch

Testing

Refer to *Continuity Testing* in this section.

Removal/installation

1. Remove the upper instrument panel (Chapter Sixteen).
2. Disconnect the two electrical connectors (**Figure 109**).
3. Remove the bolts, washers and nuts (**Figure 110**) securing the switch to the lower instrument panel.
4. Push the switch (**Figure 111**) through the lower instrument panel toward front of vehicle and remove.
5. Installation is the reverse of removal. Check the switch operation.

Brake Light Switch

Testing

1. Open the hood.
2. Trace the wiring harness from the brake light switch (A, **Figure 112**) to its connector and disconnect the connector. Note the switch wiring harness routing.
3. Use back probe pins to connect the leads of an ohmmeter or continuity tester between the connector terminals (**Figure 113**). The tester should indicate continuity when the brake pedal is depressed and infinity when the pedal is released. Refer to *Back Probe Pins* in *Measuring Tools* in Chapter One.
4. Replace the rear brake light switch if it failed to operate as described.

Removal/installation

1. Open the hood.

9

2. Disconnect the return spring (**Figure 114**) at the brake pedal.

3. Note the routing of the switch wiring harness before removing the switch.

4. Trace the wiring harness from the brake light switch (A, **Figure 112**) to its connector and disconnect the connector.

5. Loosen the nut (B, **Figure 112**) and remove the switch.

6. Installation is the reverse of removal.

7. Adjust the rear brake light switch as described in Chapter Three.

Parking Brake Switch

Testing

1. Remove the rear console (Chapter Sixteen).

2. Block the front and rear wheels so the vehicle cannot roll in either direction.

3. Trace the wiring harness from the parking brake switch (A, **Figure 115**) to its connector and disconnect the connector. Note the switch wiring harness routing.

4. Connect the leads of an ohmmeter or continuity tester between the connector terminals. The tester should indicate continuity when the parking brake lever is applied (up) and infinity when the lever is released (down).

5. Replace the parking brake switch if it failed to operate as described.

Removal/installation

1. Park the vehicle on a level surface.

2. Block the front and rear wheels so the vehicle cannot roll in either direction.

3. Remove the rear console (Chapter Sixteen).

4. Trace the wiring harness from the parking brake switch (A, **Figure 115**) to its connector and disconnect the connector. Note the switch wiring harness routing.

5. Release the parking brake lever.

6. Remove the screw (B, **Figure 115**) and switch.

7. Installation is the reverse of removal. Tighten the mounting screw (B, **Figure 115**) securely.

8. Turn the ignition switch on. The parking brake indicator should turn on when the parking brake lever is applied and turn off when the lever is released.

9. Set the parking brake and turn the ignition switch off.

Reverse Switch

Testing/removal/installation

1. Perform Steps 1-8 in *Starter Removal/Installation* in *Starter* in this chapter.

2. Lift the seat support bracket and support it with wooden blocks (**Figure 116**) to access the reverse switch.

3. Disconnect the electrical connector (**Figure 117**).

4. Connect one ohmmeter lead onto the switch lead and the other ohmmeter lead to a good engine ground (**Figure 118**).

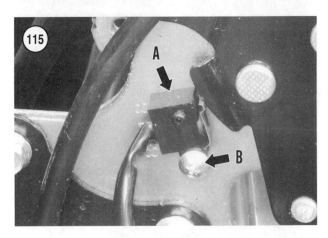

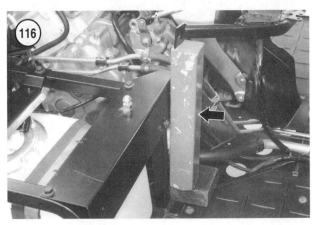

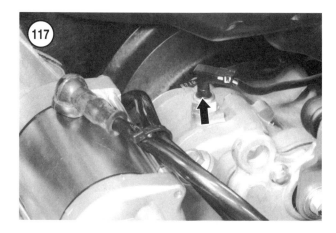

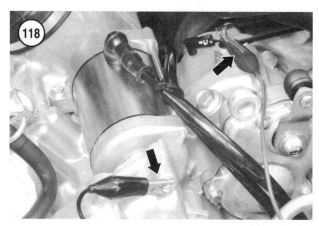

5. Lower the seat support bracket and reinstall the seat support bracket's right side mounting bolt. This bolt must be reinstalled so the shift lever can be used to shift the transmission.

6. Shift the transmission in and out of reverse and note the following:

   a. When the transmission is in reverse, the ohmmeter should read infinity.

   b. When the transmission is in neutral or any gear, the ohmmeter should read continuity.

7. Replace the reverse switch if it failed to operate as described.

8. Replace the switch as follows:

   a. Remove the switch and washer.

   b. Install a new washer on the switch.

   c. Install the reverse switch and tighten to 17 N•m (12 ft.-lb.).

9. Installation is the reverse of removal.

10. Turn the ignition switch on. The reverse indicator should turn on when the shift lever is in the reverse position.

11. Turn the ignition switch off.

Gear Position Switch

Testing/removal/installation

1. Perform Steps 1-8 in *Starter Removal/Installation* in *Starter* in this chapter.

2. Lift the seat support bracket and support it with wooden blocks (**Figure 116**) to access the gear position switch.

3. Disconnect the electrical connector (A, **Figure 119**).

4. Lower the seat support bracket and reinstall the seat support bracket's right side mounting bolt. This bolt must be reinstalled so the shift lever can be used to shift the transmission.

5. Connect the negative ohmmeter lead to a good engine ground (A, **Figure 120**).

6. Connect the positive lead to the gear position switch connector (B, **Figure 120**) blue terminal. Shift the transmission into neutral. The ohmmeter should read continuity. Shift the ohmmeter into gear. The ohmmeter should read infinity.

7. Connect the positive lead to the gear position switch connector (B, **Figure 120**) gray terminal. Shift the transmission into high gear. The ohmmeter should read continuity. Shift the ohmmeter out of high gear. The ohmmeter should read infinity.

8. Connect the positive lead to the gear position switch connector (B, **Figure 120**) white terminal. Shift the transmission into low gear. The ohmmeter should read continuity. Shift the ohmmeter out of low gear. The ohmmeter should read infinity.

9. Connect the positive lead to the gear position switch connector (B, **Figure 120**) pink terminal. The ohmmeter should read infinity when the transmission is in neutral or any gear.

10. Replace the gear position switch if it failed to operate as described.

11. Replace the switch as follows:

   a. Remove the gear position switch mounting bolts, switch (B, **Figure 119**) and O-ring.

   b. Lubricate a new O-ring with grease and install it on the gear position switch. Install the switch with its notched side facing up (**Figure 121**) and tighten the mounting bolts to 7 N•m (62 in.-lb.).

12. Installation is the reverse of removal.

13. Turn the ignition switch on and shift the transmission into neutral and each gear. The indicators on the meter assembly should turn on and off as each position is selected and changed.

14. Turn the ignition switch off.

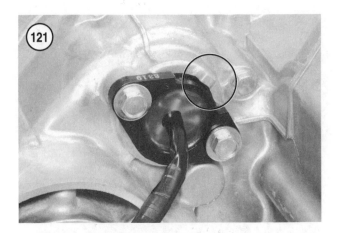

DIODE

Removal/Installation

The diode allows current to flow in one direction. The diode is plugged into the wiring harness between the electrical box and regulator/rectifier (**Figure 122**). It is also secured in place with tape.

1. Remove the air box (Chapter Eight).

2. Locate the diode in the wiring harness and remove the tape (**Figure 122**). Then disconnect and remove the diode. Refer to **Figure 123**.

3. When troubleshooting a faulty diode, install a new diode and see if the problem is solved.

4. Installation is the reverse of removal.

AUXILIARY DC JACK

Testing

1. Check the auxiliary DC jack fuse as described in this chapter. If the fuse is okay, continue with Step 2.

2. Check for voltage at the DC jack as follows:

   a. Connect the voltmeter negative test lead to a good frame ground.

   b. Insert the positive test lead into the jack (**Figure 124**).

   c. The voltmeter should read battery voltage.

   d. Remove the test leads and turn the ignition switch off.

   e. If there is no voltage reading, continue with Step 3.

3. Open the hood.

4. Disconnect the DC jack bullet connector (2008 models) or 2-pin connector (2009 and 2011-on models).

   a. Connect the voltmeter negative test lead to a good frame ground.

   b. Connect the positive test lead to the pink connector terminal (2008) or to the white/black connector terminal (2009 and 2011-on models).

   c. The voltmeter should read battery voltage.

5. Interpret the test results as follows:

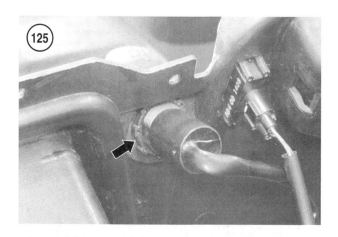

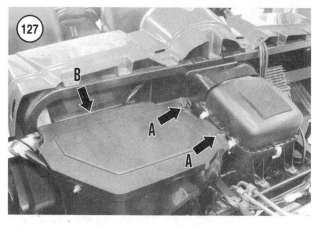

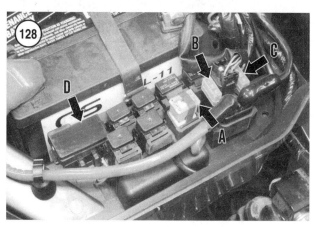

a. If voltage is recorded in Step 4 but not in Step 2, the DC jack is damaged. Replace the jack as described in this section.

b. If voltage was not recorded in Step 4, the wiring between the DC jack and battery is defective. Make the necessary repairs

Removal/Installation

1. Remove the upper instrument panel (Chapter Sixteen).
2. Disconnect the DC jack bullet connector (2008 models) or 2-pin connector (2009 and 2011-on models).
3. Remove the locknut (**Figure 125**) from inside the lower instrument panel and remove DC jack through the driver's side.
4. Installation is the reverse of removal. Note the following:

a. Install the DC jack with its LOCK POINT designation facing up (**Figure 126**).

b. Test the DC jack as described in this section.

FUSES

Whenever a fuse blows, determine the cause before replacing the fuse. Usually, the trouble is a short circuit in the wiring. This may be caused by worn-through insulation or a short to ground from a disconnected or damaged wire. Refer to **Table 8** to identify the fuses and their amperage rating.

> *CAUTION*
> *If replacing a fuse, make sure the ignition switch is turned off. This lessens the chance of a short circuit.*

> *CAUTION*
> *Never substitute any metal object for a fuse. Never use a higher amperage fuse than specified. An overload could cause a fire and the complete loss of the vehicle.*

Main Fuse

The main fuse is mounted in the electrical box.
1. Turn the ignition switch off.
2. Open the hood.
3. Turn the plastic screws (A, **Figure 127**) and remove the electrical box cover (B).
4. Slip the rubber band off the top of the main fuse (A, **Figure 128**), then grip the sides of the main fuse pull it out of its fuse holder.
5. Inspect the fuse and replace if blown or cracked.
6. Installation is the reverse of removal.

Fuel Injection Fuse

The fuel injection fuse is mounted in the electrical box.
1. Turn the ignition switch off.
2. Open the hood.

3. Turn the plastic screws (A, **Figure 127**) and remove the electrical box cover (B).

4. Pinch the locking tabs and remove the fuse cover (B, **Figure 128**). Then remove and inspect the fuel injection fuse. If the fuse is blown, replace with the spare fuse (C, **Figure 128**).

5. Installation is the reverse of removal.

Cooling Fan Fuse

1. Turn the ignition switch off.
2. Open the hood.
3. Turn the plastic screws (A, **Figure 127**) and remove the electrical box cover (B).
4. Open the fuse box cover (D, **FIgure 128**)
5. Pull the fuse (A, **Figure 129**) out of its fuse holder.
6. Remove and inspect the fuse. Replace the fuse if blown with the correct spare fuse.
7. Installation is the reverse of removal.

Fuse Box

The fuse box is mounted in the electrical box.
1. Turn the ignition switch off.
2. Open the hood.
3. Turn the plastic screws (A, **Figure 127**) and remove the electrical box cover (B).

4. Open the fuse box cover (D, **Figure 128**). Refer to the label on the bottom side of the fuse box cover to identify the fuses (B, **Figure 129**).

5. Remove and inspect the suspect fuse (C, **Figure 129**). Replace the fuse if blown with the correct spare fuse.

6. Installation is the reverse of removal.

COLOR WIRING DIAGRAMS

Color wiring diagrams for all models are located at the end of this manual.

Table 1 BATTERY SPECIFICATIONS

Type	Maintenance-free (sealed)[1]
Manufacturer	GS YUASA
Model	U1L-11
Capacity	12 volts, 28.0 amp hour
Charging current	2.8 amps × 5-10 hours
Current draw	Not specified[2]
Voltage (at 20° C [68°F])	
Fully charged	12.8 volts or higher
Needs charging	Below 12.7 volts

1. A maintenance-free battery is installed on all models described in this manual. Because this type of battery requires a high-voltage charging system, do not install a standard type battery.
2. Refer to text.

Table 2 MAINTENANCE-FREE BATTERY CHARGING TIMES

Voltage reading	State of charge	Approximate charging time
11.5 volts	0%	—[1]
11.9 volts	25%	13-20 hours
12.3 volts	50%	5-11 hours
12.7 volts	75%	3-6 hours
13.0 volts	100%[2]	—

1. Voltage readings of 11.5 volts or less require a different charging procedure and equipment. Refer to text.
2. A fully charged battery should read 12.8 volts or higher after the battery has been removed from the charger for 1 to 2 hours.

Table 3 ALTERNATOR AND CHARGING SYSTEM SPECIFICATIONS

Alternator	
Charging system output	
Amps	14.0 volts/33.5 amps @ 5000 rpm
Watts	14.0 volts/469 watts @ 5000 rpm
Charging voltage test (regulated voltage)	14.0 volts @ 5000 rpm
Stator coil resistance	0.099-0.121 ohms @ 20° C (68° F)

Table 4 IGNITION SYSTEM SPECIFICATIONS

Crankshaft position sensor resistance*	459-561 ohms
Ignition coil	
Minimum spark gap	6.0 mm (0.24 in.)
Primary coil resistance*	2.16-2.64 ohms
Secondary coil resistance*	8.64-12.96 k ohms
Ignition system	
Type	TCI (digital)
Advancer type	Throttle position sensor/electrical
Ignition timing	12° BTDC @ 1400 rpm
Lean-angle sensor output voltage	
Sensor position	
Less than 65°	3.55-4.45 volts
More than 65°	0.65-1.35 volts
Spark plug cap resistance	10.0 k ohms

*Test must be made at an ambient temperature of 20° C (68° F). Do not test when the engine or component is hot.

Table 5 STARTING SYSTEM SPECIFICATIONS

Armature coil resistance	0.0250-0.0350 ohms @ 20° C (68° F)
Brush length	
Standard	12.5 mm (0.49 in.)
Service limit	5.00 mm (0.20 in.)
Brush spring force	7.65-10.01 N (27.54-36.03 oz.)
Commutator outside diameter	
New	28.0 mm (1.10 in.)
Service limit	27.0 mm (1.06 in.)
Mica undercut depth	0.70 mm (0.03 in.)
Starter	
Manufacturer	Mitsuba
Model	SM-13

Table 6 BULB SPECIFICATIONS

Item	Specification
Headlight	30W/30W
Helmet/seat belt indicator	
2009 and 2011-on models	1.7 W
Indicator lights	
On-command four-wheel drive/differential	
gear lock indicator	LCD
All other	LED
Tail/brake light	5.0/21.0 W

Table 7 COOLING SYSTEM ELECTRICAL TEST SPECIFICATIONS

Coolant temperature sensor resistance	290-354 ohms @ 80° C (176° F)
Cooling fan circuit breaker resistance	0-0.5 ohms @ 25° C (77° F)

9

Table 8 FUSE SPECIFICATIONS

	Rating
Auxiliary DC jack fuse	10 amp
Backup fuse	10 amp
Four-wheel drive motor fuse	10 amp
Fuel injection system fuse	10 amp
Headlight fuse	15 amp
Ignition fuse	10 amp
Main fuse	40 amp
Radiator fan motor fuse	25 amp
Signal system fuse	10 amp

Table 9 ELECTRICAL SYSTEM TORQUE SPECIFICATIONS

	N•m	in.-lb.	ft.-lb.
Cargo bed panel mounting bolt/nut	7	62	–
Coolant temperature sensor	18	–	13
Crankshaft position sensor mounting bolt*	7	62	–
Engine ground cable mounting bolt	10	88	–
Flywheel nut*	60	–	44
Gear position switch mounting bolt	7	62	–
Ignition coil mounting bolt	7	62	–
Outlet pipe mounting bolt (at water pump)	10	88	–
Reverse switch	17	–	12
Right crankcase cover mounting bolts*	10	88	–
Seat support bracket mounting bolts	32	–	24
Starter clutch mounting bolt*	30	–	22
Stator coil mounting bolt*	7	62	–
Starter assembly bolts	5	44	–
Starter cable/terminal nuts			
Outer nut	5	44	–
Inner nut	11	97	–
Starter mounting bolts	10	88	–
Water pump cover mounting bolt	10	88	–
Wiring harness guide plate mounting bolt*	7	62	–

*Refer to text.

CHAPTER TEN

LIQUID COOLING AND OIL COOLER SYSTEMS

This chapter covers the liquid cooling and oil cooler systems. For routine maintenance, refer to Chapter Three.

Read *Safety* and *Service Methods* in Chapter One before servicing the vehicle in this chapter.

Table 1 and **Table 2** are at the end of this chapter.

COOLING SYSTEM SAFETY

WARNING
Do not remove the radiator cap immediately after or during engine operation. The liquid in the cooling system is hot and under pressure. Severe scalding could result if the coolant touches skin. Wait for the engine to cool and then place a shop cloth over the cap. Slowly turn the cap to relieve any pressure. Turn the cap to the safety stop and check that all pressure is relieved. To remove the cap from the radiator, press the cap down past the safety stop and twist it free. Likewise, do not remove or disconnect any cooling system component that is under pressure when the engine is hot.

COOLING SYSTEM INSPECTION

Refer to **Figure 1**.

1. If steam is observed at the muffler after the engine has sufficiently warmed up, a head gasket might be damaged. If enough coolant leaks into the cylinder, the cylinder could hydrolock. This would prevent the engine from be-

ing turned over. Coolant may also be present in the engine oil. If the oil is foamy or milky-looking, there is coolant in the oil. If so, correct the problem before returning the vehicle to service.

2. Refer *Cooling System* in Chapter Three to check the coolant level.
3. Check the radiator for clogged or damaged fins.
4. Check the radiator for loose or missing mounting bolts.
5. Check all coolant hoses and lines for cracks or damage. With the engine cold, squeeze the hoses by hand. If a hose collapses easily, it is damaged and must be replaced. Make sure the hose clamps are tight, but not so tight that they cut the hoses. Refer to *Hoses* in this section.
6. Make sure the siphon hose (6, **Figure 1**) and the reservoir breather hose (1, **Figure 1**) are not clogged or damaged.
7. To check the cooling system for leaks, pressure test it as described in this section.
8. If coolant or oil is leaking from the small hose connected to the water pump, refer to *Water Pump* in this chapter to check for a damaged seal.

Hoses

After removing any cooling system component, inspect the adjoining hoses and lines to determine if replacement is necessary. Hoses deteriorate with age and should be inspected for conditions that may cause them to fail. Loss of coolant will cause the engine to overheat, and spray from a leaking hose can cause injury. A collapsed hose prevents coolant circulation and will cause overheating. Observe the following when servicing hoses:

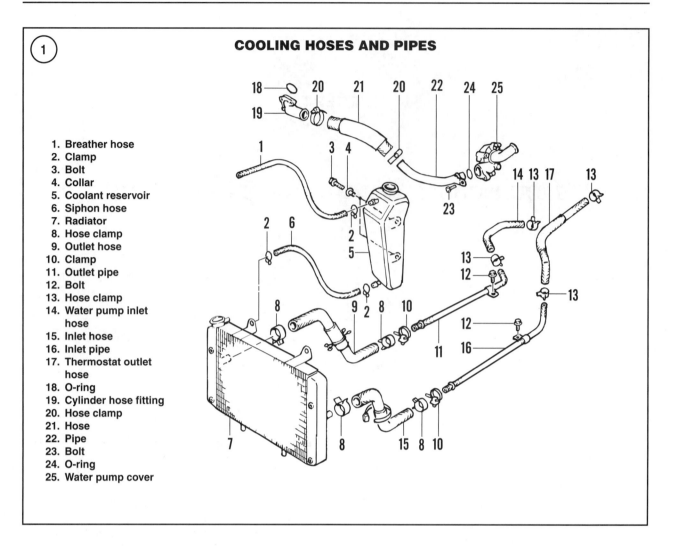

COOLING HOSES AND PIPES

1. Breather hose
2. Clamp
3. Bolt
4. Collar
5. Coolant reservoir
6. Siphon hose
7. Radiator
8. Hose clamp
9. Outlet hose
10. Clamp
11. Outlet pipe
12. Bolt
13. Hose clamp
14. Water pump inlet hose
15. Inlet hose
16. Inlet pipe
17. Thermostat outlet hose
18. O-ring
19. Cylinder hose fitting
20. Hose clamp
21. Hose
22. Pipe
23. Bolt
24. O-ring
25. Water pump cover

1. Make sure the cooling system is cool before removing any coolant hose or component.

2. Use original equipment replacement hoses and lines; they are formed to a specific shape and dimension for correct fit.

3. Loosen the hose clamps on the hose or line that is to be replaced. Slide the clamps back off the component fittings.

4. Before disconnecting a formed hose, look for a paint mark on the end of the hose. This mark usually aligns with a raised boss on the connecting part to ensure the hose is properly aligned.

CAUTION
Do not use excessive force when attempting to remove a stubborn hose. Also, use caution when attempting to loosen hoses with hose pliers. The aluminum radiator and water pump hose joints are easily damaged.

5. Twist the hose to release it from the joint. If the hose is difficult to break loose, insert a small screwdriver between the hose and joint and spray WD-40 or a similar lubricant into the opening and carefully twist the hose to break it loose.

NOTE
Remove all lubricant residue from the hose and hose fitting before reinstalling the hose.

6. Examine the fittings for cracks or other damage. Repair or replace as necessary. If the fitting is good, use a wire brush and clean off any hose residue that may have transferred to the fitting. Wipe clean with a cloth.

7. Inspect the hose clamps for rust and corrosion and replace if necessary.

8. If a hose is difficult to install on the joint, soak the end in hot water to make it more pliable. Do not use any lubricant when installing hoses.

9. Formed hoses must be properly installed. Refer to Step 4.

10. With the hose or line correctly installed, position and tighten the clamp securely. Position the clamp head so it is accessible for future removal and does not contact other parts.

Pressure Test

A cooling system tester is required to perform the following tests.

1. Raise the hood.

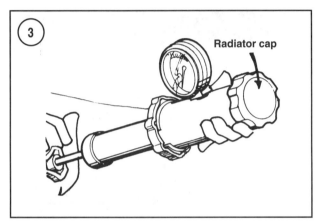

Radiator cap

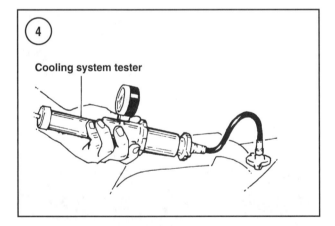

Cooling system tester

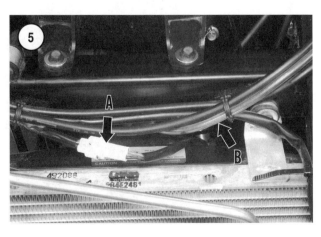

2. With the engine cold, remove the radiator cap (**Figure 2**).

3. Add coolant to the radiator to bring the level up to the filler neck.

4. Check the rubber washers on the inside of the radiator cap. Replace the cap if the washers show signs of deterioration, cracking or other damage. If the radiator cap is good, perform Step 5.

CAUTION
Do not exceed 137 kPa (20 psi) or the cooling system components may be damaged.

5. Lubricate the rubber washer on the inside of the radiator cap with coolant and install it on a cooling system pressure tester (**Figure 3**). Apply 93.3-122.7 kPa (13.5-17.8 psi) and check for a pressure drop. Replace the cap if it cannot hold this pressure for ten seconds.

6. Mount the pressure tester onto the radiator filler neck (**Figure 4**) and pressure test the cooling system to 122.7 kPa (17.8 psi). If the system cannot hold this pressure for ten seconds, check for a coolant leak:

    a. Radiator cap. If the radiator cap passed the pressure test in Step 5, but is now leaking, inspect the radiator filler neck and cap mounting flange for damage.

    b. Leaking or damaged coolant hoses.

    c. Damaged or deteriorated O-rings installed in coolant hose connectors.

    d. Damaged water pump mechanical seal.

    e. Water pump.

    f. Loose coolant drain or bleed bolts.

    g. Warped cylinder head or cylinder mating surfaces.

NOTE
*If the test pressure drops rapidly, but there are no visible coolant leaks, coolant may be leaking into the cylinder head. To check, perform a **Cylinder Leakdown Test** as described in Chapter Two. If air can be heard escaping through the radiator during the test, coolant is leaking between the cylinder head and cylinder. Another indicator of this problem is when the coolant level falls in the reservoir and radiator and there are no signs of a coolant leak.*

7. Check all cooling system hoses for damage or deterioration. Replace any questionable hose. Make sure all hose clamps are tight.

8. Remove the tester and install the radiator cap (**Figure 2**).

RADIATOR

Removal/Installation

1. Remove the hood (Chapter Sixteen).

2. Drain the cooling system (Chapter Three).

3. Disconnect the cooling fan electrical connector (A, **Figure 5**).

10

4. Remove the fan motor breather hose from its routing position along the frame and remove it with the radiator (B, **Figure 5**).

5. Disconnect the inlet hose at the radiator (**Figure 6**).

6. Disconnect the outlet hose at the radiator (A, **Figure 7**).

7. Disconnect the siphon hose at the radiator (B, **Figure 7**).

8A. If oil cooler removal is required, remove it and its mounting bracket as described in this chapter.

8B. If oil cooler removal is not required, perform the following:

    a. Cut a block of wood and place it between the bottom of the oil cooler and frame rail (A, **Figure 8**).

    b. Remove the upper and lower nuts (B, **Figure 8**) securing the oil cooler to its mounting brackets.

    c. Remove the bolts (**Figure 9**) securing the oil cooler mounting brackets to the radiator and remove the brackets.

9. Remove the radiator mounting bolts (**Figure 10**) at the top of the radiator.

10. Place a jack underneath the front of the vehicle and raise the vehicle slightly to take pressure off the front suspension. However, do not lift the vehicle so far that the front wheels are off the ground.

11. Turn the front wheel toward the right to provide clearance for radiator removal.

12. Loosen the right shock absorber's lower mounting nut.

13. Remove the right shock absorber's upper mounting nut and bolt (**Figure 11**) and pivot the shock absorber toward the right tire.

> *NOTE*
> *After draining the cooling system, there is still a considerable amount of coolant remaining in the radiator. Because the radiator will be tilted during removal, plug the radiator hose openings to prevent coolant from spilling out.*

14. Lift the radiator up to clear its lower mounting studs from the rubber dampers mounted on the frame and then move toward the rear to clear the dampers. Remove the radiator/fan assembly (**Figure 12**) from the right side of the vehicle, making sure not to damage the fins on the front bumper.

15. Installation is the reverse of removal. Note the following:

    a. Install the upper shock absorber mounting bolt from the front side of the vehicle.

    b. Tighten the upper and lower shock absorber mounting nuts to 45 N•m (33 ft.-lb.).

    c. Tighten the radiator mounting bolts to 7 N•m (62 in.-lb.).

    d. Tighten the oil cooler mounting nuts to 7 N•m (62 in.-lb.).

    e. Refill and bleed the cooling system (Chapter Three).

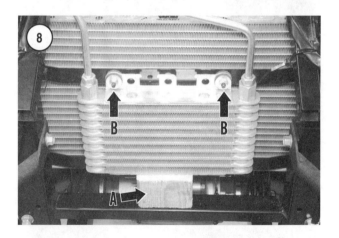

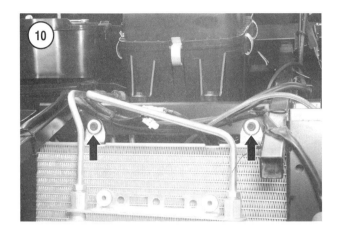

Inspection

CAUTION
Do not press too hard or the cooling fins and
tubes may be damaged.

1. Clean the exterior of the radiator with a garden hose on low pressure. Spray the front and back sides to remove all debris. Carefully use a whisk broom or stiff paint brush to remove any stubborn dirt.
2. Check for bent cooling fins. Straighten bent cooling fins with a screwdriver. If a large area of the cooling surface is damaged, replace the radiator.
3. Check the seams and other soldered connections for corrosion (green residue). If corrosion is evident, there could be a leak in that spot. Perform a cooling system pressure check as described in this chapter.
4. Fill the radiator with water and check the flow rate out of the radiator. If the flow rate is slow, or if corrosion or other buildup is seen, take the radiator to a radiator repair shop to have it flushed and pressure checked.
5. Replace the upper and lower rubber dampers if damaged.
6. Inspect the rubber seals inside the radiator cap. Replace the cap if they are hardened or starting to deteriorate.

COOLING FAN

Removal/Installation

1. Remove the radiator as described in this chapter.
2. Remove the fan bolts (A, **Figure 13**) and fan assembly (B).
3. Installation is the reverse of removal. Note the following:
   a. Install the fan onto the radiator with its wiring harness at the top.
   b. Tighten the fan assembly mounting bolts securely.
   c. Reconnect the breather hose onto the fan (C, **Figure 13**), if disconnected.

COOLANT RESERVOIR

Removal/Installation

1. Disconnect the coolant siphon hose (A, **Figure 14**) from the bottom of the coolant reservoir to drain the reservoir.
2. Disconnect the breather hose (B, **Figure 14**) from the top of the reservoir.
3. Remove the mounting bolts (C, **Figure 14**), collars and the coolant reservoir.
4. Flush the reservoir with clean water and check for cracks or other damage.
5. Inspect and replace damaged hoses. Replace weak or damaged hose clamps.
6. Install the coolant reservoir by reversing these steps. Tighten the coolant reservoir mounting bolts to 7 N•m (62 in.-lb.).

7. Fill the coolant reservoir as described in *Coolant Change* in *Cooling System* in Chapter Three. Check for leaks.

THERMOSTAT

The thermostat is located in a housing on the left side of the engine. The thermostat is a temperature sensitive valve used to control the flow of coolant into the radiator. When the engine is cold, the thermostat is closed to retain coolant in the water jackets around the engine. This helps the engine to warm up quickly. When the engine reaches a specified temperature, the thermostat opens and coolant flows between the engine and radiator, where it is cooled.

Removal/Installation

1. Remove the following as described in Chapter Sixteen:
   a. Seats.
   b. Rear console.
2. Drain coolant until the coolant level is below the thermostat housing or drain the cooling system as described in Chapter Three.
3. Place a rag underneath the thermostat to catch any residue coolant spilled from the thermostat housing.
4. Remove mounting bolts (A, **Figure 15**) and the thermostat cover (B). Remove the O-ring from the thermostat cover.
5. Remove the thermostat (A, **Figure 16**).
6. Rinse the thermostat with clean water.
7. Inspect the thermostat for damage. Make sure the spring (**Figure 17**) has not sagged or broken.
8. Inspect the thermostat valve and valve seat for any gaps. The valve should be closed when the thermostat is cold. If the valve is cold and open, replace the thermostat.
9. If necessary, test the thermostat as described in this section.
10. Remove residue from the thermostat housing and all mating surfaces.
11. Installation is the reverse of removal. Note the following:
   a. Lubricate a new O-ring with lithium grease and install on the thermostat housing shoulder.
   b. Install the thermostat with its vent hole (B, **Figure 16**) facing up.
   c. Tighten the thermostat cover mounting bolts to 10 N•m (88 in.-lb.).
   d. Fill and bleed the cooling system (Chapter Three).
   e. Start the vehicle and check for coolant leaks.

Testing

A stuck thermostat causes the engine to warm up slowly (when stuck open) or causes overheating (when stuck partially or fully closed). Check by starting the engine (when cold) and allow it to warm to normal operating temperature. During this time, carefully touch the inlet hose at the radiator (left side). If the hose becomes hot quickly, the

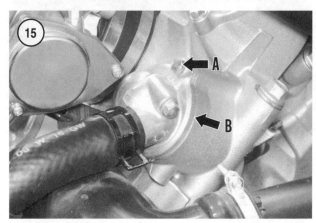

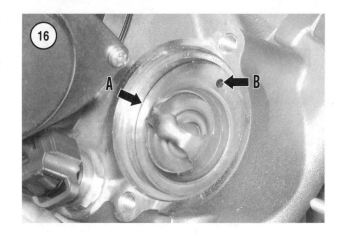

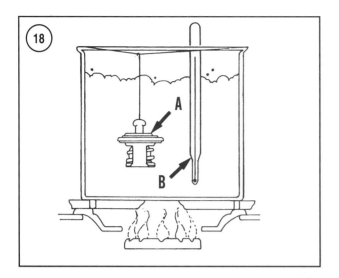

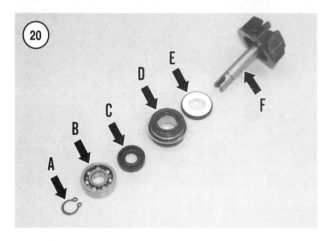

thermostat is probably stuck open. This condition causes the engine to run colder for a longer period. If the hose gradually warms and then becomes hot, the thermostat is probably operating correctly. However, if the inlet hose and radiator do not feel hot after the engine has run long enough to warm to normal operating temperature, the thermostat is probably stuck closed and is blocking coolant flow through the radiator. This condition causes the engine to overheat.

1. Support the thermostat (A, **Figure 18**) and a thermometer (B) rated higher than the test temperature in a pan of water (**Figure 18**). The thermostat and thermometer must not touch the sides or bottom of the pan or a false reading will result.

2. Gradually heat the water and continue to gently stir the water until it reaches 50-54° C (122-129.2° F). At this temperature, the thermostat valve should start to open.

3. Continue to raise the temperature to 70° C (158° F). At this temperature, the thermostat valve should be fully open, which is about 7 mm (0.28 in.).

4. If the valve fails to operate at the listed temperatures, or if the valve lift is below minimum at the specified temperature, replace the thermostat. Always replace the thermostat with one of the same temperature rating.

WATER PUMP

The water pump is mounted on the bottom, right side of the engine in the right crankcase cover. The right crankcase cover must be removed (Chapter Nine) to service the water pump.

Water Pump Seal Check

There is an inspection hose (**Figure 19**) for the water pump, located at the front bottom edge of the right crankcase cover. If a coolant leak is evident from the hose, the pump mechanical seal is leaking. If an oil leak is evident, the oil seal is leaking. When a coolant or oil leak is detected, the pump must be overhauled and both seals and bearing replaced.

Impeller Removal/Installation
And Pump Inspection

The water pump is installed in the right crankcase cover (**Figure 20**).

1. Remove the following as described in Chapter Sixteen:
   a. Seats.
   b. Rear console.

2. Drain the engine oil (Chapter Three).

3. Drain the engine coolant (Chapter Three).

4. Remove the right crankcase cover (Chapter Nine).

NOTE
Because the stator and crankshaft position sensor are installed in the right crankcase cover, handle the cover assembly carefully to prevent damage to these electrical components and their wiring harnesses. If necessary, remove the stator and crankshaft position sensor as described in Chapter Nine.

5. Remove the bolts (A, **Figure 21**) and the water pump cover (B) if it was not removed during right crankcase cover removal. Then remove the two dowel pins (A, **Figure 22**) and gasket (B).

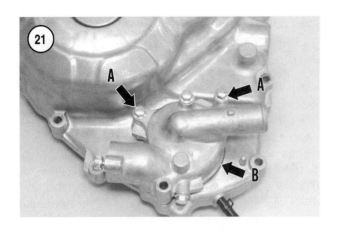

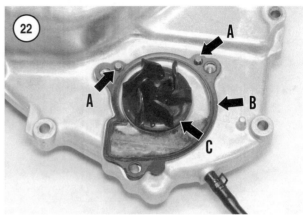

NOTE
*If damage is noted during the following inspection procedures, replace the snap ring (A, **Figure 20**), bearing (B), oil seal (C), mechanical seal (D) and impeller seal (E) as an assembly as described in this section. Also replace the impeller if damaged (F, **Figure 20**).*

6. Turn the impeller (C, **Figure 22**). The shaft should turn with noticeable resistance and have no end play. If play is detected, the mechanical seal and impeller seal assembly are probably worn or damaged.

7. Remove the snap ring (**Figure 23**) and slide the impeller (C, **Figure 22**) out of the bearing. Discard the snap ring.

8. Turn the water pump bearing (**Figure 24**) inner race by hand. The bearing race should turn smoothly.

9. Inspect the impeller blades (A, **Figure 25**) for cracks and other damage.

10. Inspect the impeller shaft (B, **Figure 25**) for scoring, bluing or other damage. Check the snap ring groove (C, **Figure 25**) for damage.

11. Inspect the contact surfaces of the mechanical seal (A, **Figure 26**) and its mating impeller seal (**Figure 27**). In order to seal properly, both surfaces must be smooth and free of damage. When installed, the impeller seal should fit squarely against the mechanical seal. Because the mechanical seal is spring loaded, it maintains pressure on the seals.

12. Check the shaft for tilt (**Figure 28**). Maximum allowable tilt is 0.15 mm (0.006 in.). If tilt is excessive, make sure the impeller seal (**Figure 27**) is seating flush in the impeller. If so, remove the impeller seal (**Figure 29**) with a hooked tool and remeasure tilt. If tilt is still excessive, replace the impeller shaft. If the measurable tilt is now less than the service limit, install a new impeller seal and mechanical seal as described in this section.

13. Inspect the water pump cover for corrosion, warpage and other damage.

NOTE
Continue with Step 14 when all worn or damaged parts have been replaced.

14. Lubricate the impeller seal and mechanical seal mating surfaces with coolant. Do not use grease or oil.

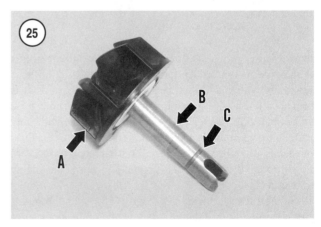

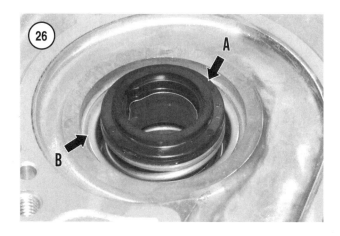

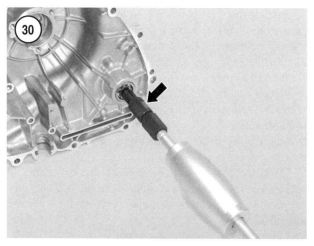

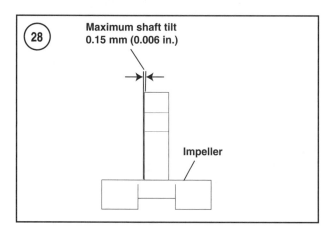

Maximum shaft tilt
0.15 mm (0.006 in.)

Impeller

15. Install the impeller through the front side of the right crankcase cover. Then push the impeller inward (against spring tension) to expose the snap ring groove and install a new snap ring (**Figure 23**) with its flat side facing out. Make sure the snap ring seats in the groove completely. Then turn the impeller (C, **Figure 22**). The shaft should turn with some resistance and have no end play.

NOTE
Do not install the water pump cover at this time. The impeller must be turned by hand and engaged to the oil pump shaft when installing the right crankcase cover. The water pump cover is installed after the right crankcase cover is installed on the engine. Refer to Chapter Nine.

16. Reverse Steps 1-5 to complete installation. Tighten the water pump cover mounting bolts to 10 N•m (88 in.-lb.).

Bearing and Seal Removal/Installation

This procedure replaces the water pump bearing (B, **Figure 20**) and the water pump seals (C-E). Refer to *Service Methods* in Chapter One.

NOTE
A blind bearing remover (Motion Pro Blind Bearing and Bushing Remover [part No. 08-0292] or equivalent) is used to remove the bearing in Step 1.

1. Insert an 8-mm bearing collet (**Figure 30**) into the bearing. Expand the collet to lock it against the bearing. Support the right crankcase cover and operate the puller to remove the bearing. Discard the bearing.
2. Pry the oil seal (**Figure 31**) out of the seal bore. Discard the seal.

NOTE
The mechanical seal has a sealer applied to its outside surface and can be difficult to remove.

3. Support the right crankcase cover (A, **Figure 32**) in a press with its inside surface facing up. Support the cover around the bearing bore with a wooden block (B, **Figure 32**). Drill a hole through the wooden block large enough for the seal to pass through.

4. Place a bearing driver (C, **Figure 32**) against the bottom of the seal and press or drive the seal out of the cover. Refer to **Figure 33**.

5. Remove the impeller seal (**Figure 29**) with a hooked tool.

6. Clean the bearing and seal bores in the cover and inspect them for scoring and other damage. If the engine overheated, check the right crankcase cover for warp and other damage.

7. Lubricate the oil seal with coolant.

8. Support the cover with the bearing side up. Place the seal over its bore with the open side of the seal facing up (**Figure 34**). Using a socket or bearing driver that fits on the outer edge of the seal, drive the seal into its bore to the depth specified in **Figure 35**. Check that the drain hole is not blocked by the seal.

9. Place the bearing over the cover bore with its manufacturer's marks facing out. Then press (**Figure 36**) or drive the bearing into its bore until it bottoms. Lubricate the bearing with engine oil.

10. Install the mechanical seal as follows:

    a. Support the cover with the bearing side down.

    b. Use a thin-walled driver (**Figure 37**) that fits onto the outer edge of the seal without contacting the seal material. If a suitable driver is not available, use the Yamaha seal installer (part No. YM-33221-A).

CAUTION
Do not remove or scratch the sealer pre-applied to the mechanical seal housing surface.

    c. Align the seal (**Figure 38**) squarely with its bore. Press or drive the seal into its bore until the seal flange bottoms squarely against the bore shoulder (B, **Figure 26**).

11. Lubricate the impeller seal with coolant and install it into the impeller with its white plastic side facing away from the impeller (**Figure 27**).

OIL COOLER LINES AND HOSES

Refer to **Figure 39**.

When servicing the oil cooler lines and hoses, note the following:

1. The oil cooler lines and hoses can be removed and replaced in sections.

2. Identify all inlet and outlet oil lines and oil hoses so they can be used to identify the new parts.

3. Always note routing and clamp positions when removing lines and hoses.

4. When disconnecting a line or hose, plug the line, hose, engine or oil cooler opening to prevent contamination.

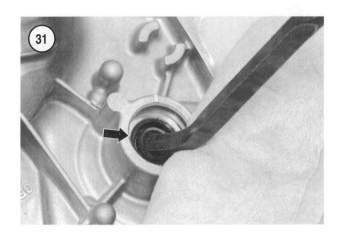

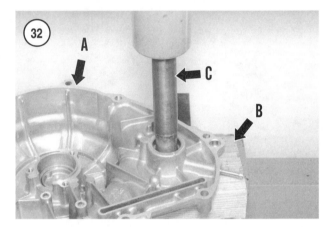

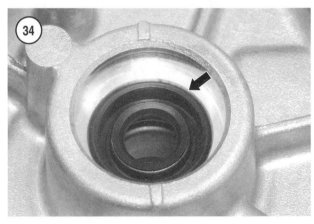

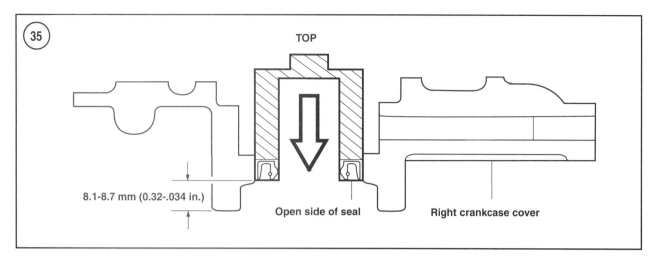

8.1-8.7 mm (0.32-.034 in.)

TOP

Open side of seal

Right crankcase cover

Front Inlet and Outlet Oil Lines and Hoses
Removal/Installation

1. Remove the following as described in Chapter Sixteen:
   a. Hood.
   b. Seats.
   c. Rear console.
   d. Corner and side panel assembly (both left and right sides).
   e. Front console.

NOTE
In Step 2, it is only necessary to free the air intake duct so that it can be repositioned in the chassis. This will allow room necessary to access and remove the front inlet and outlet oil lines and hoses.

2. Partially remove the air intake duct (Chapter Eight).
3. Loosen the oil line nuts securing the front outlet (A, **Figure 40**) and front inlet (B) oil lines at the oil cooler.
4. Remove the bolts securing the upper and lower oil line mounting brackets and remove the brackets. Refer to C, **Figure 40**, typical.
5. Open the clamps (7, **Figure 39**) securing the front inlet and outlet hoses to the front inlet and outlet oil lines. Slide the clamps away from the front oil lines.
6. Remove the front inlet and outlet oil lines.
7. Loosen the clamps (9, **Figure 39**) and remove the front inlet and outlet oil hoses.
8. If the oil lines are being replaced, remove the bolts, clamps and dampers securing the oil lines together. Identify the new oil lines then secure with the dampers, clamps and bolts and install them in their original positions.
9. Installation is the reverse of removal. Note the following:
   a. Refer to disassembly notes to make sure the oil lines and oil hoses are routed and installed in their correct position.

OIL COOLER LINES AND HOSES

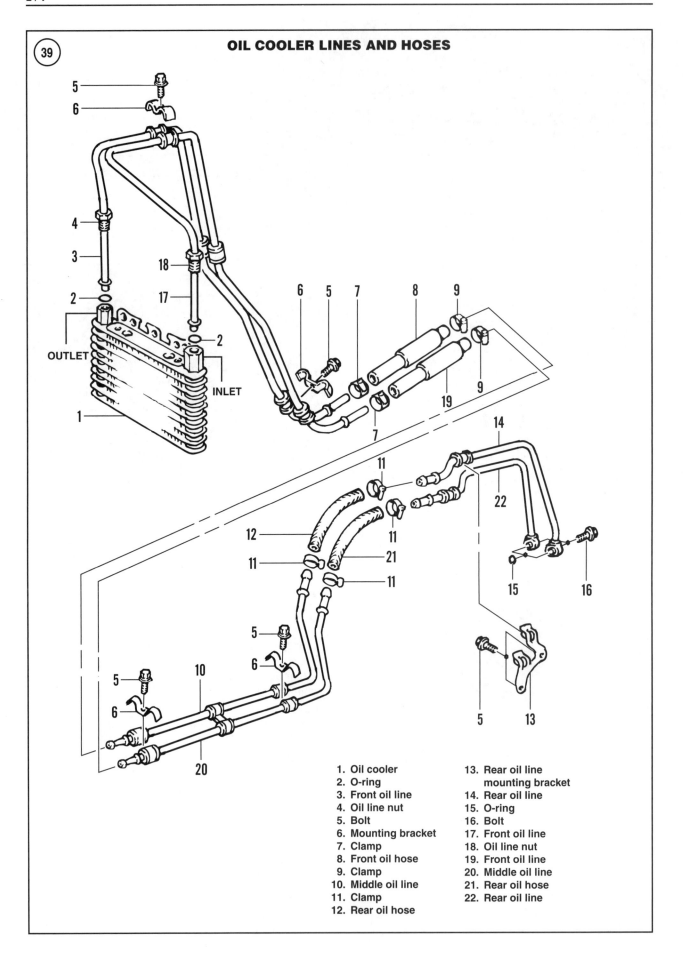

OUTLET

INLET

1. Oil cooler
2. O-ring
3. Front oil line
4. Oil line nut
5. Bolt
6. Mounting bracket
7. Clamp
8. Front oil hose
9. Clamp
10. Middle oil line
11. Clamp
12. Rear oil hose
13. Rear oil line mounting bracket
14. Rear oil line
15. O-ring
16. Bolt
17. Front oil line
18. Oil line nut
19. Front oil line
20. Middle oil line
21. Rear oil hose
22. Rear oil line

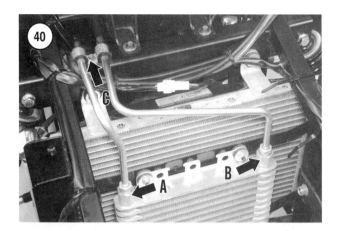

b. Lubricate new O-rings (2, **Figure 39**) with grease and install them at the oil cooler fittings.
c. Tighten the oil line mounting bracket bolts to 7 N•m (62 in.-lb.).
d. Tighten the oil line nuts to 21 N•m (15 ft.-lb.).
e. Refill the engine with oil (Chapter Three).
f. Start the engine and check for oil leaks.

Middle Oil Lines
Removal/Installation

1. Remove the following as described in Chapter Sixteen:
   a. Hood.
   b. Seats.
   c. Rear console.
   d. Right corner and side panel assembly.
   e. Front console.

NOTE
In Step 2, it is only necessary to free the air intake duct so that it can be repositioned in the chassis. This will allow room necessary to access and remove the front inlet and outlet oil lines and hoses.

2. Partially remove the air intake duct (Chapter Eight).
3. Open the clamps securing the front oil hoses to the middle oil lines.

4. Open the clamps securing the rear oil hoses (A, **Figure 41**) to the middle oil lines.
5. Remove the clamps securing the middle oil lines to the frame.
6. Remove the middle oil lines (10 and 20, **Figure 39**).
7. If the middle oil lines are being replaced, remove the bolt, clamp and damper securing the oil lines together. Identify the new oil lines then secure with the damper, clamp and bolt and install in their original position.
8. Installation is the reverse of removal. Note the following:
   a. Refer to disassembly notes to make sure the oil lines and oil hoses are routed and installed in their correct position.
   b. Tighten the oil line mounting bracket bolts to 7 N•m (62 in.-lb.).
   c. Refill the engine with oil (Chapter Three).
   d. Start the engine and check for oil leaks.

Rear Inlet and Outlet Oil Lines and Hoses
Removal/Installation

1. Drain the engine oil (Chapter Three).
2. Remove the following as described in Chapter Sixteen:
   a. Seats.
   b. Rear console.
   c. Front console.
3. Remove the rear oil hoses (12 and 21, **Figure 39**) as follows:
   a. Open the clamps (A, **Figure 41**) securing the rear inlet and outlet oil hoses to the middle inlet and outlet oil lines.
   b. Remove the clamps (B, **Figure 41**) securing the rear oil hoses to the rear oil lines.
   c. Remove the rear oil hoses.
4. Remove the rear oil lines (14 and 22, **Figure 39**) as follows:
   a. Disconnect the rear oil hoses at the lines if they were not disconnected in Step 3.
   b. Remove the Allen bolts (**Figure 42**) securing the rear oil lines to the engine.
   c. Remove the bolts securing the rear oil line bracket (13, **Figure 39**) to the engine.

10

d. Remove the rear oil lines.

5. Installation is the reverse of removal. Note the following:

    a. Refer to disassembly notes to make sure the oil lines and oil hoses are routed and installed in their correct position.

    b. Lubricate new O-rings with grease and install them onto the oil line fittings at the engine.

    c. Tighten the rear oil line Allen bolts (**Figure 42**) to 10 N•m (88 in.-lb.).

    d. Tighten the rear oil line bracket (13, **Figure 39**) mounting bolts to 10 N•m (88 in.-lb.).

    e. Refill the engine with oil (Chapter Three).

    f. Start the engine and check for oil leaks.

OIL COOLER

Removal/Installation

1. Drain the engine oil (Chapter Three).

2. Remove hood (Chapter Sixteen).

3. Clean the oil line nuts and the area around the nuts with compressed air or water.

4. Loosen the oil line nuts (A, **Figure 43**) at the top of the oil cooler.

5. Remove the oil cooler mounting nuts (B, **Figure 43**) and remove the oil cooler assembly (C). Plug the openings on top of the oil cooler to prevent contamination.

6. Discard the O-rings (2, **Figure 39**).

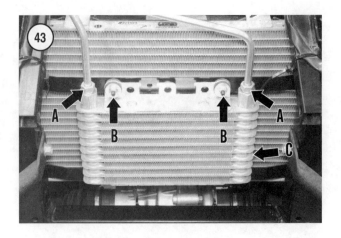

7. If necessary, remove the bolts securing the oil cooler mounting brackets to the radiator and remove oil cooler mounting brackets.

8. Replace missing or damaged oil cooler collars and dampers.

9. Installation is the reverse of removal. Note the following:

    a. Lubricate new O-rings (2, **Figure 39**) with engine oil and install them over the oil line shoulders.

    b. Tighten the oil line nuts (A, **Figure 43**) to 21 N•m (15 ft.-lb.).

    c. Tighten the oil cooler mounting nuts (B, **Figure 43**) to 7 N•m (62 in.-lb.).

    d. Refill the engine with oil (Chapter Ten).

    e. Start the engine and check for oil leaks.

Table 1 COOLING SYSTEM SPECIFICATIONS

Coolant type	Ethylene glycol containing anticorrosion inhibitors for aluminum engines
Coolant mixture	50:50 (coolant/distilled water)
Coolant capacity	
Radiator	2.35 liters (2.48 qt.)
Reservoir	
Amount between marks	0.21 liters (0.22 qt.)
Total	0.32 liters (0.34 qt.)
Cooling system test pressure	122.7 kPa (17.8 psi)
Radiator cap relief pressure	93.3-122.7 kPa (13.5-17.8 psi)
Thermostat valve	
Opening temperature	50-54° C (122-129° F)
Fully open temperature (@ 7 mm lift)	70° C (158° F)
Water pump impeller shaft tilt limit	0.15 mm (0.006 in.)

Table 2 COOLING SYSTEM TORQUE SPECIFICATIONS

	N•m	in.-lb.	ft.-lb.
Coolant drain bolt	10	88	–
Coolant hose joint mounting bolt	10	88	–
Coolant reservoir mounting bolts	7	62	–
Coolant temperature sensor	18	–	13
Front shock absorber mounting nuts	45	–	33
Oil cooler mounting nuts	7	62	–
Oil line mounting bracket bolts	7	62	–
Oil line nuts	21	–	15
Outlet pipe mounting bolt (at water pump)	10	88	–
Radiator mounting bolts	7	62	–
Rear oil line Allen bolts	10	88	–
Rear oil line bracket mounting bolt	10	88	–
Thermostat cover mounting bolt	10	88	–
Water pump cover mounting bolts	10	88	–

10

CHAPTER ELEVEN

FRONT SUSPENSION AND STEERING

This chapter covers the front wheels, hubs, suspension and steering components.

Read *Safety* and *Service Methods* in Chapter One before servicing the vehicle in this chapter.

Tables 1-4 are at the end of this chapter.

FRONT WHEELS

Removal/Installation

1. Park the vehicle on level ground and set the parking brake.

> *NOTE*
> *If both front wheels will be removed, identify their normal operating direction or locate the tires directional marks (**Figure 1**) so they can be reinstalled on the correct side of the vehicle.*

2. Loosen the front wheel lug nuts (A, **Figure 2**) before raising the vehicle.
3. Support the vehicle with both front wheels off the ground and remove the lug nuts and the front wheel.
4. Clean and dry the lug nuts and replace if damaged.
5. Refer to *Wheel Runout* in this chapter to inspect the wheels. If the tire is flat, repair it as described in *Tire Repair* in *Tires* this chapter.

6. Install the wheel with the tire's directional mark facing its normal operating direction and with the tire valve (B, **Figure 2**) facing out.
7. Install the lug nuts with their tapered side (**Figure 3**) facing the wheel and tighten finger-tight so the wheel sits squarely against the front hub.
8. Lower the vehicle so both front tires are on the ground and tighten the lug nuts in a crossing pattern and several steps to 55 N•m (41 ft.-lb.).
9. Support the vehicle again with both front wheels off the ground. Make sure the axle rotates and the front brakes are working properly.

FRONT HUB

Removal

1. Park the vehicle on level ground and set the parking brake.
2. Support the vehicle and remove the front wheel as described in this chapter.
3. Remove the center cap (**Figure 4**) from the hub nut.
4. Grind the staked portion (**Figure 5**) of the hub nut to weaken it. Do not grind through the nut as this will damage the axle threads.

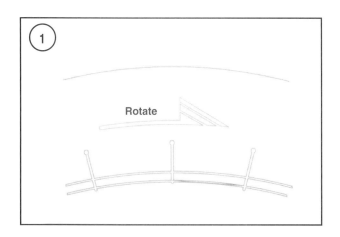

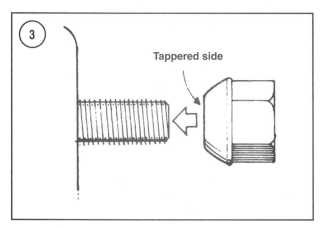

11

NOTE
The front hub nut is tightened to a high torque
value and can be difficult to remove.

5A. Use an impact wrench and remove the front hub nut (**Figure 5**). Discard the nut.

5B. If an impact wrench is unavailable, hold the hub in place with a long metal bar bolted across two of the hub studs (**Figure 6**). The metal bar must be long enough to contact the ground and lock the hub in place. Loosen the hub nut with a breaker bar and socket. Discard the nut..

6. Remove the front brake caliper (Chapter Fifteen). Do not disconnect the brake hose from the caliper unless necessary. Support the caliper with a wire. Do not let the caliper hang by the brake hose.

7. Slide the front hub (**Figure 7**) off the axle and remove it. If the hub is seized to the axle splines, remove it with a puller. Do not strike the hub or brake disc.

8. Check the O-ring (A, **Figure 8**), seated next to the knuckle bearing, for damage.

9. Inspect as described in this section.

Installation

1. If removed, lubricate the O-ring (A, **Figure 8**) with lithium grease and seat it next to the knuckle bearing.

2. Wipe the knuckle seal (B, **Figure 8**) of all old grease. Relubricate the seal lip with lithium grease.

3. Clean and dry the axle threads (C, **Figure 8**).

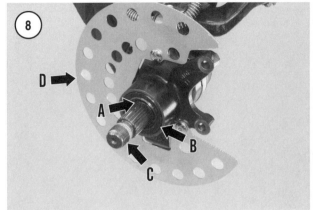

4. Clean the brake disc with brake cleaner and allow to dry.

5. Slide the front hub (**Figure 7**) onto the axle seat it against the steering knuckle.

NOTE
*Do not lubricate the axle or front hub nut threads with oil or any lubricant. The threads must be clean and dry when tightened to specification (**Table 4**).*

6. Install a new front hub nut and tighten finger-tight.

7. Mount a long metal bar (**Figure 9**) across two of the hub studs and secure in place with two lug nuts. The metal bar must be long enough to contact the ground and lock the hub in place.

8. Tighten the front hub nut to 350 N•m (255 ft.-lb.). Then use a punch and stake a portion of the nut shoulder into the notch in the axle (**Figure 5**).

9. Install the front brake caliper (Chapter Fifteen).

10. Install the center cap (**Figure 4**) over the hub nut.

11. Install the front wheel as described in this chapter.

Inspection

The front brake disc is mounted on the front hub.

1. If necessary, service the brake disc (Chapter Fifteen).

2. Inspect the front hub (**Figure 10**) for the following and replace if damaged:
    a. Cracked or damaged hub surface.
    b. Damaged hub splines.
    c. Cracks or damage around the stud mounting bores.
    d. Damaged brake disc threaded holes.

3. Inspect the front wheel studs for damage. If the studs are damaged, replace them as follows:
    a. Remove the bolts (A, **Figure 11**) and the front brake disc (B). These bolts are secured with a threadlocking compound and may be difficult to remove. Replace the bolts if the hex portion is damaged.
    b. Press the stud(s) out of the front hub.
    c. Clean the stud bore(s) in the hub and inspect for damage.
    d. Align and press in the new stud(s). Make sure the stud(s) seats fully into the hub.

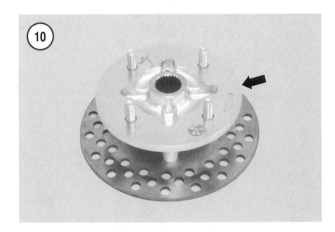

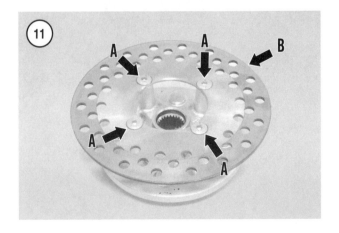

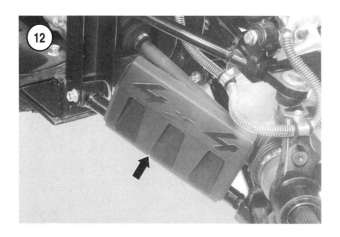

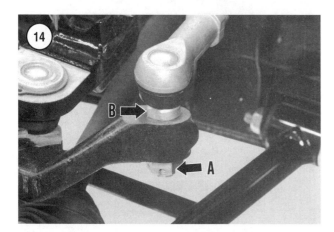

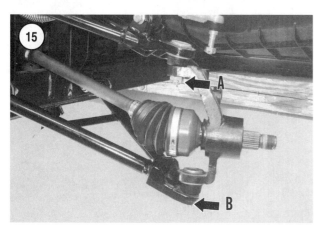

e. Install the brake disc onto the hub so the side with the chamfered mounting bolt holes faces out. Apply a medium-strength threadlocking compound onto the brake disc mounting bolts and tighten to 30 N•m (22 ft.-lb.).

STEERING KNUCKLE

Removal

1. Remove the front hub as described in this chapter.
2. Remove the bolts and the brake disc guard (D, **Figure 8**).
3. Remove the bolts and the boot guard (**Figure 12**).
4. Remove the brake hose mounting bolts at the steering knuckle (A, **Figure 13**) and upper control arm (B). Secure the brake caliper with a wire hook. Do not let the caliper hang by the brake hose.
5. Remove the cotter pin at the tie rod nut (A, **Figure 14**). Then hold the tie rod with a wrench across its flats (B, **Figure 14**) and remove the nut. Disconnect the tie rod from the steering knuckle and swing it aside. The tie rod joint is a slip fit and should lift out of the steering knuckle. Discard the cotter pin.
6. Remove the upper and lower control arm cotter pins at the steering knuckle. Then loosen both ball joint nuts (A and B, **Figure 15**) but do not remove them. Discard the cotter pins.
7. Remove the lower shock absorber mounting bolt and nut (**Figure 16**) and disconnect the shock absorber from the upper control arm.
8. Loosen the upper control arm mounting nuts (A, **Figure 17**), but do not remove them.
9. Remove the nuts and bolts (B, **Figure 17**) securing the lower control arm to the frame. Then pull the front axle outward to dislodge the O-ring (**Figure 18**) on the axle and remove it.

NOTE
*Two washers (C, **Figure 17**) are installed on the lower control arm. Account for the washers after removing the lower control arm from the frame.*

11

10. Raise the front axle with the upper and lower control arms (**Figure 19**) as required and slip the steering knuckle off of the front axle.

11. Raise the upper control arm and secure it in place with the lower shock mount and bolt or use a tie-down to raise and support the upper control arm.

12. Disconnect the upper control arm ball joint from the steering knuckle as follows:

    a. Support the lower control arm on a small jack or wooden blocks. Move the front axle aside to provide room to work on the steering knuckle. Refer to **Figure 20**.

    b. Turn the nut on the upper control arm ball joint until there is a gap between the top of the nut and the upper control arm.

NOTE
Leaving the nut on the ball joint helps to control the movement of the upper control arm once the ball joint is broken free of the steering knuckle. Also, if the threads on the ball joint are damaged during the procedure, the nut can be used as a thread chaser.

    c. Mount a 2-jaw puller (**Figure 21**) onto the upper control arm and center its pressure bolt with the ball joint stud. If the ball joint will be reused, position the tool carefully to prevent damaging the rubber boot (**Figure 22**). Apply penetrating oil onto the top of the knuckle at the ball joint stud.

    d. Operate the puller to free the ball joint stud from the steering knuckle. If the ball joint stud does not break free, relax the puller and then tighten again and leave in place. If necessary, apply additional pressure and repeat the process.

    e. Remove the puller and the tie rod nut and free the tie rod from the steering knuckle.

    f. Remove the steering knuckle with the lower control arm attached (**Figure 23**).

13. Mount the steering knuckle in a vise and repeat Step 12 to disconnect the lower control arm from the ball joint. Refer to **Figure 24**.

14. Clean and inspect the components as described in this section.

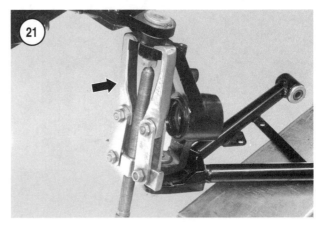

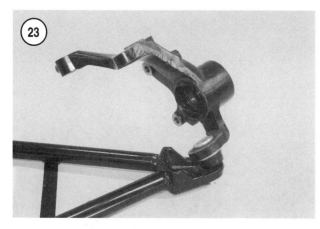

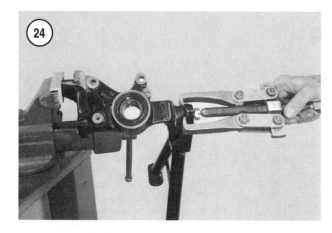

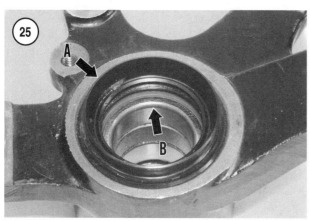

Installation

NOTE
In the following steps lubricate all of the mounting bolt shoulders with lithium grease. Do not lubricate the bolt or nut threads.

1. If removed, reconnect the shock absorber to the upper control arm and install the mounting bolt from the front side. Install the nut finger-tight.

NOTE
*Install the two washers onto the lower control arm at the positions shown in C, **Figure 17**.*

2. Install the lower control arm between the frame mounts and install the mounting bolts from the outside as shown in B, **Figure 17**. Install the nuts and tighten finger-tight. Make sure the washers (C, **Figure 17**) did not fall off.
3. Lubricate the lips on both steering knuckle seals (A, **Figure 25**) with lithium grease.

NOTE
*Make sure the front brake hose is routed above the front axle (D, **Figure 17**).*

4. Install the steering knuckle over the front axle and align it with the control arms.
5. Reconnect the upper control arm ball joint onto the steering knuckle and tighten the mounting nut finger-tight (A, **Figure 15**).
6. Reconnect the lower control arm onto the steering knuckle ball joint and tighten the mounting nut finger-tight (B, **Figure 15**).
7. When the parts are assembled, tighten the fasteners as follows:
   a. Tighten the upper control arm mounting nuts to 45 N•m (33 ft.-lb.).
   b. Tighten the lower control arm mounting nuts to 45 N•m (33 ft.-lb.).
   c. Tighten the lower shock absorber mounting nut to 45 N•m (33 ft.-lb.).
   d. Tighten the upper control arm ball joint nut to 30 N•m (22 ft.-lb.). If necessary, tighten the nut to align the cotter pin holes, then install a new cotter pin.
   e. Tighten the lower control arm ball joint nut to 30 N•m (22 ft.-lb.). If necessary, tighten the nut to align the cotter pin holes, then install a new cotter pin.
8. Pivot the steering knuckle from side to side, making sure there is no binding or roughness.
9. Reconnect the tie rod to the steering knuckle and install the mounting nut finger-tight. Hold the flat (B, **Figure 14**) on the tie rod with a wrench and tighten the nut (A) to 39 N•m (29 ft.-lb.). If necessary, tighten the nut to align the cotter pin holes, then install a new cotter pin.
10. Secure the brake hose clamps to the upper control arm (B, **Figure 13**) and steering knuckle (A) with the mounting bolts. Install the longer bolt at the steering knuckle. Tighten both bolts to 7 N•m (62 in.-lb.).

11

11. Install the boot guard (**Figure 12**) and tighten the bolts to 7 N•m (62 in.-lb.).

12. Install the brake disc guard (D, **Figure 8**) and tighten the mounting bolts to 7 N•m (62 in.-lb.).

13. Lubricate a new O-ring with lithium grease, then slide over the axle (**Figure 18**) and seat next to the knuckle bearing.

14. Install the front hub as described in this chapter.

Cleaning/Inspection

Replace worn or damaged parts.

1. Clean the knuckle with a solvent soaked rag. Do not submerge the knuckle seals, bearings or ball joint in solvent.

2. Wipe the seal lips with a rag.

3. Inspect the front knuckle for cracks and other damage.

4. Inspect the seals (A, **Figure 25**) for tearing, deterioration and other damage. If necessary, replace the seals as described in this section.

5. Turn each bearing inner race (B, **Figure 25**) and check for roughness or excessive play. If necessary, replace the bearings as described in this section. Note that a spacer is installed between the bearings.

6. Inspect the ball joint for a damaged boot (A, **Figure 26**) or stud (B). Then grasp the stud (B, **Figure 26**) and swivel in it all directions, including vertically. Check for roughness, binding and play. If damage or wear is noted, replace the ball joint as described in this section.

Seal and Bearing
Removal/Installation

The knuckle uses two seals, two bearings and a spacer.

1. To help hold the knuckle during service, mount the knuckle onto a steel bar and secure the bar in a vise as shown in **Figure 27**.

> *NOTE*
> *The inner and outer seals are different. Identify the seals so the new seals can be installed in their correct positions.*

2. Pry the seals from their bores with a tire iron (**Figure 28**) or similar tool. Make sure the tool does not contact the bore when removing the seals.

3. Mount a 30-mm collet onto a blind bearing puller (**Figure 29**). Insert the collet through the bearing and tighten it to lock against the backside of the bearing and not the spacer. Operate the puller and remove the bearing (**Figure 30**). Discard the bearing.

4. Remove the spacer (**Figure 31**).

5. Repeat Step 3 to remove the opposite bearing.

6. Clean the bearing bore of all corrosion. Then inspect for cracks and other damage.

7. Install the bearings as follows:

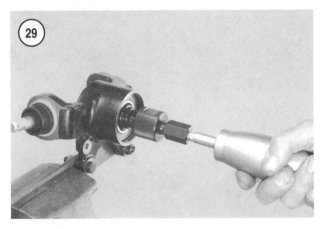

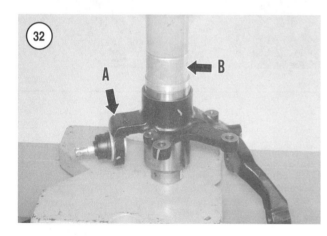

NOTE
Install the outer bearing first.

a. Support the front knuckle in a press as shown in A, **Figure 32**.

b. Center the outer bearing into the bearing bore with its manufacturer's marks facing out. Install a bearing driver (B, **Figure 32**) on the bearing's outer race and press the outer bearing into the bore until it bottoms. Refer to *Service Methods* in Chapter One.

c. Turn the bearing inner race by hand to make sure it turns smoothly.

8. Install spacer (**Figure 31**).

9. Repeat Step 7 to install the inner bearing.

NOTE
Refer to your reference notes made during removal when identifying the inner and outer seals. The inner seal has the extended lip that seats around the front axle's outer joint.

10. Insert the outer seal (**Figure 33**) into its bore with its flat side facing out. Then drive the seal into the bore with a suitable size socket until the seal seats against the bearing. Lubricate the seal lip with lithium grease.

11. Repeat Step 10 to install the inner seal (A, **Figure 25**). Make sure not to damage the extended lip on this seal during installation.

Ball Joint
Removal/Installation

The steering knuckle ball joint (**Figure 26**) is installed with a press fit and secured with a snap ring. If the ball joint is damaged, replace it with the following tools, or equivalents. Due to the shape of the steering knuckle, a hand press tool is required.

Tools

Two separate Yamaha tool sets are required to replace the steering knuckle ball joint:

1. The ball joint remover set (part No. YM-01474) consists of the following tools (**Figure 34**):

a. Hand press.

b. Long pressure screw.

2. The ball joint remover adapter set (part No. YM-01477) consists of the following tools (**Figure 34**):

a. Short pressure screw.

b. Centering plate.

c. Remover spacer.

d. Installer guide.

e. Installer spacer.

f. Spacer guide.

Procedure

1. Clean the steering knuckle and ball joint.

2. Remove the inner seal (A, **Figure 25**) from the steering knuckle so that it does not interfere with ball joint replacement.

3. Remove the rubber boot (A, **Figure 26**) from the ball joint.

4. Secure the steering knuckle in a vise and remove the snap ring (**Figure 35**) from the groove in the end of the ball joint. Remove the steering knuckle from the vise.

5. Lubricate the short and long pressure screw threads with a high pressure lubricant. This will help prevent the pressure screws from binding in the hand press when pressure is applied against the ball joint.

6. Refer to **Figure 36** and assemble the tool onto the steering knuckle and remove the ball joint as follows:

   a. Thread the short pressure screw into the hand press.

   b. Position the hand press over the steering knuckle, then secure the hand press in a vise.

   c. Install the remover spacer against the steering knuckle on the stud side and center it into the bottom of the hand press. Align the notch in the remover spacer with the short raised tab on the steering knuckle. Otherwise, the remover spacer will not align properly.

   d. Install the centering plate by aligning the depression in the centering plate with the projection on the ball joint. Turn the pressure screw until it contacts the centering plate.

   e. Check that the centering plate is properly centered against the ball joint, then tighten the pressure screw to remove the ball joint.

   f. Discard the ball joint.

7. Clean the ball joint bore in the steering knuckle and check for cracks and other damage.

8. Refer to **Figure 37** and assemble the tool onto the steering knuckle and ball joint and install the ball joint as follows:

   a. Secure the hand press in a vise.

   b. Remove the short pressure screw from the hand press and thread in the long pressure screw.

   c. Install the spacer guide through the bottom of the hand press and place the installer spacer over the spacer guide.

   d. Install the steering knuckle into the hand press and center the ball joint on top of the steering knuckle. Reposition the hand press in the vise, if required.

   e. Center the installer guide over the ball joint. Then turn the pressure screw until it contacts the installer guide and apply light pressure against the ball joint to hold it in place and to check the alignment of the ball joint with the tools and steering knuckle.

   f. Tighten the pressure screw to press the ball joint into the steering knuckle, making sure the ball joint is entering the knuckle squarely. Continue until the shoulder on the ball joint bottoms against the knuckle.

   g. Release pressure from the hand press and remove the steering knuckle.

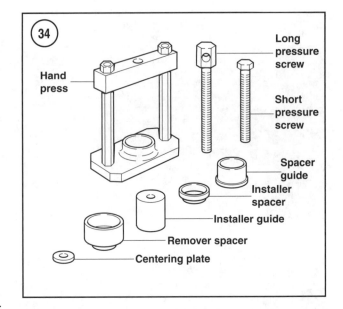

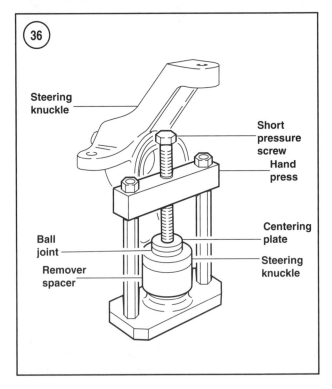

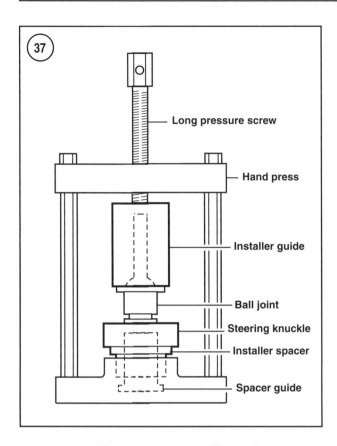

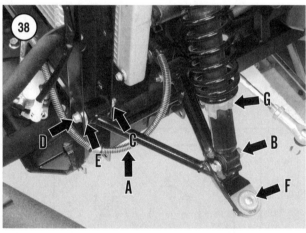

9. Install a new snap ring (**Figure 35**) into the steering knuckle groove with its flat side facing out. Check that the snap ring seats in the groove completely.

10. Lubricate the exposed part of the ball joint with lithium grease, then install the boot (A, **Figure 26**).

11. Install a new inner steering knuckle seal (A, **Figure 25**) as described in this section.

FRONT CONTROL ARMS

Removal

1. Remove the steering knuckle with the lower control arm attached as described in *Steering Knuckle* in this chapter.

2. Remove the upper control arm as follows:

a. Disconnect the front brake hose (A, **Figure 38**) at the front brake caliper (Chapter Fifteen). Cover the end of the hose to prevent brake fluid from leaking out. Note how the hose is routed before removing it through the upper control arm.

b. Remove the nut (B, **Figure 38**) and bolt and then disconnect the lower shock mount from the control arm.

c. Remove the nuts (C, **Figure 38**) and bolts (D) securing the upper control arm to the frame. Then remove the two washers (E, **Figure 38**) installed on each side of the control arm.

3. Inspect as described in this section.

Installation

1. Lubricate the control arm and lower shock absorber mounting bolt shoulders with lithium grease. Do not lubricate the mounting bolt and nut threads.

NOTE
During installation, initially finger-tighten all of the mounting nuts. Final tightening will take place when all of the components are installed and assembled onto the frame.

2. Position the upper control arm washers (A, **Figure 39**) in their original positions (E, **Figure 38**) and install the control arm between the frame brackets. Then install the upper control arm-to-frame mounting bolts (D, **Figure 38**) from the outside of the control arm. Make sure the washers did not fall off.

3. Route the front brake hose through the upper control arm as shown in A, **Figure 38**. Reconnect the brake hose at the brake caliper (Chapter Fifteen).

4. Reconnect the shock absorber onto the upper arm and install the lower shock absorber mounting bolt from the front side.

5. Install the lower control arm and steering knuckle as described in this chapter.

6. Tighten all of the fasteners as described in *Steering Knuckle* in this chapter.

7. Bleed the front brake system (Chapter Fifteen).

11

Inspection

1. Clean the control arms and all fasteners. Do not submerge the ball joint installed on the upper control arm in solvent. Wipe the ball joint with a rag soaked in solvent.

2. Inspect all welded joints and brackets on the control arms (**Figure 40**). Check for bending or other damage. If damage is evident, replace the control arm.

3. Inspect the pivot bushings (B, **Figure 39**). Inspect each bushing for play and damage. If necessary, replace damaged bushings with a press.

4. Inspect the pivot bolts, washers and nuts for damage.

5. Inspect the washers (A, **Figure 39**) for cracks and other damage.

6. Inspect the ball joint on the upper control arm (F, **Figure 38**) for a damaged boot or stud. Then grasp the stud and swivel in it all directions, including vertically (**Figure 41**). Check for roughness, binding and play. If damage or wear is noted, replace the ball joint as described in this section.

Ball Joint
Removal/Installation

The tools and procedures required to replace the upper control arm ball joint (F, **Figure 38**) are the same as described for the ball joint installed on the steering knuckle. Refer to *Ball Joint Removal/Installation* in *Steering Knuckle* in this chapter for a description of the tools and procedures. When assembling and using the tools, the short pressure screw is not required. Use the long pressure screw when replacing the ball joint.

FRONT SHOCK ABSORBERS

Vehicles were originally equipped with either oil damper shock absorbers (G, **Figure 38**) or gas-oil damper shock absorbers with a reservoir. Shock absorber service is limited to shock adjustment only. There are no replacement parts available from the manufacturer.

> *WARNING*
> *Do not attempt to disassemble the damper unit. On the gas-oil damper shock absorber, disassembly can release gas that is under pressure and cause injury.*

Adjustment
(Oil Damper Shock Absorbers)

Preload is the amount the spring is compressed from its free length. Preload is set with a five position cam-type adjuster (**Figure 42**) at the bottom of the shock (G, **Figure 38**). The least amount of spring preload is in the first position, while the most preload is in the fifth position. The standard setting is the second position. Set both shock absorbers to the same position by using a shock absorber spanner to rotate the adjuster (**Figure 43**).

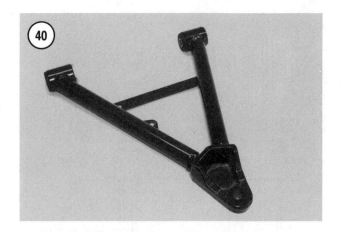

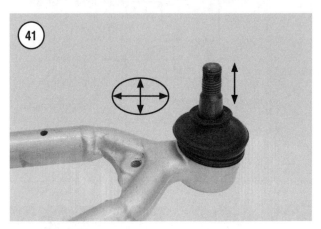

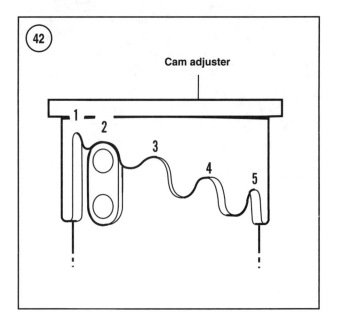

Cam adjuster

Adjustment
(Gas-Oil Damper Shock Absorbers)

> *WARNING*
> *Always adjust both front shock absorbers to the same compression, rebound and spring pre-load positions. Failure to do so may cause unstable handling and loss of control.*

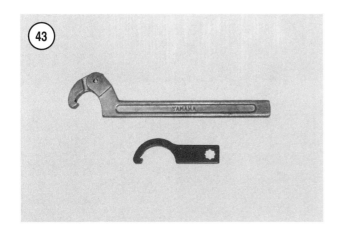

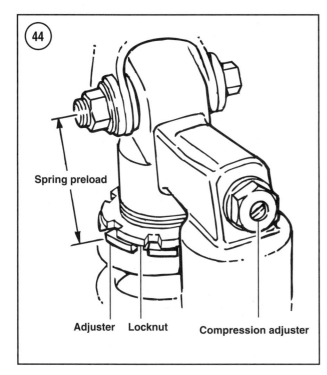

Spring preload

Adjuster   Locknut   Compression adjuster

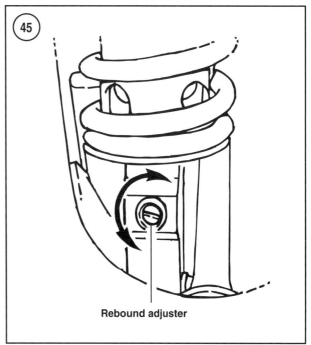

Rebound adjuster

NOTE
Make sure the compression adjuster is located in one of the detent positions and not in between any two settings.

Rebound damping

CAUTION
Do not turn the rebound adjuster past the minimum or maximum adjustment positions or the adjuster may be damaged.

The rebound damping adjustment affects the rate of shock absorber extension after it has been compressed. This adjustment has no affect on shock compression.

The rebound damping adjuster is mounted at the bottom of the shock absorber (**Figure 45**). A screw type adjuster is used. Refer to **Table 3** for adjustment positions.

For the standard setting, turn the adjuster clockwise until it stops (this is the full hard position). Then turn it counterclockwise the number of clicks listed in **Table 3**.

To increase the rebound damping, turn the adjuster clockwise. To decrease the rebound damping, turn the adjuster counterclockwise.

NOTE
Make sure the rebound adjuster is located in one of the detent positions and not in between any two settings.

Spring preload

Preload is set with the adjuster and locknut at the top of the shock absorber (**Figure 44**). Preload is the amount the

Compression damping

CAUTION
Do not turn the compression adjuster past the minimum or maximum adjustment positions or the adjuster may be damaged.

Compression damping controls the shock absorber rate, after hitting a bump. This setting has no affect on the rebound rate of the shock.

The compression adjuster is mounted near the top of the shock reservoir (**Figure 44**). A screw type adjuster is used. Refer to **Table 3** for adjustment positions.

To set the adjuster to its standard setting, turn the adjuster clockwise until it stops (this is the full hard position). Then turn it counterclockwise while counting the number of clicks listed in **Table 3**.

To increase the compression damping, turn the adjuster clockwise. To decrease the compression damping, turn the adjuster counterclockwise.

11

spring is compressed from its free length. By tightening the adjuster, spring preload is increased. By loosening the adjuster, spring preload is decreased.

1. Measure the distance between the center of the upper shock bolt to the top of the adjuster (**Figure 44**). This is the spring preload adjustment position. Compare the actual adjustment position with the specifications in **Table 3** to determine the approximate adjustment position. If adjustment is necessary, continue with Step 2.

2. Support the vehicle on a stand so the front wheels are off the ground.

NOTE
Before adjusting the spring preload, clean the threads on the locknut, adjuster and shock body to prevent thread damage.

3. Loosen the adjuster locknut with a spanner wrench (**Figure 43**).

4. Turn the adjuster to the desired spring preload position, making sure to stay within the minimum and maximum positions listed in **Table 3**.

5. Tighten the locknut to 10 N•m (88 in.-lb.).

Removal/Installation

1. Support the vehicle with both rear wheels off the ground.

2. Place wooden blocks underneath the front wheels to prevent the lower control arm from swinging down when the shock absorber mounting bolts are removed.

3. Remove the lower shock absorber nut (B, **Figure 38**) and bolt and allow the front wheel to settle against the wooden blocks.

4. Remove the upper shock absorber nut and bolt and remove the shock absorber.

5. Inspect as described in this section.

6. Install the shock absorber by reversing the removal steps. Note the following:
   a. Clean and dry the shock fasteners. Inspect and replace damaged fasteners.
   b. Lubricate the mounting bolt shoulders with lithium grease. Do not lubricate the bolt or nut threads.
   c. Install gas-oil damper shock absorbers with the reservoir positioned at the top and facing out.
   d. Install the mounting bolts from the front side and tighten the mounting nuts to 45 N•m (33 ft.-lb.).

Inspection/Lubrication

Replacement parts for the shock absorber are not available from the manufacturer. If any damage is noted, replace the shock absorber.

1. Inspect the shock absorber for leaks.

2. Inspect the shock body (**Figure 46**, typical) for severe dents that can affect shock operation.

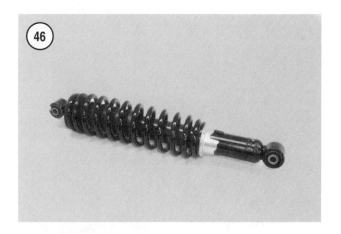

3A. On oil damper shocks, make sure the upper spring seat is locked in place against the upper shock boss and spring (**Figure 47**).

3B. On gas-oil damper shocks, make sure the locknut is tightened against the adjuster (**Figure 44**).

4. Inspect the bushing (**Figure 48**) for deterioration and damage. The rubber must be intact and the collar free of rust and corrosion.

STEERING WHEEL

Removal/Installation

NOTE
*When the front wheels are pointing straight ahead, the steering wheel's bottom spoke should be centered and positioned at the bottom as shown in **Figure 49**. If the bottom spoke is incorrectly aligned, do not remove the steering wheel to realign it without first checking the steering system. Check that the tie rods are not damaged and that the steering column and steering gearbox mounting bolts are tight. If these items are okay, check the toe-in adjustment as described in this chapter. Only after checking these items and correcting any problems should the steering wheel be readjusted.*

1. Turn the steering wheel so the front wheels are pointing straight ahead. Then check that the steering wheel's bottom spoke is centered and positioned squarely at the bottom (**Figure 49**).

2. Pry the steering wheel cover (A, **Figure 50**) off the steering wheel with a tire iron (B) or similar thin, flat-tipped tool.

3. Remove the nut (**Figure 51**) and washer that secure the steering wheel to the steering column. Then pull the steering wheel off the steering column. A puller should not be required to remove the steering wheel.

4. Clean the splines on the steering wheel and steering column.

5. Make sure the front wheels are pointing straight ahead, then install the steering wheel. The bottom spoke should be centered and positioned at the bottom as shown in **Figure 49**.

6. Install the washer and nut (**Figure 51**) and tighten to 35 N•m (26 ft.-lb.).

7. Drive the vehicle slowly on a straight level surface and make sure the steering wheel points straight ahead. Readjust the steering wheel mounting position, if necessary.

8. Push the steering wheel cover into the steering wheel so that the cover's three projections are locked on the outside of the steering wheel (**Figure 52**).

TIE ROD BOOTS AND TIE ROD ENDS

The tie rods are permanently attached to the steering gearbox. However, the tie rod ends and boots can be replaced separately and without removing the steering gearbox from the vehicle.

Removal/Installation

1. Remove the front wheel as described in this chapter.

2. Measure the length of the exposed threads (A, **Figure 53**) from the locknut to the tie rod. This dimension will be used to approximately reposition the tie rod end during assembly.

3. Hold the tie rod (B, **Figure 53**) with a wrench and loosen the tie rod end locknut (C).

11

4. Remove the cotter pin at the tie rod nut (A, **Figure 54**). Then hold the tie rod with a wrench across its flats (B, **Figure 54**) and remove the nut. Disconnect the tie rod from the steering knuckle and swing it aside. The tie rod joint is a slip fit and should lift out of the steering knuckle. Discard the cotter pin.

5. Remove the tie rod end (A, **Figure 55**) and locknut from the tie rod.

6. Open or cut the clamp on the large end of the boot and slide the boot (B, **Figure 55**) off the tie rod.

7. Clean the tie rod, tie rod end and locknut threads.

8. Lubricate the large shoulder on the steering gearbox where the tie rod enters into it with lithium grease.

9. Slide the boot (B, **Figure 55**) onto the tie rod. Seat the boot's large end onto the steering gearbox and the small end into the groove in the tie rod. Make sure the boot is not twisted, then secure the large end with a new clamp.

10. Install the locknut (C, **Figure 53**) and tie rod end onto the tie rod to the dimensions recorded in Step 2. Do not tighten the locknut as this is an approximate position only.

11. Reconnect the tie rod to the steering knuckle and install the nut finger-tight. Hold the flat (B, **Figure 54**) on the tie rod with a wrench and tighten the nut (A) to 39 N•m (29 ft.-lb.). If necessary, tighten the nut to align the cotter pin holes, then install a new cotter pin.

12. Install the front wheel as described in this chapter.

13. Repeat for the other side, if necessary.

14. Perform the *Toe-In Adjustment* as described in this chapter. After adjusting the toe-in, make sure to tighten the tie rod end locknuts (C, **Figure 53**) to 40 N•m (30 ft.-lb.).

STEERING GEARBOX, STEERING COLUMN AND STEERING SHAFT

CAUTION
Work carefully around the brake lines and coolant hoses when performing the service in this section.

Steering Gearbox

This section describes removal of the steering gearbox without removing the steering wheel, steering column or steering shaft.

Removal

1. Remove the hood (Chapter Sixteen).

2. Remove the upper instrument panel (Chapter Sixteen).

3. Remove the air box (Chapter Eight). Cover the intake tube opening with a plastic bag to prevent objects from falling into the tube and entering the engine.

4. Position the front wheels so they are pointing straight ahead and the steering wheel spoke is centered at the bottom (**Figure 49**).

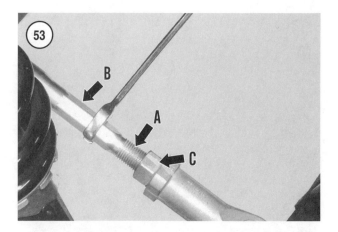

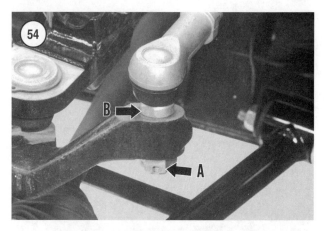

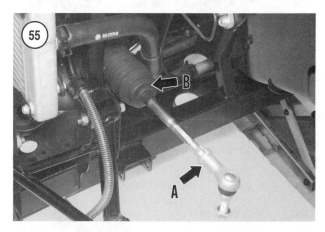

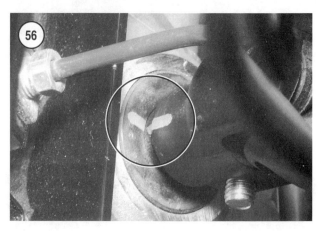

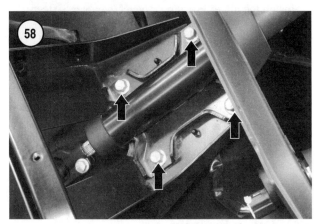

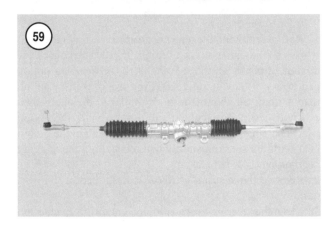

5. Locate the painted alignment marks on the steering shaft joint and on the steering gearbox seal (**Figure 56**). If the marks are undecipherable, clean the parts and make new marks with the front wheels and steering wheel pointed straight ahead. These marks will be used during installation to realign the splines on the steering shaft with the splines on the steering gearbox pinion gear.

6. Remove both front wheels as described in this chapter.

7. Remove the cotter pin at the tie rod nut (A, **Figure 54**). Then hold the tie rod with a wrench across its flats (B, **Figure 54**) and remove the nut. Disconnect the tie rod from the steering knuckle and swing it aside. The tie rod joint is a slip fit and should lift out of the steering knuckle. Discard the cotter pin. Repeat for the other tie rod.

8. Remove the bolt securing the steering shaft to the steering gearbox pinion gear (**Figure 57**).

9. Remove the bolts (**Figure 58**) securing the steering column to the frame. Then lift the steering column/steering shaft assembly and disconnect the steering shaft from the steering gearbox pinion gear.

10. Remove the bolts securing the steering gearbox to the frame and remove the steering gearbox from the left side of the vehicle (**Figure 55**). Refer to **Figure 59**.

Installation

1. Clean the mounting bolt and frame threaded holes with contact cleaner.

2. Install the steering gearbox through the frame from the left side (**Figure 55**) with the pinion gear facing toward the steering wheel. Install and tighten the mounting bolts as follows:

   a. Because the steering gearbox mounting bolts cannot be accessed with a torque wrench (unless additional parts are removed from the vehicle), apply a medium-strength threadlocking compound onto the mounting bolt threads. Install the mounting bolts and tighten securely in a crossing pattern.

   b. If the vehicle is partially disassembled where the steering gearbox mounting bolts can accessed with a torque wrench, install the mounting bolts and tighten to 48 N•m (35 ft.-lb.) in a crossing pattern.

3. Have an assistant lift and support the steering wheel (along with the steering column and steering shaft). Then install the steering shaft onto the steering gearbox pinion gear by aligning the original alignment marks (**Figure 56**) or using the new marks made prior to removal.

4. Align the steering column plate with the frame bolt holes. Then install the bolts (**Figure 58**) and tighten to 21 N•m (15 ft.-lb.) in a crossing pattern.

5. Install the lower steering shaft pinch bolt (**Figure 57**) and tighten securely.

6. If the steering shaft-to-steering column pinch bolt (**Figure 60**) was loosened or removed, tighten the bolt to 22 N•m (16 ft.-lb.).

7. Reconnect the tie rod to the steering knuckle and install the nut finger-tight. Hold the flat (B, **Figure 54**) on the tie rod with a wrench and tighten the nut (A) to 39 N•m (29 ft.-lb.). If necessary, tighten the nut to align the cotter pin holes, then install a new cotter pin.

8. Install the front wheels as described in this chapter.

9. Perform the *Toe-In Adjustment* as described in this chapter.

10. Install the air box (Chapter Eight).

11. Install the upper instrument panel (Chapter Sixteen).

12. Install the hood (Chapter Sixteen).

Steering Column and Steering Shaft

The steering column and steering shaft can be removed without removing the steering gearbox.

11

Removal

1. Remove the hood (Chapter Sixteen).
2. Remove the upper instrument panel (Chapter Sixteen).
3. Remove the steering wheel as described in this chapter.
4. Note the painted alignment marks on the steering shaft joint and on the steering gearbox seal (**Figure 56**). If the marks are undecipherable, clean the parts and make new marks with the front wheels and steering wheel pointed straight ahead. These marks will be used during installation to realign the splines on the steering shaft with the splines on the steering gearbox pinion gear.
5. Remove the steering shaft-to-steering column pinch bolt (**Figure 60**).
6. Remove the bolts (**Figure 58**) securing the steering column to the frame. Remove the steering column.
7. Remove the pinch bolt securing the steering shaft to the steering gearbox pinion gear (**Figure 57**) and remove the steering shaft.

Inspection

Replace damaged components as described in this section. Do not attempt to repair the steering column or steering shaft. Do not attempt to straighten the steering shaft.
1. Clean and dry the parts. Do not wash off any alignment marks made during removal.
2. Inspect the splines on both the steering column and steering shaft for damage.
3. Inspect the steering shaft joints for excessive wear and damage.
4. Inspect the mounting bracket on the steering column for damage.
5. Turn the steering column inner shaft and check for any roughness or binding.
6. Replace any damaged fasteners.

Installation

1. Install the steering shaft onto the steering gearbox pinion gear by aligning the original alignment marks or by using the new marks made prior to removal (**Figure 56**). Then install the lower steering shaft pinch bolt (**Figure 57**) and tighten securely.
2. Install the steering column into the steering shaft. Then align the steering column plate with the frame bolt holes. Install the bolts (**Figure 58**) and tighten to 21 N•m (15 ft.-lb.) in a crossing pattern.
3. Install the steering shaft-to-steering column pinch bolt (**Figure 60**) and tighten to 22 N•m (16 ft.-lb.).
4. Install the steering wheel as described in this chapter but do not tighten the steering wheel mounting nut.
5. Perform the *Toe-In Adjustment* as described in this chapter.
6. When the toe-in adjustment is correct and the wheels are pointing straight ahead, recheck the steering wheel alignment and readjust if necessary as described in this chapter.

7. Install the upper instrument panel (Chapter Sixteen).
8. Install the hood (Chapter Sixteen).

Steering Gearbox Disassembly/Assembly

The steering gearbox can be partially disassembled to replace components 3-10 in **Figure 61**. The tie rods (1, **Figure 61**) are permanently attached to the steering gearbox and cannot be replaced separately.

> *NOTE*
> *To service just the tie rod boots or tie rod ends, refer to **Tie Rod Boots and Tie Rod Ends** in this chapter.*

Refer to **Figure 61**.
1. Before removing the steering gearbox, position the front wheels so they are pointing straight ahead. Then check the alignment marks on the steering shaft, oil seal and pinion gear to see if they are aligned (**Figure 56**). If there are no marks, make an alignment mark similar to the one shown in **Figure 56**, while making sure to also mark the pinion gear. The pinion gear mark will be used to align the pinion gear with the steering shaft when reinstalling the steering gearbox onto the vehicle.
2. Remove the steering gearbox as described in this section.
3. Clean the steering gearbox to prevent dirt from entering the gearbox during service.

> *NOTE*
> *Use the steering shaft to turn the pinion gear in Step 4.*

4A. If there are alignment marks on the pinion gear and gearbox (A, **Figure 62**), turn the pinion gear to align them.
4B. If there are no alignment marks on the pinion gear and gearbox, turn the pinion gear back and forth while watching the tie rods. Stop when the tie rods are centered.
5. Remove the adjuster (9, **Figure 61**), spring (10) and pressure pad (11).
6. Remove the oil seal (B, **Figure 62**) by drilling a small hole through the seal. Then insert a small drift through the

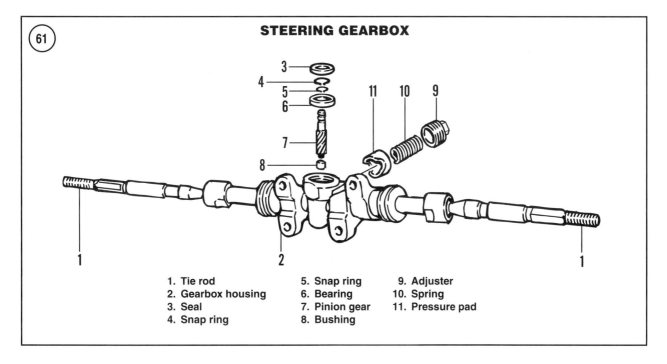

STEERING GEARBOX

1. Tie rod
2. Gearbox housing
3. Seal
4. Snap ring
5. Snap ring
6. Bearing
7. Pinion gear
8. Bushing
9. Adjuster
10. Spring
11. Pressure pad

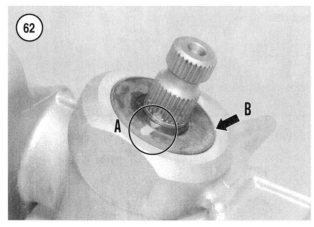

hole and pry the seal out. Remove the snap ring (4, **Figure 61**).

7. Tap the housing with a plastic hammer and remove the pinion gear and bearing.

Inspection

Replace worn or damaged parts as described in this section. If a part is not available separately, replace the steering gearbox.

1. Clean and dry the parts removed. Then remove grease from inside the gearbox.

2. Hold the bearing and turn the pinion gear by hand. If there is any binding, roughness or excessive play, replace the bearing. Remove the snap ring and remove the bearing from the pinion gear.

3. Inspect the pinion gear needle bearing pressed into the gearbox. If the bearing is damaged, replace the steering gearbox. Inspect the shoulder on the bottom of the pinion gear for excessive wear and damage.

4. Inspect the pinion gear and rack gear teeth for wear and damage. A uniform wear pattern should be evident on both parts. If not, the pinion gear-to-rack backlash adjustment may be incorrect or the pinion gear and rack lubrication is inadequate.

5. Check the pressure pad for wear and damage.

Installation

1. Lubricate the bearing with molybdenum disulfide oil and install onto the pinion gear. Secure the bearing with a new snap ring.

2. Lubricate the rack gear with approximately 5-10 g (0.2-0.4 oz.) of lithium soap based grease. Then lubricate the teeth on the pinion gear. Lubricate the shoulder on the bottom of the pinion gear that rides in the needle bearing with molybdenum disulfide oil.

3. Make sure the tie rods are centered in the gearbox.

4. Install the pinion gear while seating the bearing in the gearbox. If installing the original pinion gear, install it with its original mark lined up with the mark on the gearbox. If installing a new pinion gear, make a new mark across the pinion gear and gearbox at the point shown in A, **Figure 62**.

5. Install a new snap ring (4, **Figure 61**).

6. Lubricate the lips of a new seal with molybdenum disulfide oil and install the seal into the gearbox with its flat side facing out. Install the seal (B, **Figure 62**) until its outer surface is flush with the gearbox bore. Then scribe a mark across the seal that aligns with the mark on the pinion gear (A, **Figure 62**).

7. Lubricate the pressure pad (11, **Figure 61**) with lithium grease and install into the gearbox, then install the spring (10).

8. Install and adjust the adjuster (**Figure 63**) as follows:

11

a. Apply a medium-strength threadlocking compound onto the adjuster threads.

b. Install the adjuster and tighten to 4 N•m (35 in.-lb.).

c. Loosen the adjuster 15-25° as shown in **Figure 64**.

9. Install the steering gearbox as described in this chapter.

10. Perform the *Toe-In Adjustment* in this chapter.

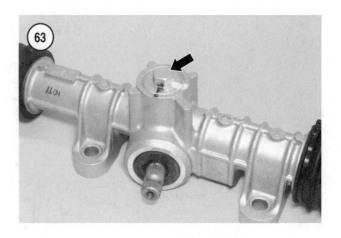

TOE-IN ADJUSTMENT

Proper toe-in adjustment cannot be achieved if the tie rods, tie rod ends (ball joints) and wheel bearings are worn or damaged. Replace worn or damaged parts before adjusting toe-in.

NOTE
*Refer to **Steering Wheel** in this chapter for additional information on steering alignment.*

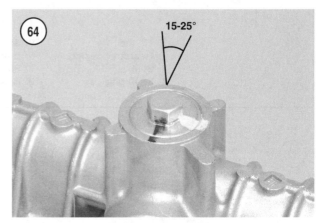

1. Inflate all tires to the recommended pressure (**Table 2**).

2. Park the vehicle on level ground. Allow space in front of and behind the vehicle so it can be rolled.

NOTE
The front wheels must be on the ground when measuring toe-in.

3. Turn the steering wheel to its centered position so the wheels are pointing forward.

4. On both front tires, make a chalk mark at the center of the tread. The mark should be level with the centerline of the axle and at the front of the tire.

5. Measure distance A between the chalk marks as shown in **Figure 65**. Record the measurement.

6. Without turning the steering wheel, roll the machine until the marks are at the back of the tire and level with the axle.

7. Measure distance B between the chalk marks as shown in **Figure 65**. Record the measurement.

8. Subtract measurement A from measurement B.

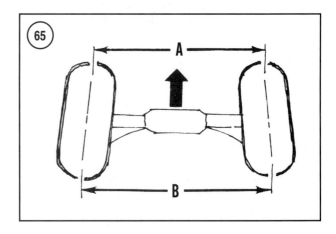

a. If the difference is 15-25 mm (0.59-0.98 in.), toe-in is correct.

b. If toe-in is not correct, perform Step 9.

WARNING
If the tie-rods are not adjusted identically, steering wheel alignment will not be correct and the vehicle will pull to one side even when the steering wheel is centered. This can cause a handling problem and loss of control.

9. Adjust both tie rods equally as follows:

a. Make a small reference mark on the top of each tie rod. Use the marks to verify that both tie rods are turned equal amounts.

b. Loosen the tie rod locknut (A, **Figure 66**) on both tie rod ends.

c. Equally turn each tie rod with a wrench fitted to the flats on the tie rod sleeve (B, **Figure 66**).

d. Recheck the measurements.

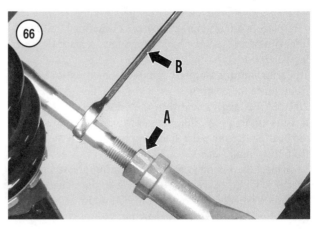

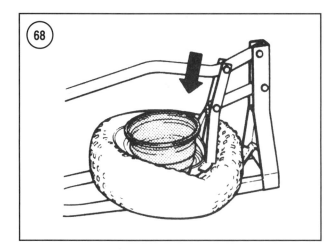

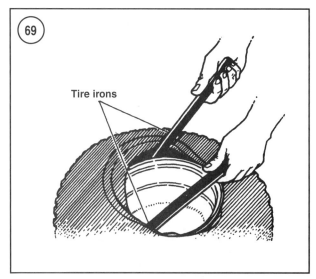

Tire irons

e. When toe-in is correct, hold each tie rod in place with a wrench (B, **Figure 66**) and use a crow's foot wrench to tighten the tie rod locknuts (A) to 40 N•m (30 ft.-lb.).

f. Turn the steering wheel from side to side and make sure all ball joints pivot properly and the boots are not twisted.

g. Test ride the vehicle *slowly* on a level surface with the steering wheel centered to ensure all adjustments are correct. The vehicle must not pull to one side.

WARNING
If the vehicle still pulls to one side while the steering wheel is centered, either the toe-in adjustment is incorrect or a steering component is worn or damaged. Do not drive the vehicle until the toe-in adjustment is correct and the vehicle does not drift. If you cannot adjust the toe-in properly, have a dealership inspect the steering assembly and front-end components and adjust the toe-in.

TIRES

The vehicle is equipped with tubeless, low pressure tires designed specifically for off-road use. Rapid tire wear will occur if the vehicle is ridden on paved surfaces. This sec-

tion describes how to remove a tire from the rim and install a plug patch and permanent cold patch.

Tire Changing

A bead breaker tool is required to change the tires. Follow the manufacturer's directions while using the following procedure as a guide.

1. Remove the valve stem cap and core and deflate the tire. Do not reinstall the core at this time.

2. Lubricate the tire bead and rim flanges with a rubber lubricant. Press the tire sidewall/bead down to allow the lubricant to penetrate the bead area. Also apply lubricant to the area where the bead breaker arm will contact the tire sidewall.

3. Position the hub into the bead breaker tool. Then lower the leverage bar so its shoe is below the rim lip (**Figure 67**). Make sure the shoe contacts the tire and not the rim lip.

4. Press the leverage bar down to break the tire bead away from the rim (**Figure 68**). Work around the rim, using the bead breaker and hand pressure to break the upper tire bead free. Relubricate the tire as required.

5. Turn the rim over and repeat Steps 2-4.

CAUTION
Failure to use rim protectors could allow the tire irons to damage the bead seating area on the rim and cause an air leak.

6. Place rim protectors or other padding on the rim edge. Position the protectors where the tire irons will be inserted.

7. Relubricate the tire beads and rim flanges.

8. Insert the tire irons between the rim and tire as shown in **Figure 69**. Pry the bead over the rim. If removal is difficult, move the tire irons closer together and work small sections at a time.

9. When the upper sidewall is free, lift the lower sidewall so it can be removed as described in Steps 6-8.

11

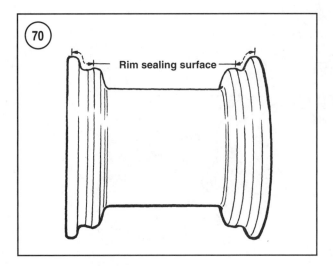

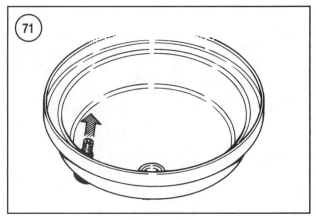

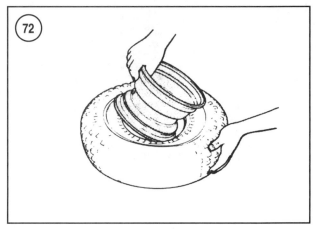

10. Clean and inspect the rim sealing surfaces (**Figure 70**). The sealing surface must be straight and smooth in order to seal properly.

11. Replace the valve stem as follows:

   a. Remove the valve stem by pulling it out from inside the rim.

   b. Clean the valve stem hole in the rim of all dirt and rubber residue.

   c. Lubricate the new valve stem with the lubricant.

   d. Insert the new valve stem through the rim hole, then pull it out until it snaps into place (**Figure 71**) using a valve stem installer.

   e. After installing the valve stem, check it for any torn rubber or other damage that may cause an air leak.

12. Check the tire sidewall for the direction arrow and orient the tire with the outside of the wheel so the arrow will point forward when the tire is mounted.

> *WARNING*
> *The sidewall arrow on the tire must be oriented properly when the tire is mounted. If the tire is installed backward (arrow pointing to the rear), the tire ply may fail during operation.*

13. Inspect the tire bead for cleanliness and the inside of the tire for any foreign objects.

14. Place the rim on the work surface with the valve stem facing up.

15. Place the tire with the sidewall directional markings pointing forward, then wet the lower tire bead and rim surface with a rubber lubricant.

16. Place the tire onto the rim (**Figure 72**) with the sidewall directional markings pointing forward and hand-fit as much of the tire into the rim as possible. Then use the rim protectors and tire irons to finish installing the lower bead.

17. Push the tire down and lubricate the upper bead and rim surface with lubricant. Then repeat Step 16 to install the upper bead over the rim.

18. Install the valve stem core, if removed.

19. Apply lubricant to both rim beads, then inflate the tire to the bead seating pressure, indicated on the sidewall.

> *WARNING*
> *Do not inflate the tire past the specified bead seating pressure. Tire explosion and severe personal injury is possible.*

> *NOTE*
> *If the tire beads will not seat because of air leakage, a tight strap placed around the perimeter of the tread will aid in driving the beads into place.*

20. After inflation, check the rim lines on both sides of the tire to ensure the beads are seated. If the beads are seated correctly, the rim lines will be parallel with the rim flanges as shown in **Figure 73**. If the beads are not seated correctly, deflate the tire and break the bead so additional lubricant can be applied to the tire bead. Reinflate the tire and check the bead alignment.

21. When the tire is properly seated, do the following:

   a. Remove the valve core to deflate the tire.

   b. Wait one hour to allow adjustment of the tire on the rim.

   c. Install the valve core and inflate the tire to the operating pressure listed in **Table 2**.

   d. Apply water to the beads and valve stem and check for leaks.

22. Install the wheel on the vehicle as described in this chapter or Chapter Thirteen.

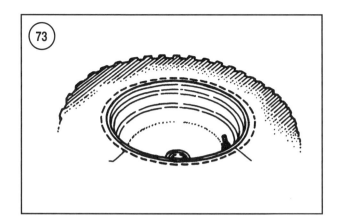

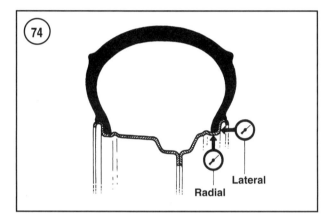

Lateral
Radial

WARNING
After installing the wheel, ride at slow to moderate speeds to make sure the tire is properly seated on the rim while stopping occasionally to check the tire and wheel. A loss of air pressure can cause loss of control.

Tire Repair

A tire can be plugged while mounted on the vehicle. A more permanent repair can be made by removing the tire from the rim and installing a cold patch inside the tire. Follow the patch manufacturer's instructions when using a rubber plug or cold patch repair kit. If instructions are not available, use the following procedures.

Rubber plug repair

This section describes repair using a universal rubber plug repair kit available at most automotive parts stores.
1. Check the tire for the object(s) that punctured the tire.
2. Mark the puncture location with chalk, then remove the object while noting its puncture path through the tire.
3. Lubricate the spiral probe on the insert tool with cement.
4. Insert the spiral probe through the puncture hole and move it up and down three times to clean and lubricate the hole.
5. Center a rubber tire plug through the hole in the spiral probe and lubricate it with cement.

6. Push the spiral probe through the puncture hole until the plug is slightly above the tire. Twist the spiral probe and remove it from the tire, leaving the plug in the puncture hole.
7. Use a razor blade and trim the plug 6 mm (1/4 in.) from the tire.
8. Allow the cement to dry. Refer to the plug manufacturer's recommendations on drying time.
9. Inflate the tire and apply a small amount of cement around the plug. The cement will bubble if there is a leak.
10. If there is a leak, perform the cold patch repair in this section.
11. If the tire holds air, inflate the tire to the pressure listed in **Table 2**.

Cold patch repair

This section describes how to install a flat rubber patch inside the tire. This type of repair works best after a rubber plug has been installed in the puncture.
1. Remove the tire from the rim as described in this chapter.
2. Check the tire for the object(s) that punctured the tire.
3. Mark the puncture location with chalk, then remove the object while noting its puncture path through the tire
4. If a plug was previously used, use a razor blade and trim its exposed end until it is flush with the inside of the tire.
5. Working inside the tire, roughen the area around the puncture that is larger than the patch. If the repair kit does not provide a tool to roughen the area, use coarse sandpaper, a wire brush or any object that will lightly scrape and roughen the surface.
6. Clean all rubber dust and dirt away from the roughened area.
7. Apply a small amount of cement to the roughened area and allow to dry until it becomes tacky. Do not touch the area with fingers.
8. Remove the backing from the patch, making sure not to touch its exposed surface.
9. Center the patch over the puncture, then press the patch into place. Do not attempt to raise or slide the patch once it contacts the cement.
10. Burnish the patch with a roller, checking that the edges are tightly sealed. If a roller is not available, use a smooth hard object (sockets work well) to burnish the patch.
11. Install the tire on the rim as described in this section.

WHEEL RUNOUT

If vibration is abnormal, check the wheels for damage and then for excessive radial and lateral runout (**Figure 74**). If okay, check the axle/knuckle bearings for wear and play.

NOTE
If the wheels have been dented or damaged, using a dial indicator to check runout may result in false readings because the indicator is not

11

reading off of a smooth surface. If this is the case, it may be necessary to remove the axle from the knuckle so the bearings can be inspected and turned by hand. If the knuckle bearings and axle are in good condition, the wheels may be damaged and require replacement.

1. Park the machine on a level surface and shift the transmission into neutral. Then raise either the front or rear end so the wheels just clear the ground. If checking the front wheels, secure the steering wheel so the wheels cannot move laterally.

2. Clean the perimeter of the wheel where it will contact the dial indicator.

3. Mount a dial indicator on a stable surface and in contact with the wheel. Either runout can be measured first. Zero the gauge so it can measure runout in both directions as the wheel is turned.

4. Maximum runout is 2 mm (0.08 in.) in either direction. If out of specification, note the following:

   a. Inspect the wheel for damage. Check for paint has cracked or peeled away, indicating possible wheel damage.

   b. If the wheel does not appear damaged, remove the axle from the steering knuckle and check the bearings for damage.

Table 1 FRONT SUSPENSION AND STEERING SPECIFICATIONS

Front shock absorber	
Type	
5B41, 5B45, 5B48, 5B49, 5B4H, 5B4M, 5BAT and 5B4H	Coil spring/oil damper
5B4B, 5B4E, 5B4P and 42SA	Gas-oil damper
Spring free length	
Oil damper shock	313.0 mm (12.32 in.)
Gas-oil damper shock	336.6 mm (13.25 in.)
Spring installed length	
Oil damper shock	247.9 mm (9.76 in.)
Gas-oil damper shock	260.5 mm (10.26 in.)
Spring rate	19.40 N/mm (110.77 lb./in.)
Front wheel travel	
2008 models	180 mm (7.1 in.)
2009 models	185 mm (7.3 in.)
2011-on models	185 mm (7.3 in.)
Front suspension type	Double wishbone
Rack and pinion gear backlash	15-25°
Steering	
Camber angle	0°
Caster angle	5.0°
Kingpin angle	
2008 models	12.0°
2009 models	11.8°
2011-on models	11.8°
Kingpin offset	0 mm (0 in.)
Trail	26.0 mm (1.02 in.)
Toe-in (tires touching ground)	15-25 mm (0.59-0.98 in.)

Table 2 TIRE AND WHEEL SPECIFICATIONS*

Tire	
Manufacturer	MAXXIS
Model	
Front	M951Y
Rear	M952Y
Size	
Front	25 × 8.00-12 NHS
Rear	25 × 10.00-12 NHS
Tire pressure (cold)	
Front	63-77 kPa (9-11 psi)
Rear	91-105 kPa (13-15 psi)
(continued)	

Table 2 TIRE AND WHEEL SPECIFICATIONS* (continued)

Wheels	
Size	
Front	12 × 6.0 AT
Rear	12 × 7.5 AT
Runout (radial and lateral)	2.0 mm (0.08 in.)

* Tire specifications are for original equipment tires only. Aftermarket tires may have different specifications.

Table 3 FRONT SHOCK ABSORBER SETTING

Oil-damper shock absorbers	
Spring preload	
Minimum	1
Maximum	5
Standard	2
Gas-oil damper shock absorbers	
Compression adjustment	
Minimum	12 clicks out
Maximum	9 clicks out
Standard	10 clicks out
Rebound adjustment	
Minimum	12 clicks out
Maximum	9 clicks out
Standard	10 clicks out
Spring preload	
Minimum	62 mm (2.44 in.)
Maximum	77 mm (3.03 in.)
Standard	67 mm (2.64 in.)

Table 4 FRONT SUSPENSION TORQUE SPECIFICATIONS

	N•m	in.-lb.	ft.-lb.
Boot guard mounting bolts	7	62	–
Brake disc guard mounting bolts	7	62	–
Brake hose clamp bolts	7	62	–
Front brake disc mounting bolts[1]	30	–	22
Front hub nut[1]	350	–	255
Front shock spring adjuster locknut[2]	10	88	–
Lower control arm ball joint nut	30	–	22
Lower control arm mounting nut	45	–	33
Lug nuts	55	–	41
Shock absorber mounting nut	45	–	33
Steering column plate mounting bolts	21	–	15
Steering gearbox adjuster[1]	4	35	–
Steering gearbox mounting bolts[1]	48	–	35
Steering shaft-to-steering column pinch bolt	22	–	16
Steering wheel mounting nut	35	–	26
Tie rod end locknut	40	–	30
Tie rod mounting nut[1]	39	–	29
Upper control arm mounting nuts	45	–	33
Upper control ball joint nut	30	–	22

1. Refer to text.
2. Gas-oil damper shock absorber.

11

CHAPTER TWELVE

FRONT AXLES AND DIFFERENTIAL

This chapter covers the front axles, differential, universal joint and front drive shaft.

Read *Safety* and *Service Methods* in Chapter One before servicing the vehicle in this chapter.

Table 1 and **Table 2** are at the end of this chapter.

FRONT AXLE

Removal

NOTE
If steering knuckle removal is also required, remove it as described in Chapter Eleven, then go to Step 14 to remove the front axle. The following procedure describes front axle removal without disconnecting the upper and lower control arms ball joints from the steering knuckle.

1. Clean the front axle area on both sides of the differential to prevent dirt from entering the differential when removing the front axle.
2. Drain the differential gear oil (Chapter Three).
3. Remove the front hub and brake disc (Chapter Eleven).
4. Remove the bolts (A, **Figure 1**) and the brake disc guard (B).
5. Remove the bolts and the boot guard (**Figure 2**).
6. Remove the brake hose mounting bolts at the steering knuckle (A, **Figure 3**) and upper arm (B). Secure the brake caliper with a wire hook. Do not let the caliper hang by the brake hose (C, **Figure 3**)
7. Remove the tie rod cotter pin and nut (A, **Figure 4**) and disconnect the tie rod from the steering knuckle. The tie rod is a slip fit. If necessary, hold the tie rod with a wrench across its flats (B, **Figure 4**) when loosening the nut.
8. Remove the front shock absorber nuts and bolts. Remove the shock absorber.
9. Loosen the upper arm mounting nuts (A, **Figure 5**), but do not remove them.

10. Remove the nuts and bolts (B, **Figure 5**) securing the lower arm to the frame. Then pull the front axle out to dislodge the O-ring (**Figure 6**) on the end of the axle and remove it.

NOTE
*Two washers (C, **Figure 5**) are installed on the lower control arm. Account for the washers after removing the lower control arm from the frame.*

11. Raise the front axle with the upper and lower arms (**Figure 7**) as required and slip the steering knuckle off of the front axle.
12. Position the lower arm/steering knuckle assembly on a stand. Then grab the front axle with both hands (**Figure 8**) and jerk the axle (not the outboard joint) sharply to disconnect it from the front differential. The circlip on the inboard side of the front axle will cause some resistance when removing the axle. The circlip will remain on the axle as it is removed from the differential. Remove and discard the circlip.
13. Inspect as described in this section.

Installation

1. Carefully wipe the differential seal (**Figure 9**) with a rag to remove all old grease. Then relubricate the seal with lithium grease.
2. Check the circlip groove on the inboard joint for any burrs or damage that would prevent the circlip from closing when installing the axle.

NOTE
The circlip used on the inboard joint is smaller than the axle outside diameter and will spread from its original size when installed over the axle. Because the circlip does not return to its original shape, it is larger and

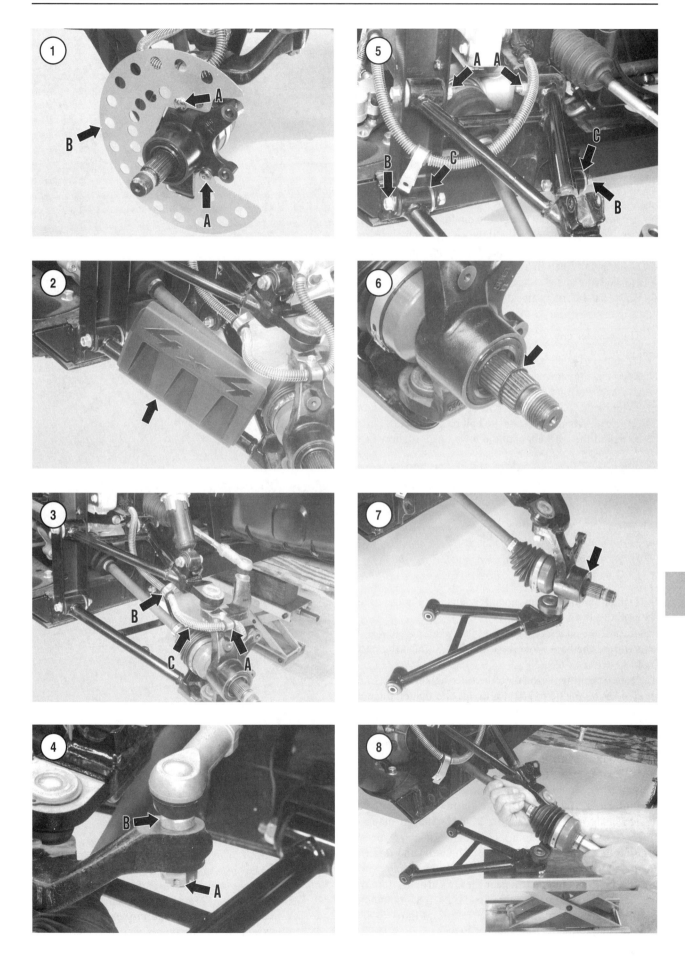

thus more difficult to compress when trying to install the axle into the differential.

3. Install a new circlip into the groove on the inboard joint axle (A, **Figure 10**). Pack the groove and circlip with lithium grease and then center the circlip in the groove. If necessary, use additional grease to help the circlip to remain centered in its groove.

4. Lubricate the inboard axle splines (B, **Figure 10**) with lithium grease.

5. Align the inboard axle splines with the differential and push the axle straight into the differential. If the axle does not enter the differential, check the circlip for damage and replace if necessary. Repeat until the circlip compresses as it passes through the differential splines and seats inside the differential. Then lightly pull on the axle to make sure it is locked in place.

6. Raise the steering knuckle and front axle as required and slip the front axle through the steering knuckle (**Figure 7**).

7. Lubricate a new O-ring (**Figure 6**) with lithium grease and install it over the axle splines.

8. Reconnect the lower arm as follows:

   a. Clean and dry the mounting bolts and nuts. Then lubricate the mounting bolt shoulders with lithium grease. Do not lubricate the bolt or nut threads.

   b. Install the washers onto the lower arm as shown C, **Figure 5**.

   c. Install the lower arm onto the frame and install the mounting bolts from the outside as shown in B, **Figure 5**. Install the nuts and tighten to 45 N•m (33 ft.-lb.).

NOTE
Make sure the washers did not fall off the lower arm.

9. Tighten the upper arm mounting nuts (A, **Figure 5**) to 45 N•m (33 ft.-lb.).

10. Install the shock absorber and its mounting bolts and nuts. Install the bolts from the front side. Tighten the nuts to 45 N•m (33 ft.-lb.).

11. Reconnect the tie rod onto the steering knuckle. Hold the flat across the tie rod (B, **Figure 4**) and tighten the nut (A) to 30 N•m (22 ft.-lb.). Install a new cotter pin and bend its arms to lock it.

12. Route the brake hose (C, **Figure 3**) around the front of the steering knuckle, making sure the hose is not twisted. Install the two brake hose clamp mounting bolts (A and B, **Figure 3**). The longer bolt is mounted on the bottom clamp (B, **Figure 3**). Tighten the bolts to 7 N•m (62 in.-lb.).

13. Install the boot guard (**Figure 2**) and tighten the mounting bolts to 7 N•m (62 in.-lb.).

14. Install the brake disc guard (B, **Figure 1**) and tighten the mounting bolts (A) to 7 N•m (62 in.-lb.).

15. Install the front hub (Chapter Eleven).

16. Install the front brake caliper and tighten its mounting bolts to 48 N•m (35 ft.-lb.).

17. Install the front wheel (Chapter Eleven).

18. When both front brake calipers are installed on the vehicle, apply the brake pedal several times to seat the pads against the disc.

19. Refill the differential gear housing with the correct type and quantity of gear oil (Chapter Three).

NOTE
If the front axle was rebuilt, make several test drives and then stop and check the axle for any grease that may have leaked out of the boots. Wipe off the axle and then repeat the checks to make sure no more grease leaks out. Usually, grease will leak one or two times and then stop after the boots are completely

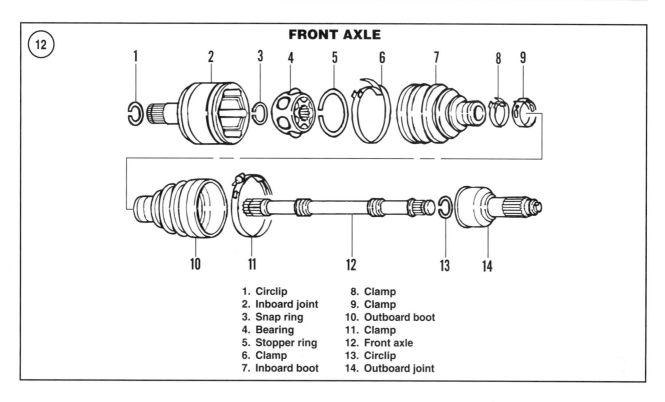

FRONT AXLE

1. Circlip
2. Inboard joint
3. Snap ring
4. Bearing
5. Stopper ring
6. Clamp
7. Inboard boot
8. Clamp
9. Clamp
10. Outboard boot
11. Clamp
12. Front axle
13. Circlip
14. Outboard joint

seated. If grease continues to leak out, check the clamps for tightness.

Inspection

Refer to **Figure 11** and **Figure 12**.

Replace the axle if damaged. The axle cannot be replaced separately.

1. Clean the axles, boots and splines. Do not submerge the axle boots in solvent. The CV joints (inside the boots) are packed with grease.

2. Inspect the axle for stripped or damaged threads.

3. Inspect for worn, distorted and broken splines on both sides of the axle.

4. Inspect the bearing and seal surfaces for scoring, galling, corrosion and other damage. If damage is evident, inspect the matching bearing in the front differential or steering knuckle.

NOTE
The axle boots encounter much abuse. Damaged boots allow dirt, mud and moisture to enter the boot, contaminate the grease and damage the bearing.

5. Inspect the boots for tearing, cracks and other damage. Check that the clamps are tight and have not slipped off of the end of the boot. A loose or torn boot will allow dirt and moisture. If necessary, replace damaged boots as described in *Disassembly/Assembly* in this section.

6. Pivot each end of the axle and check for roughness or play in the joint. If roughness is evident, disassemble the axle and inspect the parts as described in this section. If roughness or play remains after cleaning and lubrication, replace the worn parts.

7. Visually check the axle for straightness. Replace the axle if bent. A bent axle can damage the bearings in the steering knuckle and differential and cause vibration.

8. Refer to *Front Axle Inspection* in *Disassembly/Assembly* in this section to inspect the front axle after disassembly.

Disassembly/Assembly

Refer to **Figure 12**.

Before servicing the front axle, note the following:

1. The inboard and outboard joints cannot be rebuilt. The inboard joints can be disassembled for cleaning and inspection. The outboard joints cannot be disassembled, though they can be removed from the axle and partially cleaned for inspection purposes.

2. If removing both the inboard and outboard joint assemblies from the axle, remove the inboard joint first. During assembly, install the outboard joint first.

3. The boots and clamps are not identical in shape or size. Keep the clamps with their respective boots and note the boot locations in the ridges on the joints and shaft.

4. Install new boot clamps during assembly.

5. Different axle repair kits are available, depending on the parts and service required during service. Refer to a dealership for more information.

6. Install new snap rings and stopper rings during assembly.

7. Because the inboard and outboard joints are different, separate procedures are provided.

Inboard joint

Refer to **Figure 12** and A, **Figure 13**.

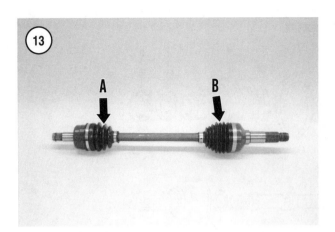

1. Note the direction the clamps face on the front axle so the new clamps can be installed facing the original direction. Pry the locking clips away from the lock, then pull and release the lock to loosen the clamp. Repeat for the other clamp. Refer to **Figure 14**.

2. Slide the boot off the inboard joint and onto the front axle.

3. Remove some of the grease from inside the inboard joint, then remove the stopper ring (**Figure 15**) from the groove in the inboard joint.

4. Pull the front axle and bearing out of the inboard joint (**Figure 16**).

5. Remove the snap ring (**Figure 17**) and slide off the bearing assembly. Be careful not to drop any of the steel balls from the bearing cage.

6. Slide the boot and clamps off the front axle. Discard the clamps as they should not be reused.

7. Clean and inspect the axle parts as described in this section.

8. If the outboard joint was also removed, install it first as described in this section.

NOTE
*The inboard boot (A, **Figure 18**) is shorter and smaller than the outboard boot (B).*

9. Install two new clamps (A, **Figure 19**) and the boot (B) onto the front axle. Face the clamps in their original directions as noted during disassembly.

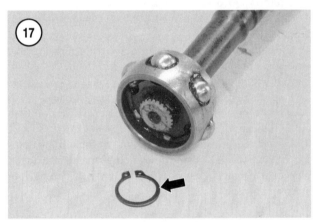

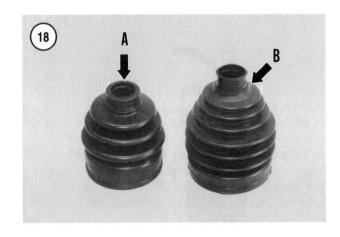

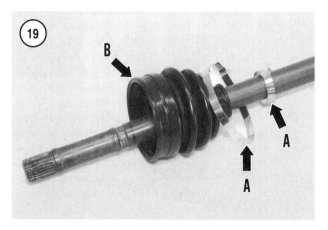

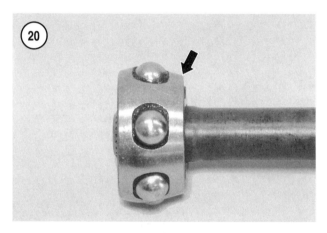

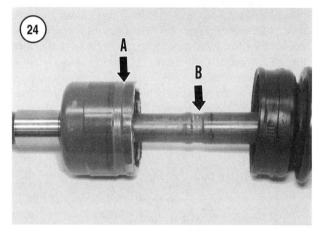

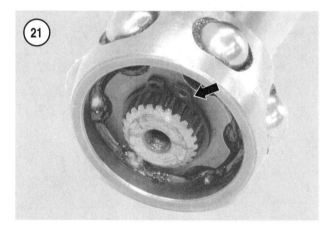

10. Pack the inboard boot with 45 g (1.6 oz.) of molybdenum disulfide grease.

11. Slide a new stopper ring (**Figure 15**) onto the front axle.

12. Install the bearing onto the front axle with the *small* end of the bearing going on first (**Figure 20**). Push the bearing onto the axle until it stops.

13. Install a new snap ring (**Figure 21**) into the groove in the front axle with the flat side of the snap ring facing out. Make sure the snap ring seats in the groove completely.

14. Apply a liberal amount of grease to the bearing assembly. Work the grease between the balls, race and case. Check for voids and fill them with grease.

15. Lubricate the inboard joint inner surface with grease.

16. Install the inboard joint into the bearing assembly by aligning the balls with the joint grooves. Then install the stopper ring (A, **Figure 22**) into the groove (B) in the inboard joint. Make sure the stopper ring seats in the groove completely.

17. After the stopper ring is in place, fill the inboard joint cavity behind the bearing assembly with grease (**Figure 23**).

18. Seat the inboard boot (A, **Figure 24**) onto the inboard joint and axle shoulders (B). Make sure the boot is not twisted.

19. Move the clamps onto the boot shoulders, then recheck that the boot is still positioned on the shoulders identified in **Figure 24**. When the boot and clamps are correctly po-

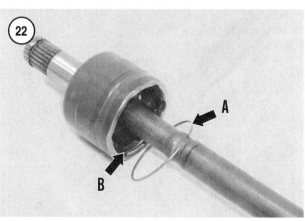

12

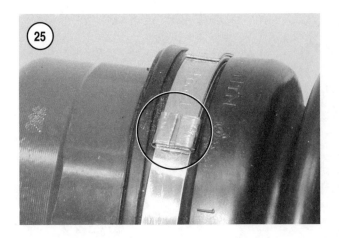

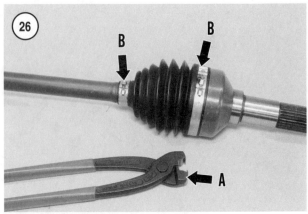

sitioned and the boot is not twisted, bend down the lock on one of the boot clamps (**Figure 14**) until it contacts the clamp. Then bend the locking clips tightly over the lock (**Figure 25**) and tap them flat with a plastic hammer. Repeat for the opposite clamp.

20. Hold the axle and pivot the joint to check its operation. The joint should move without any binding or roughness.

Outboard joint

Refer to **Figure 12** and B, **Figure 13**.

NOTE
*A boot band installing tool (Yamaha part No. YM-01527 [A, **Figure 26**] or equivalent) is required to install the outboard boot bands (B).*

1. Note the direction the clamps face on the front axle so the new clamps can be installed facing the original direction.

2. Cut the upper clamp lock across its top with a cut-off wheel mounted in a rotary grinding tool at the point shown in **Figure 27**. Do not cut all the way through the clamp. Then pry the clamp up and disconnect the clamp (**Figure 28**). Repeat for the other clamp. Discard the clamps.

3. Slide the boot off the outboard joint and onto the front axle.

NOTE
*The outboard joint is secured to the front axle with a circlip (13, **Figure 12**).*

4. Secure the front axle in a vise with soft jaws. Then tap the outboard joint with a plastic hammer (**Figure 29**) to remove it from the axle. Refer to A, **Figure 30**. As the outboard joint is driven out, the circlip will compress as the joint passes over it.

5. Remove the circlip (B, **Figure 30**) from the front axle groove and discard it.

6. Slide the boot off the front axle.

7. Clean and inspect the axle parts as described in this section.

8. If the inboard joint was also removed, install the outboard joint first.

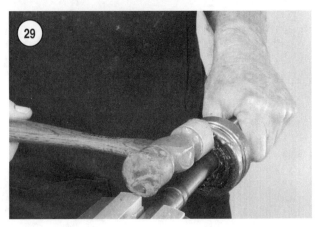

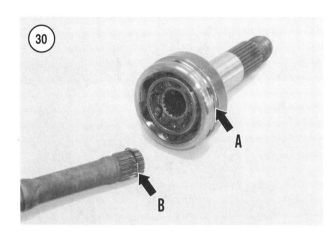

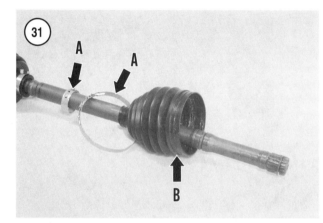

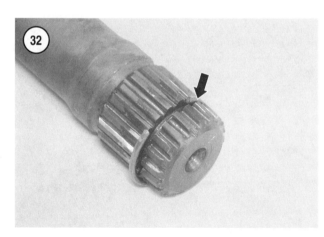

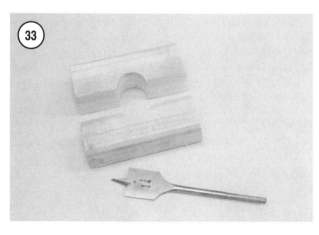

NOTE
*The outboard boot (B, **Figure 18**) is higher and larger than the inboard boot (A).*

9. Install two new clamps (A, **Figure 31**) and the boot (B) onto the front axle. Face the clamps in their original directions as noted during disassembly.

10. Pack the outboard boot with 60 g (2.1 oz.) of molybdenum disulfide grease.

11. Install a new circlip (**Figure 32**) into the front axle groove.

12. Fabricate a wooden collet clamp (**Figure 33**) to hold the outboard joint in a vise as follows:

    a. Cut a block from a 2 × 4 in. wooden board. The block should be long enough to clamp in a vise while allowing the outboard joint to hang down beside the side of the vise.

    b. Drill a 1 1/4 in. hole through the center of the wooden block with a spade bit.

    c. Cut the wooden block lengthwise in half through the drilled hole.

    d. To enable the clamp to secure the outboard joint tightly in a vise, reduce the width of the clamp halves by sanding them along their center edges where they were cut in half.

    e. Secure the outboard joint in a vise using the wooden clamp as shown in **Figure 34**. If the joint is still loose, sand the clamp halves again as required.

13. Compress the circlip and install the front axle into the outboard joint as follows:

    a. Secure the outboard joint in a vise using the wooden clamp and with the bearing side facing up (**Figure 34**).

    b. Slip the front axle into the outboard joint until the circlip contacts the joint as shown in **Figure 35**.

CAUTION
Do not drive the front axle into the outboard joint to compress the circlip. If the circlip does not immediately compress, it may damage the axle and/or the front joint splines.

    c. Tilt the front axle to seat the lower side of circlip into the joint, then use a screwdriver to push and com-

12

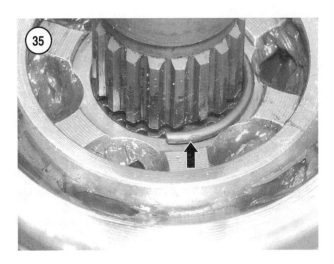

press the upper side of the circlip into the outboard joint (**Figure 36**).

   d. When the circlip is compressed inside the joint, push the front axle down until the circlip expands and locks inside the joint. Refer to **Figure 37**.

   e. Remove the front axle and outboard joint from the vise. Then pull on the parts to make sure the circlip is locked inside the outboard joint and the parts do not separate.

14. Pack the outboard joint cavity next to the bearing assembly with grease (**Figure 38**).

15. Seat the inboard boot onto the inboard joint (A, **Figure 39**) and axle shoulders (B). Make sure the boot is not twisted.

16. Move the clamps onto the boot shoulders, then recheck that the boot is still positioned on the shoulders identified in **Figure 39**. When the boot and clamps are correctly positioned and the boot is not twisted, lock the clamp with the boot band installing tool (**Figure 40**). Repeat for the opposite clamp. Refer to **Figure 41**.

17. Hold the axle and pivot the joint to check its operation. The joint should move without any binding or roughness.

18. Install the inboard joint onto the axle as described in this section if removed.

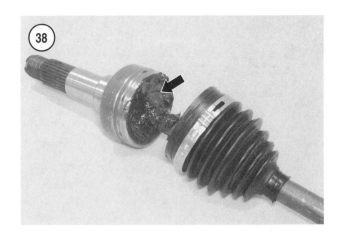

Front axle inspection

   Replace the axle if any damage is noted. The axle can be replaced separately.

1. Clean and dry the axle.
2. Check the axle splines for cracks and other damage.
3. Check the circlip grooves for damage.
4. Check the axle for bending.

Inboard joint inspection

   Replace parts that show excessive wear or damage as described in this section.

1. Clean the inboard joint bearing and housing assembly (**Figure 42**).

2. Inspect the steel balls (A, **Figure 42**), bearing cage (B) and bearing race (C) for excessive wear or damage.

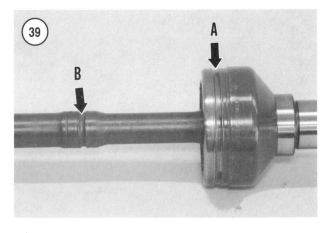

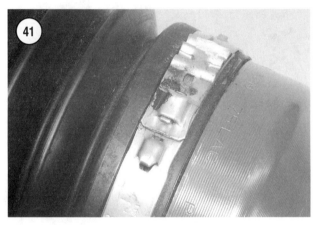

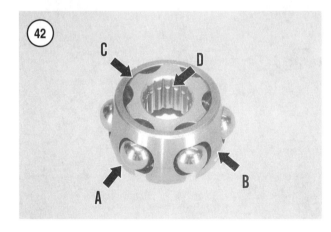

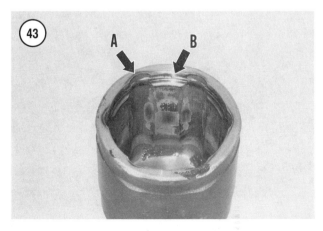

3. Check the bearing race inner splines (D, **Figure 42**) for cracks and other damage.

4. Inspect the inboard joint ball guides (A, **Figure 43**) for excessive wear, scoring or other damage.

5. Inspect the inboard joint stopper ring groove (B, **Figure 43**) for wear or damage.

6. Inspect the inboard joint outer bearing surfaces for scoring, cracks and other damage.

7. Inspect the inboard joint housing for cracks and other damage.

8. Inspect the inboard joint splines for cracks and other damage.

Outboard joint inspection

The outboard joint cannot be disassembled. If damaged, replace it as an assembly.

1. Do not clean the outboard joint (**Figure 44**) in solvent. Because the unit cannot be disassembled, the solvent will thin/contaminate the grease behind the bearing, making it difficult to thoroughly remove all grease residue and relubricate the outboard joint bearing. If the unit is contaminated with water, mud or dirt, replace it as an assembly. Use a dry rag to remove the grease from the outside of the bearing so the bearing can be inspected.

2. With the circlip removed from the front axle, insert the front axle into the outboard joint. Move the outboard joint axle through its range of motion and check for excessive play, roughness or damage (**Figure 45**).

3. Remove the front axle. Wipe off the outboard joint bearing (**Figure 44**) and inspect it for cracks, scoring and other damage.

4. Inspect the outboard joint outer bearing surfaces (A, **Figure 46**) for scoring, cracks and other damage.

5. Inspect the outboard joint housing for cracks and other damage.

6. Inspect the inner and outer outboard joint splines (B, **Figure 46**) and threads (C) for cracks and other damage.

7. Check the mating axle splines (D, **Figure 46**) and circlip groove (E) for damage.

12

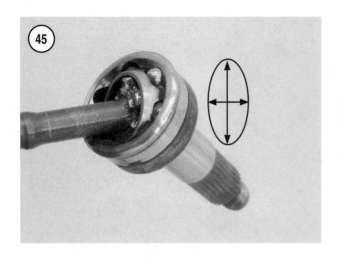

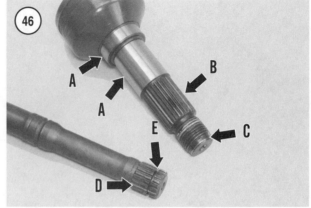

FRONT DIFFERENTIAL

This section describes service procedures for the front differential, including overhaul, seal removal/installation and gear motor service.

Differential Gear Unit Preload Check

The differential gear unit preload can be checked without removing the differential from the vehicle.

1. Park the vehicle on a level surface and shift the transmission into neutral. Block the rear wheels.

2. Raise the front of the vehicle so both front wheels are slightly off the ground.

3. Remove one of the front wheels (Chapter Eleven).

4. Mount a 32-mm socket onto a beam type torque wrench. Then place the socket onto the front axle nut and measure the break-away torque required to start the wheel rotating. Repeat several times to obtain an average reading and compare to the specifications in **Table 1**. If the reading is out of specification, replace the differential gear unit as described in this section. The differential gear unit cannot be rebuilt.

5. Reinstall the front wheel (Chapter Eleven).

6. Lower the vehicle so the front wheels are on the ground.

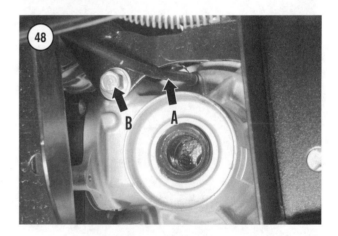

Removal

1. Shift the front differential into two-wheel drive. This will index the gear motor with the sliding gear in the front differential.

2. Remove the front axles as described in this chapter.

3. Disconnect the gear motor electrical connector (**Figure 47**) at the rear of the differential.

4. Disconnect the breather hose (A, **Figure 48**) from the right side of the differential.

5. Remove the two rear differential mounting bolts and washers. B, **Figure 48** shows the rear right side mounting bolt.

6. Remove the nut (A, **Figure 49**), washers and front differential mounting bolt.

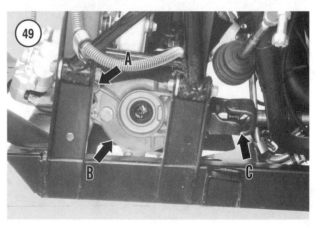

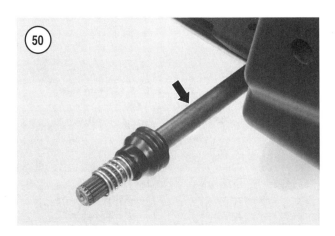

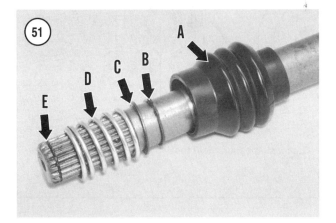

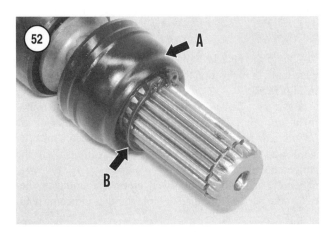

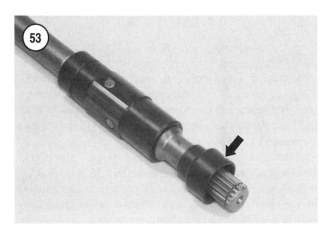

NOTE
The differential cannot be removed while connected to the front drive shaft.

7. Have an assistant hold the front drive shaft in place so it does not pull out of the universal joint at the engine, then pull the differential (B, **Figure 49**) forward to disconnect it from the drive shaft and remove it from underneath the vehicle.
8. Service the differential as described in this chapter.
9. Pull the drive shaft (**Figure 50**) forward to disconnect it from the engine and remove it.
10. Service the drive shaft as described in this chapter.

Installation

1. On the front part of the drive shaft, slide the boot (A, **Figure 51**) rearward and make sure the snap ring (B), washer (C), spring (D) and O-ring (E) are installed on the drive shaft. Slide the boot forward so that it covers these parts.
2. On the rear part of the drive shaft, fold the boot forward (A, **Figure 52**) and make sure the snap ring (B) is installed in the drive shaft groove. Then fold the boot over so it seats against the drive shaft as shown in **Figure 53**.
3. Lubricate the splines on both ends of the drive shaft with lithium grease.
4. Clean the universal joint splines at the engine and differential.
5. Install the drive shaft into the universal joint at the engine (**Figure 54**).
6. Install the differential and connect its universal joint (C, **Figure 49**) to the drive shaft.
7. Install the two rear mounting bolts (B, **Figure 48**) and washers to hold the differential in place. Then check that the drive shaft is connected to the universal joint at the engine.
8. Install the front mounting bolt and washer from the right side. Then install the washer and nut (A, **Figure 49**).
9. Tighten the front and rear differential mounting bolts and nut to 55 N•m (41 ft.-lb.).

12

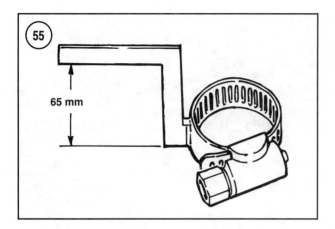

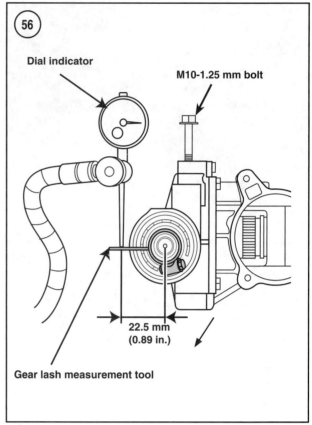

10. Reconnect the breather hose (A, **Figure 48**) onto the breather tube on the right side of the differential.

11. Reconnect the gear motor electrical connector (**Figure 47**) at the rear of the differential.

12. Install the front axles as described in this chapter.

Preliminary Inspection

If the differential is in good condition, use the following procedure to inspect the parts.

1. Plug the axle openings and clean the differential housing.

2. Inspect the housing for cracks, oil leaks and other damage. Replace damaged oil seals as described in this section.

3. Turn the universal joint and to check the differential gear unit and pinion gear for roughness, noise, play and binding. The bearings should turn smoothly and quietly. If damage or excessive play is noted, disassemble the differential as described in this section to isolate the damaged part(s).

Gear Lash Measurement/Adjustment

Perform gear lash measurement prior to disassembly to determine gear wear and whether the pinion gear shim thicknesses must be adjusted. Measuring gear lash is also necessary after replacing the pinion gear, differential gear unit, bearings or either housing. Also check the clearance whenever reusing worn parts after disassembly.

Measure gear lash with a gear lash measurement tool (Yamaha part No. YM-01475 [**Figure 55**] or equivalent) and a dial indicator.

1. Remove the universal joint assembly as described in this chapter.

2. Lock the differential housing to a vise or workbench with the drain hole facing up. Remove the differential oil drain plug. The differential housing must not move when the measurements are taken or the results will be incorrect.

3. Lock the differential gear unit in place with a suitable M10-1.25 mm bolt (**Figure 56**). Finger-tighten the bolt into the drain hole just enough to keep the ring gear from turning.

CAUTION
Overtightening the bolt may damage the ring gear.

4. Clamp the gear lash measurement tool onto the pinion gear shaft, then position the tool arm horizontally as shown in **Figure 56**.

5. Position a dial indicator in contact with the measurement tool and 22.5 mm (0.89 in.) from the center of the pinion gear shaft (**Figure 56**). The dial indicator must be stable and set to read gear lash in both directions. Zero the gauge on the dial indicator.

6. Gently rotate the pinion gear clockwise until lash between the parts is eliminated. Note the dial indicator reading.

7. Gently rotate the pinion gear shaft in the opposite direction until lash between the parts is eliminated. Note the dial indicator reading.

8. Add the indicator readings in Step 6 and 7 to determine the differential gear lash and record the number.

9. Loosen the lock bolt and rotate the pinion gear 90°. Finger-tighten the bolt, readjust the gear lash measurement tool, and repeat the check. Measure the gear lash at every 90° until the shaft has rotated one full turn (four total measurements).

10. Determine the average reading of the four checks. Differential gear lash should be 0.05-0.25 mm (0.0020-0.0098 in.). If adjustment is necessary, refer to *Disassembly* in this section to disassemble the differential housing. Adjust the differential gear lash as follows:

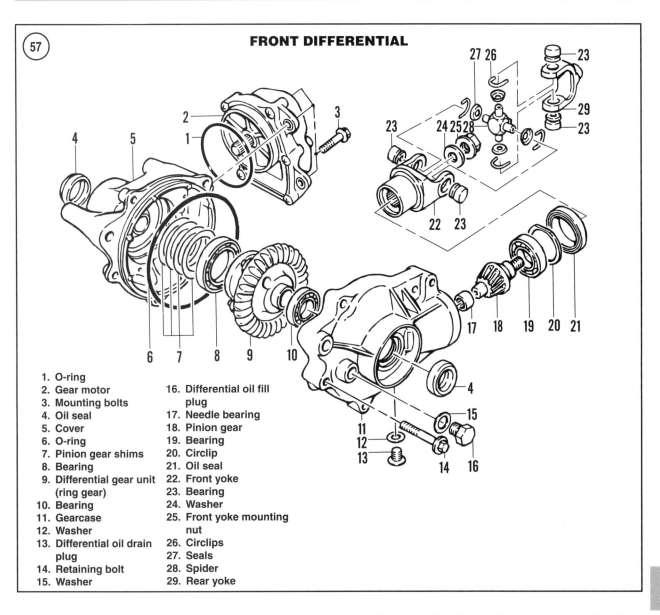

FRONT DIFFERENTIAL

1. O-ring
2. Gear motor
3. Mounting bolts
4. Oil seal
5. Cover
6. O-ring
7. Pinion gear shims
8. Bearing
9. Differential gear unit (ring gear)
10. Bearing
11. Gearcase
12. Washer
13. Differential oil drain plug
14. Retaining bolt
15. Washer
16. Differential oil fill plug
17. Needle bearing
18. Pinion gear
19. Bearing
20. Circlip
21. Oil seal
22. Front yoke
23. Bearing
24. Washer
25. Front yoke mounting nut
26. Circlips
27. Seals
28. Spider
29. Rear yoke

a. Differential gear lash is determined by the pinion gear shims (7, **Figure 57**). Four different shim thicknesses are available: 0.1 mm, 0.2 mm, 0.3 mm and 0.4 mm.

b. If the gear lash is too low, reduce the shim thickness.

c. If the gear lash is too high, increase the shim thickness.

Gear Motor
Removal/Testing/Installation

NOTE
Do not disassemble the gear motor assembly.

1. Remove the mounting bolts (A, **Figure 58**) and the gear motor (B).
2. Remove the gear motor O-ring (A, **Figure 59**).
3. Test the differential gear motor as follows:

CAUTION
Do not test the gear motor with a 12-volt battery.

a. Assemble two C-size batteries in series to create 3 volts. The Radio Shack "C" Battery Holder (part No. 270-385A) can be used as shown in **Figure 60**.

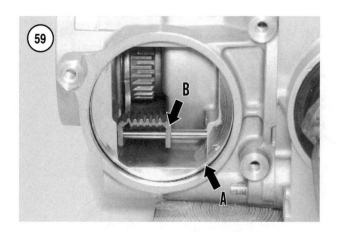

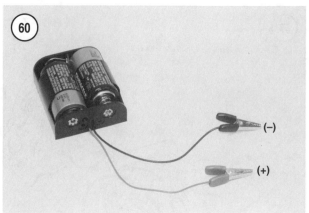

b. Connect the positive and negative battery leads to the gear motor terminals shown in **Figure 61**. The gear motor shaft should turn *counterclockwise* as shown in **Figure 61**.

c. Reverse the positive and negative battery leads at the same gear motor terminals. The gear motor shaft should turn *clockwise*.

d. Replace the gear motor if it failed to operate as described or if the gear motor shaft does not turn when battery voltage was applied to the terminals.

4. Perform the following to install the gear motor onto the differential:

a. Lubricate a new O-ring with lithium grease and install it in the housing groove (A, **Figure 59**).

b. To ensure the shift fork sliding gear does not move when installing the gear motor, make some alignment studs (A, **Figure 62**) by cutting the heads off three 6-mm bolts and threading them into the housing. The bolts must be long enough to allow removal after installing the gear motor.

c. Slide the shift fork sliding gear completely to one side as shown in B, **Figure 59**. In this position, the differential is in two-wheel drive.

CAUTION
The gear motor and the shift fork sliding gear must remain in their set positions until the parts are engaged. If the parts are not aligned properly, the indicator light and the actual differential mode may differ and the two-wheel drive or differential lock mode may not activate.

d. Check that the mark on the gear motor (A, **Figure 63**) aligns with the mark on the gear motor housing (B). If the marks do not align, connect two C-size batteries to the gear motor terminal as described in Step 3 to turn the shaft until the marks line up, then disconnect the battery terminals.

e. Install the gear motor (B, **Figure 62**) over the alignment studs and seat it against the housing while making sure the gear motor shaft engages the shift fork sliding gear.

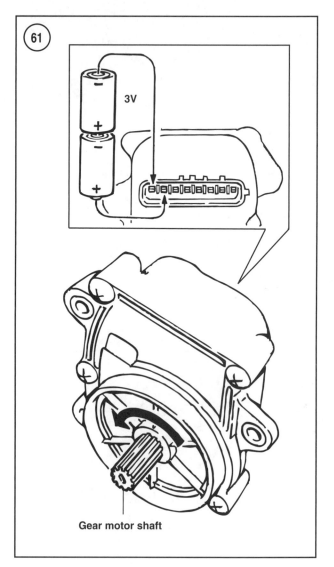

Gear motor shaft

f. Hold the gear motor in place and remove one of the studs. Install a mounting bolt finger-tight. Then remove the remaining studs and replace with the mounting bolts and tighten finger-tight one at a time.

g. Tighten the gear motor mounting bolts (A, **Figure 58**) to 11 N•m (97 in.-lb.).

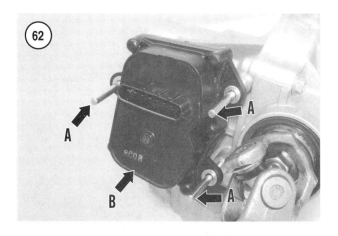

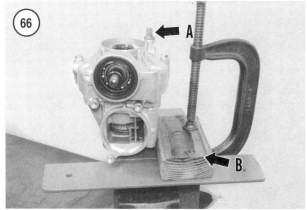

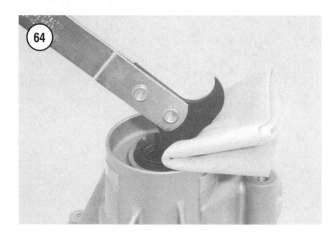

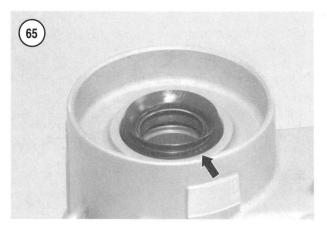

Oil Seal Removal/Installation

The two front axle seals (4, **Figure 57**) and the pinion gear seal (21) can be replaced without having to disassemble the differential housing.

Front axle seals

1. Remove the front differential as described in this section.
2. Clean the area around the seal.
3. Pry the seal out of the housing with a seal puller (**Figure 64**). Check the seal to make sure the garter spring remains in place and did not fall into the differential housing.
4. Clean the seal bore.
5. Lubricate the lips on the new seal with lithium grease.
6. Insert the new seal into the housing bore with its closed side and axle lip facing out. Drive the new seal into the housing until its outer edge is flush with the housing bore (**Figure 65**).
7. Repeat for the other seal.

Pinion gear seal

1. Remove the front differential as described in this section.
2. Clean the area around the seal and universal joint.
3. Remove the universal joint as described in this section.
4. Secure the differential housing so that it will remain steady when removing the seal. The seal can be tight and difficult to remove. **Figure 66** shows the differential housing secured to a piece of angle plate with a long bolt (A) and a wooden block (B) used to prevent the housing from turning when pressure is applied to the seal.
5. Pry the seal out of the housing with a seal puller (**Figure 67**). Check the seal to make sure the garter spring remains in place and did not fall into the differential housing.
6. Clean the seal bore.
7. Lubricate the lips on the new seal with lithium grease.
8. Insert the new seal into the housing bore with its closed side facing out. Drive or tap the seal into the housing until its outer edge is flush with the housing bore (**Figure 68**).

12

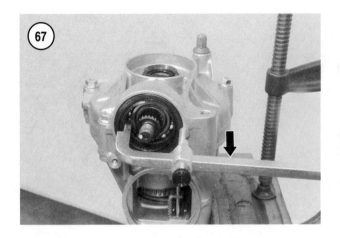

9. Before installing the universal joint yoke, check the yoke's seal operating surface for any scoring, corrosion or other defects that could damage the new seal. Remove any roughness with emery cloth or replace the yoke.

10. Install the universal joint as described in this section.

Gearcase Disassembly

Refer to **Figure 57**.

1. Remove the differential gear motor as described in this section.

2. Remove the universal joint as described in this chapter.

3. Remove the gearcase retaining bolts (**Figure 69**) in a crossing pattern.

4. Insert a prying tool in the gap between the gearcase and cover (**Figure 70**) and pry the gearcase (A, **Figure 71**) away from the cover. Remove the O-ring (B, **Figure 71**).

5. Remove the differential gear unit (C, **Figure 71**) and the pinion gear shims (**Figure 72**).

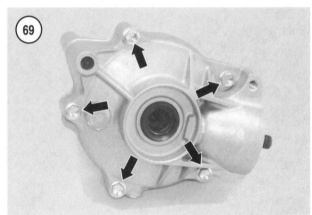

> *NOTE*
> *The shift shaft (A, **Figure 73**), shift fork (B) and clutch (C) are permanently installed in the cover. Do not attempt to remove them.*

6. Remove the pinion gear seal and front axle seals as described in this section.

> *NOTE*
> *Do not remove the pinion shaft unless damage is noted either with the pinion shaft or its needle bearing.*

7. Remove the pinion shaft as follows:

> *NOTE*
> *The snap ring (A, **Figure 74**) is difficult to remove and install.*

a. Remove the snap ring (A, **Figure 74**) from the groove in the gearcase. Discard the snap ring.

b. Remove the bearing (B, **Figure 74**) and pinion gear (C). If these parts are tight, heat the exterior of the shaft bore with a heat gun. Then tap the end of he pinion gear (**Figure 75**) to drive the gear and bearing

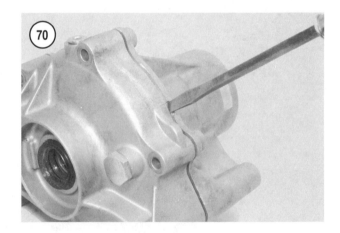

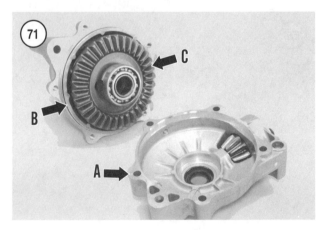

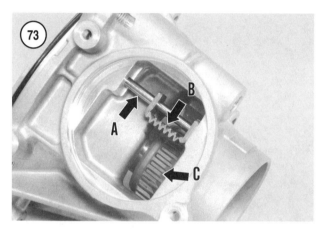

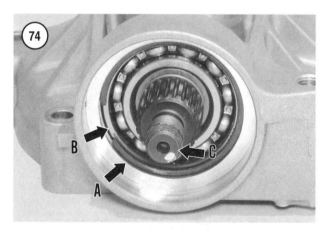

out of the housing. Use a soft drift when tapping the gear.

Inspection

1. Clean, then inspect, all components for excessive wear and damage.
2. Inspect the differential gear unit as follows:

> *NOTE*
> *Do not attempt to disassemble the differential gear unit. Replacement parts are not available.*

a. Inspect the ring gear teeth (A, **Figure 76**). If damage or uneven wear is evident, also inspect the pinion gear teeth (**Figure 75**). If the ring gear is damaged, replace the differential gear unit.

b. Inspect the differential bearings (B, **Figure 76** and A, **Figure 77**) for cracks, bluing or other damage. If there is no damage, lubricate each bearing with gear oil. Then turn each bearing and check for roughness, noise, play and binding. The bearings should turn smoothly and quietly. If damage or excessive play is evident, replace the bearings as described in this section.

c. Inspect the differential gear cluster (B, **Figure 77**). If damage or uneven wear is evident, replace the differential unit.

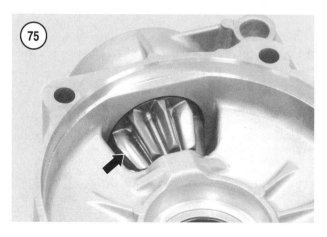

12

d. Inspect the splines (C, **Figure 77**) for cracks, roughness or other damage. Then slide the differential gear unit into the cover so the splines on the gear unit and clutch engage. The parts should slide together easily.

e. Inspect the bolts (D, **Figure 77**) for tightness.

3. Inspect the cover assembly (5, **Figure 57**) as follows:

a. Inspect the cover for cracks and damage. Check the O-ring groove for damage.

b. Inspect the different spline sets on the clutch adapter (**Figure 78**) for cracks, roughness or other damage.

c. Inspect the shift shaft (A, **Figure 73**) for damage. Then make sure the shaft is fixed in the cover and cannot slide out (**Figure 79**).

d. Slide the shift fork (B, **Figure 73**) by hand to make sure it moves smoothly and there is no roughness or binding.

4. Inspect the gearcase and pinion gear as follows:

a. Inspect the gearcase for damage. Check the mating O-ring sealing surface for signs of leakage.

b. Inspect the pinion gear teeth (**Figure 75**) for damage.

c. If the pinion gear was not removed, lubricate the bearings with gear oil. Then turn the gear and check the bearings for roughness, noise, play and binding. The shaft should turn smoothly and quietly. If damage or excessive play is evident, remove the pinion gear and replace the bearings as described in this section.

Bearing Removal/Installation

Refer to *Service Methods* in Chapter One.

Differential gear unit

Both bearings are replaced in the same way.

1. Support the bearing with a bearing splitter (**Figure 80**) in a press.

2. Press on the axle holder until the bearing is removed.

3. Clean the bearing surface on the axle holder.

4. Support the differential gear unit in a press.

5. Center the bearing on the axle holder with its manufacturer's marks facing out.

6. Place a bearing driver on the bearing's inner race and press the bearing onto the axle holder until it bottoms.

Pinion shaft needle bearing

1. Remove the pinion gear as described in this section.

2. Remove the needle bearing (17, **Figure 57**) with a blind bearing removal tool.

3. Inspect the bearing bore in the gearcase for damage.

4. Align the new bearing with the bearing bore with its manufacturer's marks facing out.

5. Press the new bearing into the bearing bore until it bottoms.

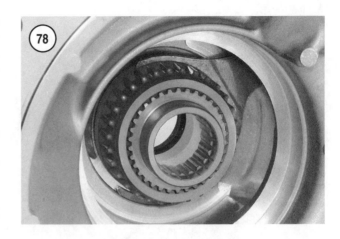

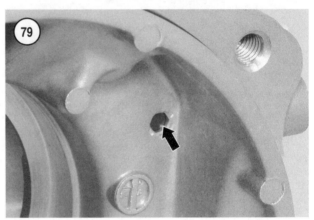

6. Install the pinion gear into the needle bearing and turn the gear to check for any damage that may have occurred when the bearing was installed.

Pinion shaft ball bearing

This bearing (19, **Figure 57**) is removed with the pinion gear (18).

Gearcase Assembly

1. If the pinion gear was removed, perform the following:

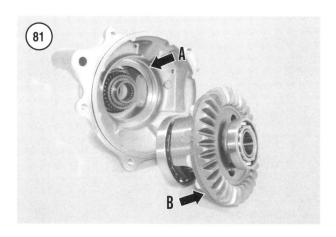

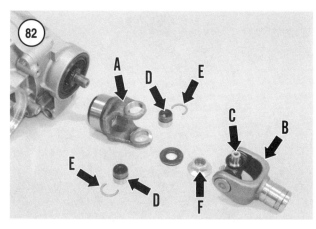

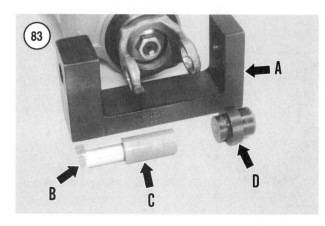

a. Lubricate the needle bearing and pinion gear bearing surfaces with gear oil.

b. Install the pinion gear (C, **Figure 74**) and ball bearing (B) into the gearcase.

c. Install a new snap ring (A, **Figure 74**) into the gearcase groove. Check the groove for damage after installing the snap ring.

2. Install the pinion gear shims (**Figure 72**) into the cover bearing bore (A, **Figure 81**).

3. Lubricate the clutch splines and the differential gear unit splines and bearings with gear oil.

4. Install the differential gear unit (B, **Figure 81**) into the cover making sure the splines on the clutch and gear unit engage. Refer to C, **Figure 71**.

5. Lubricate a new O-ring with lithium grease and install it into the cover groove (B, **Figure 71**).

6. Install the gearcase onto the cover and secure it with the mounting bolts (**Figure 69**). Then tighten the gearcase retaining bolts in a crossing pattern to 24 N•m (18 ft.-lb.).

7. If the pinion gear, differential gear unit, bearings or housings were replaced, refer to *Gear Lash Clearance/ Adjustment* in this section. Also check the clearance when wear is evident on original parts that are reused. If necessary, disassemble the differential to install different thickness shims as required. Repeat until the gear lash clearance is correct.

8. Install a new pinion gear seal and front axle seals as described in this section.

9. Install the universal joint as described in this chapter.

10. Install the gear motor as described in this section.

UNIVERSAL JOINT

The universal joint assembly consists of a front yoke (A, **Figure 82**), rear yoke (B), spider (C), four bearings (D), four circlips (E) and four seals. To remove the universal joint, it is partially disassembled by removing two opposing circlips and then pressing the two opposing bearings out of the front yoke. This will free the spider so the rear yoke/spider assembly can be removed from the front yoke. The front yoke is secured to the pinion gear and can then be removed.

NOTE
*The seal (27, **Figure 57**) and small O-ring installed on each bearing (23) are not available separately. If reusing these parts, handle them carefully during all service procedures.*

Tools

1. One of the following tools is required to hold the front yoke (A, **Figure 82**) when loosening and tightening the nut (F):

   a. A universal joint holder (Yamaha part No. YM-04062 or equivalent). This tool fits around the front yoke and uses two pins to hold the yoke in place.

   b. The Yamaha joint holder (part No. YM-04062-3 [A, **Figure 83**]). This tool has been modified to hold the front yoke with a bolt (B, **Figure 83**) and machined collar (C) along with the pin (D) that is part of the original tool. Fabricate the collar so that it fits between the holder and into one side of the yoke. Then thread the inside of the collar to accept the bolt. The bolt should be long enough to thread all the way through the collar. This tool is shown in the following sections.

2. A hydraulic press and suitable adapters are required to remove and install the universal joint bearings.

12

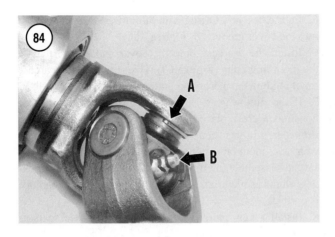

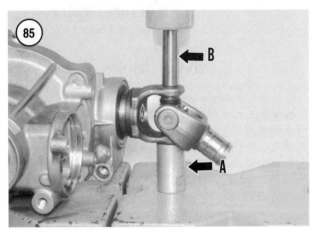

Removal

1. Remove the differential as described in this chapter.
2. Remove the gear motor as described in this chapter.

> *WARNING*
> *Because the circlips (A, **Figure 84**) may fly off when removed, wear goggles or other eye protection.*

> *NOTE*
> *Note the direction the grease nipple (B, **Figure 84**) faces so that the spider can be installed with the nipple facing in the same direction.*

3. Using a metal rod and hammer, remove a circlip (A, **Figure 84**) by driving it off one of the bearings.
4. Repeat Step 3 to remove the circlip from the opposing bearing.
5. Support the differential in a press. Then support the front yoke with a piece of pipe (A, **Figure 85**) with an inside diameter large enough to accept the bearing.
6. Position a driver (B, **Figure 85**) with an outside diameter that is small enough to pass through the yoke between the press ram and bearing.

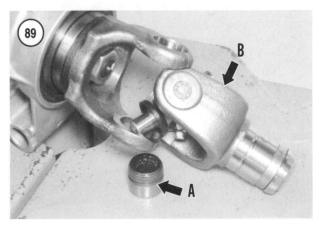

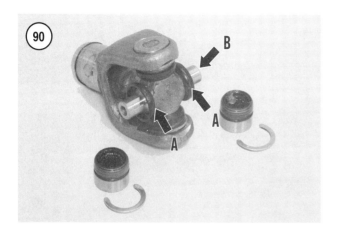

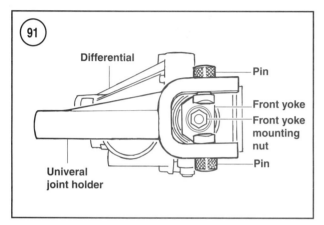

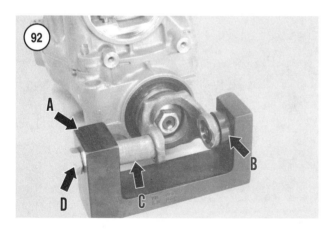

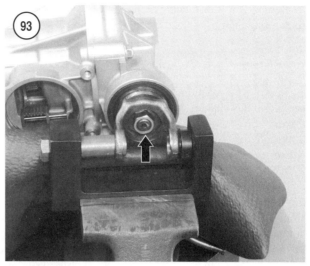

CAUTION
Before operating the press, check that the two circlips for the bearings being removed are removed.

NOTE
In Step 7, press the upper bearing just far enough to remove the lower bearing from the yoke. If the upper bearing is pressed too far, it will fall through to the inside of the yoke. Because the upper bearing must be pressed out in the same manner as the lower bearing, having to realign the bearing with the yoke bore and spider can be difficult if the parts are damaged or corroded.

7. Press the upper bearing (**Figure 86**) into the yoke to press the lower bearing out of the yoke and into the pipe. Refer to **Figure 87**.

8. Reposition the universal joint so that the upper bearing in Step 7 is now at the bottom. Center the spider in the yoke and press against the spider (**Figure 88**) to press the bearing into the pipe. Remove the bearing (A, **Figure 89**) and the rear yoke assembly (B).

9. Remove the two seals (A, **Figure 90**).

10. If necessary, repeat Steps 3-9 to remove the remaining two bearings, spider (B, **Figure 90**) and seals.

11. Remove the front yoke (A, **Figure 82**) as follows:

   a. If using joint holder part No. 04062, secure it across the front yoke with the two pins (**Figure 91**).

   b. If using joint holder part No. 04062-3 (A, **Figure 92**), secure it across the front yoke with the pin (B), machined collar (C) and bolt (D).

   c. Lock the joint holder in a vise (**Figure 93**) while using a thick blanket to protect the differential from damage. Then loosen the front yoke mounting nut (**Figure 93**).

   d. Remove the joint holder and differential from the vise. Then remove the joint holder, nut, washer and front yoke.

Inspection

1. Clean and dry all parts. Discard the circlips.

2. Inspect the yoke and spider bearing surfaces for cracks, scoring and other damage. Remove burrs with a fine-cut file.

3. Inspect the yoke housing for cracks and other damage.

4. Inspect the bearing housing and needles (A, **Figure 94**) for corrosion and other damage. If the bearing is contaminated, the seal (B, **Figure 94**) at the top of the bearing is probably distorted or damaged. Then inspect the O-ring (C, **Figure 94**) for damage. Discard the bearing if these parts are damaged or the bearing is corroded. Repeat for each bearing.

12

5. Remove all threadlocking compound residue from the pinion shaft and front yoke mounting nut threads.

Installation

1. Install a new pinion shaft seal (A, **Figure 95**) as described in this chapter. Lubricate the seal lips with lithium grease.
2. Install the front yoke (B, **Figure 95**) by aligning its splines with the pinion shaft splines. Then turn the yoke to make sure the pinion shaft seal lips are seating squarely against the yoke and are not distorted.
3. Install the washer (C, **Figure 95**) and seat it against the front yoke. Then apply a medium-strength threadlocking compound onto the front yoke mounting nut (D, **Figure 95**) and install the nut finger-tight.
4. Secure the front yoke with the same tool used during removal and tighten the front yoke mounting nut (**Figure 93**) to 62 N•m (46 ft.-lb.). Remove the joint holder and differential from the vise. Turn the yoke to make sure the pinion shaft turns smoothly.
5. If reusing the bearings, lubricate the needles with lithium grease.
6. Before installing the bearings slide each bearing (**Figure 96**) over one of the spider arms to make sure the needles are positioned against the inside of the bearing. If not, reposition the needles and recheck. The bearings should slide smoothly over the spider arm.

NOTE
*Steps 7-11 can be used to install both sets of bearings when assembling the universal joint assembly. The following photographs show assembly with the spider already installed in the rear yoke. However, if the spider was removed from the rear yoke, assemble these parts first, making sure to position the spider so the grease fitting (B, **Figure 84**) is facing in its original direction as noted prior to removal.*

7. Install a cupped seal (A, **Figure 90**) on each opposing spider arm with the cup side facing away from the spider.
8. Support the assembly in a press. Slip the spider (A, **Figure 97**) into the yoke while supporting the bottom of the yoke with a piece of pipe (B). Center the bearing (C, **Figure 97**) into the yoke bore and over the spider arm.

WARNING
Because the circlips may fly off when being installed, wear goggles or other eye protection.

CAUTION
Make sure the bearing is aligned squarely with the yoke bore. Otherwise, the bearing may enter the bore at an angle and damage the yoke. If a bearing starts moving smoothly and then tightens as it is being installed, it is probably entering the yoke at an angle. When

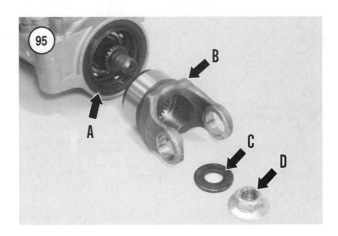

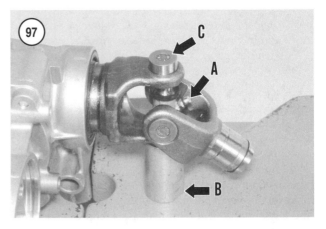

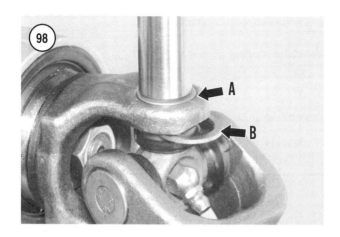

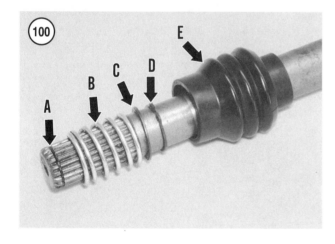

installing a bearing set, the second or opposing bearing will be harder to align squarely with the yoke.

NOTE
Install new circlips in Steps 9 and 10.

9. Using a driver on top of the bearing, press the bearing into the yoke until the top of the bearing is almost flush with the top of the yoke (A, **Figure 98**). Then check the circlip fit between the bearing shoulder and the side of the yoke (B). If there is not enough clearance, continue to press the bearing into the yoke until the circlip can be tapped

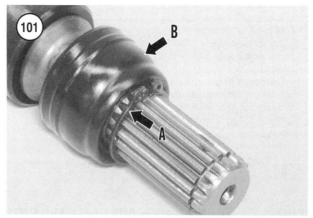

in place until it bottoms completely against the bearing (**Figure 99**).

10. Turn the universal joint over and repeat Steps 8 and 9 to install the opposing bearing and circlip.

11. After both circlips are installed, pivot the rear yoke up and down and side to side to compare the tension movement in both directions. Tension movement in both directions should be approximately the same. If the rear yoke feels tight in one or both directions, examine the circlips by trying to pry them sideways with a screwdriver (do not try to remove them) at their middle section. If a circlip feels looser than the other, support the yoke in the press with the loose circlip side down and carefully press the upper bearing until it just moves slightly. A feeler gauge can also be used to compare circlip tightness. Repeat until the yoke movement feels the same in both directions.

FRONT DRIVE SHAFT

Removal/Installation

Remove and install the front drive shaft as described in *Removal* and *Installation* in *Front Differential* this chapter.

Inspection

Refer to **Figure 57**.
The drive shaft is splined to universal joints, connected to the differential and engine.

1. At the front part of the drive shaft, inspect the splines, O-ring (A, **Figure 100**), spring (B), washer (C) and snap ring (D) for damage.

2. At the rear part of the drive shaft, inspect the splines and snap ring (A, **Figure 101**) for damage.

3. Make sure snap rings are fully seated in the shaft grooves.

4. Inspect the drive shaft for straightness. Replace the drive shaft if it is bent. A bent drive shaft can damage bearings and cause excessive vibration.

5. Inspect the boots (E, **Figure 100** and B, **Figure 100**). The boots must not be torn or damaged.

12

Table 1 FRONT AXLE AND DIFFERENTIAL SPECIFICATIONS

Ball joint lubrication	
Lubrication type	Molybdenum disulfide grease
Front axle boots lubrication	
Per dust boot	
Outboard (front wheel side)	60 g (2.1 oz.)
Inboard (differential gear side)	45 g (1.6 oz.)
Differential gear lash clearance	0.5-0.25 mm (0.0020-0.0098 in.)
Differential gear unit preload break-away torque	
New	17-25 N•m (12-18 ft.-lb.)
Minimum	10 N•m (88 in.-lb./7.2 ft.-lb.)

Table 2 FRONT AXLE AND DIFFERENTIAL TORQUE SPECIFICATIONS

	N•m	in.-lb.	ft.-lb.
Boot guard mounting bolts	7	62	–
Brake disc guard mounting bolts	7	62	–
Brake hose clamp mounting bolts	7	62	–
Differential gear motor mounting bolt	11	97	–
Differential mounting bolts and nut	55	–	41
Differential oil drain bolt	10	88	–
Differential oil fill plug	23	–	17
Front yoke mounting nut*	62	–	46
Gearcase retaining bolts	24	–	18
Lower arm mounting nuts	45	–	33
Shock absorber mounting nuts	45	–	33
Tie rod mounting nuts	30	–	22
Upper arm mounting nuts	45	–	33

*Refer to text.

REAR SUSPENSION

This chapter covers the rear wheels, hub and suspension components.

Read *Safety* and *Service Methods* in Chapter One before servicing the vehicle in this chapter.

Tables 1-4 are at the end of this chapter.

REAR WHEELS

Removal/Installation

1. Park the vehicle on level ground and set the parking brake.

> *NOTE*
> *If both rear wheels will be removed, identify their normal operating direction or locate the tires directional marks (**Figure 1**) so they can be reinstalled on the correct side of the vehicle.*

2. Loosen the rear wheel lug nuts (A, **Figure 2**).
3. Support the vehicle with both rear wheels off the ground and remove the lug nuts and the rear wheel. The wheel cap (B, **Figure 2**) is mounted inside the wheel.
4. Remove the protective plate (**Figure 3**), if necessary.
5. Clean and dry the lug nuts and replace if damaged.
6. Refer to *Wheel Runout* in Chapter Eleven. If the tire is flat, repair it as described in *Tires* in Chapter Eleven.
7. Install the protective plate (**Figure 3**), if removed.
8. Install the wheel cap (B, **Figure 2**) into the inside of the wheel, if removed.

9. Install the wheel with the tire's directional mark facing its normal operating direction and with the tire valve (C, **Figure 2**) facing out.
10. Install the lug nuts with their tapered side (**Figure 4**) facing the wheel and tighten finger-tight so the wheel sits squarely against the rear hub.
11. Lower the vehicle so both rear tires are on the ground and tighten the lug nuts in a crossing pattern to 55 N•m (41 ft.-lb.).
12. Support the vehicle again with both rear wheels off the ground.
13. Release the parking brake, then turn the rear wheel and operate the rear brake. Repeat this step several times to make sure the axle rotates and the rear brakes are working properly.

TIRES

Refer to Chapter Eleven.

REAR HUB

This section covers the rear hub and wheel spacer.

Removal

1. Park the vehicle on level ground and set the parking brake.
2. Support the vehicle and remove the rear wheels as described in this chapter.

13

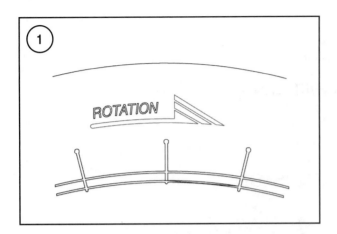

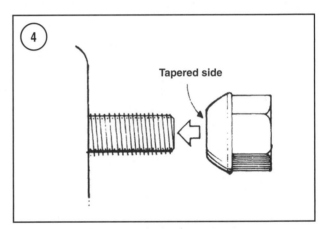

Tapered side

3. Grind the staked portion of the hub nut (**Figure 5**) to weaken it. Do not grind through the nut as this will damage the axle threads.

NOTE
The rear hub nut is tightened to a high torque value and can be difficult to remove.

4A. Use an impact wrench and remove the rear hub hub (**Figure 5**). Discard the nut.

4B. If an impact wrench is unavailable, hold the hub in place with a long metal bar bolted across two of the hub studs (**Figure 6**). The metal bar must be long enough to contact the ground and lock the hub in place. Loosen the hub nut with a breaker bar and socket. Discard the nut.

5. Remove the rear brake caliper (Chapter Fifteen). Do not disconnect the brake hose from the caliper unless necessary. Use a wire hanger to support the caliper. Do not let the caliper hang from the brake hose.

NOTE
The protective plates and wheel spacers were installed on 2008-2009 models under a free repair program sponsored by the manufacturer. All 2011 models are equipped with the protective plates and spacers at the time of manufacturer. Refer to a dealership for additional information.

6. Remove the protective plate (**Figure 3**).

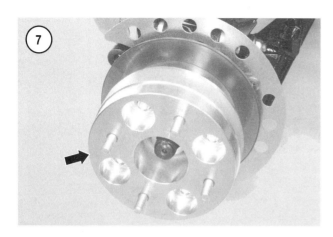

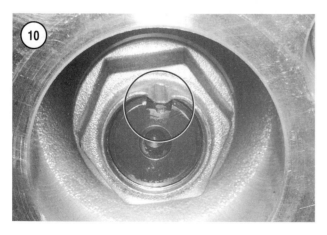

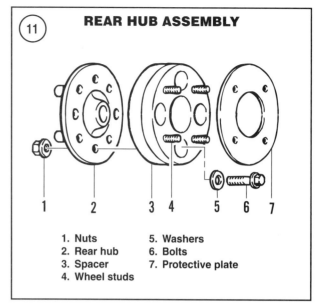

REAR HUB ASSEMBLY

1. Nuts
2. Rear hub
3. Spacer
4. Wheel studs
5. Washers
6. Bolts
7. Protective plate

7. Remove the wheel spacer/rear hub (**Figure 7**). If the rear hub is seized to the axle splines, remove the wheel spacer/ rear hub with a puller. Do not strike the wheel spacer, rear hub or brake disc.

8. Check the O-ring (A, **Figure 8**), seated next to the knuckle bearing.

9. Inspect as described in this section.

Installation

1. If removed, lubricate the O-ring (A, **Figure 8**) with lithium grease and seat it next to the knuckle bearing.

2. Wipe the knuckle seal (B, **Figure 8**) with a dry rag to remove the old grease. Relubricate the seal lip with lithium grease.

3. Clean and dry the axle threads (C, **Figure 8**).

4. Clean the brake disc with brake cleaner and allow to dry.

5. Slide the wheel spacer/rear hub (**Figure 7**) onto the axle and seat the rear hub against the knuckle.

NOTE
*Do not lubricate the axle or rear hub nut threads with oil or any lubricant. The threads must be clean and dry when tightened to specification (**Table 4**).*

6. Install a new rear hub nut and tighten finger-tight.

7. Mount a long metal bar across two of the hub studs and secure in place with two lug nuts (**Figure 9**). The metal bar must be long enough to contact the ground and lock the hub in place.

8. Tighten the rear hub nut to 350 N•m (255 ft.-lb.). Then use a punch and stake a portion of the nut shoulder into the notch in the axle (**Figure 10**).

9. Install the rear brake caliper (Chapter Fifteen).

10. Install the protective plate (**Figure 3**).

11. Install the rear wheel as described in this chapter.

13

Inspection

The rear hub is mounted on the wheel spacer and the brake disc is mounted on the rear hub. The wheel studs are installed into the wheel spacer. Refer to **Figure 11**.

1. If necessary, service the brake disc (Chapter Fifteen).
2. Inspect the rear hub and wheel spacer (**Figure 12**) for damage.
3. Inspect the rear hub nuts for looseness.
4. Inspect the rear wheel studs for damage and replace if necessary.
5. To service the rear hub and wheel spacer, perform the following:

    a. Remove the bolts (A, **Figure 13**) and the brake disc (B). These bolts are secured with a threadlocking compound and may be difficult to remove. Replace the bolts if the hex portion is damaged.

    b. Remove the nuts, bolts and washers securing the rear hub to the wheel spacer.

    c. Replace the damaged part(s).

    d. Clean and dry all parts. Replace damaged fasteners.

    e. Install the rear hub onto the wheel spacer and secure with the bolts, washers and nuts as shown in **Figure 11**. Tighten the nuts in a crossing pattern to 100 N•m (74 ft.-lb.).

    f. Install the brake disc onto the hub so the side with the chamfered mounting bolt holes faces out. Apply a medium-strength threadlocking compound onto the brake disc mounting bolts and tighten to 30 N•m (22 ft.-lb.).

REAR KNUCKLE

Removal

1. Remove the rear hub as described in this chapter.
2A. On models without cast wheels, remove the bolts (A, **Figure 14**) and the brake disc guard (B).
2B. On models with cast wheels, remove the nuts, plate, bolts and brake disc guard (B, **Figure 14**, typical).
3. Remove the nuts (A, **Figure 15**), washers and bolts securing the upper and lower arms to the rear knuckle.
4. Slide the rear knuckle out to dislodge and remove the O-ring (**Figure 16**).
5. Remove the rear knuckle (B, **Figure 15**). Account for the seal caps (A, **Figure 17**) if they fell off during removal.
6. Clean and inspect as described in this section.

Installation

1. Lubricate the collars (B, **Figure 17**) with lithium grease and slide into the rear knuckle.
2. Lubricate the inside of the seal caps (A, **Figure 17**) with lithium grease and install onto the rear knuckle.

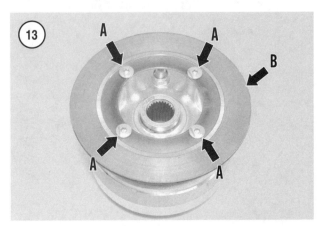

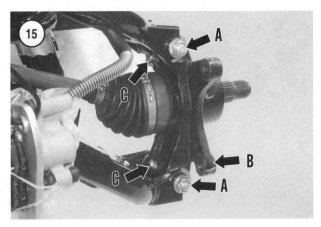

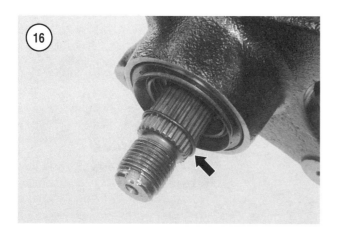

The left-hand and right-hand rear knuckles can be identified by the LH and RH (Figure 18) cast marks.

3. Lubricate the lips on both rear knuckle seals (C, **Figure 17**) with lithium grease.

4. Install the rear knuckle over the axle with the LH or RH (**Figure 18**) cast marks at the bottom. The grease nipples on the backside of the knuckle will face toward the rear of the vehicle (C, **Figure 15**).

5. Position the upper and lower arms over the rear knuckle, making sure the seal caps do not fall off.

6. Lubricate the upper and lower arm mounting bolt shoulders with lithium grease. Do not lubricate the bolt threads. Then install a washer on each bolt.

7. Install the upper and lower arm mounting bolts from the front side. Then install the washers and nuts. Finger-tighten the nuts until all parts are assembled.

8. Tighten the upper and lower control arm mounting nuts (A, **Figure 15**) at the rear knuckle to 45 N•m (33 ft.-lb.).

9. Lubricate the O-ring (**Figure 16**) with lithium grease, then slide it over the axle and seat it next to the knuckle bearing.

10A. On models without cast wheels, install the brake disc guard (B, **Figure 14**, typical) and tighten the bolts (A) to 7 N•m (62 in.-lb.).

10B. On models with cast wheels, install the brake disc guard (B, **Figure 14**) and tighten the bolts (A) to 7 N•m (62 in.-lb.). Then install the plate on the backside of the knuckle and tighten the nuts to 7 N•m (62 in.-lb.).

11. Install the rear hub as described in this chapter.

Cleaning/Inspection

Replace worn or damaged parts as described in this section.

1. Remove the seal caps and collars and clean in solvent. If rust or dirt is evident inside the knuckle bores, the seal caps are probably worn or damaged.

2. Clean the knuckle mounting bores with contact cleaner. Then clean the knuckle with a solvent soaked rag. Do not submerge the knuckle seals and bearings in solvent.

3. Wipe the seal lips with a clean, dry rag.

4. Inspect the rear knuckle for cracks and other damage.

5. Tighten the grease nipples if loose.

6. Inspect the rubber seal (A, **Figure 19**) in the seal caps for deterioration and other damage. Then fit the seal caps on the knuckle. The seal caps must fit tightly on the knuckle to prevent debris from entering past them.

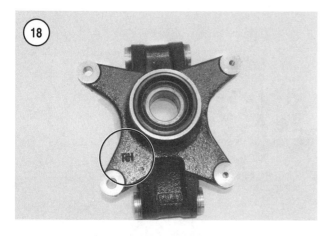

7. Inspect the collars (B, **Figure 19**) for corrosion, cracks and other damage. Then inspect the bores (C, **Figure 19**) in the knuckle for corrosion and clean if necessary. Install the collars into the knuckle to make sure they rotate smoothly and do not bind.

8. Inspect the seals (A, **Figure 20**) for tearing, deterioration and other damage. If necessary, replace the seals as described in this section.

13

9. Turn each bearing inner race (B, **Figure 20**) and check for roughness or excessive play. If necessary, replace the bearings as described in this section. Note that a spacer is installed between the bearings.

Seal and Bearing
Removal/Installation

The knuckle uses two seals, two bearings and a spacer. Refer to *Service Methods* in Chapter One.

1. To help hold the knuckle during service, mount the knuckle onto a steel bar and secure the bar in a vise as shown in **Figure 21**.

> *NOTE*
> *The inner and outer seals are different. Identify the seals so that the new seals can be installed in their correct positions.*

2. Pry the seals from their bores with a tire iron (**Figure 22**) or similar tool. Make sure the tool does not contact the bore when removing the seals.

3. Mount a 30-mm collet onto a blind bearing puller. Insert the collet through the bearing and tighten it to lock against the backside of the bearing and not the spacer (**Figure 23**). Operate the puller and remove the bearing (**Figure 24**). Discard the bearing.

4. Remove the spacer (**Figure 25**).

5. Repeat Step 3 to remove the opposite bearing.

6. Clean the bearing bore of all corrosion. Then inspect for cracks and other damage.

7. Install the bearings as follows:

> *NOTE*
> *Install the outer bearing first.*

   a. Support the rear knuckle (A, **Figure 26**) in a press.

   b. Center the outer bearing into the bearing bore with its manufacturer's marks facing out. Install a bearing driver (B, **Figure 26**) on the bearing's outer race and press the outer bearing into the bore until it bottoms.

   c. Turn the bearing inner race by hand to make sure it turns smoothly.

8. Install the spacer (**Figure 25**).

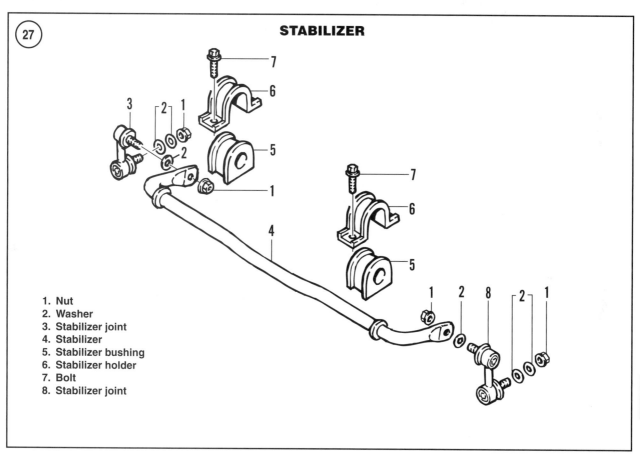

STABILIZER

1. Nut
2. Washer
3. Stabilizer joint
4. Stabilizer
5. Stabilizer bushing
6. Stabilizer holder
7. Bolt
8. Stabilizer joint

13

9. Repeat Step 7 to install the inner bearing.

NOTE
Refer to your reference notes made during removal when identifying the inner and outer seals. The inner seal has the extended lip that seats around the rear axle's outer joint.

10. Insert the outer seal into its bore with its flat side facing out (A, **Figure 20**). Then drive the seal into the bore with a suitable size socket or driver until the seal seats against the bearing. Lubricate the seal lip with lithium grease.

11. Repeat Step 10 to install the inner seal. Make sure not to damage the extended lip on this seal when installing it.

**STABILIZER
(2008-2009 MODELS)**

NOTE
The stabilizer was originally installed on 2008-2009 models and then removed under a free repair program sponsored by the manufacture. Refer to a dealership for additional information. If the stabilizer is mounted on the vehicle, service it as follows.

Removal/Inspection/Installation

Refer to **Figure 27**.

1. Remove the rear wheels as described in this chapter.

NOTE
The left and right side stabilizer joints are different. Identify them so they can be installed in their original position.

2. Remove the stabilizer joint from both lower control arms. Use a 14-mm wrench to hold the joint (**Figure 28**) so the nut can be loosened.

3. Remove the bolts securing the stabilizer holders and remove the stabilizer.

4. Clean and dry all parts. Replace damaged fasteners.

5. Inspect the stabilizer for bends, cracks and other damage.

6. Inspect the stabilizer joints. Pivot the joint in all directions, as well as vertically (**Figure 29**). Replace the joints if wear or looseness is evident.

7. Replace the stabilizer bushings if cracked or damaged.

8. Installation is the reverse of removal. Note the following:

   a. Finger-tighten the nuts and bolts until all parts are assembled. Note the position of the washers in **Figure 27** so they can be installed correctly.

   b. Tighten the stabilizer joint nuts to 60 N•m (44 ft.-lb.).

   c. Tighten the stabilizer holder bolts to 42 N•m (31 ft.-lb.).

REAR CONTROL ARMS

This section describes removal and installation of the upper and lower control arms. Each control arm can be removed independently of the other.

Removal/Installation

1. Remove the rear wheel as described in this chapter.

2. Each control arm is equipped with one washer (**Figure 30**). Identify the washer positions for each control arm as follows:

   a. Left side upper arm: A, **Figure 31**.

   b. Left side lower arm: B, **Figure 31**.

   c. Right side upper arm: A, **Figure 32**.

   d. Right side lower arm: B, **Figure 32**.

3. Remove the upper arm as follows:

   a. Disconnect the rear brake hose at the rear brake caliper (Chapter Fifteen). Then slide the brake hose out of the guides (A, **Figure 33**) on the upper arm. Cover the end of the hose to prevent brake fluid from leaking out.

   b. Remove the nut, bolt and washers (B, **Figure 33**) securing the upper arm to the rear knuckle.

   c. Remove the nuts and bolts (C, **Figure 33**) securing the upper arm to the frame and remove the upper arm (D).

4. Remove the lower arm as follows:

   a. Remove the lower arm protector mounting bolts and protector (**Figure 34**).

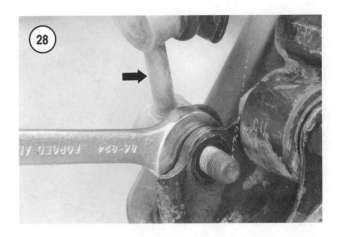

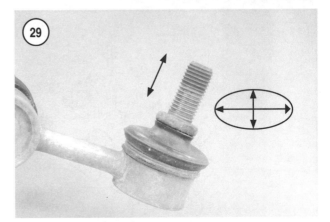

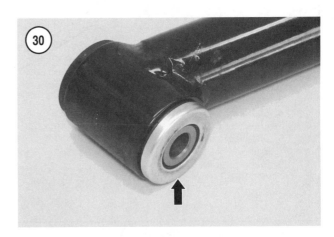

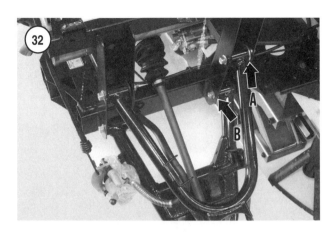

b. If so equipped, disconnect the stabilizer at the lower control arm as described in this chapter.

c. Remove the nut and bolt securing the shock absorber to the lower arm.

d. Remove the nut, bolt and washers securing the lower arm to the rear knuckle.

e. Remove the nuts and bolts (A, **Figure 35**) securing the lower arm to the frame and remove the lower arm (B).

5. Installation is the reverse of removal. Note the following:

a. Lubricate the control arm and lower shock absorber mounting bolt shoulders with lithium grease. Do not lubricate the mounting bolt and nut threads.

b. Position the washers (**Figure 30**) as described in Step 2.

c. Install all of the control arm-to-frame mounting bolts from the rear side of the control arm.

d. Install the control arm-to-rear knuckle mounting bolts from the front side of the control arm.

e. Finger-tighten the nuts until the upper and lower control arms are assembled onto the frame and rear knuckle.

f. Tighten the control arm mounting nuts to 45 N•m (33 ft.-lb.).

g. Install the lower shock absorber mounting bolt from the rear side and tighten the mounting nut to 45 N•m (33 ft.-lb.).

h. Tighten the lower arm protector mounting bolts to 7 N•m (62 in.-lb.).

i. If the upper control arm was removed, bleed the rear brake system (Chapter Fifteen). Make sure the brake hose is routed through the guides (A, **Figure 33**).

Inspection

1. Clean the control arms and all fasteners.

2. Inspect all welded joints and brackets on the control arms (**Figure 36**). Check for bending or other damage. If damaged, replace the control arm.

3. Inspect the pivot bushings (A, **Figure 37**). Inspect each bushing for play and damage. If necessary, replace damaged bushings with a press.

4. Inspect the pivot bolts, washers and nuts for damage.

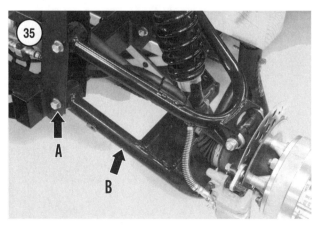

13

5. Inspect the washers (B, **Figure 37**) for cracks and other damage.

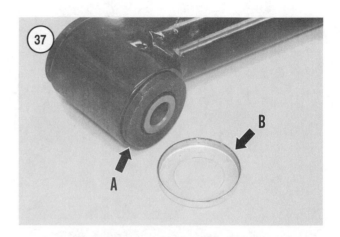

REAR SHOCK ABSORBERS

Vehicles were originally equipped with either oil damper shock absorbers (**Figure 38**) or gas-oil damper shock absorbers with a reservoir. Shock absorber service is limited to shock adjustment only. There are no replacement parts available from the manufacturer.

> *WARNING*
> *Do not attempt to disassemble the damper unit. On the gas-oil damper shock absorber, disassembly can release gas that is under pressure and cause injury.*

Adjustment
(Oil Damper Shock Absorbers)

Preload is the amount the spring is compressed from its free length. Preload is set with a five position cam-type adjuster (**Figure 39**) at the bottom of the shock. The least amount of spring preload is in the first position, while the most preload is in the fifth position (**Figure 40**). The standard setting is the second position. Set both shock absorbers to the same position by using a shock absorber spanner to rotate the adjuster (**Figure 41**).

Adjustment
(Gas-Oil Damper Shock Absorbers)

> *WARNING*
> *Always adjust both rear shock absorbers to the same compression, rebound and spring pre-load positions. Failure to do so may cause unstable handling and loss of control.*

Compression damping

> *CAUTION*
> *Do not turn the compression adjuster past the minimum or maximum adjustment positions or the adjuster may be damaged.*

Compression damping controls the shock absorber rate, after hitting a bump. This setting has no affect on the rebound rate of the shock.

The compression adjuster is mounted near the top of the shock reservoir (**Figure 42**). A screw type adjuster is used. Refer to **Table 3** for adjustment positions.

To set the adjuster to its standard setting, turn the adjuster clockwise until it stops (this is the full-hard position). Then turn it counterclockwise while counting the number of clicks listed in **Table 3**.

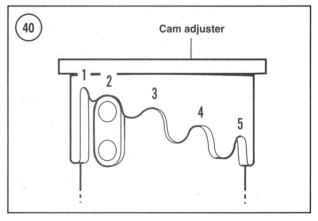

Cam adjuster

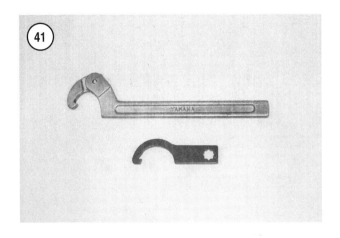

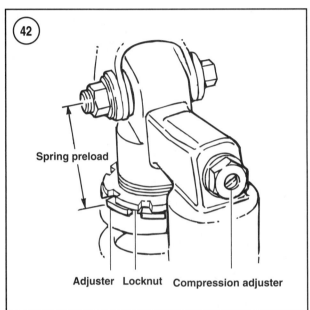

Spring preload

Adjuster Locknut Compression adjuster

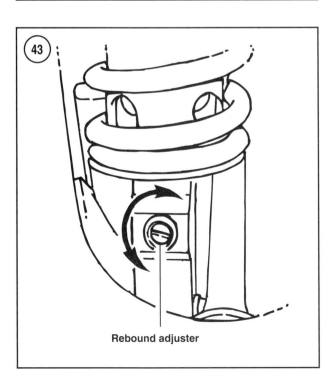

Rebound adjuster

To increase the compression damping, turn the adjuster clockwise. To decrease the compression damping, turn the adjuster counterclockwise.

NOTE
Make sure the compression adjuster is located in one of the detent positions and not in between any two settings.

Rebound damping

CAUTION
Do not turn the rebound adjuster past the minimum or maximum adjustment positions or the adjuster may be damaged.

The rebound damping adjustment affects the rate of shock absorber extension after it has been compressed. This adjustment has no affect on shock compression.

The rebound damping adjuster is mounted at the bottom of the shock absorber (**Figure 43**). A screw type adjuster is used. Refer to **Table 3** for adjustment positions.

For the standard setting, turn the adjuster clockwise until it stops (this is the full-hard position). Then turn it counterclockwise the number of clicks listed in **Table 3**.

To increase the rebound damping, turn the adjuster clockwise. To decrease the rebound damping, turn the adjuster counterclockwise.

NOTE
Make sure the rebound adjuster is located in one of the detent positions and not in between any two settings.

Spring preload

Preload is set with the adjuster and locknut at the top of the shock absorber (**Figure 42**). Preload is the amount the spring is compressed from its free length. By tightening the adjuster, spring preload is increased. By loosening the adjuster, spring preload is decreased.

1. Measure the distance between the center of the upper shock bolt to the top of the adjuster (**Figure 42**). This is the spring preload adjustment position. Compare the actual adjustment position with the specifications in **Table 3** to determine the approximate adjustment position. If adjustment is necessary, continue with Step 2.

2. Support the vehicle on a stand so the rear wheels are off the ground.

NOTE
Before adjusting the spring preload, clean the threads on the locknut, adjuster and shock body to prevent thread damage.

3. Loosen the adjuster locknut with a spanner wrench (**Figure 41**).

13

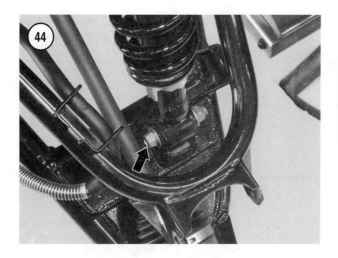

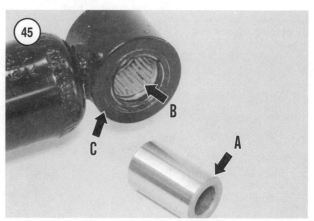

4. Turn the adjuster to the desired spring preload position, making sure to stay within the minimum and maximum positions listed in **Table 3**.

5. Tighten the locknut to 42 N•m (31 ft.-lb.).

Removal/Installation

1. Support the vehicle with both rear wheels off the ground.

2. Place wooden blocks underneath the rear wheels to prevent the lower arm from swinging down when the shock absorber mounting bolts are removed.

3. Remove the lower shock absorber nut and bolt (**Figure 44**) and allow the rear wheel to settle against the wooden blocks.

4. Remove the upper shock absorber nut and bolt and remove the shock absorber.

5. Perform *Inspection/Lubrication* in this section.

6. Install the shock absorber by reversing these removal steps. Note the following:

    a. Clean and dry the shock fasteners. Inspect and replace damaged fasteners.

    b. Install gas-oil damper shock absorbers with the reservoir positioned at the top and facing outward.

    c. Install the mounting bolts (**Figure 44**) from the rear side and tighten the mounting nuts to 45 N•m (33 ft.-lb.).

Inspection/Lubrication

Replacement parts for the shock absorber are not available from the manufacturer. If damaged, replace the shock absorber.

1. Inspect the shock absorber for gas or oil leaks.

2. Inspect the shock body for severe dents that can affect shock operation

3A. On oil damper shocks, make sure the upper spring seat is locked in place against the upper shock boss and spring.

3B. On gas-oil damper shocks, make sure the locknut is tightened against the adjuster.

4. Remove the collar (A, **Figure 45**) from the needle bearing and inspect it for rust and corrosion. Clean and dry the collar.

5. Clean and inspect the needle bearing (B, **Figure 45**). The rollers should be smooth and polished with no flat spots, burrs or other damage. Inspect the bearing cage for cracks or other damage. The collar should slide into the bearing with no interference.

6. Clean the collar, bearing and seals (C, **Figure 45**). Then lubricate the collar and needle bearing with lithium grease and install the collar into the bearing.

7. Inspect the bushing (**Figure 46**) for deterioration and damage. Check the bushing's bore and clean to remove any rust or corrosion. The rubber must be intact and the collar free of rust and corrosion.

Table 1 REAR SUSPENSION SPECIFICATIONS

Rear shock absorber	
Type	
5B41, 5B45, 5B48, 5B49, 5B4H, 5B4M, 5BAT and 5B4H	Oil damper
5B4B, 5B4E, 5B4P and 42SA	Gas-oil damper
Travel	
Oil damper shock	81.0 mm (3.19 in.)
Gas-oil damper shock	85.0 mm (3.35 in.)
Spring free length	
Oil damper shock	328.0 mm (12.91 in.)
Gas-oil damper shock	286.3 mm (11.27 in.)
Spring installed length	
Oil damper shock	273.2 mm (10.76 in.)
Gas-oil damper shock	235.0 mm (9.25 in.)
Spring rate	
K1	44.10 N/mm (251.81 lb./in.)
K2*	17.70 N/mm (672.07 lb./in.)
Rear suspension type	Double wishbone
Rear wheel travel	
2008 models	180 mm (7.1 in.)
2009 models	185 mm (7.3 in.)
2011-on models	185 mm (7.3 in.)

*Oil damper shock absorbers only.

Table 2 TIRE AND WHEEL SPECIFICATIONS*

Tire	
Manufacturer	MAXXIS
Model	
Front	M951Y
Rear	M952Y
Size	
Front	25 × 8.00-12 NHS
Rear	25 × 10.00-12 NHS
Tire pressure (cold)	
Front	63-77 kPa (9-11 psi)
Rear	91-105 kPa (13-15 psi)
Wheels	
Size	
Front	12 × 6.0 AT
Rear	12 × 7.5 AT
Runout (radial and lateral)	2.0 mm (0.08 in.)

* Tire specifications are for original equipment tires only. Aftermarket tires may have different specifications.

Table 3 REAR SHOCK ABSORBER ADJUSTMENT

Oil-damper shock absorbers	
Spring preload	
Minimum	1
Maximum	5
Standard	2
Gas-oil damper shock absorbers	
Compression dampening adjustment	
Minimum	12 clicks out
Maximum	2 clicks out
Standard	7 clicks out
Rebound dampening adjustment	
Minimum	20 clicks out
Maximum	3 clicks out
Standard	12 clicks out
Spring preload	
Minimum	63.5 mm (2.50 in.)
Maximum	78.5 mm (3.09 in.)
Standard	63.5 mm (2.50 in.)

13

Table 4 REAR SUSPENSION TORQUE SPECIFICATIONS

	N•m	in.-lb.	ft.-lb.
Brake disc guard mounting bolts	7	62	–
Brake disc mounting bolts[1]	30	–	22
Lower arm protector mounting bolts	7	62	–
Lower control arm mounting nuts	45	–	33
Lug nuts	55	–	41
Plate mounting nuts at rear knuckle[2]	7	62	–
Rear hub nut	350	–	255
Rear hub-to-wheel spacer nuts	100	–	74
Rear shock absorber mounting bolts	45	–	33
Rear shock spring adjuster locknut[3]	42	–	31
Stabilizer holder bolts	42	–	31
Stabilizer joint nuts	60	–	44
Upper control arm mounting nuts	45	–	33

1. Refer to text.
2. Models with cast wheels.
3. Gas-oil damper shock absorber.

CHAPTER FOURTEEN

REAR AXLES AND FINAL DRIVE

This chapter covers the rear axles, final drive unit and rear drive shaft.

Read *Safety* and *Service Methods* in Chapter One before servicing the vehicle in this chapter.

Table 1 and **Table 2** are at the end of the chapter.

REAR AXLE

Removal

1. Clean the final drive and rear axles to prevent dirt from entering the final drive when removing the rear axle.
2. Drain the final drive oil (Chapter Three).
3. Remove the bolts and the boot guards.
4. Remove the rear knuckle (Chapter Thirteen).
5. Loosen the upper and lower arm mounting nuts.
6. Remove the lower shock absorber mounting nut (A, **Figure 1**) and bolt (B). Refer to Chapter Thirteen.
7. Position the upper and lower arms away from the rear axle.
8. Grab the rear axle with both hands (**Figure 2**) and pull the axle (not the outboard joint) sharply to disconnect it from the final drive. The circlip on the inboard side of the rear axle will cause some resistance until it compresses and allows the axle to be removed. The circlip will remain on the axle as it is removed from the final drive unless it is broken and damaged.
9. Inspect the rear axle as described in this section.

Installation

1. Make sure the inboard and outboard joint seal mating surfaces are clean.
2. Wipe the rear axle oil seal (**Figure 3**) with a rag to remove all old grease. Then relubricate the seal lip with lithium grease.

NOTE
If the rear axle oil seal was leaking or appears damaged, replace it as described in this section.

3. Check the circlip groove on the inboard joint for any burrs or damage that would prevent the circlip from closing when installing the axle.

NOTE
The circlip used on the inboard joint is smaller than the axle outside diameter and will spread from its original size when installed over the axle. Because the circlip does not return to its original shape, it is larger and difficult to compress when trying to install the axle into the final drive.

4. Install a new circlip into the groove on the inboard joint axle (A, **Figure 4**). Pack the groove and circlip with lithium

centered in its groove. Centering the circlip helps it to compress easier when installing the axle.

5. Lubricate the inboard axle splines (B, **Figure 4**) with lithium grease.

6. Align the inboard axle splines with the final drive and push the axle straight into the final drive splines. If the axle does not enter the final drive, check the circlip for damage and replace if necessary. Repeat until the circlip compresses as it passes through the final drive splines and seats inside the final drive unit. Then lightly pull on the axle to make sure the circlip has expanded and the axle is locked in place.

7. Clean the lower shock absorber mounting bolt and nut, then lubricate the bolt shoulder with lithium grease. The threads on the bolts and nut must be dry when tightening to specification. Position the lower shock mount on the lower arm and install the mounting bolt (B, **Figure 1**) through the rear side. Install the lower shock absorber mounting nut and tighten to 45 N•m (33 ft.-lb.).

8. Tighten the upper arm mounting nuts to 45 N•m (33 ft.-lb.).

9. Tighten the lower arm mounting nuts to 45 N•m (33 ft.-lb.).

10. Install the rear knuckle (Chapter Thirteen).

11. Install the boot guard and tighten its mounting bolts to 7 N•m (62 in.-lb.).

12. Refill the final drive oil (Chapter Three).

NOTE
If the rear axle was rebuilt, make several test drives while stopping to check the axle for any grease that may have leaked out of the boots. Wipe off the axle and then repeat the checks to make sure no more grease leaks out. Usually, grease will leak one or two times and then stop after the boots are completely seated. If grease continues to leak out, make sure both ends of the boots are properly seated and the clamps are tight.

Inspection

Refer to **Figure 5** and **Figure 6**.

1. Clean the axles, boots and splines. Do not submerge the axle boots in solvent. The CV joints (inside the boots) are packed with grease.

2. Inspect the axle for stripped or damaged threads.

3. Inspect for worn, distorted and broken splines on both sides of the axle.

4. Inspect the bearing and seal surfaces for scoring, galling, corrosion and other damage. If damage is evident, inspect the matching bearing in the final drive unit or rear knuckle.

NOTE
The axle boots encounter much abuse. Damaged boots allow dirt, mud and moisture to enter the boot, contaminate the grease and damage the bearing.

5. Inspect the boots for tearing, cracks and other damage. Check that the clamps are tight and have not slipped off of the end of the boot. A loose or torn boot will allow dirt and moisture to enter the joint(s). If necessary, replace damaged boots as described in this section.

6. Pivot each end of the axle and check for roughness or play in the joint. If roughness is evident, disassemble the axle and inspect the parts as described in this section. If roughness or play remains after cleaning and lubrication, replace the worn parts.

7. Check the axle for straightness. Replace the axle if bent. A bent axle can damage the bearings in the rear knuckle and final drive unit and cause vibration.

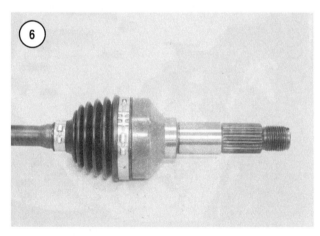

8. Refer to *Rear Axle Inspection* in *Disassembly/Assembly* in this section to inspect the axle after disassembly.

Rear Axle Oil Seal Removal/Installation

With the rear axle removed, the oil seal (**Figure 3**) can be replaced without removing the final drive unit from the frame.

1. Clean the final drive unit and the area around the rear axle. Also clean the areas above the final drive unit to prevent dirt from falling into the unit when the axle is removed.

2. Remove the rear axle as described in this section.

3. Pry the seal out of the final drive unit. If the seal is tight, pry at different points around the seal until the seal begins to move. Make sure the end of the pry tool does not gouge or score the seal bore surface. Refer to *Service Methods* in Chapter One.

4. Clean the seal bore and check it for damage.

5. Position the new seal in the seal bore with its closed side facing out and tap around the edge of the seal using a hammer and wooden block to drive it into the bore. Make sure not to damage the part of the seal that contacts the inboard joint. Continue until the edge of the seal is flush with the seal bore surface. Check that the edge of the seal seats squarely in the bore (**Figure 3**).

6. Lubricate the seal lip with lithium grease.

7. Install the rear axle as described in this section.

Disassembly/Assembly

Refer to **Figure 7**.

Before servicing the rear axle, note the following:

1. The inboard and outboard joints cannot be rebuilt. The inboard joint can be disassembled for cleaning and inspection. The outboard joint cannot be disassembled, though it can be removed from the axle and partially cleaned for inspection purposes.

2. If removing both the inboard and outboard joint assemblies from the axle, remove the inboard joint first. During assembly, install the outboard joint first.

3. The boots and clamps are not identical in shape or size. Keep the clamps with their respective boots and note the boot locations in the ridges on the joints and shaft.

4. Install new boot clamps during assembly.

5. Different axle repair kits are available, depending on the parts and service required during service. Refer to a dealership for more information.

6. Install new snap rings and stopper rings during assembly.

7. Because the inboard and outboard joints are different, separate procedures are provided.

Inboard joint

Refer to **Figure 7** and A, **Figure 8**.

1. Note the direction the clamps face on the rear axle so the new clamps can be installed facing the original direction. Pry the locking clips away from the lock, then pull and release the lock to loosen the clamp. Repeat for the other clamp. Refer to **Figure 9**.

2. Slide the boot off the inboard joint and onto the rear axle.

3. Remove some of the grease from inside the inboard joint, then remove the stopper ring (**Figure 10**) from the groove in the inboard joint.

4. Pull the rear axle and bearing out of the inboard joint (**Figure 11**).

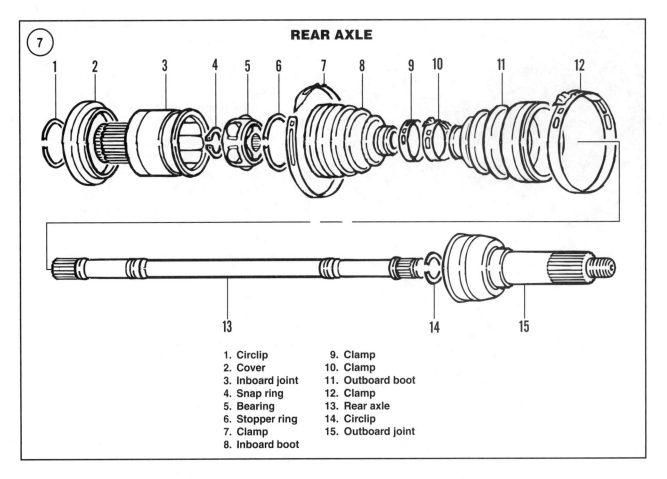

REAR AXLE

1. Circlip
2. Cover
3. Inboard joint
4. Snap ring
5. Bearing
6. Stopper ring
7. Clamp
8. Inboard boot
9. Clamp
10. Clamp
11. Outboard boot
12. Clamp
13. Rear axle
14. Circlip
15. Outboard joint

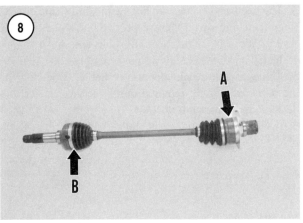

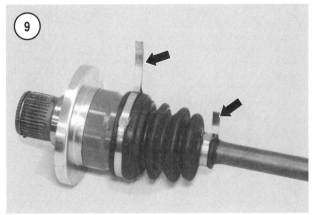

5. Remove the snap ring (**Figure 12**) and slide off the bearing assembly. Be careful not to drop any of the steel balls from the bearing cage.

NOTE
*If the bearing is tight, use a two-jaw puller to remove the bearing (**Figure 13**).*

6. Slide the boot and clamps off the rear axle. Discard the clamps as they should not be reused.
7. Clean and inspect the axle parts as described in this section.
8. If the outboard joint was also removed, install it first as described in this section.

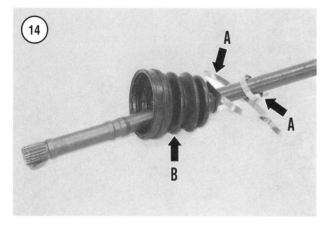

NOTE
The inboard boot (A, Figure 8) is shorter and smaller than the outboard boot (B).

9. Install two new clamps (A, **Figure 14**) and the boot (B) onto the rear axle. Face the clamps in their original directions as noted during disassembly.

10. Pack the inboard boot with 65 g (2.3 oz.) of molybdenum disulfide grease.

11. Slide a new stopper ring (**Figure 10**) onto the rear axle.

12. Install the bearing onto the rear axle with the small end of the bearing going on first (**Figure 15**). Push the bearing onto the axle until it stops.

13. Install a new snap ring into the groove in the rear axle (**Figure 16**) with the flat side of the snap ring facing out. Make sure the snap ring seats in the groove completely.

14. Apply a liberal amount of grease to the bearing assembly. Work the grease between the balls, race and case. Check for voids and fill them with grease.

15. Lubricate the inboard joint inner surface with grease.

16. Install the inboard joint into the bearing assembly by aligning the balls with the joint grooves. Then install the stopper ring into the groove in the inboard joint (**Figure 17**). Make sure the stopper ring seats in the groove completely.

17. After the stopper ring is in place, fill the inboard joint cavity behind the bearing assembly with grease (**Figure 18**).

14

18. Seat the inboard boot onto the inboard joint and axle boot ridges. Make sure the boot is not twisted.

19. Move the clamps onto the boot shoulders, then recheck that the boot is still positioned on the ridges. When the boot and clamps are correctly positioned and the boot is not twisted, bend down the lock on one of the boot clamps until it contacts the clamp. Then bend the locking clips tightly over the lock (**Figure 19**) and tap them flat with a plastic hammer. Repeat for the opposite clamp.

20. Hold the axle and pivot the joint to check its operation. The joint should move without any binding or roughness.

Outboard joint

Refer to **Figure 7** and B, **Figure 8**.

> *NOTE*
> *A boot band installing tool ([A, **Figure 20**] Yamaha part No. YM-01527 or equivalent) is required to install the outboard boot bands (B).*

1. Note the direction the clamps face on the rear axle so the new clamps can be installed facing the original direction.

2. Cut the upper clamp lock across its top with a cut-off wheel mounted in a rotary grinding tool at the point shown in **Figure 21**. Do not cut all the way through the clamp. Then pry the clamp up and disconnect the clamp (**Figure 22**). Repeat for the other clamp. Discard the clamps.

3. Slide the boot off the outboard joint and onto the rear axle.

> *NOTE*
> *The outboard joint is secured to the rear axle with a circlip (14, **Figure 7**).*

4. Secure the rear axle in a vise with soft jaws. Then tap the outboard joint with a plastic hammer (**Figure 23**) to remove it from the axle. Refer to A, **Figure 24**. As the outboard joint is driven outward, the circlip will compress as the joint passes over it.

5. Remove the circlip (B, **Figure 24**) from the rear axle groove and discard it.

6. Slide the boot off the rear axle.

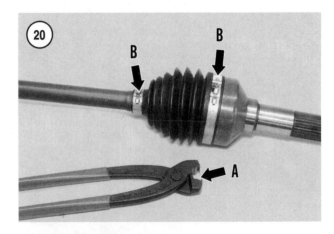

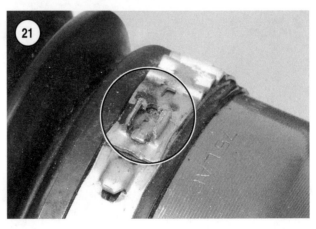

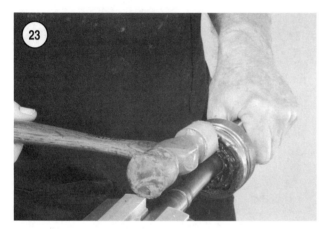

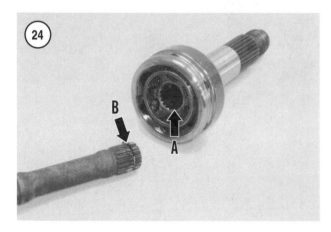

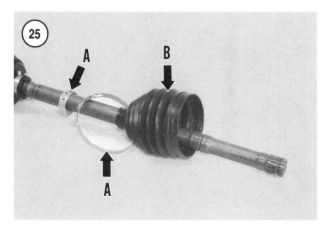

7. Clean and inspect the axle parts as described in this section.

8. If the inboard joint was also removed, install the outboard joint first.

NOTE
The outboard boot is higher and larger than the inboard boot.

9. Install two new clamps (A, **Figure 25**) and the boot (B) onto the rear axle (**Figure 25**). Face the clamps in their original directions as noted during disassembly.

10. Pack the outboard boot with 55 g (1.9 oz.) of molybdenum disulfide grease.

11. Install a new circlip (B, **Figure 24**) into the rear axle groove.

NOTE
*Refer to **Outboard Joint** in **Front Axles** in Chapter Twelve for infomration on how to fabricate a wooden clamp that can be used to hold the outboard joint when installing the axle and circlip.*

12. Compress the circlip and install the rear axle into the outboard joint as follows:

   a. Secure the outboard joint in a vise using the wooden clamps and with the bearing side facing up (**Figure 26**).

   b. Slip the rear axle into the outboard joint until the circlip contacts the joint as shown in **Figure 27**.

CAUTION
Do not drive the rear axle into the outboard joint to compress the circlip. If the circlip does not immediately compress, it may damage the axle and/or the rear joint splines.

   c. Tilt the rear axle to seat the lower side of circlip into the joint, then use a screwdriver to push and compress the upper side of the circlip into the outboard joint (**Figure 28**).

   d. When the circlip is compressed inside the joint, push the rear axle down until the circlip expands and locks inside the joint. Refer to **Figure 29**.

14

e. Remove the rear axle and outboard joint from the vise. Then pull on the parts to make sure the circlip is locked inside the outboard joint and the parts do not separate.

13. Pack the outboard joint cavity next to the bearing assembly with grease (**Figure 30**).

14. Seat the inboard boot onto the inboard joint and axle shoulders. Make sure the boot is not twisted.

15. Move the clamps onto the boot shoulders, then recheck that the boot is still positioned on the shoulders. When the boot and clamps are correctly positioned and the boot is not twisted, lock the clamp with the boot band installing tool (**Figure 31**). Repeat for the opposite clamp. Refer to **Figure 32**.

16. Hold the axle and pivot the joint to check its operation. The joint should move without any binding or roughness.

17. Install the inboard joint onto the axle if removed.

Rear axle inspection

Replace the axle if damaged. The axle can be replaced separately.

1. Clean and dry the axle.
2. Check the axle splines for damage.
3. Check the circlip grooves for damage.
4. Check the axle for bending.

Inboard joint inspection

Replace parts that show excessive wear or damage as described in this section.

1. Clean the inboard joint bearing (A, **Figure 33**) and housing (B).

2. Inspect the steel balls, bearing cage and bearing race (A, **Figure 33**) for excessive wear or damage.

3. Check the bearing race inner splines for cracks and other damage.

4. Inspect the inboard joint ball guides for excessive wear, scoring or other damage.

5. Inspect the inboard joint stopper ring groove for wear or damage.

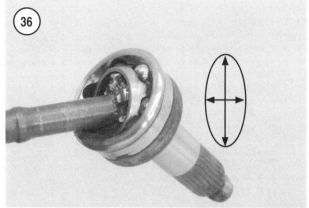

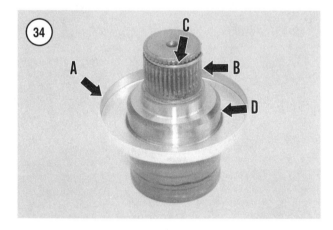

6. Inspect the dust cover (A, **Figure 34**) for bending or other damage.

7. Inspect the inboard joint housing for cracks and other damage.

8. Inspect the inboard joint splines (B, **Figure 34**) and circlip groove (C) for cracks and other damage.

9. Inspect the inboard joint outer bearing surfaces (D, **Figure 34**) for scoring, cracks and other damage.

Outboard joint inspection

The outboard joint cannot be disassembled. If damaged, replace it as an assembly.

1. Do not clean the outboard joint (**Figure 35**) in solvent. Because the unit cannot be disassembled, the solvent will thin/contaminate the grease behind the bearing, making it difficult to thoroughly remove all grease residue and relubricate the outboard joint bearing. If the unit is contaminated with water, mud or dirt, replace it as an assembly. Use a clean rag to remove the grease from the outside of the bearing so the bearing can be inspected.

2. With the circlip removed from the rear axle, insert the rear axle into the outboard joint. Move the outboard joint axle through its range of motion and check for excessive play, roughness or damage (**Figure 36**).

3. Remove the rear axle. Wipe off the outboard joint bearing (**Figure 35**) and inspect it for cracks, scoring and other damage.

4. Inspect the outboard joint outer bearing surfaces (A, **Figure 37**) for scoring, cracks and other damage.

5. Inspect the outboard joint housing for cracks and other damage.

6. Inspect the inner and outer outboard joint splines (B, **Figure 37**) and threads (C) for cracks and other damage.

7. Check the mating axle splines (D, **Figure 37**) and circlip groove for damage.

FINAL DRIVE UNIT

Removal

1. Remove the rear skid plate (Chapter Sixteen).
2. Remove the rear axles as described in this chapter.

14

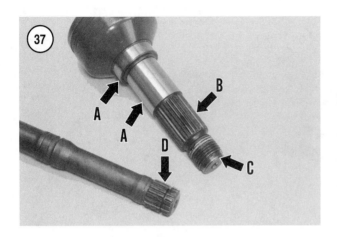

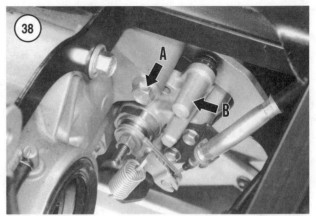

3. Remove the rear lower control arms (Chapter Thirteen).

4. Remove the rear exhaust pipe and muffler (Chapter Four). The front exhaust pipe assembly mounted on the cylinder head does not require removal.

5. Release the parking brake. Then remove the parking brake housing mounting bolts (A, **Figure 38**) and allow the housing (B) to hang down through the frame. Do not disconnect the parking brake cable unless the housing is going to be removed from the vehicle.

6. Disconnect the breather hose (A, **Figure 39**) at the final drive unit.

7. Remove the final drive unit mounting bolt nuts and washers from the left side of the unit.

8. Support the final drive assembly and remove the two mounting bolts and washers (B, **Figure 39**) from the right side.

NOTE
The drive shaft is under spring tension at the engine. Have an assistant hold the drive shaft and move it forward under spring tension while the final drive is moved rearward to disconnect it from the drive shaft.

9. Pull the final drive assembly rearward to disconnect it from the drive shaft. The parking brake disc will stay attached to the final drive unit. After disconnecting the final drive unit from the drive shaft, lower and remove the final drive unit from the bottom side of the frame.

10. Pull the drive shaft (**Figure 40**) rearward to disconnect and remove it from the engine. Account for the spring (**Figure 41**) at the front of the drive shaft and the rubber damper (**Figure 42**) at the rear of the drive shaft.

11. Service the final drive unit as described in this section.

12. Service the drive shaft as described in this chapter.

Installation

1. Lubricate the drive shaft splines and the coupling gear splines on the final drive and engine (**Figure 43**) with lithium grease.

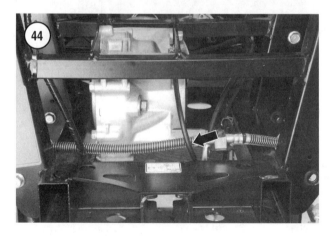

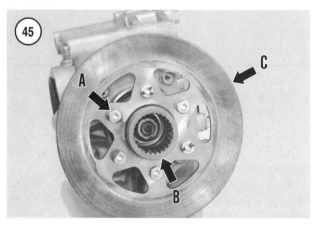

2. Clean the parking brake disc with brake cleaner and allow to dry.

3. Slide the boots over both ends of the drive shaft to seat them in place.

4. Install the spring (**Figure 41**) into the front of the drive shaft and the rubber damper (**Figure 42**) into the rear of the drive shaft.

5. Install the drive shaft (spring end) into the coupling gear at the engine.

NOTE
Have an assistant hold the drive shaft in place
and push it against the coupling gear.

6. Install the final drive unit into the frame while inserting the drive shaft into the coupling gear at the final drive unit. Make sure the rubber damper did not fall off the rear end of the drive shaft.

7. Install the bolts and washers (B, **Figure 39**) through the final drive unit from the right side. Then install the washers and nuts. Hold the bolts and tighten the nuts to 70 N•m (52 ft.-lb.).

8. Reconnect the breather hose (A, **Figure 39**) at the final drive unit. Make sure the breather hose is routed behind the brake line (**Figure 44**).

9. Reinstall the parking brake housing over the brake disc. Install the parking brake housing mounting bolts (A, **Figure 38**) and tighten to 40 N•m (30 ft.-lb.). Apply the parking brake, making sure it locks the disc.

10. Install the rear exhaust pipe and muffler (Chapter Four).

11. Install the rear lower arms (Chapter Thirteen).

12. Install the rear axles as described in this chapter.

13. Install the rear skid plate (Chapter Sixteen).

Preliminary Inspection

If the final drive unit is in good condition, use the following procedure to inspect the parts.

1. Plug the axle openings and clean the final drive unit.

2. Inspect the housing for cracks, oil leaks and other damage. Replace damaged oil seals as described in this section.

3. Check the parking brake disc mounting nuts (A, **Figure 45**) for looseness. If loose, hold the bolts and tighten the nuts to 10 N•m (88 in.-lb.).

4. Turn the coupling gear (B, **Figure 45**) to check the ring and pinion gears for roughness, noise, play and binding. The bearings should turn smoothly and quietly. If damage or excessive play is noted, disassemble the final drive unit as described in this section to isolate the damaged part(s).

Disassembly

Refer to **Figure 46**.

14

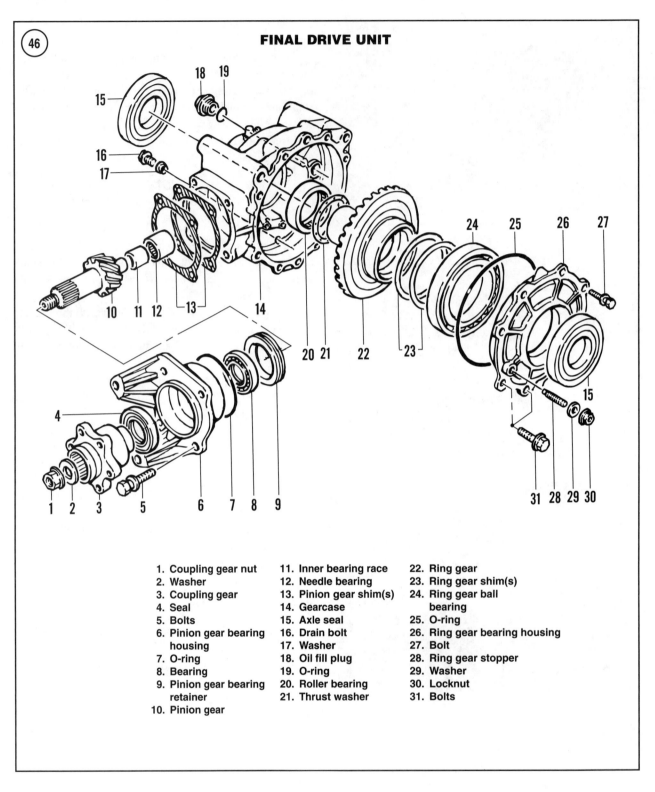

FINAL DRIVE UNIT

1. Coupling gear nut
2. Washer
3. Coupling gear
4. Seal
5. Bolts
6. Pinion gear bearing
   housing
7. O-ring
8. Bearing
9. Pinion gear bearing
   retainer
10. Pinion gear

11. Inner bearing race
12. Needle bearing
13. Pinion gear shim(s)
14. Gearcase
15. Axle seal
16. Drain bolt
17. Washer
18. Oil fill plug
19. O-ring
20. Roller bearing
21. Thrust washer

22. Ring gear
23. Ring gear shim(s)
24. Ring gear ball
    bearing
25. O-ring
26. Ring gear bearing housing
27. Bolt
28. Ring gear stopper
29. Washer
30. Locknut
31. Bolts

NOTE
*The Yamaha middle gear bearing retainer wrench (part No. YM-04128 [**Figure 47**]) is required when removing and installing the pinion gear bearing retainer (9, **Figure 46**). The other items shown in **Figure 47** are used to hold final drive unit components during service and are described in the service procedure. A hydraulic press and suitable adapt-*

ers are also required to replace the pinion gear and ring gear bearings.

1. Mark the parking brake disc's (C, **Figure 45**) outer side so it can be installed facing its original direction. Remove the nuts, bolts and the parking brake disc.
2. Remove the bolts (**Figure 48**) securing the pinion gear bearing housing to the final drive unit. Then remove the housing (A, **Figure 49**) and the pinion gear shims (B).

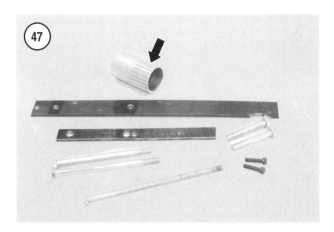

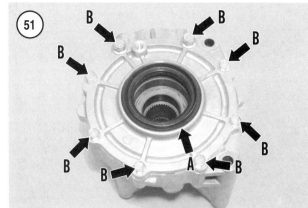

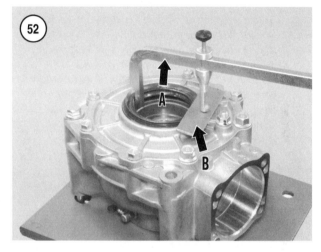

Because of the O-ring used on the housing, it may be necessary to tap the housing off with a plastic hammer. Remove and discard the O-ring (C, **Figure 49**).

3. Refer to *Coupling Gear, Pinion Gear and Seal Removal/Installation* in this section to service the pinion gear and bearing housing assembly.

4. Remove the locknut (A, **Figure 50**) and the ring gear stopper (B) with a 3-mm Allen wrench. Because sealer is applied to the stopper threads, the stopper will turn with some resistance when being removed.

5. Support the final drive unit and remove the rear axle seals (A, **Figure 51**), making sure not to scratch the seal bore with the pry tool. Refer to *Service Methods* in Chapter one. If using a seal removal tool (A, **Figure 52**, typical), make sure to support it (B) so that it does not damage the housing.

6. Remove the ring gear bearing housing retaining bolts (B, **Figure 51**) in several steps in a crossing pattern.

7. Insert a pry tool in the gap between the ring gear bearing housing and gearcase (**Figure 53**) and pry the bearing housing (A, **Figure 54**) away from the gearcase. Remove the O-ring (B, **Figure 54**).

8. Remove the ring gear shims (A, **Figure 55**) and ring gear (B).

9. Remove the thrust washer (A, **Figure 56**) from the opposite side of the ring gear.

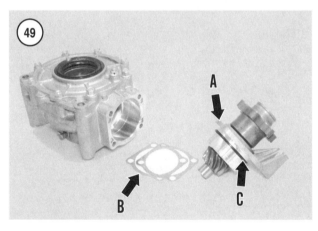

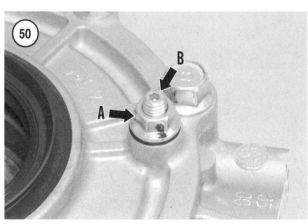

14

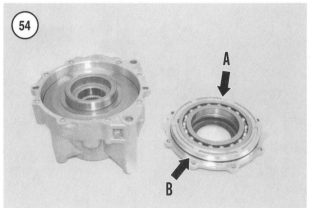

NOTE

Note the number marked on the ring gear. Record this number and indicate if it is positive or negative. This number is required when shimming the final drive unit. The number may be faint and often is removed completely when the parts are cleaned. After cleaning the ring gear, mark it again with the same number. If the number is not visible or is removed during cleaning, consult a dealership.

Coupling Gear, Pinion Gear and Seal Removal/Installation

This section services the coupling gear (3, **Figure 46**), pinion gear (10) and seal (4).

1. Remove the coupling gear as follows:
   a. Bolt a flat metal bar across the coupling gear using two bolts and nuts as shown in **Figure 57**. If necessary, grind a notch in the metal bar so that it can be moved closer to the coupling gear to provide more room to drill mounting holes through the bar.
   b. Mount the metal bar with the coupling gear in a vise to prevent the coupling gear from turning and loosen the coupling gear nut. Refer to **Figure 58**.
   c. Remove the coupling gear from the metal bar. Then remove the coupling gear nut (A, **Figure 59**), washer (B) and coupling gear (C) from the bearing housing.

2. Support the bearing housing in a press and press the pinion gear out of the housing as shown in **Figure 60**.

3. Pry the seal out of the housing as shown in **Figure 61**, making sure not to scratch the seal bore.

4. Clean and inspect the parts as described in this section.

5. If necessary, replace the pinion gear bearings and bearing race as described in this section.

6. Install a new seal (4, **Figure 46**) as follows:
   a. Lubricate the seal's lip with lithium grease.
   b. Place the seal (**Figure 62**) in its bore with its closed side facing out and drive the seal into the bore until it bottoms.

7. Install the pinion gear as follows:
   a. Support the bearing housing (A, **Figure 63**) in a press using a piece of pipe as shown in B, **Figure 63**.

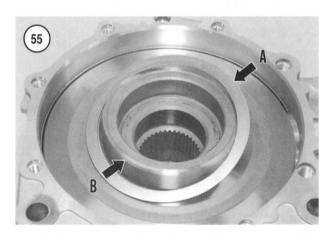

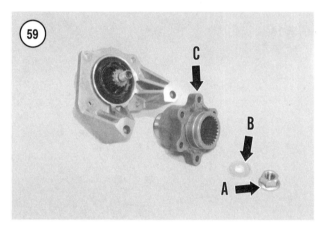

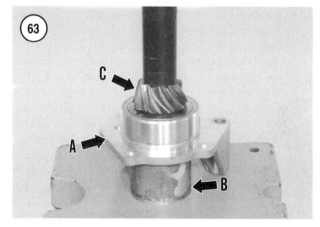

b. Press the pinion gear into the bearing until it bottoms. Refer to C, **Figure 63**.

c. Turn the pinion gear to make sure it turns smoothly.

8. Install the coupling gear as follows:

   a. Lubricate the coupling gear (C, **Figure 59**) shoulder with lithium grease and install it over the pinion gear by aligning the splines on both gears. Turn the coupling gear to make sure it seats flush against the seal lip.

   b. Install the washer (B, **Figure 59**) and coupling gear nut (A) and tighten finger-tight.

   c. Support the coupling gear with the same metal bar (**Figure 64**) used during disassembly and tighten the coupling gear nut to 80 N•m (59 ft.-lb.).

   d. Remove the coupling gear from the metal bar and turn it to make sure the pinion gear turns smoothly.

Inspection

1. Clean and dry all components.

2. Inspect the teeth on the ring gear (22, **Figure 46**) and pinion gear (10). If damage or uneven wear is evident on either part, replace the ring gear and pinion gear as a set. These parts are not available separately.

3. Inspect the bearings that support the ring gear as follows:

   a. Inspect the roller bearing (20, **Figure 46**). The rollers should be smooth and polished with no flat spots,

14

burrs or other damage. Inspect the bearing cage for cracks or other damage. Replace the bearing if necessary as described in this section.

b. Inspect the ring gear ball bearing (24, **Figure 46**) for roughness, pitting, galling and play. Also inspect the bearing for bluing, cracks and other damage.

c. Lubricate the bearings with gear oil. Then insert the ring gear into each bearing. Turn the ring gear and check for roughness, noise or excessive play. Recheck the bearings without the ring gear by turning the bearings

d. If damage is evident, replace the bearings as described in this section.

4. Inspect the bearings that support the pinion gear:

a. Inspect the needle bearing (12, **Figure 46**). The rollers should be smooth and polished with no flat spots, burrs or other damage. Inspect the bearing cage for cracks or other damage. Inspect the bearing inner race (11, **Figure 46**) for the same conditions. Replace the bearing and inner race if necessary as described in this section.

b. Inspect the pinion gear ball bearing (8, **Figure 46**) for roughness, pitting, galling and play. Also inspect the bearing for bluing, cracks and other damage.

c. Lubricate the bearings with gear oil. Then insert the pinion gear into each bearing. Turn either the pinion gear or bearing and check for roughness, noise or excessive play.

d. If damage is evident, replace the bearings as described in this section.

5. Inspect the gearcase for damage. Make sure all threaded holes are clean.

6. Inspect the ring gear bearing housing (26, **Figure 46**) for cracks and other damage. Check the O-ring groove for damage.

7. Inspect the pinion gear bearing housing (6, **Figure 46**) for cracks and other damage.

8. Inspect the thrust washer (21, **Figure 46**) and ring gear shims (23) for damage.

Bearing and Race Removal/Installation

Before removing the bearings or bearing race in this chapter, refer to *Service Methods* in Chapter One.

Pinion gear bearing

Refer to 8, **Figure 46**.

1. Remove the pinion gear bearing retainer (9, **Figure 46**) as follows:

a. Remove the pinion gear and seal from the bearing housing as described in this section.

b. Support the bearing housing with two metal bars clamped in a vise as shown in **Figure 65**.

NOTE
The bearing retainer has left-hand threads. Turn the retainer clockwise to remove it.

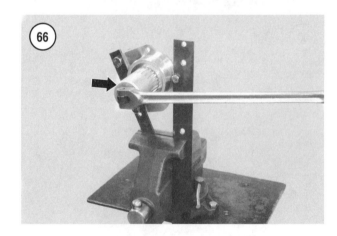

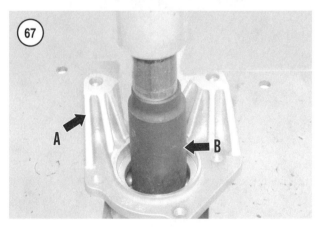

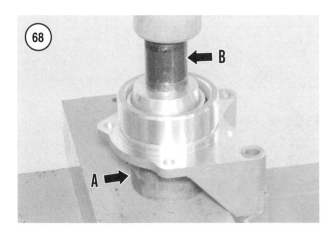

c. Loosen and remove the bearing retainer with the Yamaha middle gear bearing retainer wrench (part No. YM-04128 [**Figure 66**]).

2. Remove the bearing as follows:
   a. Support the bearing housing (A, **Figure 67**) in a press.
   b. Press the bearing out of the housing with a bearing driver (B, **Figure 67**). Discard the bearing.

3. Clean and dry the bearing housing. Remove all threadlocking compound residue from the bearing retainer and bearing housing threads.

4. Inspect the bearing bore for damage.

5. Install the new bearing as follows:

a. Support the bearing housing in a press using a piece of pipe (A, **Figure 68**), then place the bearing in its bore with its manufacturer's marks facing out.

b. Place a driver (B, **Figure 68**) on the bearing's outer race. Then press the bearing into the bearing housing until it bottoms. Turn the bearing inner race to make sure the bearing was not damaged during installation.

6. Install the bearing retainer as follows:
   a. Secure the bearing housing in the same manner used when removing the bearing retainer (**Figure 65**).

NOTE
The bearing retainer has left-hand threads. Turn the retainer counterclockwise to tighten it.

b. Apply a medium-strength threadlocking compound onto the bearing retainer threads and tighten to 170 N•m (125 ft.-lb.).

7. Install a new pinion shaft seal and the pinion shaft as described in this section.

Pinion gear needle bearing

1. Evenly heat the gearcase to 150° C (302° F) in the area around the needle bearing (**Figure 69**).

2. Insert a punch through the access hole in the gearcase (**Figure 70**) and drive the bearing out of the gearcase.

3. Allow the gearcase to cool.

4. Inspect the bearing bore for damage. Make sure there are no burrs on the bore surface that could interfere with bearing installation.

5. Evenly heat the gearcase to 150° C (302° F) in the area around the needle bearing bore.

6. Press the new bearing into the gearcase with a suitable adapter.

7. Inspect the bearing (**Figure 69**) for damage that may have occurred during installation.

8. Replace the pinion gear inner bearing race (**Figure 71**) as described in this section.

Pinion gear inner bearing race

Refer to **Figure 71**.
1. Mount a bearing splitter (**Figure 72**) against the bottom of the inner bearing race. Tighten the bearing splitter so that it seats between the bottom of the inner race and pinion gear.

2. Place a suitable driver that can pass through the inner bearing race on top of the pinion gear and press the pinion gear out of inner bearing race. Because there is not much clearance between the inner bearing race and the pinion gear for the bearing splitter to engage, removal can be difficult.

3. Clean the pinion gear and check the bearing race shoulder for scoring and other damage.

14

4. Support the pinion gear in a press. Press the new inner bearing race onto the pinion gear until it bottoms.

Ring gear roller bearing

Refer to **Figure 73**.
1. Support the final drive unit in a press with the roller bearing side facing up.
2. Place a bearing driver on the bearing as shown in **Figure 74**. Because only a small amount of the bearing is exposed to press against, it may be necessary to machine a bearing driver that contacts the bearing rollers without also contacting or damaging the area above the bearing.
3. Press the bearing out of the final drive unit. Discard the bearing.
4. Inspect the bearing bore for damage.
5. Support the final drive unit in a press with the ring gear side facing up. Then position the new bearing squarely in the bearing bore. Press the new bearing into the bearing bore until it bottoms (**Figure 73**).
6. Inspect the bearing for damage that may have occurred during installation.

Ring gear ball bearing

Refer to **Figure 75**.
1. Support the ring gear bearing housing (A, **Figure 76**) in a press.
2. Place a suitable driver (B, **Figure 76**) on the bearing's inner race and press the bearing out of the housing.
3. Inspect the bearing bore and housing for damage.
4. Support the bearing housing in a press with the bearing bore side facing up. Position the new bearing squarely into the bore with its manufacturer's marks facing up. Press the new bearing into the bearing bore until it bottoms (**Figure 75**). Use a bearing driver (**Figure 77**) that fits on the bearing's outer race.
5. Inspect the bearing for damage that may have occurred during installation.

Shim and Thrust Washer Adjustment

Whenever the ring gear, pinion gear, gearcase or ring gear bearing housing are replaced, the position of the pinion and ring gears must be adjusted using different thickness shims. New shims are selected by using the numbers stamped or marked on the ring gear, pinion gear, gearcase and ring gear bearing housing with a formula. After determining the new shims, the gearcase is assembled with the new shims and the final drive gear lash clearance is then measured. If this clearance is out of specification, the gearcase is disassembled and new ring gear shims and possibly a new thrust washer are installed. If no new components were installed, the gearcase can be assembled and the final drive gear lash measured to determine the wear of the original parts.

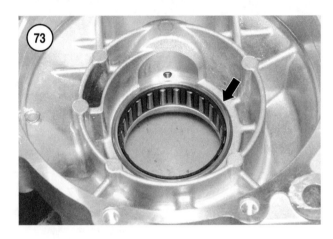

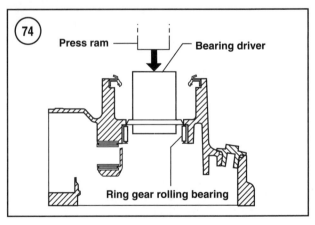

Press ram — Bearing driver

Ring gear rolling bearing

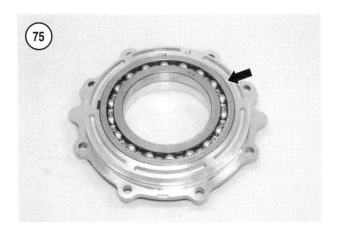

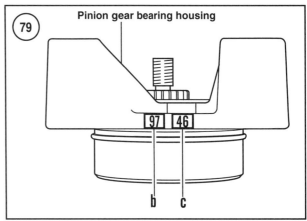

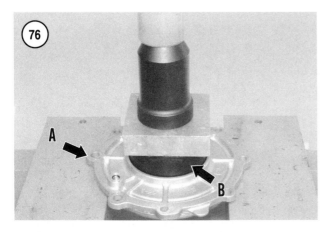

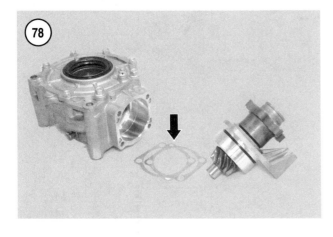

Careful adjustment is required to ensure proper operation of the final drive unit and to prevent abnormal gear noise and component wear.

CAUTION
Determine the shim/thrust washer requirements in the order presented in this procedure. While determining each shim/thrust washer size, assemble the shim(s), thrust washer and related components so the next shim or thrust washer can be calculated.

Pinion gear shim

Use the following formula and procedure to determine the shim sizes for the pinion gear assembly (**Figure 78**):
1. Determine the shim size with the formula:
$A = a + (c - b) - d$.
2. The fixed value of a in the shim formula is 92.5.
3. Note the number shown (b, **Figure 79**) on the pinion gear bearing housing for the b measurement. It indicates a decimal value. The number in this example is +97. Add this number to 34 to get the b variable of the shim formula, or 34.97 here.
4. Note the other number shown (c, **Figure 79**) on the pinion gear bearing housing for the c measurement. It indicates a decimal value. The number in this example is +46. Add this number to 55 to get the c variable of the shim formula, or 55.46 here.
5. Note the upper number shown (d, **Figure 80**) on the gearcase for the d measurement. It indicates a decimal value. The number in this example is +05. Add this number to 112 to get the d variable of the shim formula, or 112.05 here.
6. The example is now: $A = 92.5 + (55.46 - 34.97) - 112.05$. The result is $A = 0.94$. Round the hundredths numeral as follows:
   a. Round 0-2 to 0.
   b. Round 3-7 to 5.
   c. Round 8 and 9 to 10.
7. After rounding the result, the correct shim size (A) for the example is 0.95 mm thick. Pinion gear shims are available in 0.25, 0.30, 0.35, 0.40, 0.45 and 0.50 mm thicknesses.

14

8. During assembly, install the correct thickness shims (**Figure 78**) on the pinion gear assembly.

Ring gear shim

Use the following procedure to determine the shim sizes for the ring gear (A, **Figure 55**):
1. Determine the shim size with the formula:
$B = e - f - (g + h)$.
2. Note the number shown (*e*, **Figure 80**) on the gearcase for the *e* measurement. It indicates a decimal value. The number in this example is 0.98. Add this number to 50 to get the *e* variable of the shim formula, or 50.98 here.
3. Note the number shown (*f*, **Figure 81**) on the ring gear bearing housing for the *f* measurement. It indicates a decimal value. The number in this example is 0.55. Add this number to 1 to get the *f* variable of the shim formula, or 1.55 here.
4. Note the number shown (*g*, **Figure 82**) on the ring gear for the g measurement. It indicates a decimal value displayed in hundredths. The number in this example is -05. Some ring gears may display a positive number. Subtract/add this number to 35 to get the *g* variable of the shim formula. The result for the example is 34.95.
5. The fixed value of *h* (the bearing thickness) in the shim formula is 14.0.
6. The example is now: $B = 50.98 - 1.55 - (34.59 + 14.0)$. When calculated, $B = 49.43 - 48.95$. The result is:
$B = 0.48$. Round the hundredths numeral as follows:
   a. Round 0-2 to 0.
   b. Round 3-7 to 5.
   c. Round 8 and 9 to 10.
7. After rounding the results, the correct shim size (B) for the example is 0.50 mm thick. Ring gear shims are available in 0.25, 0.30, 0.35, 0.40, 0.45 and 0.50 mm thicknesses.
8. During assembly, install the correct size shim(s) (A, **Figure 55**) on the ring gear.

Ring gear thrust washer

Use the following procedure and Plastigage to determine the thrust washer (**Figure 83**) size for the ring gear:

> *NOTE*
> *The gearcase must be partially assembled to make this measurement. Make sure all of the components are clean and dry.*

1. Place the ring gear on a wooden block (**Figure 84**) so that it is raised off the workbench. This will allow the gearcase to be installed over the ring gear without bottoming against the workbench when the Plastigage strips are in place.
2. Cut four strips of 0.102-0.229 mm (0.004-0.009 in.) Plastigage (blue) and place them lengthwise on the ring gear hub (**Figure 85**). Equally space the strips around the hub. Then place the thrust washer (**Figure 86**) over the strips without turning it.

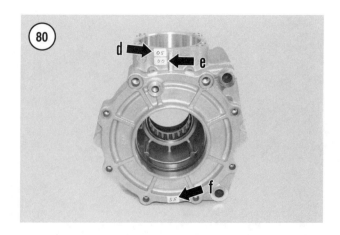

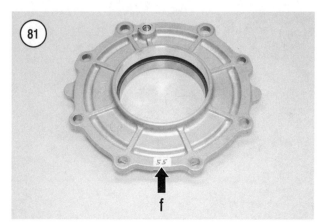

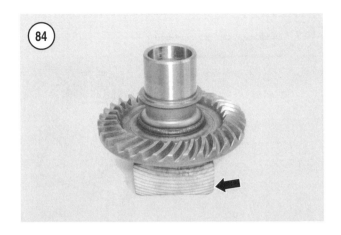

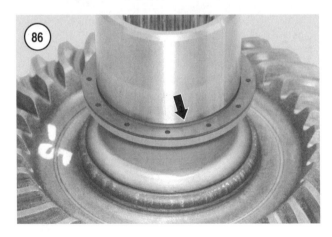

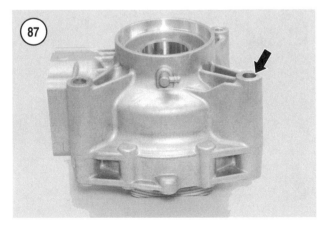

NOTE
In the following steps, do not rotate the pin-ion gear or ring gear while measuring the clearance.

3. Place the gearcase (**Figure 87**) over the ring gear. Then lift the gearcase, while at the same time holding the ring gear against the gearcase so that it cannot rotate, and turn the gearcase over. Install the ring gear shims (A, **Figure 55**) onto the ring gear. Then install the two 10-mm mount-ing bolts through the bearing housing and use them to align the bearing housing with the gearcase. Install the bearing housing without the O-ring onto the gearcase.

NOTE
To prevent the ring gear and housing from turning when tightening the bolts in Step 4, support the final drive housing in a vise.

4. Install the housing bolts and tighten as follows:
   a. Tighten all of the bolts finger-tight.
   b. Intially tighten all of the bolts in a crossing pattern to 8 N•m (71 in.-lb.).
   c. Tighten all of the bolts in a crossing pattern to 23 N•m (17 ft.-lb.).
   d. Tighten the two 10-mm bolts to 40 N•m (30 ft.-lb.).
5. Loosen all of the bolts in a crossing pattern and several steps, then remove them.
6. Remove the bearing housing and ring gear shim(s).
7. Turn the gearcase and ring gear over without allowing the ring gear to turn.
8. Lift the gearcase straight off the ring gear.
9. Remove the thrust washer (**Figure 86**). It may be slight-ly stuck because the Plastigage is now compressed and ad-hering to it. However, loosen the thrust washer by pulling it straight up. Do not turn it.
10. Examine the Plastigage. If the pieces look evenly com-pressed and do not appear smeared, continue with Step 11.
11. Measure each Plastigage strip (**Figure 88**), then aver-age the four measurements and note the following:
   a. Correct ring gear thrust clearance is 0.1-0.2 mm (0.004-0.008 in.).
   b. If necessary, resize the thrust washer and repeat the procedure until the clearance is within specification.

14

c. Ring gear thrust washers are available in 0.1 mm increments from 1.0-2.1 mm thick.

12. During assembly, install the correct size thrust washer (**Figure 86**) on the ring gear.

Final drive gear lash

After the final drive unit is assembled, check the gear lash to verify that shim selection is correct. Also check clearance whenever using worn original parts.

Measure gear lash with a gear lash measurement tool (Yamaha part No. YM-01467 [**Figure 89**] or equivalent) and a dial indicator.

1. Reassemble the final drive unit as described in this section.

2. Lock the final drive unit to a vise or workbench with the oil drain hole facing toward the side as shown in **Figure 90**. Remove the oil drain bolt. The final drive unit must not move when the measurements are taken or the results will be incorrect.

3. Lock the ring gear in place with a suitable M10-1.25 mm bolt (**Figure 90**). Finger-tighten the bolt into the drain hole just enough to keep the ring gear from turning.

> *CAUTION*
> *Overtightening the bolt may damage the ring gear.*

4. Clamp the gear lash measurement tool onto the pinion gear shaft, then position the tool arm horizontally as shown in **Figure 90**.

5. Position a dial indicator in contact with the measurement tool and 31.1 mm (1.22 in.) from the end of the measurement tool (**Figure 90**). The dial indicator must be stable and set to read gear lash in both directions. Zero the gauge on the dial indicator.

6. Gently rotate the pinion gear clockwise until lash between the parts is eliminated. Note the dial indicator reading.

7. Gently rotate the pinion gear shaft in the opposite direction until lash between the parts is eliminated. Note the dial indicator reading.

8. Add the indicator readings in Step 6 and Step 7 to determine the differential gear lash and record the number.

9. Loosen the lock bolt and rotate the pinion gear 90°. Finger-tighten the bolt, readjust the gear lash measurement tool, and repeat the check. Measure the gear lash at every 90° until the shaft has rotated one full turn (four total measurements).

10. Determine the average reading of the four checks. Final drive gear lash should be 0.1-0.3 mm (0.0040-0.0012 in.). If adjustment is necessary, refer to *Disassembly* in this section to disassemble the final gear unit. Adjust the gear lash as follows:

a. If gear lash is too low, decrease the ring gear shim thickness. If the shim adjustment needed is 0.2 mm (0.008 in.) or greater, increase the thrust washer thickness by an equal amount.

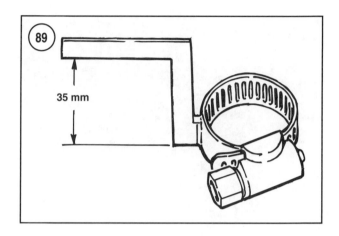

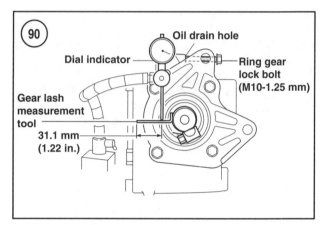

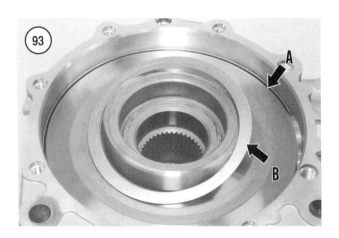

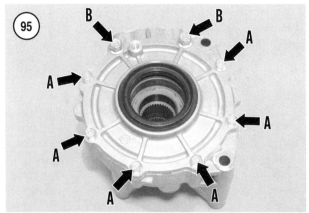

b. If gear lash is too high, increase the ring gear shim thickness. If the shim adjustment needed is 0.2 mm (0.008 in.) or greater, decrease the thrust washer thickness by an equal mount.

c. Ring gear shims (A, **Figure 55**) are available in 0.05 mm increments from 0.25-0.50 mm.

d. Ring gear thrust washers (**Figure 86**) are available in 0.1 mm increments from 1.0-2.1 mm thick.

e. After installing the replacement ring gear shim(s) or thrust washer, recheck the final drive gear lash.

Assembly

1. Make sure all parts are clean and dry before starting assembly.

2. Install a new axle seal into the gearcase with its closed side facing out. Tap the seal (**Figure 91**) in place with a wooden block until edge of the seal is flush with the seal bore surface. Check that the seal seats squarely in the bore. Refer to **Figure 92**.

3. Repeat Step 2 to install the axle seal into the ring gear bearing housing.

4. Install the thrust washer (**Figure 83**) onto the ring gear.

5. Turn the ring over while holding the thrust washer and install the ring gear (A, **Figure 93**) into the gearcase. Make sure the thrust washer did not fall off.

6. Install the ring gear shims (B, **Figure 93**) over the ring gear.

7. Lubricate a new O-ring (**Figure 94**) with lithium grease and install it in the ring gear bearing housing groove.

8. Align and install the ring gear bearing housing into the gearcase. Turn and tap the housing lightly until it seats against the gearcase. Do not force the bearing housing as resistance is caused by the O-ring and forcing the housing in place may cut and damage the O-ring.

9. Install the 8-mm (A, **Figure 95**) and 10-mm (B) ring gear bearing housing mounting bolts and tighten in the following order:

a. Tighten all of the bolts finger-tight.

b. Initially tighten all of the bolts in a crossing pattern to 8 N•m (71 in.-lb.).

c. Tighten all of the bolts in a crossing pattern to 23 N•m (17 ft.-lb.).

d. Tighten the two 10-mm bolts to 40 N•m (30 ft.-lb.).

10. Install the ring gear stopper as described in this section.

11. Install the pinion gear bearing housing as follows:

a. Lubricate a new O-ring (A, **Figure 96**) with lithium grease and install it in the bearing housing groove.

b. Install the bearing housing mounting bolts through the housing (B, **Figure 96**), then install the shim(s) (C). Installing the bolts now helps to align the shims with the bolt holes.

c. Align and install the bearing housing (A, **Figure 97**). Tighten the mounting bolts (B, **Figure 97**) finger-tight.

d. Tighten the pinion gear bearing housing mounting bolts (B, **Figure 97**) in a crossing pattern and in several steps to 32 N•m (24 ft.-lb.).

12. Install one of the rear axles into the final drive unit (**Figure 98**). Then hold the axle upright and turn the pinion shaft by hand. The assembly should turn smoothly and without any roughness or binding.

13. Clean the parking brake disc and the coupling gear surface with brake cleaner and allow to dry. Then install the brake disc (**Figure 99**) with its original side facing out, mounting bolts and nuts. Hold the bolts and tighten the nuts in a crossing pattern to 10 N•m (88 in.-lb.).

14. Install the final drive gear unit as described in this section.

14

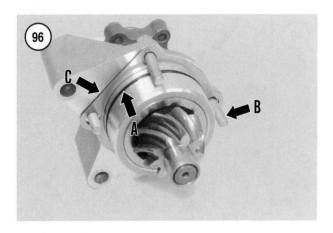

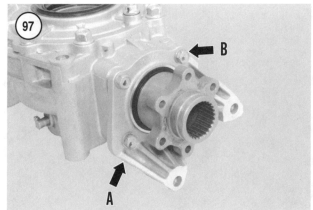

Ring Gear Stopper
Removal/Installation/Adjustment

The ring gear stopper does not normally require removal unless the final drive unit is being disassembled, it becomes loose or gear oil leaks from the stopper threads. The stopper must be adjusted during installation. If the ring gear contacts the stopper and the stopper is not loose, disassemble the final drive unit as described in this chapter to check for damage.

1. Hold the stopper with a 3-mm Allen wrench and remove the locknut (A, **Figure 100**). Then remove the stopper (B, **Figure 100**).

2. Remove all sealer from the stopper and ring gear bearing housing threads, washer and nut.

3. Install and adjust the stopper as follows:

    a. Apply a sealer onto the stopper threads. Use Yamabond No. 4 or equivalent.

    b. Thread the stopper clockwise into the bearing housing until it contacts the ring gear.

    c. Turn the stopper 120° counterclockwise.

    d. Hold the stopper to prevent it from turning and tighten the locknut to 16 N•m (12 ft.-lb.). A torque adapter (Motion Pro part No. 08-0134 or equivalent) can be used as shown in **Figure 101**. Refer to *Torque Adapters* in *Tools* in Chapter One.

    e. Turn the ring gear to make sure it does not contact the stopper. If it does and the adjustment was correctly made, disassemble the final drive gear unit as described in this section and check for damage.

REAR DRIVE SHAFT

Removal/Installation

Remove and install the rear drive shaft as described in *Final Drive Unit* in this chapter.

Inspection

1. Inspect the drive shaft (A, **Figure 102**) for straightness. Replace the drive shaft if it is bent. A bent drive shaft can damage bearings and cause excessive vibration.

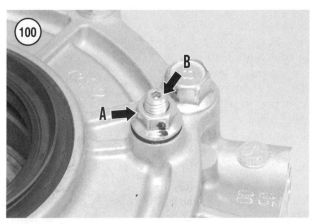

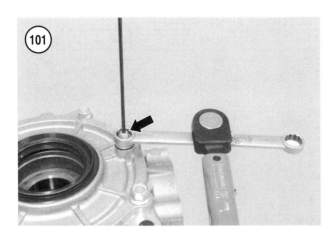

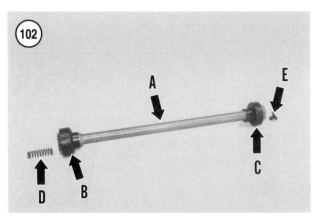

2. Inspect the splines (**Figure 103**) on both ends of the drive shaft for damage. Replace the drive shaft if the front splines are damaged. Replace the rear coupling if the splines are damage. Secure the rear coupling in place with new snap rings. Make sure the snap rings are fully seated in their grooves.

3. Replace the boots if torn or damaged. The front boot (B, **Figure 102**) is larger than the rear boot (C).

4. Replace the spring (D, **Figure 102**) if the coils are cracked or damaged.

5. Replace the damper (E, **Figure 103**) if cracked or damaged.

Table 1 REAR AXLE AND FINAL DRIVE SPECIFICATIONS

Ball joint lubrication	
Lubrication type	Molybdenum disulfide grease
Per dust boot	
Outboard (rear wheel side)	55 g (1.9 oz.)
Inboard (final drive side)	65 g (2.3 oz.)
Final drive gear lash	0.1-0.3 mm (0.004-0.012 in.)
Ring gear stopper adjustment	Refer to text.
Ring gear thrust clearance	0.1-0.2 mm (0.004-0.008 in.)

14

Table 2 REAR AXLE AND FINAL DRIVE TORQUE SPECIFICATIONS

	N•m	in.-lb.	ft.-lb.
Bearing retainer*	170	–	125
Boot guard mounting bolts	7	62	–
Coupling gear nut	80	–	59
Final drive mounting nuts	70	–	52
Final drive oil drain bolt	20	–	15
Final drive oil fill plug	23	–	17
Lower arm mounting nuts	45	–	33
Parking brake disc mounting nuts	10	88	–
Parking brake housing mounting bolts	40	–	30
Pinion gear bearing housing mounting bolts	32	–	24
Ring gear bearing housing mounting bolts*			
8-mm bolt	23	–	17
10-mm bolt	40	–	30
Ring gear stopper locknut*	16	–	12
Shock absorber mounting nut	45	–	33
Upper arm mounting nuts	45	–	33

*Refer to text.

BRAKES

This chapter covers the front and rear brake systems and the parking brake assembly. Brake maintenance intervals and routine inspection and adjustment procedures are in Chapter Three.

Read *Safety* and *Service Methods* in Chapter One before servicing the vehicle in this chapter.

Tables 1-4 are at the end of this chapter.

BRAKE SERVICE NOTES

WARNING
Do not drive the vehicle until the front and rear brakes are operating correctly.

WARNING
Only use DOT 4 brake fluid. Do not use brake fluid labeled DOT 5. This is a silicone-based brake fluid that is not compatible with glycol-based DOT 3, DOT 4 or DOT 5.1. Do not intermix two different types of brake fluid as it can cause brake component damage and lead to brake system failure.

WARNING
Never reuse brake fluid expelled during brake bleeding. Contaminated brake fluid can cause brake failure. Dispose of brake fluid properly.

WARNING
*Whenever working on the brake system, do not inhale brake dust. Do **not** use compressed air to blow off brake parts. It may contain asbestos, which can cause lung injury and cancer. Wear a face mask that meets OSHA requirements for trapping asbestos particles, and wash hands and forearms thoroughly after completing the work. Before working on the brake system, spray the components with brake cleaner. Secure and dispose of all brake dust and cleaning materials properly.*

CAUTION
Cover all parts that could become contaminated by the accidental spilling of brake fluid. Wash any spilled brake fluid from any surface immediately, as it damages the finish. Use soapy water and rinse completely.

When adding brake fluid, use DOT 4 brake fluid from a sealed container. However, because DOT 4 brake fluid is glycol-based and draws moisture, purchase brake fluid in small containers and discard any small leftover quantities. Do not store a container of brake fluid with less than 1/4 of the fluid remaining.

The brake system transmits hydraulic pressure from the master cylinder to the brake calipers. This pressure is transmitted from the calipers to the brake pads, which grip both sides of the brake discs and slows the vehicle. As the pads wear, the pistons move out of the caliper bores to automatically compensate for wear. As this occurs, the fluid level in the master cylinder reservoir goes down. This must be compensated for by occasionally adding fluid.

The proper operation of the system depends on routine inspection, a supply of clean DOT 4 brake fluid and a clean work environment when any service is performed. Any

15

debris that enters the system or contaminates the pads or brake discs can damage the components and cause poor brake performance.

Perform brake service procedures carefully. Do not use any sharp tools inside the master cylinder, calipers or on the pistons. Damage to these components could cause a loss of hydraulic pressure. If there is any doubt about your ability to correctly and safely service the brake system, have a professional technician perform the task.

Consider the following when servicing the brake system:

1. Do not allow disc brake fluid to contact any plastic parts or painted surfaces; damage will result.

2. Always keep the master cylinder reservoir and spare cans of brake fluid closed to prevent dust or moisture from entering. This contaminates the brake fluid and can cause brake failure.

3. Clean parts with an aerosol brake parts cleaner. Never use petroleum-based solvents on internal brake system components or any rubber part. They cause seals to swell and distort.

4. Do not allow any grease or oil to contact the brake pads.

5. When cleaning the brake components, wear rubber gloves to keep brake fluid off skin.

> *NOTE*
> *Removing the reservoir cover does not allow air to enter the hydraulic system unless the fluid level has dropped low enough to expose the brake fluid passage holes in the master cylinder.*

6. If the hydraulic system has been opened, bleed the system to remove air from the system. Refer to *Brake Bleeding* in this chapter.

BRAKE BLEEDING

Bleeding the brake system removes air from the brake system. Air in the brake system increases brake pedal travel while causing it to feel spongy and less responsive. Under extreme braking (heat) conditions, it can cause complete loss of brake pressure.

Read *Brake Service Notes* in this chapter.

Bleeding Tips

Before bleeding the brake system, note the following:

> *CAUTION*
> *Cover all parts that could become contaminated by the accidental spilling of brake fluid. Wash any spilled brake fluid from any surface immediately, as it damages the finish. Use soapy water and rinse completely.*

1. Always start the bleeding procedure at the caliper the farthest away from the master cylinder and bleed both the

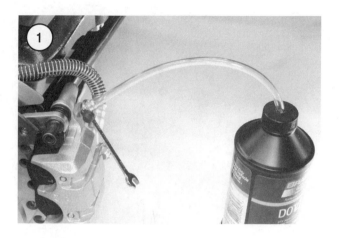

front and rear brake systems, bleed the system in the following order:

   a. Right rear.

   b. Left rear.

   c. Right front.

   d. Left front.

2. Clean the bleed valves and the area around the valves of all dirt and debris. Make sure the passageway in the end of the valve is open and clear.

3. Use a box-end wrench to open and close the bleed valves. This prevents damage to the hex-head.

4. Replace bleed valves with damaged hex-heads. These are difficult to loosen and cannot be tightened fully.

5. Install the box-end wrench on the bleed valve before installing the catch hose. This allows operation of the wrench without having to disconnect the hose.

6. Use a clear catch hose to allow visual inspection of the brake fluid as it leaves the caliper or brake unit. Air bubbles visible in the catch hose indicate that there still may be air trapped in the brake system.

7. Depending on the play of the bleed valve when it is loosened, it is possible to see air exiting through the catch hose even through there is no air in the brake system. A loose or damaged catch hose also causes air leaks. In both cases, air is being introduced into the bleed system at the bleed valve threads and catch hose connection, and not from within the brake system itself. This condition can be misleading and cause excessive brake bleeding when there is no air in the system.

8. Open the bleed valve just enough to allow fluid to pass through the valve and into the catch bottle. The farther the bleed valve is opened, the looser the valve becomes. This allows air to be drawn into the system from around the valve threads.

9. If the system is difficult to bleed, tap the brake lines on the master cylinder a few times to remove air bubbles trapped in the hose connection where the brake fluid exits the master cylinder. Also tap the banjo bolt and line connection points at the calipers and other brake units.

10. When bleeding the brakes, check the fluid level in the master cylinder frequently to prevent it from running dry, especially when using a vacuum pump. If the fluid level

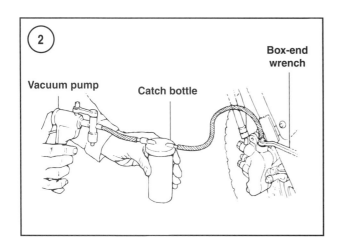

Vacuum pump   Catch bottle   Box-end wrench

drops too low, air can enter the system and it must be bled again.

Manual Bleeding

This procedure describes how to bleed the brake system with an empty bottle, length of clear hose that fits tightly onto the bleed valve, and a wrench. Two people will be required to perform the procedure. One person can open and close the bleed valve while the other person operates the brake pedal. Use the following procedure to bleed the brake system.

1. Read *Bleeding Tips* in this section.
2. Remove the front (Chapter Eleven) and rear (Chapter Thirteen) wheels.
3. Check that all brake hoses, lines and banjo bolts are tightened to specification (**Table 4**).
4. Connect the catch hose to the bleed valve on the brake caliper (**Figure 1**). Submerge the other end of the hose into the bottle partially filled with DOT 4 brake fluid. This prevents air from being drawn into the catch hose and back into the brake system.
5. Apply the brake pedal firmly (do not pump) until it stops and hold in this position. Then open the bleed valve. As air and brake fluid is forced from the system, the pedal will travel the full length of operation. When the pedal can move no farther, hold the pedal down and close the bleed valve. Do not allow the pedal to return to its up position when the bleed valve is open. Doing so will allow air to be drawn back into the system.
6. When the bleed valve is closed, release the pedal so it returns to its resting position. Check the fluid level in the reservoir and replenish, if necessary.
7. Repeat Step 5 and Step 6 until clear fluid is seen passing from the bleed valve.
8. Tighten the bleed valve to 5 N•m (44 in.-lb.).

NOTE
If small bubbles remain in the system after several bleeding attempts, close the reservoir and allow the system to stand undisturbed for a few hours. The system will stabilize and the air can be purged as large bubbles.

9. Repeat at each caliper.
10. The bleeding procedure is completed when the feel of the pedal is firm.
11. Check the brake fluid reservoir and fill the reservoir to the upper level, if necessary.
12. Reinstall the wheels as described in Chapter Eleven (front) and Chapter Thirteen (rear).
13. Test drive the vehicle slowly at first to make sure that the brakes are operating correctly.

Pressure Bleeding

This procedure uses a hand-operated vacuum pump with a hydraulic brake bleeding kit. Use the following procedure to bleed the brake system.

1. Read *Bleeding Tips* in this section.
2. Remove the front (Chapter Eleven) and rear (Chapter Thirteen) wheels.
3. Check that all brake hoses, lines and banjo bolts are tightened to specification (**Table 4**).
4. Connect the catch hose between the bleed valve and catch bottle (**Figure 2**). Connect the other hose between the catch bottle and vacuum pump. If necessary, refer to the tool manufacturer's instructions for additional information.
5. Secure the vacuum pump to the vehicle with a length of stiff wire so it will be possible to check and refill the master cylinder reservoir without having to disconnect the catch hose.
6. Pump the handle on the vacuum pump to create a vacuum in the catch hose connected to the bleed valve.
7. Open the bleed valve with a wrench to allow air and brake fluid to be drawn through the master cylinder, brake hoses and lines. Close the bleed valve *before* the brake fluid stops flowing from the system (no more vacuum in line) or the vacuum pump gauge reads zero (if so equipped). Replenish the fluid level in the reservoir.
8. Repeat Step 6 and Step 7 until clear fluid is seen passing from the bleed valve.
9. Tighten the bleed valve to 5 N•m (44 in.-lb.).

NOTE
If small bubbles remain in the system after several bleeding attempts, close the reservoir and allow the system to stand undisturbed for a few hours. The system will stabilize and the air can be purged as large bubbles.

10. Repeat at each caliper
11. The bleeding procedure is completed when the feel of the pedal is firm.
12. Check the brake fluid reservoir and fill the reservoir to the upper level, if necessary.
13. Reinstall the wheels as described in Chapter Eleven (front) and Chapter Thirteen (rear).
14. Test drive the vehicle slowly at first to make sure that the brakes are operating correctly.

15

BRAKE FLUID FLUSHING

When flushing the brake system, use only DOT 4 brake fluid as a flushing fluid. Flushing consists of pulling enough new brake fluid through the system until all of the old fluid is removed, and the fluid exiting the bleed valve appears clean and without any bubbles. To flush the brake system, use one of the bleeding procedures described in *Brake Bleeding* in this chapter.

BRAKE FLUID DRAINING

1. Read *Bleeding Tips* in *Brake Bleeding* in this chapter.
2. Remove the cap and diaphragm from the master cylinder reservoir.
3. Connect a brake bleeder to the brake caliper as described in this chapter. Operate the bleeder tool to remove as much brake fluid from the system as possible.
4. Close the bleed valve and disconnect the brake bleeder tool.
5. Service the brake components as described in this chapter.

BRAKE PADS

The pistons in the brake calipers are self-adjusting to compensate for brake pad wear. As the pads wear and the pistons move farther outward in the caliper, the brake fluid level drops.

There is no recommended mileage interval for changing the brake pads. Pad wear depends greatly on riding habits and the condition of the brake system.

Refer to *Brakes* in Chapter Three to check brake pad wear.

It is also recommended that the exposed parts of the pistons be cleaned before they are pushed back into their bores in the caliper. This prevents dirt and debris that has hardened on the pistons from damaging the caliper seals. Refer to *Brake Caliper* in this chapter.

The caliper bracket can also be removed as described in this chapter so the fixed shafts can be cleaned, lubricated and the rubber boots replaced if damaged.

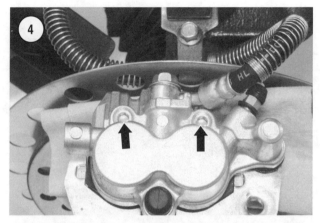

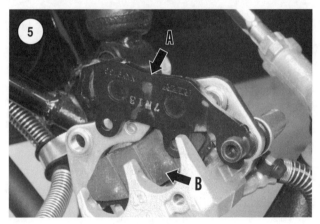

Front Brake Pads
Removal/Installation

Replace the brake pads in both front calipers.
1. Read *Brake Service Notes* in this chapter.
2. Remove the front wheel (Chapter Eleven) for the side being worked on.
3. Remove the master cylinder cover. Use a large syringe to remove and discard about 50 percent of the fluid from the reservoir. This prevents the master cylinder from overflowing when the caliper pistons are compressed for reinstallation. Do *not* drain the entire reservoir or air will enter the system. Reinstall the cover.
4. Loosen both pad pins (**Figure 3**).

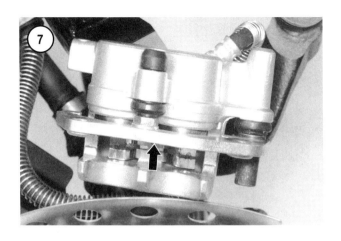

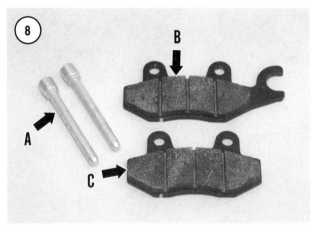

5. Remove the caliper mounting bolts and lift the caliper from the disc.

6. Remove the pad pins (**Figure 4**).

7. Remove the outer (A, **Figure 5**) and inner (B) brake pads.

8. Make sure the pad spring (**Figure 6**) is installed inside the caliper and is not damaged. Replace the pad spring if necessary.

9. Slide the caliper bracket (**Figure 7**) in and out of the caliper, checking for excessive drag or to see if it is stuck. If the bracket does not move smoothly or the boots appear damaged, service the caliper bracket fixed shafts and rubber boots as described in *Overhaul* in *Brake Caliper* in this chapter.

NOTE
*Before repositioning the caliper pistons, check the exposed parts of the caliper pistons. If the pistons are contaminated with debris, pitted or have a rough appearance, clean the pistons with a soft brush and cleaner that will not damage or swell the caliper seals. Refer to **Brake Caliper** in this chapter.*

10. Push in the caliper pistons to create room for the new pads.

11. Inspect the pad pins (A, **Figure 8**) for excessive wear, corrosion or damage. Remove corrosion and dirt from the pad pin surfaces. Dirty or damaged pad pins prevent the

brake pads from sliding properly and results in brake drag and overheating of the brake disc.

12. Inspect the brake pads (B, **Figure 8**) as follows:
   a. Inspect the friction material for light surface dirt, grease and oil contamination. Remove light contamination with sandpaper. If the contamination has penetrated the surface, replace the brake pads.
   b. Inspect the brake pads for excessive wear or damage. Replace the brake pads when the friction material is worn to the bottom of the wear indicator lines (C, **Figure 8**) or the pad material measures 1.5 mm (0.06 in.) or less.
   c. Inspect the brake pads for uneven wear. If one pad has worn more than the other, it may be binding on the pad pins, the caliper is not sliding properly or one or both pistons are stuck.

NOTE
If brake fluid is leaking from around the pistons, overhaul the brake caliper as described in this chapter.

13. Service the brake disc as follows:
   a. Use brake cleaner and a fine-grade emery cloth to remove debris and brake pad residue from the brake disc. Clean both sides of the disc.

NOTE
Cleaning the brake disc is especially important if changing brake pad compounds. Many compounds are not compatible with each other.

   b. Check the brake disc for wear as described in this chapter.

14. Install the inner pad (B, **Figure 5**) by seating it under the caliper bracket and against the piston. Make sure the friction material faces toward the brake disc.

15. Install the outer brake pad (A, **Figure 5**) by hooking its arm onto the shoulder on the caliper bracket.

16. Push both brake pads up against the pad spring and install the pad pins (**Figure 4**) through the brake caliper and brake pads and tighten finger-tight.

17. Spread the pads so there is clearance to fit the caliper over the brake disc.

18. Position the caliper over the brake disc and hub assembly, and slide the caliper down around the brake disc.

19. Install and tighten the front caliper mounting bolts to 48 N•m (35 ft.-lb.).

20. Tighten the pad pins to 17 N•m (12.5 ft.-lb.).

21. Operate the brake pedal to seat the pads against the disc, then check the brake fluid level in the reservoir. If necessary, add new DOT 4 brake fluid.

22. Check that the hub spins freely and the brake operates properly.

23. Install the front wheel (Chapter Eleven).

24. Repeat for the opposite side.

25. While riding in a safe area, break in the pads gradually following the manufacturer's instructions. Immediate

15

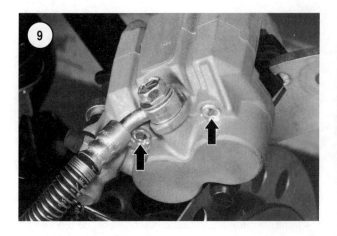

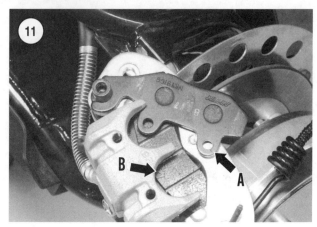

hard application glazes the new pads and reduces their effectiveness.

> *WARNING*
> *Do not drive the vehicle until the front and rear brakes and the rear brake light work properly.*

Rear Brake Pads
Removal/Installation

Replace the brake pads in both rear calipers.

1. Read *Brake Service Notes* in this chapter.

2. Remove the rear wheel (Chapter Thirteen) for the side being worked on.

3. Remove the master cylinder cover. Use a large syringe to remove and discard about 50 percent of the fluid from the reservoir. This prevents the master cylinder from overflowing when the caliper pistons are compressed for reinstallation. Do *not* drain the entire reservoir or air will enter the system. Reinstall the cover.

4. Loosen both pad pins (**Figure 9**).

5. Remove the caliper mounting bolts (**Figure 10**) and lift the caliper from the disc.

6. Remove the pad pins.

7. Remove the outer (A, **Figure 11**) and inner (B) brake pads.

8. Make sure the pad spring (**Figure 12**) is installed inside the caliper and is not damaged. Replace the pad spring if necessary.

9. Slide the caliper bracket (**Figure 13**) in and out of the caliper, checking for excessive drag or to see if it is stuck. If the bracket does not move smoothly or the boots appear damaged, service the caliper bracket fixed shafts and rubber boots as described in *Overhaul* in *Brake Caliper* in this chapter.

> *NOTE*
> *Before repositioning the caliper pistons, visually check the exposed parts of the caliper pistons. If the pistons are contaminated with debris, pitted or have a rough appearance, clean the pistons with a soft brush and cleaner that will not damage or swell the caliper seals. Refer to **Brake Caliper** in this chapter.*

10. Push in the caliper pistons to create room for the new pads.

11. Inspect the pad pins (A, **Figure 14**) for excessive wear, corrosion or damage. Remove corrosion and dirt from the pad pin surfaces. Dirty or damaged pad pins prevent the brake pads from sliding properly and results in brake drag and overheating of the brake disc.

12. Inspect the brake pads (B, **Figure 14**) as follows:

   a. Inspect the friction material for light surface dirt, grease and oil contamination. Remove light contamination with sandpaper. If the contamination has penetrated the surface, replace the brake pads.

   b. Inspect the brake pads for excessive wear or damage. Replace the brake pads when the friction material is worn to the bottom of the wear indicator lines (C, **Figure 14**) or the pad material measures 1.5 mm (0.06 in.) or less.

   c. Inspect the brake pads for uneven wear. If one pad has worn more than the other, it may be binding on the pad pins, the caliper is not sliding properly or one or both pistons are stuck.

> *NOTE*
> *If brake fluid is leaking from around the pistons, overhaul the brake caliper as described in this chapter.*

13. Service the brake disc as follows:

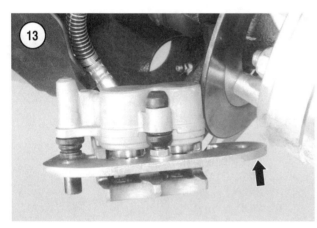

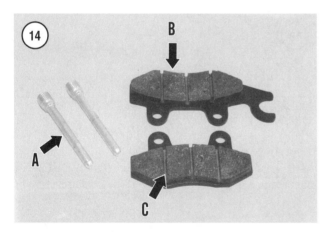

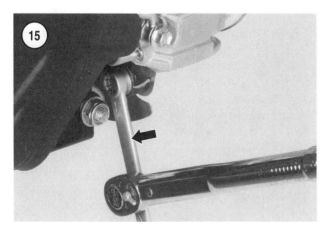

a. Use brake cleaner and a fine-grade emery cloth to remove debris and brake pad residue from the brake disc. Clean both sides of the disc.

NOTE
Cleaning the brake disc is especially important if changing brake pad compounds. Many compounds are not compatible with each other.

b. Check the brake disc for wear as described in this chapter.

14. Install the inner pad (B, **Figure 11**) by seating it under the caliper bracket and against the piston. Make sure the friction material faces toward the brake disc.

15. Install the outer brake pad (A, **Figure 11**) by hooking its arm onto the shoulder on the caliper bracket.

16. Push both brake pads up against the pad spring and install the pad pins (**Figure 9**) through the brake caliper and brake pads and tighten finger-tight.

17. Spread the pads so there is clearance to fit the caliper over the brake disc.

18. Position the caliper over the brake disc and hub assembly, and slide the caliper down around the brake disc.

19. Install and tighten the rear caliper mounting bolts (**Figure 10**) to 48 N•m (35 ft.-lb.).

NOTE
*The caliper's lower mounting bolt will require a torque adapter ([**Figure 15**] Motion Pro Torque Wrench Adapter part No. 08-0134 or equivalent) to tighten it with a torque wrench. Refer to **Torque Adapters** in **Tools** Chapter One.*

20. Tighten the pad pins (**Figure 9**) to 17 N•m (12.5 ft.-lb.).

21. Operate the brake pedal to seat the pads against the disc, then check the brake fluid level in the reservoir. If necessary, add new DOT 4 brake fluid.

22. Check that the hub spins freely and the brake operates properly.

23. Install the rear wheel (Chapter Thirteen).

24. Repeat for the opposite side.

25. While riding in a safe area, break in the pads gradually following the manufacturer's instructions. Immediate hard application glazes the new pads and reduces their effectiveness.

WARNING
Do not drive the vehicle until the front and rear brakes and the rear brake light work properly.

Parking Brake Pads
Removal/Installation

1. Park the vehicle on a level surface with the transmission shifted into low gear. Block the front wheels so the vehicle cannot roll in either direction.

15

2. Remove the rear skid plate (Chapter Sixteen).

3. Release the parking brake.

4. Remove the right rear wheel (Chapter Thirteen).

5. Clean the parking brake housing.

6. Disconnect and remove the return spring (A, **Figure 16**).

7. Remove the parking brake caliper mounting bolts (B, **Figure 16**).

8. Disconnect the parking brake cable from the parking brake lever (C, **Figure 16**) and remove the parking brake caliper.

9. Remove the pad pins (A, **Figure 17**).

10. Remove the brake pads (B, **Figure 17**).

11 Make sure the pad spring (**Figure 18**) is installed inside the caliper and is not damaged. Replace the pad spring if damaged or when installing new brake pads.

12. Slide the caliper bracket (**Figure 19**) in and out of the caliper, checking for excessive drag or to see if it is stuck. If the bracket does not move smoothly or the boots appear damaged, service the caliper and caliper bracket fixed shafts and rubber boots as described in *Parking Brake Caliper* in this chapter.

13. Inspect the pad pins (A, **Figure 20**) for excessive wear, corrosion or damage. Remove corrosion and dirt from the pad pin surfaces. Dirty or damaged pad pins prevent the brake pads from sliding properly and results in brake drag and overheating of the brake disc and brake pads.

14. Inspect the brake pads (B, **Figure 20**) as follows:

  a. Inspect the friction material for light surface dirt, grease and oil contamination. Remove light contamination with sandpaper. If the contamination has penetrated the surface, replace the brake pads.

  b. Inspect the brake pads for excessive wear or damage. Replace the brake pads when the friction material is worn to the bottom of the wear indicator lines (C, **Figure 20**) or the pad material measures 1.0 mm (0.04 in.) or less.

  c. Inspect the brake pads for uneven wear. If one pad has worn more than the other, it may be binding on its pad pins or the housing is not sliding properly.

15. Install the inner and outer brake pads (B, **Figure 17**) with the friction material facing toward the disc.

16. Apply a medium-strength threadlocking compound onto the pad pins. Push the brake pads against the pad spring and install the pad pins through the slots in the brake pads. Tighten the pad pins (A, **Figure 17**) to 17 N•m (12.5 ft.-lb.).

17. Align the parking brake caliper with the brake disc and reconnect the parking brake cable (C, **Figure 16**). Make sure the cable and housing are not twisted.

18. Spread the pads so there is clearance to fit the caliper over the brake disc.

19. Install the caliper over the brake disc.

NOTE
If there is not enough clearance between the brake pads to install them over the brake disc,

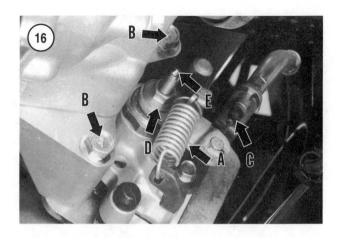

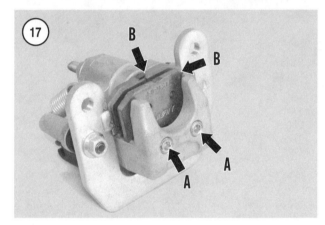

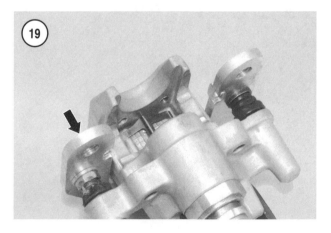

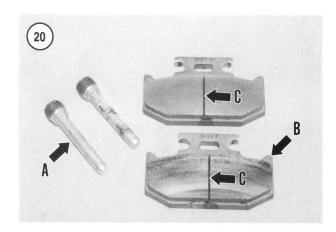

*loosen the parking brake lever nut (D, **Figure 16**) and turn the pushrod (E) outward.*

20. Install the parking brake caliper mounting bolts (B, **Figure 16**) and tighten to 40 N•m (30 ft.-lb.).

21. Reconnect the return spring (A, **Figure 16**).

22. Adjust the parking brake and tighten the parking brake lever nut as described in Chapter Three.

23. Reinstall the right rear wheel (Chapter Thirteen).

24. Reinstall the rear skid plate (Chapter Sixteen).

BRAKE CALIPER

This section covers the front and rear brake calipers. Read *Brake Service Notes* in this chapter.

NOTE
*Refer to **Parking Brake Caliper** in this chapter to service the parking brake caliper assembly.*

Removal/Installation

Front brake caliper

1. Remove the front wheel (Chapter Eleven).

2. If the brake hose will be disconnected from the caliper, drain the brake fluid from the front brake line as described in this chapter. After draining, remove the brake hose banjo

bolt (**Figure 21**) and washers at the caliper. There should be two sealing washers on each side of the brake hose. Secure a plastic bag around the end of the hose to catch any leaks or drips.

3A. If the caliper will be removed from the vehicle, remove the caliper mounting bolts and the caliper.

3B. If the caliper will be will be left attached to the brake hose:

    a. Remove the caliper mounting bolts and secure the caliper with a length of wire. Do not allow the caliper to hang by the brake hose.

    b. Insert a spacer block between the brake pads.

NOTE
The use of a spacer block will prevent the pistons from being forced out of the caliper if the brake pedal is applied with the brake caliper removed.

4. Spread the pads so there is clearance to fit the caliper over the brake disc.

5. Position the caliper over the brake disc and hub assembly, and slide the caliper down around the brake disc. Make sure the front brake hose (**Figure 22**) is not twisted.

6. Install and tighten the front caliper mounting bolts to 48 N•m (35 ft.-lb.).

7. If the brake hose was disconnected, place a new sealing washer on each side of the brake hose. Position the hose between the stopper arms (**Figure 23**) on the caliper and tighten the banjo bolt to 27 N•m (20 ft.-lb.).

8. If the brake hose was disconnected from the caliper, fill and bleed the brake system as described in this chapter.

9. Operate the brake pedal several times to seat the pads.

10. Check that the hub spins freely and the brake operates properly.

11. Install the front wheel (Chapter Eleven).

Rear brake caliper

1. Remove the rear wheel (Chapter Thirteen).

2. If the brake hose will be disconnected from the caliper, drain the brake fluid from the rear brake line as described in this chapter. After draining, remove the brake hose ban-

15

jo bolt (A, **Figure 24**) and washers at the caliper. There should be two sealing washers on each side of the brake hose. Secure a plastic bag around the end of the hose to catch any leaks or drips.

3A. If the caliper will be removed from the vehicle, remove the caliper mounting bolts (B, **Figure 24**) and the caliper.

3B. If the caliper will be will be left attached to the brake hose:

    a. Remove the caliper mounting bolts (B, **Figure 24**) and secure the caliper with a length of wire. Do not allow the caliper to hang by the brake hose.

    b. Insert a spacer block between the brake pads.

> *NOTE*
> *The use of a spacer block will prevent the pistons from being forced out of the caliper if the brake pedal is applied with the brake caliper removed.*

4. Spread the pads so there is clearance to fit the caliper over the brake disc.

5. Position the caliper over the brake disc and hub assembly, and slide the caliper down around the brake disc. Make sure the rear brake hose is not twisted.

6. Install and tighten the rear caliper mounting bolts (B, **Figure 24**) to 48 N•m (35 ft.-lb.).

> *NOTE*
> *The caliper's lower mounting bolt will require a torque adapter ([**Figure 15**] Motion Pro Torque Wrench Adapter part No. 08-0134 or equivalent) to tighten it with a torque wrench. Refer to **Torque Adapters** in **Tools** Chapter One.*

7. If the brake hose was disconnected, place a new sealing washer on each side of the brake hose. Position the hose against the caliper (C, **Figure 24**) and tighten the banjo bolt (A, **Figure 24**) to 27 N•m (20 ft.-lb.).

8. If the brake hose was disconnected from the caliper, fill and bleed the brake system as described in this chapter.

9. Operate the brake pedal several times to seat the pads.

10. Check that the hub spins freely and the brake operates properly.

11. Install the rear wheel (Chapter Thirteen).

Overhaul

These procedures apply to the front (**Figure 25**) and rear (**Figure 26**) brake calipers.

Read *Brake Service Notes* in this chapter.

Fixed shafts and boots inspection/lubrication

The brake calipers are a floating design. Fixed shafts mounted on the caliper bracket allow the brake caliper to slide or float during piston movement. The rubber boots installed over each shaft prevent dirt from entering and causing shaft wear. A grooved or damaged shaft may bind and

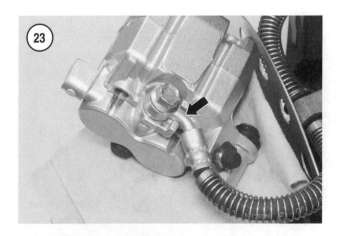

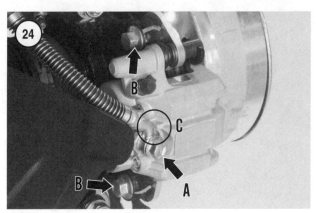

prevent caliper movement. If a caliper is not free to move, it causes the brake pads to drag on the brake disc. This will cause unnecessary pad wear and may overheat the disc and brake fluid.

The fixed shafts and boots can be serviced with the brake calipers mounted on the vehicle.

> *NOTE*
> *The rubber boots used on the front and rear brake calipers and the caliper brackets are not available separately. Handle the rubber boots carefully to prevent damage.*

1. Remove the brake pads as described in this chapter.

2A. Remove the front brake caliper boots as follows:

    a. Slide the caliper bracket (**Figure 27**) out of the caliper.

    b. Remove the caliper boots (**Figure 28**).

2B. Remove the rear brake caliper boots as follows:

    a. Slide the caliper bracket (**Figure 29**) out of the caliper.

    b. Remove the caliper boots (**Figure 30**).

3. Inspect the fixed shaft and boot assembly as follows:

    a. Inspect the rubber boots for hardness, age deterioration and damage.

    b. Inspect the caliper bracket fixed shafts (**Figure 31**, typical) for excessive wear, uneven wear, steps and other damage.

4. Installation is the reverse of these steps. Note the following:

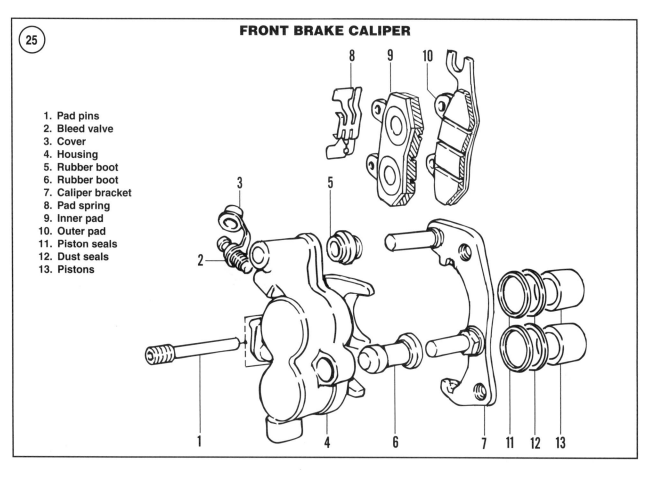

FRONT BRAKE CALIPER

25

1. Pad pins
2. Bleed valve
3. Cover
4. Housing
5. Rubber boot
6. Rubber boot
7. Caliper bracket
8. Pad spring
9. Inner pad
10. Outer pad
11. Piston seals
12. Dust seals
13. Pistons

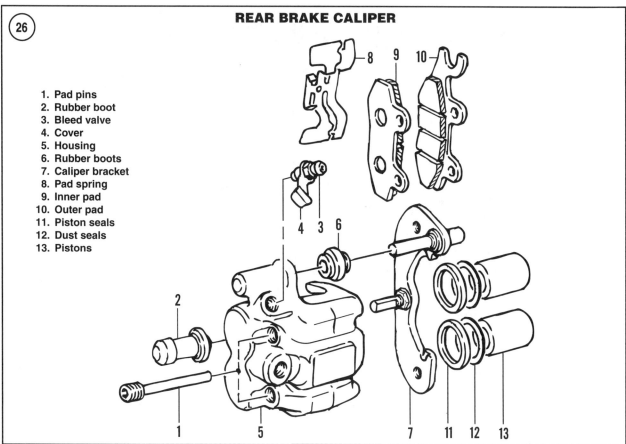

REAR BRAKE CALIPER

26

1. Pad pins
2. Rubber boot
3. Bleed valve
4. Cover
5. Housing
6. Rubber boots
7. Caliper bracket
8. Pad spring
9. Inner pad
10. Outer pad
11. Piston seals
12. Dust seals
13. Pistons

15

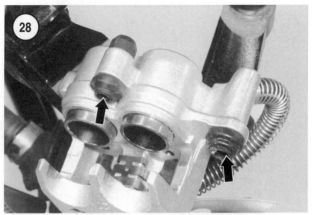

a. Partially pack the boots with silicone brake grease and install the boots facing in their original direction. Refer to **Figure 28** (front) or **Figure 30** (rear).

b. Lightly lubricate the fixed shafts with silicone brake grease.

Disassembly

1. Remove the brake pads and pad spring as described in this chapter.

2. Remove the caliper, caliper bracket and rubber boots as described in this section.

3. Close the bleed valve so air cannot escape.

> *WARNING*
> *Wear eye protection when using compressed air to remove the pistons and keep your fingers away from the pistons to prevent injury.*

> *CAUTION*
> *Do not try to pry the piston(s) out. This may damage the piston and caliper bore.*

4. Cushion the caliper piston with a shop rag and position the caliper with the piston bores facing down. Be sure to keep hands away from the pistons and apply compressed air through the brake hose port (**Figure 32**) to pop the pistons out. If only one piston came out, block its bore opening with a piece of thick rubber (old inner tube), wooden block and clamp as shown in **Figure 33**. Apply compressed air again and remove the remaining piston.

> *CAUTION*
> *Do not damage the caliper bore grooves when removing the seals in Step 5.*

5. Remove the dust (A, **Figure 34**) and piston (B) seals from the caliper bore grooves and discard them.

6. Remove the bleed valve and its cover from the caliper.

7. Clean and inspect the brake caliper assembly as described in this section.

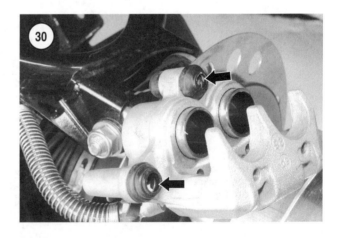

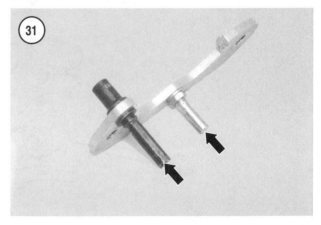

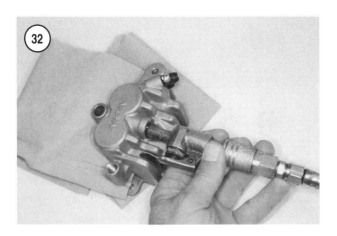

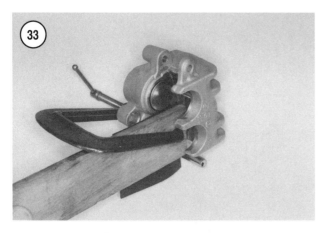

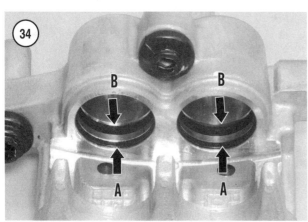

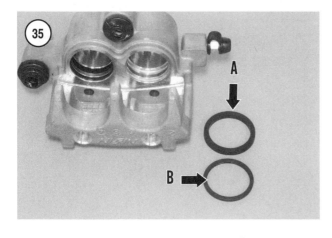

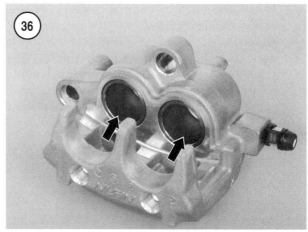

Assembly

Use new DOT 4 brake fluid when lubricating the parts in the following steps.

1. Install the bleed valve and cover into the caliper and tighten finger-tight.
2. Soak the new piston and dust seals in DOT 4 brake fluid.
3. Lubricate the piston(s) with DOT 4 brake fluid.

NOTE
*The piston seals (A, **Figure 35**) are thicker than the dust seals (B).*

4. Install new piston seals (B, **Figure 34**) into the cylinder bore rear grooves.
5. Install new dust seals (A, **Figure 34**) into the cylinder bore front grooves.

NOTE
Check that each seal fits squarely in its groove.

6. Install the pistons into the caliper bore with their open side facing out (**Figure 36**). To prevent the piston from damaging the seals, turn the pistons into the bores by hand until they bottom.
7. Service and install the rubber boots into the caliper as described in this section.
8. Install the caliper bracket as described in this section.
9. Install the brake caliper, pad spring and brake pads as described in this chapter.

Inspection

Replace worn or damaged parts.
1. Clean and dry the caliper assembly as follows:
   a. Handle the brake components carefully when servicing them.
   b. Use only DOT 4 brake fluid or isopropyl alcohol to wash rubber parts in the brake system. Never allow any petroleum-based cleaner to contact the rubber

15

parts. These chemicals cause the rubber to swell, requiring their replacement.

c. Clean the dust and piston seal grooves carefully to avoid damaging the caliper bores (**Figure 37**). Use a small pick or brush to clean the grooves. If a hard varnish residue has built up in the grooves, soak the caliper housing in solvent to help soften the residue. Then wash the caliper in soapy water and rinse completely.

d. If alcohol or solvent was used to clean the caliper, blow dry with compressed air.

e. Check the fluid passages to make sure they are clean and dry.

f. After cleaning the parts, place them on a clean lint-free cloth until reassembly.

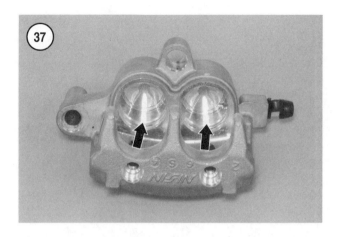

CAUTION
Do not get any oil or grease onto any of the brake caliper components. These chemicals cause the rubber parts in the brake system to swell, permanently damaging them.

2. Check each caliper bore (**Figure 37**) for corrosion, pitting and other damage. Do not hone the bores. Measure the brake caliper bore inside diameter and compare to the specification in **Table 1** or **Table 2**.

3. Inspect the pistons for pitting, corrosion, cracks or other damage. Remove light corrosion with fine emery cloth. If the piston surface (**Figure 38**) is heavily corroded and cannot be adequately cleaned, replace the piston. A corroded or pitted piston can damage the seals and cause the caliper to leak brake fluid.

4. Clean the bleed valve with compressed air. Check the valve threads for damage. Replace the dust cap if missing or damaged.

5. Clean the banjo bolt with compressed air.

6. Inspect the caliper bracket fixed shafts and rubber boots as described in this section.

MASTER CYLINDER

A single master cylinder is mounted inside the front, left part of vehicle and secured to the frame bulkhead with two bolts. A pushrod mounted on the brake pedal contacts the primary piston assembly mounted inside the master cylinder.

Read *Brake Service Notes* in this chapter.

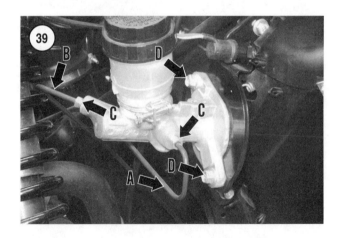

Removal

CAUTION
When removing and installing the master cylinder, make sure not to bend the metal brake lines or damage the nuts that secure the brake lines to the master cylinder.

1. Open the hood.

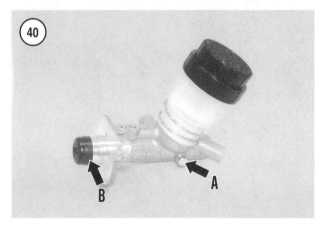

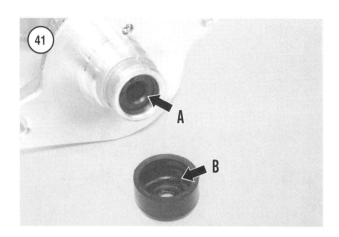

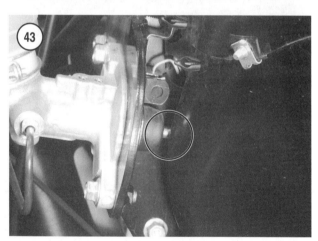

2. Remove the cap, diaphragm and float from the master cylinder. The diaphragm is secured to the cap with a plastic ring and should remain in place when the cap is removed. Use a syringe to remove brake fluid from the reservoir. Reinstall the float, cap and diaphragm to prevent debris from entering the reservoir.

3. Place a plastic sheet underneath the master cylinder to prevent spilt brake fluid from contacting other parts.

NOTE
*The front brake line (A, **Figure 39**) is mounted on the left side of the master cylinder. The rear brake line (B, **Figure 39**) is mounted*

on the right side. Note the routing before removal.

4. Loosen the nuts and disconnect the brake lines (C, **Figure 39**) from the master cylinder. Cover each pipe opening with a plastic bag to prevent contamination.

5. Remove the mounting bolts (D, **Figure 39**) and the master cylinder assembly.

NOTE
*Do not remove the stop screw (A, **Figure 40**) from the master cylinder. This screw positions the secondary piston assembly inside the master cylinder. Because the secondary piston assembly is under spring tension, if the screw is removed, the master cylinder will have to be disassembled as described in this section to reposition the secondary piston assembly and reinstall the screw.*

6. Service the master cylinder as described in this section.

7. Remove the dust boot (B, **Figure 40**) from the end of the master cylinder and check the bore (A, **Figure 41**) for any sign of brake fluid. If brake fluid is leaking from the piston bore, disassemble the master cylinder and install a new master cylinder kit as described in this section.

8. If necessary, remove the cotter pin and clevis pin (A, **Figure 42**) securing the brake pedal pushrod to the brake pedal. Then remove the brake pedal pushrod (B, **Figure 42**).

Installation

1. If the brake pedal pushrod was removed, clean the pushrod and clevis pin. Lubricate the clevis pin shoulder with lithium grease. Then reinstall the pushrod (B, **Figure 42**) through the cover and secure onto the brake pedal with the clevis pin and a new cotter pin (A). Bend the cotter pin arms over to lock it.

2. With the dust boot removed, wipe the end of the master cylinder and piston with a clean rag. Lubricate the primary piston bore (A, **Figure 41**) and the inner bore lip of the dust boot (B) with silicone brake grease. Then install the dust boot onto the master cylinder (B, **Figure 40**).

3. Wipe the brake pedal pushrod with a clean rag. Then lubricate the end of the pushrod with silicone brake grease.

4. Install the master cylinder by inserting the brake pedal pushrod through the dust boot and into the master cylinder primary piston. Refer to **Figure 43**.

5. Install the master cylinder mounting bolts (D, **Figure 39**) and tighten to 16 N•m (12 ft.-lb.).

6. Wipe off the brake line nuts and brake lines with a clean rag. Then thread the nuts into the master cylinder (C, **Figure 39**) and tighten to 19 N•m (14 ft.-lb.).

7. Fill the master cylinder with DOT 4 brake fluid and bleed the brake system as described in this chapter.

8. Check the brake pedal free play (Chapter Three).

9. Turn the ignition switch on and make sure the rear brake light comes on when operating the brake pedal.

15

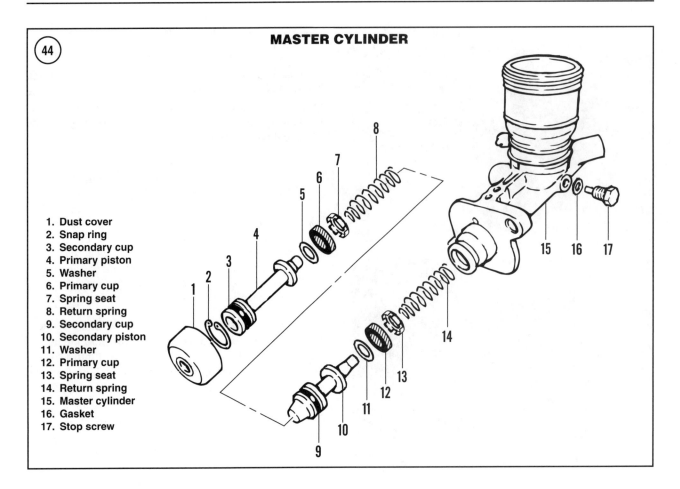

MASTER CYLINDER

1. Dust cover
2. Snap ring
3. Secondary cup
4. Primary piston
5. Washer
6. Primary cup
7. Spring seat
8. Return spring
9. Secondary cup
10. Secondary piston
11. Washer
12. Primary cup
13. Spring seat
14. Return spring
15. Master cylinder
16. Gasket
17. Stop screw

10. Slowly road test the vehicle in safe area to make sure the brakes operate correctly. If the pedal is spongy or its travel is excessive, bleed the brake system again.

Disassembly

A master cylinder kit is available from the manufacturer and contains both the primary and secondary piston assemblies. The snap ring used to secure the piston assemblies into the master cylinder is not available separately. This snap ring is only available as part of the kit. Also, do not try to remove the reservoir from the master cylinder.

Refer to **Figure 44**.

1. Remove the master cylinder as described in this section.

2. Clean the exterior of the master cylinder with soapy water and rinse with water.

3. Remove the cap (A, **Figure 45**), diaphragm (B), plastic ring (C) and float (D) from the master cylinder.

4. To service the cap assembly (**Figure 45**), perform the following:

   a. The diaphragm (B, **Figure 45**) is secured inside the cap (A) with the plastic ring (C). Remove the diaphragm (**Figure 46**) by carefully prying it off the plastic ring. The plastic ring may come off attached to the diaphragm.

   b. If the plastic ring (**Figure 47**) remained in the cap, turn it to align two of its four tabs with the two slots

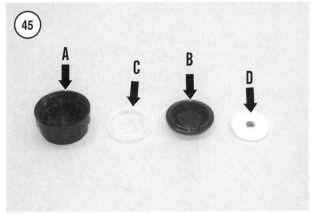

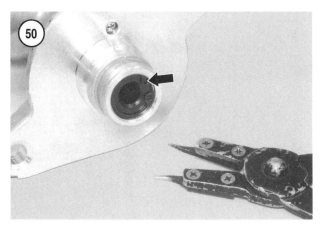

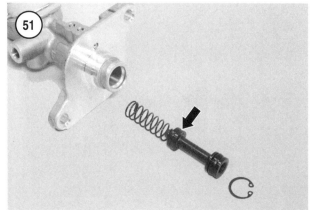

in the cap, then carefully pry the plastic ring out and remove it.

WARNING
*Inspect the relief port located inside the reservoir for any foreign matter. If this port remains closed after the brake pedal is released, pressure will build in the system and cause brake drag. The relief port is the smaller of the two ports (**Figure 48**).*

5. Remove the dust boot (**Figure 49**) from the master cylinder.

6. Compress the piston assemblies and remove the snap ring (**Figure 50**) with snap ring pliers.

7. Remove the primary piston assembly (**Figure 51**) from the master cylinder bore.

8. Remove the secondary piston assembly as follows:
   a. Insert a 3/8 in. socket extension (A, **Figure 52**) into the master cylinder and use it to compress the secondary piston assembly. Then remove the stop screw (B, **Figure 52**) and its gasket and remove the socket extension.
   b. Block off the rear brake line port with a M10 × 1.00 mm bolt (A, **Figure 53**). Do not tighten the bolt against the brake line fitting inside the port. Then block off the stop screw opening with a M6 × 1.00 bolt and washer (B, **Figure 53**).

WARNING
Wear safety goggles to protect your eyes when removing the secondary piston assembly.

   c. Cover the bore with a clean paper towel and direct low-pressure compressed air through the front brake line port (C, **Figure 53**) to remove the secondary piston assembly (D). Refer to **Figure 54**.

9. Clean and inspect the master cylinder assembly as described in this section.

Assembly

1. Open the new master cylinder kit and identify the primary (A, **Figure 55**) and secondary (B) piston assemblies.

15

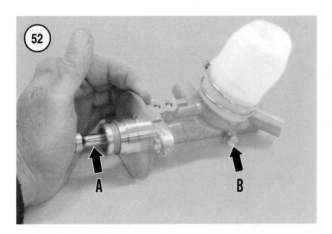

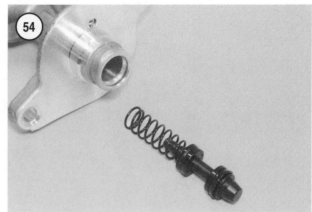

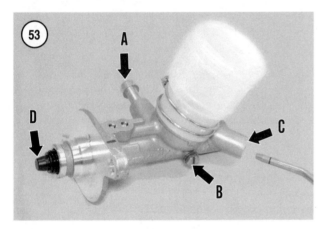

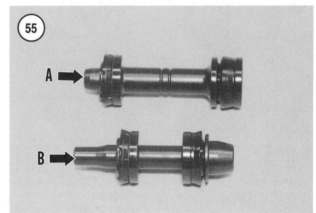

Note that the primary piston has two grooves in its middle shoulder.

2. Clean the new parts with new DOT 4 brake fluid and place on a clean, lint-free paper towel.

3. Assemble the primary piston (**Figure 56**) as follows:

    a. Install the washer (A, **Figure 56**) onto the piston.

    b. Slide the primary cup (B, **Figure 56**) onto the piston with its closed side facing toward the piston.

    c. Install the spring seat (C, **Figure 56**) with its arms facing toward and then seating onto the primary cup shoulder.

    d. Push the small end of the spring firmly onto the piston shoulder (**Figure 57**).

4. Assemble the secondary piston (**Figure 58**) as follows:

    a. Install the washer (A, **Figure 58**) onto the piston.

    b. Slide the primary cup (B, **Figure 58**) onto the piston with its closed side facing toward the piston.

    c. Install the spring seat (C, **Figure 58**) with its arms facing toward and then seating onto the primary cup shoulder.

    d. Push the small end of the spring firmly onto the piston shoulder (**Figure 59**).

5. Lubricate the master cylinder bore with new DOT 4 brake fluid.

CAUTION
Do not allow the piston cups to tear or turn inside out when installing the pistons into the

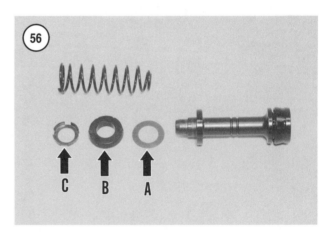

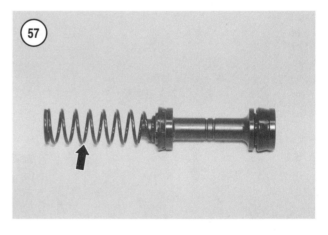

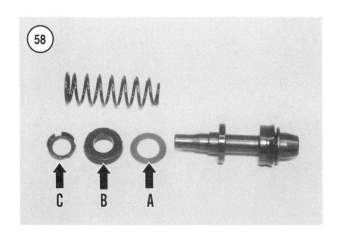

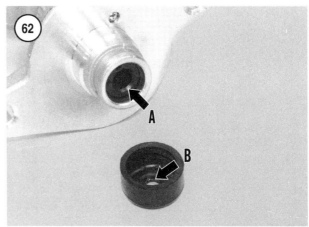

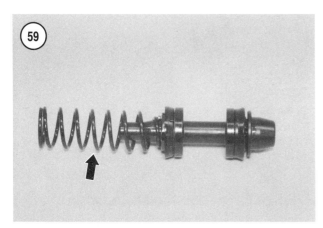

master cylinder bore. The cups are larger than the bore.

6. Install the secondary piston assembly and stop screw as follows:

    a. Install a new gasket onto the stop screw.

    b. Install the secondary piston assembly (A, **Figure 60**) into the master cylinder, spring end first.

    c. Insert a 3/8 in. socket extension (A, **Figure 52**) into the master cylinder and use it to compress the secondary piston assembly until the shoulder identified in **Figure 61** aligns with the stop screw hole in the master cylinder.

    d. Install the stop screw and tighten to 9 N•m (80 in.-lb.). Then remove the socket extension and allow the secondary piston to return and rest against the stop screw.

7. Install the primary piston assembly (B, **Figure 60**) into the master cylinder, spring end first. The open end of the spring will fit over the shoulder on the secondary piston.

8. Press the piston into the bore and install the snap ring with its flat side facing out into the groove in the master cylinder. Make sure the snap ring seats in the groove completely. Then push and release the piston assemblies to make sure they move without any binding or roughness and that the primary piston seats against the snap ring when at rest.

9. Lubricate the primary piston bore (A, **Figure 62**) and the inner bore lip of the dust boot (B) with silicone brake grease. Then install the dust boot (**Figure 49**) onto the master cylinder.

10. Assemble the cap and diaphragm assembly as follows:

    a. Install the plastic ring into the cap with its four tabs (**Figure 47**) pointing toward the cap. Align two of its tabs with the two slots in the cap and push the plastic ring until it snaps in place inside the cap.

    b. Install the diaphragm so that the side marked UP SIDE (**Figure 63**) faces toward the cap. Then seat the diaphragm's upper groove over the shoulder on the plastic ring (**Figure 46**). Make sure the diaphragm seats fully onto the plastic ring before installing the cap onto the master cylinder.

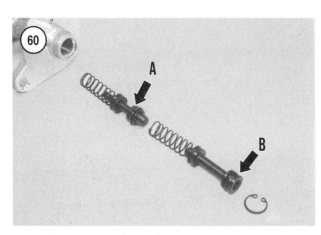

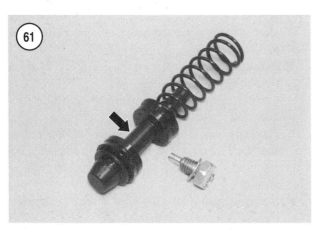

15

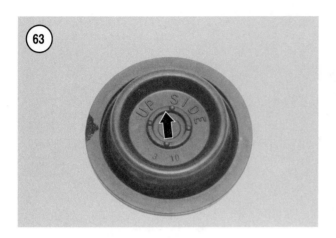

c. Install the float and cap.

11. Install the master cylinder as described in this section.

Inspection

Replace worn or damaged parts.

1. Clean and dry the master cylinder assembly as follows:

CAUTION
When cleaning and inspecting the primary and secondary piston assemblies, do not intermix the parts.

a. Do not try to remove the reservoir from the master cylinder body. Doing so will damage the reservoir and require replacement of the master cylinder assembly.

b. Handle the brake components carefully when servicing them.

WARNING
Never use petroleum-based solvents to clean brake components, or allow solvent to contact rubber parts. Petroleum-based chemicals cause the rubber parts to swell, requiring their replacement.

c. Use only DOT 4 brake fluid or isopropyl alcohol to wash rubber parts in the brake system.

d. Clean the master cylinder snap ring groove carefully with a small pick or brush. If a hard varnish residue has built up in the groove, soak the master cylinder in solvent to help soften the residue. Then wash in soapy water and thoroughly rinse in clear water.

e. Check for plugged relief and supply ports in the master cylinder reservoir. Clean with compressed air.

f. Blow the master cylinder dry with compressed air.

g. Place cleaned parts on a clean lint-free cloth until reassembly.

2. Inspect the plastic reservoir for cracks and other damage. If the reservoir is damaged, replace the master cylinder assembly. The reservoir is not available as a replacement item. Make sure the reservoir clamp is tight.

3. Inspect the primary and secondary piston assemblies (**Figure 44**) as follows:

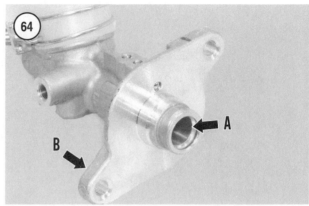

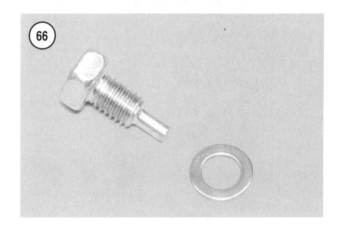

a. Refer to **Figure 56** (primary) or **Figure 58** (secondary) to partially disassemble the piston assemblies. Do not remove the secondary cup from either piston.

b. Check for a broken, distorted or collapsed piston return spring.

c. Check for worn, cracked, damaged or swollen primary and secondary cups.

d. Check the shoulders on each piston for wear, pitting and other damage. Color scuffing is acceptable, but any wear into the shoulder requires piston replacement.

e. If any of these parts show visible wear or damage, install a new master cylinder kit.

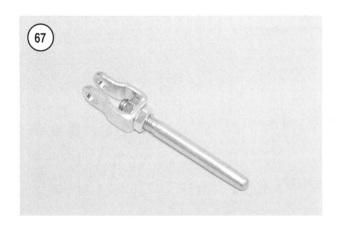

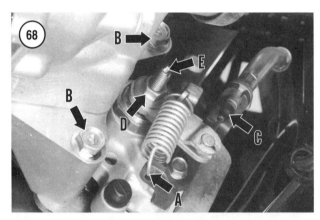

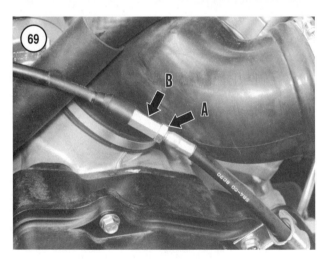

4. Check the cylinder bore (A, **Figure 64**) for corrosion, pitting and scoring. If any of these conditions are present, replace the master cylinder. Do not attempt to clean or repair the cylinder bore with a brake hone.

5. Check the master cylinder mounting flange (B, **Figure 64**) for cracks and other damage. The mating surface must be smooth.

6. Inspect the brake line fittings inside the master cylinder (**Figure 65**) for contamination, scoring and other damage.

7. Inspect the stop screw (**Figure 66**) for a worn or damaged shoulder or damaged threads. Discard the gasket.

8. Inspect the diaphragm for damage. The diaphragm prevents air from entering the reservoir and is folded so that it

can move with changes in the brake fluid level. A damaged diaphragm will allow moisture to enter the reservoir.

9. Inspect the reservoir cover for damage. Check the vent notches in the cap for contamination. These must be clear to vent the reservoir to the atmosphere.

10. Inspect the brake pedal pushrod (**Figure 67**) for scoring, cracks and other damage. The threads on the pushrod must be in good condition so the pushrod can be adjusted. Check the sides of the yoke and the clevis pin bore for damage. Replace the nuts if the shoulders are starting to round off. The end of the pushrod must be smooth as it operates against the primary piston. The pushrod parts can be replaced separately and a complete pushrod assembly is included with a new master cylinder.

PARKING BRAKE CALIPER

The parking brake is a mechanical system that locks the final drive and rear wheels only. It is independent of the hydraulic brake system. The system consists of the parking brake lever, cable, parking brake caliper, brake pads and brake disc. The brake disc is mounted onto the drive shaft coupling gear.

Pulling the parking brake lever up pulls the parking brake cable and moves the brake pads against the brake disc. Releasing the button on the parking brake lever releases the lever so it can move down and release the brake pads.

Removal

1. Park the vehicle on a level surface with the transmission shifted into low gear. Block the front wheels so the vehicle cannot roll in either direction.

2. Remove the rear skid plate (Chapter Sixteen).

3. Release the parking brake.

4. Remove the right rear wheel (Chapter Thirteen).

5. Disconnect and remove the return spring (A, **Figure 68**).

6. Remove the parking brake caliper mounting bolts (B, **Figure 68**).

> *NOTE*
> *If the parking brake cable connection is tight and cannot be disconnected at the parking brake lever, loosen the parking brake cable adjuster locknut (A, **Figure 69**) and turn adjuster (B) toward the locknut to loosen the cable free play. It is necessary to remove the rear console (Chapter Sixteen) to access the cable adjuster.*

7. Disconnect the parking brake cable from the parking brake lever (C, **Figure 68**) and remove the parking brake caliper.

Installation

1. Clean the parking brake disc with a brake cleaner and allow to dry.

15

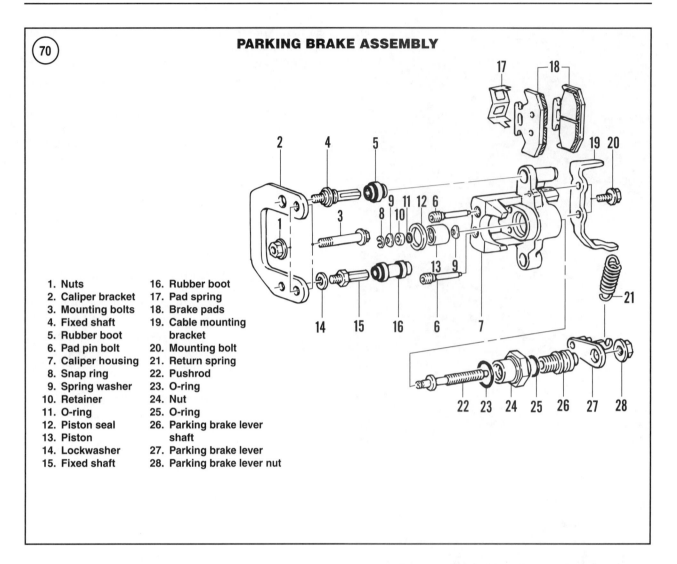

PARKING BRAKE ASSEMBLY

1. Nuts
2. Caliper bracket
3. Mounting bolts
4. Fixed shaft
5. Rubber boot
6. Pad pin bolt
7. Caliper housing
8. Snap ring
9. Spring washer
10. Retainer
11. O-ring
12. Piston seal
13. Piston
14. Lockwasher
15. Fixed shaft
16. Rubber boot
17. Pad spring
18. Brake pads
19. Cable mounting bracket
20. Mounting bolt
21. Return spring
22. Pushrod
23. O-ring
24. Nut
25. O-ring
26. Parking brake lever shaft
27. Parking brake lever
28. Parking brake lever nut

2. Align the parking brake caliper with the brake disc and reconnect the parking brake cable (C, **Figure 68**). Make sure the cable and housing are not twisted.

3. Spread the pads so there is clearance to fit the caliper over the brake disc.

4. Install the caliper over the brake disc.

NOTE
If there is not enough clearance between the brake pads to install them over the brake disc, loosen the parking brake lever nut (D, Figure 68) and turn the pushrod (E) outward.

5. Install the parking brake caliper mounting bolts (B, **Figure 68**) and tighten to 40 N•m (30 ft.-lb.).

6. Reconnect the return spring (A, **Figure 68**).

7. Adjust the parking brake and tighten the parking brake lever nut as described in Chapter Three.

8. Reinstall the right rear wheel (Chapter Thirteen).

9. Reinstall the rear skid plate (Chapter Sixteen).

Overhaul

Refer to **Figure 70**.

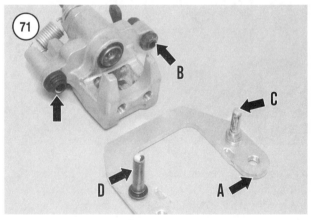

Caliper bracket, fixed shafts and boots inspection/lubrication

The parking brake caliper is a floating design. Fixed shafts mounted on the caliper bracket allow the caliper to slide or float when the parking brake is applied. The rubber boots installed over each fixed shaft prevent dirt from entering and causing shaft wear. A grooved or damaged shaft may bind and prevent caliper movement. If the caliper is

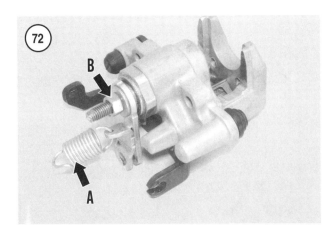

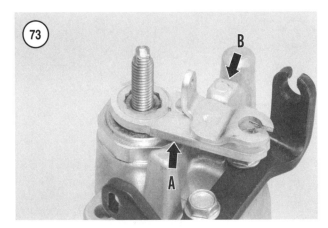

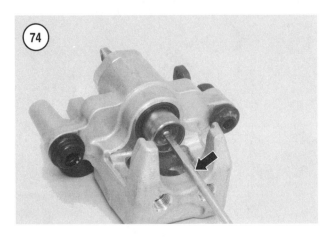

not free to float, it can cause the pads to drag on the brake disc when the parking brake lever is released. This will cause unnecessary pad wear and may overheat the disc and brake pads.

1. Remove the brake pads as described in this chapter.

2. Slide the caliper bracket (A, **Figure 71**) out of the caliper.

3. Remove the caliper boots (B, **Figure 71**).

4. Inspect the rubber boots for hardness, age deterioration and damage. Replace the boots if necessary.

5. Inspect and service the caliper bracket fixed shafts as follows:

    a. Inspect the shafts (C and D, **Figure 71**) for excessive wear, uneven wear, steps and other damage. Replace the shafts if necessary.

    b. To replace the shafts, secure the caliper bracket in a vise with soft jaws. Then loosen and remove the shaft (C, **Figure 71**) and its lockwasher or hold the shaft (D) and remove the nut. Reverse to install these shafts, making sure to clean and dry all parts. Replace the lockwasher and nut if damaged. Reinstall the parts and tighten the fixed shaft and the fixed shaft mounting nut securely.

6. Installation is the reverse of these steps. Note the following:

    a. Partially pack the boots with silicone brake grease and install the boots facing in their original direction. Refer to B, **Figure 71**.

    b. Lightly lubricate the fixed shafts with silicone brake grease.

    c. Slide the caliper bracket into the boots, making sure it slides freely.

Disassembly

1. Remove the brake pads as described in this chapter.

2. Remove the caliper bracket and rubber boots as described in this section.

3. Remove the spring (A, **Figure 72**).

4. Hold the caliper securely and remove the parking brake lever nut (B, **Figure 72**) and lever (A, **Figure 73**).

5. Turn the pushrod with a screwdriver (**Figure 74**) to remove the piston assembly (**Figure 75**).

6. Turn and remove the parking brake lever shaft (A, **Figure 76**).

7. Remove the piston seal (**Figure 77**).

8. If necessary, secure the parking brake assembly in a vise and remove the nut (B, **Figure 76**) and its O-ring.

9. If necessary, remove the snap ring and disassemble the piston/pushrod assembly as shown in **Figure 70**.

10. If necessary, unbolt and remove the cable mounting bracket from the caliper.

11. Inspect as described in this section.

15

Assembly

1. If removed install the cable mounting bracket and tighten the mounting bolts securely.

2. If the piston was removed from the pushrod, reassemble the parts in the order shown in **Figure 70** using a new O-ring and snap ring. Lubricate the O-ring with silicone brake grease. Make sure the snap ring seats in the pushrod groove completely.

3. If the nut (B, **Figure 76**) was removed, install it with a new O-ring. Lubricate the O-ring with silicone brake grease and tighten the nut securely.

4. Install a new piston seal with its open side facing out as shown in **Figure 77**. Install the seal until it bottoms squarely in its bore. Then lubricate the seal lip with silicone brake grease.

5. Lubricate a new O-ring (A, **Figure 78**) with silicone brake grease and install it onto the parking brake lever shaft.

6. Lubricate the nut bore (B, **Figure 78**) with silicone brake grease. Then turn the parking brake lever shaft into the nut until it bottoms (A, **Figure 76**).

7. Insert the piston into the caliper while threading the pushrod into the parking brake lever shaft until the pushrod extends past the end of the parking brake lever shaft by 5-6 mm (0.20-0.24 in.) as shown in **Figure 79**.

8. Install the brake lever (A, **Figure 73**) and then rotate it until it contacts the stopper (B) on the caliper housing.

9. Install the parking brake arm nut (B, **Figure 72**) and tighten finger-tight.

10. Install the piston fully (**Figure 74**) by turning the pushrod with a screwdriver.

11. Install the rubber boots and caliper bracket as described in this section.

12. Install the brake pads as described in this chapter.

13. Hook the spring (A, **Figure 72**) onto the parking brake lever (A, **Figure 69**).

14. Install the parking brake caliper as described in this section.

15. Adjust the parking brake (Chapter Three).

Inspection

1. Clean and dry the parking brake caliper.

2. Inspect the piston (A, **Figure 80**) and the caliper bore for damage.

3. The pushrod (B, **Figure 80**) must be straight so it can turn freely when adjusting the parking brake. Inspect the pushrod and parking brake lever shaft (C, **Figure 80**) threads for damage.

4. Inspect the parking brake lever shaft (C, **Figure 80**) and mating nut (B, **Figure 78**) for damage. Make sure the shaft turns easily through the nut.

5. Inspect the cable mounting bracket for cracks where the cable mounts and other damage.

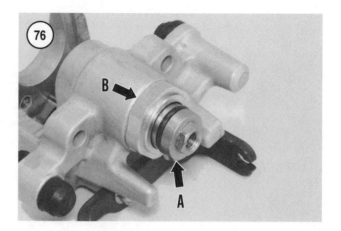

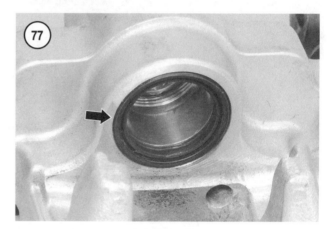

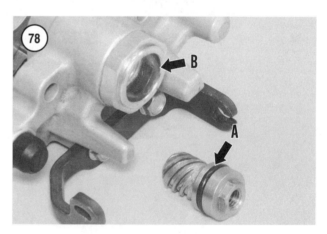

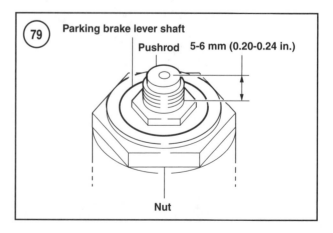

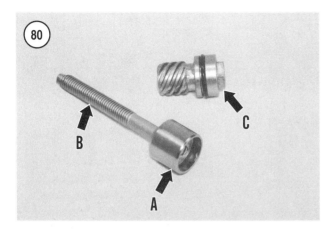

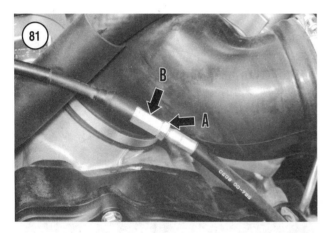

PARKING BRAKE CABLE

If the parking brake cannot be properly adjusted and the parking brake pads and brake disc thickness measurements are within specifications, the parking brake cable may have stretched beyond the service limit and should be replaced.

Removal/Installation

1. Remove the seats (Chapter Sixteen).
2. Remove the rear console (Chapter Sixteen).
3. Block the front wheels so the vehicle cannot roll
4. Remove the right rear wheel (Chapter Thirteen).
5. Release the parking brake.
6. Loosen the parking brake cable adjuster locknut (A, **Figure 81**) and adjuster (B).
7. Disconnect the return spring (A, **Figure 82**) at the parking brake lever.
8. Note the cable routing from the parking brake lever to the parking brake caliper. Then remove the cable from the frame clamps.
9. Loosen the locknut (A, **Figure 83**) securing the cable to the parking brake lever mounting bracket.
10. Disconnect the rear cable end (B, **Figure 82**) from the parking brake lever at the caliper.
11. Disconnect the front cable end (B, **Figure 83**).
12. Remove the parking brake cable.
13. Installation is the reverse of these steps.
14. Adjust the parking brake (Chapter Three).

PARKING BRAKE LEVER

Parts required to rebuild the parking brake lever are not available. If the hand lever or ratchet mechanism is damaged, replace the lever assembly.

This section describes removal of the parking brake lever from the vehicle. However, when it is only necessary to remove the parking brake lever to provide access when performing other service procedures, the lever can be removed without disconnecting it from its cable. Remove the lever and set it aside so the cable is not kinked or damaged.

Removal/Installation

1. Remove the seats (Chapter Sixteen).
2. Remove the rear console (Chapter Sixteen).
3. Block the front wheels so the vehicle cannot roll.
4. Release the parking brake.
5. Loosen the parking brake cable adjuster locknut (A, **Figure 81**) and turn the adjuster (B) inward to loosen the cable free play.
6. Loosen the locknut (A, **Figure 83**) securing the cable to the parking brake lever mounting bracket.
7. Disconnect the front cable end (B, **Figure 83**).

15

NOTE
If there is not enough free play to disconnect the cable at the release lever, perform Step 8.

8. If necessary, disconnect the cable at the parking brake lever as follows:
   a. Disconnect the return spring (A, **Figure 82**) at the parking brake lever.
   b. Disconnect the rear cable end (B, **Figure 82**) from the parking brake lever.
9. Disconnect the parking brake switch electrical connector. A, **Figure 84** shows the switch wiring harness. It is not necessary to remove the switch.
10. Remove the two mounting bolts (B, **Figure 84**) and the parking brake lever.
11. Installation is the reverse of these steps. Note the following:
   a. Install the parking brake lever so the throttle cable is routed on the left side of the lever (**Figure 85**).
   b. Tighten the parking brake lever mounting bolts to 13 N•m (115 in.-lb.).
   c. Adjust the parking brake (Chapter Three).

BRAKE HOSE AND BRAKE LINE

Brake lines connect the master cylinder to the front and rear brake hose assemblies. Refer to **Figure 86**.

Check the brake hoses and the brake lines at the brake inspection intervals listed in Chapter Three. Replace the brake hoses if they show signs of wear or damage, or if they have bulges, feel soft or signs of chafing. Replace the brake lines if they are bent, cracked or leaking.

Removal/Installation

1. Drain the brake system as described in this chapter.
2. Use a plastic drop cloth to cover areas that could be damaged by spilled brake fluid.
3. When removing a brake hose or the rear brake line, note the following:
   a. Note the hose or line routing on a piece of paper.
   b. Remove parts as required to access and replace the brake hose or rear brake line.
   c. Remove any bolts or brackets securing the brake hose or brake line to the frame or suspension component.
   d. Before removing the banjo bolts, note how the end of the brake hose is installed or indexed against the part it is threaded into. The hoses must be installed facing in their original position. Refer to **Figure 87** (front) or **Figure 88** (rear).
4. Replace damaged banjo bolts.
5. Reverse these steps to install the new brake hoses (3 and 13, **Figure 86**), while noting the following:

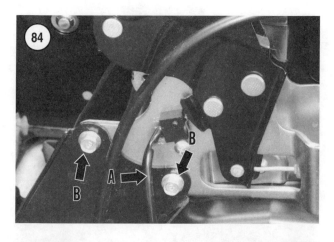

   a. Compare the new and old hoses to make sure they are the same.
   b. Clean the *new* washers, banjo bolts and hose ends to remove any contamination.
   c. Referring to the notes made during removal, route the brake hose along its original path.
   d. Tighten the brake hose joint mounting bolts (9, **Figure 86**) securely.
   e. Install a *new* banjo bolt washer on each side of the brake hose.
   f. Tighten the banjo bolts to 27 N•m (20 ft.-lb.).
   g. Tighten the front brake hose clamp mounting bolts (**Figure 89**) to 7 N•m (62 in.-lb.).
6. Reverse these steps to install new brake lines (10 and 12, **Figure 86**), while noting the following:
   a. The brake lines are available from the manufacturer and come equipped with nuts and preflared ends.
   b. Blow the new brake line out with compressed air before installing it.
   c. Wipe the brake line ends and joint nuts to remove any contamination.
   d. Do not bend the brake line or try to force it into position during installation. This creases the metal and may cause it to leak.
   e. Cover the brake line ends with a plastic bag during installation.

BRAKE HOSES AND BRAKE LINES

86

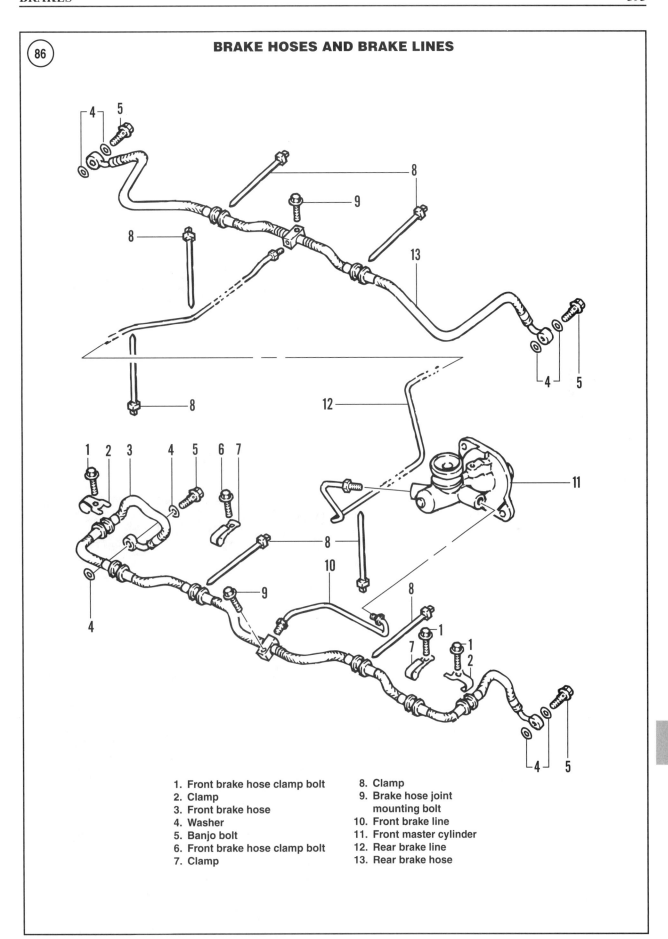

1. Front brake hose clamp bolt
2. Clamp
3. Front brake hose
4. Washer
5. Banjo bolt
6. Front brake hose clamp bolt
7. Clamp
8. Clamp
9. Brake hose joint mounting bolt
10. Front brake line
11. Front master cylinder
12. Rear brake line
13. Rear brake hose

15

f. Install the brake line following its original mounting path as noted during removal.

g. Brake lines can be damaged from vibration and heat. Install the brake lines in their original position while using original mounting fasteners and clamps.

h. Make sure there is no stress on the brake line.

i. Tighten the brake line nuts to 19 N•m (14 ft.-lb.). Refer to **Figure 90** and **Figure 91**.

7. After installing a new front brake hose assembly (3, **Figure 86**), turn the steering wheel from side to side to make sure the hose does not rub against any part or pull away from its brake unit.

8. Bleed the brake system as described in this chapter.

BRAKE DISC

Inspection

The front and rear brake discs and the parking brake disc can be inspected while installed on the vehicle. Small marks on the disc are not important, but deep scratches or other marks may reduce braking effectiveness and increase brake pad wear. If these grooves are evident and the brake pads are wearing rapidly, replace the brake disc.

Refer to **Tables 1-3** for brake disc specifications.

1A. When checking the front and rear wheel brake discs, support the vehicle with the wheel (front or rear) off the ground.

1B. When checking the parking brake disc, support the vehicle on jack stands with the rear wheels off the ground and raise the bed.

2. Measure the disc thickness at several locations around the disc (**Figure 92**, typical). Replace the disc if its thickness at any point is less than the service limit.

3. Measure brake disc runout as follows:

a. Shift the vehicle into two-wheel drive and set the select lever to neutral.

b. When measuring rear brake disc or parking brake disc runout, block the front wheels to prevent the vehicle from rolling in either direction and release the parking brake.

c. Remove the wheel(s) as described in Chapter Eleven or Chapter Thirteen.

d. Clean the disc of any rust or corrosion and wipe clean with brake cleaner. Never use an oil-based solvent that may leave an oil residue on the disc.

NOTE
It is more difficult to measure the front left side brake disc runout because the left front axle is connected directly to the differential ring gear and there is more resistance when turning the hub. When measuring the runout on this side, lower the vehicle so the right wheel is on the ground.

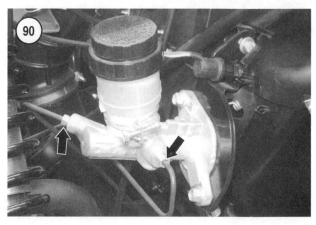

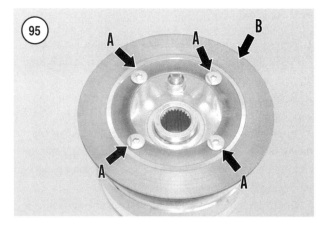

e. Position a dial indicator stem against the brake disc (**Figure 93**). Zero the dial gauge and slowly turn the wheel with a ratchet and socket to measure runout.

f. If the disc runout is out of specification, first check for loose or missing brake disc fasteners. Also check the knuckle bearings for damage.

Removal/Installation

When servicing the brake discs in this section, clean the discs and their mating surfaces of any rust or corrosion and spray clean with brake cleaner. Never use an oil-based solvent that may leave an oil residue on the disc.

Front brake discs

1. Remove the front hub (Chapter Eleven).
2. Remove the bolts (A, **Figure 94**) and the brake disc (B). These bolts are secured with a threadlocking compound and may be difficult to remove. Replace the bolts if the hex portion is damaged or starting to round out.
3. Install the brake disc onto the hub so the side with the chamfered mounting bolt holes faces out. Apply a medium-strength threadlocking compound onto the brake disc mounting bolts and tighten to 30 N•m (22 ft.-lb.).
4. Install the front hub (Chapter Eleven).

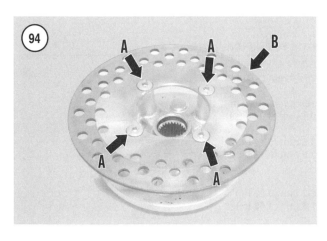

15

Rear brake discs

1. Remove the rear hub (Chapter Thirteen).
2. Remove the bolts (A, **Figure 95**) and the brake disc (B). These bolts are secured with a threadlocking compound and may be difficult to remove. Replace the bolts if the hex portion is damaged or starting to round out.
3. Install the brake disc onto the hub so the side with the chamfered mounting bolt holes faces out. Apply a medium-strength threadlocking compound onto the brake disc mounting bolts and tighten to 30 N•m (22 ft.-lb.).
4. Install the rear hub (Chapter Thirteen).

Parking brake disc

1. Remove the final drive gear unit (Chapter Fourteen).

2. Mark the disc's outer side so it can be installed facing its original direction.

3. Remove the nuts and bolts (A, **Figure 96**) and then the parking brake disc (B).

4. Install the brake disc with the side marked in Step 2 facing out. Install the brake disc, mounting bolts and nuts. Hold the bolts and tighten the nuts in a crossing pattern to 10 N•m (88 in.-lb.).

5. Install the final drive gear unit (Chapter Fourteen).

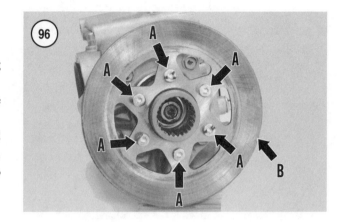

Table 1 FRONT BRAKE SERVICE SPECIFICATIONS

Brake fluid	DOT 4
Brake caliper bore inside diameter	27.0 mm (1.06 in.)
Brake disc	
Outside diameter	200.0 mm (7.87 in.)
Runout limit	0.1 mm (0.004 in.)
Thickness	
New	3.5 mm (0.14 in.)
Minimum	3.0 mm (0.12 in.)
Brake pads	
Thickness	
New	5.2 mm (0.20 in.)
Minimum	1.5 mm (0.06 in.)
Master cylinder inside diameter	17.46 mm (0.69 in.)

Table 2 REAR BRAKE SERVICE SPECIFICATIONS

Brake fluid	DOT 4
Brake caliper bore inside diameter	25.40 mm (1.00 in.)
Brake disc	
Outside diameter	184.6 mm (7.27 in.)
Runout limit	0.1 mm (0.004 in.)
Thickness	
New	3.5 mm (0.14 in.)
Minimum	3.0 mm (0.12 in.)
Brake pads	
Thickness	
New	5.2 mm (0.20 in.)
Minimum	1.5 mm (0.06 in.)

Table 3 PARKING BRAKE SERVICE SPECIFICATIONS

Brake disc	
Outside diameter	165.0 mm (6.50 in.)
Runout limit	0.1 mm (0.004 in.)
Thickness	
New	3.2 mm (0.13 in.)
Minimum	1.0 mm (0.04 in.)
Brake pads	
Thickness	
New	3.2 mm (0.13 in.)
Minimum	1.0 mm (0.04 in.)

Table 4 BRAKE TORQUE SPECIFICATIONS

	N•m	in.-lb.	ft.-lb.
Banjo bolts	27	–	20
Brake line nuts[1]	19	–	14
Caliper bleed valve	5	44	–
Front brake caliper mounting bolts	48	–	35
Front brake disc mounting bolts[2]	30	–	22
Front brake hose clamp bolts	7	62	–
Front brake pad pins	17	–	12.5
Master cylinder mounting bolts	16	–	12
Master cylinder piston stop screw	9	80	–
Parking brake disc mounting bolt	10	88	–
Parking brake caliper mounting bolts	40	–	30
Parking brake lever mounting bolt	13	115	–
Parking brake pad pins[2]	17	–	12.5
Rear brake caliper mounting bolts	48	–	35
Rear brake disc mounting bolts[2]	30	–	22
Rear brake pad pins	17	–	12.5

1. Brake line nuts are mounted on the metal brake lines.
2. Refer to text.

15

CHAPTER SIXTEEN

BODY

This chapter services the body components and the accelerator/brake pedal assembly.

Read *Safety* and *Service Methods* in Chapter One before servicing the vehicle in this chapter.

Table 1 is at the end of this chapter.

PLASTIC RIVETS

Plastic rivets (**Figure 1**) are used to position and secure many of the plastic panels on the vehicle. To remove a rivet, turn its threaded pin (A, **Figure 1**) with a Phillips screwdriver until the rivet (B) is loose and can be pulled out. If the threaded pin is stripped and will not turn out, carefully pry the rivet out of the body component with a tack tool (**Figure 2**) or equivalent automotive type rivet tool. Placing a plastic card underneath the tack tool may prevent damage to the plastic body component.

To install a rivet, remove the threaded pin from the rivet. Then install the rivet (B, **Figure 1**) into the hole until it bottoms and push the threaded pin (A) into the rivet to lock it.

If the threaded pin cannot be pushed fully into the rivet, the plastic body components that the rivet is installed through are not aligned or the rivet is damaged.

BLIND RIVETS

Refer to *Floorboard* in this chapter.

HOOD

Open/Close

1. Pull and disconnect the rubber strap (**Figure 3**) from the pin on each side of the hood.
2. Pull the left and right-side rubber straps outward to spread the outer edge of the hood (each side) and raise the hood forward.

> *NOTE*
> *Spreading the hood outward prevents the rubber strap mounting fasteners mounted on the hood from catching into the large slot in the upper instrument panel. If working alone, stuff a shop rag into one side between the rubber strap mounting fastener and panel notch helps to hold one side of the hood outward while you remove the other strap and open the hood.*

3. Close the hood by inserting the two tabs on the hood into the slots in the instrument panel cover (**Figure 4**). Pull the rubber straps over the pins to lock the hood.

Removal/Installation

1. Open the hood as described in this section.
2. Disconnect the two headlight connectors (A, **Figure 5**).

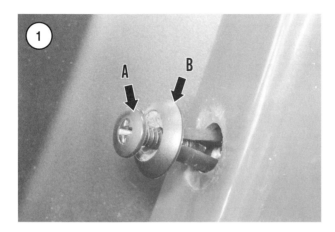

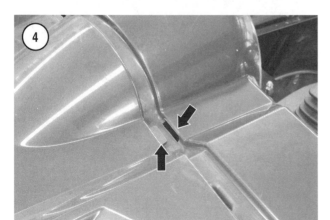

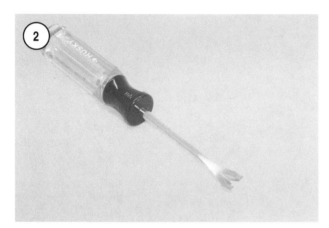

3. Remove the lock spring and pin (B, **Figure 5**) from each side of the hood.

4. Remove the hood.

5. Installation is the reverse of these steps. Note the following:

   a. Install the pins (B, **Figure 5**) from the inside so the clip holes face toward the outside. Make sure the pins slide through the hood and frame holes.

   b. Start the engine and check the headlight operation.

SEATS, SEAT SUPPORTS AND DRIVER SEAT RAIL

Driver and Passenger Seats Removal/Installation

1. For either seat, lift and hold the lever underneath the seat (**Figure 6**), then rock the lower part of the seat forward/upward and remove the seat from vehicle. The passenger grab rail is attached to the passenger seat and will come off with the seat.

2. Install the seat by placing it in the vehicle and aligning the three tabs (A, **Figure 7**) on the bottom rear of the seat with the two raised seat guides (**Figure 8**) welded onto the frame. Slide the seat rearward so the tabs are positioned underneath the guides. Then push the front part of the seat down to lock it on the pin mounted on the seat support.

3. Check the seat to make sure it is locked in place.

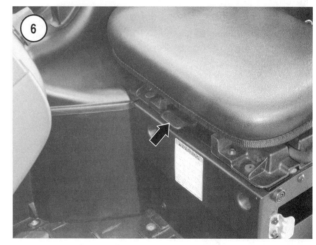

16

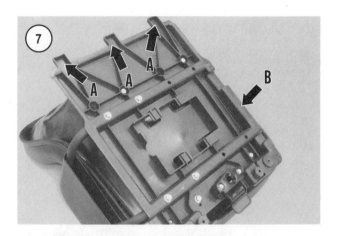

WARNING
Do not drive the vehicle until both seats are locked in place.

NOTE
If it is difficult to install the seats, the rear console is probably installed incorrectly. Check installation as described in this Chapter.

Seat Assembly Parts and Fastener Inspection

Periodically, perform the following for each seat:

1. Check the seat lock (**Figure 9**) mounted on the seat and the lock pin (A, **Figure 10**) mounted on the seat support for damage and looseness. Replace or tighten parts as required.

2. Check the bottom seat guide assembly (B, **Figure 7**), hip restraint and passenger grab rail (passenger seat only) for damage and looseness. Replace or tighten parts as required.

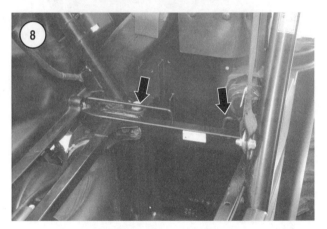

Driver Seat Support Removal/Installation

1. Remove the seat as described in this section.

2. Remove the left side corner and side panel assembly as described in this chapter.

3. Remove the seat support bracket mounting bolt (B, **Figure 10**).

4. Remove the bolts (C, **Figure 10**) securing the seat support to the frame and driver seat rail and remove the seat support (D).

5. Installation is the reverse of these steps. Note the following:

   a. Tighten the seat support mounting bolts (C, **Figure 10**) to 16 N•m (12 ft.-lb.).

   b. Tighten the seat support bracket mounting bolt (B, **Figure 10**) to 32 N•m (24 ft.-lb.).

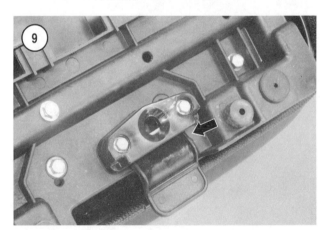

Passenger Seat Support Removal/Installation

1. Remove the seat as described in this section.

2. Remove the right side corner and side panel assembly as described in this chapter.

3. Remove the seat support bracket mounting bolt (A, **Figure 11**).

4. Remove the bolts (B, **Figure 11**) securing the seat support to the frame and remove the seat support (C).

5. Installation is the reverse of these steps. Note the following:

   a. Tighten the seat support mounting bolts (B, **Figure 10**) to 16 N•m (12 ft.-lb.).

   b. Tighten the seat support bracket mounting bolt (A, **Figure 10**) to 32 N•m (24 ft.-lb.).

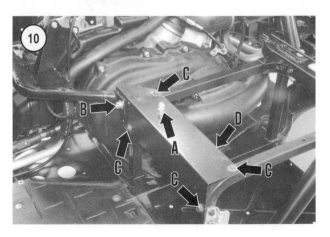

Driver Seat Rail Removal/Installation

1. Remove the driver seat support as described in this section.

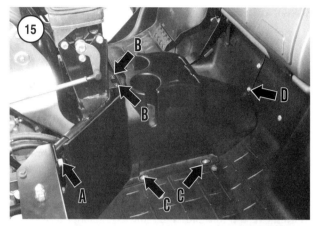

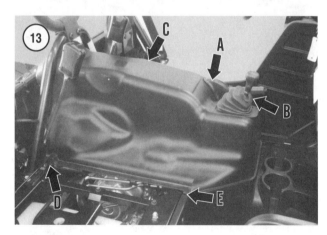

2. Remove the ignition coil (Chapter Nine).

3. Remove bolts (A, **Figure 12**) securing the driver seat rail to the frame and remove the driver seat rail (B).

4. Installation is the reverse of these steps. Tighten the driver seat rail mounting bolts to 16 N•m (12 ft.-lb.).

REAR CONSOLE

The rear console (**Figure 13**) covers the engine and is held in place by the seats.

Removal/Installation

1. Set the parking brake.

2. Remove the seats as described in this chapter.

3. Set the transmission in LOW. This positions the select lever in its most forward position and eases rear console removal.

4. Remove the parking brake lever boot (A, **Figure 13**) from around the lever and rear console.

NOTE
*The select lever boot (B, **Figure 13**) will remain on the select lever assembly. Do not attempt to remove it*

5. Lift the console (C, **Figure 13**) and slide it forward to remove it from the vehicle.

6. Install the console over the shift and parking brake levers while making sure the seats belts are positioned on the outside of the console.

7. Slide the rear console rearward, making sure its mounting tabs (**Figure 14**) fit on the inside of the front console. Then check that the front and rear sides of the console fit against the frame as shown in D and E, **Figure 13**.

8. Install the parking brake lever boot so the large hole in the boot faces forward. Fit the boot into the console.

9. Install the seats as described in this chapter.

FRONT CONSOLE

The front console (**Figure 15**) is installed between the seat support bracket and floorboard.

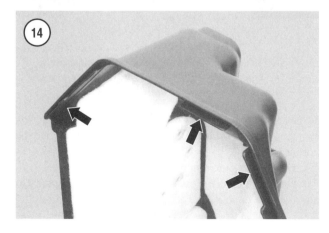

16

Removal/Installation

1. Remove the rear console as described in this chapter.

2. Remove the fasteners securing the left and right corner panel and side panel assemblies. Refer to *Corner Panels and Side Panels* in this chapter. Then lift each corner panel to disconnect its two hooks from the slots in the front console. The side and corner panel assemblies can be left in place unless removal is required.

3. Loosen the left and right side front seat support bracket mounting bolts (A, **Figure 15**).

4. Remove the two sheet metal screws (B, **Figure 15**) securing the front console to the seat support bracket.

5. Remove the left and right side bolts and washers (C, **Figure 15**) securing the front console to the floor. The washers are captured on the bolts and should not fall off.

6. Slide the front console toward the right side until its two upper bolt holes do not align with the two metal tabs welded onto the seat support bracket, then remove the console from the right side.

7. Installation is the reverse of removal. Note the following:

    a. Before installing the front console, make sure the four nut clamps on the floor align with their mounting holes.

    b. When installing the front console, make sure the front of the console is below the floor mounting screw identified in D, **Figure 15**.

    c. Tighten the two seat support bracket mounting bolts (A, **Figure 15**) to 32 N•m (23 ft.-lb.).

    d. Install the two sheet metal screws (B, **Figure 15**) securing the front console to the seat support bracket and tighten securely.

    e. Install the left and right side bolts and washers (C, **Figure 15**) securing the front console to the floor and tighten securely.

CORNER PANELS AND SIDE PANELS

The left and right side corner panels (A, **Figure 16**) and side panels (B) are removed in the same way, except it is necessary to remove the fuel cap (C) when removing the right side panel.

Removal

1. Raise the cargo bed.

2. Remove the seat for the side being serviced as described in this chapter.

3. Remove the two bolts securing the bottom of the side panel to the frame.

4. Remove the plastic rivets securing the corner panel and side panel to the frame.

5. Working behind the panels, disconnect the side panel from the corner panel. **Figure 17** shows how the hooks on the side panels fit through the slots in the corner panels.

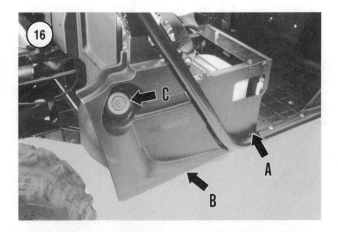

NOTE
Because of the fuel tank mounting position in the frame, it is difficult to separate the right side panel from the corner panel.

6. Lift the corner panel (A, **Figure 16**) to disconnect its two tabs from the slots in the front console and remove the corner panel.

7A. On the left side, remove the side panel.

7B. On the right side, remove the fuel cap (C, **Figure 16**) and the side panel (B). Then reinstall and tighten the fuel cap.

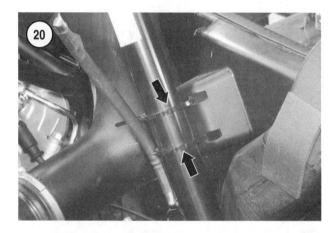

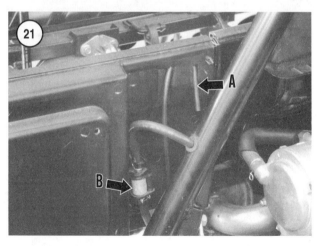

Installation

1. Install the corner panel by inserting its rear section behind the frame and then inserting its two hooks into the slots in the front console.
2. Install the side panel by inserting its hooks into the slots in the corner panel (**Figure 17**).
3. Install the two mounting bolts securing the bottom of the side panel to the frame. Do not tighten the bolts.
4. Install the corner panel and side panel plastic rivets.
5. Tighten the two mounting bolts securely.
6. Install the seat as described in this chapter.
7. Close the cargo bed.

CENTER PROTECTOR

The center protector (**Figure 18**) is mounted behind the engine.

Removal/Installation

1. Raise the cargo bed.
2. Remove the plastic rivets and the center protector (**Figure 18**).
3. Replace the rubber seal mounted on the top of the protector if damaged.
4. Reverse to install. Note the following:
   a. Place the center protector against backside of the left and right protectors.
   b. Make sure the center protector air duct aligns with the drive belt air duct.

LEFT PROTECTOR

The left protector is mounted behind the driver's seat.

Removal/Installation

1. Raise the cargo bed.
2. Remove the driver's seat as described in this chapter.
3. Remove the rear console as described in this chapter.
4. Remove the left corner panel and side panel assemblies as described in this chapter.
5. Remove the plastic rivet (A, **Figure 19**) securing the drive belt duct to the left protector.
6. Open the two plastic-ties (**Figure 20**) securing the left protector to the support frame.
7. Remove the plastic rivets securing the left protector to the frame and remove the left protector (B, **Figure 19**).
8. Replace the rubber seal mounted on the top of the protector if damaged.
9. Installation is the reverse of these steps.

RIGHT PROTECTOR

The right protector is mounted behind the passenger seat.

Removal/Installation

1. Remove the passenger seat as described in this chapter.
2. Raise the cargo bed.
3. Remove the right corner panel and side panel assemblies as described in this chapter.
4. Remove the final drive breather hose (A, **Figure 21**) from the slots in the top of the right protector.
5. Open the clamps and remove the rollover valve (B, **Figure 21**) from its position against the right protector. It is not necessary to disconnect the hoses from the rollover valve.

16

6. Remove the plastic rivets at the rear of the right protector and remove the protector (**Figure 22**).

7. Replace the rubber seal mounted on the top of the protector if damaged.

8. Installation is the reverse of these steps. Note the following:

    a. Make sure there is sufficient slack in the final drive breather hose and that the hose is not pinched along its routing path.

    b. Install the rollover valve with its UP mark facing up, then secure it with the two clamps fixed to the right protector, making sure the clamps are locked. Check that the roll over valve hose is routed properly and attached to the fuel hose clamp (**Figure 23**). Refer to Chapter Eight.

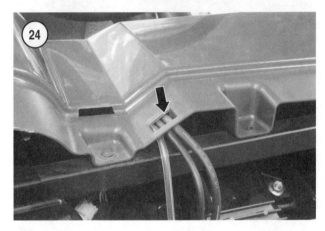

UPPER INSTRUMENT PANEL

Removal/Installation

1. Remove the hood as described in this chapter.

2. Remove the hoses from the instrument panel guide (**Figure 24**).

3. Remove the nut, fender washer, bolt and hood grommet (A, **Figure 25**) from each side of the upper instrument panel.

4. Remove the plastic rivets securing the upper instrument panel to the lower instrument panel.

5. Remove the bolts from the top of the instrument panel.

6. Remove upper instrument panel (B, **Figure 25**).

7. Installation is the reverse of these steps.

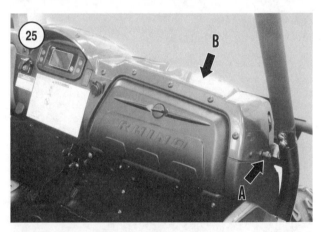

LOWER INSTRUMENT PANEL

Removal/Installation

1. Remove the upper instrument panel as described in this chapter.

2. Remove the steering wheel as described in Chapter Eleven.

3. Disconnect the electrical connectors from all of the components installed in the lower instrument panel. If it is necessary to remove the electrical components from

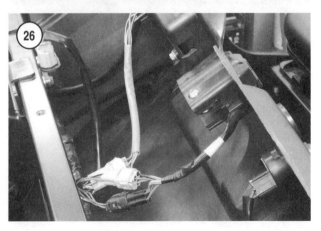

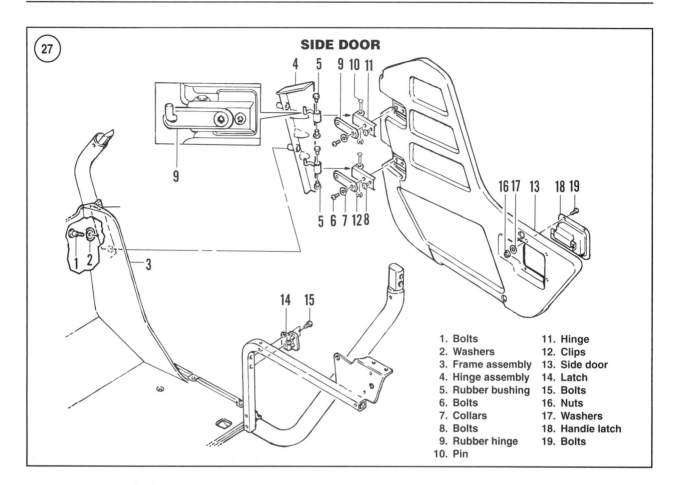

SIDE DOOR

1. Bolts
2. Washers
3. Frame assembly
4. Hinge assembly
5. Rubber bushing
6. Bolts
7. Collars
8. Bolts
9. Rubber hinge
10. Pin
11. Hinge
12. Clips
13. Side door
14. Latch
15. Bolts
16. Nuts
17. Washers
18. Handle latch
19. Bolts

the panel, refer to the service procedures in Chapter Nine. Refer to **Figure 26**, typical.

4. Remove the plastic rivets securing the pedal cover to the lower instrument panel.

5. Remove the bolts securing the lower instrument panel to the frame and remove the panel.

6. Installation is the reverse of these steps.

SIDE DOORS

Removal/Installation

Refer to **Figure 27**.

1. Remove the two side door mounting bolts (1, **Figure 27**) and washers (2) and remove the door.

2. Installation is the reverse of these steps. Apply a medium-strength threadlocking compound onto the side door mounting bolts and tighten to 23 N•m (17 ft.-lb.).

Disassembly/Reassembly

Refer to **Figure 27**.

SEAT BELTS AND BUCKLES

Removal/Installation

Seat belt

1. Remove the seat(s) as described in this chapter.

2. Remove the rear console as described in this chapter.

3. Remove the corner panel and side panel assembly as described in this chapter.

4. Remove the lower seat belt mounting nut and bolt (A, **Figure 28**).

5. Remove the seat belt reel mounting nut and bolt (B, **Figure 28**).

6. Remove the plastic cover (A, **Figure 29**) at the seat belt upper mounting bolt.

7. Remove the upper seat belt mounting nut (B, **Figure 29**) and bolt. Remove the seat belt assembly.

16

8. Replace the seat belt assembly if any part is damaged or the reel will not return the belt when released.

9. Replace damaged fasteners.

10. Installation is the reverse of these steps. Note the following:

   a. Tighten all of the seat belt mounting nuts to 59 N•m (43 ft.-lb.).

   b. After installing the seat(s), check seat belt operation by locking and unlocking the buckle. Make sure the belt moves smoothly and returns under spring tension.

Seat belt buckle

1. Remove the seat(s) as described in this chapter.

2. Note the installation angle/position of the seat belt buckle before removal (**Figure 30**).

3. Remove the rear console as described in this chapter.

4. Remove the seat belt buckle mounting bolt (**Figure 31**). Remove the buckle.

5. Installation is the reverse of these steps. Tighten the seat belt buckle mounting bolt to 59 N•m (43 ft.-lb.).

CARGO BED

Strut Removal/Installation

> *WARNING*
> *Support the cargo bed before removing the struts.*

1. Make sure the cargo bed is empty.

2. Push the cargo bed release lever down on either side of the vehicle and slowly raise the cargo bed.

> *NOTE*
> *Remove and install the struts with the cargo bed in its raised position.*

> *NOTE*
> *The area between the inner strut nut and the cargo bed strut mounting bracket is narrow.*

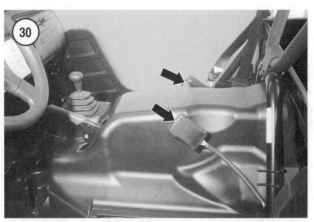

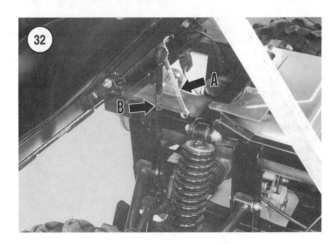

> *It may be necessary to grind an open end wrench to fit.*

3. Hold the strut's upper inner nut with a wrench (A, **Figure 32**), then loosen and remove the mounting nut.

4. Repeat Step 3 to remove the strut's lower mounting nut.

5. Remove strut from the cargo bed and frame.

6. Repeat for the other strut and lower the bed.

7. Installation is the reverse of these steps, plus the following:

   a. Install the strut with the gas damper end (B, **Figure 32**) at the top.

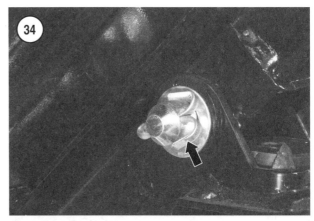

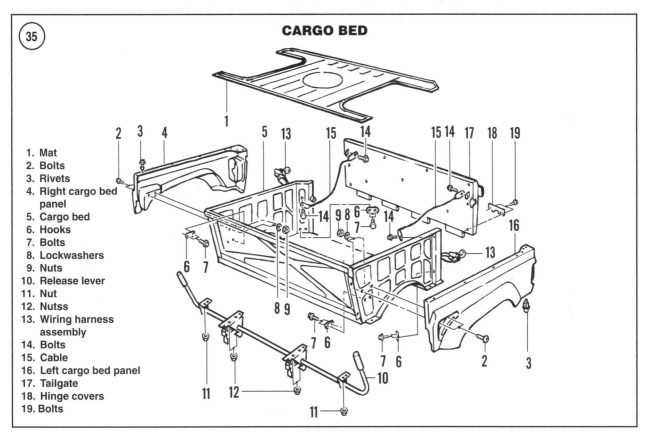

CARGO BED

1. Mat
2. Bolts
3. Rivets
4. Right cargo bed panel
5. Cargo bed
6. Hooks
7. Bolts
8. Lockwashers
9. Nuts
10. Release lever
11. Nut
12. Nutss
13. Wiring harness assembly
14. Bolts
15. Cable
16. Left cargo bed panel
17. Tailgate
18. Hinge covers
19. Bolts

b. Tighten the strut mounting nuts to 16 N•m (12 ft.-lb.).

c. Check the strut operation by lowering the cargo bed. The bed should lower under tension.

Cargo Bed Removal/Installation

1. Make sure the cargo bed is empty.

2. Disconnect the wiring harness connectors at the rear of the cargo bed (right side). Then remove the clamps as required to free the wiring harness (**Figure 33**) from the cargo bed.

3. Remove the struts as described in this section.

4. Remove the cotter pin and washer from each pivot pin (**Figure 34**). Lower the cargo bed. Discard the cotter pins.

5. Remove the pivot pins.

6. With the help of one or more assistants, remove the cargo bed, making sure the wiring harness does not interfere with removal.

7. Installation is the reverse of these steps. Note the following:

a. Secure the pivot pins with new cotter pins.

b. Make sure the cargo bed locks in place when lowered.

c. Turn the ignition switch on and check the brake light and taillight operation. Turn the ignition switch off.

Cargo Bed Disassembly/Reassembly

Refer to **Figure 35**.

16

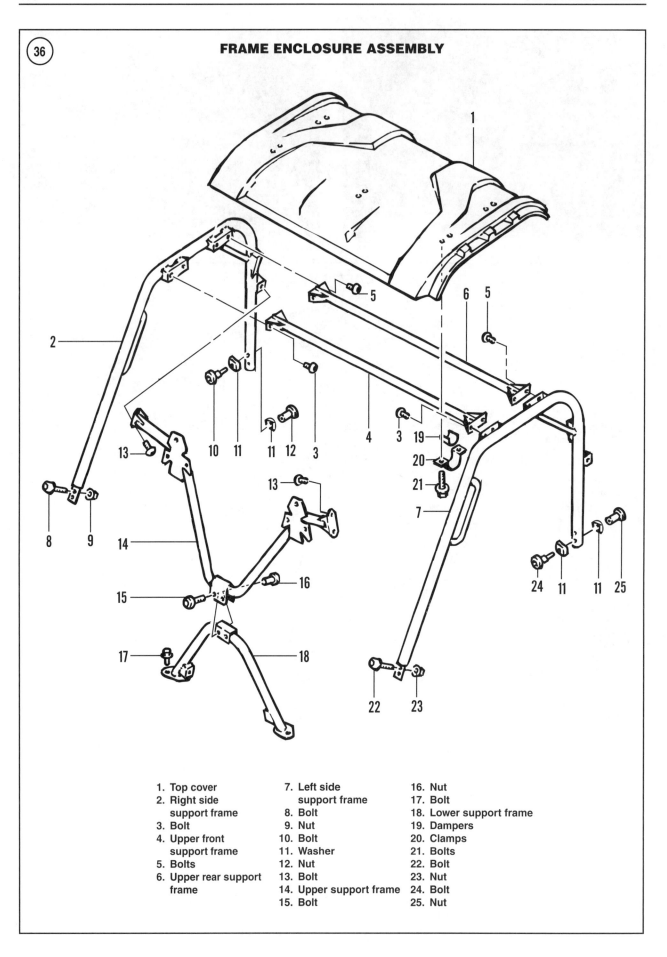

FRAME ENCLOSURE ASSEMBLY

1. Top cover
2. Right side support frame
3. Bolt
4. Upper front support frame
5. Bolts
6. Upper rear support frame
7. Left side support frame
8. Bolt
9. Nut
10. Bolt
11. Washer
12. Nut
13. Bolt
14. Upper support frame
15. Bolt
16. Nut
17. Bolt
18. Lower support frame
19. Dampers
20. Clamps
21. Bolts
22. Nut
23. Nut
24. Bolt
25. Nut

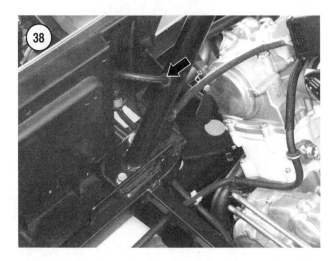

1. Remove the cargo bed as described in this section.
2. Remove the mat from inside the bed.
3. Remove the bolts securing the cables to the tailgate and cargo bed and remove them.
4. Remove the screws, hinge cover and tailgate.
5. Remove the cargo bed panels and disconnect the taillight/brake light assembly as described in *Lighting System* in Chapter Nine.
6. Remove the nuts and the release lever assembly from the bottom of the cargo bed.
7. Remove the bolts and the cargo hooks from inside the bed.
8. Installation is the reverse of these steps:
    a. Tighten the release lever 8-mm nuts (12, **Figure 35**) to 16 N•m (12 ft.-lb.).
    b. Tighten the release lever 6-mm nuts (11, **Figure 35**) to 7 N•m (62 in.-lb.).
    c. Tighten the hook bolts (7, **Figure 35**) to 7 N•m (62 in.-lb.).
    d. Tighten the cable mounting bolts (14, **Figure 35**) to 7 N•m (62 in.-lb.).

FRAME ENCLOSURE ASSEMBLY

Removal/Installation

Refer to **Figure 36**.

1. Park the vehicle on level ground and set the parking brake.
2. Remove the seats as described in this chapter.
3. Remove the seat belts as described in his chapter.
4. Remove the headrest (**Figure 37**).
5. Remove the hose (**Figure 38**) from the right side support frame.
6. Referring to **Figure 36**, remove the frame enclosure assembly in the following order:

> *NOTE*
> *Identify the mounting fasteners so they can be reinstalled in their correct positions.*

    a. Top cover (1, **Figure 36**), clamps and dampers (if so equipped).
    b. Front (4, **Figure 36**) and rear (6) upper frame supports.
    c. Upper support frame (14, **Figure 36**).
    d. Lower support frame (18, **Figure 36**).
    e. Left side support frame (7, **Figure 36**).
    f. Right side support frame (2, **Figure 36**).
7. Inspect all components for cracks, bending and other damage. If damage is found, consult with a dealership on the condition of the part and whether repair or replacement is required.
8. Clean and dry all fastener threads. Check for stripped or damaged fasteners and replace if necessary. Replace cracked or damaged washers.
9. Check for stripped or damaged frame threads.

> *NOTE*
> *Install and tighten the enclosure assembly in the following order (Steps 10-12).*

10. Install the lower support frame and tighten the mounting bolts (17, **Figure 36**) to 64 N•m (47 ft.-lb.).

> *NOTE*
> *In Step 11, install the components and tighten the fasteners finger-tight only. Final tightening will take place after the enclosure assembly is fully installed.*

11. Install the components in the following order:
    a. Left side support frame.
    b. Right side support frame.
    c. Upper support frame.
    d. Rear top frame support.
    e. Front top frame support.

> *NOTE*
> *Make sure all fasteners are properly installed before tightening them in Step 12.*

12. Tighten the components in the following order:
    a. Upper support frame side mounting bolts (13, **Figure 36**) to 65 N•m (48 ft.-lb.).
    b. Upper front support frame side mounting bolts (3, **Figure 36**) to 65 N•m (48 ft.-lb.).

16

c. Upper rear support frame side mounting bolts (5, **Figure 36**) to 65 N•m (48 ft.-lb.).

d. Left side support frame front nuts (23, **Figure 36**) to 65 N•m (48 ft.-lb.).

e. Right side support frame front nuts (9, **Figure 36**) to 65 N•m (48 ft.-lb.).

f. Upper/lower support frame nuts (16, **Figure 36**) to 22 N•m (16 ft.-lb.).

g. Left side support frame rear mounting nut (25, **Figure 36**) to 22 N•m (16 ft.-lb.).

h. Right side support frame rear mounting nut (12, **Figure 36**) to 22 N•m (16 ft.-lb.).

13. Install the headrests and tighten the mounting bolts to 7 N•m (62 in.-lb.).

14. Install the hose (**Figure 38**) into the right side support frame.

15. Install the top cover, dampers and clamps and tighten the mounting bolts securely.

16. Install the seat belts as described in his chapter.

17. Install the seats as described in this chapter.

WARNING
Do not operate the vehicle until the enclosure assembly is installed and all fasteners are properly installed and tightened.

FRONT BUMPER

Removal/Installation

1. Park the vehicle on level ground and set the parking brake.

2. Remove the bolts securing the front bumper to the frame and remove the bumper (**Figure 39**).

3. Installation is the reverse of these steps. Note the following:

a. Clean and inspect the mounting bolts.

b. Tighten the 12-mm mounting bolts to 59 N•m (43.5 ft.-lb.).

c. Tighten the 10-mm mounting bolts to 32 N•m (24 ft.-lb.).

SKID PLATES

Front Removal/Installation

1. Park the vehicle on level ground and set the parking brake.

2. Remove the bolts and washers and the front skid plate.

3. Clean and inspect the bolts and washers.

4. Installation is the reverse of these steps. Note the following:

a. Install the washers with their cupped side facing toward the skid plate (**Figure 40**). Make sure all of the washers fit into the holes in the skid plate before tightening the mounting bolts.

b. Tighten the mounting bolts to 7 N•m (62 in.-lb.).

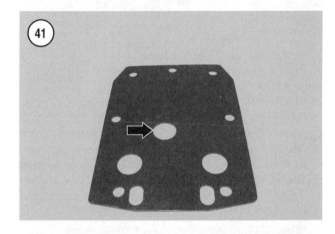

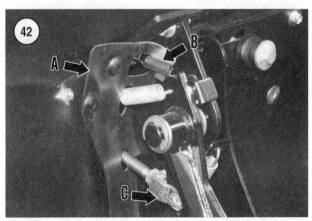

PEDAL ASSEMBLY

1. E-clip
2. Washer
3. Brake pedal
4. Pedal bracket
5. Return spring
6. Accelerator pedal
7. Return spring

Rear Removal/Installation

1. Park the vehicle on level ground and set the parking brake.
2. Remove the bolts and washers and the front skid plate.
3. Clean and inspect the bolts and washers.
4. Installation is the reverse of these steps. Note the following:
   a. Install the skid plate with the hole indicated in **Figure 41** (top view showing) facing toward the left side of the vehicle.
   b. Install the washers with their cupped side facing toward the skid plate (**Figure 40**). Make sure all of the washers fit into the holes in the skid plate before tightening the mounting bolts.
   c. Tighten the mounting bolts to 7 N•m (62 in.-lb.).

PEDAL ASSEMBLY

Removal/Installation

1. Remove the steering shaft (Chapter Eleven).
2. Remove the master cylinder (Chapter Fifteen).
3. Remove the plastic rivets and the splash plate (B, **Figure 42**).
4. Disconnect the accelerator cable at the accelerator pedal (Chapter Eight).
5. Disconnect the rear brake light switch return spring (B, **Figure 42**) at the brake pedal.

6. If necessary, remove the cotter pin and clevis pin (C, **Figure 42**) securing the brake the pedal pushrod to the brake pedal.
7. Remove the bolts securing the pedal assembly to the frame and remove it.
8. Clean and inspect the mounting bolts.
9. Installation is the reverse of these steps. Note the following:
   a. Tighten the pedal assembly mounting bolts to 16 N•m (12 ft.-lb.).
   b. If the brake pedal pushrod was removed, clean the pushrod and clevis pin. Lubricate the clevis pin shoulder with lithium grease. Then reinstall the pushrod and secure onto the brake pedal with the clevis pin and a new cotter pin (C, **Figure 42**). Bend the cotter pin arms over to lock it.
   c. Bleed the brake system (Chapter Fifteen).
   d. Adjust the accelerator pedal (Chapter Three).
   e. Check the rear brake light switch adjustment a (Chapter Three).

Disassembly/Inspection/Assembly

Replace any worn or damaged parts.
1. Refer to **Figure 43** to disassemble the pedal assembly.
2. Clean and dry all parts.
3. Inspect all pivot surfaces on the pedals and mounting bracket for excessive wear and damage.
4. Inspect the spring mounting holes for cracks, wear and other damage.

16

4. Inspect the washers for cracks and thrust wear.

5. Inspect the return springs for cracks, stretched coils and other damage.

6. During reassembly, note the following:

    a. Lubricate the pivot posts on the pedal mounting bracket and the pivot holes in the pedals with lithium grease.

    b. Make sure to install a washer (2, **Figure 43**) on each side of the pedals.

    c. Secure the pedals in place with new E-clips (1, **Figure 43**). Make sure the E-clips seats in the grooves completely.

    d. After installing the E-clips, operate the pedals by hand to make sure the pivot smoothly and with no binding or roughness.

FLOORBOARD

Removal/Installation

1. Remove the front and rear consoles as described in this chapter.

2. Remove the corner panels and side panels as described in this chapter.

3. Remove the driver seat support as described in this chapter.

4. Remove the passenger seat support as described in this chapter.

5. Remove the pedal assembly as described in this chapter.

6. Drill out the rivets (**Figure 44**).

7. Remove the bolt securing the left and right side floorboards together.

8. Remove the floorboards.

NOTE
The rivets can be installed with a hand-operated riveter but this is difficult to do if more than a few rivets must be installed. When installing more than a few rivets, install them with a pneumatic rivet tool.

9. Installation is the reverse of these steps. Align and then secure the floorboards in place with new rivets.

Table 1 BODY TORQUE SPECIFICATIONS

	N•m	in.-lb.	ft.-lb.
Cable mounting bolts	7	62	–
Driver seat rail mounting bolts	16	–	12
Front bumper mounting bolts			
10-mm	32	–	24
12-mm	59	–	43.5
Front skid plate mounting bolts	7	62	–
Headrest mounting bolts	7	62	–
Hook bolts	7	62	–
Left side support frame front nut	65	–	48
Left side support frame rear mounting nut	22	–	16
Lower support frame mounting bolts	64	–	47
Pedal assembly mounting bolts	16	–	12
Rear skid plate mounting bolts	7	62	–
(continued)			

Table 1 BODY TORQUE SPECIFICATIONS (continued)

	N•m	in.-lb.	ft.-lb.
Release lever mounting nuts			
6-mm	7	62	–
8-mm	16	–	12
Right side support frame front nut	65	–	48
Right side support frame rear mounting nut	22	–	16
Seat belt buckle mounting bolts	59	–	43.5
Seat belt mounting nuts	59	–	43.5
Seat support bracket mounting bolts	32	–	24
Seat support mounting bolts	16	–	12
Side door mounting bolts*	23	–	17
Strut mounting nuts	16	–	12
Upper front support frame side mounting bolts	65	–	48
Upper rear support frame side mounting bolts	65	–	48
Upper support frame side mounting bolt	65	–	48
Upper/lower support frame nuts	22	–	16

*Refer to text.

16

INDEX

A

Accelerator cable 217-220
   adjustment. 74
Air
   box 214
   filter. 59-61
   intake, duct 214-216
Auxiliary DC jack. 258-259
Axles
   boots inspection 81
   differential and final drive
     unit, troubleshooting. 46
   front 302-312

B

Balancer
   oil pump gears 124-127
   shaft 143
Battery. 59, 221-224
Body
   blind rivets 398
   buckles and seat belts 405-406
   cargo bed. 406-409
   console
     front 401-402
     rear 401
   floorboard 412
   frame enclosure assembly. 409-410
   front bumper. 410

hood 398-399
panel
   lower instrument. 404
   upper instrument. 404
panels, corner and side . . . 402-403
pedal assembly 411-412
plastic rivets 398
protector
   center 403
   left 403
   right 403-404
seat belts and buckles 405-406
seats, driver seat rail
   and supports 399-401
side doors 405
skid plates. 410-411
torque specifications 412
Brakes
bleeding 368-370
brake caliper 375-380
disc 394-396
fluid
   draining 370-375
   flushing. 370
hose and brake line 392-394
master cylinder 380-387
pad wear check
   front and rear 76-77

parking 78
parking brake
   cable 391
     adjustment. 78-79
   caliper. 387-390
   lever 391-392
   pad wear check. 78
   pedal adjustment. 77
rear brake light
   switch adjustment 77-78
service notes 367-368
specifications
   brakes
     front 396
     parking 397
     rear 396
     torque 397
Breather hoses inspection 73

C

Cam chain
   guides 128-129
Camshaft and
   rocker arms 97-101
Cargo bed 406-409
Center protector 403
Centrifugal clutch 179-185
Charging system 224-225
   troubleshooting. 42

Clutch
  and sheave, torque
    specifications 186
  centrifugal. 179-185
  drive belt. 167-168
    air duct assembly 164
    cover. 164-166
    left crankcase cover 179
    outer bearing housing 166-167
    troubleshooting. 45
Control cables and pedals 79-80
Coolant
  reservoir 267
Cooling
  fan. 267
  system 65-67, 252-253
    coolant reservoir. 267
    fan. 267
    inspection 263-265
    radiator 265-267
    safety 263
    specifications 276
    torque 277
    thermostat. 268-269
    water pump 269-272
Corner panels and
  side panels. 402-403
Crankcase 129-139
  seals and bearings. 139-141
  left cover. 178-179
Crankshaft. 141-143
  position sensor
    stator coil and right
      crankcase cover 226-229
Cylinder. 108-110
  leakdown test,
    troubleshooting 44
Differential, final drive
  unit and axles, troubleshooting . . 46

D

Diode. 258
Differential gear lock switch and
  four-wheel-drive motor switch . 255
Differential 312-321
Drain hoses 82-83
Drive
  belt 167-168
    adjustment 75
    air duct assembly 164
    cover. 164-166
  shaft
    front 325
    rear 364-365
    end middle gear unit,
      troubleshooting. 46-47
Duct, air intake 214-216

E

Electrical
  component replacement 221
  connectors. 221
  system
    alternator and charging
      specifications 261
    auxiliary DC jack 258-259
    battery. 221-224
    bulb specifications 261
    charging system 224-225
    component replacement 221
    connectors 221
    cooling system 251-253
      electrical test specifications 262
    crankshaft
      position sensor 226, 229 234
    diode. 258
    torque specifications. 262
    engine control unit (ECU) . . . 234
    flywheel, starter clutch
      and starter clutch gears. 229-232
    four-wheel-drive
      indicator and relays . . . 249-151
    fundamentals 17-12
    fuses 259-260, 262
    helmet/seat belt display
      (2009 and 2011-on models) . . 251
    ignition
      coil 233-334
      system. 232-233
      specifications 260, 261
      timing inspection 74
    indicator lights
      and meter assembly 247-249
    lean-angle sensor 234
    lighting system 244-247
    load control relay 253
    maintenance-free
      battery charging times 261
    meter assembly and
      indicator lights 247-249
    rectifier/regulator 225-226
    regulator/rectifier 225-226
    relays and four-wheel
      drive indicator. 249-151
    replacement 12-volt bulbs 262
    right crankcase cover,
      stator coil and crankshaft
      position sensor 226-229
    seat belt display/helmet
      (2009 and 2011-on models) . . 251
    starter 235-243
      clutch gears. 229-232
      starter clutch 229-232
      flywheel 229-232
      relay 243-244
    starting system specifications . . 261

stator coil, crankshaft
  position sensor and
  right crankcase cover . . 226-229
switches 253-258
  brake light. 255
  gear position. 257-258
  ignition 254
  light 255
  on-command four-wheel-
    drive motor and differential
    gear lock switch 255
  parking brake 256
  reverse 257
Electronic diagnostic
  system, troubleshooting 35-36
Engine
  break-in. 83-84
  compression check 71-72
  control unit (ECU) 211
  does not start,
    troubleshooting. 29-32
  filter and oil. 61-63
  installation 123-124
  lower end 162-163
    balancer
      and oil pump gears. . . . 124-127
      shaft 143
    cam chain and
      rear guide 128-129
    crankcase 129-139
      seal and bearing
        replacement. 139-141
    crankshaft. 141-143
    middle
      driven pinion gear
        bearing housing 147-150
      driven shaft. 151-153
      gear assembly shim
        and lash adjustment . 153-157
      gear bearing
        housing 145-147
      oil pipe adapter and
        relief valve 141
      pressure relief valve . . 127-128
      pump. 144-145
        gears and
          balancer. 124-127
    rear guide and cam
      chain. 128-129
    relief valve and oil
      pipe adapter 141
    shifting check. 161-162
    torque specifications. 163
    universal joint. 157-161
  mounts inspection. 79
  oil
    filter 61-62
    pressure check 62-63

Engine (continued)
  poor performance,
    troubleshooting. 29-32
  removal. 120-122
  servicing, in frame 119
  starting, troubleshooting. . . . 28-29
  top end
    bore, rings and piston
      specifications 117
    cam chain and guide. 101
    camshaft and rocker
      arms 97-101
    cylinder. 108-110
      head. 90-97
      specifications 115-116
    exhaust system 87-90
    general engine
      specifications 115
    piston, rings 11-115
      specifications 117
    rocker arms
      and camshafts. 97-101
    torque specifications. 117-118
    valves 102-108
      components 102-108
  troubleshooting. 43-44
Exhaust system 73, 87-90
External shift mechanism . . 187-190

F

Fasteners. 3-5
  inspection 83
Final drive unit, axles and
  differential, troubleshooting 46
  specifications 365
  oil. 64-65
  unit 349-364
Floorboard. 412
Flywheel, starter clutch and
  starter clutch gears 229-232
Forks and shift drums 196-197
Four-wheel-drive indicator
  and relays 249-151
Frame enclosure assembly . 409-410
Front
  axle 302-312
  bumper 410
  console 401-402
  control arms 287-288
  differential 312-321
  differential 63-64
  drive shaft. 325
  hub 278-281
  shock absorbers 288-291
  suspension. 81-82
    front shock absorber setting . . 301
    specifications 301

torque 301
steering
  specifications 300
  troubleshooting. 51
wheels. 278
Fuel
  injection system (FI). 199-201
  accelerator cable. 217-220
  air
    box 214
    intake, duct 214-216
  control unit (ECU) 211
  delivery tests. 201-202
  fuel delivery 201-202
  general specifications 220
  hose inspection. 72-73
  idle speed control unit 210
  injection system relay. 205
  injector and rail 210
  intake air
    pressure sensor 212
    temperature sensor . . . 212-213
  lean-angle sensor 213
  level sender. 205
  position sensor
    crankshaft 213
    intake air 212
  pump. 204
  rail and injector 210
  rollover valve 213-214
  tank. 202-204
  test specifications 220
  throttle
    body 205-209
    and intake joint
      inspection 73-74
    position sensor 211
  torque specifications. 220
  troubleshooting. 34-35
  requirements 59
Fuses 259-260

G

Gear
  position switch 257-258
  oil pump 124-127
General information
  conversion formulas 25
  electrical system
  fundamentals. 17-12
  fasteners 3-5
  fractional, inch and
    metric equivalents. 27
  inch, metric and
    fractional equivalents 27
  information labels and
    serial numbers. 3

metric
  tap drill sizes 26-27
  inch and fractional
    equivalents 27
model code identification 24
serial numbers and
  information labels. 3
shop supplies 6-8
storage. 23-24
technical abbreviations. 26
tools 8-13
  measuring. 13-17
torque recommendations 27
vehicle
  dimensions 24
  weight specifications 25

H

Helmet/seat belt display
  (2009 and 2011-on models) . . . 251
Hood 398-399

I

Idle speed control unit. 210
Ignition system 232-233
  coil 233-334
  timing inspection 74
  troubleshooting. 42
Ignition switch 254
Indicator lights and
  meter assembly 247-249
Information labels and
  serial numbers. 3
Intake airpressure sensor. 212
  temperature sensor 212-213

L

Lash adjustment and middle
  gear assembly 153-157
Lean-angle sensor 213, 234
Left
  crankcase cover 178-179
  protector 403
Lighting
  system. 244-247
    signal troubleshooting 50-51
Light switch 254-255
Load control relay. 253
Lower instrument panel 404
Lubricantion
  engine, oil and filter 61-63
  maintenance schedule. 84-85
  oil and fluid capacities 86
  recommended lubricants
    and fuel. 85-86

M

Maintenance
accelerator cable 74
air
filter 59-61
intake joint and
throttle body 73-74
axle boots inspection 81
battery 59
bolts, other fasteners and nuts . . 83
brakes 75-78
breather hoses inspection 73
control cables and pedals . . . 79-80
cooling system 65-67
drain hoses 82-83
drive belt inspection 75
engine
break-in 83-84
compression check 71-72
filter and oil 61-63
mounts inspection 79
oil and filter 61-62
oil pressure check 62-63
exhaust system 73
fastener inspection 83
final drive, oil 64-65
front
differential 63-64
suspension 81-82
fuel
hose inspection 72-73
requirements 59
ignition timing inspection 74
lubrication and
maintenance schedule 84-85
parking brake assembly 78-79
pedals and control cables . . . 79-80
pre-ride inspection 58-59
rear suspension 82
select lever adjustment 74-75
spark plug 67-70
specifications
torque 86
tune-up 85
steering system 80-81
throttle body and
air intake joint 73-74
tires
inflation pressure 86
wheels inspection 80
universal joint lubrication 82
valve clearance 70-71
wheel bearings 80
wheels and tires 80
Master cylinder 380-387
Measuring tools 13-17
Meter assembly and
indicator lights 247-249

Middle
driven pinion gear
bearing housing 147-150
shaft 151-153
gear
assembly shim and lash
adjustment 153-157
bearing housing 145-147
unit and drive
shafts, troubleshooting . . . 46-47

N

Nuts, bolts and
other fasteners 83

O

Oil
cooler 276
lines and hoses 272-276
hoses and lines 272-276
pipe adapter and relief valve . . . 141
pressure check 62-63
pressure relief valve 127-128
pump 143-145
On-command four-wheel-drive
motor switch and differential
gear lock switch 255
Outer bearing housing 166-167

P

Parking brake
assembly 78-79
cable 391
adjustment 78-79
caliper 387-390
lever 391-392
pad wear check 78
Pedal assembly 411-412
Piston 108-110
rings 111-115
Pre-ride, inspection 58-59

R

Radiator 265-267
Rear axle 341-350
final drive
specifications 365
torque specifications 366
Rear
console 401
control arms 334-335
drive shaft 364-365
hub 327-330
knuckle 330-333
suspension 82

troubleshooting 51
wheels 327
Regulator/rectifier 225-226
Relief valve and oil
pipe adapter 141
Reverse switch 256-257
Right
crankcase cover, stator
coil and crankshaft
position sensor 226-229
protector 403-404
Rocker arms and camshaft . . 97-101
Rollover valve 213-214

S

Seat
belt display/helmet
(2009-2011) 251
buckles and belts 405-406
driver seat rail and
supports 399-401
Select lever
adjustment 74-75
assembly 187
Serial numbers
and information labels 3
Sheave
and clutch, torque
specifications 186
drive belt specifications 186
primary and secondary . . . 168-178
Shift mechanism
drum and forks 196-197
external 187-190
Shifting check 161-162
Shock absorbers, rear 335-338
Shop supplies 6-8
Side doors 405
Signal and lighting
system, troubleshooting 50-51
Skid plates 410-411
Spark plug 67-70
Spark test 30
Specifications
alternator and charging system . 261
battery 260
bore, rings and piston 117
clutch 186
conversion formulas 25
cooling system 276
electrical test 262
torque 277
cylinder head and
valve service 115-116
diagnostic codes 55-56
drive belt and sheave 186
electrical system torque 262

17

Specifications (continued)
  lower end 162-163
  electrical system torque 262
    torque 163
    top end torque. 117-118
  final drive and rear axle 365
  front
    axle and differential 326
    brake service. 396
    shock absorber setting 301
    suspension and steering 300
    suspension torque 301
  fuel injection system test 220
    torque 220
  fuses 262
  general engine. 115
    torque specifications. 25
    vehicle dimensions. 24
    fuel injection. 220
  ignition system 261
  maintenance
    lubrication 84-85
    tune-up 85
    torque 86
  maintenance-free battery
    charging times. 261
  metric
    tap drill sizes 26-27
    inch and fractional
      equivalents 27
  model code identification 24
  oil and fluid capacities 86
  parking brake service 397
  piston, rings and bore 117
  rear
    axle and final drive. 365
    brake service. 396
    shock absorber adjustment . . 339
    suspension 339
  recommended lubricants
    and fuel. 85-86
  replacement 12-volt bulbs 262
  rings, piston and bore 117
  starting system 261
  technical abbreviations. 26
  tires
    wheels 301, 339
    tinflation pressure 86
  torque specifications. 57
    final drive and rear axle 366
    body 412
    brake. 397
    front axle and
      differential 326
    rear axle and final drive 366
    rear suspension. 340
    transmission and shift
      mechanism transmission . . 198

trouble codes 53-55
  valve service and
    cylinder head 115-116
  vehicle weight. 25
Speed sensor 213
Stabilizer
  (2008-2009 models) 333-334
Start clutch, flywheel
  and starter clutch gears . . . 229-232
Starter 235-243
  relay 243-244
  system, troubleshooting . . . 42-43
Stator coil, right crankcase
  cover and crankshaft
  position sensor 226-229
Steering
  knuckle 281-287
  system 80-81
  wheel. 291
  front
    gearbox, column
      and shaft. 292-296
    knuckle. 281-287
    shaft, column and
      gearbox. 292-296
  suspension
      specifications 300
      troubleshooting. 51
    wheel 291
Storage 23-24
Suspension
  front
    tires. 297-299
    control arms 287-288
    hub 278-281
    shock absorbers 288-291
    tie rod, boots and ends . . 291-292
    toe-in adjustment 296-297
    wheels. 278
  rear
    control arms 334-335
    hub 327-330
    knuckle. 330--333
    shock absorbers 335--338
      adjustment 339
    specifications 339
      torque 340
      tire and wheel 339
    stabilizer
      (2008-2009 models) . . . 333-334
    tires. 327
    wheels. 327
  wheel runout. 299-300
Switches 253-256
  brake light. 255
  gear position 257-258
  ignition 254
  light. 255

on-command four-wheel-
  drive motor and differential
  gear lock switch 255
  parking brake 256
  reverse. 257

                    T

Thermostat 268-269
Throttle
  body 205-209
  air intake joint
    inspection 73-74
  position sensor 211
Tie rod boots and ends 291-292
Tires 297-299
  wheels. 80
Toe-in adjustment 296-297
Tools 8-13
  measuring 13-17
Torque specifications
  body 412
  brake. 397
  cooling system 227
  clutch and sheave 186
  electrical system 262
  engine
    lower end 163
    top end 117-118
  final drive and rear axle 366
  front
    axle and differential 326
    suspension 301
  fuel injection system. 220
  general recommendations. 27
  maintenance 86
  rear
    axle and final drive. 366
    suspension troubleshooting . . . 57
  transmission and
    shift mechanism 198
Transmission. 190-196
  select lever assembly 187
  specifications 198
  shift mechanism, torque. 198
  troubleshooting. 36-42, 45-46
Troubleshooting
  axles, differential and
    final drive unit. 46
  brake system. 52-53
  charging system 42
  clutch 45
  cylinder leakdown test 44
  differential, final drive
    unit and axles 46
  drive shafts and middle
    gear unit 46-47
  electrical testing 47-50

electronic diagnostic system. 35-36
engine 43-44
  does not start 29-32
  lubrication 44
  poor performance 32-34
  starting 28-29
fastener inspection 83
final drive unit, axles
  and differential 46
front suspension and steering . . . 51
fuel system 34-35
ignition system 42
lighting and signal system . . 50-51
middle gear unit and
  drive shafts 46-47
rear suspension 51
signal and lighting 50-51
spark test 30
starter system 42-43
steering and front suspension . . . 51

torque specifications 57
transmission 45-46
rouble codes 36-42
Tune-up 58
  air filter 59-61
  brakes 75-78
  breather hose 73
  engine, oil and filter 61-63
  fastener inspection 83
  fuel hose inspection 72-73
  maintenance specifications 85
  spark plug 67-70
  tires and wheels 80
  valve clearance 70-71

U

Universal joint 157-161, 321-325
  lubrication 82
Upper instrument panel 404

V

Valve
  clearance 70-71
  rollover 213-214
  components 102-108

W

Water pump 269-272
Wheels
  bearings inspection 80
  runout 299-300
  front axle 302-312
    differential specifications 326
    torque specifications 326
  front differential 312-321
  universal joint 321-325
Wiring diagrams 420-421

17

2008-2009 AND 2011-2012 MODELS

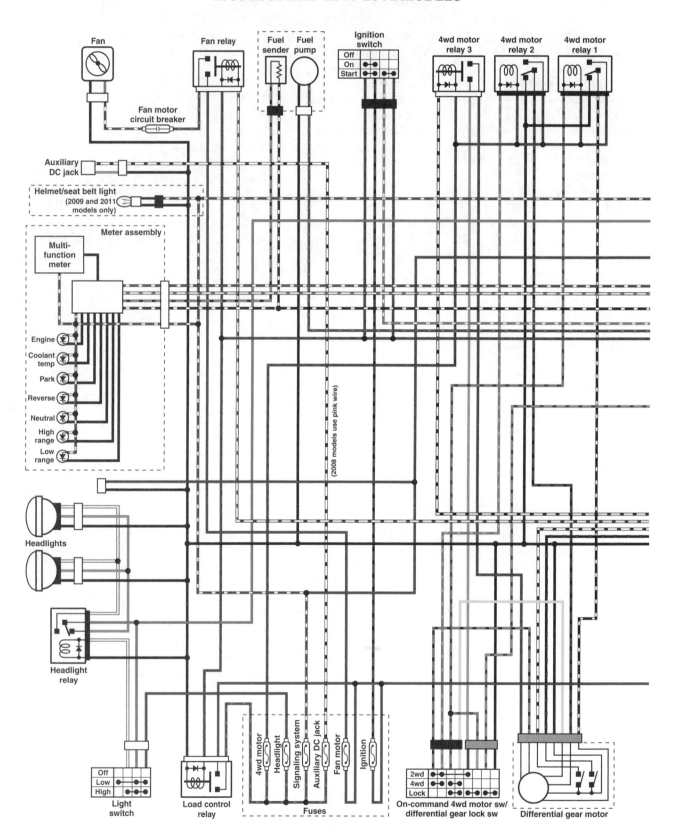

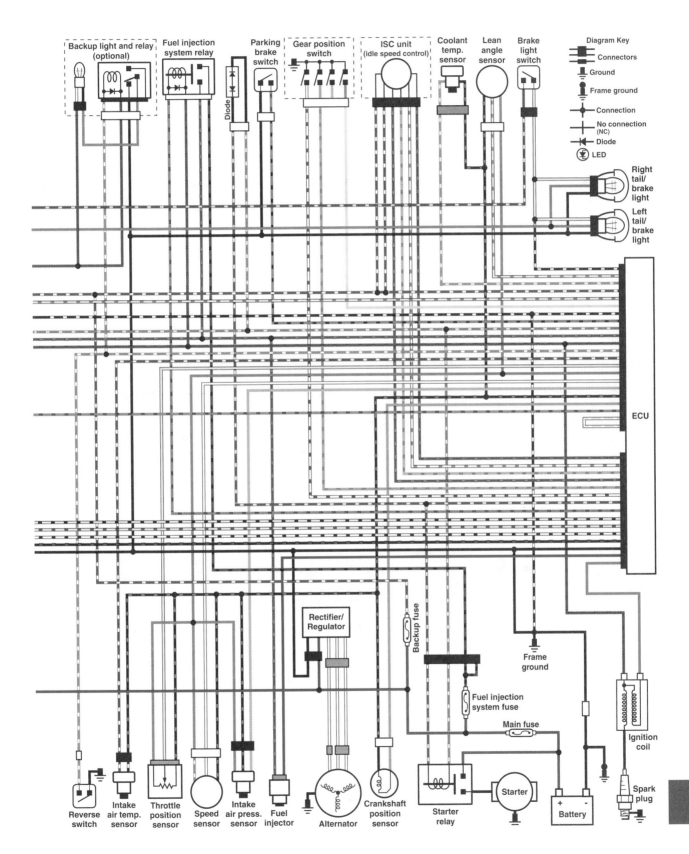

18

MAINTENANCE LOG

Date	Miles/Hours	Type of Service